D1551125

CHARLES D. SPIELBERGER, Ph.D., University of Iowa, is Professor of Psychology and Director of the Clinical Training Program at Florida State University. He previously taught at Duke University and Vanderbilt University, and was Training Specialist in Psychology for the National Institute of Mental Health.

ROBERT FOX, Ph.D., University of Cincinnati, is Associate Professor of Psychology and Director of Undergraduate Instruction at Vanderbilt University. He has also taught at the University of Cincinnati.

BRUCE MASTERTON, Ph.D., Duke University, is Associate Professor of Psychology at Florida State University. He has also taught at Wisconsin State College, Valparaiso University, and Vanderbilt University.

CONTRIBUTIONS TO
GENERAL
PSYCHOLOGY

SELECTED READINGS FOR INTRODUCTORY PSYCHOLOGY

Edited by

CHARLES D. SPIELBERGER
THE FLORIDA STATE UNIVERSITY

ROBERT FOX
VANDERBILT UNIVERSITY

BRUCE MASTERTON
THE FLORIDA STATE UNIVERSITY

THE RONALD PRESS COMPANY · NEW YORK

Library of Congress Catalog Card Number: 68–21514
PRINTED IN THE UNITED STATES OF AMERICA

PREFACE

The subject matter of psychology is traditionally covered in introductory textbooks by excellent summaries of current knowledge in the major areas of the field. However, the scientific literature of psychology is so extensive that it is generally not possible to provide a firsthand acquaintance with the original sources of this knowledge. Our primary goal in preparing this book is to provide the student who is being introduced to psychology for the first time with convenient access to original sources. The articles have been selected to complement the knowledge that is gained from textbooks, lectures, and class discussions. While most of the selections focus upon contemporary issues in psychology, a number of *classic* articles have also been included since current issues can often be better understood when viewed in historical perspective. In addition, we have included several articles that provide examples of the application of modern psychological method and theory to current social problems.

Collections of readings for courses in introductory psychology generally contain representative samples of the literature in the various major areas of psychology. While this approach permits broad coverage of the field, because of space limitations it is necessarily lacking in depth. Since many students take only an introductory course, it is our conviction that they should be provided with an opportunity to develop a deeper understanding of the subject matter of psychology in at least a few areas. Therefore, the readings included in this volume have been selected to provide intensive coverage of a limited number of important topics within major substantive areas. Although this arrangement means that some topics cannot be covered at all, we believe that the student will nevertheless gain a better overall understanding of the nature of psychology as a scientific discipline. We also feel that a more comprehensive treatment of selected topics will provide the student who plans to take advanced courses in psychology with a clearer basis for decisions regarding the selection of these courses.

The organization of this book and the selection of individual articles are particularly adapted for use with the Third Edition of *Principles of General Psychology* by Gregory A. Kimble and Norman Garmezy. The readings are divided into six parts, each corresponding to a parallel part in *Principles of General Psychology*. The articles contained in each part are all related to a central topic that is introduced by a brief essay at the beginning of the part. For each individual selection, there is also an introductory statement indicating the relationship between that particular article and the topic of the part.

While the selections in this volume enlarge upon points in *Principles of General Psychology*, the articles themselves provide basic materials that are a useful supplement to any standard textbook in general psychology. Therefore, the parts of this volume may be read in any order even though the individual articles within each part take on additional meaning if they are assigned sequentially.

We are especially grateful to the authors of the articles that have been reprinted here and to the journals and the publishers that have given us permission to use materials from their publications. In addition, we wish to thank Gregory A. Kimble and Norman Garmezy for their generous assistance, and for making available to us early drafts of the Third Edition of *Principles of General Psychology*. We would also like to express our appreciation to our colleagues at Vanderbilt University and at Florida State University for their many helpful suggestions.

The final preparation of this book was materially aided by the expert clerical and technical assistance of Patricia Harris, Pam Harrison, Karen Jensen, Cory Kelly, Martha Mercer, Olivia Riffe, Dona Tapp, and Laurette Wright. Finally, we wish to thank Jeanne Fox, Pauline Masterton, and Adele Spielberger for their patience and their help throughout our work on these readings.

CHARLES D. SPIELBERGER
ROBERT FOX
BRUCE MASTERTON

Tallahassee, Florida
Nashville, Tennessee
February, 1968

CONTENTS

PART V: BEHAVIOR DYNAMICS: ANXIETY AND CURIOSITY

PART VI: INDIVIDUALITY: INTELLIGENCE AND CREATIVITY

PART VII: PERSONALITY AND SOCIAL BEHAVIOR

CONTRIBUTIONS TO
GENERAL
PSYCHOLOGY

SELECTED READINGS FOR INTRODUCTORY PSYCHOLOGY

PSYCHOLOGY: THE OBJECTIVE STUDY OF BEHAVIOR

The goal of psychology is to provide a scientific account of the behavior of man and other animals. Of course, other fields such as literature, the arts, philosophy, and religion are also concerned with behavior and have contributed important and significant insights to our present understanding of the nature of man. While psychology shares its subject matter with these humanistic disciplines, it differs from them in its methods of observation and in its emphasis upon experimental procedures. As a branch of natural science, psychology is committed to search for comprehensive and detailed explanations of behavior that are founded on communicable and verifiable observations, and on objective and experimental methods.

Through research, psychology seeks to discover laws that specify relationships between behavior and the many different conditions and circumstances that influence it. But it is obviously not possible to investigate the infinite number of factors that affect behavior, nor is it even possible to study all the activities of only one person at any given time. Consequently, for practical reasons, the research psychologist must restrict himself to limited segments of behavior and to selected conditions and circumstances under which it occurs. Thus, in psychology, as in every science, there has developed a division of labor based on the particular aspects of behavior that are selected for study.

Some psychologists choose to investigate the dependence of behavior on biological mechanisms, others study the processes whereby people obtain knowledge about the world through the various senses, and still others are mainly concerned with individual differences in intellectual and personality characteristics. As a consequence of this division of labor, a number of major areas within the discipline have been established. These areas are defined, not only by the kind of behavior that is investigated, but also by the research methods that are used and the theoretical explanations that are given to account for experimental findings.

The major content areas of psychology are typically represented as chapter headings in introductory psychology textbooks and include such topics as physiological psychology, sensation, perception, learning, motivation, personality, abnormal psychology, and social psychology. Although it is generally useful and convenient to distinguish between areas of concentration, it should be recognized that the division is somewhat arbitrary, and that there is considerable overlap in the concepts and subject matter that are included in the various areas. Thus, the subareas are not really as different as they may appear at first glance.

While all psychologists are committed to the objective study of behavior, the research methods and procedures that are used differ markedly, depending upon the specific kinds of problems that are investigated. For example, physiological psychologists who study relationships between the structure of the brain and behavior must be highly skilled in surgical techniques and in microscopic analyses of brain tissues. They must also have an understanding of electronics in order to make use of procedures for recording complex brain potentials. Similarly, clinical psychologists who study abnormal behavior must be skilled in interpersonal relations and in the administration and interpretation of complex tests of intelligence and personality. Of course, they must also know statistics and measurement theory so that they can adapt and improve their testing procedures and develop new ones.

THE TWO DISCIPLINES OF SCIENTIFIC PSYCHOLOGY

During the past half-century, two very different approaches or orientations to the discovery of psychological laws have emerged. The first of these orientations emphasizes basic psychological processes that are found in all behaving organisms, or that are at least common to particular groups, such as all mammals, all men, or all middle-class men. The second approach is concerned with the study of individual variations in behavior, that is, the ways in which individuals in the same group differ from one another. In commenting on these two orientations in his 1957 presidential address to the American Psychological Association, Lee J. Cronbach contends that the differences between them are so extensive and so fundamental that they can be considered as "two disciplines of scientific psychology."

Psychologists who study basic processes tend to use experimental methods in which they manipulate selected variables and rigorously control others. These methods permit them to test explicit hypotheses regarding the effects on behavior of specific changes in environmental conditions, and to formulate precise laws relating behavior to its antecedents. Psychologists who are concerned with individual differences also study relationships between behavior and its antecedents. However, they seek to discover *correlations* between already existing variations in behavior and a larger number of environmental circumstances, not just those that can be experimentally manipulated. In Cronbach's words, "while the experimenter is interested only in the variation he himself creates, the correlator finds his interest in the already existing variation between individuals, social groups, and species."

An example will help to clarify some important differences in the research orientations of psychologists who are interested mainly in basic
processes and those centrally concerned with individual differences.
Imagine the reactions of a group of college students to an unexpected
announcement by their instructor that an examination will be given in the
next class period. We would expect most of the students to respond to this
announcement with a mild "anxiety" reaction. This reaction would consist of a feeling of apprehension or concern, heightened activity of the
autonomic nervous system (for example, a slight increase in heart rate or
blood pressure), and a state of increased attention or alertness to whatever additional information might be provided by the instructor regarding
the forthcoming test.

But the level of intensity and the qualitative characteristics of each
student's reaction would undoubtedly vary from student to student. This
would depend in part upon situational factors, such as the extent to which
a particular student felt he was prepared for the examination, his estimate
of the amount of time he would have to study for it, and his performance
on previous examinations. The reactions of individual students would also
depend upon particular personality characteristics. For example, a disposition to experience anxiety in classroom examinations or a tendency to
become angry when taken by surprise would probably influence the nature
and the intensity of a student's personal response to the instructor's announcement.

If an experimental and a correlational psychologist were to study the
reactions of the students, the experimental psychologist would be most interested in the average reactions of the group of students to the announcement of the forthcoming test. To him, variations in the responses of individual students would be regarded as "measurement error"—irrelevant
differences to be eliminated or controlled if possible. In contrast, the correlational psychologist would be most interested in the differences in the
reactions of individual students—precisely those differences that experimental psychologists are most likely to ignore. Of course, a more complete
explanation would take into account the behavior of the group as a whole,
as well as the reactions of each individual student.

To illustrate the advantages of this combined approach, let us assume
that most college students react to the announcement of a forthcoming test
with at least a mild elevation in anxiety level. Since college students have
had considerable experience in preparing for and taking examinations,
the average intensity of this anxiety response for the group as a whole
would probably be quite small. Consequently, if a particular student's response is relatively intense, that is, disproportionate to the objective amount
of situational stress (as defined by the average anxiety response for the
group), this can be interpreted as evidence that the student has a personal
problem, possibly of sufficient severity to require counseling or some other
form of treatment. Thus, the significance of a person's idiosyncratic responses takes on additional meaning when they are compared to the reactions of others.

Current trends in psychological research reflect frequent attempts to
combine and integrate Cronbach's two disciplines of scientific psychology.

However, emphasis on basic psychological processes and experimental manipulation of the environment is still more characteristic of research in some areas of the field, while a corresponding emphasis on individual differences and correlational methods dominates research in other areas. Therefore, in reading the scientific literature in psychology, the student should be aware of the traditional orientations of experimental and correlational psychologists. He should also keep in mind the fact that knowledge of both individual and group variation generally provides a clearer picture of the effects of an environmental change on behavior than does information from either of these sources alone.

AN OVERVIEW OF CONTRIBUTIONS TO GENERAL PSYCHOLOGY

The organization of this collection of readings is designed to represent the major areas of general psychology. The group of readings in Part II is concerned with the biological bases of behavior and contains selections that show the dependence of behavior on genetic factors, biological maturation or development, and the nervous system. The articles in Part III are related to the topics of sensation, perception, and attention. Individual selections deal with the neurophysiology of sensation and perception and the psychological processes that are involved in receiving and interpreting information about the external world. In Part IV, the topics of learning and memory are represented by a group of articles in which controlled laboratory investigations of these processes are described.

Of course, there are important individual differences in psychobiological and sensory processes and also in the ways in which different animals perceive and learn about the environment. The student should note, however, that most of the research represented in Parts II, III, and IV is devoted to obtaining knowledge about basic psychological processes. In the sections that follow, however, the emphasis on general processes diminishes, while concern with individual differences increases. This shift in emphasis parallels the shift of topics from the more fundamental and molecular psychobiological processes common to animals and man to the more complex and unique behavior of humans. There is also a corresponding shift in method from experimental procedures in which behavior and its antecedents are manipulated to observational procedures in which already existing relationships between behavior and its antecedents are studied.

Experimental and correlational psychology have contributed about equally to our understanding of motivation and behavior dynamics, the topics that are of central concern in Part V. However, rather than presenting a heterogeneous group of readings that provide information about a large number of motives, the selections in this section are limited to articles that bear upon theory and research on anxiety (or fear) and curiosity. These motivational states are selected for special emphasis for two reasons. First, as drive states, they have pervasive and profound effects on behavior, especially on human behavior. Second, anxiety and curiosity have been studied intensively during the past decade both as general psychological states or processes and as personality traits that are important sources of individual differences in behavior.

Individual differences receive greater emphasis in Parts VI and VII than in the previous sections, but the articles in these sections are also concerned with variations in psychological processes that are characteristic of particular groups of people. The selections in Part VI pertain to the nature and measurement of intelligence, the effects of heredity and environment on intellectual achievement, and the relationship between intelligence and creativity. In Part VII, most of the selections are concerned with individual differences in personality. Case histories and theoretical explanations of abnormal personality involving pathological expression of anxiety and curiosity are presented. Psychological tests and therapeutic procedures that are currently used to diagnose and to modify deviant behavior are also discussed. In addition, several studies of complex social behavior are included.

In reading this book, the student should realize that the articles contained in each section do not comprise a representative sample of the subject matter in these major areas of psychology. Instead, the readings have been selected with the aim of presenting a deeper and more detailed understanding of the facts and issues that help to illuminate important topics within major substantive areas. Thus, each section consists of a group of related articles that focus upon a similar topic but which express different points of view and demonstrate the variety of research techniques that are applicable to a particular problem area. The topical theme of each section is outlined in the editors' introduction, and there is also an introductory statement for each article that provides an overview of its specific contribution to the area.

While the majority of the readings in this volume are addressed to contemporary issues in psychology, some of these issues can be best understood in historical context. Therefore, each section contains several "classic" articles that are included to provide the student with needed perspective regarding the historical development of selected areas of psychological science. Although some of these classic articles may now seem humorous and others are frankly wrong in their conclusions, it should be recognized that they were accepted as "common knowledge" for long periods of history.

BIOLOGICAL BASES
OF BEHAVIOR

Most people accept the idea that the amazing kaleidoscope of human behavior is divisible into components such as moving, seeing, and thinking, and regard these functions as ultimately explainable by reference to the workings of specific parts of the body. Indeed, there are many facts available to us that make this idea appear quite reasonable. For example, we see with our eyes, and without eyes or with eyes covered we are blind. Thus, the concepts of "seeing" and "blindness" are not difficult to imagine and bear a direct and obvious relation to the existence of "eyes."

When we see structures in animals that look like eyes, we assume that the animal can see. If, on the other hand, an animal successfully avoids hazardous obstacles, we conclude that it sees and must have eyes even though it may not possess any structure that looks like an eye. In general, we assign functions, such as seeing, to structures, such as eyes, and we thus divide the body into parts, assigning each of these parts a function. The phenomena that constitute the subject matter of psychology may also be viewed in terms of this kind of reasoning because "structure-function" analysis is particularly applicable to descriptions of the dependence of behavior on biological mechanisms.

There are two ways in which the biological bases of behavior are usually explored. The first entails viewing a living organism as a complex structure of unknown origin. Since the structure consists of identifiable parts, the goal is to determine the contribution of each of the parts to the behavior of the whole. This point of view usually generates physiological experimentation on mature organisms and is essentially similar to the methods one would use to understand the workings of any contrivance, living or not. The second way of investigating the biological bases of behavior results from noting that living organisms have a history and that their structure and behavior depend to a large extent on past events. This point of view usually generates comparisons between organisms of different ages, or of different backgrounds, or of different species.

Because moment-to-moment behavior is so complex and its biological

9

bases are just beginning to be understood, a biological psychologist cannot ignore the potential contributions of either of these points of view. Typically, he adopts first one attitude, and then the other, hoping to gain further insight into the relations between structures and their functions through all available means. The articles in this section have been selected to reflect both experimental and comparative points of view. Although some of the authors base their conclusions strictly on comparison, others on experimentation, and still others on both, their ultimate aims are the same. Old or new, they strive to explain behavioral phenomena by showing them to be dependent on familiar biological, chemical, and physical factors.

Of the nine articles in this section, three are historical and six are modern. The first of the historical selections is an excerpt from Aristotle written in the 4th century B.C. In it he argues that the chief function of the brain is to balance the passions generated in the heart. The second article is a quotation from Vesalius. In addition to its technical contribution, it indicates that experimentation in biological psychology was not always as easy as it is today. The final historical selection is excerpted from Descartes' physiological theory of psychology. In it Descartes introduces the now famous idea that the pineal gland is the seat of man's soul.

The six modern articles are divided into two groups. The first group consists of three articles that deal with questions pertaining to the genetics of behavior. The second group contains three articles on the nervous system. In the first of the articles on genetics, Dobzhansky (Dub-jan'-ski) discusses the general question of the relation between heredity, environmental and genetic variation, and behavior. The other two articles, by Sperry and by Dennis and Dennis, are concerned with specific questions of development.

The first of the three articles on the nervous system is Lord Adrian's resolution of the apparent contradiction between the smoothness of muscular responses and the all-or-none responses of nerve cells. This is followed by Herrick's synthesis of comparative anatomy, paleontology, and psychology into a coherent and understandable picture of the origin and function of the nervous system. The final article, by Lashley, is on the contributions of the forebrain to behavior.

EARLY VIEWS OF BIOLOGY AND BEHAVIOR

1. Parts of Animals *

Aristotle

Although the critical function of the brain in the life of animals and men is now both obvious and generally accepted, it has not always been so. Aristotle applied his intellectual genius to understanding the brain with the same diligence that was characteristic of his analysis of other topics. But in contrast to his many penetrating insights, the key role of the brain eluded him. In the following excerpts from *Parts of Animals*, Aristotle argues that the chief function of the brain is cooling the blood.

The brain is present in order to preserve the animal organism as a whole. Some maintain that the Soul of an animal is Fire or some such substance. This is a crude way of putting it; and might be improved upon by saying that the Soul is carried in some body of a fiery nature. The reason for this is that the hot substance is the most serviceable of all for the activities of the Soul. *E.g.*, one of the activities of the Soul is to nourish; another is to cause motion; and these are most readily effected by means of this substance (viz. the hot). So to say that the Soul is fire is like saying that the craftsman, or his craft, is the saw or the auger which he uses, on the ground that the activity is performed while the two are near together. From what we have said this at any rate is clear: animals must of necessity have in them a certain amount of heat. Now, everything needs something to counterbalance it, so that it may achieve moderation and the mean; and it is the mean, of course, and not either of the extremes alone, which has reality and rationality. For this cause nature has contrived the brain to counterbalance the region of the heart and the heat in it; and that is why animals have a brain, the composition of which is a combination of Water and Earth. Hence, although all blooded animals have a brain, practically none of the others has (unless it be just a counterpart, as in the case of the Octopus), for since they lack blood they have but little heat.

* Reprinted by permission of The Loeb Classical Library and Harvard University Press from A. L. Park's translation of Aristotle's *Parts of Animals*, II, VII, which was written *circa* 350 B.C.

2. Dissection Procedure for the Brain *

Andreas Vesalius

During the Middle Ages, Aristotle's rationalism regarding human nature prevailed; to contradict this doctrine was to challenge God. Nevertheless, the early Renaissance counted many experimental scientists in its ranks. While such men as Vesalius, Galvani, and Volta are much less famous than the artists of the same period, they began the systematic experimentation into the life process that has culminated in modern biology and psychology. To illustrate the vagaries of experimentation in those days we quote from O'Malley's translation of Vesalius' *De Humani Corporis Fabrica,* which was written in 1543.

How the head ought to be prepared for inspection of the brain

After you have investigated the muscles of the neck, the nerves issuing from the dorsal marrow of the neck, and the organs of the body dealing with nutrition and vital spirit, I suggest that the head be removed from the body, as I mentioned at the end of the previous book, for one that has been removed can be handled with less difficulty. Heads of decapitated men are much more suitable for this purpose, especially if through the cooperation of friendly judges and prefects you can obtain them immediately after the execution and so scarcely dead. Such a judge is Marcantonio Contarini who, by Hercules, must be looked upon as a Maecenas of students. . . . A distinguished ornament of the illustrious Venetian Senate, famous every-

where for his remarkable knowledge of philosophy and languages and his many very successful diplomatic feats, and now the very vigilant podestà of Padua, he has generously supplied me with dissection material. He himself is a studious and indefatigable spectator of the structure of the human body, like another Boëthus or Sergius of Rome.

How the skull ought to be opened for dissection of the brain

Whatever sort the head may be, its bone must be sawed. First cut the skin to the bone with a razor or knife, preferably beginning a thumb's breadth above the eyebrows and continuing back from the temples to the most prominent part of the occiput. After this incision has been made, divide the skull along this line with a fine saw such as we use for amputation of a gangrenous limb or such as is used in the manufacture of ivory combs, but using great care lest the saw go deeper than the bone. It is advisable that the hair be not yet shaved from the head nor the ears removed so that, using both hands, your colleague may hold the head steady while it is being sawed. When you have sawed around the skull, draw the point of a blunt knife along the saw-cut to see whether any part of the bone still needs to be cut and, if so, saw that also. This operation is much easier with the help of another, but if you must work alone and fear lest the sawed edge may not be even, encircle the bare skull with a dyed cord such as those employed in the cutting of beams into lengths, and it will make a colored line around the skull . . .

* Reprinted by permission of the University of California Press from *Andreas Vesalius of Brussels, 1514–1564* by Charles Donald O'Malley, 1964.

3. Passions of the Soul *

René Descartes

René Descartes typifies the new breed of natural philosophers that arose in the Renaissance. He helped lead science away from explanation by the citation of authority (usually Aristotle) to explanation based on direct observation and experimentation. His contributions to mathematics and physics are well known. For example, the rectangular coordinate system of analytical geometry (cartesian coordinates) is his invention and all later developments of calculus depend heavily on this idea.

In physiology and psychology, Descartes, like his contemporary, Galileo, insisted that worldly phenomena be explained by reference to simple mechanical events. In this thesis, he rejected the idea that nature was determined by supernatural forces. This attitude resulted in his being considered as one of the first and foremost of the "mechanist" philosophers.

In the next selection, Descartes applies mechanistic principles to explain the workings of the body. Muscles are like bellows, nerves are pneumatic tubes. When it comes to thoughts, however, even Descartes found it impossible to rely on mechanics. He knew that the organs in animals and man are essentially similar, yet he felt that man possessed "something more" than beasts. Thus, he retained the idea of man's soul and free will but then, in an attempt to preserve mechanistic principles, localized the soul in a particular part of the brain. The article presented here consists of short excerpts from his treatise on physiology and psychology—the *Passions of the Soul*— written in 1649.

* Reprinted by permission of Cambridge University Press from *The Philosophical Works of Descartes*, Vol. I, 1931, translated by Elizabeth S. Haldane and G. R. T. Ross.

Article VII

A brief explanation of the parts of the body and some of its functions.

In order to render this more intelligible, I shall here explain in a few words the whole method in which the bodily machine is composed. There is no one who does not already know that there are in us a heart, a brain, a stomach, muscles, nerves, arteries, veins, and such things. We also know that the food that we eat descends into the stomach and bowels where its juice, passing into the liver and into all the veins, mingles with, and thereby increases the quantity of the blood which they contain. Those who have acquired even the minimum of medical knowledge further know how the heart is composed, and how all the blood in the veins can easily flow from the vena cava into its right side and from thence pass into the lung by the vessel which we term the arterial vein, and then return from the lung into the left side of the heart, by the vessel called the venous artery, and finally pass from there into the great artery, whose branches spread throughout all the body. Likewise all those whom the authority of the ancients has not entirely blinded, and who have chosen to open their eyes for the purpose of investigating the opinion of Harvey regarding the circulation of the blood, do not doubt that all the veins and arteries of the body are like streams by which the blood ceaselessly flows with great swiftness, taking its course from the right cavity of the heart by the arterial vein whose branches are spread over the whole of the lung, and joined to that of the venous artery by which it passes from the lung into the left side of the heart; from these, again, it goes into the great artery whose branches, spread throughout all the rest of the body, are united to the branches of the vein, which branches once more carry the same blood into the right cavity of the heart. Thus these two cavities are like sluices through each of which all the blood passes in the course of each circuit which it makes in the body. We further know that all the movements of the members depend on the muscles, and that these muscles are so mutually related one to another that when the one is contracted it draws toward itself the part of the body to which it is attached, which causes the opposite muscle at the same time to become elongated; then if at another time it happens that this last contracts, it causes the former to become elongated and it draws back to itself the part to which they are attached. We know finally that all these movements of the muscles, as also all the senses, depend on the nerves, which resemble small filaments, or little tubes, which all proceed from the brain, and thus contain like it a certain very subtle air or wind which is called the animal spirits.

ARTICLE XI

How the movements of the muscles take place.

For the sole cause of all the movements of the members is that certain muscles contract, and that those opposite to them elongate, as has already been said; and the sole cause of one muscle contracting rather than that set against it, is that there comes from the brain some additional amount of animal spirits, however little it may be, to it rather than to the other. Not that the spirits which proceed immediately from the brain suffice in themselves to move the muscles, but they determine the other spirits which are already in these two muscles, all to issue very quickly from the one of them and to pass into the other.

By this means that from which they issue becomes longer and more flaccid, and that into which they enter, being rapidly distended by them, contracts, and pulls the member to which it is attached. This is easy to understand provided that we know that there are but very few animal spirits which continually proceed from the brain to each muscle, but that there are always a quantity of others enclosed in the same muscle, which move there very quickly, sometimes by only turning about in the place where they are—that is, when they do not find any passage open from which to issue forth from it—and sometimes by flowing into the opposite muscle; and inasmuch as there are little openings in each of these muscles by which the spirits can flow from one to the other, and which are so arranged that when the spirits that come from the brain to one of them have ever so little more strength than those that proceed to the other, they open all the entrances by which the spirits of the other muscle can pass into this one, and at the same time close all those by which the spirits of this last can pass into the other. By this means all the spirits formerly contained in these two muscles very quickly collect in one of them and then distend and shorten it, while the other becomes elongated and flaccid.

ARTICLE XVI

How all the members may be moved by the objects of the senses and by the animal spirits without the aid of the soul.

We must finally remark that the machine of our body is so formed that all the changes undergone by the movement of the spirits may cause them to open certain pores in the brain more than others, and reciprocally that when some one of the pores is opened more or less than usual (to however small a degree it may be) by the action of the nerves which are employed by the senses, that changes something in the movement of the spirits and causes them to be conducted into the muscles which serve to move the body in the way in which it is usually moved when such an action takes place. In this way all the movements which we make without our will contributing thereto (as frequently happens when we breathe, walk, eat, and in fact perform all those actions which are common to us and to the brutes), only depend on the conformation of our members, and on the course which the spirits, excited by the heat of the heart, follow naturally in the brain, nerves, and muscles, just as the movements of a watch are produced simply by the strength of the springs and the form of the wheels.

Article XVII

What the functions of the soul are.

After having thus considered all the functions which pertain to the body alone, it is easy to recognise that there is nothing in us which we ought to attribute to our soul excepting our thoughts, which are mainly of two sorts, the one being the actions of the soul, and the other its passions. Those which I call its actions are all our desires, because we find by experience that they proceed directly from our soul, and appear to depend on it alone: while, on the other hand, we may usually term one's passions all those kinds of perception or forms of knowledge which are found in us, because it is often not our soul which makes them what they are, and because it always receives them from the things which are represented by them.

Article XVIII

Of the Will.

Our desires, again, are of two sorts, of which the one consists of the actions of the soul which terminate in the soul itself, as when we desire to love God, or generally speaking, apply our thoughts to some object which is not material; and the other of the actions which terminate in our body, as when from the simple fact that we have the desire to take a walk, it follows that our legs move and that we walk.

Article XIX

Of the Perceptions.

Our perceptions are also of two sorts, and the one have the soul as a cause and the other the body. Those which have the soul as a cause are the perceptions of our desires, and of all the imaginations or other thoughts which depend on them. For it is certain that we cannot desire anything without perceiving by the same means that we desire it; and, although in regard to our soul it is an action to desire something, we may say that it is also one of its passions to perceive that it desires. Yet because this perception and this will are really one and the same thing, the more noble always supplies the denomination, and thus we are not in the habit of calling it a passion, but only an action.

Article XXX

That the soul is united to all the portions of the body conjointly.

But in order to understand all these things more perfectly, we must know that the soul is really joined to the whole body, and that we cannot, properly speaking, say that it exists in any one of its parts to the exclusion of the others, because it is one and in some manner indivisible, owing to the disposition of its organs, which are so related to one another that when any one of them is removed, that renders the whole body defective; and because it is of a nature which has no relation to extension, nor dimensions, nor other properties of the matter of which the body is composed, but only to the whole conglomerate of its organs, as appears from the fact that we could not in any way conceive of the half or the third of a soul, nor of the space it occupies, and because it does not become smaller owing to the cutting off of some portion of the body, but separates itself from it entirely when the union of its assembled organs is dissolved.

Article XXXI

That there is a small gland in the brain in which the soul exercises its functions more particularly than in the other parts.

It is likewise necessary to know that although the soul is joined to the whole body, there is yet in that a certain part in which it exercises its functions more particularly than in all the others; and it is usually believed that this part is the brain, or possibly the heart: the brain, because it is with it that the organs of sense are connected, and the heart because it is apparently in it that we experience the passions. But, in examining the matter with care, it seems as though I had clearly ascertained that the part of the body in which the soul exercises its functions immediately is in nowise the heart, nor the whole of the brain, but merely the most inward of all its parts, to wit, a certain very small gland which is situated in the middle of its substance and so suspended above the duct whereby the animal spirits in its anterior cavities have communication with those in the posterior, that the slightest movements which take place in it may alter very greatly the course of these spirits; and reciprocally that the smallest changes which occur in the course of the spirits may do much to change the movements of this gland.

Article XXXII

How we know that this gland is the main seat of the soul.

The reason which persuades me that the soul cannot have any other seat in all the body than this gland wherein to exercise its functions immediately, is that I reflect that the other parts of our brain are all of them double, just as we have two eyes, two hands, two ears, and finally all the organs of our outside senses are double; and inasmuch as we have but one solitary and simple thought of one particular thing at one and the same moment, it must necessarily be the case that there must somewhere be a place where the two images which come to us by the two eyes, where the two other impressions which proceed from a single object by means of the double organs of the other senses, can unite before arriving at the soul, in order that they may not represent to it two objects instead of one. And it is easy to apprehend how these images or other impressions might unite in this gland by the intermission of the spirits which fill the cavities of the brain; but there is no other place in the body where they can be thus united unless they are so in this gland.

BEHAVIOR GENETICS AND MATURATION

4. Of Flies and Men *

Theodosius Dobzhansky

One of the most persistent and perplexing problems in psychology is the influence of hereditary factors on behavior. This general question has two specific aspects: how does an individual's genetic constitution influence his behavior? And second, how does behavior exert influence on genetic constitution? The latter question has been answered by Darwin: natural selection operates on behavioral characteristics in exactly the same manner that it operates on purely physical characteristics. The first question, however, has not been answered, nor is a concise answer yet in sight.

There is no doubt that heredity influences behavior, but how? Is behavior influenced by every gene? By the same genes that influence the color of the hair or the eyes, or perhaps height? In the next article one of America's foremost geneticists, Theodosius Dobzhansky (Dub-jan'ski), relates his work on fruit flies to these questions. In addition, he explains the nature of individual diversity and then shows how it contributes to the process of evolution. As will be seen, the diversity of human behavior is our best assurance against extinction.

One of the assertions which have gained acceptance by dint of frequent repetition is that science is competent to deal only with what recurs, returns, repeats itself. To study something scientifically, this something must be made representative of a class, group, or assemblage. A single

* Reprinted by permission of the author and the American Psychological Association from the *American Psychologist*, 1967, 22, 41-48.

Drosophila fly is of no interest whatsoever. A fly may merit some attention only if it is taken as a representative of its species. An individual person may, to be sure, merit attention. However, it is allegedly not in the province of science, but of insight, empathy, art, and literature to study and understand a person in his uniqueness.

I wish to challenge this view. Individuality, uniqueness, is not outside the competence of science. It may, in fact it must, be understood scientifically. In particular, the science of genetics investigates individuality and its causes. The singularity of the human self becomes comprehensible in the light of genetics. You may, of course, object that what science comprehends is not really a singularity but a plurality of singularities. However, an artist, no less than a biologist, becomes aware of the plurality because he has observed some singularities.

In the main, genetics is a study of differences among living beings. Genetics would be superfluous if all living beings were exactly alike. If all members of a species were exactly alike genetics could do very little. Since Mendel, the most powerful method of genetics is to observe differences among individuals in the progenies of parents which differed in some ways. Heredity and variation are the two sides of the same coin. Geneticists are always on the lookout for genetic diversity. Variety is said to be the spice of life. It is a staple necessity to geneticists.

(This applies, of course, to Mendelian genetics proper. The great discoveries of the role of chromosomes in the development, and the relationships between DNA, RNA, and protein synthesis could conceivably have been made even if Mendel's laws remained unknown).

That every person differs from every other person is so obvious that this is taken usually for granted. What continues controversial is to what extent the human differences are due to genetic and in what measure to environmental variations. Though in a new guise, the old nature-nurture problem is still with us. Now, the individuality of flies is rather less evident than human individuality. I do not claim to recognize every *Drosophila* by her face. The drosophiline individuality is nevertheless easier to analyze, and this analysis helps to throw some needed light on human individuality.

The theory of genetic individuality is simple enough. It stems directly from Mendel's second law, the law of independent assortment. An individual heterozygous for n genes has the potentiality of producing 2^n genetically different kinds of sex cells. Two parents, each heterozygous for the same n genes, can give rise to 3^n genotypes among the progeny, and parents heterozygous each for n different genes may produce 4^n genotypes. To be sure, not all of these genotypes are equally probable, because the linkage of genes in the same chromosome limits their independent assortment. Linkage disequilibrium delays but does not prevent eventual realization of the genetic variety. More important is the problem how large is n, that is, for how many genes an average individual is heterozygous, or how many genes are represented each by two or more variants in the populations of a species, such as man or a *Drosophila*.

The disagreement among geneticists on this point is rife. Those who espouse the classical theory of population structure believe that most genes are uniform, not only in all individuals of a species but even in different species not too remote in the biological system. The unfixed genes are a minority, perhaps of the order of some tens. Moreover, among the unfixed genes one variant, one allele, is normal and adaptively superior, while others are inferior and are maintained in populations by recurrent mutation. Though adherents of the classical theory are reluctant to admit this, the theory is a product of typological thinking. Lurking behind the facade of the variability, they like to envisage the Platonic archetype of the Normal Man, homozygous for all good with no bad genes.

The balance theory of population structure would assume numbers of variable genes of the order of hundreds, perhaps even thousands. An appreciable part of this variety is maintained in populations by several kinds of balancing natural selection. The kind most often discussed is the heterotic selection, operating because of hybrid vigor. There are, indeed, genetic variants which are adaptively favorable when heterozygous and unfavorable when homozygous. The gene which in homozygous condition causes sickle-cell anemia in man is a classical example; in heterozygous condition it confers a relative immunity to *falciparum* malaria. Perhaps even more important in evolution is diversifying natural selection. This can be explained most simply by pointing out that every living species faces not just one environment but a variety of environments. Human environments are certainly diverse, and moreover the diversity is growing. It is improbable that genes can be found to show optimal performance in all environments. More likely, different genes will be relatively more adaptive in different environments. Genetic variety is a method to cope with variety of environments.

Theoretical arguments cannot settle the questions for how many genes is an average individual heterozygous, and what proportion of the genes are represented by different alleles in different individuals of a species. Geneticists are busy working on these matters. I can cite here only the brilliant work of Lewontin and Hubby (1966), of the University of Chicago, as an example. Since the total number of genes is unknown, but is surely too large to have the whole set examined one by one, Lewontin and Hubby have decided to study what they believe is a random sample of genes. They chose a battery of enzymes that can be detected by electrophoresis in single individuals of the fly, *Drosophila pseudoobscura*. Some of these enzymes did and others did not show detectable genetic variations. The authors, after making a thorough examination of the possible biases and pitfalls, came to the conclusion that an individual fly was heterozygous for on the average between 10% and 15% of the genes in their sample. The numbers of kinds of genes in a sex cell can hardly be less than 10,000; an average fly may, then, be heterozygous for a number of genes of the order of 1,000.

Do these results have any bearing on man? Although man is not an overgrown *Drosophila*, he must have as many or more genes than *Drosophila* does. If the degree of heterozygosity in man is anything like it is in *Drosophila*, brothers or sisters are quite unlikely to inherit from their parents the same genes. The likelihood that any two unrelated persons are genetically identical is practically nil. Only identical twins may be genetically identical, since they arise by asexual division of a sexually produced fertilized egg. Even there the possibility of mutation and of cytoplasmic difference must be reckoned with. Human nature is, then, not unitary but multiform; the number of human natures is almost as great as the number of humans. Every person is unique, unprecedented, and unrepeatable.

The demonstration of the genetic uniqueness of individuals only opens, rather than solves, the problem as far as behavioral and social sciences are concerned. There seems little point in belaboring the truism that behavior as such is not inherited. Only genes can be inherited, in the sense of being handed down from parents to offspring. Even so, I have mostly division products, true copies of the genes I have inherited from my parents, rather than these genes themselves. The skin color is not inherited either, because the skin pigment is not carried in the sex cells. However, I am yet to meet anybody who would contend that one's genes have nothing to do with one's skin color. Human, as well as animal, behavior is the outcome of a process of development in which the genes and the environment are components of a system of feedback relationships. The same statement can be made equally validly with respect to one's skin color, the shape of one's head, blood chemistry, and somatic, metabolic, and mental diseases.

There are some authors who go so far as to question the existence of problems of genetics of behavior, distinct from genetics of anything else. They are right only inasmuch as there is not likely to exist a special brand of DNA concerned with behavior, different from that in other kinds of genes; moreover there are no genes "for" behavior, as there are no genes "for" the shape of one's nose. The problem is more subtle. It is the problem, or rather problems, of the genetic architecture of behavioral differences. We want to know how many genes are usually involved in such differences, the magnitude of their effects, the nature of their interactions, the parts played by mutation pressure, hybrid vigor, environmental heterogeneities, and by all forms of natural selection in the formation, in maintenance, and in normal and pathological variations of behavior. In this sense, the genetics and the evolution of behavior may well be different from, let us say, the genetics and the evolution of blood chemistry, or of metabolism, or of chromosomal polymorphism, or of concealing colorations, or mimetic resemblances. And in this sense, which is the only meaningful sense, the genetics of behavior, especially the experimental genetics of behavior, is not yet even a fledgling field, although it has recently begun to chirp rather lively.

In this article I can discuss only one example of a study of genetics of behavior, that made by my colleague B. Spassky and myself on phototaxis and geotaxis in *Drosophila pseudoobscura*. Hirsch and his students (Erlenmeyer-Kimling, Hirsch, & Weiss, 1962; Hirsch, 1962; Hirsch & Erlenmeyer-Kimling, 1962) have constructed a classification maze, and selected populations of *Drosophila melanogaster* which were clearly positively and others negatively geotactic in their behavior. They showed furthermore that the genetic basis of this behavior was polygenic, the three large pairs of chromosomes all influencing the result. Hadler (1964a, 1964b) made a similar maze for selection for phototaxis and succeeded in obtaining positively and negatively phototactic strains of *Drosophila melanogaster*. Dobzhansky and Spassky (1962), using Hirsch's maze, selected positively and negatively geotactic strains of *Drosophila pseudoobscura*. Their starting population was polymorphic for some inverted sections in the third chromosomes, and one of the variant chromosomes proved to favor negative geotaxis, while

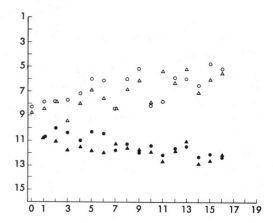

Figure 4.2 Selection for negative (light symbols) and positive (dark symbols) geotaxis. (Circles—females, triangles—males. Abscissa—generations of selection, ordinate—the geotactic score.)

chromosomal heterozygosis favored positive geotaxis.

The results of newer experiments on selection for positive and negative phototaxis and geotaxis in *Drosophila pseudoobscura* are presented in Figures 4-1 and 4-2. The ordinates show the phototactic or the geotactic scores, i.e., the averages of the 16 terminal tubes of the mazes into which the flies distribute themselves. On the geotaxis maze the tube No. 1 is the uppermost and No. 16 the lowermost, on the phototaxis maze No. 1 is reached by 15 choices of dark passages and No. 16 by 15 choices of light passages. The selection is made by running through the maze 300 females or 300 males; the 25 most positive, or most negative, individuals of each sex are selected to be the parents of the next generation. The initial populations in our experiments were photo- and geotactically neutral on the average. Or, to be more precise, these initial populations had positive, neutral, and negative individuals in such proportions that the average scores were between 8 and 9 (an average of 8.5 is exact neutrality). After 15 generations of selection, the positively phototactic line had average scores 13.4 and 14.5 for females and males respec-

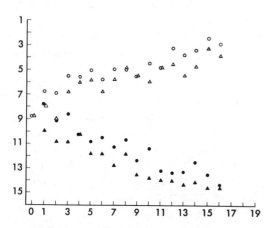

Figure 4.1 Selection for negative (light symbols) and positive (dark symbols) phototaxis. (Circles—females, triangles—males. Abscissa—generations of selection, ordinate—the phototactic score.)

tively, the negatively phototactic line 2.4 and 3.1, the positively geotactic line 12.1 and 12.5, and the negatively geotactic line 4.7 and 6.1. The frequency distributions overlap only slightly in the middle, i.e., only few flies of the selected strains end up in the terminal tubes Nos. 8 and 9.

Is it, then, the heredity which makes a *Drosophila* walk towards lights or darkness, climb up or descend? Even with flies, not only with men, the situation is more complex than that. From the effects of the selection in the first generation, the heritability of the photo- and geotactic responses can be calculated to lie between .15 and .20. This is somewhat oversimplifying the issue, but one can say that, as a first approximation, the genetic component of the behavior of the fly in our mazes is only 15% to 20%, while random chance and environment is responsible for 80% to 85%. Nor is this all. Taking the data for the 15 generations of selection as a whole, we can compute the so-called realized heritability, that is to say the efficiency of the response to the selection. This turns out to be very small, only about 9% for the phototaxis, and only about 3% for the geotaxis. In other words, a prediction of what the selection could accomplish in 15 generations, based on the initial heritability figure, would be a gross overestimate. There are several factors responsible for this situation, among which I shall single out just one, which seems most interesting.

In our first experiments (Dobzhansky & Spassky, 1962) we made selection in three populations of *Drosophila pseudoobscura* during 18 generations for positive and for negative geotaxis. After the positive and the negative populations have diverged about as much as the populations on Figure 4-2, the populations were split each into two. In one member of each pair the selection was reversed, i.e., a population formerly selected for the positive was now selected for a negative geotaxis, and vice versa. In another subpopulation the selection was relaxed, i.e., the subpopulation was propagated without selecting either

the positive or the negative individuals. The selective gains obtained through 18 generations of the original selection were almost erased in 6 generations of the reverse selection. The simple relaxation of the selection resulted in a loss of about half of the selection gains.

A partial, or even complete, loss upon abandonment of selection of what had been gained by previous selection is a phenomenon well known to breeders of agricultural plants and animals. Lerner (1954) has called this the genetic homeostasis. Very simply, the average height, weight, speed of maturation, and many other characteristics of a population which are determined by cooperation of numerous polygenes, are held by natural selection at levels near optimal for the population in the environments in which that population usually lives. When a breeder selects toward higher or toward lower levels of certain characteristics, he does so for his benefit, not necessarily for the benefit of the animal or the plant in its original environments. In other words, the artificial selection is often pitted against natural selection. As the artificial selection progresses it becomes more and more frustrated by natural selection. When the artificial selection is stopped, natural selection is given an opportunity to undo what the artificial one had gained; and reverse selection is highly effective because the artificial and the natural selections then work in the same direction, in alliance rather than in opposition.

Biologically, adaptively, this is an excellent strategy for evolution to follow. It combines high adaptedness to the existing environmental conditions with high adaptability to environmental changes. This strategy is, however, not at all what the classical theory of genetic population structure envisages. If the environment were uniform, constant, and favoring phototactically and geotactically neutral *Drosophilae*, then the simplest solution of the adaptive problem would seem to be to make all members of the species homozygous for the genes favoring photo- and geotactic neutrality. "Normal" or "typical" flies would then be neutral, and positive and negative ones would be abnormal or atypical. But this is not what is observed. The populations, though neutral on the average, contain also positive and negative genetic variants.

The availability in the populations of this genetic variance confers upon them evolutionary plasticity. A change in the environment that favors a positive or a negative photo- or geotaxis makes the population respond rapidly by adaptive genetic changes. Such responses might occur also in a genetically uniform and homozygous population, but they would be much slower. They would have to wait for the occurrence of mutations. These mutations would have to produce genetic variants which were unfavorable in the old but adaptive in the new environments. The rapidity of the genetic adjustment is, however, not the whole story. A genetically polymorphic population not only responds adaptively to environmental challenges, but in so doing it does not, so to speak, burn the bridges for retreat. It is hedged against the contingency that the environmental change to which it is adapting may only be a temporary one. If it is indeed temporary, and the original environment returns, the population can readapt itself speedily, by returning to its former genetic composition.

And yet genetic homeostasis does not stand in the way of permanent, irreversible, progressive evolutionary changes. If a new environment or a new way of life endures, a new genetic system becomes stabilized. This genetic system will be buffered against the vagaries of the new environments, but no longer able to retrace its steps to the conditions of the bygone age. If these conditions returned, the species would probably become adapted to them in some new way. One of the most interesting lessons that evolutionary biology teaches us is that there may be many more than a single method to eke out

a living from an environment. Major evolutionary changes are irreversible and unrepeatable.

This point is so central that it must be reiterated: Man is not just an overgrown *Drosophila*. We reject the belief that man is nothing but an animal. Yet he is, among other things, also an animal. Like *Drosophila*, he is a sexually reproducing, outbreeding species, and his populations are abundantly provided with genetic variability. The genetic diversity affects all kinds of traits—morphological, physiological, and behavioral. The discrete, clearcut, and usually pathological genetic variations of behavior, such as the so-called Mongoloid idiocy or phenylketonuria, need not be considered in the present discussion. The genetic variations among healthy persons are no less interesting, though much harder to study. The same situation exists also in *Drosophila*: sharp, easily distinguishable, and poorly viable mutants of classical genetics, versus slight, quantitative, polygenic variations. The difficulty, in human as well as in *Drosophila* genetics, arises because in the phenotypic variance of the second kind of traits the genetic and the environmental influences are intermingled.

Neither in the most highly selected, nor in the unselected, photo- or geotactic lines of *Drosophila* is the behavior of an individual rigidly determined. We have seen that the heritability of these behavioral traits is rather low. Whether at a given point of the maze an individual climbs upwards or downwards, takes a light or a dark passage, is in part a matter of environment, or simply of chance. The evidence is nevertheless conclusive that the genotype does bias the choices. Some flies are inclined to walk more often upward and others downward. Are the behavioral traits in human populations also conditioned by genetic variations? I shall be among the first to insist that the evidence is incomplete, and that more data must be collected. Yet the existing evidence, for a variety of traits ranging from IQ measurements to smoking habits, indicates that at least some genetic conditioning is involved, of course relatively more for some traits and less for others.

It is no secret that the study of the genetic conditioning of human behavior is hampered by the emotional reactions which this issue elicits in many people. Some wish to give an aura of scientific respectability to their race and class biases. Differences in material well-being and in social position are represented as just and necessary outcomes of the genetic differences. Others cling obstinately to the old tabula rasa theory. Man is a product of his environment and social conditions, and his genes are simply irrelevant. I submit that, irrespectively of your preconceptions, modern biology makes it necessary to state the problems of genetic conditioning of behavior in terms rather different from the traditional ones. This is because one of the most significant changes in the biological theory in the recent decades has been a shift from typological to populational models and concepts. This conceptual reformation has been discussed with admirable clarity and discernment, particularly by Simpson (1961) and by Mayr (1963), making it possible to state what is essential for us here very briefly.

To a typologist, what is real and important is the species or the race to which an organism belongs. Differences among individuals of the same species and race are, of course, too obvious to be denied. A typologist regards them, however, as merely a kind of troublesome noise in the biological system. He tries, as it were, to recognize the melody obfuscated by the noise; he seeks to identify, classify, and name the species and the races. He hopes that once he can determine to which species and race an individual belongs, that individual is thereby adequately described.

A populationist, on the contrary, regards the individuals and their diversity as the prime observable reality. The biological validity of species and races is not thereby refuted (although some extremists, try to do just that, in my opinion ill advisedly). Species and races are, however, derivative from individuals, not the other way around. Species and races are Mendelian populations, reproductive communities of sexually reproducing organisms, forms of adaptive ordering of systems of individuals, evolved because they have made the evolutionary feedback processes between the organisms and their environments most efficient and successful.

Man in the street is a spontaneous typologist. To him, all things which have the same name are therefore alike. All men have the human nature, and an alleged wisdom has it that the human nature does not change. All Negroes are alike because of their negritude, and all Jews are alike because of their jewishness. Populationalists affirm that there is no single human nature but as many human natures as there are individuals. Human nature does change. Race differences are compounded of the same ingredients as differences among individuals which compose a race. In fact, races differ in relative frequencies of genes more often than they differ qualitatively, one race being homozygous for a certain gene and the other lacking it entirely. The extremists who deny that races exist are disappointed typologists who have discovered for themselves the gene gradients between race populations. They fail to understand that such gradients elucidate the nature of race as a biological phenomenon; the facts warrant the conclusion that Platonic types of races do not exist, not that races do not exist.

The typological and populational operational approaches are characteristically different. A race of typology is described in terms of means or averages of height, weight, cephalic index, intelligence, etc. Populationists regard variances at least as important as means. Genetic variance characterizes not only the status but also the evolutionary possibilities of a population. The *Drosophila* populations with which Hirsch and his colleagues as well as ourselves began our experiments were photo- and geotactically neutral on the average. Yet the experiments have shown that the average neutrality did not mean that all individuals were neutral. Selection has attested the presence in the populations of genetic elements for positive and negative photo- and geotaxis. This does not quite mean that the original populations contained individuals as sharply positive and negative as are individuals of the selected strains. Natural and artificial selection do not act as simple sieves which isolate genotypes which were there before selection. Selection creates novelty, because it compounds genotypes the origin of which without selection would be altogether improbable.

All humans beings have certain universally recognized rights because they are members of the species Homo sapiens. Members of other species do not have the same rights. Cows are sacred to Hindus, but even in India cows are not treated exactly like humans. An imaginative French writer, Vercors, has given a thought-provoking discussion of legal and other problems that might arise if a hybrid of man and some anthropoid species were produced. Anyway, membership in a group, be that a species or a race, does not define all the characteristics of individuals. The notion that it does is implicit in race pride, exclusiveness, and bias.

Racists busy themselves attempting to scrape up any kind of evidence that Race X has a lower mean IQ, or smaller mean brain volume, or greater emotionality than Race Y. How large is the genetic component in such differences is questionable. The partitioning of the genetic and environmental variances obtained through studies on monozygotic and dizygotic twins cannot be used as a measure of the genetic and environmental components of the group differences. The basic assumption of the twin method is that the environments of the cotwins are uniform. This is obviously not true when different social classes, castes, and races are compared. Even if we had much more complete data on twins than are actually available, this would still leave the question of the magnitude of the genetic component in the group differences wide open. The argument that about one-half of the interracial variance in IQ must be genetic because this appears to be so among cotwins is a misinterpretation when it is not an intentional obfuscation.

To say that we do not know to what extent group differences in psychological traits are genetic is not the same as saying that the genetic component does not exist. It is a challenge to find out. If individuals within populations vary in some character, be that blood grouping, or stature, or intelligence, it is quite unlikely that the population means will be exactly the same. What matters is how great is the intrapopulational variance compared to the interpopulational variance. This is different for different characters. Skin pigmentation is individually variable in probably all races, but the interracial variance is evidently larger. Although precise data are not available, it is at least probable that the relation is reversed for psychological traits. In simplest terms, the brightest individuals in every class, caste, and race are undoubtedly brighter than the average in any other class, caste, or race. And vice versa—the dullest individuals in any of these groups are duller than the average of any group. There are sound biological reasons why this should be so. Very briefly, in the evolution of mankind the natural selection has worked, nearly always and everywhere, to increase and to maintain the behavioral plasticity and diversity, which are essential in all human cultures, primitive as well as advanced.

True enough, an individual taken from a population with a higher mean of some trait, say a higher intelligence, has a higher statistical probability to possess this trait more developed than an individual from a population with a lower mean. When we select *Drosophilae* for stronger or weaker photo- or geotaxis, we generally

breed the high and the low selection lines separately. Spassky and myself have, however, some experiments in progress, in which pairs of populations exchange migrants in every generation. The migrants are selected for high or for low photo- or geotaxis or for some other genetically conditioned trait. This may be considered to represent to some extent an experimental simulation of social mobility in human populations. The preliminary results of these experiments are, at least to us, fascinating. Genetically selective social mobility seems to be a powerful evolutionary agent.

A day may conceivably arise when mankind will embark on some all-out eugenical breeding program. This day is not yet in sight, because mankind has not reached a level of wisdom when it could decide with anything approaching unanimity what combination of genetic qualities should the ideal man have. It is rather easier to agree what qualities he should not have. As for positive ideals, we can only recommend that a diversity of tastes, preferences, abilities, and temperaments should be preserved and perhaps even increased. Anyway, when we consider the social implications of the human genetic diversity we are not usually preoccupied with eugenical breeding programs. The genetic diversity is, for example, most relevant to educational problems. The students are, however, selected for study, not for stud.

Insofar as the genetic component is concerned, the intelligence, or temperament, or special abilities of the parents have little predictive value for these qualities in an individual child. This does not mean that such genetic components do not exist, as some authors have overhastily concluded. It means two things. First, the heritability is fairly low, as it is low in the photo- and geotactic behavior of our flies. In other words, the environmental variance is high, and in man the parent-offspring similarities in behavioral traits may well be due more to the cultural than to the biological inheritance. Second, one cannot too often be reminded of the fact that we do not inherit the genotypes of our parents but only one half of their genes. The genes do not produce their effects in development each independently of the others. The genes interact; the genetic "nature" of an individual is an emergent product of the particular pattern or constellation of the genes he carries. This is often the reason why a child is sometimes so strikingly dissimilar to his parents in some traits, even if the environment is kept constant.

How can I summarize the contents of this article, which is itself a summary of thinking concerning a variety of issues? Perhaps the best way is to say that genetics bears out John Dewey's emphasis of "the infinite diversity of active tendencies and combinations of tendencies of which an individual [human] is capable."

REFERENCES

DOBZHANSKY, T., & SPASSKY, B. Selection for geotaxis in monomorphic and polymorphic populations of Drosophila pseudoobscura. Proceedings of the National Academy of Science, 1962, 48, 1704–1712.

ERLENMEYER-KIMLING, L., HIRSCH, J., & WEISS, J. M. Studies in experimental behavior genetics. III. Selection and hybridization analyses of individual differences in the sign of geotaxis. Journal of Comparative and Physiological Psychology, 1962, 55, 722–731.

HADLER, N. Genetic influence on phototaxis in Drosophila melanogaster. Biological Bulletin, 1964, 126, 264–273. (a)

HADLER, N. Heritability and phototaxis in Drosophila melanogaster. Genetics, 1964, 50, 1269–1277. (b)

HIRSCH, J. Individual differences in behavior and their genetic basis. In E. L. Bliss, Roots of behavior. New York: Harper, 1962. Pp. 3–23.

HIRSCH, J., & ERLENMEYER-KIMLING, L. Studies in experimental behavior genetics. IV. Chromosome analyses for geotaxis. Journal of Comparative and Physiological Psychology, 1962, 55, 732–739.

LERNER, I. M. Genetic homeostasis. Edinburgh & London: Oliver & Boyd, 1954.

LEWONTIN, R. C., & HUBBY, J. L. A molecular approach to the study of genic heterozygosity in natural populations. Genetics, 1966, 54, 595–609.

MAYR, E. Animal species and evolution. Cambridge: Harvard University Press, 1963.

SIMPSON, G. G. Principles of animal taxonomy. New York: Columbia University Press, 1961.

5. Optic Nerve Regeneration With Return of Vision in Anurans *

Roger W. Sperry

One of the amazing features of ontogenetic development is the nervous system's ability to establish an enormous number of interconnections with accuracy and precision. The axon of a developing nerve cell grows along only one of the many possible routes open to it. As it grows, it circumvents barriers and turns corners terminating abruptly on its target. Equally astonishing, two nerve cells lying side by side may develop in entirely different directions and connect to entirely different organs. This process takes place in a manner that makes it appear that the nerve cells somehow *know* where they are supposed to go or what they are supposed to do.

In mammals and man only peripheral nerves retain this intriguing property throughout life. If one of these nerves is damaged, it will regenerate itself and reconnect to its former destination, and there restore neural control once more. In primitive animals, however, even some central nerves can regenerate themselves after damage. In amphibians, for example, the optic nerve from eye to brain regenerates after damage and when it does normal vision is restored.

What determines the destination of the developing or regenerating nerve? As the new fiber grows out from the cell body, is it seeking a particular place to terminate or is it seeking a termination which will produce an adaptive effect? Does the regenerating optic nerve fiber merely reconnect to the cells to which it was formerly connected? Or does it connect to whatever cells are necessary to produce normal vision?

* Reprinted by permission of the author and the American Physiological Society from the *Journal of Neurophysiology*, 1944, 7, 57-70.

In the next article, Professor Sperry attacks these questions experimentally. He cut the optic nerve in frogs and at the same time rotated the eye about a line through the pupil. His reasoning went like this: if, after the optic nerve regenerates, the restored vision is reversed upside-down and left-to-right, then the nerve fibers must have reconnected themselves to the cells to which they had been formerly connected in spite of its maladaptive effect. In this case the course which the nerve fibers took was probably determined directly by simple chemical and physical processes. If, however, the restored vision is normal in spite of the rotated eye, the nerves must have reconnected themselves to entirely different cells than those they had been connected to previously. In that case, a more subtle factor determining their route must be sought.

The recovery of normal vision after regeneration of the optic nerve demonstrated in adult urodele amphibians (8, 9) requires that the ingrowing optic fibers reëstablish in the brain centers discriminative functional associations which are differentially suited to the diverse retinal points from which the optic fibers arise. If the relationships between retinal field and brain centers formed in regeneration were disorderly or undifferentiated, normal vision involving discrete perception of small objects and their accurate localization in space would be impossible.

Conceivably, the central reflex relations as reëstablished after regeneration might not be suitably arranged at first, but become properly adjusted only later through experience by a process of trial and error

or other means of functional adaptation. Or the adequacy of the functional effect might somehow operate during the process of regeneration to regulate the formation of appropriate central connections. Both these theoretical possibilities, however, have been ruled out in the case of the newt, *Triturus viridescens* (8), in which it has been found that the restoration of normal vision after optic nerve regeneration is quite independent of functional adaptation.

When severance of the optic nerve in this animal is combined with 180 degree rotation of the eyeball on its optic axis, visual perception after recovery is systematically reversed about the optic axis corresponding to the rotated position of the retinal field. Reversed optokinetic reactions, erroneous spatial localization of small objects, and other clear indices of reversed vision are displayed consistently and without later adjustment, just as in animals in which the eyeball has been rotated with the optic nerve left intact (7). Thus in *Triturus* reëstablishment of reflex relations in the visual centers is apparently predetermined in an orderly manner by growth factors regardless of the suitability of the functional effect for the animal.

Exactly how linkages between retina and brain centers are systematically restored by growth processes remains to be demonstrated. The work on *Triturus* suggested certain possible interpretations, however, and because of their important bearing on problems of broader significance concerning the developmental differentiation and integrative action of the nervous system it became strongly desirable to make sure that these results were not due merely to peculiarities of this one species.

The present paper deals accordingly with an extension of the previous experiments on the newt to several species of the distantly related and, so far as the visual system is concerned, more highly developed anuran amphibians, the frogs

and toads. Included also are the results of some attempts at further analysis of the problem; namely, the effects on vision of localized lesions placed in the optic lobes of the brain before and after optic nerve regeneration.

Procedure and Materials

Plan of the experiments. The general procedure was similar to that used previously in the case of *Triturus*. Severance of the optic nerve was combined with 180 degrees rotation of the eyeball on its optic axis. With eye rotation the character of visual perception after regeneration of nerve connections between retina and brain centers might be (i) normal, (ii) reversed about the optic axis corresponding to the reversal of the retinal field, or (iii) randomly blurred. If the recovered vision turned out to be normal in quality, despite the reversed position of the retinal field, it would be strong indication that function is of primary importance in regulating establishment of the central connections. Recovery of reversed vision, on the other hand, would show that the original retino-central relations are systematically restored in a predetermined manner regardless of functional effect. If visual perception on recovery should prove to be neither normal nor systematically reversed but instead a blurred confusion, it would indicate that redistribution and termination of the regenerating fibers is disorderly and nonselective, as in peripheral nerve regeneration (14).

The optic nerve was purposely pulled and teased apart in a rough manner in all cases rather than cut cleanly in order to prevent any neat approximation of the ends of individual fibers. All operations were performed under ether anesthesia with aid of a dissecting microscope with magnification of 21 times. After operation the tadpoles were kept at room temperature in 7-liter aquaria, and the frogs and toads in moist terraria of the same size.

Animals. Six species from three different families of anurans (*Bufo terrestris, Hyla cinerea, H. crucifer, H. squirella, Rana clamitans,* and *R. pipiens*) were used in the experiments.[1] All the animals were gathered in northeastern Florida. The specimens of *R. clamitans* were undergoing metamorphosis when brought into the laboratory and were operated upon shortly after. All the other

---

[1] For aid in identification of the animals acknowledgment is due Charles M. Bogert of The American Museum of Natural History.

adult animals had attained full size at the time they were gathered during their respective breeding seasons. The tadpoles were operated on in mid-larval stages. Although not identified with certainty, they were very probably all *H. crucifer*. In general the differences in the results obtained on different species were not of sufficient importance for the essential problems concerned to warrant burdening the reader throughout with the species name of each animal mentioned. Hence only the species and numbers included under each main treatment will be indicated and the species name of individual cases will be stated only where the results gave reason to believe that there might exist some significant species difference.

Criteria of vision. The ability to localize small objects in space was the principal index of visual perception used in testing recovery in the adult animals. The accuracy with which frogs, particularly the tree frogs, gauge distance and direction in leaping for prey is quite remarkable (3, 5). *H. cinerea* was frequently observed in the course of this study to capture with a single leap houseflies walking at a distance of 35 cm., a comparatively easy feat in view of some reports. This is mentioned only to furnish some indication of the efficiency of the anuran visual system. No attempt was made in the present experiments to determine the limits of such performances. The experimental tests were generally made at distances between 5 and 15 cm. Discrete localization of small objects in different sectors of the visual field furnishes of course an excellent index of the functional properties or "local signs" of different retinal areas.

In the tadpoles the optokinetic response to rotation of the visual field served as the chief criterion of visual function. Although perhaps not indicative of so great a degree of specialization in retino-central associations as is the spatial localization of small objects, the optokinetic reaction is nevertheless dependent on a certain systematic differentiation of central reflex relations. Therefore, its recovery after optic nerve regeneration, like the recovery of spatial localization, requires an orderly reëstablishment of specific functional linkages between periphery and central nervous system which was the main concern of the present experiments.

EXPERIMENTS ON TADPOLES

The regenerative capacities of anurans being less great than those of urodeles, it was not certain at the start of the experi-

ments to what extent visual function might be recovered, if at all, after section of the optic nerve. The experiments were therefore begun on tadpole stages in which chances of recovery would be greater than in adults.

Operations. In ten control cases (5 unilateral and 5 bilateral) in which the eye was left in normal position, the optic nerve with its sheaths was broken with jewelers' forceps. The stumps of the broken nerve floated rather freely in the fluid of the orbit and although some attempt was made to bring the ends close together before coagulation occurred, the broken ends in the majority of cases remained separated by a distance greater than the diameter of the nerve. Seventeen experimental cases were also prepared (7 unilateral and 10 bilateral) in which all ocular muscles were severed and the eyeball was rotated on its optic axis through 180 degrees. Several days later the nerve of the rotated eye was sectioned as in the control cases. A dorsal approach through a longitudinal incision over the eye was used both in sectioning the nerve and in rotating the eyeball. The unoperated eye of the unilateral cases in both the control and experimental groups was excised.

Recovery. During the first week after operation no optokinetic reactions could be elicited in any of the animals. The first definite signs of recovery appeared on the average 13 days after nerve section but the recovery intervals varied in different cases from 11 to 23 days. One unilateral control case never recovered vision and two bilateral experimental cases recovered vision on only one side. Histological examinaton revealed that in these three exceptional instances the regenerating optic nerve had not succeeded in reaching the chiasma. Surgical readjustment of the eyeball, which had slipped out of its intended position, was necessary in two experimental cases.

Tests of vision. The tadpoles in water in a fingerbowl were placed on a stationary platform inside a revolving upright cylindrical drum 31 cm. in diameter with opaque vertical black and white stripes on the inner wall. The stripes varied randomly in width from 2 to 7 cm. The optokinetic reaction was found to be readily and consistently elicited with this apparatus. After recovery was well established the animals were tested regularly over a five-day period and at weekly intervals thereafter. The 9 control cases and 16 experimental cases in which vision was successfully recovered displayed good optokinetic responses conforming with the following descriptions.

Results with unrotated eye. Reactions of the bilateral control cases after recovery were quite like those of normal animals. The optokinetic response, consisting of an alternate beating of the tail with the strong beats in one direction, turned the head and body in that direction in which the visual field was revolving. Sometimes the animals turned in small circles in a stationary position and at other times they swam in larger arcs and circles, always in the direction of drum rotation.

The responses of the unilateral control cases were like those of normal animals from which one eye had been excised. Reactions when drum rotation was toward the blind side were normal but those with drum rotation toward the seeing side consisted usually of only a slow sustained flexion of the tail not strong or sudden enough to cause any movement of the head and body.

Results with rotated eye. The reactions of the tadpoles with rotated eyes after recovery were essentially like those of normal and control animals except that the direction of the responses was reversed. Instead of moving the head in the same direction in which the visual field moved, the animals turned in the opposite direction. The unilateral cases responded normally toward the blind side and made only a slow, sustained tail flexion toward the seeing side just as did the unilateral control animals, but the direction of drum rotation which elicited these responses was the opposite from that which was effective in evoking the same responses in the control group.

Reversed vision was also indicated in these animals by spontaneous circus locomotion. The bilateral cases swam in circles either clockwise or counterclockwise depending on how they happened to start. The unilateral cases circled with the blind

side toward the center of the arc or circle. This tendency to swim in circles was comparable to that shown by *Triturus* after rotation of the eye (7). Both the reversed optokinetic responses and the spontaneous circling movements had been displayed in similar form by the bilateral cases during the few days immediately following eye rotation prior to optic nerve section. The results show that in these anuran larvae just as in adult *Triturus* the central reflex relations are recovered in orderly form and their reëstablishment is strictly determined by anatomical factors regardless of functional suitability.

Effect of experience. The tadpoles with rotated eyes were kept at least 1 month after recovery; four cases were retained nearly 2 months by which time the forelimbs had emerged. The reversed optokinetic reactions and circus locomotion persisted in all cases, and in no instance was any correction of the reversed responses noted.

EXPERIMENTS ON ADULT FROGS AND TOADS

Operations. In 8 control cases (all bilateral) the optic nerves were sectioned without disturbance of the eyeball or ocular muscles. In 19 experimental cases (all unilateral) severance of the optic nerve was accompanied by rotation of the eyeball. The optic nerve was sectioned with jewelers' forceps through an incision in the roof of the mouth. The inner nerve sheath was completely severed in all cases, but in most animals, at least a connecting strand of the dural sheath was left intact. The eyeball was rotated by first severing all attachments to surrounding structures except the blood vessels and the optic nerve. This was done through two incisions, one in the roof of the mouth, the other around the outside of the cornea. The globe was then grasped by the stumps of the ocular muscles and rotated anterodorsally on its optic axis through 180 degrees. Some of the blood vessels were inevitably broken in the course of rotation, but a sufficient number remained to maintain circulation through the iris. The degree of rotation was estimated by distinct landmarks in the iris and pupil which varied in the different species. After it had been adjusted, the eyeball was allowed to set and heal in its new position after which the nerve of the rotated eye was sectioned as described.

Vision in one eye is not easily tested in the presence of vision on the opposite side in anurans due to binocular overlap of the visual fields. Hence the contralateral optic nerve of the experimental group was sectioned either 3 days before rotating the eye (6 cases) or about 25 days after (13 cases). Thereafter the contralateral nerve was sectioned once or twice again after intervals of about 28 days whenever it became apparent that vision had been recovered in the unrotated eye.

Recovery. Functional regeneration of the optic nerve, though not so consistently successful as in the adult urodele, did occur readily in the great majority of these adult anurans. The first indications of recovery of vision began to appear on the average about 25 days after nerve section. The recovery period varied in different cases from 21 days to about 33 days. In two of the experimental cases the rotated eye became necrotic and was sloughed off. Two other experimental cases failed to recover vision in the rotated eye and two of the control cases recovered vision on only one side. The eye in these latter four instances retained a healthy external appearance, but microscopic examination revealed that regeneration of the optic nerve had been defective. Except for a very fine strand of fibers in one case the regenerating axons had frayed out along aberrant courses and had failed to reach the chiasma. In a fifth experimental case some signs of response to visual stimuli reappeared but the responses were too weak, infrequent, and inconsistent to permit any conclusions. A substantial strand of fibers about $\frac{1}{5}$ the size of the distal nerve stump was found in this case connecting with the chiasma but many small bundles of fibers had misregenerated along nearby structures of the orbit. The remaining 14 experimental cases which showed successful return of vision included 2 *B. terrestris*, 3 *H. cinerea*, 2 *H. crucifer*, 2 *H. squirella*, 3 *R. clamitans*, and 2 *R. pipiens*. The eight control cases included 1 *B. terrestris*, 1 *H. cinerea*, 2 *H. crucifer*, 2 *R. clamitans*, and 2 *R. pipiens*.

Tests of vision. The ability of these 22 animals to localize objects in space was tested regularly over a ten-day period beginning about one week after the first signs of recovery of function. A minimum of 8 trials per day was recorded for each animal. A housefly impaled on the end of a thin wire set endwise in a glass rod handle served as the lure. This lure was presented in different sectors of the visual field in random order. It was held with a slight oscillatory motion because the animals apparently strike almost exclusively at moving objects. Care was taken in testing visual localization to eliminate sensory cues other than visual and to avoid misleading reflections of the test object from the glass walls of the containers.

Results with unrotated eye. After recovery the control cases with eyes in normal position had no difficulty in locating and catching flies presented in any sector of the visual field. They struck with normal accuracy at the lure within the 15 cm. range tested. Although attempts to approach the lure from distances as great as 40 cm. were noticed a few times in some of the more aggressive animals, no systematic tests were conducted at these greater distances because of the great variability even among normal animals in tendency to respond. The animals made correctly directed preparatory turning movements of the head and body as the lure was moved about from one part of the visual field to another. That direction of movement was accurately perceived was further indicated by the fact that the more aggressive animals frequently struck and caught the lure as it was moving quite rapidly across the visual field in front of them.

The optokinetic response was also tested, but it proved to be rather variable in these adult anurans even before operation and not a very satisfactory index of visual recovery. Some animals showed quite good reactions while in others the response was barely discernible or lacking. Even the reactions of individual cases varied considerably from one test to another. In general the reactions were about the same in the control cases after recovery as they had been in preoperative tests. In the two animals which recovered on only one side, however, responses toward the seeing side were absent. The optokinetic reactions after recovery were always correctly correlated with the direction of rotation of the visual field. All tests indicated that the recovered vision in the control group was normal in character and not confusedly blurred as might have been expected if functional termination of the regenerating fibers in the visual centers had been random and non-selective.

It should perhaps be pointed out that the term "normal" is used in describing these results merely in a qualitative sense to distinguish normal from randomly confused vision and from reversed vision. It is quite possible that quantitatively the recovered vision was not up to normal standards. Visual acuity and intensity discrimination, for example, might well have been subnormal without noticeably affecting the animals' proficiency within the range covered by these tests. Crude tests of the size of moving objects at which the animals would strike, however, failed to reveal any significant difference between the operated and unoperated animals. Also, the term covers only the particular capacities involved in localizing small objects in space (in the adults) and in making correct optokinetic reactions (in the tadpoles). Form perception, such as it is in amphibians, color discrimination, if present (11), and any other aspect of visual function not involved in these tests may or may not have been normal in character after nerve regeneration. At the same time it must be recognized that the localization of objects in space is very probably in adult anurans the primary and most highly specialized function of vision.

Results with rotated eye. Localization of the lure by the experimental cases in which the eye had been rotated was from the start reversed about the optic axis. When a fly was held in front of the animals within easy jumping distance, they wheeled rapidly to the rear instead of striking forward. Contrariwise when the lure was held in back of them and a little to the side they struck forward into space. When the animals came to rest in such a position that the lure could be presented well below eye level, they tilted the head upward and snapped at the air above. When the lure was held above the head and a little caudad to the eye the animals struck downward in front of them and got a mouthful of mud and moss. When the lure was presented successively in front of the animals they kept shifting around in circles as if the lure had appeared behind them each time instead of in front. This brief description of the reversed reactions applies particularly to the responses of the specimens of R. clamitans and R. pipiens and also to the tree frogs when they were resting on the bottom of the terraria rather than clinging vertically to the walls. The picture was of course somewhat different in the tree frogs when responding from a vertical position and in the toads, which struck mainly with a rapid flick of the tongue. The essential reversal of the striking reactions, however, was clearly evident in all 14 cases. As in the adult urodele, Triturus, and in the tadpoles the results in these adult anurans showed that the character of the recovered vision is determined systematically by intrinsic anatomical relations irrespective of the functional adequacy for the organism.

There was a definite decrease in tendency to display the optokinetic response to movement of the visual field after eye rotation. In 12 of the 14 cases optokinetic reactions could be elicited in some degree in preoperatives tests but only four (1 R. pipiens, 1 H. crucifer, and 2 H. squirella) displayed discernible optokinetic reactions after recovery. In 5 of the 14 cases the contralateral nerve had been sectioned 8 days prior to section of the nerve of the rotated eye in order to test in the interval the effect of eye rotation alone with the original nerve connections intact. When tested all five showed nicely reversed striking responses, but only two (both H. squirella) showed any optokinetic reactions to rotation of the visual field. In both these cases the responses were reversed and abnormally exaggerated. Both animals also showed spontaneous turning movements of the head and body whenever they were aroused from their characteristic repose. These movements were made toward the blind side and were thus comparable to the spontaneous circus movements displayed by the tadpoles and adult *Triturus* (8) after eye rotation. After nerve regeneration in these 5 cases, the optokinetic responses were the same as before nerve section, *i.e.*, absent in 3 cases and reversed and abnormally exaggerated in the two *H. squirella*. Apparently the failure in the majority of cases to get as good optokinetic reactions in reverse as were made in the correct direction preoperatively was thus correlated with eye rotation and not with optic nerve regeneration. Since the spatial localization of small objects was a decidedly more critical test for the purpose of the present experiments, no further attempts were made through adaptation of the testing apparatus and method to obtain more consistent elicitation of the optokinetic reflex. In the 4 cases which exhibited the optokinetic response after recovery, it was made in reverse.

Effect of experience. After the reversed nature of the recovered vision had been ascertained, the animals were thereafter fed and tested only irregularly and no special attempt was made to determine the anurans' ability to correct reversed visual reactions by the learning process over an extended period of time. The following observations are therefore only suggestive, not conclusive.

All 14 of the adult cases with rotated eyes were kept at least 30 days after recovery of vision and four were kept longer than 70 days. Eight of the animals, never especially voracious feeders in the laboratory, showed no reliable change in their tendency to respond in reverse. Four cases, two of which had at first been quite aggressive in their misguided efforts to catch the lure, gradually became less responsive and finally refused to strike at the lure at all. After reaching this state, however, they also refused to eat even when flies were brought into direct contact with the nose, the regular method by which the animals with reverse vision were fed. It was thus not entirely clear in these four cases that the gradual decrease in frequency and vigor of reversed reactions was indicative of learning. Two other cases sacrificed at 78 and 83 days after recovery remained, on the other hand, particularly active and aggressive to the end in their misdirected attempts to catch the lure whenever it came in sight.

During the post-recovery period living flies placed periodically in the terraria with the animals with reversed vision remained uncaught except for the few that lighted or walked directly upon the animals, whereas they were immediately snatched up when placed in terraria with the animals with unrotated eyes which had recovered normal vision. The reversed optokinetic reactions and the spontaneous circus movements observed in the two *H. squirella* were still present at 40 days and 44 days after recovery when the animals were sacrificed. Thus in summary, there was a suggestion that the adult anuran may in some cases learn to inhibit the useless reversed reactions, but no indication in any case of a positive correction.

Retinal Projection on the Optic Lobe

In trying to determine how the central associations are formed in regeneration it becomes important to know whether fibers from any given retinal region have to make their way to a special localized area of the optic lobe in order to establish correct functional relations or whether it makes no difference in which region of the optic lobe the ingrowing fibers happen to terminate. If there exists an orderly projection of the retina upon the optic lobe, localized lesions therein should produce scotomas or blind spots in the visual field. Such blind spots should be detectable by noting the sectors of the visual field in which a lure can be held without eliciting any response, provided, of course, the animals respond readily when the lure is shifted into other sectors.

The anurans are exceptionally suitable for this type of test. Their tendency to remain in a set position for long intervals without any movement of head or eyes makes it easy to bring the test object into such position as to stimulate only the particular retinal area desired. The fact that responses to the lure are made primarily with the head and body without any appreciable independent exploratory movement of the eyeball also makes for clear-cut results. Walls' (11) statement, however, that "no amphibian is known to perform any eye movements other than retraction and elevation" is hardly accurate. Rotatory and turning movements of the eye in the orbit are pronounced and striking in the tadpole. Such movements are also common, though of less amplitude, in adult frogs and toads. These movements, however, seem to be associated primarily with vestibular reflexes, and if any initial exploratory movements of the eyeball occur independently of head and body movements, they are certainly so slight as to be negligible factors as far as the following experiments are concerned.

Operations. Tests were run first on 15 animals (1 *B. terrestris*, 5 *H. cinerea*, 7 *R. clamitans*, and 2 *R. pipiens*) with normal optic nerves. Lesions involving one half to two thirds of the entire lobe were made bilaterally in the anterior, dorsal and posterior portions of the lobe, each type of lesion being made in five animals. There was no attempt to produce lesions in the ventral portion, mainly because of the difficulty of avoiding injury to afferent and efferent fibers running to and from the other parts of the lobe. After the skin had been cut and reflected the cranium was broken away in small pieces and the outer meninges were cut or torn off until the dorsal aspect of the lobes was completely exposed. The lesions were begun with fine-pointed jewelers' forceps and completed by the suction method using a drawn-out point of glass tubing about 0.3 mm. inside diameter. Animals were selected which were hungry and approached and struck readily at the lure when it was presented from any direction above, below, behind, or in front of them.

When tested within an hour after operation the five animals with the anterior part of the lobe intact made no response when the lure was shown in the back part of the visual field but struck vigorously and accurately when it was shown in front. The five animals in which the ventral part of the lobe remained intact made no response when the lure was presented anywhere in the visual field above them but turned or struck forward readily when it was presented below eye level. When the lure was presented behind the five cases in which the posterior part of the lobe was intact, they turned quickly so as to face the lure in preparation to strike just as do normal animals but, when they had thus turned and the lure was directly in front of them, they made no further response until it was again moved into the back part of the visual field. By repeating the performance these animals could be made to turn around in circles without ever striking at the lure although they came into a good striking position with each turn. These 15 cases were again tested on several occasions during the following three days with similar results.

That the retina normally is projected upon the optic lobe in an orderly manner with the retinal axes reversed in the tectum is clearly indicated by these effects of tectal lesions. The results confirm the conclusions regarding tectal termination of optic fibers in anurans reached by Ströer (10) on the basis of anatomical studies. Just how precise, that is, how close to a point-to-point correlation, the retinal projection is in these anurans cannot, of course, be deduced from the above results. The observations can be taken to indicate only grossly the existence of an orderly projection of the retinal field upon the optic lobe.

Retinal Projection After Nerve Regeneration

Since the redistribution of nerve fibers in regeneration has elsewhere been shown to be indiscriminate both in mammals (4) and in amphibians (14) the question arose as to whether the systematic projection of the optic fibers on the tectum might not be drastically disarranged after regeneration, necessitating a rather complete reorganization of secondary synaptic associations in the optic lobe. Accordingly, tectal lesions similar to the preceding were made in a group of animals which had recovered vision following complete severance and regeneration of the optic nerve.

Operations. Eight cases (1 *B. terrestris*, 4 *H. cinerea*, 1 *H. squirella*, 1 *R. clamitans*, and 1 *R. pipiens*) were selected which had recovered normal vision after optic nerve regeneration and were quite aggressive in their attempts to approach and snap at the lure when it was presented in any part of the visual field. Anterior lesions were made in 4 cases, posterior in 2 cases, and medial lesions in the remaining 2. Anterior lesions were stressed because the behavioral check is more strikingly conclusive. Under normal conditions an animal partially disinclined to strike at the lure will often not shift the head and body in order to get at the lure to the rear but will strike forward where the lure is easily accessible. Thus animals that would turn around to get at the lure as they did after anterior lesions in the above cases would certainly strike at the lure directly in front of them if it could be seen. Three of the eight cases were selected from the control group and the remaining five, all unilateral, were chosen from a group of extra cases prepared especially for the purpose.

The types of scotoma produced in these cases with regenerated optic nerves conformed consistently with those which had resulted in the foregoing group of normal animals. Posterior lesions abolished responses to the lure held behind, dorsal lesions to the lure held above, and anterior lesions to the lure held in front of the animals. Two additional cases (*B. terrestris*, *H. squirella*) from the experimental group which had recovered reversed vision were also tested. A lesion in the anterior part of the optic lobe in one of them abolished responses to the lure presented behind the animal. When the lure was held in front, this animal responded by turning around to the rear in characteristic reversed manner. In the other case a medial tectal lesion

abolished responses to the lure when it was held below eye level but did not eliminate the reversed reactions to the lure when it was presented well above eye level. From the nature of the scotomas produced by tectal lesions in these ten cases with regenerated optic nerves it may be concluded that the ingrowing optic fibers reestablish functional associations in the same topographic areas of the optic lobe in which they originally terminated and that no major reorganization of secondary synaptic relations is involved in the recovery of function.

Anatomical Checks

All cases in which recovery of vision was absent or deficient, 2 tadpoles and 3 adults which recovered normal vision, and 3 tadpoles and 7 adults which recovered reversed vision were prepared for microscopic examination by the Bodian (1) method. The optic nerve was sectioned longitudinally in different planes at 10μ. The findings in those cases in which visual recovery was unsuccessful have already been mentioned.

The point at which the optic nerve had been cut was recognizable, particularly in the adult animals, by an enlargement of the nerve trunk through which individual fibers and small fiber bundles took intertwined and tortuous routes. From the entangled appearance of the neuromatous scar region it was apparent that there had not been an orderly fiber outgrowth in bridging the gap between the distal and proximal nerve stumps. The systematic restoration of proper central linkages in spite of chaotic outgrowth across the nerve gap seems unaccountable except on the assumption that fibers from different retinal regions have specific inherent properties which influence selectively the formation of central associations.

Because of the small size and great number of fibers in the optic nerve of these anurans— Breusch and Arey (2) estimate 29,000 fibers in *R. pipiens*—the histological picture was too complicated to make possible any inferences regarding the question of whether or not the regenerating fibers attain an orderly segregation in the proximal stump or in the central tracts en route to the optic lobe. The results of tectal lesions do not settle the question because it is possible that the ingrowing fibers reach the optic lobe with a random distribution but only those succeed in establishing functional synaptic connections which happen by chance to enter their proper area.

Postmortem examination of the tectal lesions revealed that their general location was as intended, but there was considerable variation in border outline. The nature of the lesions and also of the behavioral tests did not permit any detailed quantitative comparisons of the precision of retinal projection in normal and regenerated nerves.

COMMENT

The foregoing data on recovery of vision after optic nerve regeneration in six different species of anuran amphibians support the previous conclusions based on visual recovery in the urodele *Triturus* (8). These conclusions and their logical basis are, briefly, as follows: Since stimulation of different retinal areas evokes different responses, each retinal locus must possess functional connections with the brain centers differing from those of all other areas. After optic nerve regeneration these differential relations between retina and visual centers are systematically restored in their original form, as shown by tests of optokinetic responses and visual localization of small objects. This orderly restoration of central reflex relations occurs regardless of the orientation of the retina, despite a maladaptive effect for the organism, and must therefore be regulated by growth factors independently of functional adaptation. As this would otherwise be impossible the ingrowing optic fibers must possess specific properties of some sort by which they are differentially distinguished in the centers according to their respective retinal origins. The previous discussion of these points with some of their implications (8) is in large part applicable to the present data and need not be repeated.

The orderly topographical arrangement of functional relations found in the optic lobe after optic nerve regeneration is difficult to explain without assuming that the secondary neurons of the optic tectum are also biochemically dissimilar, possessing differential affinities for fibers arising from different retinal quadrants. The results thus lend further support to the supposition that neurons of the central nervous system are specified biochemically in much greater degree than is evident from their morphological variations. A degree of central neuron specification is indicated which approaches the degree of innate functional differentiation and which presumably plays an important role in the ontogenetic determination and differentiation of inherent integrating patterns.

Where the functional properties within central nuclei have an orderly distribution corresponding with anatomical dimensions as in the anuran optic lobe, it is conceivable that a basic embryonic specification arises through central self-differentiation of the nuclear mass itself. Under such conditions the conjecture that specification of the tectal neurons may be induced via the more early differentiating motor and adjustor systems becomes unnecessary, although later acquisition of afferent and efferent relations may well result in further individuation superimposed upon the initial nuclear field.

The conclusion that function is not the organizing factor in the reestablishment of systematic reflex relations in these experiments in no way contradicts the possibility that function, as a generalized, non-specific factor, may be of importance for the normal healthy maintenance and development of nerve structures. That neuron discharge acts by itself in any specific manner, in optic nerve regeneration to regulate the formation of proper rather than improper or indiscriminate reflex associations, however, seems untenable. An inherent physico-chemical differentiation of the optic fibers must be inferred.

That such neuron differentiation is extremely important in the establishment of proper linkages between centers and peripheral end organs, in amphibians at least, becomes increasingly evident. Whether these linkages are determined primarily on a physiological basis involving specific modes of excitatory discharge and selective detection as envisaged in the resonance principle (13) or depend upon specific structural associations the formation of which is regulated through the influence of peripheral differentiation on central synaptic growth, as more recently proposed (6, 8), remains uncertain. The excitatory characteristics of mononeural connections between receptor and effector organs (12) and the fact that separate muscles which function asynchronously can be excited independently in their normal action phase by branches of a single motor axon (13, 14) seem more satisfactorily explained by the resonance principle. Until these latter phenomena have been more thoroughly studied, however, it seems advisable to stress at present the alternative possibility of interpreting effects of neuron specification on a more orthodox connectionist basis.

SUMMARY

1. In larval and adult anurans of six different species regeneration of the optic nerve resulted in a return of visual perception which was well organized, not an intermingled confusion. Distinct and consistent responses to position and direction of movement of objects in the visual field were recovered.

2. The orientation of visuomotor responses after recovery, however, was dependent upon the orientation of the retina. It was normal in animals whose retinas had been left in normal position but reversed about the optic axis in animals whose retinas had been rotated through 180 degrees prior to nerve section.

3. The location of scotomas produced by localized lesions in the optic tectum after optic nerve regeneration indicated that optic fibers from different retinal loci had reestablished functional connections in the same areas of the optic lobe to which they had originally projected.

REFERENCES

1. BODIAN, D. A new method for staining nerve fibers and nerve endings in mounted paraffin sections. *Anat. Rec.*, 1936, *65:* 89–97.
2. BRUESCH, S. R., AND AREY, L. B. The number of myelinated and unmyelinated fibers in the optic nerve of vertebrates. *J. comp. Neurol.*, 1942, *77:* 631–665.
3. HARGITT, C. Behavior and color changes of tree frogs. *J. anim. Behav.*, 1912, *2:* 51–78.
4. KILVINGTON, B. Some experiments on nerve regeneration. *Aust. N. Z. J. Surg.*, 1941, *10:* 266–272.
5. NOBLE, G. K. *The biology of the Amphibia.* New York, McGraw-Hill Book Co., Inc., 1931, 577 pp.
6. SPERRY, R. The effect of crossing nerves to antagonistic muscles in the hind limb of the rat. *J. comp. Neurol.*, 1941, *75:* 1–19.
7. SPERRY, R. Effect of 180 degree rotation of the retinal field on visuomotor coördination. *J. exp. Zool.*, 1943, *92:* 263–279.
8. SPERRY, R. Visuomotor coördination in the newt (Triturus viridescens) after regeneration of the optic nerve. *J. comp. Neurol.*, 1943, *79:* 33–55.
9. STONE, L. S., and ZAUR, I. Reimplantation and transplantation of adult eyes in the salamander (Triturus viridescens) with return of vision. *J. exp. Zool.*, 1940, *85:* 243–269.
10. STRÖER, W. F. H. Zur vergleichenden Anatomie des primären optischen Systems bei Wirbeltieren. *Z. Anat. EntwGesch.*, 1939, *110:* 301–321.
11. WALLS, G. *The vertebrate eye.* Bloomfield Hills, Mich., The Cranbrook Press, 1942, 785 pp.
12. WEISS, P. Experimental innervation of muscles by the central ends of afferent nerves (establishment of a one-neurone connection between receptor and effector organ), with functional tests. *J. comp. Neurol.*, 1935, *61:* 135–174.
13. WEISS, P. Selectivity controlling the central-peripheral relations in the nervous system. *Biol. Rev.*, 1936, *11:* 494–531.
14. WEISS, P. Further experimental investigations on the phenomenon of homologous response in transplanted amphibian limbs. II. Nerve regeneration and the innervation of transplanted limbs. *J. comp. Neurol.*, 1937, *66:* 481–535.

6. The Effect of Cradling Practices upon the Onset of Walking in Hopi Children *

Wayne Dennis and Marsena G. Dennis

Although ontogenetic development proceeds along several dimensions, two are of special importance to psychology. The first of these includes the rigid and irreversible changes that occur in all organs and cells as a consequence of growth and aging. This process is called maturation. The second consists of more plastic and reversible changes that are restricted to cells in the nervous system. Such changes are brought about by practice and experience through the process called learning. Although the emergence of any behavioral capability is usually the product of a combination of these processes, some abilities are more dependent on maturation while others are more dependent on learning.

In the following article, the Dennises explode the commonsense view that a child *learns* to walk by showing that practice plays a much smaller part in determining the time at which walking begins than does aging. Their research takes advantage of an unusual child-rearing practice among the Hopi Indians and illustrates the potential contribution to psychology that can be made by the related science of anthropology.

The custom of placing the infant in a device which restrains his movements occurs in many parts of the world. A study of the effects of such restriction of movement should have considerable importance for an understanding of the factors which control the motor development of the young child.

* Reprinted by permission of Professor Wayne Dennis and the *Journal of Genetic Psychology,* 1940, *56,* 77-86.

The present paper reports such a study among the Hopi Indians of Arizona. Fortunately among the Hopi it is possible to find the conditions which are necessary to an investigation of the effects of restraint; namely, a group of people which makes use of cradles; and a second group, similar in race and culture to the first group, but which does not place its infants under the same restriction.

A. CRADLING CUSTOMS OF THE HOPI

Of the present-day Hopi villages, all make use of cradle boards, except the towns of New Oraibi and of Upper Moencopi. The latter two villages have become Americanized to the extent of giving up the use of the cradle. They have also adopted American dress, have given up some of their ceremonies, and in general are less conservative than are the other Hopi towns. Nevertheless, their diet, their nursing customs, and their child rearing practices apart from the use of the cradle board remain virtually unchanged. New Oraibi and Upper Moencopi, therefore, furnish a nearly ideal comparison group for the purpose of contrasting Hopi infants who have not been placed on the cradle with those who have been subjected to this custom.

Hopi culture has been studied extensively. Adequate bibliographies to the anthropological material may be found in the work of Beals (2) and of Murdock (9). However, the Hopi cradling practices have not been described in detail by previous writers and the following account is taken in the main from the authors' own researches.**

In former times the Hopi of all villages used a woven cradle made from the small branches of the sumac *Schmaltzia Trilobata*, but at the present time this cradle is seldom used except on First Mesa, from which only a few of our data are derived. Elsewhere the woven cradle, which required considerable labor and skill for its construction, has been replaced by a heavy board about one foot wide and about two and one-half feet long. At one end of the board is fastened a face- or head-guard of stiff heavy wire. This simple device constitutes the cradle on which the infant is firmly secured.

In order to place the infant on the board, the child, naked or wearing a shirt or diaper, is put on a cotton blanket which lies on the board. The infant's arms are extended by his sides and the right side of the blanket is pulled tight over the right arm and is put between the left arm and the left side and tucked under the infant's body. The left side of the blanket is then pulled firmly over the left arm and tucked under the right side of the child. The part of the blanket which extends beyond the feet is folded back under the infant's legs and buttocks. The infant, thus wrapped, is tied to the board by strips of cloth which encircle the baby and the board. The wrapping includes the legs which are thus fastened so that they can be flexed only to a slight degree. The infant is so firmly wrapped and tied that he cannot turn his body and cannot release his hands from the bindings. Only the head which rests on a small pillow or pad of folded cloth is relatively free to move. A piece of thin cloth is placed over the face guard in order to darken the face of the child and to exclude the flies. The cradle, with the infant upon it, lies upon the floor or upon a bed. It is never placed vertically, and is seldom carried about.

** See especially *The Hopi Child*. New York: D. Appleton-Century, 1940. P. 225.

The infant is thus bound to the board on the first day of life and for the first three months he spends nearly all of his hours in this position. Although he is taken off one or more times daily, either for bathing or for replacing soiled cloths, these operations do not consume many minutes and he is returned to the board when they are completed. The infant nurses while tied to the board, the cradle with the child attached being held to the mother's breast. He sleeps on the board at night as well as by day.

It will be seen that the cradle deprives the infant of nearly all freedom of movement during the early months. These months, of course, are largely devoted to sleep, but nevertheless the importance of "random movements" which occur during this period has been stressed by many writers.

After the early months the cradle board continues to be used in the same general manner as formerly, but the number of hours per day spent upon the board gradually decreases. In the later months the degree of freedom of the infant varies from mother to mother and from child to child. The infant may be permitted daily to spend some time unhampered upon the floor. More commonly he is held in arms or on the lap for a while each day. The amount of time spent off of the cradle gradually increases. However, night sleep and daytime naps continue to be taken while he is tied to the board, and on awaking the infant is left upon the board until he becomes restive.

The time at which the cradle is discarded varies greatly. Nearly all of those mothers who use it employ it for at least six months. Some mothers use it for more than a year. In the case of 14 of our subjects, we inquired concerning the duration of cradle board usage. With these cases the average duration of cradling was 9 months, with a range of from 4 to 14 months.

In the two progressive villages the majority of mothers use no restraining devices at all. The infant is dressed in shirt and diaper and covered loosely by a blanket, with his hands free. He is placed in a basket or bas-sinet or child's bed with no more restraint than accompanies such a position among white American children.

The present report deals only with the age at which the infants of the two groups begin to walk, although data concerning the onset of other motor performances would be desirable. Information concerning the onset of walking was obtained from moth-ers' reports. Whether or not the cradle board had been used was also determined in each case. The data were gathered in the summers of 1937 and 1938. The fact that we lived for two summers among Hopi gives us much more confidence in the data than we would have if we had obtained our material from mothers whom we did not know personally.

B. METHOD OF GATHERING DATA

In the gathering of the data for any pueblo we were accompanied by a young woman who was a native of the village. As a rule the interviews were conducted in English, but in some cases the Hopi lan-guage was used and our guide served as an interpreter.

Where it was possible, we saw all of the children of a village who were between two and six years of age. Children who were under two years of age are not included in the tabulations, as many children less than two years of age cannot walk and, hence, records of walking for this group would be necessarily incomplete. Only a few chil-dren over six years of age were included because we felt that the mother's memory would be less reliable if it covered a period of that length. In all, we secured data on 63 children who had used the board and on 42 children who had not used it.

C. RELIABILITY OF DATA

Among the Hopi, the Gregorian calendar is almost universally used, the birthdays of the children are known, and an accurate knowledge of walking ages seems to prevail.

When asked at what age a given child began to walk, the pueblo mother, after a few moments, gave a reply such as, "*A year and one month and a few days,*" or "*Two days before the first birthday,*" or something equally circumstantial. While we have no check on this point, we are of the opinion that the mothers who were interviewed gave information as accurate as that ob-tained from white mothers.[1]

One indication of the relative accuracy of the data lies in the fact that there is no unusual grouping of cases in any one month, as shown in Table 1. The cases at one year

TABLE 1

Age of Onset of Walking

Age in months	Hopi using board	Hopi not using board	Tewa
24–24.9	2	2	1
23–23.9	1	0	0
22–22.9	0	0	1
21–21.9	0	0	0
20–20.9	1	0	0
19–19.9	4	0	2
18–18.9	7	6	5
17–17.9	0	0	1
16–16.9	3	4	1
15–15.9	3	6	1
14–14.9	15	6	10
13–13.9	6	8	3
12–12.9	10	6	14
11–11.9	9	2	5
10–10.9	2	1	0
9– 9.9	0	1	2
Total cases	63	42	46
Average	14.98	15.05	14.45
Average exclud-ing cases be-yond 21.0 months	14.53	14.57	14.05
Standard deviation	2.62	2.24	2.60

[1] This is not true of the Navaho. At the present time only a few Navaho understand and make use of our calendar. We gathered the walking ages of 55 Navaho children. Of these, 43 of the re-ports were in terms of "*one year,*" "*a year and a half,*" or "*two years.*" In other words, only 12 in 55 were reported in terms of months. We have not thought it advisable to present these data. However, they agree roughly with the material here presented.

and at 18 months exceed those of the adjacent months, but scarcely more so than do the reports of white mothers (12).

In questioning the mothers, we asked how old the child was when he first began to walk by himself. If further definition was necessary, we asked when the first steps alone were taken. By examining a number of pueblo infants who were just "beginning to walk" we were able to determine that the phrase "beginning to walk" or its Indian equivalent means taking one or more steps alone which is the criterion that has been used by most investigators. This performance is a point of interest to Hopi parents and is noticed and remembered by them. There was no indication that the phrase differed in meaning for the two classes of mothers.

Our subjects were approximately evenly divided as to sex.

D. PRESENTATION OF DATA

Smith *et al.* (12) have held that children who begin to walk at an age greater than 21.0 months seem to make a separate group statistically and that all or nearly all such cases may be instances of retardation due to malnutrition or disease. We have computed averages for our data by two methods, one excluding and one including the most retarded cases among our subjects. The difference between these averages is approximately .5 of a month. Since we wished to compare our material with that of Smith *et al.*, our sigmas were computed with the retarded cases excluded, as was done by the authors just mentioned.

Table 1 presents the distribution of the ages of walking recorded by us, together with the averages and standard deviations.

It will be seen that the infants who used the cradle board and those who did not use it differ in average age of onset of walking by only seven-hundredths of a month if we include all cases (the averages being respectively 14.98 months and 15.05 months), and by only four-hundredths of a month if

we exclude the cases beyond 21.0 months. This means a difference between the averages of from one to two days. The average age at walking of those who used the cradle board, in both comparisons, is slightly less than those who did not. Since the differences are quite insignificant, there is no evidence of an effect of the cradle board upon walking. Also, included in Table 1 are the walking ages of 46 children from the Tewa villages of Santa Clara, San Ildefonso, and San Juan. These data were gathered in the same manner as the data concerning the Hopi. It will be seen that the average age of walking among the Tewa children is not significantly different from that of the Hopi groups.

We have shown in a previous communication that the Tewa use a cradle only for daytime naps, a practice which is intermediate to the customs of our two Hopi groups. The lack of a significant difference between the Tewa children and either of the Hopi groups confirms the previous finding that cradling customs do not influence the age of walking. At the same time, the close agreement between the data of the Hopi and the Tewa groups—who differ considerably in language and culture—tends to show the reliability of our method.

We feel that the results of this study are in accord with recent experimental studies on the relation of training to maturation. In general the experimental studies show that additional training or practice above a certain minimum has very little effect upon infant behavior. The Hopi infants, while restrained during many hours of the day, are not totally restrained and apparently the activity which is permitted is sufficient to provide the necessary opportunities for motor learning. We see no contradiction in the fact that the Hopi infants are not affected by the cradling practices, while two infants which the present writers subjected to restriction of practice (4) did show retardation in a few responses. In regard to a few responses our experimental subjects were entirely withheld from practice, whereas the Hopi infant who is kept on a cradle board is nevertheless free to act as he pleases several hours per day during the second half of the first year. It will be recalled that our experimental subjects, when given an opportunity, established the missing items in their repertoire with much less than the usual amount of practice.

It is our view that unhampered and healthy infants exhibit motility far in excess of the activity which at any stage of maturation leads to the establishment of the responses characteristic of that stage. Just as it has been found that nature is prodigal in that she has supplied the individual with more kidney tissue and more lung tissue than is ordinarily needed for normal functioning, so apparently has she been prodigal in eliciting in the infant more activity than is needed in the formation of new responses. That is why additional practice has little or no effect upon the infant, and it is likewise the reason why a considerable degree of restraint has no influence upon the behavioral repertoire. We do believe, however, that if activity were reduced below a certain minimum, be-

havioral development would then be affected.

No data have been published on the motor development of other Indian children, except for some casual observations by Hrdlicka (8). However, there is available a considerable body of material on the walking ages of children of other races and cultures, and it may be of interest to compare the averages of other groups with the averages of our Indian subjects.

Table 2 presents the Indian averages in comparison with the results of other studies which have used the method of mothers' reports. Since Smith *et al.* subjected several sets of data to a treatment uniform with ours, our citations in several instances are to the data as presented by Smith and her co-authors rather than to the original data.

It will be seen that the Hopi average is one month greater than the slowest of the comparison groups. This difference is statistically reliable and the other differences of course yield very high reliabilities. In comparison with the most advanced groups of white subjects, the Hopi children are practically two months retarded. While the

TABLE 2

Average Age of Walking Among
Various Groups *

Race	Location	Average	Sigma	No. of S's	Investigator
White	Seattle	12.77	2.23	831	S. Smith (13)
White	California	12.94	2.22	556	Terman, *et al.* (12)
White	United States	12.97	2.35	217	Hrdlicka (3)
White	California	13.20	1.95	61	Bayley (1)
White	Various	13.21	1.68	25	Biographies (6)
Various	Hawaii	13.25	2.27	721	Smith, *et al.* (12)
White	California	13.29	2.20	252	Pyles, *et al.* (10)
White	Iowa	13.47	1.96	108	Smith, *et al.* (12)
White	New York	13.55	1.55	49	Mead (12)
Hopi Indians	Arizona	14.55	2.51	100	
Tewa Indians	New Mexico	14.05	2.60	44	

* It may be objected that, if our table included Shirley's data, then the Indian average would not seem unusual, for the average age of walking of Shirley's subjects was 14.8 months. Her data are not listed with the others because they were gathered by a different method. In the course of periodic visits to the home, Shirley recorded whether or not she saw the child walk alone. A child might have taken a few steps sometime earlier, but unless this recurred during the examiner's visit he was not said to be walking. This definition of walking is different from the criterion here employed, and averages based on Shirley's method are necessarily greater than averages derived from mothers' reports of the first steps. The inclusion of both types of data in one table would lead to confusion and misunderstanding.

differences in central tendency are marked, it should be noted that the ranges of all groups are nearly identical, and the variability relative to the mean is quite large in all studies.

At the present time we have no information which leads to an understanding of the retardation of the Indian children. Several possible explanations suggest themselves. In the first place, the difference may be due to a constant overestimation of walking ages by the Indian mothers, or of underestimation by the women of the other groups. In our opinion, the differences are too great to be explained in this manner, although it must be admitted that the error of estimation of the Indian women is not known. Pyles *et al.* found that white American mothers, reporting on age of walking when the children were 21 months of age, underestimated the age of walking as determined by direct observation by only four-tenths of a month, whereas the difference between groups is sometimes as great as two months.

The likelihood that the groups made use of different criteria of "walking" is naturally suggested. We have already described the measures which we employed to obtain a criterion which, we feel, is comparable with that used in other studies. It is our opinion that Table 2 refers to real differences and not to differences in estimates and in criteria.

Had we not found the cradle board to be without effect, it would have been natural to turn to it as a plausible explanation of the differences. But the present evidence shows that we must turn to other causes.

One of these may be the altitude at which these Indians live, which is between 6,000 and 7,000 feet above sea level. Another environmental possibility of explanation would be a dietary one, as the diet of the pueblo child differs markedly from that of the American child. But such speculation is fruitless without further research.

However, our present data force us to point out the dubious correctness of the suggestion made by Smith and her associates (12) that age of walking is greatly influenced by the amount of sunshine and by the average annual temperature. These investigators point out that walking is earlier in Hawaii than in California, and earlier in California than in Iowa and New York, and they note that these regions differ in the same manner in respect to mean annual temperature and hours of sunshine. Yet the pueblo children are the latest walkers thus far reported, in spite of the cloudlessness and the comparative warmth of the Southwest, a fact which would seem to negate whatever evidence other data may have contributed to the theory of climatic influences on the onset of walking.

E. SUMMARY

Hopi children who are subjected to considerable restraint of movement by being bound to a cradle board for most of the day during a large part of the first year of life are no slower in beginning to walk than are the children of more acculturated Hopi mothers who have given up the use of the cradle board. The infants who are placed on the cradle board do nevertheless have some opportunities to practice coördinations which may lead to walking. Restraint of the infant is most marked in the early months, and freedom of movement is greatest in the months just preceding the onset of walking.

The lack of influence of cradling upon the onset of walking is interpreted as showing that the activity of the unhampered child is greatly in excess of the activity required to develop the characteristic infantile responses. Movement can be markedly restrained without influence upon walking, and probably without influence upon other responses. It is not held, however, that all movement or all practice could be dispensed with without effect upon behavioral development.

Hopi infants, those who are unhampered as well as those who are restrained, begin to walk at an average age which is four to eight weeks beyond the average age for this performance in any groups previously reported. The cause of this retardation of the Hopi children was not ascertained in the present study.

REFERENCES

1. BAYLEY, N. The development of motor abilities during the first three years. *Monog. Soc. Res. Child Devel.*, 1935, No. 1. Pp. 26.
2. BEALS, R. A preliminary report on the ethnography of the Southwest. Berkeley, Calif.: Nat. Park Service, Field Division of Education, 1935. Pp. 77.
3. DENNIS, W. The age at walking of children who run on all fours. *Child Devel.*, 1934, 5, 92–93.
4. ———. The effect of restricted practice upon the reaching, sitting, and standing of two infants. *J. Genet. Psychol.*, 1935, 47, 17–32.
5. ———. Infant development under conditions of restricted practice and of minimum social stimulation: A preliminary report. *J. Genet. Psychol.*, 1938, 53, 149–158.
6. DENNIS, W., & DENNIS, M. G. Behavioral development in the first year as shown by forty biographies. *Psychol., Rec.*, 1937, 1, 347–362.
7. ———. Cradles and cradling practices of the Pueblo Indians. *Amer. Anthropol.*, 1940, 42, 107–115.
8. HRDLICKA, A. Psychological and Medical Observations among Indians of Southwestern United States and Northern Mexico. Washington, D. C.: Gov't. Printing Office, 1908. Pp. 460.
9. MURDOCK, P. G. Our Primitive Contemporaries. New York: Macmillan, 1934. Pp. 614.
10. PYLES, M. K., STOLZ, H. R., & MACFARLANE, J. W. The accuracy of mothers' reports on birth and developmental data. *Child Devel.*, 1935, 6, 165–176.
11. SHIRLEY, M. M. The First Two Years: I. Locomotor Development. Minneapolis: Univ. Minn. Press, 1931.
12. SMITH, M. E., LECKER, G., DUNLAP, J. W., & CURETON, E. E. The effects of race, sex, and environment on the age at which children walk. *J. Genet. Psychol.*, 1930, 38, 489–498.
13. SMITH, S. Influence of illness during the first two years on infant development. *J. Genet. Psychol.*, 1931, 39, 284–287.

THE NERVOUS SYSTEM AND BEHAVIOR

7. Discharges in Motor Nerves *

Edgar D. Adrian

In 1912, Adrian suggested that the results of a number of his experiments could best be explained by assuming that the size or magnitude of a nerve impulse is independent of the intensity of the stimulus which elicits it. This idea has come to be known as the "all-or-none" law of neural transmission: a neuron's axon either responds with a full-blown impulse or it does not respond at all.

* Reprinted by permission of the author and the University of Pennsylvania Press from *The Mechanism of Nervous Action*, 1932, Chapter 4, 61–64.

Although the "all-or-none" law is now universally accepted, it came as a surprise to the scientific community. At first, the objections to it seemed like good ones: "If neurons do not grade their response, small responses to weak stimuli and large responses to strong stimuli, then how is it possible to sense so many gradations in the intensity of stimulation?" or "Why, then, do muscles not move in jerks and twitches instead of steady sustained contractions with graded force?"

Having started this controversy, Adrian resolved it himself in a further series of experiments. This work culminated in a small book entitled *The Mechanism of Nervous Action*, and also in the Nobel Prize. The solution to the apparently incompatible observations of ungraded responses of axons on the one hand and graded contractions of muscles on the other, is contained in the following excerpts from that book.

The chief function of the central nervous system is to send messages to the muscles which will make the body move effectively as a whole, and for this to take place the contraction of each muscle must be capable of delicate adjustment. By recording the electrical changes in the motor nerve fibres and the muscles we can see how this adjustment is brought about and how the motor nerve cells behave under varying excitation. Much of the evidence has come from other methods, and the whole subject of muscular adjustment has been discussed most clearly by Sir Charles Sherrington (1931) in a recent Hughlings Jackson lecture; for this reason we need only consider certain aspects of the motor discharge which fit in with the general picture of nerve activity. Its study will not throw much light on the problems of the central mechanism, but will at least tell us how its activity is translated into movement.

The translation depends, as with the sensory messages, on a fusion of the effects of repeated impulses, and, like sensation, the contraction is graded by changes in the frequency of the impulses in each nerve fibre and in the number of fibres which are brought into play.

THE MOTOR UNITS

A single motor nerve fibre supplies a number of muscle fibres varying from twenty to a hundred or more, and all these muscle fibres act as a single unit. Each can be made to contract independently by direct stimulation, but as the nerve impulses cannot be graded, the contraction produced by an impulse must involve all the muscles fibres which make up the 'motor unit.' But although the motor units are incapable of fractional activity, there are quite enough of them in a muscle of medium size to allow a fairly delicate gradation of the contraction. For instance Eccles and Sherrington (1930) find that there are about 430 motor nerve fibres to the gastrocnemius of the cat and 250 to the soleus. Thus the contraction of the gastrocnemius might be varied by 430 steps merely by varying the number of motor nerve fibres in action.

There is no doubt that reflex and voluntary contractions are graded mainly in this way by changes in the number of units. This can be demonstrated very easily by recording the electric changes in the muscle with a needle electrode system, for it is then possible to detect the activity of more and more motor units as the contraction increases in force. Gradation by change in number is the only form possible when the contraction is a single twitch—due to a single volley of motor impulses—and in all very rapid movements it must be by far the most important factor. But in a sustained contraction there is obviously another possibility, namely, gradation by change in the frequency of the motor impulses.

Before we deal with the evidence which shows that this kind of gradation does occur we ought to consider how it can occur. A muscle fibre, like a nerve fibre, is said to follow the all-or-none principle: how then can it give contractions of graded strength? Questions of this kind are bound to arise whenever we deal in vaguely defined Laws or Principles, and the 'all-or-none principle' has been responsible for a great deal of confusion, because it has a simple title which seems to make further definition unnecessary. It would be wiser, I believe, to say not that muscle and nerve obey the principle but, that in both of them there is an 'all-or-nothing relation between the stimulus and the propagated disturbance,' for this expresses the facts in a form which is all the better for being less attractively phrased. The facts are that a stimulus to a sense organ, a nerve, or a muscle fibre produces local effects which vary with its strength, but the explosive waves which travel away from the affected region cannot be changed in intensity by making the stimulus stronger or weaker. They are not invariable, for they depend at each point on the state of the fibre at that point; and the relation holds only for the individual waves, for clearly the total activity of a nerve fibre per second may range from nothing to several hundred impulses. In a muscle fibre the propagated disturbance itself seems to differ only in time relations from the impulse in a nerve fibre; it gives the same kind of potential change, refractory state, and so on. But it has the further effect of setting off the contractile mechanism of the fibre and this may or may not be of the explosive type. When its activity is aroused by the passage of a single disturbance the tension cannot be graded according to the strength of the stimulus, since the propagated disturbance is not graded; but if several disturbances pass over the fibre in rapid succession the tension will rise higher and higher, each disturbance causing a fresh accession of contractile activity which is added to that existing previously.

All this is merely an elaborate way of stating the fact that successive contractions may be fused into a tetanus which gives a tension much higher than that developed in a single twitch. For the present we need not consider whether the summation of contractions depends on the mechanical properties of the muscle (viscosity, etc.) or on a summation of the physical and chemical changes which cause the contraction. All that matters is that in a sustained contraction, produced by stimulating the nerve repeatedly, the average tension will vary with the frequency of the stimuli as well as with the number of units in action.

The variation with frequency comes to an end when the impulses follow so closely that the contraction is perfectly smooth; it seems only to occur during the stage of 'incomplete tetanus' when the tension fluctuates with the rhythm of the stimulus. Thus if all the motor units are acting synchronously the muscle will not give a steady contraction until the frequency of stimulation is above the range in which grading can occur; but if the different units work independently the tension developed in the whole muscle may be steady enough, although each unit gives a jerky response. This is the state of affairs in reflex or voluntary contraction, though until the last few years the evidence seemed to point in another direction.

8. The Origin and General Properties of the Nervous System *

C. Judson Herrick

In 1948 a book was published which had a most unlikely title—*The Brain of the Tiger Salamander*. Still more unlikely, the book was dedicated to the salamanders themselves. It begins, "Salamanders are shy little animals, rarely seen and still more rarely heard. If it were not so, there would be no salamanders at all . . ." Its author was the greatest of America's neuroanatomists, C. Judson Herrick, and the book is already a classic of neurology.

* Reprinted by permission of the University of Texas Press from *The Evolution of Human Nature*, 1956, Chapter 19.

In it Herrick explains his interest in neuro-anatomy: "Traditionally, comparative neurology has been regarded as a subdivision of comparative anatomy, and so it is. But it is more than this. The most refined methods of anatomical analysis cannot reveal the things that are of greatest significance for an understanding of the nervous system. Our primary interest is in the behavior of the living body, and we study brains because these organs are the chief instruments which regulate behavior."

For most of his lifetime Herrick studied salamanders in order to understand human beings. After about fifty years he returned to the problem of human behavior, organized his diverse discoveries, and just before his death, wrote another book—this one entitled *The Evolution of Human Nature.* The following article is a chapter from this second book. In it, Herrick reconstructs the evolutionary history of man's brain and man's behavior on the bases of fossil records, comparative anatomy, comparative embryology, and comparative psychology. To the picture he describes, little can be added today.

NEUROSENSORY AND NEURO-MOTOR RELATIONS

All plants and the most primitive animals get along well enough—for them—without nervous systems, for the distinctive nervous functions, viz., irritability, conductivity, and integration, are essential properties of all protoplasm, although at a low level of organization. Some nonnervous animals, e.g., the sponges, may grow to large size, but they are sessile and their local movements are slow, restricted, and incompletely integrated; in short, their behavior is essentially plantlike. A freely moving animal of large size needs a much more complicated body, with division of labor and specialized parts adapted for registering a wider variety of things and events in the surroundings, for responding to them by rapid locomotor and other movements, and for maintenance of the bodily apparatus itself and the integration of all its activities.

To meet this need the nervous and muscular tissues were gradually differentiated, at an early stage of animal evolution, from more generalized structures. In this early stage of differentiation of tissues the motor apparatus took the lead; muscles appeared before nerves (Parker, '19; for some critical comments on these observations see pp. 85-87 of my book published five years later, '24). In Parker's account of the behavior of sponges it is shown that in these large multicellular animals co-ordinated motor activity is possible without nervous control. The tissue elements which execute these movements are neuromotor cells which perform both muscular and nervous functions, but the motor apparatus is far more highly elaborated. In this prodromal stage of the evolution of the nervous system motility is the key factor. In the embryological development of higher animals this phylogenetic history is recapitulated, for muscles generally mature to functional efficiency before they have any nervous connections. The earliest movements of the embryo are generally myogenic, not neurogenic, and all muscles retain in adult life some capacity for intrinsically generated contractility.

The reason for the precocious development of the muscular tissues is that motility in its most elementary form is the cradle of all behavior, and the higher patterns of behavior are possible only through acquisition of more efficient apparatus of expression. Motility is also the cradle of mind, for mentation arises within behavior and primarily for advancement of its efficiency.

With increase in the size and complexity of animal bodies there is demand for conductors adapted for speedy communication from part to part. The flow of blood with its contained chemical messengers meets some of these requirements. Ordinary protoplasm is a conductor of physical, chemical, and electrical energies, though the transmission is slow and diffuse. Slender strands of protoplasm are spun out as nerve fibers to secure more rapid conduction without decrement for long distances by insulated pathways. These nerves keep all parts of the body in communication with one another, and in the most primitive nervous systems known this is their primary function. In the simpler polyps there is no brain to act as a dominant center of control. A diffuse network of nerves is spread almost uniformly through the entire body. Integration of the local activities is effected simply by the mutual interplay of part with part through a system of conductors, the whole thus comprising a dynamically integrated body.

The nervous systems of higher animals with larger and more complicated bodies all have more or less elaborate centers of control—ganglia and brains. These are organized on many different plans, and in all of them integration in the interest of the body as a whole is the most important nervous function. These nervous systems show progressive increase in size and complexity of structure and each of the large divisions of the animal kingdom has its own characteristic structural plan of nervous organization. The two major branches of the phylogenetic tree leading respectively to insects and mammals have nervous systems composed of similar elements— nerve cells and fibers—but these elements are combined according to radically different structural plans, so that the nervous systems of insects and men have no homologous parts. This is correlated with the fundamental difference in their patterns of behavior (Chapter 14).

The diffuse nervous network seen in polyps and jellyfish is incapable of making the refined analysis of sensory and motor experience of stimulus-response type that is essential for the more complicated patterns of behavior. In the higher animals, accordingly, the analytic apparatus necessary for sorting out the various kinds of sensory excitations and motor responses is progressively specialized and refined. This complication requires a central adjusting apparatus to canalize the different kinds of incoming messages and to direct them into the appropriate outgoing pathways. The central nervous system performs these local analytic and co-ordinating functions in addition to the general integration of all bodily activities. The importance of this distinction between the analytic and the integrative factors of behavior is explained in Chapters 7, 8, and 9.

This central control and synthesis increases progressively from lower to higher animals as the problems of behavior become more complicated, and so there is corresponding enlargement of the brain. This is true in both insect and vertebrate phyla; but in the latter the process of cephalization goes much further, reaching its culmination in the differentiation of the cortex of the cerebellum and cerebral hemispheres, which are integrators par excellence.

In the series of backboned animals from fish to man the fundamental plan of the brain is similar throughout, but the modifications of this plan in adaptation to various modes of life are amazingly great and diversified. Among the factors which determine the directions taken in these divergent lines of specialization the most important for the behaviorist is the distinction between, and the relative parts played by, the innate components of the action system and those that are acquired. This distinction we meet at every turn of our inquiry.

A second factor is the relative importance of the several senses in the economy of different species of animals depending on habitat and customary ways of making their living. For example, in most birds vision is the dominant sense and the senses of taste and smell are used but little. In dogs the sense of smell is highly developed and vision is poor. The internal structure of the brain shows corresponding differences.

A third consideration arises in connection with the various types of motor adjustment. Specialization for running, digging, climbing, flying, and swimming requires in each case a readjustment of the nervous mechanisms involved. The most striking illustration of this is seen at the transition from fishes to terrestrial animals. The simple paired fins of fishes act chiefly as rudders, not propellers. When the mudfishes emerged from the water to become amphibians these fins were transformed into legs, and quadrupedal locomotion requires much more complicated machinery than fishlike swimming. The movements at each joint of each leg must be co-ordinated and synchronized with the movements at other joints and with all movements of each of the other legs. Similarly all the other activities of land animals must be adjusted to much more diversified environmental conditions than prevail in the water.

This radical change in mode of life—from water to land and air—which began in the Devonian period about 300,000,000 years ago, marks a critical turning point in the evolution of behavior. A bigger and better brain was essential for survival and successful exploitation of the resources of the wider and more heterogeneous environment. Swimming as a total pattern requires far less refinement of central control than does walking, with its multitude of partial patterns. This change in the neuromotor apparatus is begun in the lungfishes, is carried further in the amphibians, and is completed in reptiles and all higher classes (Herrick '48, p. 14).

I think it may safely be claimed that throughout the whole course of vertebrate evolution the motor systems—the apparatus of expression—have played the leading part in setting the directions taken in the various lines of divergent specialization. This is so because every animal's success in life depends on his behavior, and this in turn must be adjusted to the motor equipment he has to work with. A larger measure of success, a richer life, may be won through improvement of the efficiency of the motor organs by the slow process of natural selection or by the acquisition of more skill in the use of the organs so provided.

MECHANISMS OF ANALYSIS AND INTEGRATION

The contrast between innate and acquired components of behavior appears in both the analytic and the integrative patterns and in the apparatus employed. The mechanism of integration in the higher vertebrates, where learned behavior plays the dominant role, is different from that found in lower animals, where most of the behavior is reflex and instinctive. So also the analytic apparatus of the stereotyped sensorimotor reactions of lower animals is inadequate to resolve the problems of behavior presented in conduct which is intelligently directed and so more individually variable. The primitive analyzers of the brain as we find them in fishes are, accordingly, in higher animals supplemented by additional nervous adjustors at a higher level of structural organization in the thalamus and cerebral hemispheres.

The analytic organs of the stereotyped inherited patterns of behavior are fixed systems of nerve cells and connecting fibers which are relatively stable and similar in all members of a race or species. The pattern of this arrangement differs from species to species in conformity with their diverse modes of life, and these arrangements have been described in great detail. The apparatus of the integrative functions and of all learned behavior, on the contrary, in the more primitive species is dispersed and hard to identify, and even in higher animals, where it is massively developed, its essential structure and method of operation are inadequately understood.

Because sensorimotor experience is concerned primarily with the adjustments of the body and its movements with reference to external things which are oriented in space and time, the organs concerned are also precisely localized in the brain. These functions are relatively uniform and predictable under standardized conditions and the temporal relations of these activities are accurately measurable. None of these statements apply with equal precision to the integrative apparatus.

Although most acquired behavior and all higher mental processes are essentially integrative, they must operate for the most part through the mediation of the analytic systems, for the data of sensory and motor experience are all they have to work with. Analysis and synthesis of experience go on hand in hand and simultaneously. It is therefore not surprising to find that the sensorimotor and the integrative tissues of the brain are closely related and intricately interwoven. Nevertheless these tissues in most regions can be distinguished when the details of structure are adequately known.

In the brains of all vertebrates it is much easier to see and describe the relatively well-defined structures which control the stereotyped reflex behavior and to test the functions performed by experiment than it is to make a similar analysis of the apparatus of integration. Because the evolution of the sensorimotor components of the nervous system has been more completely described, these components will next be examined and then the evolution of the integrative apparatus will be surveyed.

THE ANALYTIC APPARATUS

When I first began to be interested in comparative neurology I turned to the fishes and amphibians, because I anticipated that their simple stereotyped patterns of behavior would be correlated with correspondingly simple and schematic patterns of nervous structure, so that in these simple brains it would be possible to map the courses of the several reflex circuits much more clearly than can be done in the more complicated fabric of mammals. Nothing of the sort happened. To my surprise I found that the closer we approach the primitive generalized ancestral species the less well-defined and sharply localized are central pathways and nervous centers which form the analytic apparatus.

In my description of the generalized brain of a salamander ('48, chaps. 6 and 11) it is shown that although the sense organs and their peripheral nerves are highly specialized, the muscular system is at a relatively low level of differentiation. In terms of behavior this means that the salamander is well equipped for the analysis of sensory experience, but the motor responses are, for the most part, mass movements of total pattern type. The repertoire of local reflexes is less than in higher quadrupeds, and these local movements are more closely bound to the mass movements. This is especially so in the legless larvae which swim in the water; but even the locomotion of the adults when they walk on land is fishlike, for all movements of the limbs are co-ordinated with rhythmic contractions of the body musculature. In short, the sensory analyzers are much more elaborately developed than are the motor analyzers.

These features of the salamander's behavior explain the peculiar structure of the central adjusting apparatus in this brain. Because most of the activity is relatively simple mass movement, the central apparatus of motor adjustment is correspondingly simplified. The nervous impulses received from the complicated sensory analyzers have only a few motor outlets and these lead to a motor apparatus with a limited variety of possible movements.

The general plan of the primitive vertebrate brain is most clearly seen in the salamanders. The brains of two of these species I have described in detail—the mudpuppy, Necturus ('33b), and the tiger salamander, Amblystoma ('48).

Figure 8-1 is an enlarged drawing of an amphibian brain dissected so as to open the cavities (ventricles) of the cerebral hemispheres, thalamus, and medulla oblongata. Here the cerebral hemispheres, which comprise the largest part of the human brain, are very small and the medulla oblongata is relatively very large. In this brain the medulla oblongata is the central receptive station for most sensory

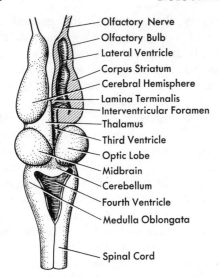

- Olfactory Nerve
- Olfactory Bulb
- Lateral Ventricle
- Corpus Striatum
- Cerebral Hemisphere
- Lamina Terminalis
- Interventricular Foramen
- Thalamus
- Third Ventricle
- Optic Lobe
- Midbrain
- Cerebellum
- Fourth Ventricle
- Medulla Oblongata
- Spinal Cord

Figure 8.1 Dorsal view of an amphibian brain. The roof of the cerebral hemisphere and thalamus has been removed on the right side to open the lateral and third ventricles. After Herrick (1924).

nerve fibers except those of smell and vision (as is true also in the human brain). The end-organs and nerves of the several senses—touch, taste, vestibular control of posture, etc.—are well developed and separately localized, but within the brain these various systems of nerve fibers converge to only two great pools, each of which extends throughout the entire length of the medulla oblongata. Precise localization of function stops at this place where the peripheral nerve fibers make contact with the central nerve cells in a dense feltwork of interlaced fibers, termed neuropil (page 51). One of these pools—the visceral sensory neuropil associated with the fasciculus solitarius—receives all fibers of gustatory and general visceral sensibility and discharges into the visceral motor mechanisms. The other pool—the somatic sensory neuropil—receives fibers of all types of cutaneous and deep sensibility that are concerned with adjustment to the external environment, i.e., the exteroceptive and proprioceptive systems of Sherrington's analysis ('48). This neuropil discharges into

somatic motor apparatus that controls the movements of the skeletal muscles.

This segregation of all sensory nerve fibers, except those of vision and olfaction, into only two receptive centers is the only well-defined localization of sensory functions present in the medulla oblongata. It corresponds with the fundamental difference in behavior between internal visceral activities and somatic sensorimotor activities that have an external reference. The visceral movements are for the most part of total pattern type. This is as true in men as in salamanders. Accordingly, there is little more specialization or separate localization of function in the fasciculus solitarius neuropil of men than of salamanders.

The evolutionary history of the somatic sensory neuropil is different. In salamanders most of the activity of the skeletal musculature is mass movement of total pattern type. No matter which sense organ excites it to activity, there are only a few things the animal can do about it. From a single pool of receptive neuropil which may be activated from any one or all of several kinds of sense organs, motor impulses go out to a limited number of motor systems, each of which is so organized as to activate the appropriate mass movement as an integrated unit. Since there are few autonomous local reflexes available, no sharply segregated and well-insulated pathways for localized reflex arcs are needed. And this is just what is found. In these generalized brains there are few clearly defined tracts for the service of local reflexes.

A man, on the contrary, has reflex and voluntary control of his separate fingers and innumerable other local movements. These separately individuated partial patterns of behavior need and have an elaborate provision of segregated cellular masses ("nuclei") connected by well-insulated tracts of fibers. The primitive diffuse receptive center seen in the somatic sensory neuropil of the salamander is here separated into many cellular areas, or nuclei, each of which receives sensory fibers of a specific modality, e.g., touch, hearing, etc. Each sensory nucleus may discharge nervous impulses by short circuits to specific motor nuclei or by longer paths (the lemniscus systems) to higher centers of correlation. In the salamander the specific localization in space of the several modalities of sense is carried only so far as the terminals of their peripheral fibers in the medulla oblongata. In the man this specificity of the analytic apparatus is carried forward as far as the thalamus and the sensory projection areas of the cerebral cortex.

It should be mentioned that the preceding description of the medulla oblongata of the salamander is somewhat oversimplified. The somatic sensory pool of neuropil is not strictly equipotential. There is an incipient localization of function of the different modalities of sense, but this is not advanced to the grade where separate reflex arcs are recognizable. From this pool of neuropil there are several outgoing pathways. These are lines of preferential discharge. Which of them will be activated in any particular situation depends on the internal physiological state of the neuropil at that time. There is nothing here that can be compared with the switchboard of an automatic telephone system with its perfectly insulated separate circuits. Just what is the mechanism by which different kinds of sensory excitation are analyzed and canalized into the appropriate neuromotor organs of response is now under active investigation.

The most primitive vertebrates now living (lampreys and their allies) have brains that are relatively smaller and less differentiated than are those of salamanders, but the general plan of internal organization is the same and so is that of the primitive ganoid fishes, like the sturgeon. The brain of the salamander is a convenient type form or standard of reference for study of the evolution of the brain because it retains many of the structural peculiarities of the most primitive brains and yet its internal differentiation has advanced sufficiently to enable us to see recognizable germinal stages of the main features of all higher brains.

The evolutionary history of the transformation of these primitive brains into the vastly more complicated human thinking machine has been so intensively studied by many people in many lands that it is now possible to record its broad outlines. These details cannot be reviewed here. They have been summarized concisely by Ariëns Kappers ('29), Schepers ('48), and others, and much more fully in an encyclopedic work by Ariëns Kappers, Huber, and Crosby ('36).

THE INTEGRATIVE APPARATUS

Turning now to the history of the differentiation of the integrative apparatus of the brain, we find a series of structural changes of radically different kind. In the most primitive fishes and amphibians the internal texture of the brain is more nearly homogeneous than in the more specialized fishes and all higher animals.

For the reasons just mentioned, the localization of function is more clear-cut on the sensory side than on the motor side, because most of the muscular activity of the unspecialized animals is mass movement. The nervous elements concerned with the analytic functions are generally recognizable and among these nerve cells and fibers there are others that are integrative in function. The latter form a very closely woven fabric of interlaced thin naked fibers, the neuropil. The bodies of all nerve cells and their widely spread dendritic branches are embedded within this fibrous mat and closely enveloped by it. Every contact of these fibers with the cell is a synaptic junction . . . , and a single cell may have a hundred or more of these contacts with fibers from near and remote parts of the brain (Figure 8-2). This web of neuropil permeates the entire brain and acts as a nonspecific conducting

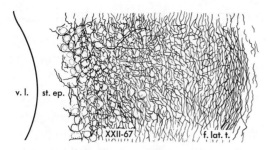

Figure 8.2 Detail of the neuropil in the anterior part of the corpus striatum of the frog, from a Golgi preparation. Magnified X 142. The lateral ventricle is marked *v. 1.;* the ependymal layer is marked *st. ep.;* the lateral forebrain bundle, which is the precursor of the human extra-pyramidal system of fibers, is marked *f. lat. t.* This tissue is a dense entanglement of very thin nerve fibers within which are embedded the cell bodies of the neurons. Only one of these neurons is stained. The clear circles mark the positions of other unstained cell bodies of the gray substance. After Herrick (1934).

system which puts every part of the brain into physiological connection with every other part. It is the primary integrating mechanism, but it is much more than this. It is germinative tissue with potentialities for further differentiation in an endless variety of ways. During subsequent stages of cerebral evolution its derivatives form the largest and most complicated structures in the brain. The details of the structure and properties of the amphibian neuropil are described more fully elsewhere ('48, pp. 29-39, 80, 88).

In the adult amphibian brain the web of neuropil binds the parts together and so does for the central nervous system what the diffuse nervous network of jellyfish does for the whole body; but it is not the first nervous tissue to reach functional maturity in vertebrate embryos. In the early development of these more complicated bodies it is essential that certain movements that have adaptive value should develop precociously, so that the newly hatched or born animal can fend

for itself as soon as possible. The moment after a salamander emerges from the egg it can swim; a newborn horse can stand and walk. To make this possible there is first laid down in the brain a system of direct nervous connections which make provision for a limited number of mass movements and local reflexes. The latter usually mature later than the former. Then there follows an outgrowth of an increasing number of collateral branches of these pioneer fibers and the central linkage of the several sensory and motor pathways by more and more complicated interconnections.

During this process some nerve cells are set apart for integrative functions only. Their fibrous processes take longer or shorter courses, branching freely, and so they form a major component of the neuropil. These nervous elements are not at any time concerned with specific reflexes, but with the co-ordination and integration of all movements. Some of the longer and thicker of these fibers may be fasciculated to form definite tracts which are tied in with one or another of the neuromotor systems for higher control of their action. In this way all the sensorimotor systems are interconnected. There are well-defined pathways of preferential discharge which activate the standardized patterns of reflex and instinctive behavior, but which ones of these will be activated in any particular situation depend on numberless factors of peripheral stimulation and central excitatory state, such as fatigue, temporary condition of the vascular and endocrine systems, etc.

The nerve cells that are concerned primarily with internal correlation and synthesis of behavior may be mingled with those which serve for analysis of sensorimotor reactions, but during the course of evolution the apparatus of each of these two classes of function becomes more and more specialized and the nerve cells set apart for integration are segregated and clustered in local nests, or nuclei, each of which serves some particular phase of the integrative process. In the human brain there are very many of these, such as the habenulae, interpeduncular and pontile nuclei, the thalamic nuclei, and the inferior olives. The three largest of these integrative centers are the cerebellum, the corpus striatum, and the cerebral cortex. These regulate all bodily movements and in addition they have vast reserves of potential nervous energy which may be discharged on occasion to reinforce, inhibit, or otherwise modify the routine activities of the brain stem and spinal cord. These nuclei must not be regarded as specific organs of the functions ascribed to them. On the contrary, they are merely critical nodal points in systems of communication of wide extent and the functions in question are performed by the system as a whole.

The undifferentiated neuropil of lower vertebrates is by no means homogeneous in texture or equipotential in function. It is under constant activation from the periphery and the physiological quality of this activity differs from region to region and from moment to moment. The same is true in those highly specialized derivatives of this neuropil that are seen in the human brain, the most complicated of which is the intricate system of thalamocortical connections.

There is localization of function in both the analytic and the integrative apparatus, but the principles of localization are radically different, as explained in Chapter 32.

It was long ago recognized by the pioneer explorers of the human brain (Meynert, Hughlings Jackson, and others) that a succession of levels of structural and functional complexity can be seen, the series extending from the peripheral end-organs through the spinal cord and brain stem to the cerebral cortex. This series is a rough register in the adult of the successive steps which were taken during the course of evolution of the integrating apparatus. This analysis, though obviously somewhat arbitrary, corresponds to levels of physiological integration. In the light of present knowledge I would list these levels as follows:

1. A low level of integration is seen at the periphery in the sensory and motor end-organs. In some of these organs, notably the eye and ear, the apparatus of both analysis and integration is elaborate.

2. A second level of integration is represented in the spinal cord and brain stem by the primary sensory and motor centers (i.e., centers directly connected with the periphery) and the systems of fibers that connect them with one another so as to provide reflex circuits for the simpler components of standardized behavior.

3. A third level is represented in the diffuse neuropil and its more specialized derivatives, such as the thalamus and the stem part of the cerebral hemispheres. This structural level serves two quite distinct sorts of physiological integration: first, the more elaborately organized instinctive complexes, including the accompanying emotional drives; and, second, conditioning of reflexes and some other kinds of individually learned behavior. The corpus striatum of reptiles and birds is the largest and most complicated structure of this level. In man this body is reduced in relative size and its action is, for the most part, ancillary to that of the cerebral cortex.

4. Historically considered, a fourth level may be recognized, characterized by the appearance of simple cerebral cortex of reptilian type. Precursors of this are found in amphibians and some fishes. Some vestiges of it remain in the human brain at the margins of the cortical field.

5. The fifth level is characterized by the mammalian type of cortex, concerned primarily with learning and the organization of learned behavior. This learned behavior is founded upon reflex and instinctive behaviors and it supplements them.

6. Finally, the human type of associational cortex carries behavior to an integrative level capable of devising and using tools and symbols and of semantic processes of reasoning.

The activities characteristic of the fifth and sixth levels are not confined to the cerebral cortex. For the most part they are circular in pattern, with the thalamus and the cortex working in reciprocal interrelationship, as clearly explained by Dusser de Barenne ('34).

The levels just mentioned are concerned primarily with adjustments to the surroundings and their integration. The internal affairs of the body are analyzed and integrated by complex systems of visceral and proprioceptive nervous organs which also may be arranged in levels of successively higher order. The cerebellum is the highest member of the proprioceptive system, as Sherrington pointed out in 1906 and I have recently ('47) again emphasized with some revision of former conceptions of its functions.

I have distinguished ('25) six levels of visceral functions: (1) Some measure of intrinsic nonnervous tonicity and automaticity is characteristic of all living substance and is especially pronounced in human muscles and viscera. (2) The visceral functions are especially susceptible to chemical control by endocrines distributed in the body fluids. (3) There is local regulation of the viscera by intrinsic autonomous sympathetic ganglionated plexuses. (4) There is central regulation of these plexuses through sympathetic nervous circuits in the cranial and spinal nerves, the efferent path going by way of preganglionic and postganglionic neurons. (5) Superposed upon these circuits there is a series of cerebral visceral centers in the brain stem, the most important of which are in the hypothalamus. (6) Finally, all of these lower levels are under some measure of control by the cerebral cortex.

Investigation of the biochemical properties of the various parts of the central nervous system reveals a metabolic gradient from cortex to spinal cord which is analyzed by Himwich ('52 and works there cited) into five functional levels. He points out that in the course of vertebrate phylogeny there has been a progressive shift of physiological dominance of several critical vital functions from the lowest level in the medulla oblongata in fishes to the cortex in man.

This analysis of the nervous system into levels, however defined, is of course artificial; it is very important to recognize that all levels of integration interpenetrate and one never operates independently of the others. Each higher level is derived from the lower and can work only with the instrumentation provided by the lower levels. Nonetheless each level has its own distinctive qualities and the laws of its operation are peculiar to it.

REFLEXOLOGY

Because the structural arrangements of cells and fibers of the analytic apparatus are most clearly revealed by the staining methods commonly used by microscopists and the experimental methods of the physiologists, attention has been directed chiefly to stimulus-response types of behavior. Much research has been devoted to mapping the courses of the reflex circuits involved in all standardized forms of behavior. This has been so successful that during the past half-century an ambitious

program of reflexology was elaborated, notably by Pavlov and the American school of behaviorism. The avowed objective was to reduce all animal and human behavior to systems of interlocking reflexes of various grades of complexity. The conditioning of these reflexes by personal experience was invoked as the mechanism of learning. The simple reflex was regarded as the unit of behavior, and all other kinds of behavior were conceived as brought about by the linkage of these units in successively more complicated patterns.

The simplicity of this scheme is attractive but illusory. In the first place, the simple reflex is a pure abstraction. There is no such thing in any living body. A more serious defect is that all the information we have about the embryology and phylogenetic development of behavior shows clearly that local reflexes are not the primary units of behavior. They are secondary acquisitions. As is clear from the researches of Coghill and many others, the actual behavior as manifested in reflexes and instincts is not developed by an additive accretion of separate reflexes; but these local partial patterns are secondarily individuated within the primordial total pattern, they are integral parts of it, and they are never completely emancipated from some measure of control by the integrative apparatus in the interest of the welfare of the body as a whole.

In current doctrines of reflexology conditioning of reflexes (learning) plays a major role. Conditioning is an observed physiological fact, but how it is done remains obscure. McCulloch (Frank et al., '48, p. 266) has suggested an ingenious hypothesis to explain some features of the mechanics of conditioning; but until this subject is further clarified there is a fatal gap in the Pavlovian system of reflexology. This much is clear: learned behavior (whether unconscious or intentionally directed) and all higher mental capacities are total patterns. Reflexes as partial patterns are used instrumentally in learning, but they do not initiate it or direct it. Learning and thinking are not analytic; they are synthetic processes; and the apparatus employed is to be sought in the integrative tissues of the brain, not in the reflex arcs.

That the local reflexes are integral and subordinate parts of the total pattern was most clearly shown by Coghill's discussion ('30; cf. also Herrick, '48, pp. 73-81) of the part played by inhibition in reflex action. He called attention to the familiar fact that for the execution of a local reflex it is essential that all antagonistic or conflicting acts must be inhibited and that in early stages of the development of salamanders it can easily be seen that the total patterns are completely inhibited before a local reflex appears. It is often equally evident that this is true also in the adult animal. He concludes, "It is then in a field of total inhibition that the local reflex emerges." We may now accept Coghill's definition: "The reflex may, therefore, be regarded as a total behavior pattern which consists of two components, one overt or excitatory, the other covert or inhibitory."

SUMMARY

All protoplasm has the properties of irritability, conductivity, and integration. The nervous tissues were first specialized for the refinement and further differentiation of these functions. The most primitive nervous systems (as seen in polyps) have nerve cells with very long fibrous extensions distributed everywhere throughout the body. These cells and fibers form a network that serves to keep all parts of the body in communication and so facilitates orderly coordination of the bodily movements. In higher animals with more complicated structure and behavior special collections of nerve cells are set apart to provide more efficient coordination and integration. These ganglia and brains take

a great variety of forms in different animals depending on the patterns of behavior manifested.

Among the general properties of the nervous system one of the most significant for behavior is the contrast between the apparatus of the stable innate components of behavior and that of the more labile individually acquired components. The mechanisms of these two kinds differ in origin, evolutionary and embryological development, and significance for problems of practical control of conduct.

The innate structural plan of the nervous system is given. The animal must accept it as it is. The larger part of this inherited structure is the sensorimotor equipment for the performance of reflex and instinctive behavior. These analytic functions are the necessary tools for the cultivation of the intrinsic values of life, the satisfactions that accrue to the organism. Satisfaction is a total pattern and the integrative apparatus is amplified and specialized as the range of needs and desires is enlarged.

The early stages in the differentiation of the nervous system have been briefly outlined, with emphasis on its primary function as integrating apparatus. The sensorimotor analytic systems are differentiated within the primary totalizing apparatus and always remain subject to control by it. The history of the progressive differentiation of the analyzers is contrasted with the quite different evolutionary development of the nervous mechanisms of integration.

Localization of function is more precise and easily demonstrated in the analytic components of the system. For this reason the reflex was long regarded as the elementary unit of behavior, but the history of both embryologic and phylogenetic development shows that it is not. Accordingly, some current doctrines of reflexology need radical revision.

9. In Search of the Engram *

Karl Lashley

For centuries it has been assumed that because man can learn there must be a part of his brain set aside for learning; since he can also remember, there must be a part of his brain set aside for memory, and so on. This pairing of parts of the brain with specific mental capacities can continue until the list of mental capacities and brain parts is exhausted. More than any other man, Karl Lashley dashed this idea once and for all.

Webster defines an engram as a "lasting trace left on an organism by psychic experience" or, in other words, a mechanism of memory. The following article is a résumé of Lashley's attempts to find the memory trace. His conclusion is compelling: a *seat of memory* and a *seat of learning* do not exist. While the engram is located in the brain, no further restriction on its locus can be made. The memory of specific things as, for example, your sweetheart's name, may be localized in a restricted region of the brain, but memory as "all things remembered" is not. Instead, memory and learning are accompanied by changes throughout the brain.

On the basis of Lashley's contribution, those who study brain functions still seek engrams (not *the* engram), but now at the cellular and subcellular level.

I. INTRODUCTION

'When the mind wills to recall something, this volition causes the little [pineal] gland, by inclining successively to different sides, to impel the animal spirits toward different parts of the brain, until they come

* Reprinted by permission of the Society for Experimental Biology from *Society for Experimental Biology Symposium No 4: Physiological Mechanisms in Animal Behavior*, 1950, 454-481.

upon that part where the traces are left of the thing which it wishes to remember; for these traces are nothing else than the circumstance that the pores of the brain through which the spirits have already taken their course on presentation of the object, have thereby acquired a greater facility than the rest to be opened again the same way by the spirits which come to them; so that these spirits coming upon the pores enter therein more readily than into the others.'

So wrote Descartes just three hundred years ago in perhaps the earliest attempt to explain memory in terms of the action of the brain. In the intervening centuries much has been learned concerning the nature of the impulses transmitted by nerves. Innumerable studies have defined conditions under which learning is facilitated or retarded, but, in spite of such progress, we seem little nearer to an understanding of the nature of the memory trace than was Descartes. His theory has in fact a remarkably modern sound. Substitute nerve impulse for animal spirits, synapse for pore and the result is the doctrine of learning as change in resistance of synapses. There is even a theory of scanning which is as least more definite as to the scanning agent and the source of the scanning beam than is its modern counterpart.

As interest developed in the functions of the brain the doctrine of the separate localization of mental functions gradually took form, even while the ventricles of the brain were still regarded as the active part. From Prochaska and Gall through the nineteenth century, students of clinical neurology sought the localization of specific memories. Flechsig defined the association areas as distinct from the sensory and motor. Aphasia, agnosia and apraxia were interpreted as the result of the loss of memory images, either of objects or of kinaesthetic sensations of movements to be made. The theory that memory traces are stored in association areas adjacent to the corresponding primary sensory areas seemed reasonable and was supported by some clinical evidence. The extreme position was that of Henschen, who speculated concerning the location of single ideas or memories in single cells. In spite of the fact that more critical analytic studies of clinical symptoms, such as those of Henry Head and of Kurt Goldstein, have shown that aphasia and agnosia are primarily defects in the organization of ideas rather than the result of amnesia, the conception of the localized storing of memories is still widely prevalent (Nielsen, 1936).

While clinical students were developing theories of localization, physiologists were analysing the reflex arc and extending the concept of the reflex to include all activity. Bechterew, Pavlov and the behaviourist school in America attempted to reduce all psychological activity to simple associations or chains of conditioned reflexes. The path of these conditioned reflex circuits was described as from sense organ to cerebral sensory area, thence through associative areas to the motor cortex and by way of the pyramidal paths to the final motor cells of the medulla and cord. The discussions of this path were entirely theoretical, and no evidence on the actual course of the conditioned reflex arc was presented.

In experiments extending over the past 30 years I have been trying to trace conditioned reflex paths through the brain or to find the locus of specific memory traces. The results for different types of learning have been inconsistent and often mutually contradictory, in spite of confirmation by repeated tests. I shall summarize to-day a number of experimental findings. Perhaps they obscure rather than illuminate the nature of the engram, but they may serve at least to illustrate the complexity of the problem and to reveal the superficial nature of many of the physiological theories of memory that have been proposed.

I shall have occasion to refer to training of animals in a variety of tasks, so shall give a very brief description of the methods used. The animals studied have been rats and monkeys with, recently, a few chimpanzees. Two lines of approach to the problem have been followed. One is purely behavioural and consists in the analysis of the sensory excitations which are actually associated with reactions in learning and which are effective in eliciting the learned reactions. The associated reactions are similarly analysed. These studies define the patterns of nervous activity at receptor and effector levels and specify certain characteristics which the memory trace must have. The second approach is by surgical destruction of parts of the brain. Animals are trained in various tasks ranging from direct sensori-motor associations to the solution of difficult problems. Before or after training, associative tracts are cut or portions of the brain removed and effects of these operations on initial learning or postoperative retention are measured. At the termination of the experiments the brains are sectioned and the extent of damage reconstructed from serial sections. The brains are also analysed for secondary degeneration, so far as available histological methods permit.

II. ELIMINATION OF THE MOTOR CORTEX

I first became sceptical of the supposed path of the conditioned reflex when I found that rats, trained in a differential reaction to light, showed no reduction in accuracy of performance when almost the entire motor cortex, along with the frontal poles of the brain, was removed. This observation led to a series of experiments designed to test the part played by the motor cortex or Betz cell area in the retention of various habits. The matter can be tested either by removing the motor cortex or by severing its connexions with the sensory areas of the brain. Both methods have been used with the rat and the monkey.

Monkeys were trained to open various latch-boxes. The motor areas were then removed. This operation produces a temporary paralysis, but after 8-12 weeks this paralysis recovers to such an extent that the animals are capable of the movements required to open the boxes. During this recovery period they did not have access to the training boxes. When sufficiently recovered, they were tested and opened the boxes promptly without random exploratory movements. The tasks require both a visual recognition of the latches and semi-skilled movements, such as turning a crank. Removal of the motor areas did not produce a loss of memory for the movements (Lashley, 1924). Jacobsen has since confirmed these observations with a chimpanzee from which the motor cortex was removed (Jacobsen, 1932).

These experiments seem to rule out the motor cortex or Betz cell area as containing any part of the conditioned reflex arc.

III. TRANSCORTICAL CONDUCTION

There is evidence, not only that the motor cortex does not participate in the transmission of the conditioned reflex pattern, but also that the transmission of impulses over well-defined, isolated paths from one part of the cortex to another is inessential for performance of complicated habits. The maze habit of the rat almost certainly involves the utilization of several sensory modalities, visual, tactile and kinaesthetic. In a rather complicated set of experiments I attempted to test the importance of connexions across the cortex for maze performance. Rats were trained on the maze, then knife cuts were made through the cortex and underlying fibres, separating different functional areas or cutting through functional areas. The incisions were long, averaging half of the entire length of the

cerebral hemispheres. After recovery the animals were tested in retention of the maze habit. In other experiments the incisions were made before training and their effect upon the rate of initial learning was tested. In neither initial learning nor in retention could any certain effect of separating the various parts of the cortex be demonstrated. If the incisions interrupted sensory tracts to the cortex, there was loss of the habit, but uncomplicated separation of cortical areas produced no effect on performance.

Such results are certainly puzzling. They leave us with almost no understanding of the function of the associative fibres which extend across from one part of the cortex to another. The results are difficult to accept, yet they are supported by various other lines of evidence. I think that they point to the conclusion that the associative connexions or memory traces of the conditioned reflex do not extend across the cortex as well-defined arcs or paths. Such arcs are either diffused through all parts of the cortex, pass by relay through lower centres, or do not exist.

IV. THE PROBLEM OF THE 'ASSOCIATION AREAS'

In anatomic theories of the memory trace the association areas of the cortex have played a major part. Frontal, parietal, occipital and temporal associative areas have been distinguished as regions of the cortex, relatively lacking in massive connexions with the lower centres of the brain. On the basis of some clinical evidence, but chiefly because of their anatomic relations, these areas have been considered as associative and as the storehouses of memory images of sensations derived from the adjacent sensory areas. Thus areas 18 and 19 of Brodmann's questionable divisions have been called the visual associative areas, areas 5 and 7 tactile associative, and areas 20, 21 and 22 of the temporal lobe the auditory association areas. The prefrontal area was considered by Hitzig to be a higher integrative region because he believed that it showed the greatest evolutionary growth in the primate brain. Special memory functions were also ascribed to it, however.

S. I. Franz reported that the removal of the frontal association areas of cats destroyed recently formed habits but left old, well-established habits unaffected (Franz, 1907). The actual observation was that the cats lost their habits of opening latch-boxes but would still come when called. His operations destroyed much of the motor areas as well as the prefrontal cortex. I later trained monkeys on latch-boxes and removed the prefrontal cortex, in an experiment designed to test the influence of the operation on learning ability. During the period allowed for recovery one of the animals found the experimental boxes piled in the corner of the room and promptly opened them. Tests of the other animals showed perfect retention of the manipulative habits. There was no indication that the recently acquired habits had been lost. Jacobsen took up the problem at this point and carried it further. He found that visual discriminative habits and simple habits of latch-box manipulation are unaffected by loss of the prefrontal association areas. Habits requiring a series of acts, such as opening a box with several independent latches, may be lost. This is not, however, a simple removal of memory traces. The animals are incapable of relearning the functions which they have lost. They fail because of a difficulty in going on from one task to the next, not from loss of memory of the individual items of the task (Jacobsen, 1936).

Loss of the delayed reaction after removal of the prefrontal lobes of the monkey has been interpreted as a loss of immediate memory. However, this task and others, which are affected by prefrontal injury, all involve a series of conflicting actions. Difficulty in maintaining a constant set or attitude is the real basis of the loss. Such an interpretation fits better with clinical findings than does the hypothesis of memory defect.

A number of experiments with the rat have shown that habits of visual discrimination survive the destruction of any part of the cerebral cortex except the primary visual projection area. Similarly for auditory habits and the auditory cortex. There is no indication of specialized memory areas outside the primary sensory fields.

It has been claimed that the differentiation of a number of cerebral areas contributes to man's superior intelligence by avoiding confusion of functions, but, if the anatomic relations in man and the rat were reversed, it would be concluded with equal assurance that, because intellectual activity requires close integration of different functions, the advantage lies with the brain in which functional areas are not sharply set off. Such *post hoc* arguments based on anatomic grounds alone have little value for functional interpretations. Many current conceptions of cerebral physiology are based upon just such dubious inferences from anatomic data.

The outcome of the experiments involving removal of the associative areas of the monkey was unexpected, in spite of the fact that it confirms the earlier results with the rat. The conclusion, which seems to be forced by the accumulated data, runs counter to the accepted tradition concerning the organization of the cerebral cortex. Memory traces, at least of simple sensorimotor associations, are not laid down and stored within the associative areas; at least not within the restricted associative area supposedly concerned with each sense modality. Memory disturbances of simple sensory habits follow only upon very extensive experimental destruction, including almost the entire associative cortex. Even combined destruction of the prefrontal, parietal, occipital and temporal areas, exclusive of the primary sensory cortex, does not prevent the animal from forming such habits, although pre-existing habits are lost and their reformation is greatly retarded.

These results, showing that the so-called associative areas are not essential to preservation of memory traces, have been obtained with rats and monkeys. Is there a

greater cortical differentiation in anthropoid apes and man? We have experimental
data only on the prefrontal associative
cortex of the chimpanzee and of man. Bilateral removal of the entire prefrontal
granular cortex in five chimpanzees in our
laboratory has not resulted in any memory
defect. One two-year-old animal, lacking
prefrontal and parietal areas, removed in
early infancy, falls well within the normal
range in all aspects of development. Adult
chimpanzees, trained in such complicated
habits as choosing an object, like a model
shown, retain the habits after removal of
the entire prefrontal cortex. We have not
been able to demonstrate loss of any memory or, in fact, of any function after such
operations.

Clinical data, with amnesias following
apparently small lesions, seem to contradict
such experimental findings. However, lesions in the human brain are mostly the
result either of tumor growth or of severe
traumatism, both of which probably produce widespread changes in addition to the
local injury. The surgical removal of parts
of the frontal lobes in the recent topectomy
studies has not produced such severe defects as usually result from traumatic destruction of the lobes (Mettler, 1949).

V. THE ROLE OF SUBCORTICAL STRUCTURES

Perhaps we have been looking in the
wrong place for the conditioned reflex arcs
or memory traces. Are they formed somewhere else than in the cortex? Experiments
on the thalamus and other subcortical structures are technically difficult, and there is
little direct evidence on this question.
Since the classical experiments of Goltz a
number of investigators have studied the
capacity of the totally decorticate animal
to learn. The outcome of these experiments
is that such animals can form simple sensori-motor associations, although with extreme slowness in comparison with the rate
of the normal animal (Polterew & Zeliony,
1930; Girden, Mettler, Finch & Culler,

1936). We must ask, however, whether
such learning occurs when the cortex is
intact.

When the sensory or associative areas of
the cerebral cortex are destroyed, the corresponding nuclei of the neo-thalamus
degenerate, so this portion of the subcortex
is eliminated from consideration by the
same experiments which rule out the cortical association areas. The only experiments bearing upon the participation of
other subcortical centres suggest that subcortical learning does not occur when the
cortex is functioning.

Fischel (1948) has maintained, solely
from comparative psychological studies,
that the basal ganglia are the seat of the
space-co-ordinate elements of motor habits.
I have destroyed the greater part of these
structures in rats, trained in the discrimination box, without producing loss of orientation. The animals may perform forced
circus movements but, in spite of this, they
maintain their orientation in the problem
box (Lashley, 1921b). The basal ganglia
in man are subject to various degenerative
diseases. The symptoms of such diseases
are, in general, tremors and other disturbances of co-ordination at a primitive level,
but without evidence of apraxia or other
disorder of the learned patterns of motor
co-ordination. The evidence seems conclusive that in mammals the basal nuclei are
not an essential link in the patterning of
learned activities.

It has been widely held that although
memory traces are at first formed in the
cerebral cortex, they are finally reduced or
transferred by long practice to subcortical
levels. The evidence for this has been the
apparently greater fragility of recently
formed habits than of old habits; the supposedly greater resistance of the latter to
brain injuries. The amnesias following
electroshock therapy indicate that it is the
age of the trace and not the amount of
practice that has built it up which determines its survival, and a difference of a few
minutes in the age of memories may suffice
to determine their loss or survival. This is

scarcely evidence for reduction to lower levels of the nervous system. The chief argument for the dropping out of memory traces from the cortex has seemingly run somewhat as follows: Consciousness is a function of the cerebral cortex; long-practised habits become automatic and are performed without conscious control; therefore they are no longer mediated by the cerebral cortex. Both premises of this syllogism are probably false, and the conclusion would not follow if they were true.

When rats are trained in a habit based upon the discrimination of intensities of light, to choose a brightly lighted alley and avoid a dimly lighted one, the removal of the striate cortex completely abolishes the habit. The animals are able to relearn the reaction and require as much practice as they did for initial learning. One group of animals was trained in this habit and given 1200 trials of overtraining, daily practice for a period of 3 months. Their behaviour strongly suggested automatization of the habit. The striate areas were then removed. The habit was lost, just as in the case of animals which are operated as soon as they give evidence of the presence of the habit. The long overtraining did not eliminate the participation of the cortex (Lashley, 1921a).

This visual habit can be formed in the absence of the visual cortex, and the rates of learning with and without the visual area are exactly the same. The average for 100 normal animals is 125 trials; for nearly 100 without the visual areas it is 123 trials. After such animals, lacking the visual cortex, have learned the brightness reaction, any other part of the cerebral cortex may be destroyed without disturbing the habit. Apparently no other part of the cortex takes over the learning function (Lashley, 1922). If, in addition to removal of the striate areas, the pretectile region of the thalamus and the optic tectum are destroyed, the animals cannot learn the discrimination reaction (Lashley, 1935b). These facts indicate that, in the absence of the visual cortex, the learning of the bright-

ness reaction is carried out by the optic tectum. However, so long as the visual cortex is intact, removal of the tectum has no effect whatever upon the performance of visual habits. The tectum apparently does not participate in visual learning so long as the cortex is intact (Lashley, 1935b).

VI. THE ENGRAM WITHIN SENSORY AREAS (EQUIPOTENTIAL REGIONS)

The experiments reported indicate that performance of habits of the conditioned reflex type is dependent upon the sensory areas and upon no other part of the cerebral cortex. What of localization within the sensory areas? Direct data upon this question are limited, but point to the conclusion that so long as some part of the sensory field remains intact and there is not a total loss of primary sensitivity, the habit mechanism can still function. Thus, in a series of experiments attempting to locate accurately the visual cortex of the rat, parts of the occipital lobes were destroyed in a variety of combinations. In these experiments it appeared that, so long as some part of the anterolateral surface of the striate cortex (the projection field of the temporal retina corresponding to the macula of primates) remained intact, there was no loss of habit. Any small part of the region was capable of maintaining the habits based on discrimination of intensities of light (Lashley, 1935b).

In a later experiment an attempt was made to determine the smallest amount of visual cortex which is capable of mediating habits based upon detail vision. The extent of visual cortex remaining after operation was determined by counting undegenerated cells in the lateral geniculate nucleus. Discrimination of visual figures could be learned when only one-sixtieth of the visual cortex remained (Lashley, 1939). No comparable data are available on postoperative retention, but from incidental observations in other experiments I am confident that retention would be possible with the same amount of tissue.

VII. FACILITATIVE FUNCTIONS IN LEARNING AND RETENTION (MASS ACTION)

The experiments thus far reported have been concerned almost entirely with discriminative habits requiring only an association between a single sensory stimulus and a motor response. A very different picture develops in experiments with other types of learning. If rats are trained in the maze and then have portions of the cortex removed, they show more or less loss of the habit. If a small amount of cortex is destroyed, 5-10%, the loss may be scarcely detectable. If large amounts, say 50% or more, are destroyed, the habit is completely lost, and relearning may require many times as much practice as did initial learning. The amount of loss, measured in terms of the practice required for relearning, is, on the average, closely proportional to the amount of cortex destroyed. There is some evidence that the more difficult the task, the greater the relative effect of the larger lesions (Lashley, 1929; Lashley & Wiley, 1933). Similar results have been obtained with latch-box learning and retention (Lashley, 1935a). So far as it is possible to analyse the data from more than 200 diverse operations, the amount of loss from a given extent of cortical destruction is about the same, no matter what part of the cerebral hemispheres is destroyed, provided that the destruction is roughly similar in both hemispheres.

The explanation of this quantitative relationship is difficult. In learning the maze the rat certainly employs a variety of sensory cues, visual, tactile, kinaesthetic, olfactory, possibly auditory. Brain injuries destroy various sensory fields and the larger the lesion the greater the reduction in available sense data. The production of different amounts of sensory deficit would thus appear to be the most reasonable explanation of the quantitative relation between habit loss and extent of lesion (Hunter, 1930; Finley, 1941). Sensory deficit certainly plays a role in it. In the experiment on effects of incisions through the cortex, which was described earlier, the severity of loss of the maze habit correlated highly with the interruption of sensory pathways, as determined from degeneration of the thalamus.

However, sensory loss will not account for all of the habit deterioration. There is evidence which shows that another more mysterious effect is involved. In the first place, destruction of a single sensory area of the cortex produces a far greater deficit in maze or latch-box performance than does loss of the corresponding sense modality. A comparison was made of the effects on retention of the latch-box habits of combined loss of vision, vibrissae touch, and the anaesthesia to touch and movement produced by sectioning the dorsal half of the spinal cord at the third cervical level. This latter operation severs the columns of Gall and Burdoch, which convey tactile and kinaesthetic impulses, and also severs the pyramidal tracts which have a dorsal position in the rat. The combined peripheral sense privation and section of the pyramids produced less loss of the latch-box habits than did destruction of a single sensory area of the cortex (Lashley, 1935a). Secondly, when blind animals are trained in the maze, the removal of the primary visual cortex produces a severe loss of the habit with serious difficulty in relearning, although the animals could have used no visual cues during the initial learning (Lashley, 1943).

A possible explanation of this curious effect was that the rat forms concepts of spatial relations in visual terms, as man seems to do, and that the space concepts are integrated in the visual cortex. The visual cortex might then function in the formation of spatial habits, even when the animal loses its sight. To test this Tsang (1934) reared rats blind from birth, trained them as adults in the maze, then destroyed the visual cortex. The resultant loss of the maze habit by these animals was as severe as in animals which had been reared with vision. The hypothesis concerning the formation of visual space concepts was not confirmed.

Our recent studies of the associative areas of the monkey are giving similar results to those gained with rats. Visual and tactile habits are not disturbed by the destruction singly, either of the occipital, parietal, or lateral temporal regions, so long as the primary sensory fields remain. However, combined destruction of these regions does produce a loss of the habits with retarded relearning. Higher level functions, such as the conditional reaction, delayed reaction, or solution of the multiple stick problem, show deterioration after extensive damage in any part of the cortex. The capacity for delayed reaction in monkeys, for example (to remember in which of two boxes food was placed), may be seriously reduced or abolished by removal either of the prefrontal lobes or of the occipital associative cortex or of the temporal lobes. That is, small lesions, embracing no more than a single associative area, do not produce loss of any habit; large lesions produce a deterioration which affects a variety of habits, irrespective of the sensori-motor elements involved.

In interpreting apparent loss of memory after cerebral damage, extreme caution is necessary. The poor performance in tasks may be due to the destruction of specific associative connexions, but is instead generally, I believe always, the result rather of interference with a higher level functional patterning. Some experiments of Dr Klüver's (personal communication) illustrate this point. Monkeys were trained in a variety of discriminative reactions calling for use of different sense modalities by a method that required them to pull in the stimulus objects by attached strings. Extensive lesions in different cortical areas all caused loss of these habits. The monkeys simply pulled the strings at random.

They were retrained in the discrimination of weights. When this was learned, the habits based on other sense modalities (reactions to intensities of light, for example) returned spontaneously. What had been disturbed by all the operations was the set or attitude to compare stimuli, not the specific memory of which one was correct.

This example perhaps illustrates at a primitive level the characteristic of amnesias as seen clinically. Apparent loss of memory is secondary to a disorder in the structuring of concepts. Some physiological mode of organizing or integrating activity is affected rather than specific associative bonds.

SUMMARY

This series of experiments has yielded a good bit of information about what and where the memory trace is not. It has discovered nothing directly of the real nature of the engram. I sometimes feel, in reviewing the evidence on the localization of the memory trace, that the necessary conclusion is that learning just is not possible. It is difficult to conceive of a mechanism which can satisfy the conditions set for it. Nevertheless, in spite of such evidence against it, learning does sometimes occur. Although the negative data do not provide a clear picture of the nature of the engram, they do establish limits within which concepts of its nature must be confined, and thus indirectly define somewhat more clearly the nature of the nervous mechanisms which must be responsible for learning and retention. Some general conclusions are, I believe, justified by the evidence.

(1) It seems certain that the theory of well-defined conditioned reflex paths from sense organ via association areas to the motor cortex is false. The motor areas are not necessary for the retention of sensori-motor habits or even of skilled manipulative patterns.

(2) It is not possible to demonstrate the isolated localization of a memory trace

anywhere within the nervous system. Limited regions may be essential for learning or retention of a particular activity, but within such regions the parts are functionally equivalent. The engram is represented throughout the region.

(3) The so-called associative areas are not storehouses for specific memories. They seem to be concerned with modes of organization and with general facilitation or maintenance of the level of vigilance. The defects which occur after their destruction are not amnesias but difficulties in the performance of tasks which involve abstraction and generalization, or conflict of purposes. It is not possible as yet to describe these defects in the present psychological terminology. Goldstein (1940) has expressed them in part as a shift from the abstract to the concrete attitude, but this characterization is too vague and general to give a picture of the functional disturbance. For our present purpose the important point is that the defects are not fundamentally those of memory.

(4) The trace of any activity is not an isolated connexion between sensory and motor elements. It is tied in with the whole complex of spatial and temporal axes of nervous activity which forms a constant substratum of behaviour. Each association is oriented with respect to space and time. Only by long practice under varying conditions does it become generalized or dissociated from these specific co-ordinates. The space and time co-ordinates in orientation can, I believe, only be maintained by some sort of polarization of activity and by rhythmic discharges which pervade the entire brain, influencing the organization of activity everywhere. The position and direction of motion in the visual field, for example, continuously modifies the spinal postural adjustments, but, a fact which is more frequently overlooked, the postural adjustments also determine the orientation of the visual field, so that upright objects continue to appear upright, in spite of changes in the inclination of the head. This substratum of postural and tonic activity is constantly present and is integrated with the memory trace (Lashley, 1949).

I have mentioned briefly evidence that new associations are tied in spontaneously with a great mass of related associations. This conception is fundamental to the problems of attention and interest. There are no neurological data bearing directly upon these problems, but a good guess is that the phenomena which we designate as attention and interest are the result of partial, subthreshold activation of systems of related associations which have a mutual facilitative action. It seems impossible to account for many of the characters of organic amnesias except in such general terms as reduced vigilance or reduced facilitation.

(5) The equivalence of different regions of the cortex for retention of memories points to multiple representation. Somehow, equivalent traces are established throughout the functional area. Analysis of the sensory and motor aspects of habits shows that they are reducible only to relations among components which have no constant position with respect to structural elements. This means, I believe, that within a functional area the cells throughout the area acquire the capacity to react in certain definite patterns, which may have any distribution within the area. I have elsewhere proposed a possible mechanism to account for this multiple representation. Briefly, the characteristics of the nervous network are such that, when it is subject to any pattern of excitation, it may develop a pattern of activity, reduplicated throughout an entire functional area by spread of excitations, much as the surface of a liquid develops an interference pattern of spreading waves when it is disturbed at several points (Lashley, 1942a). This means that, within a functional area, the neurons must be sensitized to react in certain combinations, perhaps in complex patterns of reverberatory circuits, reduplicated throughout the area.

(6) Consideration of the numerical relations of sensory and other cells in the brain

makes it certain, I believe, that all of the cells of the brain must be in almost constant activity, either firing or actively inhibited. There is no great excess of cells which can be reserved as the seat of special memories. The complexity of the functions involved in reproductive memory implies that every instance of recall requires the activity of literally millions of neurons. The same neurons which retain the memory traces of one experience must also participate in countless other activities.

Recall involves the synergic action or some sort of resonance among a very large number of neurons. The learning process must consist of the attunement of the elements of a complex system in such a way that a particular combination or pattern of cells responds more readily than before the experience. The particular mechanism by which this is brought about remains unknown. From the numerical relations involved, I believe that even the reservation of individual synapses for special associative reactions is impossible. The alternative is, perhaps, that the dendrites and cell body may be locally modified in such a manner that the cell responds differentially, at least in the timing of its firing, according to the pattern of combination of axon feet through which excitation is received.

REFERENCES

AKELAITIS, A. J. (1944). A study of gnosis, praxis and language following section of the corpus callosum and anterior commissure. *J. Neurosurgery,* 1, 94–102.

BAILEY, P., BONIN, G. v., DAVIS, F. W., GAROL, H. W. & McCULLOCH, W. S. (1944). *J. Neuropath. Exp. Neurol.* 3, 413–15.

BERGSON, H. (1896). *Matière et mémoire.* Paris.

BONIN, G. VON, GAROL, H. W. & McCULLOCH, W. S. (1942). The functional organization of the occipital lobe. *Biol. Symp.* 7, 165–92.

BUCY, P. C. (1934). The relation of the premotor cortex to motor activity. *J. Nerv. Ment. Dis.* 79, 621–30.

BUCY, P. C. & FULTON, T. F. (1933). Ipsilateral representation in the motor and premotor cortex of monkeys. *Brain,* 56, 318–42.

CLARK, W. E. L. (1941). Observations on the associative fibre system of the visual cortex and the central representation of the retina. *J. Anat., Lond.,* 75, 225–36.

DUNLAP, K. (1927). The short-circuiting of conscious responses. *J. Phil. Psychol. Sci. Meth.* 24, 263–67.

DUNLAP, K. (1930). Psychological hypotheses concerning the functions of the brain. *Sci. Mon., N.Y.,* 31, 97–112.

EBBECKE, U. (1919). *Die kortikalen psychophysischen Erregungen.* Pp. x + 306. Leipzig: Barth.

EDGELL, B. (1924). *Theories of Memory.* Pp. 1–174. Oxford: Clarendon Press.

FIELDS, P. E. (1932). Studies in concept formation. I. The development of the concept of triangularity by the white rat. *Comp. Psychol. Monogr.* 9, no. 2, pp. 1–70.

FINLEY, C. B. (1941). Equivalent losses in accuracy of response after central and after peripheral sense deprivation. *J. Comp. Neurol.* 74, 203–37.

FISCHEL, W. (1948). *Die höheren Leistungen der Wirbeltiergehirne.* Pp. iv + 96. Leipzig: Barth.

FRANZ, S. I. (1907). On the functions of the cerebrum: The frontal lobes. *Arch. Psychol.* no. 2, pp. 1–64.

FRANZ, S. I. (1911). On the functions of the cerebrum: The occipital lobes. *Psychol. Monogr.* 13, no. 4, pp. 1–118.

GAY, J. R. & GELHORN, E. (1948). Cortical projection of proprioception. *Amer. J. Physiol.* 155, 437.

GIRDEN, E., METTLER, F. A., FINCH, G. & CULLER, E. (1936). Conditioned responses in a decorticate dog to acoustic, thermal, and tactile stimulation. *J. Comp. Psychol.* 21, 367–85.

GOLDSTEIN, K. (1940). *Human Nature in the Light of Psychopathology.* Pp. x + 258. Cambridge: Harvard University Press.

HEAD, H. (1926). *Aphasia and Kindred Disorders of Speech.* Vol. 2, pp. xxxiii + 430. New York: Macmillan.

HERRICK, C. J. (1926). *Brains of Rats and Men.* Chicago: University Press.

HUNTER, W. S. (1930). A consideration of Lashley's theory of the equipotentiality of cerebral action. *J. Gen. Psychol.* 3, 455–68.

INGEBRITSEN, O. C. (1933). Coordinating mechanisms of the spinal cord. *Genet. Psychol. Monogr.* 13, no. 6, pp. 485–553.

JACOBSEN, C. F. (1932). Influence of motor and premotor area lesions upon the retention of skilled movements in monkeys and chimpanzees. *Proc. Ass. Res. Nerv. Ment. Dis.* 13, 225-47.

JACOBSEN, C. F. (1936). Studies of cerebral function in primates. *Comp. Psychol. Monogr.* 13, no. 3, pp. 1–68.

KELLOGG, W. N., DEESE, JAMES, PRONKO, N. H. & FEINBERG, M. (1947). An attempt to condition the *chronic* spinal dog. *J. Exp. Psychol.* 37, 99–117.

KENNARD, M. A. (1939). Alterations in response to visual stimuli following lesions of frontal lobe in monkeys. *Arch. Neurol. Psychiat.* 41, 1153–65.

KRECHEVSKY, I. (1936). Brain mechanisms and brightness discrimination. *J. Comp. Psychol.* 21, 405–45.

LASHLEY, K. S. (1916). The human salivary reflex and its use in psychology. *Psychol. Rev.* 23, 446–64.

LASHLEY, K. S. (1921a). Studies of cerebral function in learning. II. The effects of long continued practice upon cerebral localization. *J. Comp. Psychol.* 1, 453–68.

LASHLEY, K. S. (1921b). Studies of cerebral function in learning. III. The motor areas. *Brain,* 44, 256–86.

LASHLEY, K. S. (1922). Studies of cerebral function in learning. IV. Vicarious function after destruction of the visual areas. *Amer. J. Physiol.* 59, 44–71.

LASHLEY, K. S. (1924). Studies of cerebral function in learning. V. The retention of motor habits after destruction of the so-called motor areas in primates. *Arch. Neurol. Psychiat.* 12, 249–76.

LASHLEY, K. S. (1929). *Brain Mechanisms and Intelligence.* Pp. xiv + 186. Chicago: University Press.

LASHLEY, K. S. (1932). The mechanism of vision. V. The structure and image-forming power of the rat's eye. *J. Comp. Psychol.* 13, 173–200.

LASHLEY, K. S. (1935a). Studies of cerebral function in learning. XI. The behavior of the rat in latch-box situations. *Comp. Psychol. Monogr.* 11, 1–42.

LASHLEY, K. S. (1935b). The mechanism of vision. XII. Nervous structures concerned in the acquisition and retention of habits based on reactions to light. *Comp. Psychol. Monogr.* 11, 43–79.

LASHLEY, K. S. (1938). The mechanism of vision. XV. Preliminary studies of the rat's capacity for detail vision. *J. Genet. Psychol.* 18, 123–93.

LASHLEY, K. S. (1939). The mechanism of vision. XVI. The functioning of small remnants of the visual cortex. *J. Comp. Neurol.* 70, 45–67.

LASHLEY, K. S. (1941). Thalamo-cortical connections of the rat's brain. *J. Comp. Neurol.* 75, 67–121.

LASHLEY, K. S. (1942a). The problem of cerebral organization in vision. *Biol. Symp.* 7, 301–22.

LASHLEY, K. S. (1942b). The mechanism of vision. XVII. Autonomy of the visual cortex. *J. Genet. Psychol.* 60, 197–221.

LASHLEY, K. S. (1943). Studies of cerebral function in learning. XII. Loss of the maze habit after occipital lesions in blind rats. *J. Comp. Neurol.* 79, 431–62.

LASHLEY, K. S. (1944). Studies of cerebral function in learning. XIII. Apparent absence of transcortical association in maze learning. *J. Comp. Neurol.* 80, 257–81.

LASHLEY, K. S. (1948). The mechanism of vision. XVIII. Effects of destroying the visual 'associative areas' of the monkey. *Genet. Psychol. Monogr.* 37, 107–66.

LASHLEY, K. S. (1949). The problem of serial order in behavior. *Hixon Symposium on Cerebral Mechanisms in Behavior.*

LASHLEY, K. S. & McCARTHY, D. A. (1926). The survival of the maze habit after cerebellar injuries. *J. Comp. Psychol.* 6, 423–33.

LASHLEY, K. S. & WILEY, L. E. (1933). Studies of cerebral function in learning. IX. Mass action in relation to the number of elements in the problem to be learned. *J. Comp. Neurol.* 57, pp. 3–55.

LORENTE DE NÓ, R. (1934). Studies on the structure of the cerebral cortex. II. Continuation of the study of the Ammonic system. *J. Psychol. Neurol.* 46, 113–77.

McGEOCH, J. A. (1942). *The Psychology of Human Learning.* Pp. xviii + 633. New York: Longmans, Green.

METTLER, F. A. (1949). Physiologic effects of bilateral simultaneous removal of Brodmann's cytoarchitectural areas in the human. *Fed. Proc.* 8, 109.

NIELSEN, J. M. (1936). *Agnosia, Apraxia, Aphasia, their Value in Cerebral Localization.* Pp. vii + 210. Los Angeles: Waverly Press.

POLTEREW, S. S. & ZELIONY, G. P. (1930). Grosshirnrinde und Assoziationsfunction. *Z. Biol.* 90, 157–60.

SMITH, K. U. (1947). Bilateral integrative action of the cerebral cortex in man in verbal association and sensori-motor coordination *J. Exp. Psychol.* 37, 367–76.

SPERRY, R. W. (1947). Cerebral regulation of motor coordination in monkeys following multiple transection of sensorimotor cortex. *J. Neurophysiol.* 10, 275–94.

TSANG, YU-CHUAN (1934). The function of the visual areas of the cortex of the rat in the learning and retention of the maze. *Comp. Psychol. Monogr.* 10, 1–56.

WALKER, A. E. (1938). *The Primate Thalamus.* Pp. xxiv + 321. Chicago: University Press.

WARD, A. A. Jr., PEDEN, J. K. & SUGAR, O. (1946). Cortico-cortical connections in the monkey with special reference to Area 6. *J. Neurophysiol.* 9, 453–61.

PERCEPTION

Perception has been traditionally regarded as the process of obtaining knowledge about the world through the senses. Since both the dangerous and the desirable aspects of the immediate environment must be known before action of any kind can proceed, interest in perception comes naturally to thoughtful men who ponder their relationship to the surrounding world.

In 1890, William James defined perception as "The consciousness of particular material things present to sense." Although contemporary psychology has sharpened this definition and invented sophisticated procedures for investigating perception, the general concept has not changed. In fact, the fundamental issues in perception have been outlined for centuries, long before the development of modern experimental psychology.

Given the primacy of perception as a determinant of thought and behavior, the inquiry turns to questions of what is perceived, how it is perceived, and with what accuracy and precision. We now know, for example, that only a small portion of the available information about the environment is perceived. As would be predicted from evolutionary considerations, we tend to perceive those aspects of the environment which are most useful in guiding our behavior. Other stimuli go unheeded. Further, the existence of optical illusions shows that the objects and events which we perceive do not always faithfully reflect the realities of our environment. Differences between the perceived world and the objective world, along with evidence of the fallibility of perception, have stimulated theoretical questions that have, in turn, generated a multitude of experiments on sensation and perception, ranging from cellular physiology to social relations.

In the history of psychology, many experimenters have found it useful to draw a distinction between sensation and perception. Traditionally, sensation refers to the first stage of perception (e.g., seeing a color) that is governed largely by peripheral receptors and nerves. In contrast perception refers to more complex processes (e.g., recognizing a word) involving more central neural mechanisms. As will be seen in the articles that follow, however, the distinction between sensation and perception is not always easy nor useful to maintain.

The seven articles in this section have been chosen to illustrate several different approaches to research in perception. They are arranged in a sequence that begins with receptor mechanisms and sensory nerves and then proceeds step-by-step to more strictly psychological phenomena. The first three selections, by Müller, Pfaffman, and Hubel, deal with the nature of the neural structures involved in sensation and perception and reflect the intimate and longstanding relation between perception and neuro-physiology. As will be seen from these articles, a close correspondence between many perceptual and physiological events has already been established.

The next set of four articles is concerned with the psychological processes that are involved in perception. The experiments described by Boring deal with the perception of space; Held and Hein approach the general problem of the extent to which present action depends upon pre-viously acquired information; and Broadbent discusses the problem of selecting one perception from among several competing sources of incom-ing information. In the final article, Gibson and Pick illustrate the nature and accuracy of perception in social interaction.

SENSORY BASES OF PERCEPTION

10. The Nature of Sensation *

Johannes Müller

How do we come to know the world about us? How do we know "the sky is blue," or "the chair squeaks," and so on. One might reply, "We know those things through our senses—we look with our eyes and see the color of the sky, and with our ears we hear the squeak of the chair." But *how* do our eyes know about the colors and our ears about sounds? At this point one might say, "Our sensory receptors respond to physical stimulation, and then the nerves send the message to the brain, where it is analyzed and interpreted." This answer would be consistent with our contemporary knowledge of the nervous system and its relation to the external world.

But less than 150 years ago the process by which a physical event gave rise to a conscious sensation was still unknown. Most of the theories that were being entertained then assumed some sort of supernatural intervention although, like Descartes' theory, this feature was sometimes elaborately hidden. In 1838, Johannes Müller formulated a new theory about sensation and perception which has proved to be a valuable foundation for modern experimentation. The next article is an excerpt from his argument, written in the style typical of 19th-century scholars. Müller's major point now seems self-evident: knowledge of the environment is provided only by nerves and the signals they transmit. This means that external events must first be translated into the language of the nervous system, and it is this neural language which speaks to the mind.

* Excerpted from Book VI of *Elements of Physiology*. Translated by W. Baly. Lea and Blanchard, Philadelphia, 1843.

V. *Sensation consists in the sensorium receiving through the medium of the nerves, and as the result of the action of an external cause, a knowledge of certain qualities or conditions, not of external bodies, but of the nerves of sense themselves; and these qualities of the nerves of sense are in all different, the nerve of each sense having its own peculiar quality or energy.*

The special susceptibility of the different nerves of sense for certain influences,—as of the optic nerve for light, of the auditory nerve for vibrations, and so on,—was formerly attributed to these nerves having each a specific irritability. But this hypothesis is evidently insufficient to explain all the facts. The nerves of the senses have assuredly a specific irritability for certain influences; for many stimuli, which exert a violent action upon one organ of sense, have little or no effect upon another: for example, light, or vibrations so infinitely rapid as those of light, act only on the nerves of vision and common sensation; slower vibrations, on the nerves of hearing and common sensation, but not upon those of vision; odorous substances only upon the olfactory nerves. The external stimuli must therefore be adapted to the organ of sense—must be "homogeneous:" thus light is the stimulus adapted to the nerve of vision; while vibrations of less rapidity, which act upon the auditory nerve, are not adapted to the optic nerve, or are indifferent to it; for, if the eye be touched with a tuning-fork while vibrating, a sensation of tremors is excited in the conjunctiva, but no sensation of light. We have seen, however, that one and the same stimulus, as electricity, will produce different sensations in the different nerves of the senses; all the nerves are susceptible of its action, but the sensations in all are different. The same is the case with other stimuli, as chemical and mechanical influences. The hypothesis of a specific irritability of the nerves of the senses for certain stimuli, is therefore insufficient; and we are compelled to ascribe, with Aristotle, peculiar energies to each nerve,—energies which are vital qualities of the nerve, just as contractility is the vital property of muscle. The truth of this has been rendered more and more evident in recent times by the investigation of the so-called "subjective" phenomena of the senses by Elliot, Darwin, Ritter, Goethe, Purkinje, and Iljort. Those phenomena of the senses, namely, are now styled "subjective," which are produced, not by the usual stimulus adapted to the particular nerve of sense, but by others which do not usually act upon it. These important phenomena were long spoken of as "illusions of the senses," and have been regarded in an erroneous point of view; while they are really true actions of the senses, and must be studied as fundamental phenomena in investigations into their nature.

The sensation of sound, therefore, is the peculiar "energy" or "quality" of the auditory nerve; the sensation of light and colours that of the optic nerve; and so of the other nerves of sense. An exact analysis of what takes place in the production of a sensation would of itself have led to this conclusion. The sensations of heat and cold, for example, make us acquainted with the existence of the imponderable matter of caloric, or of peculiar vibrations in the vicinity of our nerves of feeling. But the nature of this caloric cannot be elucidated by sensation, which is in reality merely a particular state of our nerves; it must be learnt by the study of the physical properties of this agent, namely, of the laws of its radiation, its development from the latent state, its property of combining with and producing expansion of other bodies, &c. All this again, however, does not explain the peculiarity of the sensation of warmth as a condition of the nerves. The simple fact devoid of all theory is this, that warmth, as a sensation, is produced whenever the matter of caloric acts upon the nerves of feeling; and that cold, as a sensation, results from this matter of caloric being abstracted from a nerve of feeling.

So, also, the sensation of sound is produced when a certain number of impulses or vibrations are imparted, within a certain time, to the auditory nerve: but sound, as we perceive it, is a very different thing from a succession of vibrations. The vibrations of a tuning-fork, which to the ear give the impression of sound, produce in a nerve of feeling or touch the sensation of tickling; something besides the vibrations must consequently be necessary for the production of the sensation of sound, and that something is possessed by the auditory nerve alone. Vision is to be regarded in the same manner.

The essential nature of these conditions of the nerves, by virtue of which they see light and hear sound,—the essential nature of sound as a property of the auditory nerve, and of light as a property of the optic nerve, of taste, of smell, and of feeling,—remains, like the ultimate causes of natural phenomena generally, a problem incapable of solution.

The accuracy of our discrimination by means of the senses depends on the different manner in which the conditions of our nerves are affected by different bodies; but the preceding considerations show us the impossibility that our senses can ever reveal to us the true nature and essence of the material world. In our intercourse with external nature it is always our own sensations that we become acquainted with, and from them we form conceptions of the properties of external objects, which may be relatively correct; but we can never submit the nature of the objects themselves to that immediate perception to which the states of the different parts of our own body are subjected in the sensorium.

11. The Afferent Code for Sensory Quality *

Carl Pfaffman

Information regarding objects and events in the environment is translated by receptors into nerve impulses in very much the same way that a telegrapher translates words into dots and dashes. To understand how perception occurs, it is necessary to know something about the kind of code employed by the nervous system.

Certain characteristics of the neural code are already well known. For example, the more intense the stimulus, the higher the rate of nerve impulses. This aspect of the code contributes to understanding the discrimination of intensity. But what of other qualities of the stimulus such as greenness or saltiness? In the following article, Professor Pfaffman provides us with insight into the neural code for such qualities. He recorded the activity of single axons in the nerve connecting the taste buds to the brain while stimulating the tongue with a variety of simple solutions.

One of the basic problems in the psychology and physiology of sensation is that of the mechanism by which different sensory qualities are perceived. The classical dictum on this problem was propounded by Johannes Müller in his doctrine of the Specific Energies of Nerves. Actually Charles Bell had enunciated (Carmichael, 1926) the principle somewhat earlier, but Müller's version is better known. This doctrine made clear that "We are aware of the state of our nerves, not of the external stimulus itself." The eye, however stimulated, gives rise to sensations of light; the ear, to sensations of sound; and taste buds, to sensations of taste.

The further extension of the doctrine of Specific Nerve Energies to the different sensation qualities within a single modality was made by Helmholtz. According to his place theory of hearing, the perception of a particular pitch was attributed to the activity at a particular region of the basilar membrane of the inner ear, stimulation of individual nerve fibers at these specific locations gave rise to unique tonal qualities of pitch. *Pitch* depended upon *which* nerve fiber was activated (Boring, 1950). In the less complex modalities, like the cutaneous or gustatory senses, von Frey and his school propounded the view of "modalities within modalities." The cutaneous sense was said to consist of separate modalities: touch, pressure, warm, cold, and pain, each with their specific receptors. The history of research on cutaneous sensitivity is, in large measure, a history of the search for such receptors. In taste the "BIG FOUR" are familiar to all; the qualities, salty, sour, bitter, and sweet, were each mediated by a specific receptor type.

Implicit in these formulations is an isomorphism between receptor structure and phenomenology. Pure sensation as a basic psychological entity was to be reduced to a physiological entity. Psychology (at least a part thereof) was to be "explained" by the underlying physiology, hence, "Physiological Psychology." This formulation, simple and direct, dominated the field of sensory psychology from the beginning with only an occasional and sporadic dissenting voice. The fact that the psychological entities were only postulated and the question of whether they were, in fact, valid were almost forgotten in the search for the "real thing."

Many of the more recent findings in sen-

* Reprinted by permission of the author and the American Psychological Association from the *American Psychologist*, 1959, *14*, 226-232.

sory psychology and physiology derive from the application of electrophysiology to the study of sensory processes. The publication of E. D. Adrian's *The Basis of Sensation* in 1928 opened a new era. The invention of the electronic tube, appropriate amplifying circuits, and recording instruments made it possible to study directly the activity of the sense organs and their nerves. Since 1928, the advances in technique and instrumentation have been so dramatic that there is almost no part of the nervous system that cannot be probed by the inquisitive microelectrode. Psychologists have played a significant role in this development. One of their best known early discoveries was that of Wever and Bray (1930), on the cochlea and VIIIth nerve.

This paper will review some experiments with this procedure on another sense, that of taste, and will discuss their general implications for the theory of afferent coding.[1] It should be emphasized that sensation itself is not being studied. Rather the investigator "taps in" on the "basis of sensation" by recording and amplifying the nerve impulse traffic in the sensory fibers "en route" to the brain.

The sense of taste is particularly well suited to this problem because it consists of well defined differentiated structures, the taste buds, which are capable of mediating quite different sensory qualities, but the array of qualities and dimensions is not too complex for interpretation. The afferent message from receptor to brain can be studied directly in the afferent nerve fibers from the tongue, for the primary sensory nerve fibers from the receptive organs are relatively accessible with no synaptic complexities in the direct line from the receptors except for the junction between sense cell and sensory fiber.

The taste stimulus, like all stimuli, acts first upon a receptor cell. Changes in the receptor cell in turn activate or "trigger"

---

[1] Many of our experiments on taste were supported by a contract with the Office of Naval Research.

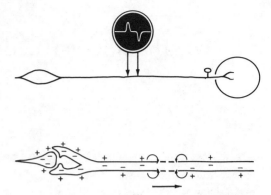

Figure 11.1 Diagram of electrophysiological recording from a single sensory nerve fiber. Upper diagram shows a single fiber in contact with a single sense cell to the left. A diphasic response on the cathode ray tube is shown as an impulse passes the recording electrodes en route to the central nervous system schematized to the right. The lower figure shows in more detail the positive and negative charges around the cell membranes associated with the passage of the nerve impulse.

impulses in the nerve fiber. Both the sense cell, as well as the nerve fiber, and in fact all living cells are like tiny batteries with a potential difference across the cell membrane. When stimulated, this membrane is depolarized, and it is this depolarization that can be recorded. Figure 11-1 schematizes such recording from a single sensory nerve fiber shown in contact with a receptor cell to the left of the figure and entering the central nervous system (CNS) to the right. The recording electrodes on the fiber connect with an appropriate recording device such as a cathode ray oscillograph shown schematically. As the impulse passes the first electrode, there is an upward deflection; as it passes the second electrode, there is a downward deflection. By an appropriate arrangement, a single or monophasic deflection only may be obtained so that at each passage of an impulse there will be a "spike" on the oscillograph tracing. The lower figure shows schematically the electrical activity associated with the passage of a nerve impulse. The message

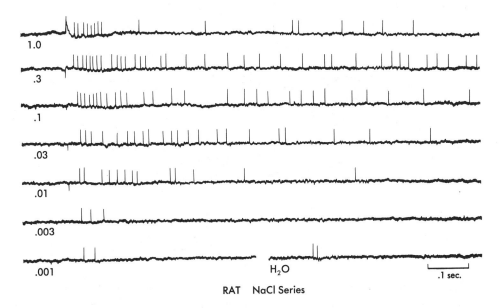

1.0

.3

.1

.03

.01

.003

.001   H₂O   .1 sec.

RAT   NaCl Series

Figure 11.2 A series of oscillograph tracings obtained from a single taste nerve fiber when different concentrations of salt solution are placed on the tongue. Note that water as well as .001 M NaCl will elicit two impulses. A concentration of .003 M NaCl will elicit three impulses and may be considered as threshold. Reproduced from the *Journal of Neurophysiology*.

delivered along any single nerve fiber therefore consists of a train of impulses, changes in excitation of the receptor are signaled by changes in the frequency of this train. Thus, changes in strength of solution bathing the tongue change the frequency of impulse discharge per second. In any one fiber, the size of the impulse is nearly constant. The sensory nerve message, therefore, is a digital process.

Figure 11-2 shows a typical series of oscillograph tracings obtained from a *single* nerve fiber when different concentrations of sodium chloride are applied to the tongue of the rat. The "spikes" signal the passage of each impulse past the recording electrode. With stronger stimuli there is a higher frequency of discharge. Threshold for this fiber lies at approximately 0.003 M. Other fibers will show similar behavior, but may possess higher thresholds for the tongue contains a population of taste receptors with thresholds of differing value.

This description applies to the impulse in the single sensory nerve fiber. Actually, the sensory nerve is a cable, made up of many different fibers each connected with one or more receptor cells. The single fiber recordings shown were obtained after the nerve cable had been dissected to a strand containing just one functional unit. Sometimes, the same effect is achieved by using microelectrodes.

The nerve fibers subserving taste travel in three nerves from the mouth region: the lingual, glossopharyngeal, and vagus nerves which contain touch, temperature, pressure, and pain fibers as well as those concerned with taste. The taste fibers from the anterior tongue branch off from the lingual nerve to form the chorda tympani nerve where it is possible to record almost exclusively from taste nerve fibers. This nerve can be exposed by appropriate surgery in the anesthetized animal and placed on the electrodes leading to the recording apparatus.

A block diagram of the apparatus to-

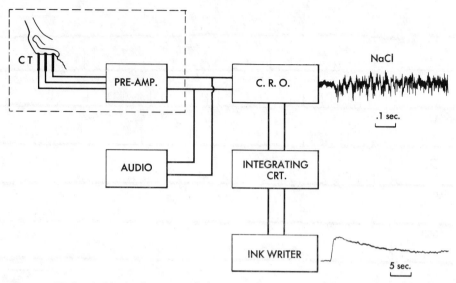

NaCl

.1 sec.

5 sec.

Figure 11.3 A block diagram of the recording apparatus, showing two types of record. The upper trace shows a typical asynchronous, multifiber discharge from a large number of active fibers; the lower trace shows the integrated record of such activity. Reproduced from the *American Journal of Clinical Nutrition*.

gether with sample records is shown in Figure 11-3. The integrated record is readily adapted to quantitative treatment by measuring the magnitude of the deflection at each response and so provides a measure of the total activity of all the fibers in the nerve. An index of over-all taste sensitivity can be obtained from such recordings. The curves in Figure 11-4 are such measures for the cat for quinine, hydrochloric acid, sodium chloride, potassium chloride, and sucrose solutions (Pfaffmann, 1955).

The basic taste stimuli can be arranged in order of thresholds from low to high as follows: quinine, hydrochloric acid, sodium chloride, potassium chloride, and sucrose. In this animal, as in man, quinine is effective in relatively low concentrations. Sugar at the other end of the scale requires relatively high concentrations, and the electrolytes are intermediate. Sugar produces a nerve response of small magnitude compared with that to other stimuli. Differences in response magnitudes are found from one species to another. In the hamster or guinea pig, for example, sugar

will elicit a strong discharge, and other species differences with quinine and the salts have been observed (Beidler, Fishman, & Hardiman, 1955; Pfaffmann, 1953). Recently, Carpenter (1956) has correlated certain of these species differences with behavioral data using the preference method.

The representation in Figure 11-4 does not show that the animal can distinguish one substance from another. Actually an animal like the rat will avoid quinine and acid, but will show a preference for NaCl and sucrose. To find how the animal can discriminate among different chemicals the single fiber analysis is required.

In the early study of the single gustatory fibers in the cat (Pfaffmann, 1941), three different kinds of fiber were found. One was responsive to sodium chloride and acid, another to quinine and acid, and a third to acid alone. Thus, acid stimulated all receptor-neural units found. This established not only that the gustatory endings were differentially sensitive to different chemicals but that the physiological receptor "types" *did not* correspond to the phenom-

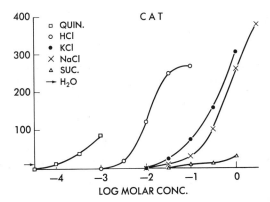

Figure 11.4 Curves of taste response in the cat to four different taste stimuli as indicated by the integrated response method. Reproduced from *Journal of Neurophysiology.*

enal categories as reported by man. In view of the more recently demonstrated species difference, this might not appear to be surprising. But, regardless of what the cat "tastes," these findings pointed to an important principle of sensory coding. This is that *the same afferent fiber may convey different information depending upon the amount of activity in another parallel fiber.* To illustrate, suppose A represents an acid-salt unit and C, an acid sensitive unit, then activity in A only would lead to salty; but activity in that same fiber, A, plus discharge in C would lead to sourness. Recent studies emphasize still another important point, namely, that some stimuli may decrease or inhibit the frequency of sensory discharge. Certain receptors, which can be stimulated by water (as well as other agents), may be inhibited by the application of dilute salt

solutions (Liljestrand & Zotterman, 1954). Taste stimuli, therefore, may either increase or decrease, i.e., modulate, the amount of afferent nerve traffic. A diminution in activity may signal, not merely the withdrawal of a particular stimulus, but the application of a different one.

Table 1 taken from a recent paper from Zotterman's laboratory (Cohen, Hagiwara, & Zotterman, 1955) illustrates the afferent code or pattern which may be described for the cat based on a compilation of the "types" so far discovered for that species.

But the use of the term "fiber type" harks back to some of the errors of classical thinking. Types are defined only by the range of stimuli sampled, the wider the range, the more difficult will it be to define pure "types." "Taste types" may turn out to be as varied and individual as "personality types." Figure 11-5 shows the variety of response patterns of nine single fiber preparations to the following standard test solutions: .03 N HCl, .1 M KCl, .1 M NaCl, .01 M quinine hydrochloride, and 1.0 M sucrose (Pfaffmann, 1955).

The bar graph shows the magnitude of response in each of the single fiber preparations in impulses per second of discharge. The central crosshatched bar graph shows the relative magnitude of response to these same solutions in the integrated response of the whole nerve. It is apparent that the individual fibers do not all have the same pattern. The sum of activity of all fibers is shown by the crosshatched diagram. Furthermore, fiber types are not immediately apparent in this array.

TABLE 1 [a]

Fiber Type Response in the Cat

Stimulus	"Water" fiber	"Salt" fiber	"Acid" fiber	"Quinine" fiber	Sensation evoked
H_2O (salt <0.03M)	+	0	0	0	→ water
NaCl (0.05M)	0	+	0	0	→ salt
HCl (*pH* 2.5)	+	+	+	0	→ sour
Quinine	+	0	0	+	→ bitter

[a] Cf., Cohen, Hagiwara, & Zotterman, 1955.

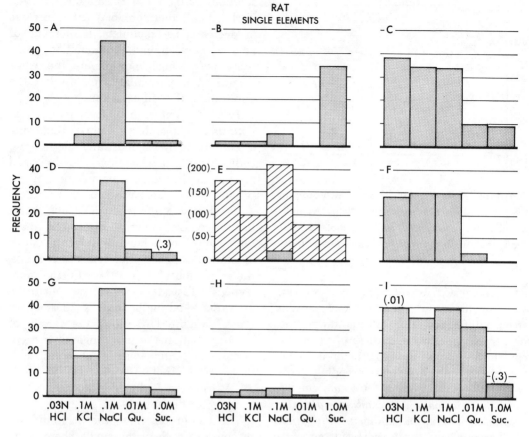

Figure 11.5 The pattern of taste responses in nine different single sensory nerve fibers of the rat. The solid bar graphs give the frequency of response in impulses per second for different taste stimuli (indicated along the abscissa). The crosshatched bar graph shows the relative response of the total nerve (integrated response) to these same solutions. Reproduced from the *Journal of Neurophysiology*.

The fact that the individual receptor cells possess combined sensitivity as salt plus acid, or salt plus sugar, cannot be dismissed as the result of multiple innervation of more than one receptor cell by a single fiber. Kimura (Beidler, 1957; Kimura & Beidler, 1956) has studied the sensitivity patterns of the individual taste cells by inserting micropipette electrodes directly into the sense cells themselves. The pattern of sensitivity found in the individual sensory cell is like that already described for the single afferent fiber. Thus, within the individual sense cell there must be different sites which are selectively sensitive

to different taste stimuli. These sites on the membrane may be determined by molecular configuration, the shape and size of pores in the membrane, or some such microcellular feature.

One additional principle must be introduced. This is that the relative rather than the absolute amount of activity in any one set of afferent fibers may determine the quality of sensation. Figure 11-6 shows frequency of discharge as a function of stimulus intensity for two units labelled A and B. Both are stimulated by both stimuli sugar and salt, but it is apparent that A is more sensitive to salt and B to sugar

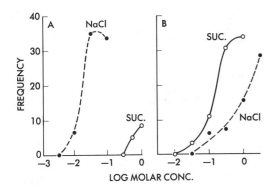

Figure 11.6 The relation between frequency of discharge and concentration in two fibers both of which are sensitive to sugar and salt. Reproduced from the *Journal of Neurophysiology.*

(Pfaffmann, 1955). Once each stimulus intensity exceeds the threshold for a particular receptor unit, the frequency of discharge increases with concentration. Thus the afferent pattern as the code for sensory quality must take account of the changing frequency of discharge with stimulus intensity. The pattern concept may be retained by recognizing that "pattern" is still apparent in the relative amount of activity of different fibers. In the two-fiber example shown in Figure 6, low concentrations of salt will discharge only A, higher concentrations will discharge both A and B, but activity in A will be greater than that in B. Low concentrations of sugar will activate only B, higher concentrations will activate both B and A, but B will be greater than A. Thus the sensory code might read:

FREQUENCY CODE
A > B = salty
B > A = sweet

where A or B may go to zero. It is not only the activity in parallel fibers that is important, it is the *relative amount* of such parallel activity.

Studies of the other senses indicate that these principles are not unique to taste. In the cutaneous senses there is a variety of different endings which overlap two or more of the classical skin modalities (Mar-

uhashi, Mizuguchi, & Tasaki, 1952). For example, some pressure receptors in the cat's tongue are activated by cold (Hensel & Zotterman, 1951), and there are several different pressure, temperature, and nociceptor endings, some serving large or small areas, some adapting slowly, others rapidly to give a variety of temporal as well as spatial "discriminanda." These findings are reminiscent of Nafe's (1934) quantitative theory of feeling, and the recent anatomical studies of Weddell (1955) and his group are of similar import.

In audition, selective sensitivity among the individual primary afferent fibers is very broad. Those fibers arising from the basal turn of the cochlea respond to tones of any audible frequency; those arising in the upper part respond only to a band of low frequency tones (Tasaki, 1954). Further, it has been suggested (Wever, 1949) that the temporal patterning of the discharge, especially in the low frequencies, provides a basis for pitch discrimination. In vision, Granit (1955) has suggested that different impulse frequencies in the *same* third order neuron from the retina may signal different spectral events at the periphery.

These electrophysiological results should not have been surprising to us. That a particular sensory dimension is not isomorphic with a particular physical dimension is well known. Auditory loudness, functionally dependent upon sound pressure level, is not synonymous with physical intensity. Pitch is not the same as frequency, although the latter is its major determinant (Stevens & Davis, 1938). Visual brightness is not the same as physical luminance. It would, indeed, have been surprising if similar nonidentities had not been found at the physiological level.

And so in attacking Müller's classic problem with modern techniques, we have found, at least, within the modalities, a solution different from that which was first anticipated. Differential sensitivity rather than specificity, patterned discharges rather than a mosaic of sensitivities is the form of our modern view. Müller's principle did not answer a problem so much as it posed one. In the answers that I have attempted to suggest, we see, not only the details of the mechanism for which we have searched, but we can discern broader implications for the principles governing the relation between psychology and physiology. Psychology cannot rest content with a pseudophysiology based solely upon phenomenology. So long as the receptor surface was conceived to be a static mosaic where phenomenal qualities were reified (in some instances in the form of specific anatomical structures), sensory psychology and physiology were reduced to the study of how the "little pictures" were transmitted via the sensory nerves to the "sensorium" located presumably somewhere "inside the head." Such a view is not only out of date, but it diverts our attention from the proper study of the afferent influx, its dynamic properties and interactions and its relevance for all levels of neural integration and behavioral organization.

REFERENCES

ADRIAN, E. D. *The basis of sensation.* New York: Norton, 1928.

BEIDLER, L. M. Facts and theory on the mechanism of taste and odor perception. In *Chemistry of natural food flavors.* Quartermaster Research and Engineering Center, 1957. Pp. 7–47.

BEIDLER, L. M., FISHMAN, I. Y., & HARDIMAN, C. W. Species differences in taste responses. *Amer. J. Physiol.,* 1955, 181, 235–239.

BORING, E. G. *A history of experimental psychology.* New York: Appleton-Century-Crofts, 1950.

CARMICHAEL, L. Sir Charles Bell: A contribution to the history of physiological psychology. *Psychol. Rev.,* 1926, 33, 188–217.

CARPENTER, J. A. Species differences in taste preferences. *J. comp. physiol. Psychol.,* 1956, 49, 139–144.

COHEN, M. J., HAGIWARA, S., & ZOTTERMAN, Y. The response spectrum of taste fibers in the cat: A single fiber analysis. *Acta. physiol., Scand.,* 1955, 33, 316–332.

GRANIT, R. *Receptors and sensory perception.* New Haven: Yale Univer. Press, 1955.

HENSEL, H., & ZOTTERMAN, Y. The response of mechano-receptors to thermal stimulation. *J. Physiol.,* 1951, 115, 16–24.

KIMURA, K., & BEIDLER, L. M. Microelectrode study of taste bud of the rat. *Amer. J. Physiol.,* 1956, 187, 610.

LILJESTRAND, G., & ZOTTERMAN, Y. The water taste in mammals. *Acta physiol., Scand.,* 1954, 32, 291–303.

MARUHASHI, J., MIZUGUCHI, K., & TASAKI, I. Action currents in single afferent nerve fibers elicited by stimulation of the skin of the toad and the cat. *J. Physiol.,* 1952, 117, 129–151.

NAFE, J. P. The pressure, pain and temperature sense. In C. Murchusion (Ed.), *Handbook of general experimental psychology.* Worcester: Clark Univer. Press, 1934. Chap. 20.

PFAFFMANN, C. Gustatory afferent impulses. *J. cell. comp. Physiol.,* 1941, 17, 243–258.

PFAFFMANN, C. Species differences in taste sensitivity. *Science,* 1953, 117, 470.

PFAFFMANN, C. Gustatory nerve impulses in rat, cat, and rabbit. *J. Neurophysiol.,* 1955, 18, 429–440.

STEVENS, S. S., & DAVIS, H. *Hearing.* New York: Wiley, 1938.

TASAKI, I. Nerve impulses in individual auditory nerve fibers of guinea pigs. *J. Neurophysiol.,* 1954, 17, 97–122.

WEDDELL, G. Somesthesis and the chemical senses. *Ann. Rev. Psychol.,* 1955, 6, 119–136.

WEVER, E. G. *Theory of hearing.* New York: Wiley, 1949.

WEVER, E. G., & BRAY, C. W. Action currents in the auditory nerve in response to acoustical stimulation. *Proc. Nat. Acad. Sci.,* 1930, 16, 344–350.

12. Integrative Processes in Central Visual Pathways of the Cat *

David H. Hubel

In the visual system of mammals, the optic nerve projects to a cluster of neurons in the brain called, collectively, the lateral geniculate body. From these cells, in turn, axons arise which carry the neural activity to cells in the neocortex. The analysis of the afferent code for vision has been extended from the retina to these more central structures in the visual system. Although technically difficult to study, the conceptual analysis of single cell activity at these stations in the visual system is quite simple. First, a single cell is located with a microelectrode, then the eye is stimulated with a variety of visual patterns, shapes, or colors in order to determine the kinds of visual stimulation to which the cell is particularly sensitive. By slowly moving the electrode about, the response of other cells can be isolated and similar determinations of sensitivity can be made.

In the next selection, Professor Hubel demonstrates that events particularly important to an animal, such as the movement of an object, are first abstracted from the barrage of stimulation striking the retina and then translated into unique neural signals. This process of abstraction and translation occurs automatically as the neural activity proceeds from retina to cortex.

An understanding of the spatial organization of the visual system relies heavily on the concept of a *receptive field*, an idea to which Hubel repeatedly refers. The receptive field of a sensory neuron is that area of the receptor surface (e.g., the retina) to which the individual neuron is specifically responsive. Hubel's analysis of the receptive fields of visual cells in the brain builds on previous work by Kuffler, who analysed the receptive fields of cells in the retina. It is the difference between the receptive fields of cells in the retina and the cortex that is the chief topic of the article.

An image falling upon the retina exerts an influence on millions of receptors. It is the task of the central nervous system to make sense of the spatial and temporal patterns of excitation in this retinal mosaic. Unless we know something of how the nervous system handles the messages it receives, we cannot easily come to grips with the problems of perception of form, movement, color, or depth.

For a study of integrative sensory mechanisms the visual system of mammals offers the advantage of a comparatively direct anatomical pathway. At each stage, from bipolar cells to the striate cortex, we can compare activity of cells with that of the incoming fibers, and so attempt to learn what each structure contributes to the visual process. In this paper I summarize a series of studies on the cat visual system made by Torsten Wiesel and myself. I concentrate mainly on experiments related to form and movement.

It is often contended that in studying a sensory system we should first learn to understand thoroughly the physiology of receptors, and only then proceed to examine more central processes. In the visual system one should presumably have a firm grasp of rod and cone physiology before looking at bipolar and retinal ganglion cells; one should thoroughly understand retinal

* Reprinted by permission of the author and the American Institute of Physics from the *Journal of the Optical Society of America*, 1963, 53, 58-66.

mechanisms before taking up studies of the brain. Unfortunately it is not always possible to be so systematic. In the case of the visual system, orderly progress is impeded by the great technical difficulties in recording from single retinal elements, especially from the rods and cones and from bipolar cells. At the single-cell level, knowledge of the electrophysiology of these structures is consequently almost entirely lacking. If we wish to learn how the brain interprets information it receives from the retina we must either struggle with retinal problems of formidable difficulty or else skip over the first two stages and begin at a point where the appropriate single-unit techniques have been worked out, i.e., the retinal ganglion cell.

The subject of retinal ganglion-cell physiology is complicated by the fact that studies have been made in a wide variety of vertebrates and under a number of different experimental conditions. Here I only describe the receptive field organization of retinal ganglion cells in the cat. This is necessary for an understanding of the integrative function of the lateral geniculate body, since the geniculate receives its main visual input directly from the retina.

Because there is convergence of a number of afferent fibers onto each cell, both for bipolar cells and for retinal ganglion cells, we are not surprised to learn that a single ganglion cell may receive its input ultimately from a large number of rods and cones, and hence from a retinal surface of considerable extent. At first glance it might seem that a progressive increase in the size of receptive fields as we follow the visual pathway centrally must lead to a wasteful and pointless blurring of detailed information acquired by the exquisitely fine receptor mosaic. To understand why fineness of discrimination is not necessarily blunted we must realize that all retinal connections are not necessarily excitatory. The existence of inhibitory connections means that when we shine a spot of light on the receptive field of a given cell we may decrease, rather than increase, the cell's rate

of firing. The effect of the stimulus will depend on the part of the receptive field we illuminate. The fineness of discrimination of a cell is determined not by the overall receptive field size, but by the arrangement of excitatory and inhibitory regions within the receptive field.

With the experiments of Kuffler (1953) it became apparent that in the light-adapted cat, retinal ganglion cells did not necessarily respond uniformly throughout their receptive fields: their discharges might be activated or suppressed by a spot of light, depending upon where on the retina the spot fell. The receptive field of a ganglion cell could thus be mapped into distinct excitatory and inhibitory regions. Two types of cells were distinguished by Kuffler: those with fields having a more or less circular excitatory center with an annular inhibitory surround, and those having the reverse arrangement. These two concentrically arranged field types were called "on"-center and "off"-center fields. The terms "off" center and "off" response refer to the empirical finding that when a spot of light suppresses a cell's firing, turning the spot off almost always evokes a discharge, termed the "off" response. Conversely when we see an "off" discharge we usually find that during the stimulus the maintained firing of a cell is suppressed.

Within the excitatory or inhibitory region of a receptive field one can demonstrate summation, i.e., for a given intensity of stimulus the response increases (number of spikes and frequency of firing increase, latency and threshold decrease) as the area stimulated is increased. On the other hand, when both types of region are included in a stimulus their separate effects tend to cancel. If the entire receptive field is illuminated, for example by diffuse light, a relatively weak response of the center type is usually obtained: an "on"-center cell thus gives a weak "on" response, and an "off"-center cell a weak "off" response. I shall use the term "peripheral suppression" to refer to this antagonistic interaction between center and periphery.

Retinal ganglion cells differ from one another in several ways besides those related to field-center type. Obviously they vary in the location of their receptive fields on the retina. In the cat (Wiesel 1960) and the monkey (Hubel and Wiesel 1960) there are considerable differences in the sizes of receptive-field centers, receptive fields near the area centralis or fovea showing a marked tendency to have smaller centers than fields in the peripheral retina. Even for a given region of the retina there is a large variation in the size of field centers. In the monkey the smallest field center so far measured had a diameter of 4 minutes of arc; this was situated 4° from the fovea. It is likely that the centers of foveal fields are much smaller than this. The total extent of a field is more difficult to determine, since the effect of a spot of light upon a cell decreases gradually with increasing distance from the field center. Measurements made by constructing area-threshold curves (Wiesel 1960) suggest that receptive fields may not greatly differ in their total size despite wide variations in center sizes.

Retinal ganglion cells differ also in the effectiveness with which the receptive-field periphery antagonizes the center response. This may be measured by determining the difference between the threshold intensity of a spot covering the receptive-field center and that of a large spot covering the entire field. The difference tends to be greater for cells with small field centers (and hence large peripheral zones) than for cells with large field centers. Since cells with small field centers are especially common in the area centralis, this ability to discriminate against diffuse light is particularly pronounced in that part of the retina.

In the cat we know of no functional retinal ganglion cell types besides the "on"-center and "off"-center cells described by Kuffler. Occasionally diffuse light evokes a discharge both at "on" and at "off." This may occur in either "on"-center cells or "off"-center cells. It depends to some extent on the state of light adaptation, stimulus in-

tensity, and other variables. The receptive fields of cells showing "on-off" responses to large spots do not seem to differ in any fundamental way from ordinary "on"-center or "off"-center cells. There thus seems to be no reason for regarding "on-off" retinal ganglion cells of cat as a distinct type.

In the cat the arrangement of excitatory and inhibitory regions within a given receptive field remains the same for all effective stimulus wavelengths. The fields thus seem to be very different from the more complex opponent-color fields described by Wolbarsht, Wagner, and MacNichol (1961) for goldfish retinal ganglion cells (see discussion of Barlow, in Wolbarsht *et al.*, 1961, p. 176). In the monkey optic nerve and lateral geniculate body there are two types of neurones, one resembling cells of the cat in having receptive-field characteristics that are independent of wavelength, the other showing color-specific responses in many ways similar to those seen in the goldfish (Hubel and Wiesel 1960; De-Valois 1960).

In the frog, Maturana, Lettvin, McCulloch, and Pitts (1960) have described retinal ganglion cells with highly complex response properties. Their records were made from unmyelinated axons or their terminal arborizations. If such axons exist in the optic nerves of cats, they have probably escaped detection in physiological studies. Unfortunately cat optic nerves have not yet been examined with the electron microscope, and it is not known whether or not they contain unmyelinated fibers.

LATERAL GENICULATE BODY

Anatomically, the dorsal lateral geniculate body differs from most other structures in the central nervous system, and certainly from the retina and cortex, in its relative simplicity. In a sense it is a one-synapse way station, since its cells receive their major input directly from the optic tract, and since most of them send their axons directly to the visual cortex. It has

often been asked whether the lateral geniculate body serves any integrative purpose
besides that of relaying incoming messages
to the cortex for further elaboration. Although in some ways the lateral geniculate
body is a simple structure, an anatomist
would hardly contend that it is nothing but
a one-to-one relay station. The existence
of convergence and divergence, complex
dendritic arborizations, and, in the cat at
least, cells with short axons terminating
within the nucleus itself, all seem to be
against such a supposition.

A strong case was made for the presence
of one-to-one synapses in the geniculate
by the microelectrode studies of Bishop,
Burke, and Davis (1958). By electrically
stimulating the severed proximal stump of
the optic nerve and recording extracel-
lularly from lateral geniculate cells they
were able to record excitatory postsynaptic
potentials (or the associated extracellular
currents) and show that they were not continuously graded, but, at least for two of
the cells they studied, were all-or-nothing.
Most excitatory postsynaptic potentials were
followed by geniculate spikes. The authors
concluded that some lateral geniculate cells
can be excited by one impulse in a single
optic-nerve fiber. They were inclined to
attribute the fact that the lateral geniculate
cell occasionally failed to fire to the effects
of anaesthesia, rather than to variation in
possible additional inputs not detected by
their electrode. Since both Bishop, Burke,
and Davis (1958) and Freygang (1958)
observed lateral geniculate cells for which
the excitatory postsynaptic potentials were
graded in several discrete steps, it is clear
that not all geniculate synapses are of a
simple one-to-one type. At least some must
have several excitatory inputs.

If there is a "straight through" connection
between some optic-nerve fibers and lateral
geniculate cells, as Bishop's findings suggest, there should be no differences in receptive fields at the two levels. A study of
lateral geniculate cells in the cat (Hubel
and Wiesel 1961) showed that lateral geniculate fields indeed have the same con-

centric center-periphery organization, and
like retinal ganglion cells, are of two types,
excitatory center and inhibitory center. It
is clear enough, then, that in the lateral
geniculate body there is no very profound
reorganization of the incoming messages.
Nevertheless, there was a suggestion that
the ability of a receptive-field periphery to
antagonize the center response was more
marked in geniculate cells than in optic-
nerve fibers. This was true even when variations in peripheral suppression with position of receptive fields on the retina (referred to above) were taken into account.

The fact that one can record geniculate
spikes together with excitatory synaptic
potentials of an all-or-none type suggested
the possibility of making a more delicate
test of geniculate function, namely, a comparison of the responses and receptive fields
of a particular geniculate cell with those of
its own excitatory postsynaptic potential
(Hubel and Wiesel 1961). When this was
done for cells with all-or-none synaptic
potentials, it was found that while almost
all lateral geniculate spikes were triggered
by an optic-nerve impulse, the converse
was not true; each synaptic potential did
not necessarily trigger a postsynaptic spike.
The success rate of the optic-nerve impulse
varied widely, depending on how the retina
was stimulated. The receptive field centers
of the optic nerve fiber and the lateral geniculate cell were, as far as one could judge,
precisely superimposed. If one shone a
restricted spot of light over the common
receptive-field center, the likelihood that
an impulse would trigger a postsynaptic
spike was very high. If, on the other hand,
the entire receptive field including the
periphery was illuminated, very few of the
synaptic potentials were followed by ge-
niculate-cell spikes. For small spots in the
center portion of the field the thresholds of
the two units were apparently identical,
but for large spots, including diffuse light,
they were often several log units apart.
Sometimes the geniculate cell would not
respond to diffuse light at any intensity.

It was thus possible not only to confirm

the impression that peripheral suppression is enhanced by lateral geniculate cells, but to obtain some notion of how the change is brought about.

This result shows clearly that even when we record a single all-or-none excitatory synaptic potential along with a geniculate cell spike, the synaptic potential we observe does not represent the only input to the cell. There must be other inputs which are influenced by illuminating the periphery of the common receptive field. Illuminating the periphery might activate retinal ganglion cells whose "on" centers were distributed over this annular region; if these neurons made inhibitory synaptic connections with the geniculate cell we could explain the cell's failure to be triggered when diffuse light was used. We might equally well suppose that lighting the periphery suppressed the firing of a set of "off"-center retinal ganglion cells making *excitatory* connections with the geniculate cell. Now inclusion of the receptive-field periphery would suppress these cells, removing the tonic asynchronous activation needed to enable the geniculate cell to follow the triggering impulses. The important point is that the geniculate cell must be receiving input from not one, but a large number of optic-nerve fibers. In a cell bound to an optic nerve fiber by a synapse having a "straight through" property, the property is a conditional one, depending on activity of other optic nerve fibers.

I have mentioned the possibility of suppressing a cell's firing by withdrawal of tonic excitation rather than by direct synaptic inhibition. The synapse that we are discussing gives us a vivid example of just that, for in illuminating the field center of an "off"-center geniculate cell we suppress firing by suppressing activity in the main optic-nerve fiber feeding into it. Of course the cell may at the same time be actively inhibited by other optic-nerve fibers (we have no evidence for or against this), but this inhibition would not be the main reason for the cessation of firing. To suppress the firing of any cell in the visual system there need only be one inhibitory link in the entire chain beginning with and including the receptor. In the case of the center of an "off"-center cell in the lateral geniculate we do not know at what stage this inhibitory link occurs. It is apparently not in the geniculate, and there is no evidence for or against its being at the retinal ganglion-cell level.

We may sum up the implications of these experiments as follows: (1) all cat geniculate cells apparently have multiple visual inputs; (2) there is often a particular relationship between a cell and one optic-nerve fiber with which it makes a powerful excitatory synapse; (3) when such a relationship exists, the receptive-field centers of the incoming fiber and the geniculate cell are of the same type, i.e., both are "on"-center or both are "off"-center; (4) the lateral geniculate body has the function of increasing the disparity, already present in the retinal ganglion cell, between responses to a small centered spot and to diffuse light.

The lateral geniculate body may have other functions besides that of increasing the effects of the receptive-field periphery. Cells in which the synaptic potential is graded in several steps must have more than one excitatory afferent. This kind of convergence might produce a geniculate receptive-field center larger than any of the field centers of the afferents. So far this has not been tested experimentally.

Some electrophysiological studies have suggested that the lateral geniculate body receives afferent fibers besides those of the optic tract (Hubel 1960; Widén and Ajmone-Marsan 1960; Arden and Söderberg 1961). Nauta and Bucher (1954) have observed a cortico-geniculate projection in the rat, and recently Nauta (personal communication) and Beresford (1961) have found in the cat a topographically precise reciprocal pathway from the striate cortex to the lateral geniculate body of the same side. So far we have found no geniculate cells with the complex properties typical of cortical cells, but fibers with these properties are frequently recorded just dorsal to the lateral geniculate body. A knowledge of the presence of a reciprocal pathway is important if we are to avoid including these units in a study of geniculate cells, particularly if there is any chance that the recording electrode is not in the geniculate but just above it.

A problem that has attracted considerable attention concerns the amount of binocular interaction in the lateral geniculate body (Bishop, Burke, and Davis 1959; Erulkar and Fillenz 1960; Grüsser and Sauer 1960; Hubel and Wiesel 1961). While there is evidence that some geniculate cells can be influenced from the two eyes, it seems to be agreed that the proportion of binocularly influenced cells in the lateral geniculate body is small. This is certainly in keeping with the anatomical findings (Silva 1956; Hayhow 1958). We have so far not succeeded in mapping out, for any geniculate cell, two receptive fields, one in each eye. The marked contrast between the scarcity of binocular interaction in the cat's geniculate and its preponderance in the visual cortex does not argue for any major role of the geniculate in binocular vision.

On anatomical grounds it is well established that alternate layers of the lateral geniculate body receive their input from alternate eyes. This has been confirmed in the cat by physiological methods (Cohn, 1956); cells in a given layer can be driven from one of the two eyes, but not from the other. A precise topographical representation of the contralateral half-fields of vision on each geniculate layer, the maps in the different layers being in register, has been established anatomically for the rhesus monkey (Polyak 1957) by noting transsynaptic atrophy following small retinal lesions. Although a similar anatomical study in the cat has not been made, the physiological evidence for a precise topographical representation in this animal is clear (Hubel and Wiesel 1961). The receptive fields of simultaneously recorded cells are near to one another and often overlap almost completely. The receptive

fields of cells recorded in sequence by an electrode passing normal to the layers are close together or almost superimposed, whereas in an oblique or tangential penetration, fields of successively recorded cells move systematically along the retina. Finally, the maps in successive layers are in register.

From what I have said about the lateral geniculate body it will be apparent that the physiological properties of even that simple structure are far from simple. The fact that a number of incoming optic-tract fibers converge upon one cell presents us with a number of possibilities. Any particular geniculate cell will have its own receptive field with center and surround. Each fiber converging upon the cell will have its own center located in the center or surround of the geniculate cell's field: the incoming fiber may have an "on" center or an "off" center; the synapse it makes may be excitatory or inhibitory. If excitatory, the synapse may be powerful, capable of setting up a spike in the geniculate cell; or it may be weak, contributing to the summed effects of a large number of other incoming fibers. Somehow these and perhaps other possibilities are made use of, to produce a mechanism in which individual incoming impulses may trigger individual postsynaptic impulses, but in which the coupling between the incoming and outgoing signals is varied. Such an ingenious piece of machinery would surely have great appeal to a mechanical or an electrical engineer. It may be worth stressing how different this synapse seems to be from that of the anterior horn cell of the spinal cord, which, because it has been so extensively studied by modern electrophysiological methods, is apt to be taken as a prototype of synapses in the central nervous system.

VISUAL CORTEX

If the lateral geniculate body is anatomically a structure of relative histological simplicity, the primary visual cortex is in contrast one of very great complexity. There is considerable order to the architectural plan of the cortex, yet our knowledge of the connections between cells gives us very little notion of how this structure functions. Of course, it has been known for years that the striate cortex is concerned with vision, and that in most mammals it is indispensable for form vision. What we have not known is how cortical cells handle the messages they receive from the lateral geniculate body. We have had insufficient evidence even to decide whether the messages are modified at all, or just handed on to some still higher centers for further elaboration (cf. Brindley 1960, p. 122).

As long as methods for single-cell recording were not available to neurophysiologists, this question of integrative cortical mechanisms could only be approached in a limited way. Since gross electrodes record only synchronous activity one could only examine attributes shared by all or most cells in a relatively large volume of tissue (the order of 1 mm³). We know now that the one important physiological quality shared by cells over such a large area of striate cortex has to do with the regions of visual field from which cells receive their projections. It is therefore not surprising that topography was one aspect of visual cortical function to be extensively explored with gross electrodes.

In a series of studies by Talbot and Marshall (1941), Talbot (1942), and Thompson, Woolsey, and Talbot (1950) the cortex was mapped in the cat, rabbit, and monkey according to the retinal areas projecting to it. These authors were able to go well beyond what was known from anatomical studies by showing that in the cat and rabbit there is a double representation of the visual half-field on the cortex of the contralateral hemisphere. The two maps lie adjacent to each other, bounded by a line which Talbot and Marshall termed the "line of decussation." This line receives projections from the vertical meridian. Any retinal region (besides the vertical meridian) projects to two regions on the cortex, one medial to the line of decussation and the other lateral to it. There has been some tendency to assume that the medial representation, called Visual Area I, is the classical striate cortex, whereas Area II is nonstriate. There is nothing in the literature to support the latter assumption, though to my knowledge it has never been questioned except by Bard (1956).

The mapping experiments of Talbot and Marshall and of Thompson, Woolsey, and Talbot have since been confirmed for the cat by single-unit techniques. We have confirmed the topographical projection scheme in the cat (Hubel and Wiesel 1962), including the presence of a second visual representation lateral to the first. Daniel and Whitteridge (1961) have repeated the experiments in the monkey and have extended the map to buried parts of the cortex. Although Talbot and Marshall did not describe a second visual area in the monkey, Wiesel and I have recently found electrophysiological evidence for a precise retinotopic projection to nonstriate visual cortex.

The introduction of microelectrodes supplies us with a powerful means of studying properties of individual cortical cells, especially those properties that are not common to cells in a large volume of nervous tissue. To learn what kinds of transformations the visual cortex makes on the incoming visual signals we may compare responses of single cortical cells with those of afferent fibers from the lateral geniculate body. If we were to find no differences in receptive fields of cells in these two structures we would indeed be disappointed, for it would mean either that in spite of its anatomical complexity the striate cortex did virtually nothing, or else that our present microelectrode techniques were not equal to the problem. The second alternative is a possible one, since the elaborative functions of the cortex might be discernible only by examining simultaneously large numbers of cells and comparing their firing patterns, perhaps with the help of computers. As it turns out, there *are* differences in receptive fields, differences which give us a fair idea of some of the functions of the cortex. Here I only attempt to summarize some of our own work (see Hubel and Wiesel 1959, 1962); for other microelectrode investigations of the visual cortex the reader may refer to several recent symposia (Rosenblith 1961; Jung and Kornhuber 1961).

In the striate cortex we have found no cells with concentric "on"- or "off"-center fields. Instead there has been an astonishing variety of new response types. These differ one from another in the details of distribution of excitatory and inhibitory regions, but they have one thing in common: that areas giving excitation and inhibition are not separated by circles, as in the retina and geniculate, but by straight lines. Some cells, for example, have receptive fields with a long narrow excitatory area flanked on either side by inhibitory areas, whereas others have the reverse arrangement, an inhibitory area flanked on the two sides by excitatory areas (Hubel and Wiesel 1962, Text-Fig. 2). Some fields have only two regions of opposite type separated by a single straight line. Summation occurs just as in the retina and geniculate, and the most effective stationary retinal stimulus for a cortical cell is one falling on either the excitatory parts of a receptive field or the inhibitory parts, but not on both simultaneously. Consequently stimuli such as long narrow dark or light rectangles, or boundaries with light to one side and darkness to the other ("edges"), are likely to be the most potent for cortical cells. Each cell will have its own optimal stimulus. Moreover the stimulus that works best in influencing a cell, exciting or inhibiting it, will do so only when shone on the appropriate part of the retina and in the correct orientation. Some cells prefer one inclination, vertical, horizontal, or oblique, others prefer another; and all inclinations seem to be about equally well represented. We have termed the inclination of the most effective stimulus the "receptive-field axis orientation" and have come to realize that this is one of a cell's most important properties. For example, if a stimulus such as a long narrow rectangle of light is shone at right angles to the optimum orientation it has little or no effect. Here the light covers portions of both the excitatory and inhibitory regions, and the two effects oppose each other.

We have already seen that turning on or off a diffuse light is not an ideal stimulus for a retinal ganglion cell. It evokes a response, but a much weaker one than that produced by a centered circular spot of just the right size. I have described how cells in the lateral geniculate body are influenced even less than retinal ganglion cells by diffuse light. In the cortex the process is apparently carried a step further. Here many cells give no response at all when one shines light on the entire receptive field. How the cat detects diffuse light and distinguishes different levels of diffuse illumination is something we do not know. Perhaps the mechanism is subcortical; it is known that the cat can make discriminations of intensity of diffuse light even when it lacks a visual cortex (Smith 1937). The information that a large patch of retina is evenly illuminated may be supplied only by cells that are activated by the boundaries of the patch; the fact that cells with fields entirely within the illuminated area are uninfluenced presumably signals the absence of contours within the patch of light—in other words, that the region is diffusely lit.

One may ask why a diffuse flash of light evokes such a large cortical slow wave, if only a small proportion of cells respond to the stimulus, and these only relatively weakly. Too little is known about slow waves to permit an entirely satisfactory answer. It is possible that a large slow wave may be produced by a small proportion of cells firing weakly but synchronously. It is interesting, however, that the visual evoked response is maximal *outside* the cortical area commonly accepted as striate (Doty 1958), and that within the primary visual area it is maximal well in front of the area centralis representation. Indeed, the area representing central vision gives only a relatively feeble response to a diffuse flash (Doty 1958). We have not thoroughly explored cortical areas representing the far periphery of the retinas: it may be that compared with cells receiving projections from centralis, those with receptive fields in the far periphery respond more actively to diffuse light. This is, in fact, the case with retinal ganglion cells (Wiesel 1960) and with geniculate cells (Hubel and Wiesel 1961).

The amazing selectivity with which cortical cells respond to a highly specific stimulus and ignore almost anything else is explained by the existence of excitatory and inhibitory receptive-field subdivisions. While these mechanisms clearly make use of inhibition, it must be stressed that we have no direct evidence that the cortex contains inhibitory synapses, just as we have none in the case of geniculate or retinal ganglion cells (see discussion of Bremer, in Jung 1960, p. 233). Whenever we suppress firing by turning on a stimulus, the effect may be produced by withdrawing tonic excitation as easily as by directly inhibiting, and so far the appropriate methods of distinguishing the two possibilities have not been used in the visual system.

In their behavior cells whose receptive fields can be divided into excitatory and inhibitory regions are probably the simplest of the striate cortex. It is therefore reasonable to suppose that at least some cells with simple fields receive their projections directly from the geniculate (Hubel and Wiesel 1962; Text-Fig. 19). In the striate cortex we find cells of a second type whose properties we have called "complex." Cells with complex receptive fields do not respond well to small spots of light, and it has not been possible to map their fields into separate excitatory and inhibitory regions. They behave as though they received their afferents from a large number of cortical cells with simple fields, all of these fields having the same axis orienta-

tion, but varying slightly from one to the next in their exact retinal positions. A complex cell thus responds to an appropriately oriented slit, edge, or dark bar, not just when it is shone in one highly critical retinal position, as we find with simple cells, but over considerable regions of retina, sometimes up to 5°–10° or more. Presumably whenever the properly oriented stimulus is applied within this area, it activates some cells with simple fields (different ones for different positions of the stimulus) and these in turn activate the complex cell. For example, a typical complex cell might be activated by a horizontal slit of light regardless of its exact position within a region several degrees in diameter. For such a cell changing the orientation by more than 5°–10° renders the stimulus ineffective, as does making it wider than some optimum width (e.g., more than ¼°). It is as though such a cell had the function of responding to the abstract quality "horizontal," irrespective of the exact retinal position.

The idea that a complex cell receives its input from a large number of simple cells all having the same receptive-field axis orientation has a remarkable parallel in the functional anatomy of the cat striate cortex. Cells that are close neighbors almost always have receptive-field axis orientations that are, as far as one can tell, identical. By making long penetrations in the manner of Mountcastle (Mountcastle 1957; Powell and Mountcastle 1959) one can show that the regions of constant axis orientation extend from surface to white matter, with walls perpendicular to the cortical layers (Hubel and Wiesel 1962). Within one of these regions, or "columns," there occur all functional types of cell, including simple and complex. All the cells in a column have their receptive fields in the same general region of retina, but there is a slight variation in exact receptive-field position from one cell to the next. If we assume that a complex cell receives its input from cells with simple fields in the same column, this constancy of receptive-field axis orientation together with the slight differences in position of fields is sufficient to account for all of the complex cell's properties. A column is thus considered to be a functional unit of cortex, to which geniculate axons project in such a way as to produce simple cortical fields all with the same axis orientation, and within which simple cells converge upon complex ones.

From the standpoint of cortical physiology it is interesting that these visual columns are in many ways analogous to the columns in the cat somatosensory cortex, described in 1957 by Mountcastle, and confirmed for the monkey by Powell and Mountcastle (1959). A columnar organization may be a feature of many cortical areas. It seems surprising that this type of organization, which must depend primarily on anatomical connections, should have no known anatomical correlate.

As far as we know all striate cortical cells in the cat can be categorized as simple or complex; there do not seem to be still higher orders of cells in this part of the brain. We are inclined to think of complex cells as representing a stage in the process of form generalization, since we can displace an image by several degrees on the retina, as long as we do not rotate it, and the population of complex cells that is influenced by the borders of the stimulus will not greatly change. The same is true if we distort the image, for instance by making it smaller or larger. As far as we know, this is the first stage in the mammalian visual pathway in which such an abstracting process occurs.

It is important to realize again that the size of a receptive field does not have any necessary bearing on a cell's ability to discriminate fine stimuli. In the cat a typical cortical receptive field in or near the area centralis may have a diameter of 1°–2°, and complex fields range in size from 2°–3° up to 10° or more. Nevertheless the optimum stimuli for these cells are likely to be of the order of 10 minutes of arc in width. In a simple field this corresponds to a dimension such as the width of a long

narrow receptive-field center. The presence of convergence at each stage of the visual pathway does lead to increased receptive-field size, but not to a loss of detail. This is the result of an interplay between inhibitory and excitatory processes.

So far I have not made any reference to one of the most important aspects of vision, namely movement. A moving stimulus commands attention more than a stationary one; clinically, movement is generally one of the first types of visual perception to return after a cortical injury (for references, see Teuber, Battersby, and Bender 1960, p. 19); even for the perception of stationary objects, eye movements are probably necessary (Ditchburn and Ginsburg 1952; Riggs, Ratliff, Cornsweet, and Cornsweet, 1953). It is not surprising, then, to find that a moving spot or pattern is in general a powerful stimulus for cortical cells. To understand why this is so we must return for a moment to a consideration of cells with simple fields. If we bring a spot from a neutral region of retina into a cell's excitatory area we produce an "on" response; if we remove a spot from the "off" region of a cell we evoke an "off" discharge. If we combine the two maneuvers by moving a spot from an "off" area into an "on" area, the two mechanisms work together to produce a greatly enhanced response. Of course, the cortical cell is most efficiently activated by the stimulus if it is a slit, dark bar, or edge, and if it is oriented in the direction appropriate for the cell. If the receptive field of the cell is not symmetrical (if one flank is smaller or produces less powerful effects than the other), the responses to two diametrically opposite directions of movement may be different. For example, a cell may fire when a spot is moved from left to right across the retina, but not when it is moved from right to left.

Now let us consider how a moving stimulus influences a complex cell. According to the scheme proposed above, a cell with complex properties receives its input from a number of cells with simple fields whose positions are staggered. Because of these differences in field position, a moving stimulus will activate first one simple cell and then another. The complex cell will thus be continuously bombarded and will fire steadily as the stimulus moves over a relatively wide expanse of retina. A stationary stimulus shone into the receptive field of a complex cell evokes as a rule only a transient response because of the adaptation which presumably occurs at the receptors and at subsequent synapses. The moving pattern would bypass much of this adaptation by activating many cells in sequence.

The same mechanism may play a part in the perception of stationary objects by making use of the saccadic eye movements which, at least in man, seem necessary for the persistence of a visual impression. A visual image as it passes across the moving retina presumably activates numbers of simple cells briefly and in sequence, leads to a more steady activation of a much smaller number of complex cells.

From what has been said so far it will be apparent that the striate cortex has a rich assortment of functions. It rearranges the input from the lateral geniculate body in such a way as to make lines and contours the most important stimuli. Directionality of stimuli must be accurately specified; the presence of a columnar system based on receptive-field axis orientation testifies to the importance of this variable. What appears to be a first step in the process of perceptual generalization results from a cell's responding to a property of a boundary (its orientation) apart from its exact position. Movement also becomes an important stimulus parameter, whose rate and direction both must be specified if a cell is to be effectively driven.

To this list one more function must be added, that of combining the pathways from the two eyes. In contrast to the lateral geniculate body, most cells in the cat cortex (probably at least 85%) receive input from the two eyes (Hubel and Wiesel 1962, Part II). By mapping out receptive fields in each eye separately and comparing them we can begin to learn about the mechanisms of binocular vision, and perhaps ultimately something about binocular depth perception and binocular rivalry.

The primary visual, or striate, cortex is probably only an early stage of the visual pathway. Yet, unfortunately, we have very little knowledge of the pathway from this point on. Except in the rat (Nauta and Bucher 1954) and cat (Beresford 1961) the points to which the striate cortex projects are not known. Even less is known about the connections of the neighboring nonstriate visual cortex, called 18 and 19, or parastriate and peristriate; we have no accurate description of what areas project to them, or of where they send their projections. There even seem to be doubts as to the validity of the distinction between the two areas (Lashley and Clark 1946). Clearly, more will have to be learned about the anatomy before neurophysiologists can make much progress in parts of the pathway beyond the striate cortex.

The work I have described may help to show how visual messages are handled by the brain, at least in the early stages of the process. The analysis takes us to what are probably at least sixth-order neurons in the visual pathway. Our understanding of cells with complex fields will be incomplete until we know how these properties are used at the next stage of integration, just as our grasp of the significance of retinal and geniculate receptive-field organization was incomplete without a knowledge of cortical receptive fields. There is no way of foreseeing what the next transformations will be, but to judge from what we have learned so far one would guess that the process of abstraction will go on, and that response specificity will increase. But it is well to remember that central nervous physiology is in a descriptive and exploratory phase. Our ignorance of CNS processes is such that the best predictions stand a good chance of being wrong.

REFERENCES

G. Arden and U. Söderberg, "The Transfer of Optic Information through the Lateral Geniculate Body of the Rabbit," in *Sensory Communication*, edited by W. A. Rosenblith (MIT Press and John Wiley & Sons, Inc., New York, 1961), pp. 521–544.

P. Bard, *Medical Physiology* (C. V. Mosby Company, St. Louis, Missouri, 1956), p. 1176.

W. A. Beresford, "Fibre Degeneration following Lesions of the Visual Cortex of the Cat," in *Neurophysiologie und Psychophysik des visuellen Systems*, edited by R. Jung and H. Kornhuber (Springer-Verlag, Berlin, 1961).

P. O. Bishop, W. Burke, and R. Davis, "Synapse Discharge by Single Fibre in Mammalian Visual System," Nature 182, 728–730 (1958).

————, "Activation of Single Lateral Geniculate Cells by Stimulation of Either Optic Nerve," Science 130, 506–507 (1959).

G. S. Brindley, *Physiology of the Retina and the Visual Pathway* (Edward Arnold, Ltd., London, 1960).

R. Cohn, "Laminar Electrical Responses in Lateral Geniculate Body of Cat," J. Neurophysiol. 19, 317–324 (1956).

P. M. Daniel and D. Whitteridge, "The Representation of the Visual Field on the Cerebral Cortex in Monkeys," J. Physiol. (London) 159, 203–221 (1961).

R. L. De Valois, "Color Vision Mechanisms in the Monkey," J. gen. Physiol. 43, Pt. 2, 115–128 (1960).

R. W. Ditchburn and B. L. Ginsburg, "Vision with Stabilized Retinal Image," Nature 170, 36–37 (1952).

R. W. Doty, "Potentials Evoked in Cat Cerebral Cortex by Diffuse and by Punctiform Photic Stimuli," J. Neurophysiol. 21, 437–464 (1958).

S. D. Erulkar and M. Fillenz, "Single-Unit Activity in the Lateral Geniculate Body of the Cat," J. Physiol. (London) 154, 206–218 (1960).

W. H. Freygang, Jr., "An Analysis of Extracellular Potentials from Single Neurons in the Lateral Geniculate Nucleus of the Cat," J. gen. Physiol. 41, 543–564 (1958).

O.-J. Grüsser and G. Sauer, "Monoculare und binoculare Lichtreizung einzelner Neurone im Geniculatum laterale der Katze," Pflüg. Arch. ges. Physiol. 271, 595–612 (1960).

W. R. Hayhow, "The Cytoarchitecture of the Lateral Geniculate Body in the Cat in Relation to the Distribution of Crossed and Uncrossed Optic Fibers," J. comp. Neurol. 110, 1–64 (1958).

D. H. Hubel, "Single Unit Activity in Lateral Geniculate Body and Optic Tract of Unrestrained Cats," J. Physiol. (London) 150, 91–104 (1960).

D. H. Hubel and T. N. Wiesel, "Receptive Fields of Single Neurones in the Cat's Striate Cortex," J. Physiol. (London) 148, 574–591 (1959).

————, "Receptive Fields of Optic Nerve Fibres in the Spider Monkey," J. Physiol. (London) 154, 572–580 (1960).

————, "Integrative Action in the Cat's Lateral Geniculate Body," J. Physiol. (London) 155, 385–398 (1961).

————, "Receptive Fields, Binocular Interaction and Functional Architecture in the Cat's Visual Cortex," J. Physiol. 160, 106–154 (1962).

R. Jung, "Microphysiologie corticaler Neurone: Ein Beitrag zur Koordination der Hirnrinde und des visuellen Systems," in *Structure and Function of the Cerebral Cortex*, edited by D. B. Tower and J. P. Schadé (Elsevier Publishing Company, Amsterdam, 1960).

R. Jung and H. Kornhuber, Editors, *Neurophysiologie und Psychophysik des Visuellen Systems* (Springer-Verlag, Berlin, 1961).

S. W. Kuffler, "Discharge Patterns and Functional Organization of Mammalian Retina," J. Neurophysiol. 16, 37–68 (1953).

K. S. Lashley and G. Clark, "The Cytoarchitecture of the Cerebral Cortex of Ateles: a Critical Examination of Architectonic Studies," J. comp. Neurol. 85, 223–305 (1946).

H. R. Maturana, J. Y. Lettvin, W. S. McCulloch, and W. H. Pitts, "Anatomy and Physiology of Vision in the Frog (*Rana pipiens*)," J. Gen. Physiol. 43, Pt. 2, 129–176 (1960).

V. B. Mountcastle, "Modality and Topographic Properties of Single Neurons of Cat's Somatic Sensory Cortex," J. Neurophysiol. 20, 408–434 (1957).

J. H. Nauta and V. M. Bucher, "Efferent Connections of the Striate Cortex in the Albino Rat," J. comp. Neurol. 100, 257–286 (1954).

S. Polyak, *The Vertebrate Visual System*, edited by H. Klüver (The University of Chicago Press, Chicago, 1957).

T. P. S. Powell and V. B. Mountcastle, "Some Aspects of the Functional Organization of the Cortex of the Postcentral Gyrus of the Monkey: a Correlation of Findings Obtained in a Single Unit Analysis with Cytoarchitecture," Johns Hopkins Hospital Bull. 105, 133–162 (1959).

L. A. Riggs, F. Ratliff, J. C. Cornsweet, and T. N. Cornsweet, "The Disappearance of Steadily Fixated Visual Test Objects," J. Opt. Soc. Am. 43, 495–501 (1953).

W. A. Rosenblith, Editor, *Sensory Communication* (MIT Press and John Wiley & Sons, Inc., New York, 1961).

P. S. Silva, "Some Anatomical and Physiological Aspects of the Lateral Geniculate Body," J. comp. Neurol. 106, 463–486 (1956).

K. U. Smith, "Visual Discriminations in the Cat: V. The Post-operative Effects of Removal of the Striate Cortex upon Intensity Discrimination," J. genet. Psychol. 51, 329–369 (1937).

S. A. Talbot, "A Lateral Localization in the Cat's Visual Cortex," Federation Proc. 1, 84 (1942).

S. A. Talbot and W. H. Marshall, "Physiological Studies on Neural Mechanisms of Visual Localization and Discrimination," Am. J. Ophthalmol. 24, 1255–1263 (1941).

H.-L. Teuber, W. S. Battersby, and M. B. Bender, *Visual Field Defects after Penetrating Missile Wounds of the Brain* (Harvard University Press, Cambridge, Massachusetts, 1960).

J. M. Thompson, C. N. Woolsey, and S. A. Talbot, "Visual Areas I and II of Cerebral Cortex of Rabbit," J. Neurophysiol. 13, 277–288 (1950).

L. Widén and C. Ajmone-Marsan, "Effects of Corticipetal and Corticifugal Impulses upon Single Elements of the Dorsolateral Geniculate Nucleus," Exptl. Neurol. 2, 468–502 (1960).

T. N. Wiesel, "Receptive Fields of Ganglion Cells in the Cat's Retina," J. Physiol. (London) 153, 583–594 (1960).

M. L. Wolbarsht, H. G. Wagner, and E. F. Mac-Nichol, Jr., "Receptive Fields of Retinal Ganglion Cells: Extent and Spectral Sensitivity," in Neurophysiologie und Psychophysik des visuellen Systems, edited by R. Jung and H. Kornhuber (Springer-Verlag, Berlin, 1961).

PERCEPTION AND ATTENTION

13. The Perception of Objects *

Edwin G. Boring

As can be seen from the previous articles, a persistent theme in the study of perception involves the concept of coding. This emphasis upon coding is directed to the problem of *how* the perceptual system does what it does. Yet a more fundamental question may be raised, namely, "Exactly *what* functions does the perceptual system perform?" To answer this question, one must investigate the output or end product of the perceptual system.

One typical technique for determining how the world actually appears to a perceiver requires the presentation of various objects to a subject. Usually the subject is then asked to report how the objects appear to him by responding to simple and unambiguous questions, for example—"Which of these two lines is longer?" or, "Do you see a light?" Similarly, the answer the subject is permitted to give is concise and unequivocal—he may say only "this one" or "that one," "yes" or "no," or he may point with his finger, or adjust a knob, etc.

The experiments described in the next paper, by Professor E. G. Boring, are examples of this general approach as it is employed in psychological research. As Boring illustrates, the end product yielded by the sensory systems is a three-dimensional world populated by stable objects. Perceptions are not determined solely by the neural coding of any single event, nor are they transmitted over any single sensory system. Rather, stable perceptions are produced by the convergence of neural activity from each of the sensory modalities and the product is integrated with our past experience.

For more than a century it has been customary to say that perception is something more than sensory impression, that perception is *of an object*, that it corresponds to a stimulating object. The modern view is that, because objects are permanent, a perception of an object tends to remain constant even when the immediate sensory impressions upon which the perception is based vary with the variety of conditions that affect stimulation.

This general rule of perception applies to all sense departments. It depends upon an integrative property of the brain and is not a function of sense organs at all. The meaning of the rule is most easily expounded in terms of particular instances, and the four examples that are best understood are the visual perception of size with distance variant, of shape with angle of

* Reprinted by permission of the author and the American Institute of Physics from the *American Journal of Physics*, 1946, *14*, 99-107.

regard variant, of brightness with intensity of illumination variant, and of hue with color of illumination variant.[1]

We know a great deal about perceived *size* with distance variant. At short distances perceived size tends not to change with distance. A man is 40 ft down the hall and walking toward you. When he is only 20 ft away, has he doubled his height? The height of the image of him on your retinas has doubled. The perception itself, however, changes very little. Or you are at a reception, standing at the end of a large hall. Are the people at the far end dwarfs, only half as tall as the people in the middle of the hall, only a tenth or a twentieth as tall as the man with whom you are talking? Do people change in size at the rate at which the images of them on your retinas change?

What happens is that, under certain circumstances, the brain corrects the perception that depends initially upon the size of the retinal image, corrects it in accordance with other sensory data that indicate the distance from which the retinal image is projected. And the brain can do an excellent job in this kind of correction. At great distances, however, the corrective mechanism becomes inadequate. A man a mile away actually does look small, in part because a mile cannot be perceived accurately. On the other hand, there is doubtless some cerebral correction for the size of a man a mile away, for even the moon— 239,000 mi away—shows a tiny correction for the smallness of its retinal image caused by its great distance.

This same tendency to preserve objective constancy happens with visually perceived *shape*. As I stand to one side and look at the top of a circular table, it does not appear as the narrow ellipse that its retinal image is, that the artist would sketch in his projection of the scene. Although every room is full of rectangles, they are perceived not as various diamonds and distorted rectangles, but approximately in their true proportions. The brain corrects the perception for the angle of projection.

So it goes with *brightnesses*. Coal looks black and white paper looks white, provided you know that you are seeing coal and white paper. The white paper may be in shadow and the coal in bright illumination, illumination so bright that the coal reflects more light than the paper. Still the coal looks black and the paper white. The brain takes account of the nature of the objects and corrects the initial impressions that are based solely on illumination.

Sir Isaac Newton observed this phenomenon. He was put to it to prove that gray is a darkish white, because gray things persist in looking gray and white things white. So he rubbed a gray powder on the floor of his chamber in the sunlight and laid nearby in the shadow a piece of white paper. Then he viewed the two objects from a distance so great that their character as objects could not be recognized and saw that the gray powder in sunlight was as white as or whiter than the white paper in shadow. A friend, pressed into service as an observer and asked to judge the patches of brightness before he knew what the objects were, corroborated him.[2]

The general rule also holds for *hue*. If you have the means of knowing from other immediately present sensory data or from past experience what color an object ought to be, then you are apt to see it in its correct color whatever the hue of the illumination. Familiar dresses and upholstery may keep their daylight hues in yellowish arti-

[1] On constancy in the perception of objects, see, for elementary accounts, E. G. Boring, H. S. Langfeld and H. P. Weld, *Introduction to psychology* (Wiley, 1939), pp. 420–427, 463f., 468f.; R. S. Woodworth, *Experimental psychology* (Holt, 1938), pp. 595–622. Another summary of the facts with historical orientation and two score references is in E. G. Boring, *Sensation and perception in the history of experimental psychology* (Appleton-Century, 1942), pp. 254–256, 262, 288–299, 308–311. The fullest and most technical discussion of the literature is in K. Koffka, *Principles of Gestalt psychology* (Harcourt Brace, 1935), pp. 211–264.

[2] I. Newton, *Opticks* (1704; reprint, Bell, 1931), bk. I, pt. ii, prop. v, exp. 15.

ficial illumination, but a new observer with no familiarity to guide him will see them with the yellows favored and the blues diminished. Twenty years ago the technicolor motion pictures were using only two component hues to make colors that should have been trichromatic. One color was put on each side of the film, and the film had only two sides. It was the blues that were cheated. The colors used were a slightly bluish red and a slightly bluish green, which will mix to give good reds and greens, poor yellows and very poor blues. What did the audiences, unused in those days to colored movies, say? That the American flag was beautiful, that the (bluish-green) skies were lovely. But the heroine never wore a pure blue dress (whatever she had on in the studio) because dresses, unlike the sky or the flag's field, can be any color and obey the laws of color mixture without this kind of cerebral mediation. Yet Little Boy [Greenish] Blue in the old-fashioned technicolor might have looked as blue as the sky.

REDUCTION AND REGRESSION

For descriptive purposes it is convenient to say that the sensory data that contribute to a perception can be divided into a core and its context. The *core* is the basic sensory excitation that identifies the perception, that connects it most directly with the object of which it is a perception. The *context* consists of all the other sensory data that modify or correct the data of the core as it forms the perception. The context also includes certain acquired properties of the brain, properties that are specific to the particular perception and contribute to the modification of its core. In other words, the context includes knowledge about the perceived object as determined by past experience, that is, by all the brain habits which affect perceiving.[3]

[3] This convenient distinction between core and context derives from the one first made by E. B. Titchener, *Textbook of psychology* (Macmillan, 1910), pp. 367–371; *A beginner's psychology* (Macmillan, 1915), pp. 114–121.

In visual perception the core is the retinal excitation, that is to say, the total optical pattern, specified with respect to the wavelengths and energies involved and the spatial distribution and temporal changes of each. Thus in the visual perception of size with distance variant, the core is the size of the retinal image. The context includes all the clues to the distance of the perceived object—clues of binocular parallax and convergence, and of lenticular accommodation and perspective, as well as the other monocular clues to the awareness of distance. If an observer has before him one disk 10 ft away and another 20 ft away, and undertakes to alter the size of one until it looks the same size as the other, he is likely to come out with two disks of the same physical size. He is obviously not then equating retinal images, for the image of the farther disk has a diameter only half that of the image of the nearer. His brain is using his awareness of distance to make the perception derived from the smaller retinal image look as large as the perception from the larger retinal image. (Whether this correction is an inference, a physiological process or both is a matter that we must consider presently.)

If the perceived object is not a disk, which is unprejudiced as to size, but a man, whose height is, of course, likely to lie between 5 and 7 ft, then this special knowledge is added to the context. Such contextual knowledge does not, however, necessarily prevail. If the visual afterimage of a 6-ft man who is 20 ft away is projected on a wall 60 ft away, the man in the afterimage will be a giant, not far from 18 ft tall—provided the observer is able to perceive the distance to the wall.

These facts of perception can be demonstrated by the *reduction* of context. When distance is fully apprehended, the perceived size of an object is likely to remain about constant, even though the distance changes greatly and the size of the retinal image changes with it. On the other hand, if you reduce the clues from which distance can be gaged, then you will find that perceived size changes with distance, getting smaller at greater distances. When this reduction of context is partial, the shrinkage of the perception with increasing distance will be less than the shrinkage of the corresponding retinal image. If the reduction could be made complete, if all clues to distance other than the changing size of the retinal image were eliminated, then presumably perceived size would be determined by the only clue remaining, the size of the retinal image. Perceived size and retinal size would then always keep the same proportional relation. With a receding object perceived size would shrink as fast as the retinal image, for the observer would be wholly unaware of the recession, unless he used his awareness of diminishing size as a clue to the perception of the distance. He might.

Some writers have preferred to think of the converse of this relationship. Reduction of context reduces perception to its bare core, but increase of context increases correspondence of the perception to the real object. If you know how far away a seen object is, you may be able to perceive its true size. If you know that that gray is coal, it may look black. This effect of context to make the perception resemble the permanent object that is being perceived rather than the perceptual core has been called by Thouless *regression toward the real object*.[4] Regression toward the object is the opposite of reduction toward the core. Regression toward the object occurs with increase of context. Reduction toward the core is secured by decrease of context.

It was Katz who in 1911 first applied this term *reduction*, not to the case of size and distance, but to color and illumination.[5] Take the illuminated coal and the shaded

white paper. The coal looks black, the paper white, although the coal reflects more light. But now interpose what Katz called a *reduction screen*, a screen with two small circular openings in it. Through one opening you see a patch of the surface of the coal, through the other a patch of the surface of the paper. You do not see enough to identify either object, and at once the patch that is the coal appears as a gray lighter than the patch that is the white paper. By the use of the screen you have reduced the context that identifies the objects, reduced it to the core of this perception, the total illumination.

PERCEIVED SIZE AND DISTANCE: HISTORY

Most persons think that the perceived size of an object varies proportionately with retinal size of its image and thus with the visual angle subtended by the object. There seem to be two reasons for this belief.

(1) To assume that visual size is measured by visual angle brings perception into the geometry of optics in a simple and logical way. Euclid in his *Optica* worked in terms of this optical geometry, equating visual angle to perceived size; yet even he noted that the magnitude of the perception does not always accord with the perceived size. Still Euclid provided the simple rule that has ever since been quite generally accepted. The principle that perceived size varies with the visual angle subtended and thus with the size of the retinal image we shall call *Euclid's rule*.

(2) Progress in understanding visual perception during the last three centuries has consisted primarily in finding out how the eye works. From the ancient belief that objects give off tiny images of themselves, images which are conducted by the optic nerve to the sensorium for perception, we have come to an understanding of optical projection upon the retina. In general, nineteenth-century physiology held that the brain perceives not the object itself but

[4] R. H. Thouless, "Phenomenal regression to the real object," *Brit. J. Psychol.* **21,** 339–359 (1931); **22,** 1–30 (1931).

[5] D. Katz, "Die Erscheinungsweisen der Farben und ihre Beeinflussung durch die individuelle Erfahrung," *Z. Psychol.*, Suppl. **7,** esp. 36–39 (1911).

its projection on the retina and the consequent excitation of the optic nerve. (Why else should there have been a problem as to why we see right side up when the retinal image is upside down?) When perception was found not to correspond exactly with the stimulus object, one looked —all through the nineteenth century—to the eye for the explanation of the illusion, for but little was known about the supraretinal physiology of vision.

Nevertheless, there have been constant reminders that visual angle (retinal size) and perceived size do not always correspond. There were the eighteenth-century philosophers who tried to figure out the curve along which trees, bordering on an avenue, should be planted in order that the two lines of trees might look parallel and everywhere equidistant, when viewed from a specified end. And there were the psychologists in the period 1889–1913 who determined these curves experimentally. Various scientists remarked in the middle nineteenth century that Euclid's rule does not hold. If you view a length l at a distance d and compare it with a length $2l$ at a distance $2d$, then l and $2l$ form retinal images of the same size and should, by Euclid's rule, appear to be the same size. Actually, it is easily noted that $2l$ looks longer than l; yet that observation seldom excites curiosity since, it can be said, if $2l$ really is longer than l, why should it not look longer? Euclid gave a reason why it should not, but plainly he was wrong.

Then there was Emmert's law in 1881, the law that the perceived linear size of an afterimage is proportional to the distance of the background on which the image is projected. Emmert's law contradicts Euclid's. In an afterimage the size of the retinal image is fixed; how then does the size of the perception alter so greatly? Yet the fact is that the afterimage of a near object projected on a far background looks gigantic when retinal size does not change at all.

In the present century there has arisen in connection with the tenets of Gestalt psychology the conception of *size constancy*, the hypothesis that the perceived size of an object remains constant irrespective of the distance at which the object is perceived. There has been a great deal of misunderstanding and controversy about this matter; but that need not concern us, for the facts are plain.[6]

PERCEIVED SIZE AND DISTANCE: MEASUREMENT

Let me now summarize an experiment that Holway and I completed a few years ago, an experiment that measures the dependence of perceived size upon distance, and that also shows how the resulting functions depend upon the context and how the effective context can be analyzed by successively reducing it.[7]

We seated the observer at the right-angled junction of two halls, facing the convex corner at 45° from the longitudinal axes of the halls. By turning his head from side to side he could look down one hall or the other, alternating at will. We worked at night in complete darkness except for the light that came from the two illuminated stimulus disks.

The standard stimulus was a disk of light, projected from a lantern on a translucent screen. It was placed in the hall at the right at distances from the observer varying from 10 to 120 ft. The size of the disk was made proportional to the distance so that it always subtended at the observer an angle of 1°. It was the perceived size of this disk at different distances that was the subject of investigation.

In the hall at the left was a comparison stimulus for measuring perceived size. It consisted of a projected disk of light which remained always at 10 ft from the observer. Its size could be changed by the use of a

[6] For the history of research and observation, see Boring, reference 1 (1942), pp. 288–299, 308–311.

[7] A. H. Holway and E. G. Boring, "Determinants of apparent visual size with distance variant," *Am. J. Psychol.* **54**, 21–37 (1941).

long series of apertures with which the
projection lantern was provided. The observer varied the size of this comparison
stimulus until he was satisfied that he had
made it the same perceived size as the
standard stimulus. This judgment is not
always easy when the disks are at different
distances, but the difficulty arises only in
the final adjustments of the comparison
stimulus. Great differences in perceived
size at great differences in distance are
easily observed with immediate certainty,
even when the judgment departs widely
from Euclid's rule of the visual angle.

The results of this procedure are plotted
in Fig. 13-1. The two dashed lines, B and
F, represent theoretical relationships.

The function B is for perceived size constant, irrespective of distance. The reason
this line rises (slope = tan 1°) is that we
increased the size of the standard stimulus
in proportion to its distance, keeping its
angular subtension constant at 1°. We did
this in order to avoid any physiological distortion that might arise from exciting different sizes of retinal areas. The straight
line B is thus the function for perceived
size constancy because it is the function for
a comparison stimulus increasing with the
standard stimulus and remaining equal to
it, when the standard stimulus is increased
with distance in order to keep angular subtension constant.

The horizontal line F is the function for
proportionality of perceived size to retinal
size (visual angle). It represents *Euclid's
rule.* Since the visual angle was kept constant at 1°, proportionality of perceived
size to visual angle would in this case be
constant.

The other four functions show what happens with reduction. Although the observed points are not shown here, the fits to
straight lines are close.

Free binocular regard is shown in function A. If size constancy were to be the
rule, we should expect A to coincide with
B. To our surprise it lay slightly above B,
for the four more reliable of the five ob-

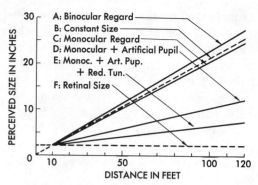

Figure 13.1 Visually perceived size as a
function of the distance of the perceived object. The perceived standard disk at every distance is of such physical size that its diameter
subtends an angle of 1° to the observer. Its
perceived size (ordinate scale) is the diameter,
in inches, of a comparison disk 10 ft from the
observer and equated in perceived size to the
standard disk. The six functions shown are as
follows: A, free binocular regard; the perceived size increased slightly with distance;
B, constant size, the function for no change of
perceived size with distance; C, monocular regard; the perceived diminished slightly with
distance; D, monocular regard with use of artificial pupil; great decrease of perceived size
with distance; E, monocular regard, with use
of artificial pupil and reduction tunnel; still
greater decrease in perceived size; F, retinal
size, the function for decrease in perceived
size proportional to the actual size of the
retinal image (visual angle subtended).

servers. A receding object tends (under
these conditions) to get a little larger in
perception while its retinal image is becoming very much smaller. Perceived size,
in other words, is not only constant; it is
"more than constant!" The position of this
function suggests that the binocular mechanism is set to compensate immediately for
shrinkage of the retinal image by increasing
distance and that under these conditions
it overcompensates slightly. That finding
might be an argument for the phenomenon's
being the consequence of a property of the
brain and not a matter of inference. It is
doubtful, however, that any good can come

from trying to distinguish between inference and its brain physiology.

Our first step was to reduce binocular to monocular vision by putting a patch over one of the observer's eyes. Function C resulted, a close approximation to size constancy. Some of the individual functions for C lay just above B, some below, and the average, as shown, was a little below. Later experiments by Taylor and myself with two men, each of whom had lost the use of one eye more than ten years earlier, gave functions similar to those on which C in Fig. 13-1 is based.[8] For this reason we assumed that monocular vision, either temporary or permanent, follows closely the law of size constancy, and that overcompensation may sometimes result when the use of a second eye is added.

The next reduction of the distance context was to add to monocular observation an artificial pupil, which eliminated accommodation of the iris diaphragm and reduced the effectiveness of the lenticular accommodation by stopping the lens down to 1.8 mm. With this situation there were more individual differences among observers, but the reliability of each observer remained high. Function D in Fig. 13-1 is the average result. It shows that reduction toward the proportionality to retinal size (Euclid's rule, function F) has progressed greatly.

The use of monocular vision with an artificial pupil still left some visible clues to the distance of the stimulus. The faint light from the two stimuli showed vaguely to the dark-adapted eye the perspective of the walls, floor and ceiling of the corridor. To get rid of these clues we constructed a "reduction tunnel" of heavy black cloth, 3 ft square in cross section and capable of being extended to 100 ft long. The observer viewed the standard stimulus through it, and a further reduction resulted, as shown by function E in Fig. 13-1.

Complete reduction should give an observed function that coincides with F. We were unable to obtain it. Not with all this effort and artifice could we make Euclid's commonly accepted law of perceived size as proportional to visual angle come true! Yet the function F must be found if all clues to distance are eliminated. The results plotted in E show the observers discriminating different distances fairly accurately. If the function E were known, then the distance could be told from a knowledge of the equations of perceived size. The failure to reduce to F means that there are still clues to distance left.

Figure 13-1 is confusing because the standard stimulus was kept constant in angular size instead of in linear size. Figure 13-2 is simpler, showing how the size of a constant disk would appear to change if it approached the observer or receded from him. The contractions and expansions are shown as ratios to the linear size of the disk at 10 ft away from the observer. Figure 13-2 is derived from Fig. 13-1 by making the assumption that the relationships of Fig. 13-1 would hold for areas of the retina

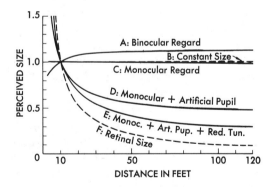

Figure 13.2 Visually perceived size as a function of the distance of the perceived object. These curves are derived from those of Fig. 13-1 by the use of certain simple assumptions. Perceived size is shown as ratios to the perceived size of the stimulus object at a distance of 10 ft and subtending an angle of 1°. See legend to Fig. 13-1 for further specification of the six functions shown.

[8] D. W. Taylor and E. G. Boring, "Apparent size as a function of distance for monocular observers," *Am. J. Psychol.* **55**, 102–105 (1942).

differing considerably from 1°, and the further assumption that difference in perceived size is proportional to the amount of change necessary in the stimulus to abolish difference in perceived size. This last statement means, for example, that if two disks at different distances looked the same size and one had a diameter four times the diameter of the other, then, if the diameters were made actually equal, one of them would appear to be one-quarter the length of the other. It is a plausible assumption, but not necessarily correct. The functions of Fig. 13-2 yield curves because they are reciprocal to linear functions.

In view of these consistent results there cannot be much doubt that perceived size depends upon more than the size of the retinal image, that the clue from the retinal image is corrected by those contexts that establish the distance of the perceived object, and that the correction can be fully adequate when the context is not too greatly reduced. Monocular vision in the near-dark is good enough to keep size constant. Binocular vision in the near-dark may do too good a job. We have no measurements to show what happens with the perspective clues that good illumination in a furnished hall would produce.

These functions hold up to a distance of 120 ft, and possibly up to 200 ft. What happens at great distances? We have only casual observation and one experiment to show. A man a mile away looks small, even though seen with two eyes in broad daylight over a terrain that furnishes excellent perspective clues. Is he reduced as much in perceived size as is his image on my retina? We do not know. The experiments on great distances have yet to be made, and should be made.

There is, however, one experiment on the perceived size of a distant object—the moon. The moon's disk subtends about ½°, but the horizon moon may be matched to a comparison stimulus that is 12 ft away and that subtends an angle of 3°, and a moon in elevation to a comparison stimulus of 2°.[9] In other words, a disk, 2160 mi in diameter and 239,000 mi away, appears the same size as a disk 7½ in. in diameter 12 ft away. If Euclid's law held, the moon would match in size a disk 1¼ in. in diameter at 12 ft distance, because this little disk and the moon would each subtend an angle of ½°. There is for the moon no size constancy. The real moon does not look so big as a 239,000-mi disk 12 ft away! The lack of distance contexts for the moon nearly reduces its perception to the law of retinal size, yet not quite. The perceived dummy moon 12 ft away regresses toward the real object to an amount six times what its retinal size would justify, although it is still only one 18-millionth of the size of the real moon. It seems that the great but nearly indeterminate distance of the moon provides just enough context to shift the perceptual size a little bit away from what retinal size alone would give, shifting it in the direction of size constancy, in the direction of regression toward the real object.

LOGIC OR PHYSIOLOGY?

It is an interesting question as to just what is going on when an organism uses the totality of available relevant clues or cues in modeling a perception so that it resembles as nearly as possible the permanent object which is being perceived. From one point of view, the conscious organism seems to be using *clues* to form an inference as to the real nature of the object which is revealed to it through various sense data. From another point of view, the organism seems to be using the various sensory excitations as *cues* to bring a given perception onto the stage of consciousness in accordance with a script in which the stage directions are the integrative properties of the brain. *Clues* and *cues*—both words are used, and they represent two

[9] E. G. Boring, "The moon illusion," *Am. J. Physics* 11, 55–60 (1943), and references there cited.

theories of perception, which are often opposed to each other without their being truly incompatible.

Helmholtz recognized this dilemma when, in 1866, he undertook to explain these perceptual phenomena by an appeal to the concept of *unconscious inference* (*unbewusster Schluss*).[10] The perception is essentially, he said, a conclusion formed from evidence by inductive inference. The process of its formation, while like a conscious inference, is actually unconscious. It is normally irresistible and instantaneous, although, Helmholtz thought, it can be unlearned and was therefore probably learned in the first place.

On that last matter Helmholtz certainly made too large a generalization. That coal is black is doubtless learned, and perhaps an artist might unlearn coal's color enough to see it in sunlight as light gray. That is not certain, though. It is possible that the artist sees his light-gray paint as black when he realizes it is coal. Some of the optical illusions break down or diminish under critical inspection, but others persist as inevitably compulsory. No amount of inspection, thought or knowledge will teach you to see the circles of Fig. 13-3 as anything other than spirals. They are circles though—perfect circles. That they are closed figures appears at once if you start at *a* and follow the circle around until you come back to *a* again.

An illusion is, however, not a good example of unconscious inference, for it involves faulty logic or physiologic, whichever it is. It does not produce a perception that is faithful to its true object. A much better instance of compulsory unconscious inference is the stereoscopic perception of depth.

[10] H. Helmholtz, *Physiological optics* (1866, tr., Optical Society of America, 1925), vol. III, pp. 1–35; *Die Thatsachen in der Wahrnehmung* (Hirschwald, 1879). Helmholtz seems to have had the idea of unconscious inference as early as 1855. See E. G. Boring, *A history of experimental psychology* (Appleton-Century, 1929), pp. 300–304.

Figure 13.3 Twisted cord illusion. The perceived spirals are actually perfect circles, as can be found by starting at *a* and following the apparent spiral back to *a* again. Adapted from J. Fraser, *Brit. J. Psychol.* 2, 307–20 (1908).

In stereoscopic vision the evidence for depth or solidity lies in that slight disparity of the two retinal images which is furnished by binocular parallax. Given a few constants of the binocular system, the forms and sizes of the two disparate images, and the assignment of one image to the left eye and the other to the right, and you can figure out geometrically by conscious inference what the dimensions in depth are. The visual mechanism, however, makes this inference instantaneously and unconsciously. If the stereograms are photographs, rich in detail, it is as impossible ever to see the disparity between them, as it is to be aware of disparity in the binocular observation of a solid object. Only in very simple stereoscopic images, such as the outline drawings of geometric figures, does one sometimes see the disparity as doubled lines first, before the doubling disappears and the images pull together into a single solid figure. In the perception the brain reaches a correct inferential conclusion as to the depth of the perceived object, but the process is no more conscious than is the inference of an electronic computer which calculates almost instantly from relevant data a range and elevation and correctly aims a gun.

It is in fact this electric analogy that answers quite well the question as to whether the integrative process in perceiving is logical or physiological. It is both. There is no contradiction. The inference is as logical and as unconscious as it is when made electrically in a machine.

The Gestalt psychologists—Wertheimer, Köhler and Koffka—have emphasized the notion that perceptual integration in the brain is due to the operation of certain dyanmic patterns of "force" that often correct or alter the perceptual form in ways that resemble closely the operation of mechanical or electric field forces.[11] Frequently this process results in what might be called a simplification. Two disparate images, one on each retina, constitute a confusion and make no sense. Put them together and you have both simplicity and sense—a single tridimensional object. Helmholtz would have called that unconscious inference, but the Gestalt psychologists eschew *inference* in favor of *field forces*.

Figure 13-4 is similar to a figure of Koffka's. Above, at *A*, you see three sets of four lines each. At *B* you see the three sets superposed, and the 12 lines arranged in this relation give you the perception of depth. It is practicably impossible to see them any more as lying flat in the plane of the paper, as they did in *A*. The cube of *B*

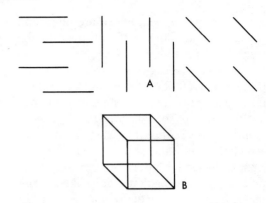

Figure 13.4 Dynamics of the visual field. The 12 lines of A, three sets of four lines each, all seen as lying in the plane of the paper, when superposed to make B, form a perceived solid in which the 12 lines no longer appear to lie on the plane of the paper.

insists on appearing solid, although it is reversible and may be seen in either of two perspectives. Is the cube simpler than the 12 lines? Well, there is only one cube, and perhaps one is simpler than 12. At any rate the cube is more sensible than the 12 lines because it is an object. The brain has here integrated an object. For binocular parallax it redintegrates an object.

There is, then, no objection to be raised to the idea that brain properties should operate to establish the conclusions to inferences. Physical properties do in the electric computer. They might in the brain. It takes a brain to do any conscious inferring, and the brain operates always under natural physical law. There is no real contradiction between Helmholtz and the Gestalt psychologists.

It is, moreover, clear that these integrative properties of the brain are both native and acquired, dependent upon both *heredity* and *learning*. The dynamics of stereoscopy and of the perceptions of Figs. 13-3 and 13-4 seem almost certainly native neural properties and not acquired. Seeing objects in their true colors and brightnesses irrespective of the illumination, must be learned. The chromosomes take no account of what colors are in the American flag.

[11] The leaders of the movement called Gestalt psychology are Max Wertheimer (1880–1943), Kurt Koffka (1886–1941) and Wolfgang Köhler (1887–). The movement began in Germany with experiments on perception and with the development of a theory of perception. See reference 1 for Koffka's discussion and the books that give other references to this large literature. A very important contribution is W. Köhler, *Die physischen Gestalten in Ruhe und im stationären Zustand* (Vieweg, 1920); see also his *The place of value in a world of facts* (Liveright, 1938), *Dynamics in psychology* (Liveright, 1940), and Köhler and H. Wallach, "Figural after-effects," *Proc. Am. Phil. Soc.* 88, 269–357 (1944).

It would be a bold man who would assert at present that constancy of perceived shape is either wholly learned or wholly native. We do not know. What then about the correction of retinal size for distance?

There are experiments which show that chickens can learn to choose larger grains of corn and reject smaller, when the difference in size is of the order of only 10 percent. When they have acquired this discrimination, then they will choose remote large grains in preference to small grains near-by, although the retinal images of the remote large grains may be only one-fifth the size of the retinal images of the near small grains.[12] Still the chickens may have learned to take distance into account.

Children do not do so well as adults, nor young children so well as older, in matching boxes for actual size when the boxes lie on the floor at different distances away.[13] There are individual differences among adults, and anything that tends to distort the perception of distance seems to affect the perception of size, whereas the best judgments of objective size are got from the observers who can estimate the distances most correctly.[14] Such findings suggest that learning plays a role.

On the other hand, it is somewhat implausible that, in learning to compensate for changing size of the retinal image with changing distance, one should acquire a habit for overcompensation (function A in Figs. 13-1 and 13-2). Overcompensation

seems to imply the operation of more basic mechanisms than those that are learned. Still there is no conclusive evidence. One might acquire separately by learning a number of corrective processes which, all working concurrently, would then overshoot the mark. If that conclusion is correct, we are still left with the problem as to why the organism would learn to compensate just a little bit for the small size of the moon's image on the retina. If that correction is learned, it must have been carried over from some other experience.

Actually the decision on this question does not matter. No inherited function is ever quite unaffected by learning, and no learned function is ever able to operate entirely without dependence on what is given it by inheritance. If the perception of size with distance variant depends on both chromosomes and practice, it will be like almost every other psychophysiological function.

BIOLOGICAL USE OF PERCEPTION

The physiology of perception is uncertain, but its biology is clear. The function of perception is to transform chaotic sense experience into the relative stability of permanent objects, the objects which cause the experience or are implied by the experience, whichever way you like to look at it. An object can be regarded as an as-if theory of experience. Experience would be as it is if there were permanent objects. And the properties of the objects thus become generalizations about experience. So perception, in getting back of experience to the objects, is performing even in primitive man and the animals the same function that science performs in man's civilization. As the purpose of scientific theories is economy of thought, so the purpose of perception is economy of thinking. It picks out and establishes what is permanent and therefore important to the organism for its survival and welfare.

To see a gray as coal is useful. It is to know that this gray will burn and give

[12] W. Köhler, "Optische Untersuchungen am Schimpansen und am Haushuhn," *Abhandl. preuss. Akad. Wiss., Phys.-math. Klasse,* No. 3, 18–139 (1915); W. Götz, "Experimentelle Untersuchungen zum Problem der Sehgrössenkonstanz beim Haushuhn," *Z. Psychol.* **99,** 247–260 (1926).

[13] F. Beyrl, "Über die Grössenauffassung bei Kindern," *Z. Psychol.* **100,** 344–371 (1926); H. Frank, "Die Sehgrössenkonstanz bei Kindern," *Psychol. Forsch.* **10,** 102–106 (1928).

[14] R. H. Thouless, "Individual differences in phenomenal regression," *Brit. J. Psychol.* **22,** 216–241 (1932); M. R. Sheehan, "A study of individual consistency in phenomenal constancy," *Arch. Psychol.,* No. 222 (1938); B. E. Holaday, "Die Grössenkonstanz der Sehdinge bei Variation der inneren und äusseren Wahrnehmungsbedingungen," *Arch. ges. Psychol.* **88,** 419–486 (1933).

heat. To see a verdigris as blue is to recognize your country's flag. To see a diamond as square is to recognize the book or the table for what it is, which is important, and to ignore the effect of your own angular relation to it, which, since it changes as you move, is unimportant. To see a distant object with a small retinal image as large and a near object with a large retinal image as small is to get away from the unimportant retinal images to the great importance of the sizes of objects. A chicken by that means gets all the big grains of corn,

no matter how far away they are. Perhaps the greatest perceptual achievement of the organism is the way in which it receives on bidimensional retinas optical projections of the tridimensional world, losing, it would seem, all the tridimensionality, and then, taking immediate physiological account of the disparity of binocular parallax and other clues when they are available, instantaneously puts the solid object together again in perception, recovering the tridimensionality of the real object which had seemed irrevocably lost.

14. Movement-Produced Stimulation in the Development of Visually Guided Behavior *

Richard Held and Alan Hein

When you reach for an object, your brain gambles that your eyes have correctly signalled its position. The brain usually wins such wagers because, as can be seen in the previous articles, the location of objects in space is reliably encoded by the visual system.

While it is obvious that accurate localization is biologically adaptive, it is by no means obvious how this accuracy is achieved. There are two broad possibilities: vision and action may become synchronized through repeated encounters with the environment (i.e., learning), or the coordination may be completely innate and thus independent of experience. In the next selection, Professors Held and Hein describe a test of these alternatives with respect to the coordination of vision and locomotion in kittens.

* Reprinted by permission of the authors and the American Psychological Association from the *Journal of Comparative and Physiological Psychology*, 1963, 56, 872-876.

Full and exact adaptation to sensory rearrangement in adult human Ss requires movement-produced sensory feedback. Riesen's work suggested that this factor also operates in the development of higher mammals but he proposed that sensory-sensory associations are the prerequisite. To test these alternatives, visual stimulation of the active member (A) of each of 10 pairs of neonatal kittens was allowed to vary with its locomotor movements while equivalent stimulation of the second member (P) resulted from passive motion. Subsequent tests of visually guided paw placement, discrimination on a visual cliff, and the blink response were normal for A but failing in P. When other alternative explanations are excluded, this result extends the conclusions of studies of adult rearrangement to neonatal development.

Hebb's writing (1949) has stirred interest in the effects of exposure to the environment on the development of spatial perception and coordination. The main experimental attack on the problem has used the technique of rearing animals in restricted environments (deprivation) from the time of birth or shortly thereafter. An alternative approach consists in experimentally analyzing the conditions for modifying certain sensorimotor coordinations in adults on the assumption that they are similarly plastic during the entire exposure-history of the organism (Hein & Held, 1962; Held, 1955, 1961). If this supposition is true, the analysis carried out on adults must also define the kind of contact with the environment required for development. Use of the rearrangement technique for studying plasticity in adult human Ss has yielded results which suggest its complementarity to the procedures of neonatal deprivation (Held & Bossom, 1961). This experiment demonstrates the convergence of the two approaches.

In the human adult, change in stimulation dependent upon the natural movements of S has been shown essential to the achievement of full and exact compensation for sensory rearrangements (Hein & Held, 1958; Held, 1955; Held & Bossom, 1961; Mikaelian & Held, in press). A suggestive parallel between these findings and those of deprivation studies comes from two experiments on kittens reared under different conditions of deprivation. In one experiment Ss were allowed visual experience in an illuminated and patterned environment only while they were restrained in holders which prevented them from freely moving about (Reisen & Aarons, 1959). When subsequently tested they showed deficiencies in visually guided behavior compared with their normally reared litter mates. Related deficits followed rearing in a second experiment in which Ss were allowed to move about freely in light but with diffusing hoods over their eyes (Reisen, 1961c). The exposure factor lacking under both conditions was the variation in visual stimulation produced by the full range of S's movement in normal circumstances; a result consistent with our findings.

Riesen has suggested that his deprived Ss showed deficits because they lacked sufficient opportunity for developing sensory-sensory associations in the manner proposed by Hebb (Riesen, 1961c)—even the patterned surroundings viewed by the holder-restrained Ss may not have provided sufficient variation in visual stimulation for forming the necessary associations. This interpretation agrees with ours in asserting that the variation in visual stimulation accompanying movement is essential for the development of certain coordinations but it omits our qualification that this variation can be effective only when it is concurrent with and systematically dependent upon self-produced movements (Hein & Held, 1962; Held, 1961). The alternative to our interpretation asserts that changes in stimulation irrespective of their relation to self-produced movements are sufficient. To decide between these two alternatives, we reared different sets of kittens from birth under the two implied conditions of exposure and subsequently compared their development. Under one condition stimulation varied as a result of Ss own locomotion whereas under the other it was equivalently varied by transporting Ss through an equivalent range of motion while they were restrained from locomoting.

METHOD

Subjects

Ten pairs of kittens were used; each pair from a different litter.

Exposure Apparatus and Procedure

The exposure apparatus diagramed in Figure 14-1 was designed to equate the visual stimulation received by each member of a pair of Ss. Stimulation varied with the locomotor movements of the active S (A in Figure 14-1) but varied with equivalent motion of the passive S (P). To attain this equivalence, the gross motions of A were mechanically transferred to P. These movements were restricted to rotations around three axes. The radial symmetry

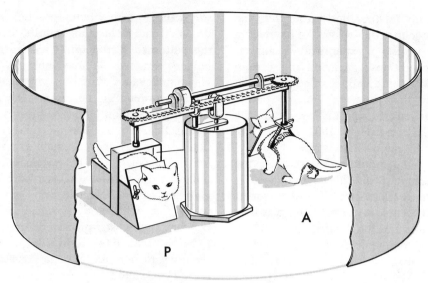

Figure 14.1 Apparatus for equating motion and consequent visual feedback for an actively moving (A) and a passively moved (P) S.

of the visible environment made variations in visual stimulation, contingent upon these movements, equal over time for the two Ss.

The P was placed in the gondola and held there by a neckyoke and body clamp. The lever from which the gondola was suspended was then balanced by appropriate placement of a counterweight. When attached to the opposite end of the lever by a second neckyoke and body-clamp assembly, A was free to move itself in both directions around the three axes of rotation a-a, b-b, and c-c while pulling P through the equivalent movements around a-a, b-b, and d-d by means of the mechanical linkages to the gondola. The distance between c-c and d-d was 36 in. The range of motions normally performed by Ss was somewhat reduced by the experimental apparatus. Use of ball bearings and aluminum in the construction of the apparatus reduced friction and inertia insofar as possible. The importance of these restraints is mitigated, we believe, by previous findings in rearrangement studies which indicate that similar restraints, and constant changes in the inertia overcome by muscular movement, do not affect the adaptation process (Held & Hein, 1958; Held & Schlank, 1959).

Head motion was not restricted for either A or P. This restriction seemed unnecessary since Riesen and Aarons (1959) have shown that kittens reared from birth with variation in visual stimulation consequent upon free head motions, but otherwise restricted, failed to learn a simple spatial discrimination. Because of its constraints, P could not locomote. However, its limbs were free to move and to slide along the smooth floor of the gondola. According to our observations these movements frequently occurred.

The apparatus was surrounded by a galvanized iron cylinder that was 24 in. high with a diameter of 48 in. The lever support mechanism was enclosed within a second cylinder that was 11 in. high with a diameter of 12 in. The smaller cylinder served to obscure each S's view of its mate. Patterning was provided by vertically oriented 1 in. wide stripes of black and white masking tape separated by 1 in. of bare metal. Additional texture was provided by the rough side of a piece of masonite which served as the floor. The floor was uniform throughout thus providing equivalent visual stimulation for the two Ss. Sight of the paws and other body parts was excluded by appropriate extensions of the neck stocks.

Testing Apparatus and Procedure

We used tests of visually guided behavior that minimized S's gross movements in the visible environment in order not to confound the conditions of testing with those of exposure, a confusion which past investigators have generally disregarded. For this purpose responses to stimuli were used that require no conditioning with repetition of movements but which are nonetheless contingent upon a capacity to make visual-spatial discriminations. Following the leads of earlier work, we have used three such tests:

1. Visually-guided paw placement (Riesen, 1961c). S's body was held in E's hands so that its head and forelegs were free. It was slowly carried forward and downward towards the edge of a table or some other horizontal surface. A normally-reared S shows visually-mediated anticipation of contact by extending its paws as it approaches the edge.

2. Avoidance of a visual cliff (Walk & Gibson, 1961). The visual cliff consists essentially of a narrow platform supported by vertical sides that drop a few inches to a large plate of glass. The S placed on the platform can descend to the glass on either one of two sides. Its view on the "deep" side is through the glass to a patterned surface 30 in. below. On the other side it views a similarly patterned surface attached to the underside of the glass. In our apparatus, both surfaces were illuminated from below and hence the clean glass surface was practically invisible. For the vertical sides of the platform, we substituted planes inclined 35° from the vertical.

3. Blink to an approaching object (Riesen, 1958). The S was held in a standing position in a neckyoke and body clamp with a large sheet of Plexiglas positioned directly in front of its face. The E moved his hand quickly toward S, stopping just short of contact with the Plexiglas.

Several additional tests were performed to check the status of peripheral receptor and response mechanisms. These included observations of pupillary reflex to light, the tactual placing response, and visual pursuit of a moving object. The S, held in a standing position in a neckyoke and body clamp, was light-adapted in the normally illuminated laboratory prior to observation of the pupillary reflex. Change in pupillary size was then noted when a light beam from a penlight was moved across the eye from outer to inner canthus. To determine the presence of the tactual paw-placing response S was supported as in the visual paw-placing test. It was then carried to the edge of a table where the dorsa of its front paws were brought into contact with the vertical edge of the table. Observations of experimental Ss were compared with those of normals which, in response to this stimulus, place the paws on the horizontal surface of the table. Visual pursuit was elicited by E's hand moving slowly across S's visual field.

General Procedure

The 10 pairs of Ss were divided into two Groups, X and Y, whose members were reared with minor differences. Each of the eight pairs of Group X was reared in darkness from birth until member A attained the minimal size and coordinational capacity to move itself and its mate in the apparatus. This age varied between 8 and 12 weeks. They then began exposure in the apparatus for 3 hr. daily. The two pairs of Group Y received 3 hr. daily exposure, beginning at 2 and ending at 10 weeks of age, to the patterned interior of the laboratory while restrained in holders that allowed some head movement but prevented locomotion. They then began exposure in the apparatus for 3 hr. daily. When not exposed, all Ss were kept in lightless cages together with their mothers and litter mates. We had found in pilot studies that Ss reared in this fashion did not show the freezing, agitation, or fear responses reported to follow social isolation by Melzack (1962) and Riesen (1961a).

Six repetitions of the paw-placement test were performed after each daily exposure period for all Ss. On the first day that one S of each pair in Group X displayed visual paw placing, both were tested on the visual cliff. They were retested on the following day. For each test and retest S was required to descend from the central platform six times. Immediately following trials on the visual cliff on the second day, member P of each pair was put in a continuously illuminated room for 48 hr. Retesting of visual placing and renewed trials on the visual cliff followed this unrestricted exposure. The testing procedure differed slightly for pairs of Group Y. On the first day that A displayed visual paw placing, it was tested on the visual cliff and retested on the following day. However, its mate (P) was not placed on the cliff at this time; instead, the passive exposure procedure was continued for 3 hr. daily for a total of 126 hr. The paw placing and visual cliff tests were then administered to P.

RESULTS

The principal results of this experiment are summarized in Table 1. The amount of time required for the development of a visually-guided paw-placement in the members of each pair of litter mates is indicated in the column under the heading Exposure in Apparatus. After those periods of exposure required by A, every P mate failed to display the response. Observations suggest a tendency for the placing response to develop in the livelier of the active Ss with fewer hours of exposure than required by the quieter ones. The blink response to an approaching hand developed concurrently with the placing response. Pupillary reflex to light, tactual placing response, and visual pursuit were each noted on first elicitation, just prior to the initial exposure in the apparatus.

TABLE 1

Ratio of Descents to Shallow and Deep Sides of Visual Cliff

Pair number	Age in weeks[a]	Exposure in apparatus (in hr.)		Ratio of descents shallow/deep	
		A	P	A	P
1X	8	33	33	12/0	6/6
2X	8	33	33	12/0	4/8
3X	8	30	30	12/0	7/5
4X	9	63	63	12/0	6/6
5X	10	33	33	12/0	7/5
6X	10	21	21	12/0	7/5
7X	12	9	9	12/0	5/7
8X	12	15	15	12/0	8/4
1Y	10	30	126	12/0	6/6
2Y	10	33	126	12/0	8/4

[a] At the beginning of exposure in the experimental apparatus.

On the day that the visually-guided placing response was shown by A, he was tested on the modified visual cliff. All As behaved like normally reared Ss which had been observed previously in a pilot experiment. As shown by the totals of Table 1, each A descended to the shallow side of the cliff on every trial of the first day and repeated this performance on the trials of the following day. The P members of Group X were tested on the cliff on the same days as their actively exposed litter mates. They showed no evidence of discriminating the shallow from the deep side. Observations of the P members of Group Y on the cliff, after their prolonged passive exposure, gave similar results and they also failed to perform visual paw placement. Following the 48 hr. period of freedom in an illuminated room, the P members of Group X were retested. They then displayed normal visually-guided paw-placement and performed all descents to the shallow side of the visual cliff.

DISCUSSION

The results are consistent with our thesis that self-produced movement with its concurrent visual feedback is necessary for the development of visually-guided behavior. Equivalent, and even greatly increased, variation in visual stimulation produced by other means is not sufficient. However, before concluding that our thesis is valid we must consider other alternative explanations of the deficits in the behavioral development of neonates following deprivation. These alternatives assert that loss of function does not reflect deficiencies in a process of the central nervous system that depends upon exposure for its development. Instead, the capacity to perform is allegedly present but prevented from operating by either peripheral blockage or other suppressive effects of the special rearing conditions. Such negative effects fall into two categories: (a) anatomical or physiological deterioration and (b) behavioral inhibition.

Included under anatomical or physiological deterioration said to result from deprivation, are the findings of atrophy in peripheral parts of the visual nervous system, a literature reviewed by Riesen (1961b); the assumption that maturation of the retina is prevented (Walk & Gibson, 1961); and the suggestion that general debility results from lack of use of various organs (Hess, 1962). In the present experiment, the relevance of peripheral atrophy is contraindicated by the presence of pupillary and pursuit reflexes and the rapid recovery of function of the passive Ss once given their freedom. Debility specific to the motor systems of these Ss can be ruled out on the grounds that their tactual placing responses and other motor activities were indistinguishable from those of normals. In addition, differential losses in the periphery or differential debility could hardly be expected to result from those differences between active and passive exposures which occurred in the experimental apparatus.

Inhibition of performance attributable to the effects of shock, fright, or overactivation upon exposure to the novel and increased stimulation that follows release from the deprived state has been suggested by Sutherland (1959) and Melzack (1962). Sutherland has also suggested that habits developed during deprivation may compete with and inhibit the normal response. However, both our active and passive Ss were raised under very similar conditions insofar as restriction was concerned and under the rather mild conditions of deprivation of this experiment we did not observe any signs of shock, excitement, or fright. Moreover, the passive Ss were not observed performing responses that might have competed with the expected response.

These findings provide convincing evidence for a developmental process, in at least one higher mammal, which requires for its operation stimulus variation concurrent with and systematically dependent upon self-produced movement. This conclusion neither denies nor affirms that other processes, such as maturation, occur concomitantly. The results demonstrate the complementarity of studies of adult rearrangement and neonatal deprivation.

REFERENCES

HEBB, D. O. *The organization of behavior.* New York: Wiley, 1949.

HEIN, A., & HELD, R. Minimal conditions essential for complete re-learning of hand-eye coordination with prismatic distortion of vision. Paper read at Eastern Psychological Association. Philadelphia, 1958.

HEIN, A., & HELD, R. A neural model for labile sensorimotor coordinations. In E. E. Bernard & M. R. Kare (Eds.), *Biological prototypes and synthetic systems.* Vol. 1, New York: Plenum Press, 1962. Pp. 71–74.

HELD, R. Shifts in binaural localization after prolonged exposures to atypical combinations of stimuli. *Amer. J. Psychol.,* 1955, 68, 526–548.

HELD, R. Exposure-history as a factor in maintaining stability of perception and coordination. *J. nerv. ment. Dis.,* 1961, 132, 26–32.

HELD, R., & BOSSOM, J. Neonatal deprivation and adult rearrangement: Complementary techniques for analyzing plastic sensory-motor coordinations. *J. comp. physiol. Psychol.,* 1961, 54, 33–37.

HELD, R., & HEIN, A. Adaptation of disarranged hand-eye coordination contingent upon re-afferent stimulation. *Percept. mot. Skills,* 1958, 8, 87–90.

HELD, R., & SCHLANK, M. Adaptation to optically-increased distance of the hand from the eye by re-afferent stimulation. *Amer. J. Psychol.*, 1959, 72, 603–605.

HESS, E. H. Ethology: An approach toward the complete analysis of behavior. In R. Brown, E. Galanter, E. H. Hess, & G. Mandler (Eds.). *New directions in psychology.* New York: Holt, Rinehart & Winston, 1962. Pp. 159–266.

MELZACK, R. Effects of early perceptual restriction on simple visual discrimination. *Science*, 1962, 137, 978–979.

MIKAELIAN, H., & HELD, R. Two types of adaptation to an optically-rotated visual field. *Amer. J. Psychol.*, in press.

RIESEN, A. H. Plasticity of behavior: Psychological aspects. In H. F. Harlow & C. N. Woolsey (Eds.), *Biological and biochemical bases of behavior.* Madison: Univer. Wisconsin Press, 1958. Pp. 425–450.

RIESEN, A. H. Excessive arousal effects of stimulation after early sensory deprivation. In P. Solomon, P. E. Kubzansky, P. H. Leiderman, J. H. Mendelson, R. H. Trumbull, & D. Wexler (Eds.), *Sensory deprivation.* Cambridge: Harvard Univer. Press, 1961. Pp. 34–40. (a)

RIESEN, A. H. Stimulation as a requirement for growth and function in behavioral development. In D. W. Fiske & S. R. Maddi (Eds.). *Functions of varied experience.* Homewood: Dorsey Press, 1961. Pp. 57–80. (b)

RIESEN, A. H. Studying perceptual development using the technique of sensory deprivation. *J. nerv. ment. Dis.*, 1961, 132, 21–25. (c)

RIESEN, A. H., & AARONS, L. Visual movement and intensity discrimination in cats after early deprivation of pattern vision. *J. comp. physiol. Psychol.*, 1959, 52, 142–149.

SUTHERLAND, N. S. Stimulus analyzing mechanisms. In, *Mechanization of thought processes: National physical laboratory symposium No. 10.* Vol. 2. London: Her Majesty's Stationery Office, 1959. Pp. 575–609.

WALK, R. D., & GIBSON, E. J. A comparative and analytical study of visual depth perception. *Psychol. Monogr.*, 1961, 75 (15, Whole No. 519).

15. A Mechanical Model for Human Attention and Immediate Memory *

D. E. Broadbent

Most persons have encountered models at some point during their scientific education. The model of an atom with sun-like nucleus and planetary electrons circling in orbits is one example; an organic molecule composed of sticks and balls is another. In everyday life, road maps serve as useful models.

Models are helpful because they make explicit the relationships and assumptions intrinsic to events not readily visualized. They can be constructed out of any material at hand, and the concreteness of their existence conveniently reminds one that the explanation inherent in the model is strictly an analogy, not to be confused with the fabric of the real event. These virtues of models are especially attractive to psychologists, who must necessarily deal with complex processes largely through indirect means.

One of the most fundamental problems for psychology is the phenomenon of attention. A model of the attention process is described by Professor Broadbent in the next selection. Although the model appears to be rather simple, it profitably organizes and effectively integrates a large body of data.

Many people have a natural distaste for model building. A mechanical model is essentially a theory expressed in material parts rather than in abstract symbols such as words or mathematical expressions. Its logical standing is the same: that is, it stands or falls by the degree to which it fits the results of experiments on human or other animals. Yet many models in the past have been somewhat undistinguished in the closeness with which experiment has

* Reprinted by permission of the author and the American Psychological Association from the *Psychological Review*, 1957, 64, 205-215.

been considered in their design. It is difficult to avoid feeling that this is because a model is unduly laborious to build as compared with a verbal theory, so that the builder tends to become obsessed with the properties of his model rather than those of the organism. Consequently there is much to be said for building theories verbally, and especially for using the qualitative terms of information theory in the hypothetico-deductive fashion ably set out by Mackay (29). Such an approach has certain advantages over the other popular alternative of quantitative S-R terms; these advantages have been considered elsewhere (11).

For example, the writer holds that the human perceptual system has a limited capacity, that in consequence a selective operation is performed upon all inputs to the system, and that this operation takes the form of selecting all inputs having some characteristic in common. Such an operation extracts little information from the signal and thus should be economical of nervous mechanism. Characteristics on which the selection can operate may be named "sensory channels." The particular selection made at any one time will depend partly on characteristics of the input itself (physical intensity, earliness in time, absence of recent inputs on that channel, position of the channel in the hierarchy of all channels) and partly on information in a more permanent store. The change from one selection to another will take a determinate time.

Incoming information may be held in a more temporary store at a stage previous to that of the selective operation. Such information will pass through the perceptual system on the next subsequent selection of the sensory channel of its arrival, if it is still in store; but the probability of the latter condition being fulfilled will decline with time spent in store. After passage through the perceptual system, information may be returned to the same temporary store, the selection of information for such return being determined by information in a more permanent store.

But although such a purely verbal theory may fit experimental results, it is difficult to communicate to others without putting them to the trouble of learning the necessary vocabulary. And if the theory is rephrased, still abstractly, it is open to misinterpretation; thus Deese (19), in a paper which makes a number of valuable contributions to the theory of prolonged work, has described the writer as postulating an inhibitory construct in human performance. This misunderstanding probably arises from the fact that the theory outlined in the last two paragraphs is intended to apply both to conditioning and to human watch keeping; in neither case is it thought necessary to find an inhibitory construct of orthodox learning theory type. To say that conditioning and perception are related is not to apply a particular interpretation of the former to the latter.

Clearly, then, some sort of expository device is needed for an abstract theory using unfamiliar terms. And it is even difficult for the theorist to remember in abstract form the results of the many different experiments which a good theory should consider. A simple mechanical model has the virtue of avoiding these difficulties. It has other vices: it may have accidental properties which mislead research. Perhaps the best compromise is to state a theory in abstract terms, and also to give a model which can be described by the same verbal theory. Information concepts are applicable to any system, whatever its physical nature, and so may equally fit a model or a man. This is the approach of Deutsch (20, 21), and it has real advantages, independent of the value of his particular theory. The present paper is therefore intended to describe an extremely simple model of the human perceptual system. It may serve both as an easy introduction to the formal theory in information flow terms and also as a convenient mnemonic for the results of a number of experiments.

THE BASIC MODEL

The necessary requirements are a Y-shaped tube (Fig. 15-1) mounted vertically, and a set of small balls. Each ball bears a number so that all are individually recognizable. The Y tube has a narrow stem which will just take only one ball, though the branches are wider. At the junction of stem and branches is a hinged flap which normally hangs straight downward, but which can be pivoted about its upper edge so as to close off either of the branches of the Y. This pivoting can be done by a handle from outside the tube, controlled by stored information; purists may wish to control the handle by a punched-tape system, but a human being is an adequate substitute. When the handle is left alone the flap moves freely so that a ball dropped into one arm of the Y will knock the flap aside and fall into the stem of the Y.

In this model the balls represent the information from various stimuli. The branching arms represent different sensory channels; thus one might be one ear and one the other ear. Alternatively, one might be the ear and one the eye. (Sensory channel is not, however, quite equivalent to sense-organ, since we would treat sounds localized in different places as being on different channels.) The bottom of the Y represents a response output, so that the process of dropping a ball into the arms and observing its emergence at the bottom is analogous to that of delivering a stimulus and observing a response. The behavior of the model resembles that of man in the following ways:

(a) If two balls are dropped simultaneously, one into each of the branches, they will strike the flap on both sides; it will not move and therefore they will jam in the junction. Numerous experiments show this "distraction" effect, but there are certain advantages in citing an auditory

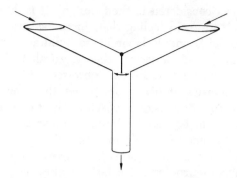

Figure 15.1 The simple model for attention.

experiment (5, 33). These same experiments show that if the handle is used to shut off one branch before the balls are inserted, then the ball entering the other branch will emerge successfully, which is analogous to previous instructions.

(b) If the two balls are not strictly simultaneous, the first to arrive will obtain an advantage by knocking the flap over and shutting out the other. This had been shown to be analogous with competing auditory stimuli by Spieth, Curtis, and Webster (36).

(c) If the Y is not perfectly vertical, the ball in the more vertical branch will have an advantage over a simultaneous ball in the other because the door will hang to one side. Equally, one sensory channel may have an advantage over another, as has been shown for high-pitched noise as compared with low (10).

(d) If one ball is flung violently down its branch, it may succeed in forcing over the door against the unassisted weight of a ball on the opposite branch. Equally, an intense stimulus may have an advantage (2, 10).

(e) After a single ball has been passed through the system, the door will swing back from the position into which it has been pushed. Naturally it will overswing, and temporarily close the branch which has just been used. A stimulus has similarly an extra advantage for response if it comes on a previously quiet channel as opposed to a previously busy one. This has been shown by Poulton (34) for auditory signals, and a related finding is that of Hyman (25) for visual reaction times. In the latter case, stimuli of different frequencies of occurrence were delivered, and it was found that average reaction time to a set of stimuli was proportional to the information conveyed by them; but the infrequent signals, while giving long reaction times, did not give times as long as those to be expected from information theory calculations. Note, however, that the time taken for a swing is important in the model; this will probably also be true in man, to judge from data which are best considered below. It may also be connected with Hyman's finding that, for numbers of alternatives greater than two, the second of two identical signals received an unduly fast reaction.

(f) If a given number of balls are to be put through the tube, it is best to deliver them asymmetrically, the majority to one branch. There is then less risk of jamming than if equal numbers are admitted by both branches. The analogous finding for auditory messages has been reported by Webster and Thompson (37). This point is related to another, that if balls are being inserted into one branch at random intervals the effect of increasing the rate of delivery of balls through that same branch (the "speed" of work) is not the same as that of adding the same number of extra balls to the other branch (the "load" of work). There is more risk of jamming in the latter case. This point was first clearly emphasized by Conrad, using visual signals (16). Obviously the effect of using two branches rather than one will be more serious if the rate of delivery of balls is high, since this increases the probability of a jam. Conrad showed such an interaction of speed and load. Mackworth and Mackworth (28) have shown a similar effect in a different type of task, and have demonstrated that the fluctuating difficulty of this complex task at any instant can be represented by the amount by which each signal is overlapped by other simultaneous ones.

At this point we may pause to consider the cynical reader who is wicked enough to be doubtful of the existence of a Y-shaped tube somewhere in the region of the thalamus. Such a reader will probably have noticed already a situation which will follow when two balls are dropped into the model and jamming is avoided by the door being to one side for one of the reasons listed. The favored ball will descend the stem of the Y, but the impeded ball will not therefore disappear. It will emerge later, when the door next swings back to the opposite branch. Surprisingly enough, this also happens with man. Simultaneous stimuli either jam or produce successive responses.[1] It has been shown for three different combinations of sensory channels (7, 8), and is probably an effect identical with the "prior entry" of classical psychology. In the same way Conrad has not only shown complete failures to respond (17) but also shifts in the time at which responses appear (18).

Having thus demolished the cynic, we must add that a slight complication should be added to the model in order to cover perfectly the results of experiments on successive response to simultaneous stimuli. But this will be left until the section on immediate memory; let us first deal with the effects of speed and of prolonged performance on the simple model.

(g) As the stem of the Y is so narrow, there will be a certain amount of delay between the insertion and emergence of each ball. At slow rates of insertion each ball will, however, emerge before the next is

[1] At the risk of complicating the issue, we must say that "stimuli" in this sentence means "stimuli not of low information content." A familiar predictable sequence of stimuli may quite well produce responses simultaneous with other responses (1). And the same S-R unit interferes less with another task when drawn from a smaller ensemble of possibilities (12). This point is of course implied in the statement that the perceptual mechanism has a limited capacity in the sense of information theory.

inserted. At faster rates there will develop a lag such that one ball may be inserted before the previous one emerges. With still faster rates balls will begin to accumulate in the branch; response will get further and further behind stimulus as the task proceeds. But this is a desperate expedient and will lead to breakdown when the branch is full unless the rate slows down again. These stages have been shown by Vince (35) for visual stimuli; a related effect has also been shown in less detail in hearing (4). A result of the piling up of balls in the branch when the rate is too high is that a ball inserted at a very short interval after another will remain in the tube longer than is normal: the "psychological refractory period" (38). It must be remembered that balls are analogous to information and not to stimulation; highly probable stimuli will not give an unduly long reaction under these conditions (22).

(h) Now suppose that we wish to operate the handle in such a way that one branch always has priority: prolonged performance of a task involving only one sensory channel. If there is a fairly rapid flow of balls down the selected branch, the handle will hardly need holding after the initial setting, since the beginning of any swing back will probably be checked by another ball. But if the selected branch is not very busy, the weight of the door must be held by a positive force on the handle. In this case the fingers holding the handle will fatigue; for purists, the punched-tape machine will only hold one branch shut for a limited period. When the handle is released the door will swing back to close the opposite branch, and then return pendulum-wise to the desired position when it will again be held. The result will be that prolonged tasks in which unexpected stimuli appear for less than a certain period (the "swings of the door") will show marked decrements in performance. But similar tasks in which the stimuli are present for longer times will show much less decrement.

The earlier evidence for this view of prolonged performance has been summarized elsewhere (6). But earlier presentations have misled Deese (19) into supposing that this view implied a decrement with continued performance of *any* vigilance task. He employed tasks in which a signal was either presented repeatedly until seen, or else painted on a tube face by a sweep line which did not return to obliterate the signal for nearly three seconds. It was in fact predicted by the writer (6, p. 300) that such tasks would show little or no decrement, and this was found by Deese to be the case. The latter type of task gave more signs of decrement, probably being a borderline case, since the trace left on the phosphor screen decayed until scarcely visible at the end of the three seconds. It should be noted that an expectancy theory of the type favored by Deese, while undoubtedly applicable to some aspects of vigilance, is not able to account for the effects of varying the length of signal presentation. In our Y-tube model, the role of expectancy is incorporated by describing the balls as representing information rather than stimulation; the more probable signals receive more efficient response. But the swinging of the flap is also necessary.

To summarize the writer's present views on vigilance, the efficiency of a man asked to detect infrequent signals should be described by both a mean and a variance. The mean level is determined by such factors as the rate at which signals arrive but not necessarily by the length of time since the session began. The variance, on the other hand, increases as the session progresses, short intervals of extremely low efficiency being interspersed with fairly long periods of normal or supernormal efficiency. The score from any given task may depend on one or on the other of these quantities. Thus, for example, the earlier British work has been mostly concerned with the instants of very low efficiency; the type of results reported by Deese and by later British workers (6) mostly with the mean over appreciable periods of time.

To return to our model, two further points should be made. The first is that the door need not swing the whole way over when the handle is released; it may reach a central position just as two balls arrive. There will then be a jam rather than passage of the wrong ball. Equally, failure of reaction to a task need not imply overt reaction to some irrelevant stimulus.

Secondly, as the balls represent information rather than stimulation, tasks in which the sequence of stimuli is predictable will not show fatigue decrements of this type. To show decrements, the signals must be unpredictable either in content, as were those of Bills (3), whose "blocks" are instances of this effect, or else in time of occurrence, as were those of Mackworth (27); this, however, is only one of the necessary conditions.

IMMEDIATE MEMORY

Our Y tube does seem at this stage to have related a number of facts about perception and put them in a way which most people can understand. It is admittedly ludicrous as a description of what really happens in the brain, but this is a positive advantage. Psychologists are not likely to mistake this model for speculative neurology, and so they should concentrate their experiments on the essentials of the theory rather than the irrelevant properties of the model. As a device for communicating the outline of the theory, however, the model seems sufficiently adequate to justify an extra complication in order to express a theory of immediate memory. This theory is in a slightly different position from the views on perception which have been given so far; the latter are entailed by the experiments, but the theory of immediate memory is not the only conceivable explanation of the observed facts. Yet it has a fairly high probability and is worth discussing.

The complication is twofold. First, a device must be supposed fitted to each branch of the Y tube, such that if any individual ball remains in the branch for more than a certain time continuously it is removed from the system completely. This could be done by filling the tube with acid, but the writer does not wish to encourage the development of a race of fingerless psychologists. Mechanical devices are quite possible, though complicated to describe, and the details will therefore be left unspecified and available from the author. The second complication is that from the foot of the stem two return tubes lead back to the branches (Fig. 15-2). Admission to these return tubes is controlled by a lower door which again is operated by a handle. The latter is dependent on an outside operator, or the familiar punched-tape machine —in brief, some form of stored information. Finally, as the return tubes are operating against gravity they must contain some form of conveyor, but this has no particular psychological significance.

In immediate memory experiments, as usually performed, a stream of stimuli is delivered completely before any overt response is required. Thus all the information in the stream is within the organism at one time; all the balls are somewhere in

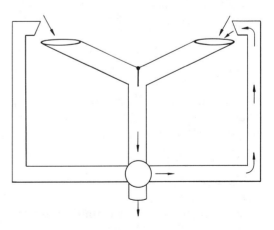

Figure 15.2 The model modified to illustrate the theory of immediate memory as a recurrent circuit; or, in other terms, as a fading trace periodically revived by rehearsal.

the tubes. Yet with small numbers of balls the time between insertion and emergence can be varied without any apparent effect on efficiency (13). Let us consider some of the methods which may be adopted.

(a) In the first place, let us suppose a short series of balls to be waiting in one of the branches. If they stay there indefinitely, the critical time will be exceeded and the ball which has been there longest will leave the system. Thus the branch will not serve as a store during an unlimited period of delay before response is allowed. What is perfectly possible, however, is for the series of balls to pass down the stem and, by the lower door, back up a return tube to the other branch. As soon as the full series has completed this round the process can be repeated, so that the set of balls can be kept in the system for any desired time. But note that insertion of any other ball during that time will either mean that the extra ball will never emerge, or else that the circulation of the series will meet interference. Note also that the system will only operate with a limited number of balls; above that number each ball will have to wait in the branch for more than the critical time, and there will therefore be a severe breakdown of storage. These are well-known characteristics of immediate memory. Less obvious is the suggestion that the interfering effect of an extra ball during the delay will depend on the size of the series circulating, being most serious near the limit. This has been shown by Brown (14). He also demonstrated that the interval before or after the interpolated stimuli had little effect, as one would expect, and that if the extra stimuli came before the memory span stimulus there was little effect. It is Brown's explanation of his results which has prompted the present account.

(b) If both branches contain balls, movements of the door will put one group into circulation before the other; to move the door over while a group is actually passing would be to risk a jam. So all balls on one branch will pass down the stem before

any on the other. As has been said, the memory analogy is in fact true, if a digit memory span is obtained with half the digits on one ear and half on the other, or half on the eye and half the ear (7, 8). In addition, the first branch to be dealt with undergoes less risk of any ball reaching the critical time; equally, performance is better on the first set of digits to be recalled (9, 13).

(c) So far we have considered only the case in which the branches start with balls in them. But in practice these balls will be inserted into the branch one after another, and the extra time intervals thus produced will have their effect. Thus, for example, if balls are inserted rapidly into both branches simultaneously, the difficulty of moving the door will apply, as mentioned in the last paragraph; and so all the balls in one branch will be dealt with before any in the other. But if there is a sizeable interval between successive balls in each branch, the door may be swung back and forth so as to deal with each branch alternately. A slow presentation of stimuli may equally allow them to be dealt with in the actual order of arrival rather than channel by channel (7, 8). It should be noted that the time allotted to "swings of the door," as measured by these experiments, agrees with that determined by the experiments on prolonged performance mentioned previously (6).

(d) Again, suppose a lengthy series of balls is inserted through one branch, the door being held open for them by the handle. If a couple of balls are meanwhile delivered to the other branch and wait there till the stem is clear for them to pass, there is naturally some risk that this extra pair of balls will exceed the critical time. The risk will be greater if they are inserted with the earlier balls of the long series than if inserted with the later balls. This also is true of immediate memory for spoken digits arriving at the two ears (9). A point of interest concerns the effect of "irrelevant" balls which arrive on the second branch during a long series on the first. If all the balls in the second branch are irrelevant, the door may be kept closed against them and they will eventually exceed the critical time and be removed (15). But if some relevant balls are also on the second branch, the door will have to be opened and the mixture of relevant and irrelevant balls passed down the stem. The former can be recirculated in the usual immediate memory fashion, and the latter removed by the lower door. The presence of irrelevant balls either before or after relevant ones will therefore produce a greater risk of jamming or of the critical time being exceeded. This also is true of immediate memory (9).

(e) Now consider cases in which the order of the balls emerging at the bottom of the stem is different from that of their insertion. The extreme case is that of "backward memory span." With our simple model, the easiest situation to consider is that in which the first half of a series of balls is to emerge after the second half. This can be arranged on the first circulation by passing the first balls down the stem and back up the return tube to the branch opposite to that in which they were inserted. The later balls are returned to the same branch which they entered, and on the second circulation are the first to be admitted to the stem. After they have passed the flap the other balls can follow them. This will mean that the first balls have stayed in the branch longer than will normally be necessary for simple recirculation, and so are more likely to exceed the critical time. Therefore such a rearrangement of order will reduce the "memory span." Furthermore it will alter the order of difficulty, since the first members of the series will suffer more than the later ones. These effects have been shown by Kay and Poulton (26), and are supported by Brown (13). The reduced memory span for a rearranged list is of course familiar from intelligence testing, but the change in the serial-order effect is a more important deduction.

(f) Serial-order effects will clearly depend very considerably on the rates of presentation of stimuli and of required re-sponse, as compared to the rate of recirculation. They will also depend on the way in which stored information is used to operate the two handles—that is, on the strategy of the subject. They will certainly not be completely determined by the primitive learning process, as is supposed by some existing theories. In fact it has been shown by Kay and Poulton (26) that the serial-order effect is altered by the subject's absence of knowledge about the order in which recall will be required, even though the actual order remains the same as in a control experiment. (Knowledge of the amount to be recalled will also affect the efficiency of recall as well as the order, as has been shown by Brown [13]. This is because the uninformed subject must recirculate material which is not in fact to be recalled later; retention is an active process.)

Some general points about serial-order effect may be made, however. First, if the rate of response is below that of recirculation, but not so slow as to allow complete recirculation between responses, the first items in response will have stayed in store less long than the later items. So, as in (b) above, the earlier part of a list recalled in the order of presentation will be better recalled than the later part. Second, if the time taken to respond is eliminated—for instance, by requiring recall of only one item in the series—then the time taken to present the stimuli will be the chief factor influencing serial-order effects. The last stimuli to arrive will then be those which have been stored for the shortest time, and will be best recalled. This is the result of Gibson and Raffel (23).

Third, a special case of some importance arises when fresh material is being presented while earlier material is being recalled. Considering the model, suppose a short series of balls are inserted and recirculated to the branch opposite that by which they arrived. If they are now to be passed down the stem during the arrival of fresh balls on the original branch, the earliest of the second series of balls will suffer the longest delay. Consequently the end of the first series and the beginning of the second series will be the points of greatest difficulty. If the two series are considered as one long one, the familiar U-shaped serial-order effect will appear. This has been demonstrated by Poulton (32). In conventional learning experiments subjects are not instructed to rehearse (recirculate) the earlier items during presentation of the later ones. But it seems plausible that, during the presentation of a long series at a medium rate, the presence of the earlier balls in the second branch should normally encourage a tendency to recirculate them while the later balls are still arriving. This would be comparable to the higher priority of a previously quiet channel, which was mentioned in the section on perception. It would result in the U-shaped curve of difficulty being the usual one for serially presented material; but the curve will be subject to great modification by instructions. Furthermore a very slow rate of presentation, resulting from allowing recirculation during gaps between presentations, will minimize the effect. This is the case (24).

LIMITATIONS OF THE MODEL

Certain properties of the model are likely to be misleading. Of these the most important has been stated several times above, but is worth repeating. The balls represent information, not stimulation. The reader must not contemplate the Y tube and decide that two stimuli cannot be dealt with simultaneously. They can if they convey sufficiently little information. Clearly, many reflexes are compatible with one another, and it is likely that simple "voluntary" reactions are equally capable of being carried on simultaneously. It is only with unpracticed reactions involving a choice between several alternatives that we find an interference between two stimuli; but this is a very normal case outside the laboratory. Theories such as that put forward by

Welford (38) for the "refractory period" undoubtedly need the qualification that highly probable stimulus sequences may not show these effects (22). But this does not disprove their general value.

A related point is more serious. The length of the immediate memory span is roughly constant whatever the size of the ensemble from which the items are chosen (31): one cannot remember enough binary digits to make the information in immediate memory equal to that stored in memorizing ordinary decimal digits (30). Yet the model makes the limit on memory span dependent on the time taken to pass the items through a limited capacity system, which will in turn depend on the information per item. Perhaps this difficulty may be resolved by suggesting that each possible item represents an extra branch on the stem, and an incoming ball is always recirculated to its appropriate branch. The time taken to withdraw all the balls again would then depend on the time taken by the flap to operate, which is not dependent on the information per item. But this is clearly leading us into complications; for the present we may merely note that the point is an important one about immediate memory but not impossible to handle with a model of this type. A minor caution which should be added is that the model is deterministic while all the experimental results quoted are statistical.

Finally, we have put forward this model as one which may be described by an exactly worded theory which applied also to man. The present paper is directed largely at those who find such a theory unintelligible in its original form, but it should be borne in mind that the theory under test is the abstract one given in the first section. Otherwise the error of identifying the model with the organism may be made, if only to discredit the theory by its obvious absurdity. The formulation given earlier is not complete, but it indicates the way in which the model and the man may be described by the same abstract theory. There should therefore be no excuse for treating the Y tube as anything more than an expository device and a mnemonic for recalling the results of numerous experiments. The writer's freedom from such an error is demonstrated by the fact that he has never built his model in any physical sense.

SUMMARY

A mechanical model is described, to act as an easy introduction to a formal theory of attention and immediate memory in information theory terms. A number of deductions from the theory which agree with experimental results on human beings are given as descriptions of the behavior of the model.

REFERENCES

1. BAHRICK, H. P., NOBLE, M., & FITTS, P. M. Extra task performance as a measure of learning a primary task. *J. exp. Psychol.*, 1954, **48**, 298–302.
2. BERLYNE, D. E. Stimulus intensity and attention in relation to learning theory. *Quart. J. exp. Psychol.*, 1950, **2**, 71–75.
3. BILLS, A. G. Blocking: a new principle in mental fatigue. *Amer. J. Psychol.*, 1931, **43**, 230–245.
4. BROADBENT, D. E. Speaking and listening simultaneously. *J. exp. Psychol.*, 1952, **43**, 267–273.
5. BROADBENT, D. E. Listening to one of two synchronous messages. *J. exp. Psychol.*, 1952, **44**, 51–55.
6. BROADBENT, D. E. Noise, paced performance and vigilance tasks. *Brit. J. Psychol.*, 1953, **44**, 295–303.
7. BROADBENT, D. E. The role of auditory localization in attention and memory span. *J. exp. Psychol.*, 1954, **47**, 191–196.
8. BROADBENT, D. E. Successive responses to simultaneous stimuli. *Quart. J. exp. Psychol.*, 1956, **8**, 145–152.
9. BROADBENT, D. E. Immediate memory and simultaneous stimuli. *Quart. J. exp. Psychol.*, 1957, **9**, 1–11.
10. BROADBENT, D. E. Effects on behaviour from noises of high and low pitch. Brit. Med. Res. Council, *Appl. Psychol. Unit Rep. No. 222*, 1954.
11. BROADBENT, D. E. The concept of capacity and the theory of behaviour. In *Proc. 3rd London Symposium on Information Theory.* London: Butterworths, 1956.
12. BROADBENT, D. E. Listening between and during practised auditory distractions. *Brit. J. Psychol.*, 1956, **47**, 51–60.
13. BROWN, J. The nature of set-to-learn and of intra-material interference in immediate memory. *Quart. J. exp. Psychol.*, 1954, **6**, 141–148.
14. BROWN, J. Immediate memory. Unpublished doctoral thesis, Univer. of Cambridge, 1955.
15. CHERRY, E. C. Some experiments on the recognition of speech, with one and with two ears. *J. Acoust. Soc. Amer.*, 1953, **25**, 975–979.
16. CONRAD, R. Speed and load stress in a sensorimotor skill. *Brit. J. indust. Med.*, 1951, **8**, 1–7.
17. CONRAD, R. Missed signals in a sensori-motor skill. *J. exp. Psychol.*, 1954, **48**, 1–9.
18. CONRAD, R. Adaptation to time in a sensorimotor skill. *J. exp. Psychol.*, 1955, **49**, 115–121.
19. DEESE, J. Some problems in the theory of vigilance. *Psychol. Rev.*, 1955, **62**, 359–368.
20. DEUTSCH, J. A new type of behaviour theory. *Brit. J. Psychol.*, 1953, **44**, 304–317.
21. DEUTSCH, J. A machine with insight. *Quart. J. exp. Psychol.*, 1954, **6**, 6–11.
22. ELITHORN, A., & LAWRENCE, C. Central inhibition—some refractory observations. *Quart. J. exp. Psychol.*, 1955, **7**, 116–127.
23. GIBSON, J. J., & RAFFEL, G. A technique for investigating retroactive and other inhibitory effects in immediate memory. *J. gen. Psychol.*, 1936, **15**, 107–116.
24. HOVLAND, C. I. Experimental studies in rote learning theory. II. Reminiscence with varying speed of syllable presentation. *J. exp. Psychol.*, 1938, **22**, 338–353.
25. HYMAN, R. Stimulus information as a determinant of reaction time. *J. exp. Psychol.*, 1953, **45**, 188–196.
26. KAY, H., & POULTON, E. C. Anticipation in memorizing. *Brit. J. Psychol.*, 1951, **42**, 34–41.
27. MACKWORTH, N. H. Researches on the measurement of human performance. *M.R.C. Spec. Rep. No. 268.* Her Majesty's Stationery Office, 1950.
28. MACKWORTH, J. F., & MACKWORTH, N. H. The overlapping of signals for decisions. *Amer. J. Psychol.*, 1956, **69**, 26–47.
29. MACKAY, D. M. In symposium on cybernetics. *Advanc. Sci.*, 1954, **40**, 402–406.
30. MILLER, G. A. The magical number seven, plus or minus two: some limits on our capacity for processing information. *Psychol. Rev.*, 1956, **63**, 81–97.
31. POLLACK, I. Assimilation of sequentially encoded information. *Amer. J. Psychol.*, 1953, **66**, 421–435.
32. POULTON, E. C. Memorization during recall. *Brit. J. Psychol.*, 1953, **44**, 173–176.
33. POULTON, E. C. Two-channel listening. *J. exp. Psychol.*, 1953, **46**, 91–96.
34. POULTON, E. C. Listening to overlapping calls. *J. exp. Psychol.*, 1956, **52**, 334–339.
35. VINCE, M. A. Rapid response sequences and the psychological refractory period. *Brit. J. Psychol.*, 1949, **40**, 23–40.
36. SPIETH, W., CURTIS, J. F., & WEBSTER, J. C.

Responding to one of two simultaneous messages. *J. Acoust. Soc. Amer.*, 1954, **26**, 391–
396.
37. WEBSTER, J. C., & THOMPSON, P. O. Some
audio considerations in air control towers.

J. Audio. Eng. Soc., 1953, **1**, 171–175.
38. WELFORD, A. T. The psychological refractory
period and the timing of high-speed performance—a review and a theory. *Brit. J. Psychol.*,
1952, **43**, 2–19.

16. Perception of Another Person's Looking Behavior *

James J. Gibson and Anne D. Pick

Experiments in perception often investigate the effects of simple stimuli presented under highly controlled conditions. This procedure is usually employed when specific hypotheses about particular perceptual mechanisms are under test and it is desirable to study the mechanism in relative isolation. But perceptual research can also be extended to more natural or more complex situations. Consider, for example, the many social interactions between people that involve an exchange of glances. Surprising as it may seem at first, some reflection on this common phenomenon reveals that it is indeed important to know when someone is looking at you and when he is not.

In the final article of this section, Professors Gibson and Pick determine how this discrimination is made and then measure its accuracy.

The classical senses in normal use require not only receptors but also muscles for adjusting them.[1] Touching, sniffing and tasting, listening, and above all, looking, involve some degree of motor activity. These responses have no effect on the en-vironment, it is true, but they do have an effect on the stimulation which controls behavior. In different ways, they explore the possibilities of stimulation, maximizing, refining, and sharpening its content of information. Focused, stabilized, and appropriately centered retinal images, for instance, are the product of a whole complex of ocular responses which have been recorded and are fairly well understood. The sense-organ adjustments, in short, are a form of observable behavior. The act of visual attention in another person can be perceived simply by watching his face, and we do in fact notice where a person is looking.

The act of looking can be treated as a source of stimulation as well as a type of response. The eyes not only look, but are looked at. The direction of a person's gaze usually indicates what object he is interested in or what person he is responding to in the sphere of the environment, and a shift of his fixation may indicate what he is going to do next, as the boxer and the fencer know. The fact of *being looked at*, that is, a line of gaze fixed on the body of the observer himself, is especially significant.

That men do discriminate, or try to discriminate, the postures and movements of the eyes of another person is strongly suggested by the number of words used in ordinary speech to distinguish modes of looking. Variants of

* Reprinted by permission of the authors and *The American Journal of Psychology* from Volume 76, 1963, 386-394.

[1] This research was supported in part by the Office of Naval Research under Contract 401 (14) with Cornell University. Special thanks are due to Jane Danielson for serving as the 'looker' in this experiment. The work has benefited greatly from a previous unpublished study by Elinor Wardwell.

the verb 'to look' include *stare, watch, peer, glance, peep, glare, glower, gaze, contemplate,* and *scan.* Adverbial modifiers of the verb are frequent. A person can be said to look *directly* or *askance, overtly* or *covertly, boldly* or *bashfully, sternly* or *mildly, critically* or *kindly,* or even *unseeingly.* Among the many idiomatic expressions or metaphors are, *he caught my eye,* or *held my eye,* or *looked me up and down,* or *his eyes dropped,* or *flickered,* or *his gaze wandered.* A person may either *cast an eye on,* or *fasten his eyes on,* or *look down his nose at.* He may *steal a glance,* give a *sidelong glance,* or a *guarded glance,* or have a *discerning glance,* a *piercing glance,* or a *fixed stare.* He may also give one a *sly look,* an *open look,* or a *black look.* These examples suggest that the task of judging expressions of emotion entails a separate and distinct problem, that of judging what might be called the expression of *attention.*

When we observe that one person looks at another angrily (or sadly, fearfully, or happily), we are observing a space as well as an emotion. A face is normally seen surrounded by an environment in three dimensions. The instigator of emotion is visible as well as the face. A portrait, therefore, can render an emotion but not the object or event provoking it, as evidenced by the direction of the line of regard.

The facial patterns for the perception of emotion have been studied in many experiments, but the ocular patterns for the perception of the act of looking at something have been neglected. Only a few studies are even relevant.

Cline investigated the perception aroused by a pair of schematic faces in three-quarters profile whose eyes were so drawn as to appear to be looking at each other.[2] He systematically varied the expressive features of the two drawings and noted the social situations perceived in accordance with these combinations. But he did not vary the apparent gaze-line of either face.

Wardwell, assuming that being looked at is a potent social stimulus, studied the effect on the behavior of a child of an adult who stared at him most of the time, part of the time, or none of the time.[3] In a test-situation, although the children were preoccupied with the task, they proved to be very conscious of whether they were or were not being observed, and for what proportion of the time.

Recently, Wada has noted that rhesus monkeys are aware of being looked at by a human individual, the criterion being a specific change in electrical activity recorded from the brainstem.[4] Cornell rhesus monkeys also seem to behave differently when a pair of eyes is fixed on them than when the same pair of eyes is fixed away from them, as determined by an invisible observer looking through a one-way screen. Perhaps all primates perceive whether or not they are being looked at. If so, they must have acute discrimination for the line of gaze of another individual.

Stimulus for the Perception of the Act of Looking

The potential stimulus for the perception of the act of looking must be distinguished from the *source* of the stimulus, although experimenters often do not do so. The stimulus proper is the light reflected from the 'looker,' more exactly, the differential rays of light which can enter the eyes of the O. The source of stimulation is the head and eyes of the looker in their surroundings. The posture of the eyes relative to the head and the surroundings is what has to be perceived by O. It can only be given in the bidimensional array of light reflected by these surfaces. The face itself is an elastic mobile surface of skin, and the visible eyes are the bulging frontal surfaces of spheres. The face has its 'features,' and the eyes have a pupil and sclera within a frame formed by the eyelids. These shapes are projected to O as an arrangement of forms within larger forms.

As a first approximation, one might suppose that the stimulus-information for the perception of the looker's gaze is a form-variable connected with 'centering,' that is,

---

[2] M. G. Cline, Some perceived properties of social interaction. Unpublished Doctoral dissertation, Cornell University, 1954.

[3] Elinor Wardwell, Children's reactions to being watched during success and failure. Unpublished Doctoral dissertation, Cornell University, 1960.

[4] J. A. Wada, Modification of cortically induced responses in brain stem of shift of attention in monkeys, *Science,* 133, 1961, 40–42.

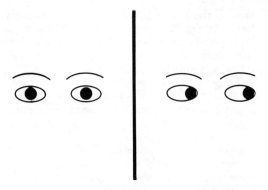

Figure 16.1 Schematic centering or off-centering of the pupil in the sclera as the stimulus for the impression of being or not being looked at.

the concentricity of the pupil in the sclera, the 'white of the eye.' When it is centered, the gaze will be seen to be directed at *O;* when it is off-centered in either direction, the gaze is perceived correspondingly to deviate toward the right or left of *O.* Fig. 16-1 isolates this variable and illustrates the hypothesis. One might in fact study experimentally the acuity with which iris-centering and off-centering are detected. This approximate hypothesis, however, is insufficient. On further consideration, one realizes that it holds for the special case when the looker's head is pointing in the same direction as his eyes, in the frontal or facing position. The fact is that a person does not always face in the same direction as he looks. A face can be recognized in a series of stimulus-transformations varying from full-face to profile. Hence this form-variable, the face-form, must also be taken into account in analyzing the stimulus-information. Fig. 16-2 illustrates the fact that the stimulus-meaning of the eye-forms depends on the face-form that surrounds it. The illustration brings up the whole question of the influence of one form on another included within it; we need only note here a quite simple relation—that the asymmetry of the projected face is equal and opposite to that of the projected eyes when the eyes are perceived to be looking at 'me.'

Physiologically, a turning of the eyes normally compensates for the opposite turning of the head, this being the reflex mechanism by which the eyes of all vertebrates are stabilized relative to the optical environment. Exploratory or saccadic eye-turning could not occur except for this fundamental stabilization of the eyes to the ambient light. There is an invariant reciprocal relationship between compensatory eye-turning and head-turning. Hence, in the stimulus-array there will be an invariant reciprocal relationship between the projected form of the iris in the eye and that of the face for any fixed direction of gaze.

From all this we are led to a more promising hypothesis about the stimulus for the perception of the direction of gaze: it is not the eye-form as such but the eye-form relative to the face-form. More exactly, the information is given by a constant relation of the asymmetry of the iris to the opposite asymmetry of the face. The eye-pattern can be variable in the manner of Fig. 16-1, but since this variation is reciprocal to the variation of the larger pattern around it, an invariant exists. The value of this invariant specifies the direction in which the eyes are looking.

In short, the problem is one of spatial

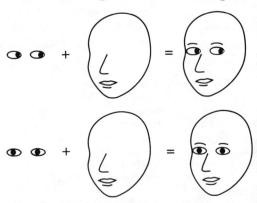

Figure 16.2 The same eye-forms as in Fig. 16-1 surrounded by a face-form which shifts the apparent direction of the eyes. Eyes formerly gazing to the right now seem to gaze forward, and those formerly gazing forward now gaze to the left.

perception. One perceives the orientation of the head in space just as one perceives the orientation of other mobile objects in the environment, and because one also registers the posture of the eyes in the head, one can perceive the *absolute* orientation of the eyes in space. So considered, the problem has implications for the classical puzzle of shape-constancy. According to our hypothesis, the stimulus for *being looked at* would be a nearly equal asymmetry of the two linked variables. Unequal asymmetry would specify a direction of gaze to one side or the other. It is this part of the hypothesis that we propose to test. Is such an invariant relation among forms detectable, and with what accuracy?

THE EXPERIMENT

For a study of the psychophysics of the perception of the gaze of another, we might use as stimuli drawings of objects, photographs, models, or the postures of a real person. Since the experiment was exploratory, we chose the last. A student was employed and trained as an impersonal source of controlled social stimulation. At the request of E, she would adopt one of seven eye-postures in one of three head-postures relative to the O. The method of constant stimuli was used. The task of O was to judge whether he was or was not being looked at. How accurate would these judgments be? Specifically, we measured the smallest deviation of the looker's line of regard from the bridge of O's nose that could just be noticed. We wished to be able to compare the acuity of this discrimination with other types of visual acuity.

The 'looker' had large brown eyes. She had been carefully drilled in the procedure to be used, and maintained the same passive facial expression on all trials. Her eyes had been tested and shown to be free of ocular imbalance, since a preliminary unpublished experiment by Wardwell had shown that even a slight phoria affected O's judgments adversely. The looker sat opposite O at a distance of 2 m., in ordinary room-illumination—at a level less than optimal for other types of acuity.

The variable stimuli, the absolute orientations of her eyes in the room, were established by having her look steadily at one of seven fixation-points on or near the face of the O.

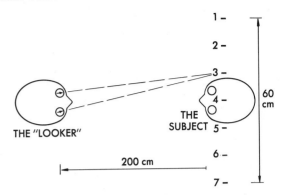

Figure 16.3 View of the experimental arrangement from above. The horizontal distance is shortened relative to the vertical.

A scale of seven numbered spots was marked on the wall just behind O's head, as shown in Fig. 16–3. The middle spot was the bridge of O's nose and the others were to the right or left of his head. The spots were 10 cm. apart, the angular separation being 2.9° for the central part of the scale at a distance of 200 cm. The seven eye-postures were presented at each of three head-postures: facing the O, turned 30° right, and turned 30° left.

The procedure was as follows: The looker assumed one of the 21 eye-fixations in accordance with a prearranged random order, maintaining the fixation steadily, until the judgment was made, usually 5-6 sec. O noted the appearance of her eyes and face and then made a judgment of *yes* or *no*, meaning "You are looking directly at me," or "You are not looking directly at me." O then turned away and the looker prepared for the next trial. Judgments were recorded by E. Each O made 25 judgments for each of 7 fixations in each of 3 head-positions, a total of 525. Six adult O's, all with presumably normal vision, were used.

Results

The 'yes' judgments were counted and tabulated. Some Os gave more than others did, but the accuracy of perception could be measured by the degree to which the 'yeses' clustered around Point 4, on the scale of 7 fixation-points, the point corresponding to the bridge of O's nose. The frequency-distributions of 'yes' judgments over the scale were plotted for each of the

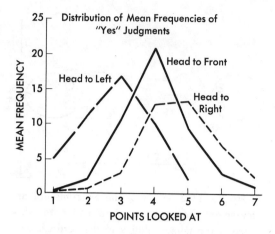

Figure 16.4 Pooled distributions of the judgments of "yes" at seven different eye-positions for each of three head-postures.

three head-positions, for each O separately. Individual differences were not large; hence the Os were pooled and the three mean distributions are shown in Fig. 16-4. The SDs are 0.92, 0.80, and 0.93, reading from left to right.

It can be noted that for the frontal head-position the pooled distribution is centered very close to Point 4, indicating no constant error in the group as a whole. For the other head-postures the distributions are shifted significantly, showing consistent constant errors. The shift is in the direction of head-pointing. Evidently the perception of eye-pointing is somewhat influenced by the perception of head-pointing.

The SDs are a measure of the precision of judgments. They are all less than one step on the scale of fixation-points. The peaked distributions show a clustering of the 'yeses' around a certain stimulus-presentation which indicates acute perception of being looked at.

The SDs for the different head-positions are not significantly different from one another. This means that acuity for the perception of gaze is independent of head-pointing. We conclude that the absolute orientation of the eyes in space is detectable, although with some constant error.

The invariant postulated as existing between the two reciprocal form-variables must be effective for perception or, if not this precise invariant, something equivalent to it.

Comparison with Other Types of Acuity

We take the mean SD of the distribution of all 'yes' judgments in this experiment to be a measure of a threshold, the just noticeable deviation of the looker's line of regard from O's nose. This deviation corresponds to a distance of about 9 cm. seen from 200 cm. It is roughly the distance from the nose to the edge of the face. The angular deviation of the looker's eyes is 2.8° for the SD with head front. The corresponding linear displacement of the looker's iris (the frontal displacement of the eyeball corresponding to a rotation of 2.8°) is less than 1 mm. This degree of asymmetry is slight. A displacement of 1 mm. at a distance of 2000 mm. is a very small angle of intercept, about 1 min. of arc. The minimal separation of the elements of a printed letter necessary for its identification is usually taken to be 1 min. of arc in the Snellen test. If it is remembered that the level of illumination on the looker's face was not as high as is customary on an acuity-chart, and that acuity depends on illumination, we may safely conclude that this type of acuity is at least as good as Snellen acuity.

The pattern-variable by which one detects the line of regard of a person is geometrically complex, as Fig. 16-2 shows. It is not a 'form' but a high-order relation between forms. Evidently this does not mean, however, that acuity for such optical information is any less than it is for some of the geometrically 'simpler' variables measured in standard acuity-tests. Very subtle properties of visual pattern are known to be stimuli for perception. When, as in our experiment, they specify the state of another person, they may come to be discriminated with the greatest efficiency possible for the visual receptive system.

Discussion and Conclusions

This experiment should no doubt be repeated without using a live person as the source of stimulation, perhaps with a realistic model having movable calibrated eyes, or with a set of photographs, or with schematic drawings. Conceivably, our looker unconsciously betrayed the act of fixating the center of O's face by some slight change in facial expression, despite training to the contrary. No such changes could be observed by E. Furthermore, if such a minimal cue had been utilized exclusively by the Os, it would have been as effective in the deviated head-positions as in the frontal head-position, and the constant errors would not have occurred. We believe that a real person can be used successfully to produce the stimuli for a psychophysical experiment. Nevertheless, a model or pictures would yield direct control by E of the stimulus-variable and would guarantee the elimination of all other cues.

The possibility of separating the ocular expression of the direction of attention from the facial expression of emotion at least has been demonstrated. This should be considered in future studies of the perception of human heads. The stimulus-variable corresponding to the direction of gaze, in fact, can be analyzed and experimentally controlled more easily than the stimulus-variables corresponding to emotional expressions. The families of elastic deformations of the face that we see as frowning, smiling, and the like are hard to dimensionalize, although Schlosberg has started to do so.[5] The rotations of the eyes and head, on the contrary, are mechanical movements to a close approximation, which are geometrically simpler. The elastic movements of the facial surface provide optical transformations of a group belonging to topology but not to perspective geometry.[6] The rotary movements of the eyes and head, being rigid instead of elastic, provide transformations corresponding to different perspectives of the same object. The stimulus-information is of a mathematically different order, and the corresponding perception is typically one of orientation, not deformation.[7]

The results suggest that we have good discrimination for the line of gaze of another person, at least with respect to whether or not we are being looked at. The ability to read the eyes seems to be as good as the ability to read fine print on an acuity-chart, according to our first determination.

The variable error of judgment does not appear to be significantly greater when the eyes look 'askance' at me than when they look directly at me, although a constant error is produced under the former conditions. This result is consistent with the hypothesis of a relational stimulus-variable for the perception of gaze.

Finally, we have shown the possibility of using a psychophysical method for studying a seemingly complex stimulus-variable —but a variable which conveys information for meaningful perception. All the various styles of looking that were listed at the beginning are properly meaningful in social life. We have isolated only one of the variables in this complex, the temporary line of gaze. Other qualities of looking behavior might be amenable to experimental control if the attempt were made. The study of the expressive reactions of men and animals in general, the basis of social interaction, might profit by this analytical approach.

[5] R. S. Woodworth, and Harold Schlosberg, *Experimental Psychology*, 1954, Ch. 5.

[6] Kai von Fieandt and J. J. Gibson, The sensitivity of the eye to two kinds of continuous transformation of a shadow-pattern, *J. exp. Psychol.*, 57, 1959, 344–347.

[7] J. J. Gibson, and E. J. Gibson, Continuous perspective transformations and the perception of rigid motion, *J. exp. Psychol.*, 54, 1957, 129–138.

LEARNING AND FORGETTING

The majority of animals survive by sharply limiting their behavioral repertoire to those actions that maximize the opportunities provided by their peculiar environments. In marked contrast, the higher primates and man have staked their survival on a highly developed brain which allows quick learning and long memory. Because of this fundamental distinction, learning and memory hold a central position in the subject matter of psychology. In fact, until very recently, a major portion of experimental psychology has been concerned with the variables that affect the speed of learning and the permanence of memories. It is upon these topics that the next group of readings is focused.

The first three articles, by Pavlov, Skinner, and by Spielberger and DeNike, describe investigations of learning under controlled laboratory conditions. The work of Pavlov and Skinner reflect relatively independent lines of inquiry. The kind of learning discovered by Pavlov and described in the first article is known now as classical or respondent conditioning. In the second article Skinner builds on Edward L. Thorndike's earlier work on instrumental learning. He describes the complex modifications of animal behavior that can be obtained through operant conditioning—a special form of instrumental learning that he used to investigate the behavior of rats and pigeons. In the final article of this group, Spielberger and DeNike apply the techniques of operant conditioning to the verbal behavior of humans, and demonstrate the critical role of conscious awareness in human learning.

Memory is the main theme of the next two selections. Underwood describes some of the factors which influence forgetting within the framework of interference theory and provides an explanation of memory that is derived directly from more general principles of learning. Brown and McNeill report one of the first experimental attacks upon a common subjective phenomenon of memory—the frustrating failure to recall something we know that we know, or, as Brown and McNeill put it, the "tip of the tongue" phenomenon.

The last two articles in the section are concerned with two facets of the larger problems of thinking and language. In the first article of this pair, McNeill outlines the conditions that influence the acquisition of language in man. In the final paper Woodworth and Sells arrange a confrontation between the mechanics of Aristotelian logic and the process of rational analysis. Their results show that deductive reasoning is not independent of emotional and social factors.

CLASSICAL CONDITIONING AND INSTRUMENTAL LEARNING

17. Conditioned Reflexes *

Ivan P. Pavlov

By the second half of the 19th century many of the conceptual barriers to the development of a scientific psychology had been removed. For instance, one could now assert that the operations of the mind were determined by related operations of the brain. Moreover, one could specify with some certainty the portions of the brain that were most directly involved in the production of mind; the most promising candidate appeared to be the most recently acquired portions, called the neocortex. But given the relationship between mind and cortex, the next necessary step was the development of a method which permitted objective observation of the mind-cortex interplay, for science can deal only with events open to public inspection.

Ivan Pavlov, an eminent Russian physiologist who received the Nobel Prize in 1904 for his work on the process of digestion, was aware of the need for appropriate objective methods with which to study neural activity. When he noted that salivary secretions could be produced in lawful ways by a variety of stimuli such as bells and flashing lights, the critical elements of an appropriate method were at hand. Pavlov devoted the rest of his career to the intensive investigation of these "psychic reflexes"—with a method we now know as classical conditioning. In 1924, Pavlov presented a series of general lectures reviewing the first

* This is excerpted from Lecture II of *Conditioned Reflexes: An investigation of the physiological activity of the cerebral cortex* as translated and edited by G. V. Anrep in 1927 and reprinted by Dover Publications, New York, 1960.

twenty years of his work on conditioning. The next selection is an excerpt from his second lecture.

In the previous lecture I gave an account of the reasons which led us to adopt, for the investigation of the functions of the cerebral hemispheres, the purely objective method used for investigating the physiological activity of the lower parts of the nervous system. In this manner the investigation of the cerebral hemispheres is brought into line with the investigations conducted in other branches of natural science, and their activities are studied as purely physiological facts, without any need to resort to fantastic speculations as to the existence of any possible subjective state in the animal which may be conjectured on analogy with ourselves. From this point of view the whole nervous activity of the animal must be regarded as based firstly on inborn reflexes. These are regular causal connections between certain definite external stimuli acting on the organism and its necessary reflex reactions. Such inborn reflexes are comparatively few in number, and the stimuli setting them in action act close up, being as a rule the general physical and chemical properties of the common agencies which affect the organism. The inborn reflexes by themselves are inadequate to ensure the continued existence of the organism, especially of the more highly organized animals, which, when deprived of their highest

127

nervous activity, are permanently disabled, and if left to themselves, although retaining all their inborn reflexes, soon cease to exist. The complex conditions of everyday existence require a much more detailed and specialized correlation between the animal and its environment than is afforded by the inborn reflexes alone. This more precise correlation can be established only through the medium of the cerebral hemispheres; and we have found that a great number of all sorts of stimuli always act through the medium of the hemispheres as temporary and interchangeable signals for the comparatively small number of agencies of a general character which determine the inborn reflexes, and that this is the only means by which a most delicate adjustment of the organism to the environment can be established. To this function of the hemispheres we gave the name of "signalization."

Before passing on to describe the results of our investigation it is necessary to give some account of the purely technical side of the methods employed, and to describe the general way in which the signalizing activity of the hemispheres can be studied. It is obvious that the reflex activity of any effector organ can be chosen for the purpose of this investigation, since signalling stimuli can get linked up with any of the inborn reflexes. But, as was mentioned in the first lecture, the starting point for the present investigation was determined in particular by the study of two reflexes—the food or "alimentary" reflex, and the "defence" reflex in its mildest form, as observed when a rejectable substance finds its way into the mouth of the animal. As it turned out, these two reflexes proved a fortunate choice in many ways. Indeed, while any strong defence reflex, e.g. against such a stimulus as a powerful electric current, makes the animal extremely restless and excited; and while the sexual reflexes require a special environment—to say nothing of their periodic character and their dependence upon age—the alimentary reflex

and the mild defence reflex to rejectable substances are normal everyday occurrences.

It is essential to realize that each of these two reflexes—the alimentary reflex and the mild defence reflex to rejectable substances—consists of two distinct components, a motor and a secretory. Firstly the animal exhibits a reflex activity directed towards getting hold of the food and eating it or, in the case of rejectable substances, towards getting rid of them out of the mouth; and secondly, in both cases an immediate secretion of saliva occurs, in the case of food, to start the physical and chemical processes of digestion and, in the case of rejectable substances, to wash them out of the mouth. We confined our experiments almost entirely to the secretory component of the reflex: the allied motor reactions were taken into account only where there were special reasons. The secretory reflex presents many important advantages for our purpose. It allows of an extremely accurate measurement of the intensity of reflex activity, since either the number of drops in a given time may be counted or else the saliva may be caused to displace a coloured fluid in a horizontally placed graduated glass tube. It would be much more difficult to obtain the same accuracy of measurement for any motor reflex, especially for such complex motor reactions as accompany reflexes to food or to rejectable substances. Even by using most delicate instruments we should never be able to reach such precision in measuring the intensity of the motor component of the reflexes as can easily be attained with the secretory component. Again, a very important point in favour of the secretory reflexes is the much smaller tendency to interpret them in an anthropomorphic fashion—i.e. in terms of subjective analogy. Although this seems a trivial consideration from our present standpoint, it was of importance in the earlier stages of our investigation and did undoubtedly influence our choice.

For the purpose of registering the intensity of the salivary reflex all the dogs employed in the experiments are subjected to a preliminary minor operation, which consists in the transplantation of the opening of the salivary duct from its natural place on the mucous membrane of the mouth to the outside skin. For this purpose the terminal portion of the salivary duct is dissected and freed from the surrounding tissue, and the duct, together with a small portion of the mucous membrane surrounding its natural opening, is carried through a suitable incision, to the outside of the cheek in the case of the parotid gland, or under the chin in the case of the submaxillary gland. In this new position the duct is fixed by a few stitches which are removed when the wound has healed. As a result of the operation the saliva now flows to the outside, on to the cheek or chin of the animal, instead of into the mouth, so that the measurement of the secretory activity of the gland is greatly facilitated. It is only necessary for this purpose to adjust a small glass funnel over the opening of the duct on to the skin, and for this we find a special cement prepared according to a formula of Mendeléeff[1] most useful. As an alternative, very suitable and accurate as a recording apparatus is a hemispherical bulb which also can be hermetically sealed on to the skin. From the bulb project two tubes, one pointing up and the other pointing down. The latter tube is used for drawing off the saliva which collects during each observation, while the former tube connects by air transmission with a horizontal graduated glass tube filled with coloured fluid. As the saliva flows into the hemispherical bulb the coloured fluid is displaced along the graduated tube, where the amount of secretion can be read off accurately. Further, it is not difficult to fix up an automatic electrically-recording device which will split up the displaced fluid

into drops of exactly equal volume and reduce any lag in the movement of the fluid to a minimum.[2]

To come to the general technique of the experiments, it is important to remember that our research deals with the highly specialized activity of the cerebral cortex, a signalizing apparatus of tremendous complexity and of most exquisite sensitivity, through which the animal is influenced by countless stimuli from the outside world. Every one of these stimuli produces a certain effect upon the animal, and all of them taken together may clash and interfere with, or else reinforce, one another. Unless we are careful to take special precautions the success of the whole investigation may be jeopardized, and we should get hopelessly lost as soon as we began to seek for cause and effect among so many and various influences, so intertwined and entangled as to form a veritable chaos. It was evident that the experimental conditions had to be simplified, and that this simplification must consist in eliminating as far as possible any stimuli outside our control which might fall upon the animal, admitting only such stimuli as could be entirely controlled by the experimenter. It was thought at the beginning of our research that it would be sufficient simply to isolate the experimenter in the research chamber with the dog on its stand, and to refuse admission to anyone else during the course of an experiment. But this precaution was found to be wholly

[1] *Mendeléeff's cement:* Colophonium, 50 grammes; ferric oxide, 40 grammes; yellow beeswax, 25 grammes.

[2] In almost all the experiments quoted in these lectures the amount of salivary secretion is, for the sake of uniformity, given in drops. It was, however, only in the very earliest period of the research—before the separation of the experimenter from the animal was made—that the actual number of drops falling from a small funnel fixed over the fistula was counted, and only a few of these experiments are given. In the great majority of the experiments the salivary secretion was measured by the displacement of water in a graduated tube or by the electric recorder, allowing a much greater accuracy of measurement. The readings so obtained have been converted, in the tables, into drops. Thus, in some experiments it will be noticed that the number of drops is given to an accuracy of one-tenth.

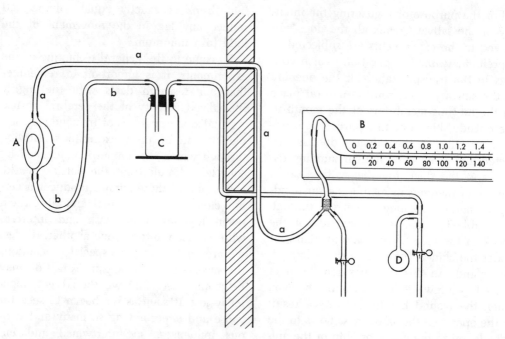

Figure 17.1 The apparatus used for recording the salivary secretion in experiments on conditioned reflexes. A, hemispherical bulb which is fixed over the fistula. a, connecting tube leading through the partition separating the animal's room from the experimenter and connecting the bulb A to the registering apparatus, B. b, tube connecting the bulb with bottle, C. After each observation, a vacuum is created in the bottle C by depression of the rubber balloon D; the saliva accumulating in A is thus sucked away. During the observation, A is automatically disconnected from C and connected with the registering apparatus. During the aspirations of the saliva from bulb A, the latter is automatically disconnected from the registering apparatus.

inadequate, since the experimenter, however still he might try to be, was himself a constant source of a large number of stimuli. His slightest movements—blinking of the eyelids or movement of the eyes, posture, respiration and so on—all acted as stimuli which, falling upon the dog, were sufficient to vitiate the experiments by making exact interpretation of the results extremely difficult. In order to exclude this undue influence on the part of the experimenter as far as possible, he had to be stationed outside the room in which the dog was placed, and even this precaution proved unsuccessful in laboratories not specially designed for the study of these particular reflexes. The environment of the animal, even when shut up by itself in a room, is perpetually changing. Footfalls of a passer-by, chance conversations in neighbouring rooms, slamming of a door or vibration from a passing van, street-cries, even shadows cast through the windows into the room, any of these casual uncontrolled stimuli falling upon the receptors of the dog set up a disturbance in the cerebral hemispheres and vitiate the experiments. To get over all these disturbing factors a special laboratory was built at the Institute of Experimental Medicine in Petrograd, the funds being provided by a keen and public-spirited Moscow business man. The primary task was the protection of the dogs from uncontrolled extraneous stimuli, and this was effected by surrounding the building with an isolating trench and employing other special structural devices. Inside the building all the research rooms (four to each floor) were isolated from one another by a cross-shaped corridor; the top and ground floors, where these rooms were situated, were separated by an intermediate floor. Each research room was carefully partitioned by the use of sound-proof materials into two compartments—one for the animal, the other for the experimenter. For stimulating the animal, and for registering the corresponding reflex response, electrical methods or pneumatic transmission were used. By means of these arrangements it was possible to get something of that stability of environmental conditions so essential to the carrying out of a successful experiment.

Another point should be mentioned—although in this respect the means at our disposal still leave something to be desired. In analysing the exceedingly complex influence of the external environment upon the animal, the experimenter must be able to exercise full control over all the conditions obtaining during the course of any experiment. He should therefore have at his disposal various instruments for affecting the animal by different kinds of stimuli, singly or combined, so as to imitate simple natural conditions. But we were often handicapped by the conditions in which we had to work and by the shortcomings of the instruments at our disposal, for we always found that the cerebral hemispheres were sensitive to far finer gradations of stimulus than we could furnish.

It is possible that the experimental conditions I have described may raise somewhere the objection of being abnormal and artificial. However it is hardly likely, in view of the infinite variety of stimuli met with under natural conditions, that we shall hit on one that is quite unprecedented in the life of the animal. Moreover, in dealing with any phenomenon of vast complexity it is absolutely necessary to isolate the different single factors involved, so as to study them independently, or in arbitrary groups in which we can keep the individual units

under control. But as a matter of fact the same objection and the same answer apply equally to the whole of animal physiology. For instance, the methods of vivisection and of the study of isolated organs and tissues, which aim at the same isolation of different individual functions, have been constantly employed, and we may safely say that the greater part of the achievements of physiology are due to the successful application of such methods of control. In our experiments it is the whole animal which is placed under a limited number of rigidly defined conditions, and only by this method is it possible to study the reflexes independently of one another.

*   *   *

In our general survey we characterized a reflex as a necessary reaction following upon a strictly definite stimulus under strictly defined conditions. Such a definition holds perfectly true also for signalization; the only difference is that the type of the effective reaction to signals depends upon a greater number of conditions. But this does not make signalization differ fundamentally from the better known reflexes in any respect, since in the latter, variations in character or force, inhibition and absence of reflexes, can also be traced to some definite change in the conditions of the experiment.

Thorough investigation of the subject shows that accident plays no part whatever in the signalizing activity of the hemispheres, and all experiments proceed strictly according to plan. In the special laboratory I have described, the animal can frequently be kept under rigid experimental observation for 1 to 2 hours without a single drop of saliva being secreted independently of stimuli applied by the observer, although in the ordinary type of physiological laboratory experiments are very often distorted by the interference of extraneous and uncontrolled stimuli.

All these conditions leave no grounds for regarding the phenomena which we have termed "signalization" as being any-thing else than reflex. There is, however, another aspect of the question which at a first glance seems to point to an essential difference between the better known re-flexes and signalization. Food, through its chemical and physical properties, evokes the salivary reflex in every dog right from birth, whereas this new type claimed as re-flex—"the signal reflex"—is built up grad-ually in the course of the animal's own individual existence. But can this be con-sidered as a fundamental point of differ-ence, and can it hold as a valid argument against employing the term "reflex" for this new group of phenomena? It is certainly a sufficient argument for making a definite distinction between the two types of reflex and for considering the signal reflex in a group distinct from the inborn reflex. But this does not invalidate in any way our right logically to term both "reflex," since the point of distinction does not concern the character of the response on the part of the organism, but only the mode of forma-tion of the reflex mechanism. We may take the telephonic installation as an illustration. Communication can be effected in two ways. My residence may be connected di-rectly with the laboratory by a private line, and I may call up the laboratory whenever it pleases me to do so; or on the other hand, a connection may have to be made through the central exchange. But the re-sult in both cases is the same. The only point of distinction between the methods is that the private line provides a per-manent and readily available cable, while the other line necessitates a preliminary central connection being established. In the one case the communicating wire is al-ways complete, in the other case a small addition must be made to the wire at the central exchange. We have a similar state of affairs in reflex action. The path of the inborn reflex is already completed at birth; but the path of the signalizing reflex has still to be completed in the higher nervous centres. We are thus brought to consider the mode of formation of new reflex

mechanisms. A new reflex is formed in-evitably under a given set of physiological conditions, and with the greatest ease, so that there is no need to take the subjective states of the dog into consideration. With a complete understanding of all the factors involved, the new signalizing reflexes are under the absolute control of the experi-menter; they proceed according to as rigid laws as do any other physiological proc-esses, and must be regarded as being in every sense a part of the physiological ac-tivity of living beings. I have termed this new group of reflexes conditioned reflexes to distinguish them from the inborn or un-conditioned reflexes. The term "condi-tioned" is becoming more and more gen-erally employed, and I think its use is fully justified in that, compared with the inborn reflexes, these new reflexes actually do de-pend on very many conditions, both in their formation and in the maintenance of their physiological activity. Of course the terms "conditioned" and "unconditioned" could be replaced by others of arguably equal merit. Thus, for example, we might retain the term "inborn reflexes," and call the new type "acquired reflexes"; or call the former "species reflexes" since they are characteristic of the species, and the latter "individual reflexes" since they vary from animal to animal in a species, and even in the same animal at different times and under different conditions. Or again we might call the former "conduction reflexes" and the latter "connection reflexes."

There should be no theoretical objection to the hypothesis of the formation of new physiological paths and new connections within the cerebral hemsipheres. Since the especial function of the central nervous system is to establish most complicated and delicate correspondences between the or-ganism and its environment we may not unnaturally expect to find there, on the analogy of the methods used by the tech-nician in everyday experience, a highly developed connector system superimposed on a conductor system. The physiologist certainly should not object to this conception seeing that he has been used to employing the German conception of "Bahnung," which means a laying down of fresh physiological paths in the centres. Conditioned reflexes are phenomena of common and widespread occurrence: their establishment is an integral function in everyday life. We recognize them in ourselves and in other people or animals under such names as "education," "habits," and "training;" and all of these are really nothing more than the results of an establishment of new nervous connections during the post-natal existence of the organism. They are, in actual fact, links connecting definite extraneous stimuli with their definite responsive reactions. I believe that the recognition and the study of the conditioned reflex will throw open the door to a true physiological investigation probably of all the highest nervous activities of the cerebral hemispheres, and the purpose of the present lectures is to give some account of what we have already accomplished in this direction.

We come now to consider the precise conditions under which new conditioned reflexes or new connections of nervous paths are established. The fundamental requisite is that any external stimulus which is to become the signal in a conditioned reflex must overlap in point of time with the action of an unconditioned stimulus. In the experiment which I chose as my example the unconditioned stimulus was food. Now if the intake of food by the animal takes place simultaneously with the action of a neutral stimulus which has been hitherto in no way related to food, the neutral stimulus readily acquires the property of eliciting the same reaction in the animal as would food itself. This was the case with the dog employed in our experiment with the metronome. On several occasions this animal had been stimulated by the sound of the metronome and immediately presented with food—*i.e.* a stimulus which was neutral of itself had been superimposed upon the action of the inborn alimentary reflex. We observed that, after several repetitions of

the combined stimulation, the sounds from the metronome had acquired the property of stimulating salivary secretion and of evoking the motor reactions characteristic of the alimentary reflex. The first demonstration was nothing but an example of such a conditioned stimulus in action. Precisely the same occurs with the mild defence reflex to rejectable substances. Introduction into the dog's mouth of a little of an acid solution brings about a quite definite responsive reaction. The animal sets about getting rid of the acid, shaking its head violently, opening its mouth and making movements with its tongue. At the same time it produces a copious salivary secretion. The same reaction will infallibly be obtained from any stimulus which has previously been applied a sufficient number of times while acid was being introduced into the dog's mouth. Hence a first and most essential requisite for the formation of a new conditioned reflex lies in a coincidence in time of the action of any previously neutral stimulus with some definite unconditioned stimulus. Further, it is not enough that there should be overlapping between the two stimuli; it is also and equally necessary that the conditioned stimulus should begin to operate before the unconditioned stimulus comes into action.

* * *

As regards the condition of the hemispheres themselves, an alert state of the nervous system is absolutely essential for the formation of a new conditioned reflex. If the dog is mostly drowsy during the experiments, the establishment of a conditioned reflex becomes a long and tedious process, and in extreme cases is impossible to accomplish. The hemispheres must, however, be free from any other nervous activity, and therefore in building up a new conditioned reflex it is important to avoid foreign stimuli which, falling upon the animal, would cause other reactions of their own. If this is not attended to, the establishment of a conditioned reflex is very difficult, if not impossible. Thus, for example, if the dog has been so fastened up that anything causes severe irritation, it does not matter how many times the combination of stimuli is repeated, we shall not be able to obtain a conditioned reflex. A somewhat similar case was described in the first lecture—that of the dog which exhibited the *freedom reflex* in an exaggerated degree. It can also be stated as a rule that the establishment of the first conditioned reflex in an animal is usually more difficult than the establishment of succeeding ones. It is obvious that this must be so, when we consider that even in the most favourable circumstances the experimental conditions themselves will be sure to provoke numerous different reflexes—*i.e.* will give rise to one or other disturbing activity of the hemispheres. But this statement must be qualified by remarking that in cases where the cause of these uncontrolled reflexes is not found out, so that we are not able to get rid of them, the hemispheres themselves will help us. For if the environment of the animal during the experiment does not contain any powerful disturbing elements, then practically always the extraneous reflexes will with time gradually and spontaneously weaken in strength.

The third factor determining the facility with which new conditioned reflexes can be established is the health of the animal. A good state of health will ensure the normal functioning of the cerebral hemispheres, and we shall not have to bother with the effects of any internal pathological stimuli.

The fourth, and last, group of conditions has to do with the properties of the stimulus which is to become conditioned, and also with the properties of the unconditioned stimulus which is selected. Conditioned reflexes are quite readily formed to stimuli to which the animal is more or less indifferent at the outset, though strictly speaking no stimulus within the animal's range of perception exists to which it would be absolutely indifferent. In a normal animal the slightest alteration in the environment—even the very slightest sound or faintest odour, or the smallest change in intensity of illumination—immediately evokes the reflex which I referred to in the first lecture as the investigatory reflex —"What is it?"—manifested by a very definite motor reaction. However, if these neutral stimuli keep recurring, they spontaneously and rapidly weaken in their effect upon the hemispheres, thus bringing about bit by bit the removal of this obstacle to the establishment of a conditioned reflex. But if the extraneous stimuli are strong or unusual, the formation of a conditioned reflex will be difficult, and in extreme cases impossible.

It must also be remembered that in most cases we are not acquainted with the history of the dog before it came into the laboratory, and that we do not know what sort of conditioned reflexes have been established to stimuli which appear to be of the simplest character. But in spite of this we have, in a large number of cases, found it possible to take a strong stimulus which evoked some strong unconditioned response of its own, and still succeed in converting it into a conditioned stimulus for another reflex. Let us take for example a nocuous stimulus, such as a strong electric current or wounding or cauterization of the skin. These are obviously stimuli to vigorous unconditioned defence reflexes. The organism responds by a violent motor reaction directed towards removal of the nocuous stimulus or to its own removal from it. But we may, nevertheless, make use even of these stimuli for the establishment of a new conditioned reflex. Thus in one particular experiment a strong nocuous stimulus—an electric current of great strength—was converted into an alimentary conditioned stimulus, so that its application to the skin did not evoke the slightest defence reaction. Instead, the animal exhibited a well-marked alimentary conditioned reflex, turning its head to where it usually received the food and smacking its lips, at the same time producing a profuse secretion of saliva.

Time	Distance of secondary coil in cms.	Part of Skin Stimulated	Secretion of Saliva in drops during 30 secs.	Motor Reaction
4.23 p.m.	4	usual place	6	In all cases the motor
4.45 ”	4	” ”	5	reaction displayed was
5.7 ”	2	new place	7	that characteristic of
5.17 ”	0	” ”	9	an alimentary reflex;
5.45 ”	0	” ”	6	there was no slightest
				trace of any motor de-
				fence reflex.

After each stimulation the dog was allowed to eat food for a few seconds.

The above is a record taken from a research by Dr. Eroféeva.

Similar results were obtained from dogs in which cauterization or pricking of the skin deep enough to draw blood was made to acquire the properties of an alimentary conditioned stimulus. These experiments have been apt to upset very sensitive people; but we have been able to demonstrate, though without any pretension of penetrating into the subjective world of the dog, that they were labouring under a false impression. Subjected to the very closest scrutiny, not even the tiniest and most subtle objective phenomenon usually exhibited by animals under the influence of strong injurious stimuli can be observed in these dogs. No appreciable changes in the pulse or in the respiration occur in these animals, whereas such changes are always most prominent when the nocuous stimulus has not been converted into an alimentary conditioned stimulus. Such a remarkable phenomenon is the result of diverting the nervous impulse from one physiological path to another. This transference is dependent, however, upon a very definite condition—namely, upon the relative strengths of the two unconditioned reflexes.

Successful transformation of the unconditioned stimulus for one reflex into the conditioned stimulus for another reflex can be brought about only when the former reflex is physiologically weaker and biologically of less importance than the latter. We are led to this conclusion from a consideration of Dr. Eroféeva's experiments. A nocuous stimulus applied to the dog's skin was transformed into a conditioned stimulus for the alimentary reflex. This, we consider, was due to the fact that the alimentary reflex is in such cases stronger than the defence reflex. In the same way we all know that when dogs join in a scuffle for food they frequently sustain skin wounds, which however play no dominant part as stimuli to any defence reflex, being entirely subordinated to the reflex for food. Nevertheless there is a certain limit—there are stronger reflexes than the alimentary reflex. One is the reflex of self-preservation, of existence or non-existence, life or death. To give only one example, it was found impossible to transform a defence reaction into an alimentary conditioned reflex when the stimulus to the unconditioned defence reaction was a strong electric current applied to skin overlying bone with no muscular layer intervening. This signifies that the afferent nervous impulses set up by injury to the bone, and signalizing far greater danger than those set up by injury to the skin, cannot acquire even a temporary connection with the part of the brain from which the alimentary reflex is controlled. Nevertheless, on the whole, the foregoing considerations emphasize the advantage of using the alimentary reflex for most of our experiments, since in the hierarchy of reflexes this holds a very high place.

While, as we have seen, very strong and even specialized stimuli can under certain conditions acquire the properties of conditioned stimuli, there is, on the other hand, a minimum strength below which stimuli cannot be given conditioned properties. Thus a thermal stimulus of 45° C. applied to the skin can be made into an alimentary conditioned reflex, whereas at 38° to 39° C. (approximately 2° C. above the skin temperature in the dog) a thermal stimulus is ineffective [experiments of Dr. Solomonov]. Similarly, while with the help of a very strong unconditioned stimulus it is possible to convert a very unsuitable stimulus—for example, one which naturally evokes a different unconditioned reflex—into a conditioned stimulus, it is exceedingly difficult or even impossible with the help of only a weak unconditioned stimulus to transform even a very favourable neutral stimulus into a conditioned stimulus. Even where such a conditioned reflex is successfully established, its occurrence results only in a very small reflex response. Some unconditioned stimuli may be permanently weak, others may display a weakness which is only temporary—varying with the condition of the animal. As an example of the last we may take food. In the hungry animal food naturally brings about a powerful unconditioned reflex, and the conditioned reflex develops quickly. But in a dog which has not long been fed the unconditioned stimulus has only a small effect, and alimentary conditioned reflexes either are not formed at all or are established very slowly.

By complying with all the conditions which I have enumerated—which is not a very difficult task—a new conditioned reflex is infallibly obtained. We apply to the receptors of the animal rigidly defined stimuli; these stimuli necessarily result in the formation of a new connection in the hemispheres with a consequent development of a typical reflex reaction.

To sum up, we may legitimately claim the study of the formation and properties of conditioned reflexes as a special department of physiology. There is no reason for thinking about all these events in any other way, and it is my belief that in these questions prejudices blunt the intellect and that generally speaking the preconceptions of the human mind stand in the way of any admission that the highest physiological activity of the hemispheres is rigidly determined. The difficulty is mainly due to the tremendous complexity of our subjective states; and, of course, these cannot yet be traced to their primary causations.

18. Pigeons in a Pelican *

B. F. Skinner

Since the pioneering investigations of Pavlov and Thorndike the main thrust of research on learning has been directed toward the development of more adequate theoretical formulations, but a more immediate dividend of this enterprise has been the acquisition of a large store of information about the variables which govern the efficiency of learning in specific situations. These data have provided the basis for the development of a powerful training technique, called operant conditioning, whereby the desired response is acquired step by step through the systematic and judicious administration of a reward immediately following each appropriate response. The format of many recent "programmed texts" and "teaching

* Reprinted by permission of the author and the American Psychological Association from the *American Psychologist*, 1960, *15*, 28-37.

machines" has grown out of principles of operant training. In the next selection, Professor B. F. Skinner, the inventor of operant conditioning, describes one of the early demonstrations of how complex behavior can be shaped and controlled by operant methods.

This is the history of a crackpot idea, born on the wrong side of the tracks intellectually speaking, but eventually vindicated in a sort of middle class respectability. It is the story of a proposal to use living organisms to guide missiles—of a research program during World War II called "Project Pigeon" and a peacetime continuation at the Naval Research Laboratory called "ORCON," from the words "organic control." Both of these programs have now been declassified.

Man has always made use of the sensory capacities of animals, either because they are more acute than his own or more convenient. The watchdog probably hears better than his master and in any case listens while his master sleeps. As a detecting system the dog's ear comes supplied with an alarm (the dog need not be taught to announce the presence of an intruder), but special forms of reporting are sometimes set up. The tracking behavior of the bloodhound and the pointing of the hunting dog are usually modified to make them more useful. Training is sometimes quite explicit. It is said that sea gulls were used to detect submarines in the English Channel during World War I. The British sent their own submarines through the Channel releasing food to the surface. Gulls could see the submarines from the air and learned to follow them, whether they were British or German. A flock of gulls, spotted from the shore, took on special significance. In the seeing-eye dog the repertoire of artificial signaling responses is so elaborate that it has the conventional character of the verbal interchange between man and man.

The detecting and signaling systems of lower organisms have a special advantage when used with explosive devices which can be guided toward the objects they are to destroy, whether by land, sea, or air. Homing systems for guided missiles have now been developed which sense and signal the position of a target by responding to visible or invisible radiation, noise, radar reflections, and so on. These have not always been available, and in any case a living organism has certain advantages. It is almost certainly cheaper and more compact and, in particular, is especially good at responding to patterns and those classes of patterns called "concepts." The lower organism is not used because it is more sensitive than man—after all, the kamikaze did very well—but because it is readily expendable.

PROJECT PELICAN

The ethical question of our right to convert a lower creature into an unwitting hero is a peacetime luxury. There were bigger questions to be answered in the late thirties. A group of men had come into power who promised, and eventually accomplished, the greatest mass murder in history. In 1939 the city of Warsaw was laid waste in an unprovoked bombing, and the airplane emerged as a new and horrible instrument of war against which only the feeblest defenses were available. Project Pigeon was conceived against that background. It began as a search for a homing device to be used in a surface-to-air guided missile as a defense against aircraft. As the balance between offensive and defensive weapons shifted, the direction was reversed, and the system was to be tested first in an air-to-ground missile called the "Pelican." Its name is a useful reminder of the state of the missile art in America at that time. Its detecting and servomechanisms took up so much space that there was no room for explosives: hence the resemblance to the pelican "whose beak can hold more than its belly can." My title is perhaps now clear.

At the University of Minnesota in the spring of 1940 the capacity of the pigeon to steer toward a target was tested with a moving hoist. The pigeon, held in a jacket and harnessed to a block, was immobilized except for its neck and head. It could eat grain from a dish and operate a control system by moving its head in appropriate directions. Movement of the head operated the motors of the hoist. The bird could ascend by lifting its head, descend by lowering it, and travel from side to side by moving appropriately. The whole system, mounted on wheels, was pushed across a room toward a bull's-eye on the far wall. During the approach the pigeon raised or lowered itself and moved from side to side in such a way as to reach the wall in position to eat grain from the center of the bull's-eye. The pigeon learned to reach any target within reach of the hoist, no matter what the starting position and during fairly rapid approaches.

The experiment was shown to John T. Tate, a physicist, then Dean of the Graduate School at the University of Minnesota, who brought it to the attention of R. C. Tolman, one of a group of scientists engaged in early defense activities. The result was the first of a long series of rejections. The proposal "did not warrant further development at the time." The project was accordingly allowed to lapse. On December 7, 1941 the situation was suddenly restructured; and, on the following day, with the help of Keller Breland, then a graduate student at Minnesota, further work was planned. A simpler harnessing system could be used if the bomb were to rotate slowly during its descent, when the pigeon would need to steer in only one dimension: from side to side. We built an apparatus in which a harnessed pigeon was lowered toward a large revolving turntable across which a target was driven according to contacts made by the bird during its descent. It was not difficult to train a pigeon to "hit" small ship models during fairly rapid descents. We made a demonstration film showing hits on various kinds of targets, and two psychologists then engaged in the war effort in Washington, Charles Bray and Leonard Carmichael, undertook to look

for government support. Tolman, then at the Office of Scientific Research and Development, again felt that the project did not warrant support, in part because the United States had at that time no missile capable of being guided toward a target. Commander (now Admiral) Luis de Florez, then in the Special Devices Section of the Navy, took a sympathetic view. He dismissed the objection that there was no available vehicle by suggesting that the pigeon be connected with an automatic pilot mounted in a small plane loaded with explosives. But he was unable to take on the project because of other commitments and because, as he explained, he had recently bet on one or two other equally long shots which had not come in.

The project lapsed again and would probably have been abandoned if it had not been for a young man whose last name I have ungratefully forgotten, but whose first name—Victor—we hailed as a propitious sign. His subsequent history led us to refer to him as Vanquished; and this, as it turned out, was a more reliable omen. Victor walked into the Department of Psychology at Minnesota one day in the summer of 1942 looking for an animal psychologist. He had a scheme for installing dogs in antisubmarine torpedoes. The dogs were to respond to faint acoustic signals from the submarine and to steer the torpedo toward its goal. He wanted a statement from an animal psychologist as to its feasibility. He was understandably surprised to learn of our work with pigeons but seized upon it eagerly, and citing it in support of his contention that dogs could be trained to steer torpedoes he went to a number of companies in Minneapolis. His project was rejected by everyone he approached; but one company, General Mills, Inc., asked for more information about our work with pigeons. We described the project and presented the available data to Arthur D. Hyde, Vice-President in Charge of Research. The company was not looking for new products, but Hyde thought that it might, as a public service, develop the pigeon system to the point at which a governmental agency could be persuaded to take over.

Breland and I moved into the top floor of a flour mill in Minneapolis and with the help of Norman Guttman, who had joined the project, set to work on further improvements. It had been difficult to induce the pigeon to respond to the small angular displacement of a distant target. It would start working dangerously late in the descent. Its natural pursuit behavior was not appropriate to the characteristics of a likely missile. A new system was therefore designed. An image of the target was projected on a translucent screen as in a camera obscura. The pigeon, held near the screen, was reinforced for pecking at the image on the screen. The guiding signal was to be picked up from the point of contact of screen and beak.

In an early arrangement the screen was a translucent plastic plate forming the larger end of a truncated cone bearing a lens at the smaller end. The cone was mounted, lens down, in a gimbal bearing. An object within range threw its image on the translucent screen; and the pigeon, held vertically just above the plate, pecked the image. When a target was moved about within range of the lens, the cone continued to point to it. In another apparatus a translucent disk, free to tilt slightly on gimbal bearings, closed contacts operating motors which altered the position of a large field beneath the apparatus. Small cutouts of ships and other objects were placed on the field. The field was constantly in motion, and a target would go out of range unless the pigeon continued to control it. With this apparatus we began to study the pigeon's reactions to various patterns and to develop sustained steady rates of responding through the use of appropriate schedules of reinforcement, the reinforcement being a few grains occasionally released onto the plate. By building up large extinction curves a target could be tracked continuously for a matter of minutes without reinforcement. We trained pigeons to follow a variety of land and sea targets, to neglect large patches intended to represent clouds or flak, to concentrate on one target while another was in view, and so on. We found that a pigeon could hold the missile on a particular street intersection in an aerial map of a city. The map which came most easily to hand was of a city which, in the interests of international relations, need not be identified. Through appropriate schedules of reinforcement it was possible to maintain longer uninterrupted runs than could conceivably be required by a missile.

We also undertook a more serious study of the pigeon's behavior, with the help of W. K. Estes and Marion Breland who joined the project at this time. We ascertained optimal conditions of deprivation, investigated other kinds of deprivations, studied the effect of special reinforcements (for example, pigeons were said to find hemp seed particularly delectable), tested the effects of energizing drugs and increased oxygen pressures, and so on. We differentially reinforced the force of the pecking response and found that pigeons could be induced to peck so energetically that the base of the beak became inflamed. We investigated the effects of extremes of temperature, of changes in atmospheric pressure, of accelerations produced by an improvised centrifuge, of increased carbon dioxide pressure, of increased and prolonged vibration, and of noises such as pistol shots. (The birds could, of course, have been deafened to eliminate auditory distractions, but we found it easy to maintain steady behavior in spite of intense noises and many other distracting conditions using the simple process of adaptation.) We investigated optimal conditions for the quick development of discriminations and began to study the pigeon's reactions to patterns, testing for induction from a test figure to the same figure inverted, to figures of different sizes and colors, and to figures against different grounds. A simple device using carbon paper to record the points at which a pigeon pecks a figure showed a promise which has never been properly exploited.

We made another demonstration film and renewed our contact with the Office of Scientific Research and Development. An observer was sent to Minneapolis, and on the strength of his report we were given an opportunity to present our case in Washington in February 1943. At that time we were offering a homing device capable of reporting with an on-off signal the orientation of a missile toward various visual patterns. The capacity to respond to pattern was, we felt, our strongest argument, but the fact that the device used only visible radiation (the same form of information available to the human bombardier) made it superior to the radio controlled missiles then under development because it was resistant to jamming. Our film had some effect. Other observers were sent to Minneapolis to see the demonstration itself. The pigeons, as usual, behaved beautifully. One of them held the supposed missile on a particular intersection of streets in the aerial map for five minutes although the target would have been lost if the pigeon had paused for a second or two. The observers returned to Washington, and two weeks later we were asked to supply data on (a) the population of pigeons in the United States (fortunately, the census bureau had some figures) and (b) the accuracy with which pigeons struck a point on a plate. There were many arbitrary conditions to be taken into account in measuring the latter, but we supplied possibly relevant data. At long last, in June 1943, the Office of Scientific Research and Development awarded a modest contract to General Mills, Inc. to "develop a homing device."

At that time we were given some information about the missile the pigeons were to steer. The Pelican was a wing steered glider, still under development and not yet successfully steered by any homing device. It was being tested on a target in New Jersey consisting of a stirrup shaped pattern bulldozed out of the sandy soil near the coast. The white lines of the target stood out clearly against brown and green cover. Colored photographs were taken from various distances and at various angles, and the verisimilitude of the reproduction was checked by flying over the target and looking at its image in a portable camera obscura.

Because of security restrictions we were given only very rough specifications of the signal to be supplied to the controlling system in the Pelican. It was no longer to be simply on-off; if the missile was badly off target, an especially strong correcting signal was needed. This meant that the quadrant-contact system would no longer suffice. But further requirements were left mainly to our imagination. The General Mills engineers were equal to this difficult assignment. With what now seems like unbelievable speed, they designed and constructed a pneumatic pickup system giving a graded signal. A lens in the nose of the missile threw an image on a translucent plate within reach of the pigeon in a pressure sealed chamber. Four air valves resting against the edges of the plate were jarred open momentarily as the pigeon pecked. The valves at the right and left admitted air to chambers on opposite sides of one tambour, while the valves at the top and bottom admitted air to opposite sides of another. Air on all sides was exhausted by a Venturi cone on the side of the missile. When the missile was on target, the pigeon pecked the center of the plate, all valves admitted equal amounts of air, and the tambours remained in neutral positions. But if the image moved as little as a quarter of an inch off-center, corresponding to a very small angular displacement of the target, more air was admitted by the valves on one side, and the resulting displacement of the tambours sent appropriate correcting orders directly to the servosystem.

The device required no materials in short supply, was relatively foolproof, and delivered a graded signal. It had another advantage. By this time we had begun to realize that a pigeon was more easily controlled than a physical scientist serving on a committee. It was very difficult to convince the latter that the former was an orderly system. We therefore multiplied the probability of success by designing a multiple bird unit. There was adequate space in the nose of the Pelican for three pigeons each with its own lens and plate. A net signal could easily be generated. The majority vote of three pigeons offered an excellent guarantee against momentary pauses and aberrations. (We later worked out a system in which the majority took on a more characteristically democratic function. When a missile is falling toward *two* ships at sea, for example, there is no guarantee that all three pigeons will steer toward the same ship. But at least two must agree, and the third can then be punished for his minority opinion. Under proper contingencies of reinforcement a punished bird will shift immediately to the majority view. When all three are working on one ship, any defection is immediately punished and corrected.)

The General Mills engineers also built a simulator—a sort of Link trainer for pigeons—designed to have the steering characteristics of the Pelican, in so far as these had been communicated to us. Like the wing steered Pelican, the simulator tilted and turned from side to side. When the three-bird nose was attached to it, the pigeons could be put in full control—the "loop could be closed"—and the adequacy of the signal tested under pursuit conditions. Targets were moved back and forth across the far wall of a room at prescribed speeds and in given patterns of oscillation, and the tracking response of the whole unit was studied quantitatively.

Meanwhile we continued our intensive study of the behavior of the pigeon. Looking ahead to combat use we designed methods for the mass production of trained birds and for handling large groups of trained subjects. We were proposing to train certain birds for certain *classes* of targets, such as ships at sea, while special squads were to be trained on special targets, photographs of which were to be ob-

tained through reconnaissance. A large crew of pigeons would then be waiting for assignment, but we developed harnessing and training techniques which should have solved such problems quite easily.

By December 1943, less than six months after the contract was awarded, we were ready to report to the Office of Scientific Research and Development. Observers visited the laboratory and watched the simulator follow a target about a room under the control of a team of three birds. They also reviewed our tracking data. The only questions which arose were the inevitable consequence of our lack of information about the signal required to steer the Pelican. For example, we had had to make certain arbitrary decisions in compromising between sensitivity of signal and its integration or smoothness. A high vacuum produced quick, rather erratic movements of the tambours, while a lower vacuum gave a sluggish but smooth signal. As it turned out, we had not chosen the best values in collecting our data, and in January 1944 the Office of Scientific Research and Development refused to extend the General Mills contract. The reasons given seemed to be due to misunderstandings or, rather, to lack of communication. We had already collected further data with new settings of the instruments, and these were submitted in a request for reconsideration.

We were given one more chance. We took our new data to the radiation lab at the Massachusetts Institute of Technology where they were examined by the servo-specialists working on the Pelican controls. To our surprise the scientist whose task it was to predict the usefulness of the pigeon signal argued that our data were inconsistent with respect to phase lag and certain other characteristics of the signal. According to his equations, our device could not possibly yield the signals we reported. We knew, of course, that it had done so. We examined the supposed inconsistency and traced it, or so we thought, to a certain nonlinearity in our system. In pecking an image near the edge of the plate, the pigeon strikes a more glancing blow; hence the air admitted at the valves is not linearly proportional to the displacement of the target. This could be corrected in several ways: for example, by using a lens to distort radial distances. It was our understanding that in any case the signal was adequate to control the Pelican. Indeed, one servo authority, upon looking at graphs of the performance of the simulator, exclaimed: "This is better than radar!"

Two days later, encouraged by our meeting at MIT, we reached the summit. We were to present our case briefly to a committee of the country's top scientists. The hearing began with a brief report by the scientist who had discovered the "inconsistency" in our data, and to our surprise he still regarded it as unresolved. He predicted that the signal we reported would cause the missile to "hunt" wildly and lose the target. But his prediction should have applied as well to the closed loop simulator. Fortunately another scientist was present who had seen the simulator performing under excellent control and who could confirm our report of the facts. But reality was no match for mathematics.

The basic difficulty, of course, lay in convincing a dozen distinguished physical scientists that the behavior of a pigeon could be adequately controlled. We had hoped to score on this point by bringing with us a demonstration. A small black box had a round translucent window in one end. A slide projector placed some distance away threw on the window an image of the New Jersey target. In the box, of course, was a pigeon—which, incidentally, had at that time been harnessed for 35 hours. Our intention was to let each member of the committee observe the response to the target by looking down a small tube; but time was not available for individual observation, and we were asked to take the top off the box. The translucent screen was flooded with so much light that the target was barely visible, and the peering scientists offered conditions much more unfa-

miliar and threatening than those likely to be encountered in a missile. In spite of this the pigeon behaved perfectly, pecking steadily and energetically at the image of the target as it moved about on the plate. One scientist with an experimental turn of mind intercepted the beam from the projector. The pigeon stopped instantly. When the image again appeared, pecking began within a fraction of a second and continued at a steady rate.

It was a perfect performance, but it had just the wrong effect. One can talk about phase lag in pursuit behavior and discuss mathematical predictions of hunting without reflecting too closely upon what is inside the black box. But the spectacle of a living pigeon carrying out its assignment, no matter how beautifully, simply reminded the committee of how utterly fantastic our proposal was. I will not say that the meeting was marked by unrestrained merriment, for the merriment was restrained. But it was there, and it was obvious that our case was lost.

Hyde closed our presentation with a brief summary: we were offering a homing device, unusually resistant to jamming, capable of reacting to a wide variety of target patterns, requiring no materials in short supply, and so simple to build that production could be started in 30 days. He thanked the committee, and we left. As the door closed behind us, he said to me: "Why don't you go out and get drunk!"

Official word soon came: "Further prosecution of this project would seriously delay others which in the minds of the Division would have more immediate promise of combat application." Possibly the reference was to a particular combat application at Hiroshima a year and a half later, when it looked for a while as if the need for accurate bombing had been eliminated for all time. In any case we had to show, for all our trouble, only a loftful of curiously useless equipment and a few dozen pigeons with a strange interest in a feature of the New Jersey coast. The equipment was scrapped, but 30 of the pigeons were kept to see how long they would retain the appropriate behavior.

In the years which followed there were faint signs of life. Winston Churchill's personal scientific advisor, Lord Cherwell, learned of the project and "regretted its demise." A scientist who had had some contact with the project during the war, and who evidently assumed that its classified status was not to be taken seriously, made a good story out of it for the *Atlantic Monthly*, names being changed to protect the innocent. Other uses of animals began to be described. The author of the *Atlantic Monthly* story also published an account of the "incendiary bats." Thousands of bats were to be released over an enemy city, each carrying a small incendiary time bomb. The bats would take refuge, as is their custom, under eaves and in other out-of-the-way places; and shortly afterwards thousands of small fires would break out practically simultaneously. The scheme was never used because it was feared that it would be mistaken for germ warfare and might lead to retaliation in kind.

Another story circulating at the time told how the Russians trained dogs to blow up tanks. I have described the technique elsewhere (Skinner, 1956). A Swedish proposal to use seals to achieve the same end with submarines was not successful. The seals were to be trained to approach submarines to obtain fish attached to the sides. They were then to be released carrying magnetic mines in the vicinity of hostile submarines. The required training was apparently never achieved. I cannot vouch for the authenticity of probably the most fantastic story of this sort, but it ought to be recorded. The Russians were said to have trained sea lions to cut mine cables. A complicated device attached to the sea lion included a motor driven cable-cutter, a tank full of small fish, and a device which released a few fish into a muzzle covering the sea lion's head. In order to eat, the sea lion had to find a mine cable and swim along side it so that the cutter was automatically triggered, at which point a few fish were released from the tank into the muzzle. When a given number of cables had been cut, both the energy of the cutting mechanism and the supply of fish were exhausted, and the sea lion received a special stimulus upon which it returned to its home base for special reinforcement and reloading.

ORCON

The story of our own venture has a happy ending. With the discovery of German accomplishments in the field of guided missiles, feasible homing systems suddenly became very important. Franklin V. Taylor of the Naval Research Laboratory in Washington, D. C. heard about our project and asked for further details. As a psychologist Taylor appreciated the special capacity of living organisms to respond to visual patterns and was aware of recent advances in the control of behavior. More important, he was a skillful practitioner in a kind of control which our project had conspicuously lacked: he knew how to approach the people who determine the direction of research. He showed our demonstration film so often that it was completely worn out—but to good effect, for support was eventually found for a thorough investigation of "organic control" under the general title ORCON. Taylor also enlisted the support of engineers in obtaining a more effective report of the pigeon's behavior. The translucent plate upon which the image of the target was thrown had a semiconducting surface, and the tip of the bird's beak was covered with a gold electrode. A single contact with the plate sent an immediate report of the location of the target to the controlling mechanism. The work which went into this system contributed to the so-called Pick-off Display Converter developed as part of the Naval Data Handling System for human observers. It is no longer necessary for the radar operator to give a verbal report of the location of a pip on the screen. Like the pigeon, he has only to touch the pip with a special contact. (He holds the contact in his hand.)

At the Naval Research Laboratory in Washington the responses of pigeons were studied in detail. Average peck rate, average error rate, average hit rate, and so on were recorded under various conditions. The tracking behavior of the pigeon was analyzed with methods similar to those employed with human operators. Pattern perception was studied, including generalization from one pattern to another. A simulator was constructed in which the pigeon controlled an image projected by a moving-picture film of an actual target: for example, a ship at sea as seen from a plane approaching at 600 miles per hour.

The publications from the Naval Research Laboratory which report this work (Chernikoff & Newlin, 1951; Conklin, Newlin, Taylor, & Tipton, 1953; Searle & Stafford, 1950; Taylor, 1949; White, 1952) provide a serious evaluation of the possibilities of organic control. Although in simulated tests a single pigeon occasionally loses a target, its tracking characteristics are surprisingly good. A three- or seven-bird unit with the same individual consistency should yield a signal with a reliability which is at least of the order of magnitude shown by other phases of guided missiles in their present stage of development. Moreover, in the seven years which have followed the last of these reports, a great deal of relevant information has been acquired. The color vision of the pigeon is now thoroughly understood; its generalization along single properties of a stimulus has been recorded and analyzed; and the maintenance of behavior through scheduling of reinforcement has been drastically improved, particularly in the development of techniques for pacing responses for less erratic and steadier signals (Skinner, 1957). Tests made with the birds salvaged from the old Project Pigeon showed that even after six years of inactivity a pigeon will immediately and correctly strike a target

to which it has been conditioned and will continue to respond for some time without reinforcement.

The use of living organisms in guiding missiles is, it seems fair to say, no longer a crackpot idea. A pigeon is an extraordinarily subtle and complex mechanism capable of performances which at the moment can be equalled by electronic equipment only of vastly greater weight and size, and it can be put to reliable use through the principles which have emerged from an experimental analysis of its behavior. But this vindication of our original proposal is perhaps the least important result. Something happened during the brief life of Project Pigeon which it has taken a long time to appreciate. The practical task before us created a new attitude toward the behavior of organisms. We had to maximize the probability that a given form of behavior would occur at a given time. We could not enjoy the luxury of observing one variable while allowing others to change in what we hoped was a random fashion. We had to discover all relevant variables and submit them to experimental control whenever possible. We were no doubt under exceptional pressure, but vigorous scientific research usually makes comparable demands. Psychologists have too often yielded to the temptation to be content with hypothetical processes and intervening variables rather than press for rigorous experimental control. It is often intellectual laziness rather than necessity which recommends the *a posteriori* statistical treatment of variation. Our task forced us to emphasize prior experimental control, and its success in revealing orderly processes gave us an exciting glimpse of the superiority of laboratory practice over verbal (including some kinds of mathematical) explanation.

THE CRACKPOT IDEA

If I were to conclude that crackpot ideas are to be encouraged, I should probably be told that psychology has already had more than its share of them. If it has, they have been entertained by the wrong people. Reacting against the excesses of psychological quackery, psychologists have developed an enormous concern for scientific respectability. They constantly warn their students against questionable facts and unsupported theories. As a result the usual PhD thesis is a model of compulsive cautiousness, advancing only the most timid conclusions thoroughly hedged about with qualifications. But it is just the man capable of displaying such admirable caution who needs a touch of uncontrolled speculation. Possibly a generous exposure to psychological science fiction would help. Project Pigeon might be said to support that view. Except with respect to its avowed goal, it was, as I see it, highly productive; and this was in large measure because my colleagues and I knew that, in the eyes of the world, we were crazy.

One virtue in crackpot ideas is that they breed rapidly and their progeny show extraordinary mutations. Everyone is talking about teaching machines nowadays, but Sidney Pressey can tell you what it was like to have a crackpot idea in that field 40 years ago. His self-testing devices and self-scoring test forms now need no defense, and psychomotor training devices have also achieved a substantial respectability. This did not, however, prepare the way for devices to be used in verbal instruction—that is, in the kinds of teaching which are the principal concern of our schools and colleges. Even five short years ago that kind of instruction by machine was still in the crackpot category. (I can quote official opinion to that effect from high places.) Now, there is a direct genetic connection between teaching machines and Project Pigeon. We had been forced to consider the mass education of pigeons. True, the scrap of wisdom we imparted to each was indeed small, but the required changes in behavior were similar to those which must be brought about in vaster quantities in human students. The techniques of shaping behavior and of bringing it under stimulus control which can be traced, as I have suggested elsewhere (Skinner, 1958), to a memorable episode on the top floor of that flour mill in Minneapolis needed only a detailed reformulation of verbal behavior to be directly applicable to education.

I am sure there is more to come. In the year which followed the termination of Project Pigeon I wrote *Walden Two* (Skinner, 1948), a utopian picture of a properly engineered society. Some psychotherapists might argue that I was suffering from personal rejection and simply retreated to a fantasied world where everything went according to plan, where there never was heard a discouraging word. But another explanation is, I think, equally plausible. That piece of science fiction was a declaration of confidence in a technology of behavior. Call it a crackpot idea if you will; it is one in which I have never lost faith. I still believe that the same kind of wide-ranging speculation about human affairs, supported by studies of compensating rigor, will make a substantial contribution toward that world of the future in which, among other things, there will be no need for guided missiles.

REFERENCES

CHERNIKOFF, R., & NEWLIN, E. P. ORCON. Part III. Investigations of target acquisition by the pigeon. *Naval Res. Lab. lett. Rep.*, 1951, No. S-3600-629a/51 (Sept. 10).

CONKLIN, J. E., NEWLIN, E. P., JR., TAYLOR, F. V., & TIPTON, C. L. ORCON. Part IV. Simulated flight tests. *Naval Res. Lab. Rep.*, 1953, No. 4105.

SEARLE, L. V., & STAFFORD, B. H. ORCON. Part II. Report of phase I research and bandpass study. *Naval Res. Lab. lett. Rep.*, 1950, No. S-3600-157/50 (May 1).

SKINNER, B. F. *Walden two.* New York: Macmillan, 1948.

SKINNER, B. F. A case history in scientific method. *Amer. Psychologist*, 1956, **11**, 221–233.

SKINNER, B. F. The experimental analysis of behavior. *Amer. Scient.*, 1957, **45**, 343–371.

SKINNER, B. F. Reinforcement today. *Amer. Psychologist*, 1958, **13**, 94–99.

TAYLOR, F. V. ORCON. Part I. Outline of proposed research. *Naval Res. Lab. lett. Rep.*, 1949, No. S-3600-157/50 (June 17).

WHITE, C. F. Development of the NRL ORCON tactile missile simulator. *Naval Res. Lab. Rep.*, 1952, No. 3917.

19. Descriptive Behaviorism Versus Cognitive Theory in Verbal Operant Conditioning *

Charles D. Spielberger and L. Douglas DeNike

The power of the scientific method has turned upon the ability to identify the small number of critical variables which underlie ostensibly complicated events. Faced with the complexity of human behavior, some psychologists have adapted the strategy of working with simpler animals in situations where environmental factors can be carefully controlled. Thus, our understanding of the learning process has been profitably advanced by the investigation of laboratory animals (e.g., rats and pigeons) engaged in simple learning tasks.

Having established laws of animal learning it is then necessary to determine their breadth of generality and applicability to humans. Thus, attempts to apply the principles of reinforcement derived from animal research to complex human learning represent a natural extension of the inquiry. However, it is not surprising that, with man, some modification of these principles is necessary. The next selection, by Professors Spielberger and DeNike, demonstrates how the cognitive variable of "awareness" must be incorporated into the theoretical network in order to account for instrumental learning in man.

Operant behavior generally refers to responses which an organism in a given environment displays spontaneously without special training.[1] Operant conditioning usually implies a variety of experimental techniques wherein a subject is rewarded after engaging in operant behavior of a selected kind. The successful conditioning of an operant response is inferred from an increase in its rate of occurrence as a function of reward (reinforcement) administered by the experimenter. Through the efforts of those who have used operant conditioning procedures, significant advances in our knowledge of animal learning have been made possible, and widespread interest has been generated in the use of such procedures for investigating human learning. The purpose of the present paper is to examine theoretical and methodological issues which have arisen in recent applications of operant conditioning techniques to verbal learning.

In verbal operant conditioning, hereafter termed verbal conditioning, the subject is typically instructed to speak in accordance with a particular task. He is not told that this task involves reinforcement or learning. The experimenter attempts to change the rate of emission of certain responses by the systematic application of a reinforcing stimulus, usually some form of social reward, such as the experimenter saying "Mmm-hmm" or "Good." Studies of verbal conditioning originated in close connection with the concepts and procedures developed by Skinner (1938) with infrahuman species. Greenspoon, a pioneer in verbal conditioning research, maintains that

... it should be possible to work with verbal behavior in much the same way that experimenters have worked with the behavior of rats, pigeons, etc. It should also be possible to investigate the same kinds of variables that

* Reprinted by permission of the authors and the American Psychological Association from the *Psychological Review*, 1966, 73, 306-326.

[1] Work on this paper was supported in part by grants to the first author from the National Institutes of Mental Health (MH 7446) and Child Health and Human Development (HD 947), United States Public Health Service. We are indebted to Norman Cliff, Jum C. Nunnally, Henry Slucki, and Donald L. Thistlethwaite for their critical comments on the manuscript.

have been investigated with the non-verbal be-havior of humans and infrahumans [1962, p. 511].

Thus, the Skinnerian (1957, 1963a, 1963b) approach has been clearly apparent both in the methods employed and the variables investigated in most verbal conditioning experiments.

In keeping with Skinner's emphasis on the "experimental analysis of behavior," many verbal conditioners have largely ig-nored the possibility that subjects' aware-ness of response-reinforcement contingen-cies might influence their conditioning per-formance. Investigators who have exam-ined subjects' verbal reports in relation to their conditioning performance have dis-covered considerable evidence suggesting that cognitive processes mediate perform-ance gains in verbal conditioning. But de-scriptive behaviorists have been quick to rejoin that the relationships between awareness and performance observed by cognitively oriented researchers have arisen from artifacts associated with the verbal report procedures from which awareness was inferred. Thus, in verbal conditioning, broadly opposed theoretical systems lock horns: Descriptive behaviorists argue for learning without awareness, those of cog-nitive persuasion argue against it, and proponents of each point of view generate methodological criticisms of the experimen-tal work carried on in the opposing camp.

It would appear that radically different epistemologies underlie the theoretical dif-ferences between Skinnerian and cognitive researchers. The epistemological issues, which revolve around the admissibility of conscious awareness as a desideratum for psychological science, have been discussed in detail elsewhere (Spielberger, 1965). Therefore, rather than restating these issues here, a simple analogy may better serve to illustrate how varying pretheoreti-cal assumptions about the general nature and scope of science can lead to highly disparate approaches to a concrete scientific problem.

It seems reasonable to conjecture that

biologists of an earlier generation who did not believe in protozoa probably contended at times that objects too small to be ob-served by the naked eye were *irrelevant to scientific analysis* (of disease, for instance). Attempts to explore the domain of the microscopic world might have been dis-dained by such observers as revealing only illusory effects traceable to light diffusion in the microscope, and so on. Similarly, we might expect that present-day psychol-ogists who consider thoughts and hy-potheses to be beyond the limits of "scien-tific" inquiry would not vigorously search for them in experimental subjects. Further-more, we should not be surprised to find that such psychologists were uninterested and unskilled in evaluating cognitive phe-nomena which for them do not exist. On the other hand, early biologists who be-lieved in protozoa might occasionally have "seen" them when they were not there. Similarly, we might expect, as has been suggested by Farber (1963), that cogni-tively oriented verbal conditioning re-searchers, in their eagerness to attribute behavior to mediating conscious processes, would sometimes inadvertently suggest (or erroneously infer) awareness in questioning subjects who show performance gains.

One obvious implication of the above analogy is that competing scientific theories lead to different experimental procedures and often to observational errors which support the theoretical predilections of the investigator (Rosenthal, 1963). In most cases, however, such methodological dif-ferences and observational errors are even-tually resolved since competing theories generally lead to more sensitive experi-ments. Furthermore, good experiments contribute to the accumulation of a com-posite set of facts which facilitate the con-vergence of theoretical schools and the establishment of an organized body of scientific knowledge (Campbell, 1963). But, if the epistemological assumptions which underlie competing scientific theo-ries differ, the methodological consequences of such differences may lead to the collection of noncomparable data about which pointless theoretical controversy is generated. Unfortunately, this seems to be the case in verbal conditioning.

In this paper, we propose to examine the relative merits of cognitive and Skinnerian interpretations of verbal conditioning and the methodological assumptions on which these interpretations are based. The organization of the paper is as follows: In Section I the use of verbal report measures as indexes of awareness (mediating cognitive processes) will be discussed, and the various objections which investigators of a Skinnerian bent have raised concerning these measures will be enumerated and analyzed. In Section II methodological problems associated with the assessment of awareness from postconditioning interviews will be considered, and procedures for assessing awareness during conditioning will be described along with the results of two experiments in which such procedures were utilized. A theoretical analysis of verbal conditioning in terms of cognitive concepts will be presented in Section III. In Section IV the significance of the verbal conditioning paradigm for the more general question of learning without awareness will be taken up. [Section I, which consists of philosophical objections to verbal report methodology, has been omitted.]

❂   ❂   ❂

II. THE USE OF VERBAL REPORTS IN VERBAL CONDITIONING

The questioning techniques employed to assess awareness in verbal conditioning studies have included both oral interviews and written-response questionnaires. These have been utilized both during and after conditioning trials. In this section, we will first consider methodological factors associated with the assessment of awareness from postconditioning interviews. We will then describe procedures developed for assessing awareness during conditioning and the findings of two experiments in which such procedures were employed.

The Assessment of Awareness after Conditioning

The assessment of awareness from postconditioning interviews is influenced by the style of questioning, the wording of questions and the number of questions asked, the interpolation of extinction trials, and the experimenter's concern with correlated hypotheses. Each of these factors will be discussed below in terms of its potential effect on reports of awareness obtained in postconditioning interviews.

Oral interview versus written questionnaire procedures. Both oral interviews and written-response questionnaires have been utilized for assessing awareness after the completion of conditioning trials. Either style of questioning would appear to have certain characteristic advantages and disadvantages. Written-response questionnaires eliminate the potential biasing influence of the experimenter who conducts an oral interview. However, the responses elicited by this procedure may not be as complete as those obtained from questions asked and answered orally, and clarification of unclear replies through additional inquiry is not generally feasible. Furthermore, some subjects may be inclined to avoid being incorrect by not responding when they are unsure of their hypotheses.

Number and wording of questions. In early verbal conditioning studies, awareness interviews were very brief, and the questions were vaguely worded. For example, in one study (Sidowski, 1954) the postconditioning interview consisted of only two questions: (a) "Were you aware of the purpose of the experiment?" and (b) "Were you aware of the purpose of the light?" (the contingent reinforcing stimulus). In response to these questions, a subject who might have been perfectly aware of the response-reinforcement contingency might not have had any idea of the "scientific purpose" of the experiment nor of the reinforcing stimulus. Furthermore, questions asked in this form make it easier to say

"No" than "Yes" since the latter response will obviously require elaboration. A series of questions in which subjects were asked to state their thoughts about when and why the light was blinking would have been more satisfactory.

Given minimal questioning, subjects tend to respond according to their own preconceptions about what is important and refer to the reinforcing stimulus only when asked about it. For example, after the conclusion of a pseudo-ESP verbal conditioning experiment, Krieckhaus and Eriksen (1960) held informal conversations with subjects who showed performance gains, but failed to verbalize a correct response-reinforcement contingency in a structured interview. They reported:

Two (subjects) verbalized very clearly their awareness of the effects of reinforcement upon their behavior. When asked why they had not stated this in response to the postconditioning interview questions, both of them commented that they hadn't understood that this was what E was asking. They both stated that they thought E was concerned with whether or not they were getting ESP messages, rather than trying to find out whether the reinforcement of "good" had affected their choice of responses [p. 515].

Thus, the requirement of asking for information with clear and adequately worded questions is coordinate with the necessity of asking a sufficient number of questions.

Although more detailed questioning might in some cases increase the likelihood of suggesting awareness indiscriminately (Farber, 1963), a series of questions of gradually increasing specificity enables the interviewer to assess awareness and motivation while providing minimal *surplus* information. Furthermore, in studies in which such interviews were employed (see Spielberger, 1962), it has been demonstrated that: (*a*) Substantial numbers of subjects were identified as aware of correct response-reinforcement contingencies who were not so classified on the basis of brief interviews; and (*b*) performance gains were limited essentially to aware subjects

and specific to those responses for which the individual subject was aware of a correct contingency.

Extinction trials. In verbal conditioning, the practice of interpolating extinction trials (e.g., Cohen, Kalish, Thurston, & Cohen, 1954; Greenspoon, 1955) or other tasks (Gergen, 1965; Sassenrath, 1959) between acquisition trials and the interview in which awareness is assessed probably reduces the likelihood that awareness will be detected. Subjects who are aware of a correct contingency during conditioning may either forget their hypotheses, interpret the withdrawal of the reinforcing stimulus during extinction as a sign that they were wrong, or both. We have observed that, even during acquisition trials, instances of *accidental* nonreinforcement due to experimenter error sometimes suffice to disconfirm subjects' hypotheses (Spielberger & DeNike, 1963).

Correlated hypotheses. The problem of assessing correlated hypotheses in learning experiments was first raised by Postman and Jarrett (1952). In verbal conditioning, a subject is considered to have a correlated hypothesis if he verbalizes a contingency which is different from, but correlated with, the reinforcement principle employed by the experimenter (Dulany, 1961). Thus, a subject need not be aware of the *experimenter's* definition of the contingency in order to show performance gains through conscious pursuit of his *own* hypotheses. For example, suppose one spring a whimsical millionaire were to emplace a few gold nuggets on some fertile ground on his estate and announce magnanimously to the townsfolk that all were welcome to come there and shovel around on the surface. Anyone inquiring among these townsfolk as they labored would find them highly aware that they were "digging for gold" and highly unaware that they were "spading a garden."

In the traditional verbal conditioning task in which plural nouns are reinforced

(Greenspoon, 1955), a subject would receive 100% reinforcement if he said serially, "apples, oranges, peaches," etc. When interviewed, he might report as his hypothesis that reinforcement is contingent upon his naming "fruits." While the response class "fruits" is formally different from "plural nouns," the subject who named fruits would be reinforced for acting on this hypothesis and would be likely to develop the conviction that he was being encouraged to say words of similar meaning, as Dulany (1961) has convincingly shown. That subjects sometimes develop and pursue correlated ideas in response to less than 100% reinforcement points up the importance of *random* reinforcement rather than *no* reinforcement for control groups in verbal conditioning experiments (DeNike & Spielberger, 1963; Spielberger, DeNike, & Stein, 1965). And as Adams (1957) has pointed out, correlated hypotheses are typically *not* evaluated in investigations which have reported evidence for learning without awareness.

Thus far, we have discussed methodological factors which influence reports of awareness obtained from interviews or questionnaires conducted after the completion of the conditioning task. As previously noted, in recent verbal conditioning experiments in which such factors were taken into account, performance gains were limited essentially to subjects who verbalized a correct or correlated contingency. However, in these experiments, awareness was inferred from responses to interview questions asked *after* performance measures had been taken. Therefore, it could be argued that the performance gains of aware subjects were automatically produced by reinforcement and that the awareness-performance relationship could be accounted for by noncognitive explanations. The assessment of awareness during conditioning would provide a firmer basis for evaluating the temporal relationship between performance and awareness in verbal conditioning. Such procedures will now be considered.

The Assessment of Awareness during Conditioning

Most noncognitive explanations of verbal conditioning implicitly assume that increments in performance initially result from the direct and automatic effects of reinforcement and that performance gains occur prior to the time that the subject becomes aware of a correct response-reinforcement contingency. On the other hand, it is argued in cognitive explanations of verbal conditioning that awareness precedes performance increments. Thus, reinforcement theory and cognitive theory lead to differential predictions with regard to the temporal relationship between the development of awareness and the inception of performance gains. But in order to evaluate temporal factors in verbal conditioning, a procedure is required which will permit determination of whether or not subjects become aware of a correct contingency *during conditioning*, and if so, when. The results of two studies in which awareness was assessed during conditioning are discussed below.

Experiment I. DeNike (1964) reinforced female college students for giving *human-noun responses* in a word-naming task (Matarazzo, Saslow, & Pareis, 1960). His subjects were required to write down their "thoughts about the experiment" after each block of 25 response words. As a signal for the subject to record her thoughts, a light was turned on which remained lit until the subject indicated she was ready to resume saying words. No reinforcement was given during the first two word blocks, which provided a measure of operant rate. Beginning with the third word block, subjects in the Experimental Group were reinforced with "Mmm-hmm" for each human-noun response; those in the Control Group were reinforced with "Mmm-hmm" for 10% of their response words, according to a predetermined random schedule.

Awareness of the contingency between human-noun responses and the experimenter's "Mmm-hmm" was inferred from the thoughts (notes) which each subject recorded during conditioning. On the basis of these notes, subjects were independently rated by four judges

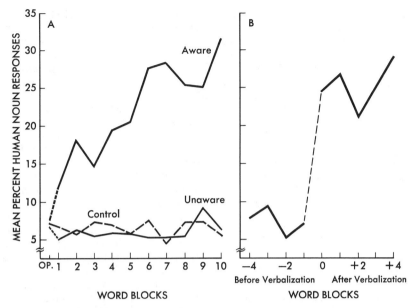

Figure 19.1 Conditioning curves. A, mean percentage of human-noun responses given by the *Aware, Unaware,* and *Control* groups on the conditioning task. B, conditioning curve for the *Aware* group in which the data for preverbalization and postverbalization word blocks have been separately Vincentized. Adapted from DeNike (1964).

as either *aware* or *unaware* of a correct contingency. Agreement between pairs of judges ranged from 90–95%, and there was unanimity or a 3–1 consensus among the judges with respect to the classification of 59 of the 61 subjects in the Experimental Group. For each aware subject, the judges also indicated the word block on which a correct contingency was first recorded.

If performance gains in verbal conditioning are automatically produced by reinforcement, it would be expected that gradual increments in performance would occur for all subjects, and that performance gains for aware subjects would occur prior to the word block on which they recorded a correct contingency in their notes. However, if acquisition of the reinforced response class in verbal conditioning is mediated by awareness, performance gains would be expected only for aware subjects, and these should occur on or subsequent to the word block on which such subjects recorded a correct contingency. The performance curves of DeNike's Aware, Unaware, and Control Groups are presented in Figure 19–1A. It may be noted that the output of human nouns for the Aware Group increased markedly over the reinforced word blocks and that the Unaware and Control Groups failed to show

any performance gains. However, although only subjects who recorded correct contingencies in their notes gave more human nouns, it cannot be determined from the data as arrayed in Figure 19–1A whether or not aware subjects showed increments in performance prior to the word block on which they recorded a correct contingency.

In order to evaluate the temporal relationship between performance gains and awareness, the conditioning data for the aware subjects were examined as a function of the word block on which each first recorded a correct contingency in her notes. This word block was designated the "0" block. Word blocks prior to and subsequent to Block 0 were designated the preverbalization and postverbalization blocks and were labeled respectively with negative and positive integers, after the practice of Philbrick and Postman (1955). The 0 blocks of the aware subjects were then aligned, and the data for the preverbalization and postverbalization blocks were separately Vincentized (Munn, 1950). The Vincentized conditioning curve for the Aware Group is given in Figure 19–1B in which it may be noted that performance on the conditioning task: (*a*) remained at essentially the same level in the preverbalization blocks as in the operant blocks, (b) increased markedly on the 0 block, and (c) was maintained at a relatively high level during the postverbalization blocks. The finding that the performance increments of aware subjects first occurred during the word block on which they first recorded a correct contingency in their notes would appear to indicate that their increased output of human-noun responses was cognitively mediated. The absence of preverbalization performance gains would appear particularly difficult to explain by the use of learning theories which ascribe automatic trans-situational reinforcing effects to verbal stimuli.

Although it was possible, according to a cognitive theoretical interpretation of verbal conditioning, for aware subjects in DeNike's study to give essentially 100% human-noun responses on each postawareness word block, it may be noted in Figure 19–1 that the mean number of such responses given by these subjects never exceeded 35%. Interview data obtained by DeNike after the conclusion of the conditioning task revealed some aware subjects for whom the reinforcing stimulus had no incentive value, and these subjects failed to show performance gains (DeNike, 1965). In contrast, aware subjects who reported that they wanted to receive reinforcement showed a marked increase in their output of human nouns on postawareness word blocks. In the next study to be reported, a uniformly high level of motivation to receive reinforcement was induced during conditioning in all subjects.

Experiment II. Using similar conditioning procedures to those described for Experiment I, female college students were reinforced with "Mmm-hmm" for giving human-noun responses (Spielberger, Bernstein, & Ratliff, 1966). Also, as in Experiment I, awareness of a correct response-reinforcement contingency was evaluated from the thoughts about the experiment (notes) which subjects recorded after each word block. However, the procedures differed from those of the previous experiment in that, between the seventh and eighth reinforced word blocks of the conditioning task, each subject was told: "As you may have noted, there is a rule under which I say 'Mmm-hmm.' Try to act on that rule so as to make me say 'Mmm-hmm' as often as you can." The purpose of this instruction was to increase the incentive value of the reinforcing stimulus. Immediately after conditioning a different experimenter conducted an interview which checked on the incentive manipulation and provided additional data on subjects' awareness.

The notes which subjects recorded during conditioning were rated by two judges who had no contact with the subjects nor any knowledge of their performance on the conditioning task. The judges agreed perfectly in classifying each subject as either aware or unaware of a correct contingency. For the subjects rated aware, the judges also indicated the word block on which a correct contingency was first reported. Those subjects who recorded a correct contingency prior to the incentive-inducing instruction were designated the Aware-Pre Group; those who did so subsequent to this instruction were designated the Aware-Post Group; subjects who failed to record a correct contingency during conditioning were called the Unaware Group. The mean percentage of human-noun responses given by the three groups in the operant blocks and the reinforced blocks prior to the incentive-inducing instruction are given in Figure 19–2A in which the Aware-Pre Group's conditioning data have been Vincentized. Statistical analyses of these data indicated that: (a) The three groups did not differ during the operant blocks; (b) the performance gains of the Aware-Pre Group first occurred on the word block on which these subjects first recorded a correct contingency; and (c) the Aware-Post and Unaware Groups failed to show performance gains. Thus, prior to the incentive-inducing instruction, aware and unaware subjects performed much as did their counterparts in DeNike's study (see Figure 19–1).

Data obtained in the postconditioning interview indicated that the instruction to try to make the experimenter say "Mmm-hmm" had the desired effect on the subjects' motivation to receive reinforcement. Almost all the subjects indicated that, as a consequence of the instruction, they wanted more for the experimenter to say "Mmm-hmm," and they tried harder to make him say it. The performance of the Aware-Pre, the Aware-Post, and Unaware Groups in the word blocks subsequent to the instruction are indicated in Figure 19–2B. The immediate marked increase in the number of human nouns given by the Aware-Pre Group on Block 8 suggested that the incentive manipulation increased the motivation of these subjects to receive reinforcement and that their prior awareness of a correct contingency permitted them at once to give more human-noun responses. The somewhat less marked increase in human nouns for the Aware-Post Group subsequent to the instruction may be interpreted as indicating that these subjects, most of whom recorded a correct contingency in their notes on Block 8, had to become aware before heightened motivation induced by the instruction could influence their performance. Consistent with this interpretation, examination of the conditioning data for individual subjects in the Aware-Post Group revealed that initial performance increments tended to occur on the word block on which a correct contingency was first recorded.

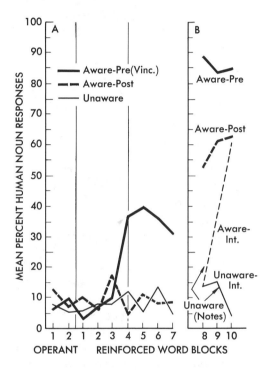

Figure 19.2 Conditioning curves. A, mean percentage of human-noun responses given by the *Aware-Pre, Aware-Post,* and *Unaware* groups on the operant word blocks and the reinforced word blocks prior to the incentive-inducing instruction. B, mean percentage of human-noun responses given by the *Aware-Pre, Aware-Post, Aware-Int.,* and *Unaware-Int.* groups on the word blocks subsequent to the incentive-inducing instruction. Adapted from Spielberger, et al. (1966).

The mean percentage of human-noun responses given by the Unaware Group increased gradually in the postinstruction word blocks, from 15% on Block 8 to 30% on Block 10 (not shown in Figure 19–2B), suggesting that these subjects conditioned without awareness. In order to evaluate this possibility further, the postconditioning interview protocols of all subjects who failed to record a correct contingency in their notes were examined by two judges who had neither contact with the subjects nor knowledge of their performance on the conditioning task. The judges agreed perfectly in rating approximately half of these subjects as aware of a correct contingency solely on the basis of their verbal reports in the interview.

The performance of subjects rated aware on the basis of their interview responses, but unaware on the basis of their notes (Aware-Int. Group), is compared, in Figure 19–2B, with the performance of subjects rated unaware on the basis of *both* their interview responses and their notes (Unaware-Int. Group). For the latter group, the output of human-noun responses subsequent to the instruction did not increase. Indeed, by the final word block, the number of human nouns given by the Unaware-Int. Group was below what it had been prior to the instruction. In contrast, the conditioning curve for the Aware-Int. Group showed a significant rise subsequent to the instruction, and performance increments for individual subjects tended to correspond with the word block on which they claimed they became aware. Furthermore, several of these subjects spontaneously reported that they had not recorded a correct response-reinforcement contingency in their notes because they did not become aware of it until the final word block and did not have sufficient confidence in their hypothesis to report it.

In sum, the findings in Experiments I and II are consistent with the hypothesis that "what is learned" in verbal conditioning is awareness of a correct response-reinforcement contingency. These findings would also appear to indicate that the reinforcing stimulus in verbal conditioning has both information and incentive value (Dulany, 1962), and that the latter influences the degree to which subjects who are aware of a correct contingency act on their awareness.

The findings in Experiments I and II would appear difficult to account for in terms of a theory which does not include a concept of awareness as a mediating cognitive state or process. In these investigations, only subjects who were judged to be aware of a correct response-reinforcement contingency showed performance gains, and these tended to correspond with the word block on which each aware subject first recorded a correct contingency.

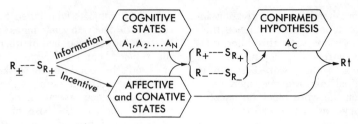

Figure 19.3 Schematic diagram indicating the hypothetical processes which are assumed to mediate performance gains in verbal conditioning for subjects who show "conditioning" effects.

III. AN ANALYSIS OF VERBAL CONDITIONING IN TERMS OF COGNITIVE CONCEPTS

The schematic diagram presented in Figure 19-3 reflects a general formulation of the sequence of hypothetical events which we believe mediate performance gains in verbal conditioning for subjects who show "conditioning" effects. The diagram is not intended to represent any particular cognitive theory in detail. Rather, it is offered to account for the findings of recent investigations of verbal conditioning, such as those described in Section II. A similar more detailed and sophisticated theoretical analysis of verbal conditioning has been recently advanced by Dulany (1962).

The temporal sequence of events in Figure 19-3 is from left to right. Those events which are merely temporally contiguous are indicated by dotted lines; presumed causal relationships between events are represented by solid arrows. The symbol R_+ indicates that in verbal conditioning the subject initially emits a variety of responses, some of which belong to the reinforced class, R_+, and some of which do not, R_-. These are followed respectively by reinforcement, S_{R+}, and nonreinforcement, S_{R-}, which convey differential information and provide differential incentive to the subject.

The information provided by the reinforcing stimulus gives rise to one or more cognitive states, represented as A_1, A_2, . . .

A_N. For example, the sequence of cognitive states developed by a subject in a word-naming verbal conditioning task might be: "The experimenter sometimes says 'good' after some of my words" (A_1); "Perhaps his saying 'good' depends on what words I say" (A_2); "Perhaps he wants me to figure out what words he is saying 'good' to, and give more of those" (A_3), etc. Depending upon the pattern and amount of reinforcement which they receive and recall, some subjects may be able to skip some of these early logical steps and go directly to a tentative formulation of the correct hypothesis, A_N: "Perhaps he is saying 'good' when I say words denoting people." We have observed that subjects who verbalize a correct hypothesis approach the experiment essentially as a problem-solving task. Furthermore, in verbal conditioning experiments in which subjects are given explicitly a problem-solving set, they proceed more directly to test out their hypotheses, and a larger proportion verbalize a correct contingency (DeNike & Spielberger, 1963; Spielberger & Levin, 1962).

Concurrent with the concept-formation activity involved in arriving at a correct hypothesis, subjects also develop affective and conative states based on the *incentive* provided by the reinforcing stimulus. For example, if the reinforcing stimulus has positive incentive value for a particular subject, he will *want* to receive reinforcement, and generally will *try* to elicit it from the experimenter. On the other hand, if the reinforcing stimulus has neutral or negative incentive value for the subject, he may be indifferent to it or attempt to avoid it (Mandler & Kaplan, 1956). Thus, the subject's affective and conative states in conjunction with his cognitive states (hypotheses) lead him to give responses, R_+, which he believes are in the reinforced response class, intermixed with a few responses, R_-, which are not expected to elicit reinforcement. Following these responses, the selective administration of the reinforcing stimulus, S_{R+}, or the absence of the reinforcing stimulus, S_{R-}, either confirms the subject's hypothesis, A_C, or leads him to modify it. The confirmed hypothesis, if accompanied by appropriate affective and conative states, results in increased output of the reinforced response class, $R \uparrow$.

It should be noted that the schematic diagram in Figure 19-3 massively oversimplifies our view of verbal conditioning. In it, we have treated affective and conative states as essentially constant and independent of cognitive states; there is much reason to suspect that these fluctuate and interact with the subjects' hypotheses. We have diagramed the process for the successful subject and ignored the numerous blind alleys explored by both successful and unsuccessful subjects; such processes should receive consideration in any theory which claims completeness. The nature of the conditioning task, the status of the experimenter, the instructions given to the subject, the characteristics of the subject population—all of these have demonstrable influence on mediating states and performance in verbal conditioning. In the final section of this paper, the significance of the verbal conditioning paradigm for the more general question of human learning without awareness will be considered.

IV. VERBAL CONDITIONING AND THE QUESTION OF LEARNING WITHOUT AWARENESS

Few persons doubt that behavior occurs without awareness, as in, for example, shifting gears, fingernail biting, facial tics, etc. (Eriksen, 1960). Of theoretical interest, however, is the extent to which such behaviors are initially *learned* without the mediation of cognitive processes. Kimble (1962) has suggested that the question of whether learning without awareness is possible may not have the same answer for all forms of learning. In classical eyelid conditioning, according to Kimble, it would appear that the subject need only be aware of the unconditioned stimulus for learning to take place.

In verbal conditioning, the evidence for learning without awareness reported in early experiments (e.g., Cohen et al., 1954; Greenspoon, 1955; Taffel, 1955) now appears suspect because of shortcomings in the evaluation of awareness in these studies. In recent experiments in which awareness was more carefully and thoroughly assessed (e.g., DeNike, 1964; Dulany, 1961, 1962; Spielberger, 1962), the absence of learning-without-awareness effects all but compels the conclusion that performance gains in verbal conditioning are consciously mediated. However, for the reasons indicated below, the verbal conditioning paradigm may not provide an appropriate framework for clarifying the more general question of whether human operant learning can occur without awareness.

Subject Vigilance

Most subjects in psychological experiments, as Orne (1962) has pointed out, tend to be alert to manipulations that the experimenter may impose upon them and vigilant vis-à-vis their own behavior. In almost all verbal conditioning research, the subject is aware that he is participating in a psychological experiment. Thus, subjects in verbal conditioning experiments ordinarily notice the reinforcing stimulus and attempt to ascribe some meaning to it, making learning without awareness unlikely.

Response Monitoring

Despite reinforcement and no admonition to the contrary, reinforced words are rarely repeated in word-naming verbal conditioning tasks. This almost universal tendency not to repeat words would be difficult to explain by automatic reinforcement theories. When asked why they did not repeat reinforced words, subjects usually indicate that they believed they were supposed to give a variety of words. It would appear that the subject keeps both his past responses and their consequences in mind and monitors new responses according to his hypotheses about the experiment. Thus, on the assumption that selective responding is guided by response monitoring in accordance with the subjects' hypotheses, the tendency not to repeat reinforced words in verbal conditioning becomes understandable, and learning without awareness seems improbable.

Response Sets

Some subjects approach verbal conditioning with a problem-solving set, while others interpret the conditioning task as either a personality test or an attempt to make them "conform." When a problem-solving set is combined with response monitoring in a vigilant subject, the subject notices the reinforcing stimulus, proceeds to test out successive hypotheses about the experiment, and is likely to become aware of a correct or correlated response-reinforcement contingency. In contrast, subjects with a personality-test set may get so involved in their free associations (on a word-naming verbal conditioning task) that they are oblivious to the reinforcing stimulus or tend to regard it as annoying and disruptive. Other subjects with personality-test sets devote considerable effort to the selection of "innocuous" or "unrevealing" words or otherwise defensively edit their responses so that they will not reveal personal secrets or shortcomings. Subjects who believe the experimenter is attempting to manipulate their behavior often report that they deliberately ignored the reinforcing stimulus or tried to avoid it. Thus, while a "conformity" or "personality" interpreta-

tion of the verbal conditioning task tends to prevent learning without awareness by causing subjects to ignore or avoid the reinforcing stimulus and/or to perceive it as unpleasant, a problem-solving approach tends to preclude learning without awareness by making it easier for the subjects to become aware.

The foregoing analysis of the "demand characteristics" (Orne, 1962) of verbal operant conditioning suggests that it is unlikely that learning without awareness will be found in laboratory experiments which employ the methods traditionally associated with the verbal conditioning paradigm. Under such conditions, it might be expected on a priori grounds that subjects will be particularly vigilant about their own verbal responses which are likely to be more carefully monitored than most other behavior. Or, in Eriksen's (1960) words, ". . . any situation where the cues and the reinforcements are salient enough to produce learning, will not escape detection by awareness [p. 298]."

It would appear more plausible to seek evidence of learning without awareness in situations where subjects are not aware that they are participating in a psychological experiment and on tasks which do not induce intensive response monitoring or defensive response sets. A likely place to look for such evidence might be in settings where subjects are motivated not to be aware, as, for example, in experimental situations involving processes such as repression, dissonance reduction, conformity, and ingratiation. At present, only scattered attempts have been made to investigate human operant learning with research designs representative of some of the forenamed conditions (e.g., Centers, 1963; Gergen, 1965; Goldiamond, 1965; Hefferline, Keenan, & Harford, 1959; Kimmel & Baxter, 1964; Verplanck, 1956; Vogel-Sprott, 1964). In such studies, however, the role of awareness has ordinarily not been the focus of investigation, and, consequently, the methods employed to assess awareness are subject to the criticisms discussed earlier. Therefore, where learning-without-awareness effects have been found, little confidence may be placed in such results. This in no way implies that human operant learning cannot take place without awareness, but merely affirms Adams' (1957) observation that such learning has not been demonstrated convincingly in the laboratory.

Some Final Considerations

We have endeavored in this paper to compare the relative adequacy with which descriptive behaviorism and cognitive learning theory can account for the findings of verbal operant conditioning experiments. We have argued that the descriptive behaviorists' implicit rejection of awareness as a concept has had serious methodological consequences which have retarded the convergence of empirical findings and the development of adequate theory. We have also contended that the utilization of awareness as a systematic concept has led to experimental findings which the Skinnerian approach would not have predicted. Finally, we have presented evidence to support the view that the reinforcing stimulus in verbal conditioning has both information and incentive value and that "what is learned" in verbal conditioning is awareness of a correct (or correlated) response-reinforcement contingency.

With respect to whether human operant learning can occur without awareness, it should be noted that although this question would appear to have an empirical answer, in verbal conditioning the answer turns out to be inextricably tied to an investigator's theoretical orientation and, more fundamentally, to his epistemological assumptions concerning awareness as a concept (Spielberger, 1962, 1965). The issue is further complicated by the fact that different learning theories imply different operational definitions of the learned response (Campbell, 1954), leading in verbal conditioning to the collection of noncomparable data and to fruitless theoretical controversy. This controversy, which revolves about the role of awareness in verbal conditioning, is reminiscent of earlier disagreements among S–R and cognitive theorists concerning the role of reinforcement in learning. It has since been recognized that much of the controversy and confusion with respect to reinforcement stemmed from the failure of learning theorists to differentiate conceptually between the law of effect as an empirical statement and as a general theory of reinforcement (Spence, 1951).

On an empirical level, most would agree with the observation that performance in a variety of tasks is facilitated by reinforcement, but S–R and cognitive learning theories are still sharply divided on the question of whether reinforcement is required for learning to take place. Similarly, it is generally accepted that performance will be facilitated by the presence of appropriate cognitive states; that is, an "empirical law of cognition" is as supportable as the empirical law of effect,[2] but whether cognitive processes mediate any and all forms of learning is as dubious as a general theory of reinforcement. Thus, while a "theoretical law of cognition" might well serve to explain the findings in verbal conditioning experiments with human adults, it is quite another matter to demonstrate the role of cognitive processes in the learning of animals and preverbal children.

Nevertheless, the careful investigation of subjects' awareness in relation to other behavior is, we believe, requisite to the development of an adequate theory of human learning. Progress in this direction will depend upon the general acceptance of experimental procedures which permit sensitive evaluation of cognitive processes. These procedures must surely include subjects' verbal reports and must provide nec-

[2] We are grateful to Donald L. Thistlethwaite for suggesting the analogy between an empirical law of cognition in verbal conditioning and the empirical law of effect in traditional discussions of learning theory.

essary safeguards against biasing or distorting such reports. Furthermore, it must be clearly recognized that the validity of verbal reports in any experimental context rests upon the willingness and linguistic competence of subjects to describe their mediating states when properly questioned (Dulany, 1961), and that verbal reports are but imperfectly related to the subjects' internal states (Eriksen, 1960). Paradoxically, perhaps the most significant contribution of verbal conditioning research has been the stimulation of interest in verbal report procedures and in concepts such as awareness among psychologists who are inclined to insist that thoughts and ideas are beyond the limits of scientific inquiry.

REFERENCES

ADAMS, J. K. Laboratory studies of behavior without awareness. *Psychological Bulletin,* 1957, **54,** 383–405.

CAMPBELL, D. T. Operational delineation of "what is learned" via the tranposition experiment. *Psychological Review,* 1954, **61,** 167–174.

CAMPBELL, D. T. Social attitudes and other acquired behavioral dispositions. In S. Koch (Ed.), *Psychology: A study of a science.* Vol. 6. New York: McGraw-Hill, 1963. Pp. 94–172.

CENTERS, R. A. Laboratory adaptation of the conversational procedure for the conditioning of verbal operants. *Journal of Abnormal and Social Psychology,* 1963, **67,** 334–339.

COHEN, B. D., KALISH, H. I., THURSTON, J. R., & COHEN, E. Experimental manipulation of verbal behavior. *Journal of Experimental Psychology,* 1954, **47,** 106–110.

DeNIKE, L. D. The temporal relationship between awareness and performance in verbal conditioning. *Journal of Experimental Psychology,* 1964, **68,** 521–529.

DeNIKE, L. D. Recall of reinforcement and conative activity in verbal conditioning. *Psychological Reports,* 1965, **16,** 345–346.

DeNIKE, L. D., & SPIELBERGER, C. D. Induced mediating states in verbal conditioning. *Journal of Verbal Learning and Verbal Behavior,* 1963, **1,** 339–345.

DULANY, D. E. Hypotheses and habits in verbal "operant conditioning." *Journal of Abnormal and Social Psychology,* 1961, **63,** 251–263.

DULANY, D. E. The place of hypotheses and intentions: An analysis of verbal control in verbal conditioning. In C. W. Eriksen (Ed.), *Behavior and awareness.* Durham: Duke University Press, 1962. Pp. 102–129.

ERIKSEN, C. W. Discrimination and learning without awareness: A methodological survey and evaluation. *Psychological Review,* 1960, **67,** 279–300.

FARBER, I. E. The things people say to themselves. *American Psychologist,* 1963, **18,** 185–197.

GERGEN, K. J. The effects of interaction goals and personalistic feedback on the presentation of self. *Journal of Personality and Social Psychology,* 1965, **1,** 413–424.

GOLDIAMOND, I. Stuttering and fluency as manipulable operant response classes. In L. Krasner & L. P. Ullmann (Eds.), *Research in behavior modification: New developments and their clinical implications.* New York: Holt, Rinehart, & Winston, 1965. Pp. 106–156.

GREENSPOON, J. The reinforcing effect of two spoken sounds on the frequency of two responses. *American Journal of Psychology,* 1955. **68,** 409–416.

HEFFERLINE, R. F., KEENAN, B., & HARFORD, R. A. Escape and avoidance conditioning in human subjects without their observation of the response. *Science,* 1959, **130,** 1338–1339.

KIMBLE, G. A. Classical conditioning and the problem of awareness. In C. W. Eriksen (Ed.), *Behavior and awareness.* Durham: Duke University Press, 1962. Pp. 27–45.

KIMMEL, H. D., & BAXTER, R. Avoidance conditioning of the GSR. *Journal of Experimental Psychology,* 1964, **68,** 482–485.

KRIECKHAUS, E. E., & ERIKSEN, C. W. A study of awareness and its effect on learning and generalization. *Journal of Personality,* 1960, **28,** 503–517.

MANDLER, G., & KAPLAN, W. K. Subjective evaluation and reinforcing effect of a verbal stimulus. *Science,* 1956, **124,** 582–583.

MATARAZZO, J. D., SASLOW, G., & PAREIS, E. N. Verbal conditioning of two response classes: Some methodological considerations. *Journal of Abnormal and Social Psychology,* 1960, **61,** 190–206.

MUNN, N. L. *Handbook of psychological research on the rat: An introduction to animal psychology.* Boston: Houghton Mifflin, 1950.

ORNE, M. T. On the social psychology of the psychological experiment: With particular reference to demand characteristics and their implications. *American Psychologist,* 1962, **17,** 776–783.

PHILBRICK, E. B., & POSTMAN, L. A further analysis of "learning without awareness." *American Journal of Psychology,* 1955, **68,** 417–424.

POSTMAN, L., & JARRETT, R. F. The experimental analysis of "learning without awareness." *American Journal of Psychology,* 1952, **65,** 244–255.

ROSENTHAL, R. On the social psychology of the psychological experiment: The experimenter's hypothesis as unintended determinant of experimental results. *American Scientist,* 1963, **51,** 268–283.

SASSENRATH, J. M. Learning without awareness and transfer of learning sets. *Journal of Educational Psychology,* 1959, **50,** 205–212.

SIDOWSKI, J. B. Influence of awareness of reinforcement on verbal conditioning. *Journal of Experimental Psychology,* 1954, **48,** 355–360.

SKINNER, B. F. *The behavior of organisms: An experimental analysis.* New York: Appleton-Century-Crofts, 1938.

SKINNER, B. F. *Verbal behavior.* New York: Appleton-Century-Crofts, 1957.

SKINNER, B. F. Behaviorism at fifty. *Science,* 1963, **140,** 951–958. (a)

SKINNER, B. F. Operant behavior. *American Psychologist,* 1963, **18,** 503–515. (b)

SPENCE, K. W. Theoretical interpretations of learning. In S. S. Stevens (Ed.), *Handbook of experimental psychology.* New York: Wiley, 1951. Pp. 690–729.

SPIELBERGER, C. D. The role of awareness in verbal conditioning. In C. W. Eriksen (Ed.), *Behaviorism and awareness.* Durham: Duke University Press, 1962. Pp. 73–101.

SPIELBERGER, C. D. Theoretical and epistemological issues in verbal conditioning. In S. Rosenberg (Ed.), *Directions in psycholinguistics.* New York: Macmillan, 1965. Pp. 149–200.

SPIELBERGER, C. D., BERNSTEIN, I. H., & RATLIFF, R. G. Information and incentive value of the reinforcing stimulus in verbal conditioning. *Journal of Experimental Psychology,* 1966, **71,** 26–31.

SPIELBERGER, C. D., & DeNIKE, L. D. Implicit epistemological bias and the problem of awareness in verbal conditioning: A reply to Greenspoon. *Psychological Reports,* 1963, **12,** 103–106.

SPIELBERGER, C. D., DeNIKE, L. D., & STEIN, L. S. Anxiety and verbal conditioning. *Journal of Personality and Social Psychology,* 1965, **1,** 229–239.

SPIELBERGER, C. D., & LEVIN, S. M. What is learned in verbal conditioning? *Journal of Verbal Learning and Verbal Behavior,* 1962, **1,** 125–132.

TAFFEL, C. Anxiety and the conditioning of verbal behavior. *Journal of Abnormal and Social Psychology,* 1955, **51,** 496–501.

VERPLANCK, W. S. The operant conditioning of human motor behavior. *Psychological Bulletin,* 1956, **53,** 70–83.

VOGEL-SPROTT, M. E. Response generalization under verbal conditioning in alcoholics, delinquents, and students. *Behaviour Research and Therapy,* 1964, **2,** 135–141.

MEMORY AND FORGETTING

20. Interference and Forgetting *

Benton J. Underwood

The relatively permanent changes in behavior that occur as a consequence of experience demonstrate beyond question that animals *retain* and *utilize* information acquired through learning—in short, animals have memories. Although the concepts of learning and memory may seem essentially interdependent, analysis of underlying processes is facilitated by drawing a logical distinction between the two concepts. Learning emphasizes the process of response acquisition, and the variable of major importance is the number of trials or experiences required to reach some performance level. Memory emphasizes the storage and recovery of responses; the major variables are time and the events which intervene between learning trials.

Research on memory, then, is concerned with the fate of responses that have been previously learned. The most obvious fact for which a theory of memory must account is that forgetting occurs—many new responses enter the system, yet only a few survive. One major theoretical formulation explains the loss of these responses in terms of "interference." In this view, the response or memory trace does not simply evaporate over time—rather, its integrity is destroyed by the interference result-

* Reprinted by permission of the author and the American Psychological Association from the *Psychological Review,* 1957, *64,* 49-60.

ing from other contemporaneous memories. The next selection, by Professor Underwood, describes some of the major variables which influence the interference process.

I know of no one who seriously maintains that interference among tasks is of no consequence in the production of forgetting.[1] Whether forgetting is conceptualized at a strict psychological level or at a neural level (e.g., neural memory trace), some provision is made for interference to account for at least some of the measured forgetting. The many studies on retroactive inhibition are probably responsible for this general agreement that interference among tasks must produce a sizable proportion of forgetting. By introducing an interpolated interfering task very marked decrements in recall can be produced in a few minutes in the laboratory. But there is a second generalization which has resulted from these studies, namely, that most forgetting must be a function of the learning of tasks which interfere with that which has already been learned (19). Thus, if a single task is learned in the laboratory and retention measured after a week, the loss has been attributed to the interference from activities learned outside the laboratory during the week. It is this generalization with which I am concerned in the initial portions of this paper.

Now, I cannot deny the data which show large amounts of forgetting produced by an interpolated list in a few minutes in the laboratory. Nor do I deny that this loss may be attributed to interference. But I will try to show that use of retroactive inhibition as a paradigm of forgetting (via interference) may be seriously questioned. To be more specific: if a subject learns a single task, such as a list of words, and retention of this task is measured after a day, a week, or a month, I will try to show that very little of the forgetting can be attributed to an interfering task learned outside the laboratory during the retention interval. Before pursuing this further, I must make some general comments by way of preparation.

Whether we like it or not, the experimental study of forgetting has been largely dominated by the Ebbinghaus tradition, both in terms of methods and materials used. I do not think this is due to sheer perversity on the part of several generations of scientists interested in forgetting. It may be noted that much of our elementary knowledge can be obtained only by rote learning. To work with rote learning does not mean that we are thereby not concerning ourselves with phenomena that have no counterparts outside the laboratory. Furthermore, the investigation of these phenomena can be handled by methods which are acceptable to a science. As is well known, there are periodic verbal revolts against the Ebbinghaus tradition (e.g., 2, 15, 22). But for some reason nothing much ever happens in the laboratory as a consequence of these revolts. I mention these matters neither by way of apology nor of justification for having done some research in rote learning, but for two other reasons. First, it may very well be true, as some have suggested (e.g., 22), that studies of memory in the Ebbinghaus tradition are not getting at all of the important phenomena of memory. I think the same statement—that research has not got at all of the important processes—could be made about all areas in psychology; so that the criticism (even if just) should not be indigenous to the study of memory. Science does not deal at will with all natural events. Science deals with natural events only when ingenuity in developing methods and techniques of measurement allow these events to be brought within the scope of science. If, therefore, the studies of mem-

[1] Address of the president, Midwestern Psychological Association, St. Louis, Missouri, May, 1956. Most of the data from my own research referred to in this paper were obtained from work done under Contract N7 onr-45008, Project NR 154-057, between Northwestern University and The Office of Naval Research.

ory which meet scientific acceptability do not tap all-important memorial processes, all I can say is that this is the state of the science in the area at the moment. Secondly, because the bulk of the systematic data on forgetting has been obtained on rote-learned tasks, I must of necessity use such data in discussing interference and forgetting.

Returning to the experimental situation, let me again put in concrete form the problem with which I first wish to deal. A subject learns a single task, such as a list of syllables, nouns, or adjectives. After an interval of time, say, 24 hours, his retention of this list is measured. The explanatory problem is what is responsible for the forgetting which commonly occurs over the 24 hours. As indicated earlier, the studies of retroactive inhibition led to the theoretical generalization that this forgetting was due largely to interference from other tasks learned during the 24-hour retention interval. McGeoch (20) came to this conclusion, his last such statement being made in 1942. I would, therefore, like to look at the data which were available to McGeoch and others interested in this matter. I must repeat that the kind of data with which I am concerned is the retention of a list without formal interpolated learning introduced. The interval of retention with which I am going to deal in this, and several subsequent analyses, is 24 hours.

First, of course, Ebbinghaus' data were available and in a sense served as the reference point for many subsequent investigations. In terms of percentage saved in relearning, Ebbinghaus showed about 65 per cent loss over 24 hours (7). In terms of recall after 24 hours, the following studies are representative of the amount forgotten: Youtz, 88 per cent loss (37); Luh, 82 per cent (18); Krueger, 74 per cent (16); Hovland, 78 per cent (11); Cheng, 65 per cent and 84 per cent (6); Lester, 65 per cent (17). Let us assume as a rough average of these studies that 75 per cent forgetting was measured over 24 hours. In

all of these studies the list was learned to one perfect trial. The percentage values were derived by dividing the total number of items in the list into the number lost and changing to a percentage. Thus, on the average in these studies, if the subject learned a 12-item list and recalled three of these items after 24 hours, nine items (75 per cent) were forgotten.

The theory of interference as advanced by McGeoch, and so far as I know never seriously challenged, was that during the 24-hour interval subjects learned something outside the laboratory which interfered with the list learned in the laboratory. Most of the materials involved in the investigations cited above were nonsense syllables, and the subjects were college students. While realizing that I am viewing these results in the light of data which McGeoch and others did not have available, it seems to me to be an incredible stretch of an interference hypothesis to hold that this 75 per cent forgetting was caused by something which the subjects learned outside the laboratory during the 24-hour interval. Even if we agree with some educators that much of what we teach our students in college is nonsense, it does not seem to be the kind of learning that would interfere with nonsense syllables.

If, however, this forgetting was not due to interference from tasks learned outside the laboratory during the retention interval, to what was it due? I shall try to show that most of this forgetting was indeed produced by interference—not from tasks learned outside the laboratory, but from tasks learned previously in the laboratory. Following this I will show that when interference from laboratory tasks is removed, the amount of forgetting which occurs is relatively quite small. It then becomes more plausible that this amount could be produced by interference from tasks learned outside the laboratory, although, as I shall also point out, the interference very likely comes from prior, not interpolated, learning.

In 1950 a study was published by Mrs. Greenberg and myself (10) on retention as a function of stage of practice. The orientation for this study was crassly empirical; we simply wanted to know if subjects learn how to recall in the same sense that they learn how to learn. In the conditions with which I am concerned, naive subjects learned a list of ten paired adjectives to a criterion of eight out of ten correct on a single trial. Forty-eight hours later this list was recalled. On the following day, these same subjects learned a new list to the same criterion and recalled it after 48 hours. This continued for two additional lists, so that the subjects had learned and recalled four lists, but the learning and recall of each list was complete before another list was learned. There was low similarity among these lists as far as conventional symptoms of similarity are concerned. No words were repeated and no obvious similarities existed, except for the fact that they were all adjectives and a certain amount of similarity among prefixes, suffixes, and so on must inevitably occur. The recall of these four successive lists is shown in Fig. 20-1.

As can be seen, the more lists that are learned, the poorer the recall, from 69 per cent recall of the first list to 25 per cent recall of the fourth list. In examining errors at recall, we found a sufficient number of intrusion responses from previous lists to lead us to suggest that the increasing decrements in recall were a function of proactive interference from previous lists. And, while we pointed out that these results had implications for the design of experiments on retention, the relevance to an interference theory of forgetting was not mentioned.

Dr. E. J. Archer has made available to me certain data from an experiment which still is in progress and which deals with this issue. Subjects learned lists of 12 serial adjectives to one perfect trial and recalled them after 24 hours. The recall of a list always took place prior to learning the next list. The results for nine succes-

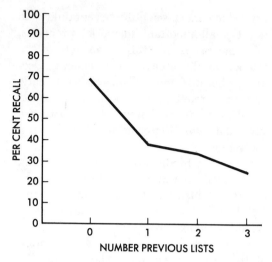

Figure 20.1 Recall of paired adjectives as a function of number of previous lists learned (10).

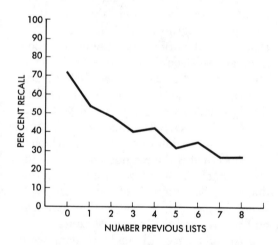

Figure 20.2 Recall of serial adjective lists as a function of number of previous lists learned. Unpublished data, courtesy of Dr. E. J. Archer.

sive lists are shown in Fig. 20-2. Let me say again that there is no laboratory activity during the 24-hour interval; the subject learns a list, is dismissed from the laboratory, and returns after 24 hours to recall the list. The percentage of recall falls from 71 per cent for the first list to 27 per cent for the ninth.

In summarizing the more classical data on retention above, I indicated that a rough estimate showed that after 24 hours 75 per cent forgetting took place, or recall was about 25 per cent correct. In viewing these values in the light of Greenberg's and Archer's findings, the conclusion seemed inescapable that the classical studies must have been dealing with subjects who had learned many lists. That is to say, the subjects must have served in many conditions by use of counterbalancing and repeated cycles. To check on this I have made a search of the literature on the studies of retention to see if systematic data could be compiled on this matter. Preliminary work led me to establish certain criteria for inclusion in the summary to be presented. First, because degree of learning is such an important variable, I have included only those studies in which degree of learning was one perfect recitation of the

list. Second, I have included only studies in which retention was measured after 24 hours. Third, I have included only studies in which recall measures were given. (Relearning measures add complexities with which I do not wish to deal in this paper.) Fourth, the summary includes only material learned by relatively massed practice. Finally, if an investigator had two or more conditions which met these criteria, I averaged the values presentation in this paper. Except for these restrictions, I have used all studies I found (with an exception to be noted later), although I do not pretend to have made an exhaustive search. From each of these studies I got two facts: first, the percentage recalled after 24 hours, and second, the average number of previous lists the subjects had learned before learning the list on which recall after 24 hours was taken. Thus, if a subject had served in five experimental conditions via counter-

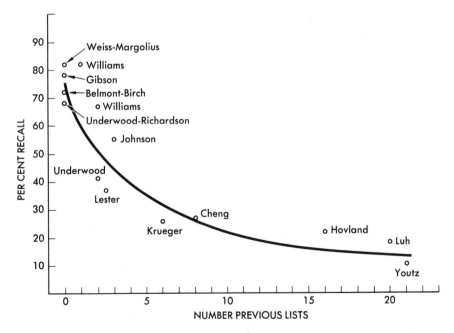

Figure 20.3 Recall as a function of number of previous lists learned as determined from a number of studies. From left to right: Weiss and Margolius (35), Gibson (9), Belmont and Birch (3), Underwood and Richardson (33), Williams (36), Underwood (27, 28, 29, 30), Lester (17), Johnson (14), Krueger (16), Cheng (6), Hovland (11), Luh (18), Youtz (37).

balancing, and had been given two practice lists, the average number of lists learned before learning the list for which I tabulated the recall was four. This does not take into account any previous experiments in rote learning in which the subject might have served.

For each of these studies the two facts, average number of previous lists learned and percentage of recall, are related as in Fig. 20-3. For example, consider the study by Youtz. This study was concerned with Jost's law, and had several degrees of learning, several lengths of retention interval, and the subjects served in two cycles. Actually, there were 15 experimental conditions and each subject was given each condition twice. Also, each subject learned six practice lists before starting the experimental conditions. Among the 15 conditions was one in which the learning of the syllables was carried to one perfect recitation and recall was taken after 24 hours. It is this particular condition in which I am interested. On the average, this condition would have been given at the time when the subject had learned six practice lists and 15 experimental lists, for a total of 21 previous lists.

The studies included in Fig. 20-3 have several different kinds of materials, from geometric forms to nonsense syllables to nouns; they include both paired-associate and serial presentation, with different speeds of presentation and different lengths of lists. But I think the general relationship is clear. The greater the number of previous lists learned the greater the forgetting. I interpret this to mean that the greater the number of previous lists the greater the *proactive* interference. We know this to be true (26) for a formal proactive-inhibition paradigm; it seems a reasonable interpretation for the data of Fig. 20-3. That there are minor sources of variances still involved I do not deny. Some of the variation can be rationalized, but that is not the purpose of this report. The point I wish to make is the obvious one

of the relationship between number of previous lists learned—lists which presumably had no intentionally built-in similarity —and amount of forgetting. If you like to think in correlational terms, the rank-order correlation between the two variables is —.91 for the 14 points of Fig. 20-3.

It may be of interest to the historian that, of the studies published before 1942 which met the criteria I imposed, I did not find a single one in which subjects had not been given at least one practice task before starting experimental conditions, and in most cases the subjects had several practice lists and several experimental conditions. Gibson's study (1942) was the first I found in which subjects served in only one condition and were not given practice tasks. I think it is apparent that the design proclivities of the 1920s and 1930s have been largely responsible for the exaggerated picture we have had of the rate of forgetting of rote-learned materials. On the basis of studies performed during the 1920s and 1930s, I have given a rough estimate of forgetting as being 75 per cent over 24 hours, recall being 25 per cent. On the basis of modern studies in which the subject has learned no previous lists—where there is no proactive inhibition from previous laboratory tasks—a rough estimate would be that forgetting is 25 per cent; recall is 75 per cent. The values are reversed. (If in the above and subsequent discussion my use of percentage values as if I were dealing with a cardinal or extensive scale is disturbing, I will say only that it makes the picture easier to grasp, and in my opinion no critical distortion results.)

Before taking the next major step, I would like to point out a few other observations which serve to support my general point that proactive inhibition from laboratory tasks has been the major cause of forgetting in the more classical studies. The first illustration I shall give exemplifies the point that when subjects have served in several conditions, forgetting after relatively short periods of time is greater than after

24 hours if the subject has served in only one condition. In the Youtz study to which I have already referred, other conditions were employed in which recall was taken after short intervals. After 20 minutes recall was 74 per cent, about what it is after 24 hours if the subject has not served in a series of conditions. After two hours recall was 32 per cent. In Ward's (34) well-known reminiscence experiment, subjects who on the average had learned ten previous lists showed a recall of only 64 per cent after 20 minutes.

In the famous Jenkins-Dallenbach (13) study on retention following sleep and following waking, two subjects were used. One subject learned a total of 61 lists and the other 62 in addition to several practice lists. Roughly, then, if the order of the conditions was randomized, approximately 30 lists had been learned prior to the learning of a list for a given experimental condition. Recall after eight waking hours for one subject was 4 per cent and for the other 14 per cent. Even after sleeping for eight hours the recall was only 55 per cent and 58 per cent.

I have said that an interpolated list can produce severe forgetting. However, in one study (1), using the A-B, A-C paradigm for original and interpolated learning, but using subjects who had never served in any previous conditions, recall of the original list was 46 per cent after 48 hours, and in another comparable study (24), 42 per cent. Thus, the loss is not nearly as great as in the classical studies I have cited where there was no interpolated learning in the laboratory.

My conclusion at this point is that, in terms of the gross analysis I have made, the amount of forgetting which might be attributed to interference from tasks learned outside the laboratory has been "reduced" from 75 per cent to about 25 per cent. I shall proceed in the next section to see if we have grounds for reducing this estimate still more. In passing on to this section, however, let me say that the study of fac-

tors which influence proactive inhibition in these counterbalanced studies is a perfectly legitimate and important area of study. I mention this because in the subsequent discussion I am going to deal only with the case where a subject has learned a single list in the laboratory, and I do not want to leave the impression that we should now and forevermore drop the study of interference produced by previous laboratory tasks. Indeed, as will be seen shortly, it is my opinion that we should increase these studies for the simple reason that the proactive paradigm provides a more realistic one than does the retroactive paradigm.

When the subject learns and recalls a single list in the laboratory, I have given an estimate of 25 per cent as being the amount forgotten over 24 hours. When, as shown above, we calculate percentage forgotten of lists learned to one perfect trial, the assumption is that had the subjects been given an immediate recall trial, the list would have been perfectly recalled. This, of course, is simply not true. The major factor determining how much error is introduced by this criterion-percentage method is probably the difficulty of the task. In general, the overestimation of forgetting by the percentage method will be directly related to the difficulty of the task. Thus, the more slowly the learning approaches a given criterion, the greater the drop on the trial immediately after the criterion trial. Data from a study by Runquist (24), using eight paired adjectives (a comparatively easy task), shows that amount of forgetting is overestimated by about 10 per cent. In a study (32) using very difficult consonant syllables, the overestimation was approximately 20 per cent. To be conservative, assume that on the average the percentage method of reporting recall overestimates the amount forgotten by 10 per cent. If we subtract this from the 25 per cent assumed above, the forgetting is now re-estimated as being 15 per cent over 24 hours. That is to say, an interference theory, or any other form of theory, has to account for a very small amount of forgetting as compared with the amount traditionally cited.

What are the implications of so greatly "reducing" the amount of forgetting? There are at least three implications which I feel are worth pointing out. First, if one wishes to hold to an interference theory of forgetting (as I do), it seems plausible to assert that this amount of forgetting could be produced from learning which has taken place outside of the laboratory. Furthermore, it seems likely that such interference must result primarily from proactive interference. This seems likely on a simple probability basis. A 20-year-old college student will more likely have learned something during his 20 years prior to coming to the laboratory that will interfere with his retention than he will during the 24 hours between the learning and retention test. However, the longer the retention interval the more important will retroactive interference become relative to proactive interferences.

The second implication is that these data may suggest greater homogeneity or continuity in memorial processes than hitherto supposed. Although no one has adequately solved the measurement problem of how to make comparisons of retention among conditioned responses, prose material, motor tasks, concept learning, and rote-learned tasks, the gross comparisons have indicated that rote-learned tasks were forgotten much more rapidly than these other tasks. But the rote-learning data used for comparison have been those derived with the classical design in which the forgetting over 24 hours is approximately 75 per cent. If we take the revised estimate of 15 per cent, the discrepancies among tasks become considerably less.

The third implication of the revised estimate of rate of forgetting is that the number of variables which appreciably influence rate of forgetting must be sharply limited. While this statement does not in-

evitably follow from the analyses I have made, the current evidence strongly supports the statement. I want to turn to the final section of this paper which will consist of a review of the influence of some of the variables which are or have been thought to be related to rate of forgetting. In considering these variables, it is well to keep in mind that a variable which produces only a small difference in forgetting is important if one is interested in accounting for the 15 per cent assumed now as the loss over 24 hours. If appropriate for a given variable, I will indicate where it fits into an interference theory, although in no case will I endeavor to handle the details of such a theory.

Time

Passage of time between learning and recall is the critical defining variable for forgetting. Manipulation of this variable provides the basic data for which a theory must account. Previously, our conception of rate of forgetting as a function of time has been tied to the Ebbinghaus curve. If the analysis made earlier is correct, this curve does not give us the basic data we need. In short, we must start all over and derive a retention curve over time when the subjects have learned no previous materials in the laboratory. It is apparent that I expect the fall in this curve over time to be relatively small.

In conjunction with time as an independent variable, we must, in explanations of forgetting, consider why sleep retards the processes responsible for forgetting. My conception, which does not really explain anything, is that since forgetting is largely produced by proactive interference, the amount of time which a subject spends in sleep is simply to be subtracted from the total retention interval when predicting the amount to be forgotten. It is known that proactive interference increases with passage of time (5); sleep, I believe, brings to a standstill whatever these processes are which produce this increase.

Degree of Learning

We usually say that the better or stronger the learning the more or better the retention. Yet, we do not know whether or not the *rate* of forgetting differs for items of different strength. The experimental problem is a difficult one. What we need is to have a subject learn a single association and measure its decline in strength over time. But this is difficult to carry out with verbal material, since almost of necessity we must have the subject learn a series of associations, to make it a reasonable task. And, when a series of associations are learned, complications arise from interaction effects among associations of different strength. Nevertheless, we may expect, on the basis of evidence from a wide variety of studies, that given a constant degree of similarity, the effective interference varies as some function of the strength of associations.

Distribution of Practice

It is a fact that distribution of practice during acquisition influences retention of verbal materials. The facts of the case seem to be as follows. If the subject has not learned previous lists in the laboratory, massed practice gives equal or better retention than does distributed practice. If, on the other hand, the subject has learned a number of previous lists, distributed practice will facilitate retention (32). We do not have the theoretical solution to these facts. The point I wish to make here is that whether or not distribution of learning inhibits or facilitates retention depends upon the amount of interference from previous learning. It is reasonable to expect, therefore, that the solution to the problem will come via principles handling interference in general. I might also say that a theoretical solution to this problem will also provide a solution for Jost's laws.

Similarity

Amount of interference from other tasks is closely tied to similarity. This similarity must be conceived of as similarity among materials as such and also situational similarity (4). When we turn to similarity within a task, the situation is not quite so clear. Empirically and theoretically (8) one would expect that intratask similarity would be a very relevant variable in forgetting. As discussed elsewhere (31), however, variation in intratask similarity almost inevitably leads to variations in intertask similarity. We do know from a recent study (33) that with material of low meaningfulness forgetting is significantly greater with high intralist similarity than with low. While the difference in magnitude is only about 8 per cent, when we are trying to account for a total loss of 15 per cent, this amount becomes a major matter.

Meaningfulness

The belief has long been held that the more meaningful the material the better the retention—the less the forgetting. Osgood (21) has pointed out that if this is true it is difficult for an interference theory to handle. So far as I know, the only direct test of the influence of this variable is a recent study in which retention of syllables of 100 per cent association value was compared with that of zero association value (33). There was no difference in the recall of these syllables. Other less precise evidence would support this finding when comparisons are made among syllables, adjectives, and nouns, as plotted in Fig. 20–3. However, there is some evidence that materials of very low meaningfulness are forgotten more rapidly than nonsense syllables of zero association value. Consonant syllables, both serial (32) and paired associates (unpublished), show about 50 per cent loss over 24 hours. The study using serial lists was the one mentioned earlier as knowingly omitted from Fig. 20–3. These syllables, being extremely difficult to learn, allow a correction of about 20 per cent due to criterion overestimation, but even with this much correction the forgetting (30 per cent) is still appreciably more than the estimate we have made for other materials. To invoke the interference theory to account for this discrepancy means that we must demonstrate how interference from other activities could be greater for these consonant syllables than for nonsense syllables, nouns, adjectives, and other materials. Our best guess at the present time is that the sequences of letters in consonant syllables are contrary to other well-established language habits. That is to say, letter sequences which commonly occur in our language are largely different from those in consonant syllables. As a consequence, not only are these consonant syllables very difficult to learn, but forgetting is accelerated by proactive interference from previously well-learned letter sequences. If subsequent research cannot demonstrate such a source of interference, or if some other source is not specified, an interference theory for this case will be in some trouble.

Affectivity

Another task dimension which has received extensive attention is the affective tone of the material. I would also include here the studies attaching unpleasant experiences to some items experimentally and not to others, and measuring retention of these two sets of items. Freud is to a large extent responsible for these studies, but he cannot be held responsible for the malformed methodology which characterizes so many of them. What can one say by way of summarizing these studies? The only conclusion that I can reach is a statistical one, namely, that the occasional positive result found among the scores of studies is about as frequent as one would expect by sampling error, using the 5 per cent

level of confidence. Until a reliable body of facts is established for this variable and associated variables, no theoretical evaluation is possible.

Other Variables

As I have indicated earlier, I will not make an exhaustive survey of the variables which may influence rate of forgetting. I have limited myself to variables which have been rather extensively investigated, which have immediate relevance to the interference theory, or for which reliable relationships are available. Nevertheless, I would like to mention briefly some of these other variables. There is the matter of *warm-up* before recall; some investigators find that this reduces forgetting (12); others, under as nearly replicated conditions as is possible to obtain, do not (23). Some resolution must be found for these flat contradictions. It seems perfectly reasonable, however, that inadequate set or context differences could reduce recall. Indeed, an interference theory would predict this forgetting if the set or context stimuli are appreciably different from those prevailing at the time of learning. In our laboratory we try to reinstate the learning set by careful instructions, and we simply do not find decrements that might be attributed to inadequate set. For example, in a recent study (33) subjects were given a 24-hour recall of a serial list after learning to one perfect trial. I think we would expect that the first item in the list would suffer the greatest decrement due to inadequate set, yet this item showed only .7 per cent loss. But let it be clear that when we are attempting to account for the 15 per cent loss over 24 hours, we should not overlook any possible source for this loss.

Thus far I have not said anything about forgetting as a function of characteristics of the subject, that is, the personality or intellectual characteristics. As far as I have been able to determine, there is not a single valid study which shows that such variables have an appreciable influence on forgetting. Many studies have shown differences in learning as a function of these variables, but not differences in rate of forgetting. Surely there must be some such variables. We do know that if subjects are severely insulted, made to feel stupid, or generally led to believe that they have no justification for continued existence on the earth just before they are asked to recall, they will show losses (e.g., 25, 38), but even the influence of this kind of psychological beating is short lived. Somehow I have never felt that such findings need explanation by a theory used to explain the other facts of forgetting.

Concerning the causes of forgetting, let me sum up in a somewhat more dogmatic fashion than is probably justified. One of the assumptions of science is finite causality. Everything cannot influence everything else. To me, the most important implication of the work on forgetting during the last ten years is that this work has markedly *reduced* the number of variables related to forgetting. Correspondingly, I think the theoretical problem has become simpler. It is my belief that we can narrow down the cause of forgetting to interference from previously learned habits, from habits being currently learned, and from habits we have yet to learn. The amount of this interference is primarily a function of similarity and associative strength, the latter being important because it interacts with similarity.

SUMMARY

This paper deals with issues in the forgetting of rote-learned materials. An analysis of the current evidence suggests that the classical Ebbinghaus curve of forgetting is primarily a function of interference from materials learned previously in the laboratory. When this source of interference is removed, forgetting decreases from about 75 per cent over 24 hours to about 25 per cent. This latter figure can be reduced by at least 10 per cent by other methodologi-

cal considerations, leaving 15 per cent as an estimate of the forgetting over 24 hours. This estimate will vary somewhat as a function of intratask similarity, distributed practice, and with very low meaningful material. But the overall evidence suggests that similarity with other material and situational similarity are by far the most critical factors in forgetting. Such evidence is consonant with a general interference theory, although the details of such a theory were not presented here.

REFERENCES

1. ARCHER, E. J., & UNDERWOOD, B. J. Retroactive inhibition of verbal associations as a multiple function of temporal point of interpolation and degree of interpolated learning. *J. exp. Psychol.*, 1951, **42**, 283–290.
2. BARTLETT, F. C. *Remembering: a study in experimental and social psychology.* London: Cambridge Univer. Press, 1932.
3. BELMONT, L., & BIRCH, H. G. Re-individualizing the repression hypothesis. *J. abnorm. soc. Psychol.*, 1951, **46**, 226–235.
4. BILODEAU, I. McD., & SCHLOSBERG, H. Similarity in stimulating conditions as a variable in retroactive inhibition. *J. exp. Psychol.*, 1951, **41**, 199–204.
5. BRIGGS, G. E. Acquisition, extinction, and recovery functions in retroactive inhibition. *J. exp. Psychol.*, 1954, **47**, 285–293.
6. CHENG, N. Y. Retroactive effect and degree of similarity. *J. exp. Psychol.*, 1929, **12**, 444–458.
7. EBBINGHAUS, H. *Memory: a contribution to experimental psychology.* (Trans. by H. A. Ruger, and C. E. Bussenius) New York: Bureau of Publications, Teachers College, Columbia Univer., 1913.
8. GIBSON, ELEANOR J. A systematic application of the concepts of generalization and differentiation to verbal learning. *Psychol. Rev.*, 1940, **47**, 196–229.
9. GIBSON, ELEANOR J. Intra-list generalization as a factor in verbal learning. *J. exp. Psychol.*, 1942, **30**, 185–200.
10. GREENBERG, R., & UNDERWOOD, B. J. Retention as a function of stage of practice. *J. exp. Psychol.*, 1950, **40**, 452–457.
11. HOVLAND, C. I. Experimental studies in rote-learning theory. VI. Comparison of retention following learning to same criterion by massed and distributed practice. *J. exp. Psychol.*, 1940, **26**, 568–587.
12. IRION, A. L. The relation of "set" to retention. *Psychol. Rev.*, 1948, **55**, 336–341.

13. JENKINS, J. G., & DALLENBACH, K. M. Oblivescence during sleep and waking. *Amer. J. Psychol.*, 1924, **35**, 605–612.

14. JOHNSON, L. M. The relative effect of a time interval upon learning and retention. *J. exp. Psychol.*, 1939, **24**, 169–179.

15. KATONA, G. *Organizing and memorizing: studies in the psychology of learning and teaching.* New York: Columbia Univer. Press, 1940.

16. KRUEGER, W. C. F. The effect of overlearning on retention. *J. exp. Psychol.*, 1929, **12**, 71–78.

17. LESTER, O. P. Mental set in relation to retroactive inhibition. *J. exp. Psychol.*, 1932, **15**, 681–699.

18. LUH, C. W. The conditions of retention. *Psychol. Monogr.*, 1922, **31**, No. 3 (Whole No. 142).

19. McGEOCH, J. A. Forgetting and the law of disuse. *Psychol. Rev.*, 1932, **39**, 352–370.

20. McGEOCH, J. A. *The psychology of human learning.* New York: Longmans, Green, 1942.

21. OSGOOD, C. E. *Method and theory in experimental psychology.* New York: Oxford Univer. Press, 1953.

22. RAPAPORT, D. Emotions and memory. *Psychol. Rev.*, 1943, **50**, 234–243.

23. ROCKWAY, M. R., & DUNCAN, C. P. Pre-recall warming-up in verbal retention. *J. exp. Psychol.*, 1952, **43**, 305–312.

24. RUNQUIST, W. Retention of verbal associations as a function of interference and strength. Unpublished doctor's dissertation, Northwestern Univer., 1956.

25. RUSSELL, W. A. Retention of verbal material as a function of motivating instructions and experimentally-induced failure. *J. exp. Psychol.*, 1952, **43**, 207–216.

26. UNDERWOOD, B. J. The effect of successive interpolations on retroactive and proactive inhibition. *Psychol. Monogr.*, 1945, **59**, No. 3 (Whole No. 273).

27. UNDERWOOD, B. J. Studies of distributed practice: VII. Learning and retention of serial nonsense lists as a function of intralist similarity. *J. exp. Psychol.*, 1952, **44**, 80–87.

28. UNDERWOOD, B. J. Studies of distributed practice: VIII. Learning and retention of paired nonsense syllables as a function of intralist similarity. *J. exp. Psychol.*, 1953, **45**, 133–142.

29. UNDERWOOD, B. J. Studies of distributed practice: IX. Learning and retention of paired adjectives as a function of intralist similarity. *J. exp. Psychol.*, 1953, **45**, 143–149.

30. UNDERWOOD, B. J. Studies of distributed practice: X. The influence of intralist similarity on learning and retention of serial adjective lists. *J. exp. Psychol.*, 1953, **45**, 253–259.

31. UNDERWOOD, R. J. Intralist similarity in verbal learning and retention. *Psychol. Rev.*, 1954, **3**, 160–166.

32. UNDERWOOD, B. J., & RICHARDSON, J. Studies of distributed practice: XIII. Interlist interference and the retention of serial nonsense lists. *J. exp. Psychol.*, 1955, **50**, 39–46.

33. UNDERWOOD, B. J., & RICHARDSON, J. The influence on meaningfulness, intralist similarity, and serial position on retention. *J. exp. Psychol.*, 1956, **52**, 119–126.

34. WARD, L. B. Reminiscence and rote learning. *Psychol. Monogr.*, 1937, **49**, No. 4 (Whole No. 220).

35. WEISS, W., & MARGOLIUS, G. The effect of context stimuli on learning and retention. *J. exp. Psychol.*, 1954, **48**, 318–322.

36. WILLIAMS, M. The effects of experimentally induced needs upon retention. *J. exp. Psychol.*, 1950, **40**, 139–151.

37. YOUTZ, ADELLA C. An experimental evaluation of Jost's laws. *Psychol. Monogr.*, 1941, **53**, No. 1 (Whole No. 238).

38. ZELLER, A. F. An experimental analogue of repression: III. The effect of induced failure and success on memory measured by recall. *J. exp. Psychol.*, 1951, **42**, 32–38.

21. The "Tip of the Tongue" Phenomenon *

Roger Brown and David McNeill

What is Li'l Abner's last name? What is the name of the faithful pet that belongs to Little Orphan Annie? If you have attempted to recall these well-known facts and failed, then you may have experienced the "tip of the tongue" phenomenon, that tantalizing state in which a memory trace simmers just below the threshold of conscious awareness. This commonplace but unpredictable memory state has been investigated experimentally by Professors Brown and McNeill. On the basis of a careful analysis of errors made by persons in a "tip of the tongue" state, the authors develop interesting inferences about the mechanism of memory storage.

William James wrote, in 1893: "Suppose we try to recall a forgotten name. The state of our consciousness is peculiar. There is a gap therein; but no mere gap. It is a gap that is intensely active. A sort of wraith of the name is in it, beckoning us in a given direction, making us at moments tingle with the sense of our closeness and then letting us sink back without the longed-for term. If wrong names are proposed to us, this singularly definite gap acts immediately so as to negate them. They do not fit into its mould. And the gap of one word does not feel like the gap of another, all empty of content as both might seem necessarily to be when described as gaps" (p. 251).

The "tip of the tongue" (TOT) state involves a failure to recall a word of which

one has knowledge. The evidence of knowledge is either an eventually successful recall or else an act of recognition that occurs, without additional training, when recall has failed. The class of cases defined by the conjunction of knowledge and a failure of recall is a large one. The TOT state, which James described, seems to be a small subclass in which recall is felt to be imminent.

For several months we watched for TOT states in ourselves. Unable to recall the name of the street on which a relative lives, one of us thought of *Congress* and *Corinth* and *Concord* and then looked up the address and learned that it was *Cornish.* The words that had come to mind have certain properties in common with the word that had been sought (the "target word"): all four begin with *Co;* all are two-syllable words; all put the primary stress on the first syllable. After this experience we began putting direct questions to ourselves when we fell into the TOT state, questions as to the number of syllables in the target word, its initial letter, etc.

Woodworth (1934), before us, made a record of data for naturally occurring TOT states and Wenzl (1932, 1936) did the same for German words. Their results are similar to those we obtained and consistent with the following preliminary characterization. When complete recall of a word is not presently possible but is felt to be imminent, one can often correctly recall the general type of the word; *generic* recall may succeed when particular recall fails. There seem to be two common varieties of generic recall. (a) Sometimes a part of the target word is recalled, a letter or two, a syllable,

* Reprinted by permission of the authors and Academic Press, Inc. from the *Journal of Verbal Learning and Verbal Behavior*, 1966, 5, 325-337.

or affix. Partial recall is necessarily also *generic* since the class of words defined by the possession of any *part* of the target word will include words other than the target. (b) Sometimes the abstract form of the target is recalled, perhaps the fact that it was a two-syllable sequence with the primary stress on the first syllable. The whole word is represented in *abstract form recall* but not on the letter-by-letter level that constitutes its identity. The recall of an abstract form is also necessarily *generic*, since any such form defines a class of words extending beyond the target.

Wenzl and Woodworth had worked with small collections of data for naturally occurring TOT states. These data were, for the most part, provided by the investigators; were collected in an unsystematic fashion; and were analyzed in an impressionistic nonquantitative way. It seemed to us that such data left the facts of generic recall in doubt. An occasional correspondence between a retrieved word and a target word with respect to number of syllables, stress pattern or initial letter is, after all, to be expected by chance. Several months of "self-observation and asking-our-friends" yielded fewer than a dozen good cases and we realized that an improved method of data collection was essential.

We thought it might pay to "prospect" for TOT states by reading to S definitions of uncommon English words and asking him to supply the words. The procedure was given a preliminary test with nine Ss who were individually interviewed for 2 hrs each.[1] In 57 instances an S was, in fact, "seized" by a TOT state. The signs of it were unmistakable; he would appear to be in mild torment, something like the brink of a sneeze, and if he found the word his relief was considerable. While searching for the target S told us all the words that came to his mind. He volunteered the information that some of them resembled the

---

[1] We wish to thank Mr. Charles Hollen for doing the pretest interviews.

target in sound but not in meaning; others he was sure were similar in meaning but not in sound. The E intruded on S's agony with two questions: (a) How many syllables has the target word? (b) What is its first letter? Answers to the first question were correct in 47% of all cases and answers to the second question were correct in 51% of the cases. These outcomes encouraged us to believe that generic recall was real and to devise a group procedure that would further speed up the rate of data collection.

METHOD

Subjects

Fifty-six Harvard and Radcliffe undergraduates participated in one of three evening sessions; each session was 2 hrs long. The Ss were volunteers from a large General Education Course and were paid for their time.

Word List. The list consisted of 49 words which, according to the Thorndike-Lorge *Word Book* (1952) occur at least once per four million words but not so often as once per one million words. The level is suggested by these examples: *apse, nepotism, cloaca, ambergris,* and *sampan.* We thought the words used were likely to be in the passive or recognition vocabularies of our Ss but not in their active recall vocabularies. There were 6 words of 1 syllable; 19 of 2 syllables; 20 of 3 syllables; 4 of 4 syllables. For each word we used a definition from *The American College Dictionary* (Barnhart, 1948) edited so as to contain no words that closely resembled the one being defined.

Response Sheet. The response sheet was laid off in vertical columns headed as follows:

Intended word (+ One I was thinking of).
            (— Not).
Number of syllables (1–5).
Initial letter.
Words of similar sound.
            (1. *Closest in sound*)
            (2. *Middle*   )
            (3. *Farthest in Sound*)
Words of similar meaning.
Word you had in mind if not intended word.

Procedure

We instructed Ss to the following effect.

In this experiment we are concerned with that state of mind in which a person is unable to think of a word that he is certain he knows, the state of mind in which a word seems to be on the tip of one's tongue. Our technique for precipitating such states is, in general, to read definitions of uncommon words and ask the subject to recall the word.

(1) We will first read the definition of a low-frequency word.

(2) If you should happen to know the word at once, or think you do, or, if you should simply not know it, then there is nothing further for you to do at the moment. Just wait.

(3) If you are unable to think of the word but feel sure that you know it and that it is on the verge of coming back to you then you are in a TOT state and should begin at once to fill in the columns of the response sheet.

(4) After reading each definition we will ask whether anyone is in the TOT state. Anyone who is in that state should raise his hand. The rest of us will then wait until those in the TOT state have written on the answer sheet all the information they are able to provide.

(5) When everyone who has been in the TOT state has signalled us to proceed, we will read the target word. At this time, everyone is to write the word in the leftmost column of the response sheet. Those of you who have known the word since first its definition was read are asked not to write it until this point. Those of you who simply did not know the word or who had thought of a different word will write now the word we read. For those of you who have been in the TOT state two eventualities are possible. The word read may strike you as definitely the word you have been seeking. In that case please write '+' after the word, as the instructions at the head of the column direct. The other possibility is that you will not be sure whether the word read is the one you have been seeking or, indeed, you may be sure that it is not. In this case you are asked to write the sign '—' after the word. Sometimes when the word read out is not the one you have been seeking your actual target may come to mind. In this case, in addition to the minus sign in the leftmost column, please write the actual target word in the rightmost column.

(6) Now we come to the column entries themselves. The first two entries, the guess as to the number of syllables and the initial letter, are required. The remaining entries should be filled out if possible. When you are in a TOT state, words that are related to the target word do almost always come to mind. List them as they come, but separate words which you think resemble the target in sound from words which you think resemble the target in meaning.

(7) When you have finished all your entries, but before you signal us to read the intended target word, look again at the words you have listed as 'Words of similar sound.' If possible, rank these, as the instructions at the head of the column direct, in terms of the degree of their seeming resemblance to the target. This must be done without knowledge of what the target actually is.

(8) The search procedure of a person in the TOT state will sometimes serve to retrieve the missing word before he has finished filling in the columns and before we read out the word. When this happens please mark the place where it happens with the words "Got it" and *do not provide any more data.*

RESULTS

Classes of Data

There were 360 instances, across all words and all Ss, in which a TOT state was signalled. Of this total, 233 were positive TOTs. A positive TOT is one for which the target word is known and, consequently, one for which the data obtained can be scored as accurate or inaccurate. In those cases where the target was not the word intended but some other word which S finally recalled and wrote in the rightmost column his data were checked against that word, his effective target. A negative TOT is one for which the S judged the word read out not to have been his target and, in addition, one in which S proved unable to recall his own functional target.

The data provided by S while he searched for the target word are of two kinds: explicit guesses as to the number of syllables in the target and the initial letter of the target; words that came to mind while he searched for the target. The words that came to mind were classified by S into 224 words similar in sound to the target (hereafter called "SS" words) and 95 words similar in meaning to the target (hereafter called "SM" words). The S's information about the number of syllables in, and the initial letter of the target may be inferred from correspondences between the target and his SS words as well as directly discovered from his explicit guesses. For his knowledge of the stress pattern of the target and of letters in the target, other than the initial letter, we must rely on the SS words alone since explicit guesses were not required.

To convey a sense of the SS and SM words we offer the following examples. When the target was *sampan* the SS words (not all of them real words) included: *Saipan, Siam, Cheyenne, sarong, sanching,* and *sympoon.* The SM words were: *barge, houseboat,* and *junk.* When the target was *caduceus* the SS words included: *Casadesus, Aeschelus, cephalus,* and *leucosis.* The SM words were: *fasces, Hippocrates, lictor,* and *snake.* The spelling in all cases is S's own.

We will, in this report, use the SM words to provide baseline data against which to evaluate the accuracy of the explicit guesses and of the SS words. The SM words are words produced under the spell of the positive TOT state but judged by S to resemble the target in meaning rather than sound. We are quite sure that the SM words are somewhat more like the target than would be a collection of words produced by Ss with no knowledge of the target. However, the SM words make a better comparative baseline than any other data we collected.

General Problems of Analysis

The data present problems of analysis that are not common in psychology. To begin with, the words of the list did not reliably precipitate TOT states. Of the original 49 words, all but *zither* succeeded at least once; the range was from one success to nine. The Ss made actual targets of 51 words not on the original list and all but five of these were pursued by one S only. Clearly none of the 100 words came even close to precipitating a TOT state in all 56 Ss. Furthermore, the Ss varied in their susceptibility to TOT states. There were nine who experienced none at all in a 2-hr period; the largest number experienced in such a period by one S was eight. In out data, then, the entries for one word will not usually involve the same Ss or even the same number of Ss as the entries for another word. The entries for one S need not involve the same words or even the same number of words as the entries for another S. Consequently for the tests we shall want to make there are no significance tests that we can be sure are appropriate.

In statistical theory our problem is called the "fragmentary data problem." [2] The best thing to do with fragmentary data is to report them very fully and analyze them in several different ways. Our detailed knowledge of these data suggests that the problems are not serious for, while there is some variation in the pull of words and the susceptibility of Ss there is not much variation in the quality of the data. The character of the material recalled is much the same from word to word and S to S.

Number of Syllables

As the main item of evidence that S in a TOT state can recall with significant success the number of syllables in a target word he has not yet found we offer Table 1. The entries on the diagonal are instances in which guesses were correct. The order of the means of the explicit guesses is the same as the order of the actual numbers of syllables in the target words. The rank order correlation between the two is 1.0 and such a correlation is significant with a $p < .001$ (one-tailed) even when only five items are correlated. The modes of the guesses correspond exactly with the actual numbers of syllables, for the values one through three; for words of four and

TABLE 1

Actual Numbers of Syllables and Guessed Numbers for all TOTs in the Main Experiment

	Guessed numbers					No guess	Mode	Mean
Actual numbers	1	2	3	4	5			
1	9	7	1	0	0	0	1	1.53
2	2	55	22	2	1	5	2	2.33
3	3	19	61	10	1	5	3	2.86
4	0	2	12	6	2	3	3	3.36
5	0	0	3	0	1	1	3	3.50

[2] We wish to thank Professor Frederick Mosteller for discussing the fragmentary data problem with us.

five syllables the modes continue to be three.

When all TOTs are combined, the contributions to the total effects of individual Ss and of individual words are unequal. We have made an analysis in which each word counts but once. This was accomplished by calculating the mean of the guesses made by all Ss for whom a particular word precipitated a TOT state and taking that mean as the score for that word. The new means calculated with all words equally weighted were, in order: 1.62; 2.30; 2.80; 3.33; and 3.50. These values are close to those of Table 1 and *rho* with the actual numbers of syllables continues to be 1.0.

We also made an analysis in which each S counts but once. This was done by calculating the mean of an S's guesses for all words of one syllable, the mean for all words of two syllables, etc. In comparing the means of guesses for words of different length one can only use those Ss who made at least one guess for each actual length to be compared. In the present data only words of two syllables and three syllables precipitated enough TOTs to yield a substantial number of such matched scores. There were 21 Ss who made guesses for both two-syllable and three-syllable words. The simplest way to evaluate the significance of the differences in these guesses is with the Sign Test. In only 6 of 21 matched scores was the mean guess for words of two syllables larger than the mean for words of three syllables. The difference is significant with a $p = .039$ (one-tailed). For actual words that were only one syllable apart in length, Ss were able to make a significant distinction in the correct direction when the words themselves could not be called to mind.

The 224 SS words and the 95 SM words provide supporting evidence. Words of similar sound (SS) had the same number of syllables as the target in 48% of all cases. This value is close to the 57% that were correct for explicit guesses in the main experiment and still closer to the 47% correct

already reported for the pretest. The SM words provide a clear contrast; only 20% matched the number of syllables in the target. We conclude that S in a positive TOT state has a significant ability to recall correctly the number of syllables in the word he is trying to retrieve.

In Table 1 it can be seen that the modes of guesses exactly correspond with the actual numbers of syllables in target words for the values one through three. For still longer target words (four and five syllables) the means of guesses continue to rise but the modes stay at the value three. Words of more than three syllables are rare in English and the generic entry for such words may be the same as for words of three syllables; something like "three or more" may be used for all long words.

Initial Letter

Over all positive TOTs, the initial letter of the word S was seeking was correctly guessed 57% of the time. The pretest result was 51% correct. The results from the main experiment were analyzed with each word counting just once by entering a word's score as "correct" whenever the most common guess or the only guess was in fact correct; 62% of words were, by this reckoning, correctly guessed. The SS words had initial letters matching the initial letters of the target words in 49% of all cases. We do not know the chance level of success for this performance but with 26 letters and many words that began with uncommon letters the level must be low. Probably the results for the SM words are better than chance and yet the outcome for these words was only 8% matches.

We did an analysis of the SS and SM words, with each S counting just once. There were 26 Ss who had at least one such word. For each S we calculated the proportion of SS words matching the target in initial letter and the same proportion for SM words. For 21 Ss the proportions were not tied and in all but 3 cases the larger value was that of the SS words. The difference is significant by Sign Test with $p = .001$ (one-tailed).

The evidence for significantly accurate generic recall of initial letters is even stronger than for syllables. The absolute levels of success are similar but the chance baseline must be much lower for letters than for syllables because the possibilities are more numerous.

Syllabic Stress

We did not ask S to guess the stress pattern of the target word but the SS words provide relevant data. The test was limited to the syllabic location of the primary or heaviest stress for which *The American College Dictionary* was our authority. The number of SS words that could be used was limited by three considerations. (a) Words of one syllable had to be excluded because there was no possibility of variation. (b) Stress locations could only be matched if the SS word had the same number of syllables as the target, and so only such matching words could be used. (c) Invented words and foreign words could not be used because they do not appear in the dictionary. Only 49 SS words remained.

TABLE 2

Syllables Receiving Primary Stress in Target Words and SS Words

		Target words	
		1st syllable	*2nd syllable*
SS Words	1st syllable	25	6
	2nd syllable	6	12

As it happened all of the target words involved (whatever their length) placed the primary stress on either the first or the second syllable. It was possible, therefore, to make a 2×2 table for the 49 pairs of target and SS words which would reveal the correspondences and noncorrespondences. As can be seen in Table 2 the SS words tended to stress the same syllable as the target words. The χ^2 for this table is 10.96 and that value is significant with $p < .001$. However, the data do not meet the independence requirement, so we cannot be sure that the matching tendency is significant. There were not enough data to permit any other analyses, and so we are left suspecting that S in a TOT state has knowledge of the stress pattern of the target, but we are not sure of it.

Letters in Various Positions

We did not require explicit guesses for letters in positions other than the first, but the SS words provide relevant data. The test was limited to the following positions: first, second, third, third-last, second-last, and last. A target word must have at least six letters in order to provide data on the six positions; it might have any number of letters larger than six and still provide data for the six (relatively defined) positions. Accordingly we included the data for all target words having six or more letters.

Figure 21–1 displays the percentages of letters in each of six positions of SS words which matched the letters in the same positions of the corresponding targets. For comparison purposes these data are also provided for SM words. The SS curve is at all points above the SM curve; the two are closest together at the third-last position. The values for the last three positions of the SS curve quite closely match the values for the first three positions. The values for the last three positions of the SM curve, on the other hand, are well above the values for the first three positions. Consequently the *relative* superiority of the SS curve is greater in the first three positions.

The letter-position data were also analyzed in such a way as to count each target word just once, assigning each position in the target a single score representing the

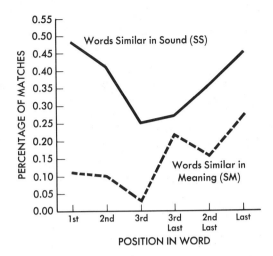

Figure 21.1 Percentages of letter matches between target words and SS words for six serial positions.

proportion of matches across all Ss for that position in that word. The order of the SS and SM points is preserved in this finer analysis. We did Sign Tests comparing the SS and SM values for each of the six positions. As Fig. 21–1 would suggest the SS values for the first three positions all exceeded the SM values with p's less than .01 (one-tailed). The SS values for the final two positions exceeded the SM values with p's less than .05 (one-tailed). The SS values for the third-last position were greater than the SM values but not significantly so.

The cause of the upswing in the final three positions of the SM curve may be some difference in the distribution of information in early and late positions of English words. Probably there is less variety in the later positions. In any case the fact that the SS curve lies above the SM curve for the last three positions indicates that S in a TOT state has knowledge of the target in addition to his knowledge of English word structure.

Chunking of Suffixes

The request to S that he guess the initial letter of the target occasionally elicited a response of more than one letter; e.g., *ex*

in the case of *extort* and *con* in the case of *convene*. This result suggested that some letter (or phoneme) sequences are stored as single entries having been "chunked" by long experience. We made only one test for chunking and that involved three-letter suffixes.

It did not often happen that an S produced an SS word that matched the target with respect to all of its three last letters. The question asked of the data was whether such three-letter matches occurred more often when the letters constituted an English suffix than when they did not. In order to determine which of the target words terminated in such a suffix, we entered *The American College Dictionary* with final trigrams. If there was an entry describing a suffix appropriate to the grammatical and semantic properties of the target we considered the trigram to be a suffix. There were 20 words that terminated in a suffix, including *fawning, unctuous,* and *philatelist.*

Of 93 SS words produced in response to a target terminating in a suffix, 30 matched the target in their final three letters. Of 130 SS words supplied in response to a target that did not terminate in a suffix only 5 matched the target in their final three letters. The data were also analyzed in a way that counts each S just once and uses only Ss who produced SS words in response to both kinds of target. A Sign Test was made of the difference between matches of suffixes and matches of endings that were not suffixes; the former were more common with $p = .059$ (one-tailed). A comparable Sign Test for SM words was very far from significance. We conclude that suffix-chunking probably plays a role in generic recall.

Proximity to the Target and Quality of Information

There were three varieties of positive TOT states: (1) Cases in which S *recognized* the word read by E as the word he had been seeking; (2) Cases in which S *re-*

called the intended word before it was read out; (3) Cases in which S *recalled* the word he had been seeking before E read the intended word and the recalled word was not the same as the word read. Since S in a TOT state of either type 2 or type 3 reached the target before the intended word was read and S in a TOT state of type 1 did not, the TOTs of the second and third types may be considered "nearer" the target than TOTs of the first type. We have no basis for ordering types 2 and 3 relative to one another. We predicted that Ss in the two kinds of TOT state that ended in recall (types 2 and 3) would produce more accurate information about the target than Ss in the TOT state that ended in recognition (type 1).

The prediction was tested on the explicit guesses of initial letters since these were the most complete and sensitive data. There were 138 guesses from Ss in a type 1 state and 58 of these, or 42%, were correct. There were 36 guesses from Ss in a type 2 state and, of these, 20, or 56%, were correct. There were 59 guesses from Ss in a type 3 state and of these 39, or 66%, were correct. We also analyzed the results in such a way as to count each word only once. The percentages correct were: for type 1, 50%; type 2, 62%; type 3, 63%. Finally, we performed an analysis counting each S just once but averaging together type 2 and type 3 results in order to bring a maximum number of Ss into the comparison. The combining action is justified since both type 2 and type 3 were states ending in recall. A Sign Test of the differences showed that guesses were more accurate in the states that ended in recall than in the states that ended in recognition: one-tailed $p < .01$. Supplementary analyses with SS and SM words confirmed these results. We conclude that when S is nearer his target his generic recall is more accurate than when he is farther from the target.

Special interest attaches to the results from type 2 TOTs. In the method of our experiment there is nothing to guarantee that when S said he recognized a word he had really done so. Perhaps when E read out a word, S could not help thinking that that was the word he had in mind. We ourselves do not believe anything of the sort happened. The single fact that most Ss claimed fewer than five positive TOTs in a 2-hr period argues against any such effect. Still it is reassuring to have the 36 type 2 cases in which S recalled the intended word *before* it was read. The fact that 56% of the guesses of initial letters made in type 2 states were correct is hard-core evidence of generic recall. It may be worth adding that 65% of the guesses of the number of syllables for type 2 cases were correct.

Judgments of the Proximity of SS Words

The several comparisons we have made of SS and SM words demonstrate that when recall is imminent S can distinguish among the words that come to mind those that resemble the target in form from those that do not resemble the target in form. There is a second kind of evidence which shows that S can tell when he is getting close (or "warm").

In 15 instances Ss rated two or more SS words for comparative similarity to the target. Our analysis contrasts those rated "most similar" (1) with those rated next most similar (2). Since there were very few words rated (3) we attempted no analysis of them. Similarity points were given for all the features of a word that have now been demonstrated to play a part in generic recall—with the single exception of stress. Stress had to be disregarded because some of the words were invented and their stress patterns were unknown.

The problem was to compare pairs of SS words, rated 1 and 2, for overall similarity to the target. We determined whether each member matched the target in number of syllables. If one did and the other did not, then a single similarity point was assigned the word that matched. For each word, we counted, beginning with the initial letter, the number of consecutive letters in common with the target. The word having the longer sequence that matched the target earned one similarity point. An exactly comparable procedure was followed for sequences starting from the final letter. In sum, each word in a pair could receive from zero to three similarity points.

We made Sign Tests comparing the total scores for words rated most like the target (1) and words rated next most like the target (2). This test was only slightly inappropriate since only two target words occurred twice in the set of 15 and only one S repeated in the set. Ten of 12 differences were in the predicted direction and the one-tailed $p = .019$. It is of some interest that similarity points awarded on the basis of letters in the middle of the words did not even go in the right direction. Figure 1 has already indicated that they also do not figure in Ss' judgments of the comparative similarity to the target of pairs of SS words. Our conclusion is that S at a given distance from the target can accurately judge which of two words that come to mind is more like the target and that he does so in terms of the features of words that appear in generic recall.

Conclusions

When complete recall of a word has not occurred but is felt to be imminent there is likely to be accurate generic recall. Generic recall of the *abstract form* variety is evidenced by S's knowledge of the number of syllables in the target and of the location of the primary stress. Generic recall of the *partial* variety is evidenced by S's knowledge of letters in the target word. This knowledge shows a bowed serial-position effect since it is better for the ends of a word than for the middle and somewhat better for beginning positions than for final positions. The accuracy of generic recall is greater when S is near the target (complete recall is imminent) than when S is far from the target. A person experiencing generic recall is able to judge the relative similarity to the target of words that occur to him

and these judgments are based on the features of words that figure in partial and abstract form recall.

DISCUSSION

The facts of generic recall are relevant to theories of speech perception, reading, the understanding of sentences, and the organization of memory. We have not worked out all the implications. In this section we first attempt a model of the TOT process and then try to account for the existence of generic memory.

A Model of the Process

Let us suppose (with Katz and Fodor, 1963, and many others) that our long-term memory for words and definitions is organized into the functional equivalent of a dictionary. In real dictionaries, those that are books, entries are ordered alphabetically and bound in place. Such an arrangement is too simple and too inflexible to serve as a model for a mental dictionary. We will suppose that words are entered on keysort cards instead of pages and that the cards are punched for various features of the words entered. With real cards, paper ones, it is possible to retrieve from the total deck any subset punched for a common feature by putting a metal rod through the proper hole. We will suppose that there is in the mind some speedier equivalent of this retrieval technique.

The model will be described in terms of a single example. When the target word was *sextant*, Ss heard the definition: "A navigational instrument used in measuring angular distances, especially the altitude of sun, moon, and stars at sea." This definition precipitated a TOT state in 9 Ss of the total 56. The SM words included: *astrolabe, compass, dividers,* and *protractor*. The SS words included: *secant, sextet,* and *sexton*.

The problem begins with a definition rather than a word and so S must enter his dictionary backwards, or in a way that would be backwards and quite impossible for the dictionary that is a book. It is not impossible with keysort cards, providing we suppose that the cards are punched for some set of semantic features. Perhaps these are the semantic "markers" that Katz and Fodor (1963) postulate in their account of the comprehension of sentences. We will imagine that it is somehow possible to extract from the definition a set of markers and that these are, in the present case: "navigation, instrument, having to do with geometry." Metal rods thrust into the holes for each of these features might fish up such a collection of entries as: *astrolabe, compass, dividers,* and *protractor.* This first retrieval, which is in response to the definition, must be semantically based and it will not, therefore, account for the appearance of such SS words as *sextet* and *sexton.*

There are four major kinds of outcome of the first retrieval and these outcomes correspond with the four main things that happen to Ss in the TOT experiment. We will assume that a definition of each word retrieved is entered on its card and that it is possible to check the input definition against those on the cards. The first possible outcome is that *sextant* is retrieved along with *compass* and *astrolabe* and the others and that the definitions are specific enough so that the one entered for *sextant* registers as matching the input and all the others as not-matching. This is the case of correct recall; S has found a word that matches the definition and it is the intended word. The second possibility is that *sextant* is not among the words retrieved and, in addition, the definitions entered for those retrieved are so imprecise that one of them (the definition for *compass,* for example) registers as matching the input. In this case S thinks he has found the target though he really has not. The third possibility is that *sextant* is not among the words retrieved, but the definitions entered for those retrieved are specific enough so that none of them will register a match with the input. In this case, S does not know the word and realizes the fact. The above three outcomes are the common ones and none of them represents a TOT state.

In the TOT case the first retrieval must include a card with the definition of *sextant* entered on it but with the word itself incompletely entered. The card might, for instance, have the following information about the word: two-syllables, initial s, final t. The entry would be a punchcard equivalent of S___ ___T. Perhaps an incomplete entry of this sort is James's "singularly definite gap" and the basis for generic recall.

The S with a correct definition, matching the input, and an incomplete word entry will know that he knows the word, will feel that he almost has it, that it is on the tip of his tongue. If he is asked to guess the number of syllables and the initial letter he should, in the case we have imagined, be able to do so. He should also be able to produce SS words. The features that appear in the incomplete entry (two-syllables, initial s, and final t) can be used as the basis for a second retrieval. The subset of cards defined by the intersection of all three features would include cards for *secant* and *sextet.* If one feature were not used then *sexton* would be added to the set.

Which of the facts about the TOT state can now be accounted for? We know that Ss were able, when they had not recalled a target, to distinguish between words resembling the target in sound (SS words) and words resembling the target in meaning only (SM words). The basis for this distinction in the model would seem to be the distinction between the first and second retrievals. Membership in the first subset retrieved defines SM words and membership in the second subset defines SS words.

We know that when S had produced several SS words but had not recalled the target he could sometimes accurately rank-order the SS words for similarity to the target. The model offers an account of this ranking performance. If the incomplete entry for *sextant* includes three features of the word then SS words having only one or two of these features (e.g., *sexton*) should be judged less similar to the target than SS words having all three of them (e.g., *secant*).

When an SS word has all of the features of the incomplete entry (as do *secant* and *sextet* in our example) what prevents its being mistaken for the target? Why did not the S who produced *sextet* think that the word was "right?" Because of the definitions. The forms meet all the requirements of the incomplete entry but the definitions do not match.

The TOT state often ended in recognition; i.e., S failed to recall the word but when E read out *sextant* S recognized it as the word he had been seeking. The model accounts for this outcome as follows. Suppose that there is only the incomplete entry S___ ___T in memory, plus the definition. The E now says (in effect) that there exists a word *sextant* which has the definition in question. The word *sextant* then satisfies all the data points available to S; it has the right number of syllables, the right initial letter, the right final letter, and it is said to have the right definition. The result is recognition.

The proposed account has some testable implications. Suppose that E were to read out, when recall failed, not the correct word *sex-*

tant but an invented word like *sekrant* or *saktint* which satisfies the incomplete entry as well as does *sextant* itself. If S had nothing but the incomplete entry and E's testimony to guide him then he should "recognize" the invented words just as he recognizes *sextant*.

The account we have given does not accord with intuition. Our intuitive notion of recognition is that the features which could not be called were actually in storage but less accessible than the features that were recalled. To stay with our example, intuition suggests that the features of *sextant* that could not be recalled, the letters between the first and the last, were entered on the card but were less "legible" than the recalled features. We might imagine them printed in small letters and faintly. When, however, the E reads out the word *sextant*, then S can make out the less legible parts of his entry and, since the total entry matches E's word, S recognizes it. This sort of recognition should be "tighter" than the one described previously. *Sekrant* and *saktint* would be rejected.

We did not try the effect of invented words and we do not know how they would have been received but among the outcomes of the actual experiment there is one that strongly favors the faint-entry theory. Subjects in a TOT state, after all, sometimes recalled the target word without any prompting. The incomplete entry theory does not admit of such a possibility. If we suppose that the entry is not S___ ___T but something more like S*ex tan*T (with the italicized lower-case letters representing the faint-entry section) we must still explain how it happens that the faintly entered, and at first inaccessible, middle letters are made accessible in the case of recall.

Perhaps it works something like this. The features that are first recalled operate as we have suggested, to retrieve a set of SS words. Whenever an SS word (such as *secant*) includes middle letters that are matched in the faintly entered section of the target then those faintly entered letters become accessible. The match brings out the missing parts the way heat brings out anything written in lemon juice. In other words, when *secant* is retrieved the target entry grows from S*ex tan*T to SE*x t*ANT. The retrieval of *sextet* brings out the remaining letters and S recalls the complete word—*sextant*.

It is now possible to explain the one as yet unexplained outcome of the TOT experiment. Subjects whose state ended in recall had, before they found the target, more correct information about it than did Ss whose state ended in recognition. More correct information means fewer features to be brought out by duplication in SS words and so should mean a greater likelihood that all essential features will be brought out in a short period of time.

All of the above assumes that each word is entered in memory just once, on a single card. There is another possibility. Suppose that there are entries for *sextant* on several different cards. They might all be incomplete, but at different points, or, some might be incomplete and one or more of them complete. The several cards would be punched for different semantic markers and perhaps for different associations so that the entry recovered would vary with the rule of retrieval. With this conception we do not require the notion of faint entry. The difference between features commonly recalled, such as the first and last letters, and features that are recalled with difficulty or perhaps only recognized, can be rendered in another way. The more accessible features are entered on more cards or else the cards on which they appear are punched for more markers; in effect, they are wired into a more extended associative net.

The Reason for Generic Recall

In adult minds words are stored in both visual and auditory terms and between the two there are complicated rules of translation. Generic recall involves letters (or phonemes), affixes, syllables, and stress location. In this section we will discuss only letters (legible forms) and will attempt to explain a single effect—the serial position effect in the recall of letters. It is not clear how far the explanation can be extended.

In brief overview this is the argument. The design of the English language is such that one word is usually distinguished from all others in a more-than-minimal way, i.e., by more than a single letter in a single position. It is consequently *possible* to recognize words when one has not stored the complete letter sequence. The evidence is that we do not store the complete sequence if we do not have to. We begin by attending chiefly to initial and final letters and storing these. The order of attention and of storage favors the ends of words because the ends carry more information than the middles. An incomplctc cntry will serve for recognition, but if words are to be produced (or recalled) they must be stored in full. For most words, then, it is eventually necessary to attend to the middle letters. Since end letters have been attended to from the first they should always be more clearly entered or more elaborately connected than middle letters. When recall is required, of words that are not very familiar to S as it was in our experiment, the end letters should often be accessible when the middle are not.

In building pronounceable sequences the English language, like all other languages, utilizes only a small fraction of its combinatorial possibilities (Hockett, 1958). If a language used all possible sequences of phonemes (or letters) its words could be shorter, but they would be much more vulnerable to misconstruction. A change of any single letter would result in reception of a different word. As matters are actually arranged, most changes result in no word at all; for example: *textant, sixtant, sektant.* Our words are highly redundant and fairly indestructible.

Underwood (1963) has made a distinction for the learning of nonsense syllables between the "nominal" stimulus which is the syllable presented and the "functional" stimulus which is the set of characteristics of the syllable actually used to cue the response. Underwood reviews evidence showing that college students learning paired-associates do not learn any more of a stimulus trigram than they have to. If, for instance, each of a set of stimulus trigrams has a different initial letter, then Ss are not likely to learn letters other than the first, since they do not need them.

Feigenbaum (1963) has written a computer program (EPAM) which simulates the selective-attention aspect of verbal learning as well as many other aspects. ". . . EPAM has a *noticing order for letters of syllables*, which prescribes at any moment a letter-scanning sequence for the matching process. Because it is observed that subjects generally consider end letters

before middle letters, the noticing order is initialized as follows: first letter, third letter, second letter" (p. 304). We believe that the differential recall of letters in various positions, revealed in Fig. 21-1 of this paper, is to be explained by the operation in the perception of real words of a rule very much like Feigenbaum's.

Feigenbaum's EPAM is so written as to make it possible for the noticing rule to be changed by experience. If the middle position were consistently the position that differentiated syllables, the computer would learn to look there first. We suggest that the human tendency to look first at the beginning of a word, then at the end and finally the middle has "grown" in response to the distribution of information in words. Miller and Friedman (1957) asked English speakers to guess letters for various open positions in segments of English text that were 5, 7, or 11 characters long. The percentages of correct first guesses show a very clear serial position effect for segments of all three lengths. Success was lowest in the early positions, next lowest in the final positions, and at a maximum in the middle positions. Therefore, information was greatest at the start of a word, next greatest at the end, and least in the middle. Attention needs to be turned where information is, to the parts of the word that cannot be guessed. The Miller and Friedman segments did not necessarily break at word boundaries but their discovery that the middle positions of continuous text are more easily guessed than the ends applies to words.

Is there any evidence that speakers of English do attend first to the ends of English words? There is no evidence that the eye fixations of adult readers consistently favor particular parts of words (Woodworth and Schlosberg, 1954). However, it is not eye fixation that we have in mind. A considerable stretch of text can be taken in from a single fixation point. We are suggesting that there is selection within this stretch, selection accomplished centrally; perhaps by a mechanism like Broadbent's (1958) "biased filter."

Bruner and O'Dowd (1958) studied word perception with tachistoscopic exposures too brief to permit more than one fixation. In each word presented there was a single reversal of two letters and the S knew this. His task was to identify the *actual* English word responding as quickly as possible. When the *actual* word was AVIATION, Ss were presented with one of the following: VAIATION, AVITAION, AVIATINO. Identification of the actual word as AVIATION was best when S saw AVITAION, next best when he saw AVIA-TINO, and most difficult when he saw VAIA-TION. In general, a reversal of the two initial letters made identification most difficult, reversal of the last two letters made it somewhat less difficult, reversal in the middle made least difficulty. This is what should happen if words are first scanned initially, then finally, then medially. But the scanning cannot be a matter of eye movements; it must be more central.

Selective attention to the ends of words should lead to the entry of these parts into the mental dictionary, in advance of the middle parts. However, we ordinarily need to know more than the ends of words. Underwood has pointed out (1963), in connection with paired-associate learning, that while partial knowledge may be enough for a stimulus syllable which need only be recognized it will not suffice for a response item which must be produced. The case is similar for natural language. In order to speak one must know all of a word. However, the words of the present study were low-frequency words, words likely to be in the passive or recognition vocabularies of the college-student Ss but not in their active vocabularies; stimulus items, in effect, rather than response items. If knowledge of the parts of new words begins at the ends and moves toward the middle we might expect a word like *numismatics*, which was on our list, to be still registered as NUM__ __ICS. Reduced entries of this sort would in many contexts serve to retrieve the definition.

The argument is reinforced by a well-known effect in spelling. Jensen (1962) has analyzed thousands of spelling errors for words of 7, 9, or 11 letters made by children in the eighth and tenth grades and by junior college freshmen. A striking serial position effect appears in all his sets of data such that errors are most common in the middle of the word, next most common at the end, and least common at the start. These results are as they should be if the order of attention and entry of information is first, last, and then, middle. Jensen's results show us what happens when children are forced to produce words that are still on the recognition level. His results remind us of those bluebooks in which students who are uncertain of the spelling of a word write the first and last letters with great clarity and fill in the middle with indecipherable squiggles. That is what should happen when a word that can be only partially recalled must be produced in its entirety. End letters and a stretch of squiggles may, however, be quite adequate

for recognition purposes. In the TOT experiment we have perhaps placed adult Ss in a situation comparable to that created for children by Jensen's spelling tests.

There are two points to clarify and the argument is finished. The Ss in our experiment were college students, and so in order to obtain words on the margin of knowledge we had to use words that are very infrequent in English as a whole. It is not our thought, however, that the TOT phenomenon occurs only with rare words. The absolute location of the margin of word knowledge is a function of S's age and education, and so with other Ss we would expect to obtain TOT states for words more frequent in English. Finally the need to produce (or recall) a word is not the only factor that is likely to encourage registration of its middle letters. The amount of detail needed to specify a word uniquely must increase with the total number of words known, the number from which any one is to be distinguished. Consequently the growth of vocabulary, as well as the need to recall, should have some power to force attention into the middle of a word.

REFERENCES

BARNHART, C. L. (Ed.) *The American college dictionary.* New York: Harper, 1948.

BROADBENT, D. E. *Perception and communication.* New York: Macmillan, 1958.

BRUNER, J. S., AND O'DOWD, D. A note on the informativeness of words. *Language and Speech,* 1958, 1, 98–101.

FEIGENBAUM, E. A. The simulation of verbal learning behavior. In E. A. Feigenbaum and J. Feldman (Eds.) *Computers and thought.* New York: McGraw-Hill, 1963. Pp. 297–309.

HOCKETT, C. F. *A course in modern linguistics.* New York: Macmillan, 1958.

JAMES, W. *The principles of psychology,* Vol. I. New York: Holt, 1893.

JENSEN, A. R. Spelling errors and the serial-position effect. *J. educ. Psychol.,* 1962, 53, 105-109.

KATZ, J. J., AND FODOR, J. A. The structure of a semantic theory. *Language,* 1963, 39, 170–210.

MILLER, G. A., AND FRIEDMAN, ELIZABETH A. The reconstruction of mutilated English texts. *Inform. Control,* 1957, 1, 38–55.

THORNDIKE, E. L., AND LORGE, I. *The teacher's word book of 30,000 words.* New York: Columbia Univer., 1952.

UNDERWOOD, B. J. Stimulus selection in verbal learning. In C. N. Cofer and B. S. Musgrave (Eds.) *Verbal behavior and learning: problems and processes.* New York: McGraw-Hill, 1963. Pp. 33–48.

WENZL, A. Empirische und theoretische Beiträge zur Erinnerungsarbeit bei erschwerter Wortfindung. *Arch. ges. Psychol.,* 1932, 85, 181–218.

WENZL, A. Empirische und theoretische Beiträge zur Erinnerungsarbeit bei erschwerter Wortfindung. *Arch. ges. Psychol.,* 1936, 97, 294–318.

WOODWORTH, R. S. *Psychology.* (3rd ed). New York: Holt, 1934.

WOODWORTH, R. S., AND SCHLOSBERG, H. *Experimental psychology.* (Rev. ed.). New York: Holt, 1954.

LANGUAGE AND THINKING

22. The Creation of Language *

David McNeill

The use of language by adult human beings is so natural and automatic a naive person might conclude language is innate. But we know from observations of very young children that language is not present initially and does not begin to appear in a form that we can readily understand until around the age of two. However, if deprived of the opportunity to practice, a child may never begin talking. Therefore, language must require learning as well as an adequate nervous system and speech apparatus.

But what is learned and how is it learned? Careful analysis of the structure of language suggests that speakers act as though they know a fairly complicated set of rules, like the rules for a game, even though they may not be able to state these rules. It would seem that the language game cannot be played without the rules, for the words alone are not sufficient.

Since rules appear to be essential in language acquisition it is difficult to apply the theories of learning that are used to explain animal behavior. In fact, there is reason to believe that a quite different kind of learning may be operative. In the next selection, Professor McNeill describes the acquisition of spoken language by young children and discusses the kinds of problems an adequate theory must accommodate.

At the age of about one, a normal child, not impaired by hearing loss or speech impediment, will begin to say words. By one-and-one half or two years, he will begin to form simple two- and three-word sentences. By four years, he will have mastered very nearly the entire complex and abstract structure of the English language. In slightly more than two years, therefore, children acquire full knowledge of the grammatical system of their native tongue. This stunning intellectual achievement is routinely performed by every pre-school child, but what is known about the process underlying it? The process is, as the title of this article implies, one of invention. On the basis of fundamental biological characteristics (of which only slight understanding is presently available), each generation creates language anew.

In order to understand the creation of language, one must understand something of what is created. The structure of language is not obvious to introspection, as

* Reprinted by permission of the author and *Discovery,* now incorporated with *Science Journal,* from *Discovery,* 1966, 27, 34-37.

any who have suffered through elementary school courses in "grammar" will attest. However, the appropriate portrayal of language is a linguistic description, not an elementary school "grammar". The grammars of modern linguistics aim to describe the linguistic *knowledge* possessed by fluent speakers of a language—their linguistic "competence", as the M.I.T. linguist Noam Chomsky calls it. A recent article by John C. Marshall introduced readers to some aspects of these grammars (*see* 'The language of man,' Discovery, October, 1964) so the nature of linguistic competence will be treated only briefly here.

Let us think about a single sentence. By so restricting our attention, we eliminate discourse, dialogue, and the exchange of ideas, all of which are important questions for understanding the development of language. In return we shall gain relative simplicity without losing an accurate vision of linguistic knowledge. A sentence consists of words arranged in a particular order, but it is much more than this. In addition, a sentence has structure; the words fall together in certain definite ways. As an example, take the sentence, *the professor berated the student*. It contains two major constituents (*the professor*) and (*berated the student*); the second of these, moreover, is itself made up of constituents, (*berated*) and (*the student*). The entire sentence, therefore, possesses a hierarchical structure in which some constituents contain others. This pattern can be represented by means of a tree-diagram in which lower-order constituents branch downward from higher-order ones. This much linguistic notation fulfills a fairly obvious purpose. Less obvious but equally important is the fact that sentences also possess a 'deep' or 'underlying' structure.

The importance of deep structure derives from its intimate involvement with our ability to extract meaning from sentences. Consider, for example, the similarities and differences between the two sentences, *John is easy to please* and *John is eager to please*. Superficially, these sentences are

constructed in the same way, but the sentences clearly differ profoundly. In the first *John* is the object of the verb, whereas in the second *John* is the subject of the sentence. Every English speaker automatically understands this difference and yet it is not represented in the surface form of the two sentences. Instead, the two sentences differ in deep structure.

Grammatical relations, such as subject and object, are carried by structures *not* directly apparent in the surface form of sentences. We know something of 'abstract' linguistic features, aspects of sentences that lie behind their manifest form. The deep structure of sentences carries such abstract knowledge. Deep structures must, accordingly, be different from the corresponding surface structures, and even the simplest sentence has an underlying structure that differs in some respect from its manifest form. The problem for a theory of language acquisition is to explain the development of such abstractions.

A key linguistic concept is the notion of a grammatical transformation. A transformation is a rule of grammar that relates deep structures to surface structures. Our intuitions about sentences include abstract knowledge precisely because we have learned to use a transformational grammar. Without rules of transformation, all linguistic knowledge would have to be manifest in the surface form of sentences, and a sentence like *John is easy to please* would be impossible. The acquisition of transformations then, is importantly involved in the acquisition of language.

ACQUIRING A UNIVERSAL GRAMMAR

Let us think, not about children for the moment, but about an abstract 'Language Acquisition Device', which we shall call LAD for short (alternatively, a 'Language Acquisition System', or LAS—the feminine form). LAD receives a *corpus* of speech, which is a set of utterances, some grammatical, some not. The corpus may be large, but it is not unlimited in size. It contains, let us say, the number of utterances ordinarily overheard by a two-year old child. Upon receipt of this corpus, LAD creates a *grammatical system*. This, in turn, may be regarded as LAD's theory about the regularities that appear in the corpus of speech. As with any theory, LAD's grammatical system will allow predictions of future observations—predictions of which utterances will be grammatical sentences. It will also allow LAD to distinguish the aspects of utterances that are unimportant from the aspects that are grammatically significant.

LAD creates a grammar by passing the evidence contained in the corpus through some kind of internal structure. The sequence can be represented by a simple flow diagram:

corpus of speech   LAD   grammatical system

If we understood LAD's internal structure, we would understand how LAD invents a grammar. The problem is not unlike those exercises given to engineering students in which they must infer the internal wiring of a 'black box'. Its input is a corpus of speech: its output is a grammatical system. Just as an engineering student, we need a theory of its internal structure.

One hint about LAD's internal structure arises from the fact that it must be able to acquire any natural language. We do not want LAD to find Bantu easier than, say, English, or Russian, or Japanese. Whatever is contained in LAD, therefore, must be universally applicable, so our theory of LAD will be (in part) a theory of linguistic universals. One way to portray some of the internal structure of LAD is to portray the structure common to all languages. This conclusion yields an important insight into the acquisition of language.

For notice that the problem of understanding LAD is exactly like the problem of understanding real children. Like LAD, children are exposed to a corpus of speech, and like LAD they develop grammatical competence on the basis of this corpus. Moreover, in the case of both LAD and children some kind of internal structure converts a corpus of speech into a grammatical system. Since the same corpus is input and the same grammatical system is output, LAD and children must have the same internal structure. LAD's internal structure therefore corresponds to the fundamental human capacity for language.

The abstract grammatical relations of subject-predicate and verb-object are linguistically universal. If they reflect a fundamental capacity for language, then children must impose these abstract relations on their earliest speech. The grammatical relations must appear early because a capacity for language *is* the reason (we suppose) that children acquire language quickly. The problem now is to find evidence on behalf of this hypothesis.

Two kinds may be mentioned. One comes from a small American child observed by Roger Brown, the other from a small Japanese child whom I have observed. We shall take up the American child first, a boy Brown calls Adam.

When Adam was two years old, he produced large numbers of word combinations. These were sentences in Adam's grammar. Two-word combinations were most common, three-word combinations somewhat less so, and four-word combinations were very rare. These sentences were the first that Brown recorded, and probably were among the first that Adam ever produced. A small sample is given below:

> Two boot
> Hear tractor
> See truck, mommy
> Adam make tower
> A gas

Roger Brown and his colleague Colin Fraser have called these sentences "telegraphic", aptly capturing their abbreviated quality. Analyzing many hundreds of such sentences, Brown and a second colleague, Ursula Bellugi, concluded that Adam possessed three different grammatical classes, two of which resembled classes of adult English. There were nouns (*boot, tractor, truck, mommy, Adam, tower, gas*), verbs (*hear, see, make*), and a third class of "modifiers" (*two* and *a* in the sentences above, plus adjectives, plus the words *this, that, other* and *'nother*). Adam's class of modifiers thus comprised several adult classes, but even his noun and verb classes failed to observe certain adult distinctions —for example, the difference between count (*boot*) and mass (*gas*) nouns.

Looking at Adam's sentences, an adult feels intuitively that they honour the basic grammatical relations of subject-predicate and verb-object. *Hear tractor* appears to be a verb and an object. *Adam make tower* appears to be a subject and a predicate, and the predicate in turn appears to be a verb and object. And so on. These intuitions are quite compelling, but of course they might also be quite wrong. Adam may not have intended these sentences in the way we interpret them. We need another means of examining Adam's speech that does not depend on our understanding of what he wanted to say.

One approach is based on the following calculations. With three grammatical classes, there are $(3)^2 = 9$ different two-word combinations, and $(3)^3 = 27$ different three-word combinations. If Adam were combining words at random, we should expect to find all (or nearly all) these nine and 27 different combinations. However, they do not all honour the basic grammatical relations. Only four of the two-word combinations directly express one or another grammatical relation, and only eight of the three-word combinations do so. If Adam were attempting to use the basic grammatical relations from the first, he would restrict himself to these admissible patterns. That is exactly what he did. In eight hours of recorded speech, involving some four hundred sentences, there were examples of every admissible combination but no examples of inadmissible ones.

It is not obvious that this should be the case on *a priori* grounds. Parental speech presents many examples of inadmissible combinations of Adam's grammatical classes. Take, for example, the combination, verb-verb-modifier. Because of the double verb, it does not express a grammatical relation, and sentences of this type —for example, *come eat this*—did not appear in Adam's early speech. But *come and eat this* is surely a common sentence-type in adult speech. It did not serve as a model for Adam because the adult sentence contains several transformations not yet part of Adam's grammatical competence. Lacking the appropriate transformations, there was no way for Adam to express the basic grammatical relations, so the sentence-type did not appear.

Adam's restriction of the variety of sentence-types is one kind of evidence that children include abstract relations in their earliest speech. A second kind of evidence comes from a child acquiring a radically different language, Japanese.

Unlike English, Japanese is a postpositional language. Very roughly, postpositions correspond to English prepositions, but not all postpositions can be translated into prepositions, and conversely. Among the postpositions without an equivalent in English are two, *wa* and *ga*, that indicate the grammatical subject of sentences. According to the linguist S.-Y. Kuroda, *wa* and *ga* are carried into the surface structure by transformations that operate on the deep structure. In order for a child to acquire these transformations, therefore, the abstract relation of 'subject' must already be available. If it were not, a child would not be able to use *wa* or *ga* appropriately.

The child whose speech I have observed is a little girl living in Tokyo, who hears only Japanese and, at the time of writing, is two years old. In the interest of maintaining the tradition begun by Brown, I shall call her Izanami, after the goddess of Japanese mythology who helped create the world.

Izanami's sentences at this time are all two-, three-, and occasionally four-words long. She is, therefore, at the same stage as Adam, still within the earliest phase of grammatical development. In eight hours of recorded speech, there were 100 occurrences of *ga*, but only 6 occurrences of *wa*. All Izanami's uses of *ga* were appropriate, and she rarely omitted the postposition when it was needed. Clearly Izanami can express the basic grammatical relation of 'subject' by means of the *ga*-transformation. Her earliest speech contains an abstract feature, as it must if a linguistic universal reflects an aspect of the fundamental capacity for language.

But what of *wa?* It is quite clear that Izanami does not know how to use it. Since she has the relation of 'subject' available to her, something must be blocking the *wa*-transformation itself. In parental speech, *wa* and *ga* appear in the same places, after the subject, so parental speech cannot explain the absence of *wa* from Izanami's grammar. Moreover, *wa* is used by Izanami's mother twice as often as *ga*, which if anything would favour the acquisition of *wa*. The explanation of *wa*'s absence seems to be the different uses to which *wa* and *ga* are put by Japanese grammar. Although both mark the subject of a sentence, their semantic implications are very different, and children do appear to be sensitive only to those embodied in *ga*.

The postposition *wa* is required whenever the predicate of a sentence is something attributed to the subject. It is the postposition for permanent conditions, the semantic significance of which is often translated into English by the expression "as for . . . . ."; *as for this, it is a flower*, or *as for cats, they eat goldfish*. In such cases, the sentence presents an unchanging and 'inherent' connection between the subject and the predicate.

The postposition *ga*, in contrast, is required whenever the subject of a sentence is merely linked to the predicate, the two standing in an *equal* and temporary rela-

tion. It is the postposition for momentary description, as in *a man is standing on the corner* or *the cat ate the goldfish*. In such cases, the sentence presents a fortuitous 'non-inherent' connection between the subject and the predicate.

Therefore, children apparently attempt to express momentary description when employing the abstract relation of 'subject', not permanent connections. This is a surprising result for several reasons.

One of the examples calling for *wa* above is a definition. In Japanese it would be, roughly, *this-wa is a flower*. We can be certain that Izanami understands sentences of this type in her mother's speech. They are the only way in which she receives new information and new vocabulary. Yet, *wa* does not appear in Izanami's grammar. Related to the use of *wa* in definitions is its use in describing stable relationships. One would say to a recalcitrant child, *people-wa eat their supper*. It is often assumed that children first develop grammar in an effort to *name* stable relationships in the physical world. Izanami belies this hypothesis. In fact, on Izanami's evidence, naming and grammatical development have nothing whatsoever to do with each other. All instances of appellation require *wa* in Japanese. Because Izanami, just as all children, names objects a great deal, her postposition would have to be *wa*, not *ga*, if there were a connection between the acquisition of names and the acquisition of grammar. In fact, however, they are entirely independent.

Children exposed to English and children exposed to Japanese both include abstract grammatical relations in their earliest speech. To these children may be added a third child exposed to Russian. According to Dan I. Slobin, here too, abstract grammatical relations appear in early speech. In spite of radical differences in the conditions of learning, therefore, children are found to do similar things. They do so because of their shared inborn capacity for language.

ACQUIRING A PARTICULAR GRAMMAR

Our account of language acquisition is not yet complete. Ultimately, children do different things when the conditions of learning are different. Exposure to English does not lead to competence in Japanese! What has been left out of account is the acquisition of transformations. In considering this aspect of development, we shall see something of how a child brings his capacity for language into contact with the speech of his local community.

The general idea of a transformation is an instance of what Chomsky calls a "formal" universal of language. Transformations appear in all languages, but the *particular* transformations of each language are peculiar to that language. Aside from sound, in fact, transformations are the main source of linguistic uniqueness.

How do children acquire transformations? Unfortunately, there is no definite answer. However, one view is that the process takes place in the same manner as scientific inference. On the basis of their capacity for language, children formulate hypotheses about regularities observed in parental speech. Each hypothesis is evaluated against further evidence, such as additional parental speech and parental reactions to a child's own speech. In pursuing this empirical programme, children may even perform linguistic experiments, the equivalent in most respects of the experiments conducted in scientific laboratories.

The experimental aspect is perhaps the most interesting, for it involves a symbiotic exchange between a child and his parent. Roger Brown has called attention to a common phenomenon in parent-child dialogues. Very often parents imitate children, and in so doing, enlarge a child's sentence into completely well-formed English. If a child says *doggie bite*, a parent may reply *yes, he is biting*, adding the auxiliary verb, *is*, and the progressive inflection, *-ing*. Both additions exemplify details of English transformation, and do so within the context of the child's own speech. Brown calls this process "expansion". He finds that parents expand approximately 30% of what two year old children say.

Expansions provide a natural experiment for a child. Suppose a child does say *doggie bite*. There are many possible expansions. In addition to *yes, he is biting*, an adult might say *he bit, he will bite, his biting. . . . . .*, and probably more. Each expansion holds constant the elements preserved in the child's sentence while varying a particular transformation, just as a real experiment holds some factors constant while varying others. Moreover, the observations in a real experiment are relevant to the hypothesis under test and the same is true in expansion. Suppose that context indicates to the parent that the child is talking about an event going on at the moment. The only possible expansion would then be *yes, he is biting*. If the child were in fact talking about this event as it occurred, and if he were looking for some way to express this idea, the expansion would provide relevant information.

There is one respect in which expansions and real experiments differ. An experimenter has some control over his observations, but a child does not. The child above may have meant that this dog always bites, in which event the expansion *yes he is biting* would have provided mis-information. It is unlikely that this happens often. Presumably, one reason that adults do not expand more than 30% of the time is that 70% of the contexts are not clear, and so offer no guidance as to what a child means. Parents play safe with this powerful tool of science.

A capacity for language would contain a great deal more than the matters discussed in this article—the basic grammatical relations and the general idea of a transformation. It would certainly include, in addition, an ability to construct a dictionary of some kind as well as certain rules for using it. There are also universal phonetic principles, such as the stock of 'distinctive features' into which all speech sounds may be resolved, which probably correspond to a part of the capacity for language. There are probably universal principles whereby linguistic knowledge is converted into actual speaking or listening, although very little is known about this at the present time. (It is significant, nonetheless, that all children speak fluently, no matter how primitive their grammars may be.) All these things, plus still others not yet imagined, may make up the capacity for language, and may, therefore, contribute to the astonishing speed with which children acquire their native tongue.

However, the possibility is worth considering that very little of this is, in fact, a capacity for *language*. Much of what I have discussed may actually be the linguistic manifestation of a very general, though still inborn, cognitive capacity—cognition is the process by which the mind gets knowledge. If this is true, then the study of how language is acquired may provide insight into the very basis of mental life. For if the capacity for language is a special case of more general cognitive capacity, it would follow that the latter must have all the universal properties of the former. In short, the appropriate theory of mind may be a transformational system in which a vast range of complex ideas is converted into a much smaller range of abstract cognitive structures, just as a true grammar converts an infinite range of sentences into a limited number of abstract deep structures. Needless to say, the exploration of this possibility has only begun.

THE BASIS FOR THE RAPID ACQUISITION OF LANGUAGE

Nonetheless, if for the moment we accept this view, the creation of language can be considered in a larger sense, speculating on an aspect of the evolution of language. Our speculations may shed some light on the basis of children's ability to acquire language in a very short period of time. The argument will be that language has come to mirror cognition through a long period of evolution which consisted of the addition of specific transformations—the rules that distinguish one language from another. The primaeval grammar may have been mainly free of transformations, just as systems of animal communication are free of transformations. It may have been a system in which the features now contained in the deep structure of sentences were very nearly all located in the surface structure. As such, it would have been very different from the cognitive system of primitive language users.

Moreover, if primaeval grammar was mostly free of transformation, it would need to have been very complex in order to have communicated a wide range of information. Without transformations to relate a large variety of surface structures to a limited number of abstract structures, all the different surface types must have been understood directly instead of indirectly through deep structures. A grammar of that degree of complexity would have taken many years to acquire. The suggestion, therefore, is this: specific transformations evolved in order to make acquisition of grammar possible at earlier ages. The pressure for evolution would have arisen from the need to express great conceptual variety through economic means. The consequence of evolution would have been a vast reduction in the complexity of language without loss of expressive power. In the end, the conceptual and linguistic systems would have been brought into alignment by making language abstract at precisely those points where cognition is abstract.

The innovators of such evolutionary change could only have been children attempting to acquire language. Adults had nothing to do with it. Language slowly became transformational because an occasional child reformulated the speech received from adults by inventing a transformation. This, of course, is what contemporary children do, too—invent transformations. The process of invention would be the same for children of the remote past as for children of today. The difference is that a contemporary child is presented with sentences that reflect the presence of transformations (whereas a child of antiquity was not). But if the basic intellectual abilities of children in antiquity were roughly the same as now, this very fact—that transformed sentences signal the presence of transformations—explains how each innovation in the evolution of language could have been passed on to the next generation. The process of evolution would have been the process of language acquisition. Each new transformation would have slightly changed the corpus of speech that the innovator, now mature, presented to his progeny. His progeny then could have acquired the transformation in the usual manner, just as do contemporary children, and so language would have advanced.

The direction of evolution, according to the account just given, must have been toward simplicity. It was not toward complexity, as most theories of linguistic evolution have it. According to the present view, language changed from an extremely complex system, largely free of transformations and taking many years to acquire, to a much simpler system, rich in transformations and taking only a few years to acquire. Thus, the presence of transformations in contemporary language allows children to develop language with the great speed that they do. Indeed, transformations may have evolved precisely in order to enable every child as young as two to acquire a language—an achievement so commonplace that few people ever stop to question this remarkable act of creation.

FURTHER READING

The Genesis of Language: In Children and Animals. By F. Smith and G. A. Miller (MIT Press, Cambridge, Mass., 1966).

New Directions in the Study of Language. By E. H. Lenneberg (MIT Press, Cambridge, Mass., 1964).

Aspects of the Theory of Syntax. By N. Chomsky (MIT Press, Cambridge, Mass., 1965).

Social Psychology. By R. Brown (Free Press, Glencoe, Ill., 1965).

23. An Atmosphere Effect in Formal Syllogistic Reasoning *

Robert S. Woodworth and Saul B. Sells

By formal logic the validity of any argument can be tested independently of the truth or falsity of the initial premise. The method of testing is perfectly rigorous and completely rational. The existence of an ideal system of logic (and mathematics) naturally invites comparison with deductive thought as it actually occurs in man. At one time the formal rules of logic and mathematics were thought to be the "laws of thinking." But investigations of thinking suggest that human thought processes are far more labile and irrational than a respectable system of logic could accept. In the next selection, Professors Woodworth and Sells describe a now classic experiment which examines one source of illogical thought.

* Reprinted by permission of Dr. Sells and the American Psychological Association from the Journal of Experimental Psychology, 1935, 18, 451-460.

True though it certainly is that the syllogism is a tool of logical analysis rather than a diagram of any typical reasoning process, the use of syllogisms as problems appears to be a promising lead in the experimental study of thinking. Especially syllogisms with purely symbolic terms, such as

All S is M;
All P is M;
Therefore, all S is P,

have some of the advantages possessed by lists of nonsense syllables in memory experiments, in their freedom from extraneous associations and from factual truth or falsity. When such symbolic syllogisms, valid and invalid, are presented in an experiment, as has been done by Störring (2-7) and by Wilkins (8), they are found to be very unequal in difficulty. Certain of the standard logical fallacies, like that of Undistributed Middle, offer much more difficulty than some others, as Universal Conclusion from Particular Premise. Why some syllogisms make easy problems and others difficult ones is a question for psychological inquiry.

In scrutinizing the detailed reports of Störring and Wilkins, we have succeeded in formulating three hypotheses which, taken together, seem to account for the observed differences in difficulty, the presence of difficulty being indicated either by the subject's introspective report or by the objective fact of his acceptance of an invalid conclusion.

The first hypothesis will be readily accepted. It is simply that difficulty arises from the ambiguity of the language in which syllogisms are expressed. Ambiguity attaches especially to the word 'some,' as in "Some X is Y." By the conventions of formal logic 'some' means 'at least some,' *i.e.* 'some and perhaps all,' while in ordinary speech it often carries the implication, 'some but not all.' A person not familiar with formal logic may therefore regard it as perfectly correct to infer from "Some X is Y" that "Some (other) X is not Y."

The second hypothesis is that of caution or wariness on the part of the subject in an experiment. It is evidently more incautious to accept a universal than a particular conclusion, and probably it is more incautious to accept an affirmative than a negative proposition. At any rate a larger percent of invalid particular conclusions are accepted than of universal, and of negative than of affirmative.

The third hypothesis, that of 'atmosphere,' demands fuller explanation and defence. The atmosphere of the premises may be affirmative or negative, universal or particular. Whatever it is, according to the hypothesis, it creates a sense of validity for the corresponding conclusion. An affirmative atmosphere in the premises makes it easy to accept an affirmative conclusion, etc.

An analogous kind of 'atmosphere' accounts for many grammatical errors. A heedless speaker or writer often makes the verb agree in number with the general atmosphere of the subject phrase instead of with the noun which is the formal subject. For instance:

"The laboratory equipment in these situations were in many instances essentially the same as those used before."
"A common background of emotional conflict, repression, and abnormal reactions of a motor, visceral or perceptual nature, have justified an inherent relationship."

Still another analogy is found in the 'confluxion' illusions, such as the Müller-Lyer, in which the observer sees one of two equal lines as longer than the other because the total impression of one part of the figure is bulkier than that of the other part. He finds it difficult in the figure and in the sentence, as in the syllogism, to analyze out the precise fact or relationship with which he is trying to deal.

The atmosphere hypothesis was first suggested by the difficulties of 'simple conversion,' as brought out by Eidens (1) and by Wilkins. If we use the customary symbols for the four standard propositions, we have the following table, derived from the data of Wilkins.

PERCENT OF COLLEGE STUDENTS ACCEPTING THE SIMPLE CONVERSE OF SYMBOLIC PROPOSITIONS

A = universal affirmative, as "All X is Y"	. .	24%
E = universal negative, as "No X is Y"	. . . .	72
I = particular affirmative, as "Some X is Y"		90
O = particular negative, as "Some X is not Y"	. . . .	53

'Atmosphere' can account for the acceptance of the simple converse of A or O, which is invalid, as well, no doubt, as for some of the acceptances of the valid converse of E or I. 'Caution' can explain the failure of a considerable percent to accept the converse of E, and the less frequent acceptance of the converse of A than of I.

According to the atmosphere hypothesis,

A has an all-yes atmosphere
E has an all-no atmosphere
I has a some-yes atmosphere
O has a some-no atmosphere

When the subject does not *see* the relationships clearly, he is influenced by the atmosphere of the premise, and is inclined to accept the simple converse of any symbolic proposition.

The hypothesis needs to be supplemented or elaborated in order to cover the case of the syllogism with its two premises. If they are both of one kind, A, E, I or O, atmosphere clearly calls for a similar conclusion. But if one premise is A and the other I, the atmosphere is partly universal and partly particular, a blend of *all* and *some*, which would certainly be weaker than a straight *all*, and thus would amount to a *some*.

In general formulation the secondary hypotheses suggested for application to syllogistic reasoning are (1) that a particular premise creates a *some* atmosphere, even though the other premise be universal, and (2) that a negative premise creates a negative atmosphere even though the other premise be affirmative.

In detail, the secondary atmosphere hypotheses are that:

with premises AA, atmosphere calls for an A conclusion;

with premises AE or EE, it calls for an E conclusion;

with premises AI or II, it calls for an I conclusion;

with premises AO, EI, EO, IO or OO, it calls for an O conclusion.

The reader can judge for himself whether there is any prima facie case for atmosphere by glancing through the following list of syllogisms, asking himself simply which conclusions seem easiest to accept.

AA If all X's are Y's, and all Z's are Y's, then:
    A All X's are Z's
    I Some X's are Z's
    O Some X's are not Z's
    E No X's are Z's

AI If all X's are Y's, and some Y's are Z's, then:
    A All X's are Z's
    I Some X's are Z's
    O Some X's are not Z's
    E No X's are Z's

AO If all X's are Y's, and some Z's are not X's, then:
    A All Z's are Y's
    I Some Z's are Y's
    O Some Z's are not Y's
    E No Z's are Y's

AE If all X's are Y's, and no X's are Z's, then:
    A All Z's are Y's
    I Some Z's are Y's
    O Some Z's are not Y's
    E No Z's are Y's

II If some X's are Y's, and some Y's are Z's, then:
    A All X's are Z's
    I Some X's are Z's
    O Some X's are not Z's
    E No X's are Z's

IO If some X's are Y's, and some Y's are not Z's, then:
    A All X's are Z's
    I Some X's are Z's
    O Some X's are not Z's
    E No X's are Z's

IE If some X's are Y's, and no Y's are Z's, then:
    A All Z's are X's
    I Some Z's are X's
    O Some Z's are not X's
    E No Z's are X's

OO If some X's are not Y's, and some X's are not Z's, then:
    A All Y's are Z's
    I Some Y's are Z's
    O Some Y's are not Z's
    E No Y's are Z's

OE If some X's are not Y's, and no Y's are Z's, then:

    A All Z's are X's
    I Some Z's are X's
    O Some Z's are not X's
    E No Z's are X's

EE If no X's are Y's, and no X's are Z's, then:

    A All Y's are Z's
    I Some Y's are Z's
    O Some Y's are not Z's
    E No Y's are Z's

The more definite evidence which we have to present as a check on the atmosphere hypothesis comes from two syllogism experiments, one being that of Wilkins, already cited, and the other an unpublished study by Sells. Wilkins had as subjects 81 Columbia College undergraduates, while Sells had 90 educated adults who were regularly employed as subjects on the Civil Works Administration project in Adult Learning, conducted at the Institute of Educational Research, Teachers College, Columbia University, under the direction of Dr. Irving Lorge, in 1934.

The syllogisms were presented somewhat differently in the two experiments, and in neither exactly as shown in the above list. Wilkins presented three conclusions with each of 35 pairs of premises, as for example:

No a's are b's; some a's are c's; therefore

    a. some c's are not b's
        (accepted by 71 percent)
    b. no c's are b's
        (accepted by 23 percent)
    c. some b's are not c's
        (accepted by 47 percent)

Here the first conclusion is valid, and usually in the Wilkins experiment one or more of the suggested conclusions was valid (instead of all being invalid as in our list above). The subjects were instructed to mark each separate conclusion as valid or invalid. The results of this experiment, so far as they have to do with the acceptance of invalid conclusions from purely symbolic premises, have been extracted by the authors from the Wilkins data and are presented here in Table I.

Tables Showing the Effect of Atmosphere on Acceptance of Invalid Conclusions

Entries indicate average percent accepting each type of false conclusion from given premises. Blanks mean that the corresponding types were not tried in the experiments.

TABLE I
($n = 81$)

Premises	Types of Invalid Conclusion			
	A	E	I	O
AA	36		33	11
AE	4	45	4	34
EE	3	21		13
AI	6		62	39
II			51	29
AO			33	47
EI		23	8	44
OO			18	32

TABLE II
($n = 90$)

Premises	Types of Invalid Conclusion			
	A	E	I	O
AA	51		66	27
AE	8	51	19	54
EA		56		59
EE		41		37
AI	18		66	
IA	21		70	
II			68	
AO		18	41	71
OA		21	43	74
EI		31		58
IE		32		59
IO				60
OI				63
EO				53
OE				49
OO				54

In the Sells experiment 300 syllogisms were presented, each with a single conclusion to be marked as 'true' or 'false,' as in the example,

    If no x's are y's,
    And if all z's are y's;
    Then no z's are x's.

The results of this experiment by Sells are shown in Table II.

The question answered by Tables I and II is this: Given two premises of the types shown in the left-hand column, and a suggested conclusion of the type shown at the top of a column, what percent of the subjects accept the conclusion as valid when, logically, it is invalid? Each entry shows the responses of the 81–90 subjects to one or more problems; but where there are blanks in the tables, no problems of the corresponding type were presented.

The bold-faced numbers in the tables show the percent accepting invalid conclusions which are favored by 'atmosphere'; and it will be seen that these percents are always substantial, and larger, with few exceptions, than the percents accepting invalid conclusions not favored by atmosphere. The exceptions, and indeed nearly all the acceptances not accounted for by atmosphere, can be brought under the other two hypotheses of 'caution' and of the ambiguity of *some*. For many subjects, "Some are" implies "Some are not" and vice versa. When therefore an *I* conclusion is favored by atmosphere, we can expect an *O* conclusion also to be often accepted; and vice versa.

'Caution' would lead to the acceptance of a particular conclusion when atmosphere favors the corresponding universal. Thus, with the premises *AA*, we find fully as many subjects accepting the *I* as the *A* conclusion; and similarly when atmosphere calls for an *E* conclusion we find large percents accepting the *O* conclusion as well. There is however excellent logical ground for such acceptances, once 'atmosphere' is recognized; for an *A* proposition logically implies its subordinate *I*, an *E* its subordinate *O*. Whenever a subject would have accepted an *A* conclusion, he should be willing to accept an *I* also. (He would not do so, of course, if and when he took *some* to mean *not all*.) Thus nearly all the acceptances not referable to mere atmosphere can be explained by atmosphere plus a little logic, or by atmosphere weakened by caution, or by the ambiguity of *some*. The only remaining exception of any importance is the fairly large percent accepting conclusion *E* from premises *EI*, where

atmosphere favors *O* and not *E*. A syllogism in which this occurred is quoted from Wilkins on page 452 above.

The order of the premises seems to have little effect on their atmosphere or on the acceptance of the conclusion. Table II affords a comparison of six pairs of premises presented in both orders. We observe that, with premises *AE*, 51 percent accepted a false *E* conclusion, as against 56 percent accepting this conclusion from premises in the reverse order, *EA*. The other comparisons show similar small differences.

An interesting corollary of the atmosphere hypothesis has to do with *valid conclusions*. Since the secondary hypotheses of atmosphere (page 193) correspond with certain formal rules of the syllogism, to the effect that if one premise is negative the conclusion must be negative, and if one premise is particular the conclusion must be particular, atmosphere should function to facilitate the drawing or acceptance of a valid conclusion. Therefore the valid conclusions should be less difficult than the invalid. In the Sells experiment with 300 syllogisms the average percent of errors for the 71 valid items was 16, while for the 229 invalid items it was 40. For 48 items presenting the Fallacy of Universal Conclusion from a Particular Premise, which proved to be the least difficult of the nine formal fallacies presented, the average percent of errors was 20.

A further bit of evidence for atmosphere can be drawn from the Wilkins data on acceptance of *valid* conclusions. Premises *AA* are capable of yielding valid conclusions in either *A* or *I*, and premises *AE* (or *EA*) can yield valid conclusions in *E* or *O*. Atmosphere should give the advantage to the *A* conclusions from *AA*, and to the *E* conclusions from *AE*, whether valid or invalid. The percents of acceptance are as shown on the next page.

Reading horizontally in this table we see that valid conclusions, as well as invalid, are more often accepted when favored by atmosphere than otherwise. Reading vertically we see that the valid conclusions are

Premises	AA			AE		
Conclusions	A	I	S.D.$_{diff.}$	E	O	S.D.$_{diff.}$
Valid	96	76	3.5	80	59	3.0
Invalid	36	33	3.2	45	34	4.9
Valid–Invalid	60	43		35	25	

more often accepted than the invalid. The difference, Valid-Invalid (like the difference Right-Wrong in a True-False test) can be regarded as a measure of the amount of acceptance of the valid conclusions which is due to seeing the logical relationship. That is, while this group of college students showed a 96 percent acceptance of the valid A conclusions from AA premises, they also showed a 36 percent acceptance of invalid A conclusions from the same type of premises, because of atmosphere or other illogical factors, and therefore they can be credited only with a 96 − 36 = 60 percent net score for genuine understanding of the relationships in AAA syllogisms. Their understanding was much less in AEE syllogisms.

The evidence for the atmosphere hypothesis falls short of what would be demanded for a complete demonstration. The gaps in the tables need to be filled in by further experiments now in progress. These gaps represent types of syllogisms which are usually considered too absurd to deserve a trial, and reference back to our first list of sample syllogisms will show how absurd many of them are. Still they should be tried and may prove to be more deceptive than they seem.

SUMMARY

The problem is that of discovering psychological factors operating towards the acceptance of invalid conclusions in a syllogism test. Three such factors are suggested: the ambiguity of the word *some*, which is used in a distributive sense in logic ('at least some') and very often in a partitive sense in ordinary speech ('only some'); 'caution' or wariness, favoring the acceptance of weak and guarded rather than of strong conclusions; and 'atmosphere,' the global impression or 'feel' of the premises, which is affirmative or negative, universal or particular. Examination of the data from two experiments indicates that nearly all the acceptances of invalid conclusions can possibly be explained by these three hypothetical factors.

REFERENCES

1. EIDENS, H., Experimentelle Untersuchungen über den Denkverlauf bei unmittelbaren Folgerungen, *Arch. f. d. ges. Psychol.*, 1929, **71**, 1–66.
2. STÖRRING, G., Experimentelle Untersuchungen über einfache Schlussprozesse, *Arch. f. d. ges. Psychol.*, 1908, **11**, 1–127.
3. STÖRRING, G., Allgemeine Bestimmungen über Denkprozesse und kausale Behandlung einfacher experimentell gewonnener Schlussprozesse, *Arch. f. d. ges. Psychol.*, 1925, **52**, 1–60.
4. STÖRRING, G., Psychologie der disjunktiven und hypothetischen Urteile und Schlüsse, *Arch. f. d. ges. Psychol.*, 1926, **54**, 23–84.
5. STÖRRING, G., Psychologie der zweiten und dritten Schlussfigur und allgemeine Gesetzmässigkeiten der Schlussprozesse, *Arch. f. d. ges. Psychol.*, 1926, **55**, 47–110.
6. STÖRRING, G., *Das urteilende und schliessende Denken in kausaler Behandlung*, Leipzig, Akademische Verlagsgesellschaft, 1926. Pp. xv + 232.
7. STÖRRING, W., Experimentelle Untersuchungen über einfache und komplexere Schlussprozesse, *Arch. f. d. ges. Psychol.*, 1925, **50**, 467–512.
8. WILKINS, M. C., The effect of changed material on ability to do formal syllogistic reasoning, *Arch. of Psychol.*, 1928, **16** (whole no. 102), pp. 83.
9. WILHELM, W., Über Mittel und Fehler beim Schliessen, *Arch. f. d. ges. Psychol.*, 1934, **92**, 175–192.

BEHAVIOR DYNAMICS:
ANXIETY AND CURIOSITY

In common sense terms, the topic of behavior dynamics is concerned with the question of "why" people do what they do. Why does one decide to become a scientist, an engineer, or an artist? Why do students select a particular major, or study harder in some courses than in others? Why does the coed buy the red dress rather than the blue one, and choose to wear it on one occasion but not on another? The scientific study of behavior dynamics is concerned with the motivational determinants of these actions, that is, with the investigation of factors that instigate, energize, and sustain behavior. Thus, behavior dynamics involves processes that may be described by words such as motives, drives, needs, goals, purposes, aims, and intentions.

It is customary in the study of behavior dynamics to identify two general classes of motives or drives, conventionally referred to as physiological or primary drives and acquired or secondary drives. Primary drives are based on vital organic needs that result when an organism lacks something essential to its survival. For example, deprivation of food or water energizes and sustains a variety of behavioral responses designed to eliminate or alleviate these conditions. In a similar manner, sex hormones help to activate complex patterns of behavior that bring about sexual satisfaction.

The motivations most significant for human adjustment, however, do not generally come from deprivations of vital needs, but instead they arise from the social interactions of people. Beginning with the extreme dependency of human infants and young children on their parents, a variety of social motives may be acquired, depending upon the manner in which the child's needs for nurturance and love are handled. Through learning, the intensity of social motives can become so strong that individuals will endure extreme degrees of pain and deprivation, often risking their lives for causes that cannot be understood solely in terms of man's biological nature. Such strongly motivated behaviors, marked by strivings to escape or to attack and by widespread changes in the viscera and skeletal muscles, are called emotions. Fear and anger are examples of intense emotional states that may have profound effects upon behavior.

The idea that fear or anxiety is a pervasive emotion in man and animals is not new and it is generally accepted that anxiety is a fundamental factor in neurotic symptom formation. In contrast to the long history of concern with the motivational effects of anxiety, psychologists did not begin to consider curiosity as a drive state until the early 1950's, and the legitimacy of this interpretation is still open to question. As motivational states, anxiety and curiosity are quite different from the physiological drives that are based on states of deprivation. Like physiological drives, anxiety and curiosity seem to involve activation of the autonomic nervous system. But these emotional states differ from physiological drives in that they seem to have a much broader range of effects on human behavior.

The nine articles in this section are all related to theory and research on anxiety (fear) and curiosity. The first three articles provide historical accounts of early concerns with these emotional states. In the first selection, Darwin gives a vivid description of the properties of fear in man and animals. Like Darwin, William James regarded fear as an instinctive reaction to certain stimuli that once posed a threat to the survival of man's ancient ancestors. James also considered curiosity to be an instinctive response to novel objects, and he was among the first to recognize the intrinsic antagonistic relationship between curiosity and fear. In the final article in this group, Watson and Rayner describe one of the first laboratory investigations of fear. Their results show that neutral stimuli can acquire the power to elicit this powerful emotional response through classical conditioning.

The next three articles are concerned with current theory and research on anxiety. Freud discusses some of the complexities associated with the problem of anxiety, the relationship between fear and anxiety, and the difference between objective and neurotic anxiety. Spence describes a number of experiments that show the effects of anxiety, conceptualized as "emotionally-based drive," on different learning tasks. Finally, Spielberger cites evidence from the research literature that provides a basis for distinguishing between concepts of anxiety as an emotional state and as a dispositional personality trait.

The last three articles in the section are concerned with theory and research on curiosity. Berlyne reviews experiments in which exploratory behavior was aroused by novel or complex situations, and he interprets the results of these studies as demonstrating a curiosity drive. Maw and Maw first identified children who were rated by themselves and others as high in curiosity, and then showed that these children preferred to hear stories about unusual designs or symbols. In the final article of this section, Penney investigates the relationship between anxiety and curiosity as personality traits. His finding that these traits are negatively correlated suggests that anxious children tend to inhibit exploratory behavior.

EARLY CONCERN WITH FEAR AND CURIOSITY

24. Fear and Terror *

Charles Darwin

Fear is generally regarded as one of the most basic human emotions. Everyone experiences fear from time to time when circumstances pose a threat to personal well-being. If experienced in moderate amounts, fear is adaptive because it energizes the actions necessary to cope with an immediate danger. However, in excessive amounts, fear is maladaptive since it leads to ineffective behavior and debility and can even cause death.

In order to study fear in detail, its properties must be identified and described. This has been done by Charles Darwin, perhaps the greatest naturalistic observer of all time. In the following selection from *The Expression of Emotions in Man and Animals*, first published in 1872, Darwin describes the most typical manifestations of fear—rapid palpitation of the heart, trembling, erection of the hair, dilation of the pupils, dryness of the mouth, increased perspiration, peculiar facial expression, change in voice quality, etc.

An important characteristic of fear noted by Darwin is that it varies in level of intensity, ranging from mild apprehension or surprise to an extreme "agony of terror." For Darwin, the potential for experiencing fear was an inherent characteristic of animals and men, evolved over countless generations through the process of natural selection.

* Excerpted from Chapter XII of *The Expression of Emotions in Man and Animals*. D. Appleton and Company, New York, 1896.

The word 'fear' seems to be derived from what is sudden and dangerous;[1] and that of terror from the trembling of the vocal organs and body. I use the word 'terror' for extreme fear; but some writers think it ought to be confined to cases in which the imagination is more particularly concerned. Fear is often preceded by astonishment, and is so far akin to it, that both lead to the senses of sight and hearing being instantly aroused. In both cases the eyes and mouth are widely opened, and the eyebrows raised. The frightened man at first stands like a statue motionless and breathless, or crouches down as if instinctively to escape observation.

The heart beats quickly and violently, so that it palpitates or knocks against the ribs; but it is very doubtful whether it then works more efficiently than usual, so as to send a greater supply of blood to all parts of the body; for the skin instantly becomes pale, as during incipient faintness. This paleness of the surface, however, is probably in large part, or exclusively, due to the vasomotor centre being affected in such a manner as to cause the contraction of the small arteries of the skin. That the skin is much affected under the sense of

[1] H. Wedgwood, Dict. of English Etymology, vol. ii. 1862, p. 35. See, also, Gratiolet ('De la Physionomie,' p. 135) on the sources of such words as 'terror, horror, rigidus, frigidus,' &c.

great fear, we see in the marvellous and inexplicable manner in which perspiration immediately exudes from it. This exudation is all the more remarkable, as the surface is then cold, and hence the term a cold sweat; whereas, the sudorific glands are properly excited into action when the surface is heated. The hairs also on the skin stand erect; and the superficial muscles shiver. In connection with the disturbed action of the heart, the breathing is hurried. The salivary glands act imperfectly; the mouth becomes dry,[2] and is often opened and shut. I have also noticed that under slight fear there is a strong tendency to yawn. One of the best-marked symptoms is the trembling of all the muscles of the body; and this is often first seen in the lips. From this cause, and from the dryness of the mouth, the voice becomes husky or indistinct, or may altogether fail. "Obstupui, steteruntque comæ, et vox faucibus hæsit."

Of vague fear there is a well-known and grand description in Job:—"In thoughts from the visions of the night, when deep sleep falleth on men, fear came upon me, and trembling, which made all my bones to shake. Then a spirit passed before my face; the hair of my flesh stood up. It stood still, but I could not discern the form thereof: an image was before my eyes, there was silence, and I heard a voice, saying, Shall mortal man be more just than God? Shall a man be more pure than his Maker?" (Job iv. 13.)

As fear increases into an agony of terror, we behold, as under all violent emotions, diversified results. The heart beats wildly, or may fail to act and faintness ensue; there is a death-like pallor; the breathing is laboured; the wings of the nostrils are wildly dilated; "there is a gasping and convulsive motion of the lips, a tremor on the hollow cheek, a gulping and catching of the throat;"[3] the uncovered and protruding eyeballs are fixed on the object of terror; or they may roll restlessly from side to side, *huc illuc volvens oculos totumque pererrat*.[4] The pupils are said to be enormously dilated. All the muscles of the body may become rigid, or may be thrown into convulsive movements. The hands are alternately clenched and opened, often with a twitching movement. The arms may be protruded, as if to avert some dreadful danger, or may be thrown wildly over the head. The Rev. Mr. Hagenauer has seen this latter action in a terrified Australian. In other cases there is a sudden and uncontrollable tendency to headlong flight; and so strong is this, that the boldest soldiers may be seized with a sudden panic.

As fear rises to an extreme pitch, the dreadful scream of terror is heard. Great beads of sweat stand on the skin. All the muscles of the body are relaxed. Utter prostration soon follows, and the mental powers fail. The intestines are affected. The sphincter muscles cease to act, and no longer retain the contents of the body.

Dr. J. Crichton Browne has given me so striking an account of intense fear in an insane woman, aged thirty-five, that the description though painful ought not to be omitted. When a paroxysm seizes her, she screams out, "This is hell!" "There is a black woman!" "I can't get out!"—and other such exclamations. When thus screaming, her movements are those of alternate tension and tremor. For one instant she clenches her hands, holds her arms out before her in a stiff semiflexed position; then suddenly bends her body forwards, sways rapidly to and fro, draws her fingers through her hair, clutches at

---

[2] Mr. Bain ('The Emotions and the Will,' 1865, p. 54) explains in the following manner the origin of the custom "of subjecting criminals in India to the ordeal of the morsel of rice. The accused is made to take a mouthful of rice, and after a little time to throw it out. If the morsel is quite dry, the party is believed to be guilty,—his own evil conscience operating to paralyse the salivating organs."

[3] Sir C. Bell, Transactions of Royal Phil. Soc. 1822, p. 308. 'Anatomy of Expression,' p. 88 and pp. 164–169.

[4] See Moreau on the rolling of the eyes, in the edit. of 1820 of Lavater, tome iv. p. 263. Also, Gratiolet, De la Phys. p. 17.

her neck, and tries to tear off her clothes. The sterno-cleido-mastoid muscles (which serve to bend the head on the chest) stand out prominently, as if swollen, and the skin in front of them is much wrinkled. Her hair, which is cut short at the back of her head, and is smooth when she is calm, now stands on end; that in front being dishevelled by the movements of her hands. The countenance expresses great mental agony. The skin is flushed over the face and neck, down to the clavicles, and the veins of the forehead and neck stand out like thick cords. The lower lip drops, and is somewhat everted. The mouth is kept half open, with the lower jaw projecting. The cheeks are hollow and deeply furrowed in curved lines running from the wings of the nostrils to the corners of the mouth. The nostrils themselves are raised and extended. The eyes are widely opened, and beneath them the skin appears swollen; the pupils are large. The forehead is wrinkled transversely in many folds, and at the inner extremities of the eyebrows it is strongly furrowed in diverging lines, produced by the powerful and persistent contraction of the corrugators.

Mr. Bell has also described[5] an agony of terror and of despair, which he witnessed in a murderer, whilst carried to the place of execution in Turin. "On each side of the car the officiating priests were seated; and in the centre sat the criminal himself. It was impossible to witness the condition of this unhappy wretch without terror; and yet, as if impelled by some strange infatuation, it was equally impossible not to gaze upon an object so wild, so full of horror. He seemed about thirty-five years of age; of large and muscular form; his countenance marked by strong and savage features; half naked, pale as death, agonized with terror, every limb strained in anguish, his hands clenched convulsively, the sweat breaking out on his bent and contracted brow, he kissed incessantly the figure of our

Saviour, painted on the flag which was suspended before him; but with an agony of wildness and despair, of which nothing ever exhibited on the stage can give the slightest conception."

I will add only one other case, illustrative of a man utterly prostrated by terror. An atrocious murderer of two persons was brought into a hospital, under the mistaken impression that he had poisoned himself; and Dr. W. Ogle carefully watched him the next morning, while he was being handcuffed and taken away by the police. His pallor was extreme, and his prostration so great that he was hardly able to dress himself. His skin perspired; and his eyelids and head drooped so much that it was impossible to catch even a glimpse of his eyes. His lower jaw hung down. There was no contraction of any facial muscle, and Dr. Ogle is almost certain that the hair did not stand on end, for he observed it narrowly, as it had been dyed for the sake of concealment.

With respect to fear, as exhibited by the various races of man, my informants agree that the signs are the same as with Europeans. They are displayed in an exaggerated degree with the Hindoos and natives of Ceylon. Mr. Geach has seen Malays when terrified turn pale and shake; and Mr. Brough Smyth states that a native Australian "being on one occasion much frightened, showed a complexion as nearly approaching to what we call paleness, as can well be conceived in the case of a very black man." Mr. Dyson Lacy has seen extreme fear shown in an Australian, by a nervous twitching of the hands, feet, and lips; and by the perspiration standing on the skin. Many savages do not repress the signs of fear so much as Europeans; and they often tremble greatly. With the Kafir, Gaika says, in his rather quaint English, the shaking "of the body is much experienced, and the eyes are widely open." With savages, the sphincter muscles are often relaxed, just as may be observed in much frightened dogs, and as I have seen with monkeys when terrified by being caught.

[5] 'Observations on Italy,' 1825, p. 48, as quoted in 'The Anatomy of Expression,' p. 168.

THE ERECTION OF THE HAIR

Some of the signs of fear deserve a little further consideration. Poets continually speak of the hair standing on end; Brutus says to the ghost of Cæsar, "that mak'st my blood cold, and my hair to stare." And Cardinal Beaufort, after the murder of Gloucester exclaims, "Comb down his hair; look, look, it stands upright." As I did not feel sure whether writers of fiction might not have applied to man what they had often observed in animals, I begged for information from Dr. Crichton Browne with respect to the insane. He states in answer that he has repeatedly seen their hair erected under the influence of sudden and extreme terror. For instance, it is occasionally necessary to inject morphia under the skin of an insane woman, who dreads the operation extremely, though it causes very little pain; for she believes that poison is being introduced into her system, and that her bones will be softened, and her flesh turned into dust. She becomes deadly pale; her limbs are stiffened by a sort of tetanic spasm, and her hair is partially erected on the front of the head.

Dr. Browne further remarks that the bristling of the hair which is so common in the insane, is not always associated with terror. It is perhaps most frequently seen in chronic maniacs, who rave incoherently and have destructive impulses; but it is during their paroxysms of violence that the bristling is most observable. The fact of the hair becoming erect under the influence both of rage and fear agrees perfectly with what we have seen in the lower animals. Dr. Browne adduces several cases in evidence. Thus with a man now in the Asylum, before the recurrence of each maniacal paroxysm, "the hair rises up from his forehead like the mane of a Shetland pony." He has sent me photographs of two women, taken in the intervals between their paroxysms, and he adds with respect to one of these women, "that the state of her hair is a sure and convenient criterion of her mental condition." The extraordinary condition of the hair in the insane is due, not only to its erection, but to its dryness and harshness, consequent on the subcutaneous glands failing to act. Dr. Bucknill has said [6] that a lunatic "is a lunatic to his finger's ends;" he might have added, and often to the extremity of each particular hair.

Dr. Browne mentions as an empirical confirmation of the relation which exists in the insane between the state of their hair and minds, that the wife of a medical man, who has charge of a lady suffering from acute melancholia, with a strong fear of death, for herself, her husband and children, reported verbally to him the day before receiving my letter as follows, "I think Mrs. ———— will soon improve, for her hair is getting smooth; and I always notice that our patients get better whenever their hair ceases to be rough and unmanageable."

Dr. Browne attributes the persistently rough condition of the hair in many insane patients, in part to their minds being always somewhat disturbed, and in part to the effects of habit,—that is, to the hair being frequently and strongly erected during their many recurrent paroxysms. In patients in whom the bristling of the hair is extreme, the disease is generally permanent and mortal; but in others, in whom the bristling is moderate, as soon as they recover their health of mind the hair recovers its smoothness.

In a previous chapter we have seen that with animals the hairs are erected by the contraction of minute, unstriped, and involuntary muscles, which run to each separate follicle. In addition to this action, Mr. J. Wood has clearly ascertained by experiment, as he informs me, that with man the hairs on the front of the head which slope forwards, and those on the back which slope backwards, are raised in opposite directions by the contraction of the occipito-frontalis or scalp muscle. So that this

[6] Quoted by Dr. Maudsley, 'Body and Mind,' 1870, p. 41.

muscle seems to aid in the erection of the hairs on the head of man, in the same manner as the homologous *panniculus carnosus* aids, or takes the greater part, in the erection of the spines on the backs of some of the lower animals.

❀   ❀   ❀

DILATATION OF THE PUPILS

Gratiolet [7] repeatedly insists that the pupils are enormously dilated whenever terror is felt. I have no reason to doubt the accuracy of this statement, but have failed to obtain confirmatory evidence, excepting in the one instance before given of an insane woman suffering from great fear. When writers of fiction speak of the eyes being widely dilated, I presume that they refer to the eyelids. Munro's statement,[8] that with parrots the iris is affected by the passions, independently of the amount of light, seems to bear on this question; but Professor Donders informs me, that he has often seen movements in the pupils of these birds which he thinks may be related to their power of accommodation to distance, in nearly the same manner as our own pupils contract when our eyes converge for near vision. Gratiolet remarks that the dilated pupils appear as if they were gazing into profound darkness. No doubt the fears of man have often been excited in the dark; but hardly so often or so exclusively, as to account for a fixed and associated habit having thus arisen. It seems more probable, assuming that Gratiolet's statement is correct, that the brain is directly affected by the powerful emotion of fear and reacts on the pupils; but Professor Donders informs me that this is an extremely complicated subject. I may add, as possibly throwing light on the subject, that Dr. Fyffe, of Netley Hospital, has observed in two patients that the pupils were distinctly dilated during the cold stage of an ague fit. Professor Donders has also often seen dilatation of the pupils in incipient faintness.

HORROR

The state of mind expressed by this term implies terror, and is in some cases almost synonymous with it. Many a man must have felt, before the blessed discovery of chloroform, great horror at the thought of an impending surgical operation. He who dreads, as well as hates a man, will feel, as Milton uses the word, a horror of him. We feel horror if we see any one, for instance a child, exposed to some instant and crushing danger. Almost every one would experience the same feeling in the highest degree in witnessing a man being tortured or going to be tortured. In these cases there is no danger to ourselves; but from the power of the imagination and of sympathy we put ourselves in the position of the sufferer, and feel something akin to fear.

Sir C. Bell [9] remarks, that "horror is full of energy; the body is in the utmost tension, not unnerved by fear." It is, therefore, probably that horror would generally be accompanied by the strong contraction of the brows; but as fear is one of the elements, the eyes and mouth would be opened, and the eyebrows would be raised, as far as the antagonistic action of the corrugators permitted this movement. A tortured man, as long as his sufferings allowed him to feel any dread for the future, would probably exhibit horror in an extreme degree.

Horror is generally accompanied by various gestures, which differ in different individuals. Judging from pictures, the whole body is often turned away or shrinks; or the arms are violently protruded as if to push away some dreadful object. The most frequent gesture, as far as can be inferred from the action of persons who endeavour to express a vividly-imagined scene of horror, is the raising of both shoulders, with the bent arms pressed closely against the

[7] 'De la Physionomie,' pp. 51, 256, 346.
[8] As quoted in White's 'Gradation in Man,' p. 57.

[9] 'Anatomy of Expression,' p. 169.

sides or chest. These movements are nearly the same with those commonly made when we feel very cold; and they are generally accompanied by a shudder, as well as by a deep expiration or inspiration, according as the chest happens at the time to be expanded or contracted. The sounds thus made are expressed by words like *uh* or *ugh*.[10] It is not, however, obvious why, when we feel cold or express a sense of horror, we press our bent arms against our bodies, raise our shoulders, and shudder.

CONCLUSION

I have now endeavoured to describe the diversified expressions of fear, in its gradations from mere attention to a start of surprise, into extreme terror and horror. Some of the signs may be accounted for through the principles of habit, association, and inheritance,—such as the wide opening of the mouth and eyes, with upraised eyebrows, so as to see as quickly as possible all around us, and to hear distinctly whatever sound may reach our ears. For we have thus habitually prepared ourselves to discover and encounter any danger. Some of the other signs of fear may likewise be accounted for, at least in part, through these same principles. Men, during numberless generations, have endeavoured to escape from their enemies or danger by headlong flight, or by violently struggling with them; and such great exertions will have caused the heart to beat rapidly, the breathing to be hurried, the chest to heave,

and the nostrils to be dilated. As these exertions have often been prolonged to the last extremity, the final result will have been utter prostration, pallor, perspiration, trembling of all the muscles, or their complete relaxation. And now, whenever the emotion of fear is strongly felt, though it may not lead to any exertion, the same results tend to reappear, through the force of inheritance and association.

Nevertheless, it is probable that many or most of the above symptoms of terror, such as the beating of the heart, the trembling of the muscles, cold perspiration, &c., are in large part directly due to the disturbed or interrupted transmission of nerve-force from the cerebro-spinal system to various parts of the body, owing to the mind being so powerfully affected. We may confidently look to this cause, independently of habit and association, in such cases as the modified secretions of the intestinal canal, and the failure of certain glands to act. With respect to the involuntary bristling of the hair, we have good reason to believe that in the case of animals this action, however it may have originated, serves, together with certain voluntary movements, to make them appear terrible to their enemies; and as the same involuntary actions are performed by animals nearly related to man, we are led to believe that man has retained through inheritance a relic of them, now become useless. It is certainly a remarkable fact, that the minute unstriped muscles, by which the hairs thinly scattered over man's almost naked body are erected, should have been preserved to the present day; and that they should still contract under the same emotions, namely, terror and rage, which cause the hairs to stand on end in the lower members of the Order to which man belongs.

[10] See remarks to this effect by Mr. Wedgwood, in the Introduction to his 'Dictionary of English Etymology,' 2nd edit. 1872, p. xxxvii. He shows by intermediate forms that the sounds here referred to have probably given rise to many words, such as *ugly, huge,* &c.

25. Fear and Curiosity *

William James

William James, regarded by many as the greatest of American psychologists, is best remembered for his theory of emotion. In this theory, first reported in *Mind* in 1884, James was strongly influenced by Darwin's views of the evolution of mankind. Carl Georg Lange of Copenhagen published a similar conception of emotion in 1885 and the two theories combined are now generally referred to as the James-Lange Theory of Emotion.

The instinctive nature of emotions and the contribution of glandular and muscular processes to emotional states are emphasized by James. He argues that having an emotional experience involves a two-stage process. In the first stage, stimuli which evoke emotion lead to automatic changes in the visceral organs and skeletal muscles. In the second stage, these bodily changes are perceived and interpreted. The emotion *is* the perception of changes in the body, not the cause of such changes. Thus, according to James, "we feel afraid *because* we tremble," and not vice-versa.

Fear was regarded by James as a "genuine instinct," that is, a response which is reliably elicited by certain stimuli such as strange noises, strange people, black things, high places, or supernatural phenomena. He thought the tendency for people to react with fear when faced by such stimuli could be explained by reference to the conditions which threatened the survival of our ancient ancestors, both human and animal.

For James, curiosity was also instinctive. He believed that novel objects and events had the power to arouse attention. He was also among the first to recognize an inherent antagonistic relationship between fear and curiosity that resulted in the alternative arousal of these two emotions by novel stimuli. Attraction to a novel stimulus was seen as adaptive in that the new object might be used to advantage, but fear of a novel object was also adaptive in that the object could be dangerous or harmful.

Fear is a reaction aroused by the same objects that arouse ferocity. The antagonism of the two is an interesting study in instinctive dynamics. We both fear, and wish to kill, anything that may kill us; and the question which of the two impulses we shall follow is usually decided by some one of those *collateral circumstances* of the particular case, to be moved by which is the mark of superior mental natures. Of course this introduces uncertainty into the reaction; but it is an uncertainty found in the higher brutes as well as in men, and ought not to be taken as proof that we are less instinctive than they. Fear has bodily expressions of an extremely energetic kind, and stands, beside lust and anger, as one of the three most exciting emotions of which our nature is susceptible. The progress from brute to man is characterized by nothing so much as by the decrease in frequency of proper occasions for fear. In civilized life, in particular, it has at last become possible for large numbers of people to pass from the cradle to the grave without ever having had a pang of genuine fear. Many of us need an attack of mental disease to teach us the meaning of the word. Hence the possibility of so much blindly optimistic

* Excerpted from Chapter 24 of *Principles of Psychology*, Volume II, Henry Holt & Co., New York, 1890.

philosophy and religion. The atrocities of life become 'like a tale of little meaning though the words are strong;' we doubt if anything like *us* ever really was within the tiger's jaws, and conclude that the horrors we hear of are but a sort of painted tapestry for the chambers in which we lie so comfortably at peace with ourselves and with the world.

Be this as it may, fear is a genuine instinct, and one of the earliest shown by the human child. *Noises* seem especially to call it forth. Most noises from the outer world, to a child bred in the house, have no exact significance. They are simply startling. To quote a good observer, M. Perez:

Children between three and ten months are less often alarmed by visual than by auditory impressions. In cats, from the fifteenth day, the contrary is the case. A child, three and a half months old, in the midst of the turmoil of a conflagration, in presence of the devouring flames and ruined walls, showed neither astonishment nor fear, but smiled at the woman who was taking care of him, while his parents were busy. The noise, however, of the trumpet of the firemen, who were approaching, and that of the wheels of the engine, made him start and cry. At this age I have never yet seen an infant startled at a flash of lightning, even when intense; but I have seen many of them alarmed at the voice of the thunder. . . . Thus fear comes rather by the ears than by the eyes, to the child without experience. It is natural that this should be reversed, or reduced, in animals organized to perceive danger afar. Accordingly, although I have never seen a child frightened at his first sight of fire, I have many a time seen young dogs, young cats, young chickens, and young birds frightened thereby. . . . I picked up some years ago a lost cat about a year old. Some months afterward at the onset of cold weather I lit a fire in the grate of my study, which was her reception-room. She first looked at the flame in a very frightened way. I brought her near to it. She leaped away and ran to hide under the bed. Although the fire was lighted every day, it was not until the end of the winter that I could prevail upon her to stay upon a chair near it. The next winter, however, all apprehension had disappeared. . . . Let us, then, conclude that there are hereditary dispositions to fear, which are independent of experience, but which experiences may end by attenuating very considerably. In the human

infant I believe them to be particularly connected with the ear.*

The effect of noise in heightening any terror we may feel in adult years is very marked. The *howling* of the storm, whether on sea or land, is a principal cause of our anxiety when exposed to it. The writer has been interested in noticing in his own person, while lying in bed, and kept awake by the wind outside, how invariably each loud gust of it arrested momentarily his heart. A dog, attacking us, is much more dreadful by reason of the noises he makes.

Strange men, and *strange animals,* either large or small, excite fear, but especially men or animals advancing toward us in a threatening way. This is entirely instinctive and antecedent to experience. Some children will cry with terror at their very first sight of a cat or dog, and it will often be impossible for weeks to make them touch it. Others will wish to fondle it almost immediately. Certain kinds of 'vermin,' especially spiders and snakes, seem to excite a fear unusually difficult to overcome. It is impossible to say how much of this difference is instinctive and how much the result of stories heard about these creatures. That the fear of 'vermin' ripens gradually, seemed to me to be proved in a child of my own to whom I gave a live frog once, at the age of six to eight months, and again when he was a year and a half old. The first time he seized it promptly, and holding it, in spite of its struggling, at last got its head into his mouth. He then let it crawl up his breast, and get upon his face, without

* Psychologie de l'Enfant, pp. 72–74. In an account of a young gorilla quoted from Falkenstein, by R. Hartmann ('Anthropoid Apes,' International Scientific Series, vol. LII (New York, 1886), p. 265), it is said: "He very much disliked strange noises. Thunder, the rain falling on the skylight, and especially the long-drawn note of a pipe or trumpet, threw him into such agitation as to cause a sudden affection of the digestive organs, and it became expedient to keep him at a distance. When he was slightly indisposed, we made use of this kind of music with results as successful as if we had administered purgative medicine."

showing alarm. But the second time, although he had seen no frog and heard no story about a frog between whiles, it was almost impossible to induce him to touch it. Another child, a year old, eagerly took some very large spiders into his hand. At present he is afraid, but has been exposed meanwhile to the teachings of the nursery. One of my children from her birth upwards saw daily the pet pug-dog of the house, and never betrayed the slightest fear until she was (if I recollect rightly) about eight months old. Then the instinct suddenly seemed to develop, and with such intensity that familiarity had no mitigating effect. She screamed whenever the dog entered the room, and for many months remained afraid to touch him. It is needless to say that no change in the pug's unfailingly friendly conduct had anything to do with this change of feeling in the child.

Preyer tells of a young child screaming with fear on being carried near to the *sea*. The great source of terror to infancy is solitude. The teleology of this is obvious, as is also that of the infant's expression of dismay—the never-failing cry—on waking up and finding himself alone.

Black things, and especially *dark places,* holes, caverns, etc., arouse a peculiarly gruesome fear. This fear, as well as that of solitude, of being 'lost,' are explained after a fashion by ancestral experience. Says Schneider:

It is a fact that men, especially in childhood, fear to go into a dark cavern or a gloomy wood. This feeling of fear arises, to be sure, partly from the fact that we easily suspect that dangerous beasts may lurk in these localities—a suspicion due to stories we have heard and read. But, on the other hand, it is quite sure that this fear at a certain perception is also directly inherited. Children who have been carefully guarded from all ghost-stories are nevertheless terrified and cry if led into a dark place, especially if sounds are made there. Even an adult can easily observe that an uncomfortable timidity steals over him in a lonely wood at night, although he may have the fixed conviction that not the slightest danger is near. This feeling of fear occurs in many men

even in their own house after dark, although it is much stronger in a dark cavern or forest. The fact of such instinctive fear is easily explicable when we consider that our savage ancestors through innumerable generations were accustomed to meet with dangerous beasts in caverns, especially bears, and were for the most part attacked by such beasts during the night and in the woods, and that thus an inseparable association between the perceptions of darkness of caverns and woods, and fear took place, and was inherited.*

High places cause fear of a peculiarly sickening sort, though here, again, individuals differ enormously. The utterly blind instinctive character of the motor impulses here is shown by the fact that they are almost always entirely unreasonable, but that reason is powerless to suppress them. That they are a mere incidental peculiarity of the nervous system, like liability to sea-sickness, or love of music, with no teleological significance, seems more than probable. The fear in question varies so much from one person to another, and its detrimental effects are so much more obvious than its uses, that it is hard to see how it could be a selected instinct. Man is anatomically one of the best fitted of animals for climbing about high places. The best psychical complement to this equipment would seem to be a 'level head' when there, not a dread of going there at all. In fact, the teleology of fear, beyond a certain point, is very dubious. Professor Mosso, in his interesting monograph, 'La Paura' (which has been translated into French), concludes that many of its manifestations must be considered pathological rather than useful; Bain, in several places, expresses the same opinion; and this, I think, is surely the view which any observer without *a priori* prejudices must take. A certain amount of timidity obviously adapts us to the world we live in, but the *fear-paroxysm* is surely altogether harmful to him who is its prey.

Fear of the supernatural is one variety of fear. It is difficult to assign any normal object for this fear, unless it

* Der Menschliche Wille, p. 224.

were a genuine ghost. But, in spite of psychical research-societies, science has not yet adopted ghosts; so we can only say that certain *ideas* of supernatural agency, associated with real circumstances, produce a peculiar kind of horror. This horror is probably explicable as the result of a combination of simpler horrors. To bring the ghostly terror to its maximum, many usual elements of the dreadful must combine, such as loneliness, darkness, inexplicable sounds, especially of a dismal character, moving figures half discerned (or, if discerned, of dreadful aspect), and a vertiginous baffling of the expectation. This last element, which is *intellectual,* is very important. It produces a strange emotional 'curdle' in our blood to see a process with which we are familiar deliberately taking an unwonted course. Any one's heart would stop beating if he perceived his chair sliding unassisted across the floor. The lower animals appear to be sensitive to the mysteriously exceptional as well as ourselves. My friend Professor W. K. Brooks, of the Johns Hopkins University, told me of his large and noble dog being frightened into a sort of epileptic fit by a bone being drawn across the floor by a thread which the dog did not see. Darwin and Romanes have given similar experiences.* The idea of the supernatural involves that the usual should be set at naught. In the witch and hobgoblin supernatural, other elements still of fear are brought in—caverns, slime and ooze, vermin, corpses, and the like.† A

human corpse seems normally to produce an instinctive dread, which is no doubt somewhat due to its mysteriousness, and which familiarity rapidly dispels. But, in view of the fact that cadaveric, reptilian, and underground horrors play so specific and constant a part in many nightmares and forms of delirium, it seems not altogether unwise to ask whether these forms of dreadful circumstance may not at a former period have been more normal objects of the environment than now. The ordinary cocksure evolutionist ought to have no difficulty in explaining these terrors, and the scenery that provokes them, as relapses into the consciousness of the cave-men, a consciousness usually overlaid in us by experiences of more recent date.

There are certain other pathological fears, and certain peculiarities in the expression of ordinary fear, which might receive an explanatory light from ancestral conditions, even infra-human ones. In ordinary fear, one may either run, or remain semi-paralyzed. The latter condition reminds us of the so-called death-shamming instinct shown by many animals. Dr. Lindsay, in his work 'Mind in Animals,' says this must require great self-command in those that practise it. But it is really no feigning of death at all, and requires no self-command. It is simply a terror-paralysis which has been so useful as to become hereditary. The beast of prey does not think the motionless bird, insect, or crustacean dead. He simply fails to notice them at all; because his senses, like ours, are much more strongly excited by a moving object than by a still one. It is the same instinct which leads a boy playing 'I spy' to hold his very breath when the seeker is near, and which makes the beast of prey

* Cf. Romanes, Mental Evolution, etc., p. 156.
† In the 'Overland Monthly' for 1887, a most interesting article on Laura Bridgman's writings has been published by Mr. E. C. Sandford. Among other reminiscences of her early childhood, while she still knew nothing of the sign-language, the wonderful blind deaf-mute records the following item in her quaint language: "My father [he was a farmer and probably did his own butchering] used to enter his kitchen bringing some killed animals in and deposited them on one of sides of the room many times. As I perceived it it make me shudder with terror because I did not know what the matter was. I hated to approach the dead. One morning I went to take a short walk with my Mother. I went into a snug house for

some time. They took me into a room where there was a coffin. I put my hand in the coffin & felt something so queer. It frightened me unpleasantly. I found something dead wrapped in a silk h'd'k'f so carefully. It must have been a body that had had vitality. . . . I did not like to venture to examine the body for I was confounded."

himself in many cases motionlessly lie in wait for his victim or silently 'stalk' it, by rapid approaches alternated with periods of immobility. It is the opposite of the instinct which makes us jump up and down and move our arms when we wish to attract the notice of some one passing far away, and makes the shipwrecked sailor frantically wave a cloth upon the raft where he is floating when a distant sail appears. Now, may not the statue-like, crouching immobility of some melancholiacs, insane with general anxiety and fear of everything, be in some way connected with this old instinct? They can give no *reason* for their fear to move; but immobility makes them feel safer and more comfortable. Is not this the mental state of the 'feigning' animal?

Again, take the strange symptom which has been described of late years by the rather absurd name of *agoraphobia*. The patient is seized with palpitation and terror at the sight of any open place or broad street which he has to cross alone. He trembles, his knees bend, he may even faint at the idea. Where he has sufficient self-command he sometimes accomplishes the object by keeping safe under the lee of a vehicle going across, or joining himself to a knot of other people. But usually he slinks round the sides of the square, hugging the houses as closely as he can. This emotion has no utility in a civilized man, but when we notice the chronic agoraphobia of our domestic cats, and see the tenacious way in which many wild animals, especially rodents, cling to cover, and only venture on a dash across the open as a desperate measure—even then making for every stone or bunch of weeds which may give a momentary shelter—when we see this we are strongly tempted to ask whether such an odd kind of fear in us be not due to the accidental resurrection, through disease, of a sort of instinct which may in some of our ancestors have had a permanent and on the whole a useful part to play?

CURIOSITY

Already pretty low down among vertebrates we find that any object may excite attention, provided it be only *novel,* and that attention may be followed by approach and exploration by nostril, lips, or touch. Curiosity and fear form a couple of antagonistic emotions liable to be awakened by the same outward thing, and manifestly both useful to their possessor. The spectacle of their alternation is often amusing enough, as in the timid approaches and scared wheelings which sheep or cattle will make in the presence of some new object they are investigating. I have seen alligators in the water act in precisely the same way towards a man seated on the beach in front of them—gradually drawing near as long as he kept still, frantically careering back as soon as he made a movement. Inasmuch as new objects *may* always be advantageous, it is better that an animal should not *absolutely* fear them. But, inasmuch as they may also possibly be harmful, it is better that he should not be quite indifferent to them either, but on the whole remaining on the *qui vive,* ascertain as much about them, and what they may be likely to bring forth, as he can, before settling down to rest in their presence. Some such susceptibility for being excited and irritated by the mere novelty, as such, of any movable feature of the environment must form the instinctive basis of all human curiosity; though, of course, the superstructure absorbs contributions from so many other factors of the emotional life that the original root may be hard to find. With what is called scientific curiosity, and with metaphysical wonder, the practical instinctive root has probably nothing to do. The stimuli here are not objects, but ways of conceiving objects; and the emotions and actions they give rise to are to be classed, with many other æsthetic manifestations, sensitive and motor, as *incidental* features of our mental life. The philosophic brain responds to an inconsistency or a gap in its knowledge, just as the musical brain responds to a discord in what it hears. At certain ages the sensitiveness to particular gaps and the pleasure of resolving particular puzzles reach their maximum, and then it is that stores of scientific knowledge are easiest and most naturally laid in. But these effects may have had nothing to do with the uses for which the brain was originally given; and it is probably only within a few centuries, since religious beliefs and economic applications of science have played a prominent part in the conflicts of one race with another, that they may have helped to 'select' for survival a particular type of brain.

26. Conditioned Emotional Reactions *

John B. Watson and Rosalie Rayner

Although fear and anxiety are among the most pervasive and widely experienced human emotions, they are extremely difficult to study. One reason is that people differ greatly in the things they fear. Another reason is that most individuals develop elaborate mechanisms for protecting themselves from these unpleasant and often painful emotional states. Consequently, it is difficult to separate fear and anxiety from the learned reactions that help us escape or reduce the intensity of these emotions whenever they occur.

In the next selection, John B. Watson and Rosalie Rayner describe one of the earliest laboratory investigations of fear. This study was based on Watson's theory that fear is one of three basic emotions (fear, rage, and love) that are automatically aroused by appropriate stimuli. The purpose of the experiment is to show that neutral stimuli can acquire the power to elicit fear through classical conditioning. (See the selection by I. P. Pavlov in Part IV.)

In this study, the unconditioned stimulus (UCS) was a loud tone that evoked a strong fear response the first time it was presented to the subject. The conditioned stimulus (CS) was a tame and harmless white rat. By presenting the white rat and then sounding the tone, the authors demonstrate that the rat, which previously elicited no fear, soon acquired that power. They also demonstrate that this acquired fear generalized to a number of other similar stimuli and that it persisted over a considerable period of time.

In recent literature various speculations have been entered into concerning the possibility of conditioning various types of emotional response, but direct experimental evidence in support of such a view has been lacking. If the theory advanced by Watson and Morgan[1] to the effect that in infancy the original emotional reaction patterns are few, consisting so far as observed of fear, rage and love, then there must be some simple method by means of which the range of stimuli which can call out these emotions and their compounds is greatly increased. Otherwise, complexity in adult response could not be accounted for. These authors without adequate experimental evidence advanced the view that this range was increased by means of conditioned reflex factors. It was suggested there that the early home life of the child furnishes a laboratory situation for estab-

* Reprinted from the *Journal of Experimental Psychology*, 1920, 3, 1-12.

[1] 'Emotional Reactions and Psychological Experimentation,' *American Journal of Psychology*, April, 1917, Vol. 28, pp. 163–174.

lishing conditioned emotional responses. The present authors have recently put the whole matter to an experimental test.

Experimental work has been done so far on only one child, Albert B. This infant was reared almost from birth in a hospital environment; his mother was a wet nurse in the Harriet Lane Home for Invalid Children. Albert's life was normal: he was healthy from birth and one of the best developed youngsters ever brought to the hospital, weighing twenty-one pounds at nine months of age. He was on the whole stolid and unemotional. His stability was one of the principal reasons for using him as a subject in this test. We felt that we could do him relatively little harm by carrying out such experiments as those outlined below.

At approximately nine months of age we ran him through the emotional tests that have become a part of our regular routine in determining whether fear reactions can be called out by other stimuli than sharp noises and the sudden removal of support. Tests of this type have been described by the senior author in another place.[2] In brief, the infant was confronted suddenly and for the first time successively with a white rat, a rabbit, a dog, a monkey, with masks with and without hair, cotton wool, burning newspapers, etc. A permanent record of Albert's reactions to these objects and situations has been preserved in a motion picture study. Manipulation was the most usual reaction called out. *At no time did this infant ever show fear in any situation.* These experimental records were confirmed by the casual observations of the mother and hospital attendants. No one had ever seen him in a state of fear and rage. The infant practically never cried.

Up to approximately nine months of age we had not tested him with loud sounds. The test to determine whether a fear reaction could be called out by a loud sound

was made when he was eight months, twenty-six days of age. The sound was that made by striking a hammer upon a suspended steel bar four feet in length and three-fourths of an inch in diameter. The laboratory notes are as follows:

One of the two experimenters caused the child to turn its head and fixate her moving hand; the other, stationed back of the child, struck the steel bar a sharp blow. The child started violently, his breathing was checked and the arms were raised in a characteristic manner. On the second stimulation the same thing occurred, and in addition the lips began to pucker and tremble. On the third stimulation the child broke into a sudden crying fit. This is the first time an emotional situation in the laboratory has produced any fear or even crying in Albert.

We had expected just these results on account of our work with other infants brought up under similar conditions. It is worth while to call attention to the fact that removal of support (dropping and jerking the blanket upon which the infant was lying) was tried exhaustively upon this infant on the same occasion. It was not effective in producing the fear response. This stimulus is effective in younger children. At what age such stimuli lose their potency in producing fear is not known. Nor is it known whether less placid children ever lose their fear of them. This probably depends upon the training the child gets. It is well known that children eagerly run to be tossed into the air and caught. On the other hand it is equally well known that in the adult fear responses are called out quite clearly by the sudden removal of support, if the individual is walking across a bridge, walking out upon a beam, etc. There is a wide field of study here which is aside from our present point.

The sound stimulus, thus, at nine months of age, gives us the means of testing several important factors. I. Can we condition fear of an animal, *e.g.*, a white rat, by visually presenting it and simultaneously striking a steel bar? II. If such a conditioned emotional response can be established, will

[2] 'Psychology from the Standpoint of a Behaviorist,' p. 202.

there be a transfer to other animals or other objects? III. What is the effect of time upon such conditioned emotional responses? IV. If after a reasonable period such emotional responses have not died out, what laboratory methods can be devised for their removal?

I. THE ESTABLISHMENT OF CONDITIONED EMOTIONAL RESPONSES

At first there was considerable hesitation upon our part in making the attempt to set up fear reactions experimentally. A certain responsibility attaches to such a procedure. We decided finally to make the attempt, comforting ourselves by the reflection that such attachments would arise anyway as soon as the child left the sheltered environment of the nursery for the rough and tumble of the home. We did not begin this work until Albert was eleven months, three days of age. Before attempting to set up a conditioned response we, as before, put him through all of the regular emotional tests. *Not the slightest sign of a fear response was obtained in any situation.*

The steps taken to condition emotional responses are shown in our laboratory notes.

11 Months 3 Days

1. White rat suddenly taken from the basket and presented to Albert. He began to reach for rat with left hand. Just as his hand touched the animal the bar was struck immediately behind his head. The infant jumped violently and fell forward, burying his face in the mattress. He did not cry, however.

2. Just as the right hand touched the rat the bar was again struck. Again the infant jumped violently, fell forward and began to whimper.

In order not to disturb the child too seriously no further tests were given for one week.

11 Months 10 Days

1. Rat presented suddenly without sound. There was steady fixation but no tendency at first to reach for it. The rat was then placed nearer, whereupon tentative reaching movements began with the right hand. When the rat nosed the infant's left hand, the hand was immediately withdrawn. He started to reach for the head of the animal with the forefinger of the left hand, but withdrew it suddenly before contact. It is thus seen that the two joint stimulations given the previous week were not without effect. He was tested with his blocks immediately afterwards to see if they shared in the process of conditioning. He began immediately to pick them up, dropping them, pounding them, etc. In the remainder of the tests the blocks were given frequently to quiet him and to test his general emotional state. They were always removed from sight when the process of conditioning was under way.

2. Joint stimulation with rat and sound. Started, then fell over immediately to right side. No crying.

3. Joint stimulation. Fell to right side and rested upon hands, with head turned away from rat. No crying.

4. Joint stimulation. Same reaction.

5. Rat suddenly presented alone. Puckered face, whimpered and withdrew body sharply to the left.

6. Joint stimulation. Fell over immediately to right side and began to whimper.

7. Joint stimulation. Started violently and cried, but did not fall over.

8. Rat alone. *The instant the rat was shown the baby began to cry. Almost instantly he turned sharply to the left, fell over on left side, raised himself on all fours and began to crawl away so rapidly that he was caught with difficulty before reaching the edge of the table.*

This was as convincing a case of a completely conditioned fear response as could have been theoretically pictured. In all seven joint stimulations were given to bring about the complete reaction. It is not unlikely had the sound been of greater intensity or of a more complex clang character that the number of joint stimulations might have been materially reduced. Experiments designed to define the nature of the sounds that will serve best as emotional stimuli are under way.

II. WHEN A CONDITIONED EMOTIONAL RESPONSE HAS BEEN ESTABLISHED FOR ONE OBJECT, IS THERE A TRANSFER?

Five days later Albert was again brought back into the laboratory and tested as follows:

11 Months 15 Days

1. Tested first with blocks. He reached readily for them, playing with them as usual. This shows that there has been no general transfer to the room, table, blocks, etc.

2. Rat alone. Whimpered immediately, withdrew right hand and turned head and trunk away.

3. Blocks again offered. Played readily with them, smiling and gurgling.

4. Rat alone. Leaned over to the left side as far away from the rat as possible, then fell over, getting up on all fours and scurrying away as rapidly as possible.

5. Blocks again offered. Reached immediately for them, smiling and laughing as before.

The above preliminary test shows that the conditioned response to the rat had carried over completely for the five days in which no tests were given. The question as to whether or not there is a transfer was next taken up.

6. Rabbit alone. The rabbit was suddenly placed on the mattress in front of him. The reaction was pronounced. Negative responses began at once. He leaned as far away from the animal as possible, whimpered, then burst into tears. When the rabbit was placed in contact with him he buried his face in the mattress, then got up on all fours and crawled away, crying as he went. This was a most convincing test.

7. The blocks were next given him, after an interval. He played with them as before. It was observed by four people that he played far more energetically with them than ever before. The blocks were raised high over his head and slammed down with a great deal of force.

8. Dog alone. The dog did not produce as violent a reaction as the rabbit. The moment fixation occurred the child shrank back and as the animal came nearer he attempted to get on all fours but did not cry at first. As soon as the dog passed out of his range of vision he became quiet. The dog was then made to approach the infant's head (he was lying down at the moment). Albert straightened up immediately, fell over to the opposite side and turned his head away. He then began to cry.

9. The blocks were again presented. He began immediately to play with them.

10. Fur coat (seal). Withdrew immediately to the left side and began to fret. Coat put close to him on the left side, he turned immediately, began to cry and tried to crawl away on all fours.

11. Cotton wool. The wool was presented in a paper package. At the end the cotton was not covered by the paper. It was placed first on his feet. He kicked it away but did not touch it with his hands. When his hand was laid on the wool he immediately withdrew it but did not show the shock that the animals or fur coat produced in him. He then began to play with the paper, avoiding contact with the wool itself. He finally, under the impulse of the manipulative instinct, lost some of his negativism to the wool.

12. Just in play W. put his head down to see if Albert would play with his hair. Albert was completely negative. Two other observers did the same thing. He began immediately to play with their hair. W. then brought the Santa Claus mask and presented it to Albert. He was again pronouncedly negative.

11 Months 20 Days

1. Blocks alone. Played with them as usual.

2. Rat alone. Withdrawal of the whole body, bending over to left side, no crying. Fixation and following with eyes. The response was much less marked than on first presentation the previous week. It was thought best to freshen up the reaction by another joint stimulation.

3. Just as the rat was placed on his hand the rod was struck. Reaction violent.

4. Rat alone. Fell over at once to left side. Reaction practically as strong as on former occasion but no crying.

5. Rat alone. Fell over to left side, got up on all fours and started to crawl away. On this occasion there was no crying, but strange to say, as he started away he began to gurgle and coo, even while leaning far over to the left side to avoid the rat.

6. Rabbit alone. Leaned over to left side as far as possible. Did not fall over. Began to whimper but reaction not so violent as on former occasions.

7. Blocks again offered. He reached for them immediately and began to play.

All of the tests so far discussed were carried out upon a table supplied with a mattress, located in a small, well-lighted dark-room. We wished to test next whether conditioned fear responses so set up would appear if the situation were markedly altered. We thought it best before making this test to freshen the reaction both to the rabbit and to the dog by showing them at the moment the steel bar was struck. It will be recalled that this was the first time any effort had been made to directly condition response to the dog and rabbit. The experimental notes are as follows:

8. The rabbit at first was given alone. The reaction was exactly as given in test (6) above.

When the rabbit was left on Albert's knees for a long time he began tentatively to reach out and manipulate its fur with forefingers. While doing this the steel rod was struck. A violent fear reaction resulted.

9. Rabbit alone. Reaction wholly similar to that on trial (6) above.

10. Rabbit alone. Started immediately to whimper, holding hands far up, but did not cry. Conflicting tendency to manipulate very evident.

11. Dog alone. Began to whimper, shaking head from side to side, holding hands as far away from the animal as possible.

12. Dog and sound. The rod was struck just as the animal touched him. A violent negative reaction appeared. He began to whimper, turned to one side, fell over and started to get up on all fours.

13. Blocks. Played with them immediately and readily.

On this same day and immediately after the above experiment Albert was taken into the large well-lighted lecture room belonging to the laboratory. He was placed on a table in the center of the room immediately under the skylight. Four people were present. The situation was thus very different from that which obtained in the small dark room.

1. Rat alone. No sudden fear reaction appeared at first. The hands, however, were held up and away from the animal. No positive manipulatory reactions appeared.

2. Rabbit alone. Fear reaction slight. Turned to left and kept face away from the animal but the reaction was never pronounced.

3. Dog alone. Turned away but did not fall over. Cried. Hands moved as far away from the animal as possible. Whimpered as long as the dog was present.

4. Rat alone. Slight negative reaction.

5. Rat and sound. It was thought best to freshen the reaction to the rat. The sound was given just as the rat was presented. Albert jumped violently but did not cry.

6. Rat alone. At first he did not show any negative reaction. When rat was placed nearer he began to show negative reaction by drawing back his body, raising his hands, whimpering, etc.

7. Blocks. Played with them immediately.

8. Rat alone. Pronounced withdrawal of body and whimpering.

9. Blocks. Played with them as before.

10. Rabbit alone. Pronounced reaction. Whimpered with arms held high, fell over backward and had to be caught.

11. Dog alone. At first the dog did not produce the pronounced reaction. The hands were held high over the head, breathing was checked, but there was no crying. Just at this moment the dog, which had not barked before, barked three times loudly when only about six inches from the baby's face. Albert immediately fell over and broke into a wail that continued until the dog was removed. The sudden barking of the hitherto quiet dog produced a marked fear response in the adult observers!

From the above results it would seem that emotional transfers do take place. Furthermore it would seem that the number of transfers resulting from an experimentally produced conditioned emotional reaction may be very large. In our observations we had no means of testing the complete number of transfers which may have resulted.

III. THE EFFECT OF TIME UPON CONDITIONED EMOTIONAL RESPONSES

We have already shown that the conditioned emotional response will continue for a period of one week. It was desired to make the time test longer. In view of the imminence of Albert's departure from the hospital we could not make the interval longer than one month. Accordingly no further emotional experimentation was entered into for thirty-one days after the above test. During the month, however, Albert was brought weekly to the laboratory for tests upon right and left-handedness, imitation, general development, etc. No emotional tests whatever were given and during the whole month his regular nursery routine was maintained in the Harriet Lane Home. The notes on the test given at the end of this period are as follows:

1 Year 21 Days

1. Santa Claus mask. Withdrawal, gurgling, then slapped at it without touching. When his hand was forced to touch it, he whimpered and cried. His hand was forced to touch it two more times. He whimpered and cried on both tests. He finally cried at the mere visual stimulus of the mask.

2. Fur coat. Wrinkled his nose and withdrew both hands, drew back his whole body and began to whimper as the coat was put

nearer. Again there was the strife between withdrawal and the tendency to manipulate. Reached tentatively with left hand but drew back before contact had been made. In moving his body to one side his hand accidentally touched the coat. He began to cry at once, nodding his head in a very peculiar manner (this reaction was an entirely new one). Both hands were withdrawn as far as possible from the coat. The coat was then laid on his lap and he continued nodding his head and whimpering, withdrawing his body as far as possible, pushing the while at the coat with his feet but never touching it with his hands.

3. Fur coat. The coat was taken out of his sight and presented again at the end of a minute. He began immediately to fret, withdrawing his body and nodding his head as before.

4. Blocks. He began to play with them as usual.

5. The rat. He allowed the rat to crawl towards him without withdrawing. He sat very still and fixated it intently. Rat then touched his hand. Albert withdrew it immediately, then leaned back as far as possible but did not cry. When the rat was placed on his arm he withdrew his body and began to fret, nodding his head. The rat was then allowed to crawl against his chest. He first began to fret and then covered his eyes with both hands.

6. Blocks. Reaction normal.

7. The rabbit. The animal was placed directly in front of him. It was very quiet. Albert showed no avoiding reactions at first. After a few seconds he puckered up his face, began to nod his head and to look intently at the experimenter. He next began to push the rabbit away with his feet, withdrawing his body at the same time. Then as the rabbit came nearer he began pulling his feet away, nodding his head, and wailing "da da." After about a minute he reached out tentatively and slowly and touched the rabbit's ear with his right hand, finally manipulating it. The rabbit was again placed in his lap. Again he began to fret and withdrew his hands. He reached out tentatively with his left hand and touched the animal, shuddered and withdrew the whole body. The experimenter then took hold of his left hand and laid it on the rabbit's back. Albert immediately withdrew his hand and began to suck his thumb. Again the rabbit was laid in his lap. He began to cry, covering his face with both hands.

8. Dog. The dog was very active. Albert fixated it intensely for a few seconds, sitting very still. He began to cry but did not fall over backwards as on his last contact with the dog. When the dog was pushed closer to him he at first sat motionless, then began to cry, putting both hands over his face.

These experiments would seem to show conclusively that directly conditioned emotional responses as well as those conditioned by transfer persist, although with a certain loss in the intensity of the reaction, for a longer period than one month. Our view is that they persist and modify personality throughout life. It should be recalled again that Albert was of an extremely phlegmatic type. Had he been emotionally unstable probably both the directly conditioned response and those transferred would have persisted throughout the month unchanged in form.

ANXIETY AND COPING BEHAVIOR

27. Anxiety *

Sigmund Freud

Freud regarded the phenomenon of anxiety as the central problem in neurosis, "a riddle, of which the solution must cast a flood of light upon our whole mental life." To Freud, anxiety was "something felt," a painful affective experience distinguishable from other strong emotions such as anger and grief by its unique combination of "unpleasurable" qualities. These unpleasant qualities include feelings of apprehension or dread and heightened autonomic nervous system activity. But Freud was not interested in analyzing the properties of anxiety states. His main concern was identifying the sources of stimulation which precipitated anxiety reactions.

In his early theoretical formulations, Freud believed anxiety to be the result of a discharge of sexual energy (libido) associated with repressed somatic sexual tensions. He later discarded this view in favor of a conception of anxiety as a signal indicating the presence of a dangerous situation, and this led him to distinguish between *objective* and *neurotic* anxiety on the basis of the source of the danger. Objective anxiety is a normal reaction to a real danger in the external world, while neurotic anxiety is an irrational reaction to an imagined danger that might result from the expression of sexual or aggressive impulses.

The following selection is excerpted from a lecture presented by Freud to medical students at the University of Vienna in the winter sessions of 1915–17. The entire series of 28 lectures was subsequently published in 1920 and the resulting book has become the most widely read work of Freud. In it Freud presents his basic theories of human personality on which most psychoanalytic methods of treatment are still based today.

You will certainly have judged the information that I gave you in the last lecture about ordinary nervousness as the most fragmentary and most inadequate of all my accounts. I know that it was; and I expect that nothing surprised you more than that I made no mention of the 'anxiety' which most nervous people complain of and themselves describe as their most terrible burden. Anxiety or dread can really develop tremendous intensity and in consequence be the cause of the maddest precautions. But in this matter at least I wished not to cut you short; on the contrary, I had determined to put the problem of nervous anxiety to you as clearly as possible and to discuss it at some length.

Anxiety (or *dread*) [1] itself needs no description; everyone has personally experienced this sensation, or to speak more cor-

---

[1] [*Angst.* The German word denotes a more intense feeling than the English 'anxiety'; the latter, however, derived from the same root, has become established as the technical English term.—Tr.]

rectly this affective condition, at some time or other. But in my opinion not enough serious consideration has been given to the question why nervous persons in particular suffer from anxiety so much more intensely, and so much more altogether, than others. Perhaps it has been taken for granted that they should; indeed, the words "nervous" and "anxious" are used interchangeably, as if they meant the same thing. This is not justifiable, however; there are anxious people who are otherwise not in any way nervous and there are, besides, neurotics with numerous symptoms who exhibit no tendency to dread.

However this may be, one thing is certain, that the problem of anxiety is a nodal point, linking up all kinds of most important questions; a riddle, of which the solution must cast a flood of light upon our whole mental life. I do not claim that I can give you a complete solution; but you will certainly expect psychoanalysis to have attacked this problem too in a different manner from that adopted by academic medicine. Interest there centres upon the anatomical processes by which the anxiety condition comes about. We learn that the medulla oblongata is stimulated, and the patient is told that he is suffering from a neurosis in the vagal nerve. The medulla oblongata is a wondrous and beauteous object; I well remember how much time and labour I devoted to the study of it years ago. But to-day I must say I know of nothing less important for the psychological comprehension of anxiety than a knowledge of the nerve-paths by which the excitations travel.

One may consider anxiety for a long time without giving a thought to nervousness. You will understand me at once when I describe this form of anxiety as OBJECTIVE ANXIETY, in contrast to neurotic anxiety. Now *real* anxiety or dread appears to us a very natural and rational thing; we should call it a reaction to the perception of an external danger, of an injury which is expected and foreseen; it is bound up with the reflex of flight, and may be regarded as an expression of the instinct of self-preservation. The occasions of it, i.e. the objects and situations about which anxiety is felt, will obviously depend to a great extent upon the state of the person's knowledge and feeling of power regarding the outer world. It seems to us quite natural that a savage should be afraid of a cannon or of an eclipse of the sun, while a white man who can handle the weapon and foretell the phenomenon remains unafraid in the same situation. At other times it is knowledge itself which inspires fear, because it reveals the danger sooner; thus a savage will recoil with terror at the sight of a track in the jungle which conveys nothing to an ignorant white man, but means that some wild beast is near at hand; and an experienced sailor will perceive with dread a little cloud on the horizon because it means an approaching hurricane, while to a passenger it looks quite insignificant.

The view that objective anxiety is rational and expedient, however, will on deeper consideration be admitted to need thorough revision. In face of imminent danger the only expedient behaviour, actually, would be first a cool appraisement of the forces at disposal as compared with the magnitude of the danger at hand, and then a decision whether flight or defence, or possibly attack, offered the best prospect of a successful outcome. Dread, however, has no place in this scheme; everything to be done will be accomplished as well and probably better if dread does not develop. You will see too that when dread is excessive it becomes in the highest degree inexpedient; it paralyses every action, even that of flight. The reaction to danger usually consists in a combination of the two things, the fear-affected and the defensive action; the frightened animal is afraid *and* flees, but the expedient element in this is the 'flight,' not the 'being afraid.'

One is tempted therefore to assert that the development of anxiety is never expedient; perhaps a closer dissection of the situation in dread will give us a better insight into it. The first thing about it is the 'readiness' for danger, which expresses itself in heightened sensorial perception and in motor tension. This expectant readiness is obviously advantageous; indeed, absence of it may be responsible for grave results. It is then followed on the one hand by a motor action, taking the form primarily of flight and, on a higher level, of defensive action; and on the other hand by the condition we call a sensation of 'anxiety' or dread. The more the development of dread is limited to a flash, to a mere signal, the less does it hinder the transition from the state of anxious readiness to that of action, and the more expediently does the whole course of events proceed. The *anxious readiness* therefore seems to me the expedient element, and the *development* of anxiety the inexpedient element, in what we call anxiety or dread.

I shall not enter upon a discussion whether the words anxiety, fear, fright, mean the same or different things in common usage. In my opinion, *anxiety* relates to the condition and ignores the object, whereas in the word *fear* attention is directed to the object; *fright* does actually seem to possess a special meaning—namely, it relates specifically to the condition induced when danger is unexpectedly encountered without previous anxious readiness. It might be said then that anxiety is a protection against fright.

It will not have escaped you that a certain ambiguity and indefiniteness exists in the use of the word 'anxiety.' It is generally understood to mean the subjective condition arising upon the perception of what we have called 'developed' anxiety; such a condition is called an affect. Now what is an affect, in a dynamic sense? It is certainly something very complex. An affect comprises first of all certain motor innervations or discharges; and, secondly, certain sensations, which moreover are of two kinds —namely, the perceptions of the motor actions which have been performed, and the directly pleasurable or painful sensations which give the affect what we call its dominant note. But I do not think that this de-

scription penetrates to the essence of an affect. With certain affects one seems to be able to see deeper, and to recognize that the core of it, binding the whole complex structure together, is of the nature of a *repetition* of some particular very significant previous experience. This experience could only have been an exceedingly early impression of a universal type, to be found in the previous history of the species rather than of the individual. In order to be better understood I might say that an affective state is constructed like an hysterical attack, i.e. is the precipitate of a reminiscence. An hysterical attack is therefore comparable to a newly formed individual affect, and the normal affect to a universal hysteria which has become a heritage.

Do not imagine that what I am telling you now about affects is the common property of normal psychology. On the contrary, these conceptions have grown on the soil of psychoanalysis and are only indigenous there. What psychology has to say about affects—the James-Lange theory, for instance—is groups. Many of the objects and situations feared are rather sinister, even to us normal people, they have some connection with danger; and these phobias are not entirely incomprehensible to us, although their intensity seems very much exaggerated. Most of us, for instance, have a feeling of repulsion upon encountering a snake. It may be said that the snake-phobia is universal in mankind. Charles Darwin has described most vividly how he could not control his dread of a snake that darted at him, although he knew that he was protected from it by a thick plate of glass The second group consists of situations that still have some relation to danger, but to one that is usually belittled or not emphasized by us; most situation-phobias belong to this group. We know that there is more chance of meeting with a disaster in a railway train than at home—namely, a collision; we also know that a ship may sink, whereupon it is usual to be drowned; but we do not brood upon these dangers and we travel without anxiety by train and boat. Nor can it be denied that if a bridge were to break at the moment we were crossing it we should be hurled into the torrent, but that only happens so very occasionally that it is not a danger worth considering. Solitude too has its dangers, which in certain circumstances we avoid, but there is no question of never being able to endure it for a moment under any conditions. The same thing applies to crowds, enclosed spaces, thunderstorms, and so on. What is foreign to us in these phobias is not so much their content as their intensity. The anxiety accompanying a phobia is positively indescribable! And we sometimes get the impression that neurotics are not really at all fearful of those things which can, under certain conditions, arouse anxiety in us and which they call by the same names.

There remains a third group which is entirely unintelligible to us. When a strong full-grown man is afraid to cross a street or square in his own so familiar town, or when a healthy well-developed woman becomes almost senseless with fear because a cat has brushed against her dress or a mouse has scurried through the room, how can we see the connection with danger which is obviously present to these people? With this kind of animal-phobia it is no question of an increased intensity of common human antipathies; to prove the contrary, there are numbers of people who, for instance, cannot pass a cat without attracting and petting it. A mouse is a thing that so many women are afraid of, and yet it is at the same time a very favourite pet name; [2] many a girl who is delighted to be called so by her lover will scream with terror at the sight of the dainty little creature itself. The behaviour of the man who is afraid to cross streets and squares only suggests one thing to us—that he behaves like a little child. A child is directly taught that such situations are dangerous, and the man's anxiety too is allayed when he is led by

someone across the open space.

The two forms of anxiety described, the 'free-floating' expectant dread and that attached to phobias, are independent of each other. The one is not the other at a further stage; they are only rarely combined, and then as if fortuitously. The most intense general apprehensiveness does not necessarily lead to a phobia; people who have been hampered all their lives by agoraphobia may be quite free from pessimistic expectant dread. Many phobias, e.g. fear of open spaces, of railway travelling, are demonstrably acquired first in later life; others, such as fear of darkness, thunder, animals, seem to have existed from the beginning. The former signify serious illness, the latter are more of the nature of idiosyncrasies, peculiarities; anyone exhibiting one of these latter may be suspected of harbouring others similar to it. I must add that we group all these phobias under *anxiety-hysteria*, that is, we regard them as closely allied to the well-known disorder called conversion-hysteria.

The third form taken by neurotic anxiety brings us to an enigma; there is no visible connection at all between the anxiety and the danger dreaded. This anxiety occurs in hysteria, for instance, accompanying the hysterical symptoms; or under various conditions of excitement in which, it is true, we should expect some affect to be displayed, but least of all an anxiety-affect; or without reference to any conditions, incomprehensible both to us and to the patient, an unrelated anxiety-attack. We may look far and wide without discovering a danger or an occasion which could even be exaggerated to account for it. These spontaneous attacks show therefore that the complex condition which we describe as anxiety can be split up into components. The whole attack can be represented (as a substitute) by a single intensively developed symptom—shuddering, faintness, palpitation of the heart, inability to breathe— and the general feeling which we recognize as anxiety may be absent or may have become unnoticeable. And yet these states

2 [In Germany it replaces the use of "duck" for this purpose in English.—Tʀ.]

which are termed 'anxiety equivalents' have the same clinical and ætiological validity as anxiety itself.

Two questions arise now: Is it possible to bring neurotic anxiety, in which such a small part or none at all is played by danger, into relation with 'objective anxiety,' which is essentially a reaction to danger? And, how is neurotic anxiety to be understood? We will at present hold fast to the expectation that where there is anxiety there must be something of which one is afraid.

Clinical observation yields various clues to the comprehension of neurotic anxiety, and I will now discuss their significance with you.

(a) It is not difficult to see that expectant dread or general apprehensiveness stands in intimate relation to certain processes in the sexual life—let us say, to certain modes of libido-utilization. The simplest and most instructive case of this kind arises in people who expose themselves to what is called frustrated excitation, i.e. when a powerful sexual excitation experiences insufficient discharge and is not carried on to a satisfying termination. This occurs, for instance, in men during the time of an engagement to marry, and in women whose husbands are not sufficiently potent, or who perform the sexual act too rapidly or incompletely with a view to preventing conception. Under these conditions the libidinal excitation disappears and anxiety appears in place of it, both in the form of expectant dread and in that of attacks and anxiety-equivalents. The precautionary measure of *coitus interruptus*, when practised as a customary sexual régime, is so regularly the cause of anxiety-neurosis in men, and even more so in women, that medical practitioners would be wise to enquire first of all into the possibility of such an ætiology in all such cases. Innumerable examples show that the anxiety-neurosis vanishes when the sexual malpractice is given up.

So far as I know, the fact that a connection exists between sexual restraint and anxiety conditions is no longer disputed, even by physicians who hold aloof from psychoanalysis. Nevertheless I can well imagine that they do not neglect to invert the connection, and to put forward the view that such persons are predisposed to apprehensiveness and consequently practice caution in sexual matters. Against this, however, decisive evidence is found in the reactions in women, in whom the sexual function is essentially passive, so that its course is determined by the treatment accorded by the man. The more 'temperament,' i.e. the more inclination for sexual intercourse and capacity for satisfaction, a woman has, the more certainly will she react with anxiety manifestations to the man's impotence or to *coitus interruptus;* whereas such abuse entails far less serious results with anæsthetic women or those in whom the sexual hunger is less strong.

Sexual abstinence, which is nowadays so warmly recommended by physicians, of course only has the same significance for anxiety conditions when the libido which is denied a satisfactory outlet is correspondingly insistent, and is not being utilized to a large extent in sublimation. Whether or not illness will ensue is indeed always a matter of the quantitative factor. Even apart from illness, it is easy to see in the sphere of character-formation that sexual restraint goes hand in hand with a certain anxiousness and cautiousness, whereas fearlessness and a boldly adventurous spirit bring with them a free tolerance of sexual needs. However these relations may be altered and complicated by the manifold influences of civilization, it remains incontestible that for the average human being anxiety is closely connected with sexual restriction.

I have by no means told you all the observations which point to this genetic connection between libido and anxiety.

28. A Theory of Emotionally-Based Drive (D) and Its Relation to Performance in Simple Learning Situations *

Kenneth W. Spence

The results of the previous study, by Watson and Rayner, show that people can be conditioned to fear a neutral stimulus by simply pairing it with a fear-producing stimulus. This means that emotions such as fear and anxiety are partly determined by an individual's past learning experiences. But emotions are related to learning in still another way because once an emotional state is aroused, it can have important effects on the learning process itself.

In the following article, Kenneth W. Spence describes a series of experiments that show how anxiety influences performance on such diverse tasks as eyelid conditioning and verbal learning. In these experiments, Professor Spence utilizes an anxiety questionnaire to select subjects. He assumes that scores on this questionnaire reflect individual differences in generalized drive, D, a major variable in Hull's learning theory. The performance on different learning tasks of subjects who differed in anxiety level was consistent with the interpretation that these subjects also differed in D.

Because of ethical considerations, it is not generally possible to induce painful emotional states in the laboratory. It should be noted, however, that Spence's procedure of selecting subjects who already differed in anxiety (or drive) makes it possible to study the effects of strong emotions on behavior under controlled laboratory conditions.

* Reprinted by permission of the American Psychological Association from the *American Psychologist*, 1958, *13*, 131-141.

A number of years ago we instituted at the University of Iowa a series of experiments concerned with the role of aversive motivational factors in learning situations. In addition to the more usual direct manipulation of variables influencing the motivational state of an individual, such, for example, as varying the intensity of a noxious stimulus, degree of motivation was also varied in these studies by employing selected subjects who differed in terms of their performance on a so-called scale of emotional responsiveness or manifest anxiety (31). That these experiments have aroused considerable interest among both clinical and experimental psychologists is readily evident, not only from the large number of published studies that have attempted either to check or extend our experimental findings, but also from the not infrequent critical reactions they have elicited. Now, while some of the criticisms directed against our studies undoubtedly have merit, it has been rather dismaying to discover the extent to which many of them reflect a serious lack of understanding of the structure and purpose of the basic theoretical framework underlying the experiments.

While some of the responsibility for this failure to understand the nature and objectives of the theory can be assigned to the critics, I hasten to acknowledge that our theoretical treatments have been quite inadequate. The major difficulty is that the studies have appeared only in experimental journals in which space limitations have required that theoretical discussions be kept to a minimum. Since each article tended to limit the discussion to those portions of the theory relevant to the particular phenomena being reported, the theory has been presented only in a very piecemeal fashion. Apparently our hope that the interested reader, particularly the critic, would familiarize himself with the theory as a whole by considering all of the articles has not been realized.

THEORETICAL SCHEMA

One of the purposes of this paper is to provide a more systematic presentation of our basic theory, or, to use an expression recently introduced by Cronbach and Meehl (4), of the nomological network underlying our studies. Following this the experimental evidence bearing on the theory will be presented and discussed. Fig. 28-1 presents the main concepts employed, at least in so far as one kind of learning situation, classical conditioning, is concerned.

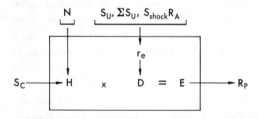

Figure 28.1 Diagram representing portion of theoretical schema relevant to data for classical conditioning. (See text for explanation of symbols.)

At the top of the figure are shown the experimentally manipulated independent variables such as N, the number of paired conditioning trials; S_u, the unconditioned stimulus; ΣS_u, the number of previous presentations of the unconditioned stimulus; R_A, score on the anxiety or emotional responsiveness scale. The empirical response measure at the lower right-hand corner is the dependent variable. Inside the rectangle are represented the several theoretical concepts (intervening variables) and the interrelations assumed among them. The arrows indicate the functions relating the dependent response measure to the intervening variables, and the latter to the experimentally manipulated variables. Details of the portion of the theory between the intervening variable E and the empirical response measure (R_p), involving such theoretical concepts as oscillatory inhibition and response threshold, have been omitted since our present purpose does not require them. It is sufficient to state that response frequency (R_p) is some positive monotonic function of excitatory potential E.

That the schema presented in Fig. 28-1 conforms to the Cronbach and Meehl concept of a nomological net is readily apparent. Thus to quote these writers: "The laws in a nomological network may relate (a) observable properties or quantities to each other; or (b) theoretical constructs to observables; or (c) different theoretical constructs to one another" (4, p. 290). One may readily find examples in our schema of each of these "laws," or as I would prefer to call them, "relations," since the term "law" typically has a narrower meaning than these authors have given it.

The theory takes its start from Hull's basic assumption that the excitatory potential, E, determining the strength of a response is a multiplicative function of a learning factor, H, and a generalized drive factor, D, i.e., $E = H \times D$ (9). We have assumed, further, that the drive level, D, in the case of aversive situations at least, is a function of the magnitude or strength of a hypothetical response mechanism—a persisting emotional response in the organism, designated as r_e, that is aroused by any form of aversive stimulation. That is, aversive, stressful stimulation is assumed to arouse activity under the control of the autonomic nervous system, which, according to some neurophysiological evidence, may act as an energizer of cortical mechanisms. Those of you who are familiar with the theoretical writings of Miller (13) and Mowrer (14) will recognize that this mechanism is similar to one these writers have postulated in connection with their investigations of acquired motivation. Thus they assumed that aversive stimuli arouse a hypothetical pain (emotional) response which, when conditioned to previously neutral stimulus events, provides the basis for an acquired drive of fear.

On the basis of analogy with overt reflexes to noxious stimulation, there were a number of properties that could be assigned to our hypothetical response mechanism. Three, in particular, will be discussed here. The first and most obvious is based on our knowledge that the magnitude or strength of observable reflexes to noxious stimulation (e.g., the corneal reflex to an air puff, the GSR to an electric shock) varies directly with the intensity or degree of noxiousness of the stimulus. Assuming our hypothetical emotional response, r_e, would exhibit the same property, it followed that the level of drive, D, present in classical defense conditioning would be a positive function of the intensity of the US. From the remaining portion of the theory, it could be deduced that the performance level, e.g., frequency of CR's, would vary positively with the intensity of the US employed. At the time of the original formulation of our theory there was some evidence, in particular an experiment by Passey (15), which supported this implication of the theory.

A second implication of our hypothetical mechanism was based on the adaptive property of observable reflexes to noxious stimuli: namely, that such responses characteristically exhibit adaptation or weakening with repeated stimulation. On the assumption that our hypothetical emotional response would behave in an analogous manner, it followed that, if a series of trials employing the US alone were given *prior* to conditioning, a lower level of D would be present during the subsequent conditioning than if no such adaptation trials were given. But if D were lower, the level of performance in the conditioning situa-

tion would also be lower following such adaptation trials than without them. This assumption or hypothesis, if you wish, is represented in Fig. 28-1 by $r_e = f(\Sigma S_u)$. At the time of formulation of the theory, we found a study by MacDonald (12) that gave results precisely in line with this implication.

The third implication of our theoretical mechanism was based on the well-known fact or observation that individuals differ in the magnitude of their reflex responses to a given intensity of stimulation. By analogy, again, we were led to assume that individuals would differ characteristically in the magnitude of this response, r_e, to the same intensity of stressful stimulation. If now there were available some means of assessing differences in this emotional responsiveness of individuals, our theoretical schema would lead to the prediction that highly emotional subjects, as assessed by the measuring device, would exhibit a higher level of performance in aversive forms of conditioning than subjects who scored low on the device.

The problem thus became one of attempting to develop a test for identifying individual differences in the responsiveness of this hypothetical emotional mechanism. Such a test, of course, would have to be defined independently of the measures that were to be employed in testing the theoretical network, i.e., the measures of performance in conditioning and other learning situations. It was in connection with this portion of our theory that the Manifest Anxiety or A-scale was developed. The idea of using a self-inventory test that would differentiate subjects in terms of the degree to which they admitted to possessing overt or manifest symptoms of emotionality was suggested by Taylor in a doctoral dissertation (30).

At this point I should like to make a methodological digression and comment on a criticism recently made concerning this aspect of our research. One pair of critics, inspired, but unfortunately not too enlightened, by the excellent article of Cronbach and Meehl (4) on construct validity, insisted that we should have developed our scale for measuring D on the basis of a theory so that, and I quote them, "performance on it might be a basis for inferring drive (differences) independently of the outcome of subsequent experiments" (10, p. 162). While there are a number of highly questionable methodological points in the arguments of these critics, I should like to call attention here merely to the fact that it is simply not true that no theorizing guided us in the development of the A-scale. As has just been recounted, we did have some very definite theoretical notions as to what lay behind differences in level of generalized drive, D, especially in the case of classical defense types of conditioning.

This theory, that D is a function of the strength of the emotional response made by the organism to the noxious stimulation, had already received considerable support. Its extension in the present instance to the individual difference variable logically demanded that we measure the emotional responsiveness of individuals under comparable environmental conditions. Naturally, so-called physiological indices of emotionality, such as, for example, changes in pulse rate or in the GSR, were indicated; and we have conducted some research along this line. However, it occurred to Taylor that it might be both interesting and valuable to investigate the possibility of making use of the presumed behavioral symptoms of emotionality that clinicians have described. That the questionnaire type of test developed turned out as well as it apparently has is to the credit, I think, of the clinical psychologists who selected the behavioral items as indicative of emotionally over-reactive individuals.

In this connection a further comment is in order concerning a surprising question that was asked by these same critics. Thus the problem was posed as to what the consequences would have been for either the theory or the test had the experiments using the A-scale been negative. The answer to the question, at least regards the theory, should be obvious. The implications of the other portions of our theory with respect to our response mechanism, r_e, were sufficiently well confirmed that we would have had no hesitancy about abandoning the A-scale as being related to D in our theory. Since, however, the implications of this aspect of our theoretical net were confirmed, we have continued to employ the A-scale as one operational definition of this emotional responsiveness variable. That a more satisfactory scale, even one of this questionnaire type, can be developed, I have no doubt. Indeed, I would recommend that some of the time and energy now being squandered in the many distorted, even mendacious, criticisms that seem to find such ready acceptance in our current discussion-type journals be directed at this more constructive task. If the main purpose of these attacks is to discredit and eliminate the theory, they will fail in this objective, for the history of science clearly reveals that a theory is usually discarded only when a better theory is advanced. The same goes for the constructs within a theory.

EXPERIMENTAL EVIDENCE

With these methodological remarks out of the way, let us turn now to the experimental evidence bearing on our theoretical schema. I shall spend the major part of my limited space presenting and discussing the findings of our eyelid conditioning experiments, for it was in connection with data from this type of learning situation that the schema was originally formulated. With regard to performance curves of conditioning, e.g., frequency curves, the implications of the theory are, as we have seen, that level of performance will be a positive function of (a) the intensity of the US, (b) the level of score on the A-scale, and (c) the intensity of an extra stressful stimulation. We shall take up the first two of these variables together; since space is so limited, I shall present only those studies which had the largest sample of subjects and hence have provided the most reliable and stable data.

Eyelid Conditioning Experiments

In Fig. 28-2 are presented the findings of two experiments (one unpublished; the other, 27), one of which involved 120 subjects and the other 100 subjects. Both studies employed two levels of puff intensity, .6 lb. and 2.0 lbs./sq. in., in the one represented in the lower graph; .25 lb. and 1.5 lbs./sq. in., in the upper graph. Each study also involved two levels of emotionality (upper and lower 20% of subjects on the A-scale). Examination of the curves in both graphs shows clearly that at each of the four puff intensities, the High A group (shown by solid curves) was well above the Low A group (broken curves). Statistical analysis over all of the conditioning trials revealed the differences were significant at the .01 level in the lower graph and at the .025 level in the upper.[1]

A second point to be noted in these data is relevant to the assumption that the learning or habit factor (H) and the drive factor (D) combine in a multiplicative manner to determine response strength. This assumption leads to the further implication that frequency curves of conditioning for different values of the anxiety variable will exhibit a gradual divergence over the course of training.[2] That this prediction was borne out may be seen by inspecting the graphs. Statistical confirmation of the divergence is revealed by the fact that the trials-×-anxiety interaction terms for both sets of data were highly significant (.005 and .025 levels).

The findings with respect to the intensity of US variable also supported the impli-

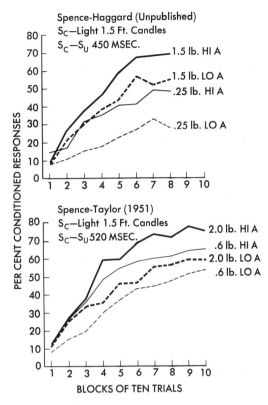

Figure 28.2 Performance in eyelid conditioning as function of A-score and intensity of US.

cations of our theory. Thus it may be seen in both studies that the subjects that had the strong puff performed at a higher level than those with the weak puff. The divergence between the curves is also apparent.

As an indication of the stability of our findings involving these two experimental variables, Fig. 28-3 presents data from these same two studies along with some relevant data from four other investigations recently conducted in our laboratory (26). Shown on the ordinate of this graph are the percentage of CR's given in the block of Trials 41–80 as a function of the intensity of the unconditioned stimulus employed. The uppermost curve in this graph represents the results for subjects selected from the high end of the A-scale; the lowest curve, subjects selected from the low end. The middle curve represents data obtained in

[1] Since unequal numbers of each sex were used in both of these studies and because women consistently exhibit a greater difference than men, the curves have been weighted equally for male and female subjects.

[2] This prediction must be qualified to the extent that the frequency measure has a ceiling of 100% and thus may not always reflect the continued growth of E. This is particularly the case at high levels of D in which E also is high.

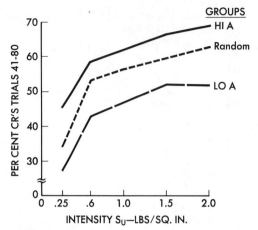

Figure 28.3 Showing relation between conditioning performance and intensity of US for unselected and high and low A-score subjects.

four different experiments in which unselected subjects, so far as A-score, were conditioned under highly comparable conditions to those used with the selected subjects (i.e., similar visual CS and very comparable S_c–S_u intervals). The consistency of the results from experiment to experiment, particularly the relation of the curve for the unselected subjects to those for the High and Low A subjects, is, I believe, quite impressive.

In addition to the data presented in these graphs, four other investigations have reported finding that High A subjects responded at a significantly higher level than Low A subjects in eyelid conditioning (21, 22, 28, 30). One additional study (8) also found superior performance by High A subjects, although the difference in this instance was not significant. A reasonable interpretation of the failure to obtain a significant difference in this latter study, especially to anyone familiar with the variability of individual conditioning data, is that there were only ten subjects in each group.

Mention was made earlier of the fact that in addition to the anxiety scale we have also attempted to employ a number of physiological measures as further operational definitions of our emotional respon-

siveness variable. One of the most discouraging aspects of this work has been the lack of consistency, i.e., unreliability from day to day, of such measures. Especially has this been the case with the GSR, on which, unfortunately, we concentrated most of our time and energy. Recently, however, we have obtained results (to be published) with these measures that are rather more promising. Using changes in GSR and heart rate made to a mildly noxious stimulus and converting the measures into a so-called autonomic lability score by means of a formula suggested by Lacey (11), two groups of subjects who fell in the upper and lower third of the distribution of such scores were subsequently conditioned. Shown in Fig. 28-4 are the frequency curves of eyelid conditioning for these two groups of subjects. As may be seen, the subjects with the high autonomic lability index performed at a higher level than those with a low index. The difference is significant at the .02 level.

In addition to varying performance by manipulating the A-scale and US variables, it should be possible to produce a higher level of conditioning performance by presenting a strong extra stimulus, such as an

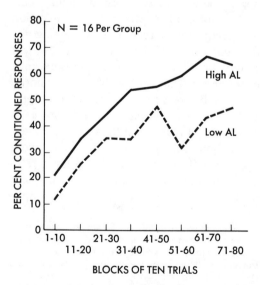

Figure 28.4 Percentage of CR's for the high and low autonomic lability (AL) groups in blocks of ten trials.

electric shock, during the course of conditioning. Similarly, after a subject has experienced a strong electric shock just prior to conditioning, the mere threat of further shocks during the conditioning should arouse a strong and persisting emotional response that would raise the level of D and hence the level of performance. We have already published the results of one such experiment with unselected subjects which corroborated, in part, these theoretical expectations (25).

Recently a further experiment (to be published) studying the effects of shock threat on High and Low A subjects was completed in our laboratory. Some idea of the nature of the findings can be gained from Fig. 28-5 which presents the frequency curves of conditioning for four groups of Low A subjects (20th percentile). The two top curves in this graph are for subjects conditioned with a relatively strong air puff (1.5 lbs./sq. in.); the lower two, for subjects who had a weak puff (.25 lb./sq. in.). It will be seen that at both puff levels the threatened group (solid curve) was consistently above the nonthreatened group (broken curve) throughout the whole 80 trials. A similar experiment with high anxious subjects revealed a difference between the threat and nonthreat groups throughout the conditioning in the case of groups which had a weak puff. In the strong puff groups, however, the curves for the threat and nonthreat group, after separating in the early trials, came together in the later stages of the conditioning (last 40 trials). This latter effect undoubtedly results, in part, from the ceiling imposed by the frequency measure.

Space will not permit a detailed presentation of the experimental evidence with respect to that portion of our theory concerned with the assumption that the emotional response to the noxious US would be weaker if adaptation trials are given prior to conditioning. It is sufficient to state that the original finding of MacDonald (12), that such preadapted subjects exhibited a lower level of performance in conditioning

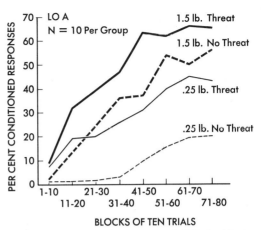

Figure 28.5 Percentage of CR's in blocks of ten trials as a function of shock or no-shock threat and intensity of the US for subjects who score low on A-scale.

than nonadapted subjects, has been corroborated by Taylor (32). The latter experimenter also found that conditioning performance was inversely related to the intensity of the US employed during the preconditioning adaptation period. Thus the implications of this part of the theoretical network have also received further support.

The final set of conditioning data that I would like to present are concerned with the effect of level of D on differential conditioning. Without going into the theoretical derivation, it may be shown that one of the implications of our theory is that the higher the drive level, D, of the subjects, the greater should be the differentiation between the positive and the negative, i.e., nonreinforced, stimulus in such differential conditioning. Two studies from our laboratory have reported finding that, in five separate comparisons, high anxious subjects showed better discrimination than low anxious subjects (21, 23). Although none of the differences were significant, four closely approached being so. More recently we have investigated the effect of varying the level of D on differential conditioning by direct manipulation of the intensity of the US. The graph in Fig. 28-6 presents the findings of this study (17) in

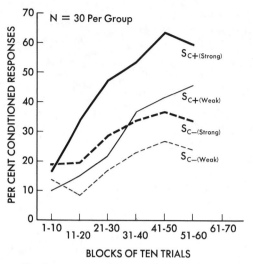

Figure 28.6 Percentage of CR's to the positive and negative stimuli for groups conditioned with a strong and weak US.

terms of the frequency of CR's given to the two stimuli, positive and negative. As may be seen, the subjects conditioned with the strong US not only showed a higher level of response to the positive and negative stimuli, but, as predicted from our theory, the difference between the conditioned responses to the two stimuli was greater in the case of the group that had the strong US. Again this latter difference approached, but did not quite reach, statistical significance. Unfortunately, conditioning data are plagued by high individual variability, produced in part by a few subjects who show very little or no conditioning. In an effort to ascertain what the finding would be for subjects who showed considerable conditioning, a separate analysis was made of the upper two-thirds of each of the two groups run in the experiment. In the case of these subjects discrimination was significantly better for the high drive group at the .05 level.

So much for the findings in our eyelid conditioning studies. On the whole, we believe they are in fair accord with our theoretical schema, including the portion of it that involves the A-scale. While not all of the results have met acceptable levels of significance, the fact that the direction of the differences in such instances has almost invariably been in accord with the theory has encouraged us to continue to hold to it. Attention might also be called here to the fact that this theoretical model, particularly the hypothetical emotional response mechanism, has also been quite successful in connection with a wide variety of other behavioral situations involving noxious stimulation with animals. Examples are to be found in the many studies cited by Miller (13) on the motivating and reinforcing roles of acquired fear in learning situations. The experiments of a number of investigators on the persisting motivational effects of emotionality aroused by electric shock on the consummatory behavior of rats provide yet another example (1, 2, 18, 19).

Complex Human Learning

Turning now to our studies involving the more complex types of human learning, let me begin by saying that it is in this area that the limitations of space in experimental journals for theoretical elaboration have been most unfortunate. Certainly we recognize that these treatments have been quite inadequate, particularly from the point of view of discussing the many factors that complicate efforts at theorizing in this area. By way of example let me mention two important points that need to be recognized but, unfortunately, have not always been so.

First, it should be realized that in order to derive implications concerning the effects of drive variation in any type of complex learning task, it is necessary to have, in addition to the drive theory, a further theoretical network concerning the variables and their interaction that are involved in the particular learning activity. It is perhaps unnecessary to point out here that theoretical schemas for such types of learning are as yet in a very primitive state of development, indeed almost nonexistent. As a consequence of this, one has considerable difficulty in drawing conclusions about the motivational part of the new, combined theory from supposedly negative findings, for the defect may be in the part of the network specifying the action of the variables in the complex learning situation.

The second point is that our theory of the mechanism underlying D was developed in connection with experimental situations involving some form of noxious stimulation. Complex human learning tasks, on the other hand, typically do not involve the use of a noxious stimulus. Whatever stress is present in these situations is usually produced by instructions that aim to create in the subject the desire or need to make as good a showing as possible. While it is true that this stress may be greatly augmented by introducing failure or punishment into the situation, so far as the usual type of human learning experiment is concerned, the question as to whether High A subjects would be more emotional than Low A subjects, and hence have a higher D level, is a moot one. In this connection two alternative subhypotheses have been proposed: (a) the chronic hypothesis: that High A subjects react emotionally in a chronic manner to all situations, whether stressful or not; and (b) the emotional reactivity hypothesis: that High A subjects have a lower threshold of emotional responsiveness and react with a stronger emotional response than Low A subjects to situations containing some degree of stress (16, 20, 25). As may be seen, according to the first of these hypotheses, mild nonthreatening situations would produce a differential drive (D) level in subjects scoring at extremes of the scale; whereas according to the second, there would not be a difference. These two examples are sufficient, I believe, to point up the fact that the problems involved in the extension of the theory to these more complex types of learning are quite formidable and that at this stage there necessarily must be a considerable amount of trial and error in our theorizing.

Now it will be recalled that the theoretical schema presented in Fig. 28-1 assumed that in classical conditioning habit strength to but a single response was established to the CS. In this circumstance, as we have seen, an increase in drive level implied an increase in response strength. In more complex, selective learning tasks, on the other hand, there are, typically, a hierarchy of competing response tendencies. Actually most of the complex learning situations employed with humans involve a number or sequence of such response hierarchies which involve competing responses, e.g., a number of choice points in the maze, whether verbal or spatial. To show what the implications of variation of drive level will be in such competing response situations, let us begin by considering the simplest conceivable case: one in which there is but a single response hierarchy involving two alternative responses. The single choice point maze involving turning left or right is one example of such a situation. If now the habit strength of the correct to-be-learned response is, at the beginning of the learning, somewhat stronger than that of the incorrect response, it may be shown that the higher the drive level, D, the greater will the difference between the competing excitatory potentials be and, *neglecting all other considerations*, the higher should be the percentage of correct responses at the start of learning, the sooner should the learning criterion be attained, and the smaller should be the total number of errors.[3]

[3] As discussed in my Silliman Lectures (21), there are a number of other considerations that need to be taken into account in extending the theory to such competing response situations. Thus the particular composition rule (law) assumed in these lectures to describe the manner in which the competing responses interacted with each other led to the implication that the percentage of occurrence of the competing responses is a function, not only of the magnitude of the difference between the competing Es, but also of their absolute level above the threshold L. As a consequence in the low range of E values, there may actually be an inverse relation between performance level (percent choice of the response with stronger E) and the level of drive. Still other considerations involve whether habit strength (H) in learning situations is or is not assumed to be dependent on the reinforcer and whether drive strength (D) determines the inhibitory factor (I_n). Different combinations of these alternative

The reverse situation, that in which the correct response is at the outset weaker than the incorrect one, is, from the theoretical viewpoint, even more complex. In this instance the stronger the drive, the greater will be the percent choice of the wrong response, or, in other words, the poorer will be the performance at this initial stage. But, as training proceeds, sooner or later the habit strength of the correct, reinforced response will overtake that of the wrong, unreinforced response and from this point on the percent choice of the correct response should in general be higher for the high drive group than for the low drive group. In other words, the performance curves should be expected to cross. Precise predictions about the total number of errors, number of trials, etc. in this situation will depend to a considerable extent upon the particular functions and parameter values assigned to the assumed habit and inhibitory factors. Actually we have never got around to working out in detail the implications of the various possibilities for the total learning period even in this simplest case.

Recalling now that such a learning task as the serial verbal or spatial maze involves a number of such competing response hierarchies, we see that the problem of predicting the effect on performance of variation of the drive in such situations becomes even more complicated. On the assumption that anticipatory and perseverative associative tendencies would develop in such a manner as to make the incorrect response the stronger in the case of many of the choice points of a maze, it was hoped that it would be possible to demonstrate that high drive (i.e., High A) subjects would perform more poorly in such serial learning situations than low drive (i.e., Low A) subjects. Two experiments, one with a verbal

assumptions, including even other possible composition rules, lead to different behavior consequences. Critical evaluation of the different conceivable theoretical models will require considerably more empirical data obtained under a wide variety of experimental conditions than is now available.

form of maze (35) and one using a finger maze (5) actually did provide results in agreement with this theoretical expectation. However, as was pointed out at the time, there was a serious discrepancy between the theory and the obtained results in these studies in that the anxious subjects made more errors at all but one of the choice points in both studies. In view of the ease of learning many of these choice points, and hence evidence for little or no strong competing response tendencies, the theory would have led us to expect that the High A subjects would have made fewer errors on them than the Low A subjects. Obviously the theory was wrong in some respect, but just in what way—an incorrect assumption or failure to include an important relevant variable—was not clear.

At this point in our work we realized that such serial learning tasks are, for a variety of reasons, quite unsatisfactory. Among the most important from our viewpoint was the fact that one has little or no knowledge of the relative strengths of the competing responses in each of the hierarchies. Accordingly we abandoned this type of situation and attempted to develop learning tasks in which it would be possible to specify or manipulate in some known manner the relative strengths of the competing responses in each hierarchy. Probably the chief value of these earlier experiments is that they did point up the fact that a higher anxiety score (and hence possibly a higher drive level) does not necessarily always lead to a higher level of performance.

Among the types of learning problems that we turned to was paired-associates learning. This type of learning task may be conceived as consisting of the formation of a set of more or less isolated S-R associations or habit tendencies. In one type of list, which we have referred to as a noncompetitive list, an attempt is made to isolate as much as possible the paired items by minimizing the degree of synonymity or formal similarity among both the stimulus and response words. As learning proceeds and the habit strengths of the stimulus words to their paired response words increase, high drive subjects should, according to our theory, perform at a higher level than low drive subjects. An important condition in this derivation is that the associative connections between each stimulus word and the nonpaired response words are lower than that to the paired response word.

Two lists of this type have been employed. In one the associative connections between the paired words were initially zero or at least very low. In this type of list it would be predicted that there would be little or no difference between high and low drive subjects at the start of learning, but that as learning progressed the curve of correct responses would diverge, that for the high drive group being the higher. Using nonsense syllables of low association value and low intralist similarity, Taylor has reported two experiments in which this type of list was employed (33, 34). The lower pair of curves in Fig. 28-7 present the data from one of these studies (34). Both curves, it will be observed, began at a very low level with the curve for the High A group (solid line) rising above that for the Low A group (broken line). An unpublished study from our laboratory employing nonassociated paired adjectives has given similar results, although the superiority of the High A over the Low A subjects was significant only on a single tailed hypothesis.

The second type of noncompetitive list differs from the first in that the associative strengths of the paired words are, as the result of past experiences, considerably above zero. Under this condition it would be predicted that the performance curves would, on the first anticipation trial, be considerably above 0% and that the curve for the high drive group would be above that for the low drive group. Employing paired adjectives that had been scaled by Haagen (7) as having high "closeness of association" values, two studies (24, 29) have reported results which support these implications. The upper pair of curves in

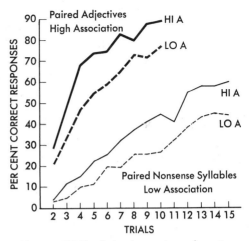

Figure 28.7 Paired-associates learning as a function of A-score under conditions of unusual interword pair competition.

Fig. 28-7 shows the findings of one of these studies (29). As may be seen, the initial level of performance was well above 0 and the High A subjects started out and continued at a higher level than the Low A subjects. On the other hand, a recently completed doctoral dissertation (6) using this type of list failed to obtain results in accord with the theory. There was little or no difference between the two groups at any stage of practice.

In contrast to these noncompetitive type lists we have also designed a competitive list which includes some paired items in which the initial habit strength of the stimulus word to call out the paired word is weaker than the habit strengths to one or more other response words in the list. In the case of these items it would be predicted from our theory that high drive subjects would at the start of learning perform more poorly than low drive subjects. Here again we should have emphasized that the theory of paired-associates learning has as yet not been developed sufficiently to predict what will happen beyond the first few trials, and it would have been more appropriate, as far as implications for our drive theory are concerned, if we had used at most only the data from the first four or five trials. Precise predictions concerning performance beyond this point must await the development of a more adequate theory of the variables determining the weakening of these stronger, incorrect responses in paired-associates learning. Two published studies (24, 29) and one doctoral dissertation (6) have reported data with respect to the implication of our theory for this type of list; while all three found, as predicted, that the High A subjects were inferior to Low A subjects in the first four trials, none of the results was statistically significant. However, the implication of the theory that there would be an interaction between level of A-score and performance on the two kinds of lists, competitive and noncompetitive, was confirmed.

Summarizing the results with these paired-associates lists, I would say that the batting average of our theory is fairly high but by no means perfect. It is clearly evident from the data that differences in level of A-score (and hence level of D), if it is a factor determining performance on such tasks, is a relatively unimportant one. Certainly individual differences in verbal learning ability play a much more decisive role. Moreover, there are as yet many factors that play important roles in such complex behavior situations, about which we have as yet little or no knowledge. Among those of a motivational nature is the type of task-irrelevant response that Child and his group have studied (3). We think of these interfering responses as being elicited by drive stimuli (s_D), and hence they would be incorporated in a more complete motivational theory of learned behavior. On the basis of evidence in the literature and some recently completed studies of our own, we believe this factor is especially important when shock is introduced into verbal learning situations.

I should like to conclude this presentation by stating very briefly the purpose of such theoretical schemas as has been presented here. As I conceive them, their primary function is to provide for the unification of what, without the theory, would be a multiplicity of isolated or unconnected facts and laws. Thus, in the present instance, such phenotypically different phenomena as behavior in eyelid conditioning under various stimulus conditions, degree of emotionality as revealed by a personality questionnaire and physiological measures, and such opposite performance differentials in paired-associates tasks as just described have been interrelated by means of the theory. That much work, both of a theoretical and experimental nature, remains to be done in this area of behavior study is clearly revealed by the many gaps and deficiencies in the present attempt. It is my firm belief, however, that progress in the development of this, as in any other scientific field of knowledge, is greatly facilitated by such theoretically oriented research endeavors.

REFERENCES

1. AMSEL, A. The effect upon level of consummatory response of the addition of anxiety to a motivational complex. *J. exp. Psychol.*, 1950, **40**, 709–715.
2. AMSEL, A., & MALTZMAN, I. The effect upon generalized drive strength of emotionality as inferred from the level of consummatory response. *J. exp. Psychol.*, 1950, **40**, 563–569.
3. CHILD, I. L. Personality. *Annu. Rev. Psychol.*, 1954, **5**, 149–170.
4. CRONBACH, L. J., & MEEHL, P. E. Construct validity in psychological tests. *Psychol. Bull.*, 1955, **52**, 281–302.
5. FARBER, I. E., & SPENCE, K. W. Complex learning and conditioning as a function of anxiety. *J. exp. Psychol.*, 1953, **45**, 120–125.
6. FREDENBURG, NORMA C. Paired-associates learning as a function of anxiety level and shock. Unpublished doctoral dissertation, State Univer. of Iowa, 1956.
7. HAAGEN, C. H. Synonymity, vividness, familiarity, and association value ratings of 400 pairs of common adjectives. *J. Psychol.*, 1949, **27**, 453–463.
8. HILGARD, E. R., JONES, L. V., & KAPLAN, S. J. Conditioned discrimination as related to anxiety. *J. exp. Psychol.*, 1951, **42**, 94–99.
9. HULL, C. L. *Principles of behavior.* New York: Appleton-Century, 1943.
10. JESSOR, R., & HAMMOND, K. R. Construct validity and the Taylor anxiety scale. *Psychol. Bull.*, 1957, **54**, 161–170.
11. LACEY, O. L. The evaluation of autonomic responses toward a general solution. *Ann. N. Y. Acad. Sci.*, 1956, **67**, 123–164.

12. MacDonald, Annette. The effect of adaptation to the unconditioned stimulus upon the formation of conditioned avoidance response. *J. exp. Psychol.*, 1946, 36, 1–12.

13. Miller, N. E. Learnable drives and rewards. In S. S. Stevens (Ed.), *Handbook of experimental psychology.* New York. Wiley, 1951. Pp. 435–472.

14. Mowrer, O. H. A stimulus response analysis of anxiety and its role as a reinforcing agent. *Psychol. Rev.*, 1939, 46, 553–565.

15. Passey, G. E. The influence of intensity of unconditioned stimulus upon acquisition of a conditioned response. *J. exp. Psychol.*, 1948, 38, 420–428.

16. Rosenbaum, G. Stimulus generalization as a function of clinical and experimentally induced anxiety. Unpublished doctoral dissertation, State Univer. of Iowa, 1950.

17. Runquist, W. N., Spence, K. W., & Stubbs, D. W. Differential conditioning and intensity of the US. *J. exp. Psychol.*, in press.

18. Siegel, P. S., & Brantley, J. J. The relationship of emotionality to the consummatory response of eating. *J. exp. Psychol.*, 1951, 42, 304–306.

19. Siegel, P. S., & Siegel, Helen S. The effect of emotionality on the water intake of the rat. *J. comp. physiol. Psychol.*, 1949, 42, 12–16.

20. Spence, K. W. *Behavior theory and conditioning.* New Haven: Yale Univer. Press, 1956.

21. Spence, K. W., & Beecroft, R. S. Differential conditioning and level of anxiety. *J. exp. Psychol.*, 1954, 48, 399–403.

22. Spence, K. W., & Farber, I. E. Conditioning and extinction as a function of anxiety. *J. exp. Psychol.*, 1953, 45, 116–119.

23. Spence, K. W., & Farber, I. E. The relation of anxiety to differential eyelid conditioning. *J. exp. Psychol.*, 1954, 47, 127–134.

24. Spence, K. W., Farber, I. E., & McFann, H. H. The relation of anxiety (drive) level to performance in competitional and noncompetitional paired-associates learning. *J. exp. Psychol.*, 1956, 52, 296–305.

25. Spence, K. W., Farber, I. E., & Taylor, Elaine. The relation of electric shock and anxiety to level of performance in eyelid conditioning. *J. exp. Psychol.*, 1954, 48, 404–408.

26. Spence, K. W., & Ross, L. E. Experimental evidence on the relation between performance level in eyelid conditioning and anxiety (drive) level. USN Office of Naval Research *Tech Rep.*, 1957, No. 5 (Contract N9 onr-93802).

27. Spence, K. W., & Taylor, Janet A. Anxiety and strength of the US as determiners of the amount of eyelid conditioning. *J. exp. Psychol.*, 1951, 42, 183–188.

28. Spence, K. W., & Taylor, Janet A. The relation of conditioned response strength to anxiety in normal, neurotic, and psychotic subjects. *J. exp. Psychol.*, 1953, 45, 265–272.

29. Spence, K. W., Taylor, J., & Ketchel, Rhoda. Anxiety (drive) level and degree of competition in paired-associates learning. *J. exp. Psychol.*, 1956, 52, 306–310.

30. Taylor, Janet A. The relationship of anxiety to the conditioned eyelid response. *J. exp. Psychol.*, 1951, 41, 81–92.

31. Taylor, Janet A. A personality scale of manifest anxiety. *J. abnorm. soc. Psychol.*, 1953, 48, 285–290.

32. Taylor, Janet A. Level of conditioning and intensity of the adaptation stimulus. *J. exp. Psychol.*, 1956, 51, 127–131.

33. Taylor, Janet A. The effects of anxiety level and psychological stress on verbal learning. *J. abnorm. soc. Psychol.*, in press.

34. Taylor, Janet A., & Chapman, J. P. Paired-associate learning as related to anxiety. *Amer. J. Psychol.*, 1955, 68, 671.

35. Taylor, Janet A., & Spence, K. W. The relationship of anxiety level to performance in serial learning. *J. exp. Psychol.*, 1952, 44, 61–64.

36. Taylor, Janet A., & Spence, K. W. Conditioning level in behavior disorders. *J. abnorm. soc. Psychol.*, 1954, 49, 497–502.

29. State Anxiety and Trait Anxiety *

Charles D. Spielberger

Anxiety is a major explanatory concept in almost every contemporary theory of personality. Yet, there is considerable ambiguity and semantic confusion regarding the definition of anxiety and little agreement on the methods by which anxiety should be measured. Differences of opinion on the nature of anxiety, the particular stimulus conditions that arouse it, and the kinds of past experiences that make

* Reprinted by permission of the author and the publisher from Chapter 1 of *Anxiety and Behavior,* Academic Press, Inc., New York, 1966.

individuals more or less vulnerable to it, are the rule rather than the exception.

In the following selection, Professor Spielberger suggests that it is necessary to distinguish between two quite different and distinct concepts of anxiety, which he calls *state anxiety* and *trait anxiety*. State anxiety is an emotional response, that is, an experience or condition characterized by feelings of apprehension and heightened activity in the autonomic nervous system. Trait anxiety refers to differences between people in "anxiety proneness." Persons high in trait anxiety are more strongly and frequently disposed to experience a state of anxiety because they tend to perceive greater danger in the world in which they live.

Although contemporary interest in anxiety phenomena has historical roots in the philosophical and theological views of Pascal and Kierkegaard (May, 1950), it was Freud who first attempted to explicate the meaning of anxiety within the context of psychological theory. He regarded anxiety as "something felt," an unpleasant affective *state* or condition. This state, as observed in patients with anxiety-neurosis, was characterized by "all that is covered by the word 'nervousness'," apprehension or anxious expectation, and efferent discharge phenomena (Freud, 1924). Specific symptoms of the latter included heart palpitation (transitory arythmia, tachycardia), disturbances of respiration ("nervous dyspnoea"), sweating, tremor and shuddering, vertigo, and numerous other physiological and behavioral manifestations.

Anxiety was distinguishable from other unpleasant affective (emotional) states such as anger, grief, or sorrow by its unique combination of phenomenological and physiological qualities. These gave to anxiety a special "character of unpleasure" which, although difficult to describe, seemed "to possess a particular note of its own" (Freud, 1936, p. 69). The subjective, phenomenological qualities of anxiety— the feelings of apprehensive expectation or

dread—were emphasized by Freud, especially in his later formulations, while the physiological-behavioral (efferent) discharge phenomena, although considered an essential part of the anxiety state and an important contributor to its unpleasantness, were of little theoretical interest to him. Freud was mainly concerned with identifying the sources of stimulation which precipitated anxiety rather than with analyzing the properties of such states; he hoped to discover, in prior experience, "the historical element . . . which binds the afferent and efferent elements of anxiety firmly together" (1936, p. 70).

In his early theoretical formulations, Freud believed that anxiety resulted from the discharge of repressed, unrelieved somatic sexual tensions (libido). He held that when libidinal excitation produced mental images (lustful ideas) that were perceived as dangerous, these ideas were repressed. The libidinal energy, thus blocked from normal expression, accumulated and was automatically transformed into anxiety, or into symptoms that were anxiety equivalents. Freud later modified this view in favor of a more general conceptualization of anxiety in which its functional utility to the ego was emphasized. He conceived of anxiety as a signal indicating the presence of a danger situation and differentiated between objective anxiety and neurotic anxiety largely on the basis of whether the source of the danger was from the external world or from internal impulses.

Objective anxiety, which was regarded by Freud as synonymous with fear, involved a complex internal reaction to anticipated injury or harm from some external danger. A real danger situation existed in the external world, was consciously perceived as threatening, and this perception of danger evoked an anxiety reaction. Thus:

external danger ⟶ perception of danger ⟶
objective anxiety

With objective anxiety, the intensity of the anxiety reaction was proportional to the magnitude of the external danger that evoked it: the greater the external danger, the stronger the perceived threat, the more intense the resulting reaction. The unpleasantness of the anxiety reaction, coupled with cues provided by the perception of its source, was generally sufficient to mobilize an individual either to flee the danger situation or in some way to protect himself from it.

Neurotic anxiety, like objective anxiety, was characterized by feelings of apprehension and physiological arousal. But neurotic anxiety differed from objective anxiety in that the source of the danger that evoked this reaction was internal rather than external, and this source was not consciously perceived because it had been repressed. In essence, neurotic anxiety was the historical product of an aversive conditioning process (Mowrer, 1939) involving instinctual impulses and repression, and commonly occurring in childhood. The etiology of neurotic anxiety entailed: (1) the expression of aggressive or sexual impulses for which the child was strongly and consistently punished (external danger); (2) the evocation of objective anxiety, i.e., the apprehensive expectation of punishment, by cues associated with the forbidden impulses when these were later experienced; (3) an attempt to alleviate or reduce objective anxiety by repressing (banishing from awareness) those stimuli associated with the punished impulses that elicited this unpleasant reaction; and (4) the evocation of neurotic anxiety when a partial breakdown in repression results in "derivatives" of repressed impulses (internal stimuli) erupting into awareness. Thus:

Since most of the cues associated with the punished impulses remained repressed, neurotic anxiety was experienced as "objectless," or, as in the case of phobias, the relationship between the object that was feared and the original danger situation was not recognized.

Neurotic anxiety, according to Freud, was experienced by everyone to some extent, from time to time, but when manifested in pathological amounts, it defined the clinical syndrome, anxiety-neurosis. Anxiety was the "fundamental phenomenon and the central problem of neurosis" (1936, p. 85), and understanding anxiety was considered "the most difficult task that has been set us," a task whose solution required "the introduction of the right abstract ideas, and of their application to the raw material of observation so as to bring order and lucidity into it" (1933, p. 113). Both the complexity of this task and Freud's personal commitment to it were reflected in the fact that his theoretical views on the subject of anxiety evolved over a period of nearly 50 years, were continually modified, and were never regarded as complete.

Other personality theorists have since joined the search for the "right abstract ideas" with which to illuminate and clarify anxiety phenomena, but order and lucidity have not resulted. Lack of agreement regarding the nature of anxiety, the particular stimulus conditions that arouse it, and the sorts of past experiences that make individuals more or less vulnerable to it, is the rule rather than the exception. Consider, for example, the differences among the concepts of anxiety advanced by Mowrer (1950), Sullivan (1953), and May (1950):

1. As an alternative to Freud's "impulse theory" of anxiety, Mowrer has proposed a

$$\text{internal impulses} \longrightarrow \text{external danger (punishment)} \longrightarrow \text{objective anxiety} \longrightarrow \text{repression}$$

$$\text{partial breakdown of repression} \longrightarrow \text{derivatives of internal impulses} \longrightarrow \text{neurotic anxiety}$$

"guilt theory" in which it is contended that ". . . anxiety comes, not from acts which the individual would commit but dares not, but from acts which he has committed but wishes that he had not" (1950, p. 537). Thus, neurotic anxiety results from the repudiation of the demands of the conscience, not the instincts, from repression that has been turned toward the superego rather than the id.[1] If one behaves irresponsibly, with too much self-indulgence and too little self-restraint, then anxiety is experienced.

2. For Sullivan, anxiety was an intensely unpleasant state of tension arising from the experience of disapproval in interpersonal relations. Through an empathic linkage between an infant and its mother, "The tension of anxiety, when present in the mothering one, induces anxiety in the infant" (Sullivan, 1953, p. 41). Once aroused, anxiety distorts the individual's perception of reality, limits the range of stimuli that are perceived, and causes those aspects of the personality that are disapproved to be dissociated.

3. According to May, anxiety was "the apprehension cued off by a threat to some value which the individual holds essential to his existence as a personality" (1950, p. 191). While the capacity to experience anxiety was innate, the particular events or stimulus conditions which evoked it were largely determined by learning. An anxiety reaction was *normal* if it was proportionate to the objective danger and did not involve repression or other defense mechanisms. Neurotic anxiety reactions were disproportionate to the objective danger (but not the subjective danger) and involved repression and neurotic defenses. Fear was a learned response to a localized danger which did not constitute a threat to the basic values of the individual.

What is the nature of anxiety? Is anxiety innate or learned? What basis is there

for differentiating between anxiety and fear? Between anxiety and guilt? How many different kinds of anxiety can be identified, and by what operational criteria may these be distinguished? What sorts of stimulus conditions elicit anxiety, and do these differ for different kinds of anxiety? Is it meaningful to speak of *conscious* and *unconscious* anxiety? Of *bound* and *free-floating* anxiety? The answers to such questions will differ depending upon one's theoretical conception of anxiety, and this, in turn, will determine the inferences and the operations which give anxiety empirical meaning in the clinic and the laboratory. Given the conceptual ambiguities in anxiety theory, it is perhaps not surprising that anxiety research is characterized by semantic confusion and contradictory findings.

STATE ANXIETY AND TRAIT ANXIETY

Ambiguity in the conceptual status of anxiety arises from the more or less indiscriminate use of the term to refer to two very different types of concepts. Anxiety is perhaps most commonly used in an empirical sense to denote a complex reaction or response—a transitory state or condition of the organism that varies in intensity and fluctuates over time. But the term anxiety is also used to refer to a personality trait—to individual differences in the extent to which different people are characterized by anxiety states and by prominent defenses against such states. For example, consider the statement: "Mr. Smith is anxious." This may be interpreted as meaning either that Smith is anxious *now* or that Smith is an *anxious person*. If the statement is meant to imply that Smith is anxious now, at this very moment, then the validity of the statement may be ascertained by making appropriate measurements to determine whether or not Smith is manifesting (experiencing) a particular state with specifiable properties. On the other hand, if the statement is intended to signify that Smith

---

[1] Freud, too, identified a form of "moral anxiety," experienced as shame or guilt, as arising from the superego, but he differentiated moral anxiety from neurotic anxiety.

is an anxious person, the same measurements should reveal that Smith's level of state anxiety is *chronically* higher than that of most other people, as would be the case if he were suffering from anxiety-neurosis.

Empirical evidence of different types of anxiety concepts has emerged from the factor analytic studies of Cattell and Scheier (1958; 1961). These investigators identified two distinct anxiety factors which they labeled *trait anxiety* and *state anxiety* on the basis of the procedures by which these factors were isolated and the variables which loaded on them. The trait anxiety factor was interpreted as measuring stable individual differences in a unitary, relatively permanent personality characteristic. The state anxiety factor was based on a pattern of variables that covaried over occasions of measurement, defining a transitory state or condition of the organism which fluctuated over time. Component characterological variables that loaded the trait anxiety factor included: "ergic tension," "ego weakness," "guilt proneness," "suspiciousness," and "tendency to embarrassment" (1961, pp. 57 and 182); anxiety neurotics obtained high scores on this factor. Physiological variables such as respiration rate and systolic blood pressure markedly loaded the state anxiety factor, but had only slight loadings on trait anxiety (1961, p. 82). Thus, if Smith were anxious *now*, he would presumably score high on Cattell and Scheier's state anxiety factor, and if he were characterologically or chronically anxious, it is probable that his trait anxiety score would also be elevated.

Anxiety as a Transitory State

Most empirical work on transitory anxiety has been concerned with delineating the properties of the anxiety state and identifying the stimulus conditions which evoke it. After reviewing the psychological and psychiatric literature, Krause (1961) concluded that transitory anxiety is conventionally inferred from six different types of evidence: introspective reports, physiological signs, "molar" behavior (e.g., body posture, gesturing, speech characteristics), task performance, clinical intuition, and the response to stress. Of these, according to conventional usage, introspective reports provide the most widely accepted basis for inferring transitory anxiety. For example, Basowitz *et al.* (1955, p. 3) define anxiety as "the conscious and reportable experience of intense dread and foreboding, conceptualized as internally derived and unrelated to external threat." In other words, to report that one feels "anxious" is to be anxious, provided of course that the subject is capable of distinguishing between different feeling states and is motivated to report accurately and honestly.

As a check upon the honesty of introspective reporting, Krause recommends measuring physiological signs or, to use his terminology, adrenosympathetic (a-s) activation. He questions, however, the evidential sufficiency of physiological measures, molar behavior, task performance, or clinical intuition as independent criteria for defining (inferring) transitory anxiety unless used in conjunction with introspective reports. Thus, some combination of introspective reports and physiological-behavioral signs would seem to be required in order to define unambiguously the presence of anxiety states in humans. Schachter and Singer (1962) provide impressive evidence that emotional states consist of two factors: physiological arousal and socially determined cognitions. The latter lead the individual to describe his feelings with particular emotional labels and provide the basis for his introspective reports about them.

With regard to the convention of defining transitory anxiety in terms of response to stress, Krause (1961) reasons that, in the absence of introspective or physical criteria, this logically requires the identification of stressor stimuli on grounds other than the anxiety response itself. But responses of individual subjects to various stressors are known to be highly idiosyncratic, due in part to the fact that the anxiety response is readily conditioned to stimuli with which it is associated. Consequently, the response to a particular stressor stimulus will depend on an individual's previous experience, and any stimulus can have anxiety-producing effects if it is interpreted as threatening or dangerous, irrespective of the real danger involved. Nevertheless, it is important to determine classes of stimuli or situations (stressors) that are likely to induce anxiety states, and to distinguish these from stimuli that are unlikely to evoke anxiety (Basowitz *et al.*, 1955, pp. 7-9). Both types of stimuli are required in anxiety research (Krause, 1961).

Martin (1961) proposes that anxiety should be defined as a complex pattern of response and should be distinguished conceptually and operationally from the external or internal stimuli which elicit it. This approach dispenses with the traditional, stimulus-defined difference between fear as a response to a real external danger and anxiety as a reaction to some unknown threat, and emphasizes the importance of identifying and measuring the observable physiological and behavioral response patterns which distinguish anxiety (fear) from other emotional states. Martin also maintains that anxiety reactions should not be confused with "defenses" against anxiety, i.e., the reactions that have been learned in order to eliminate or mitigate anxiety states. This would seem to be especially important in research on older children and adults since persons characterized by chronic anxiety tend to develop a host of mechanisms or symptoms which help them to avoid unpleasant anxiety states.

In sum, research on anxiety phenomena would seem to require that anxiety reactions or states be operationally and conceptually distinguished from the stimulus conditions that arouse them and the cognitive and behavioral maneuvers that are learned because they lead to anxiety reduction. It would appear that research on anxiety also requires that a distinction be made between anxiety as a transitory state that fluctuates over time and as a personality trait that remains relatively stable over time.

Anxiety as a Personality Trait

Experimental work relevant to the concept of trait anxiety has been concerned primarily with investigating differences between groups of subjects who are presumed to differ in anxiety level. One research strategy involves the selection of patient groups characterized by high levels of chronic anxiety and comparing them with normal control groups under stressful and nonstressful conditions. Using this approach, Malmo (1950; 1957) and his colleagues have concluded that patient groups characterized by high levels of chronic anxiety show greater reactivity and wider variability than normals on many different physiological and behavioral measures, irrespective of the stress situation.

Trait anxiety has also been investigated in studies in which subjects who are presumed to differ in anxiety level are selected from normal populations (Spence, 1958; Taylor, 1956), typically on the basis of extreme scores on a personality questionnaire such as the Taylor (1953) Manifest Anxiety Scale (MAS).[2] The performance of high anxious and low anxious subjects are then compared on a variety of learning tasks. It was at first generally assumed that subjects with high scores on the MAS were chronically more anxious or emotionally responsive than those with low MAS scores. Recent findings have suggested, however, that subjects with high MAS scores react with higher anxiety levels in situations that contain some degree of stress, but not in the absence of stress (e.g., Spence, 1964; Spielberger & Smith, 1966).

Such findings suggest that trait anxiety measures reflect anxiety-proneness—differences between individuals in the probability

[2] The MAS, a self-report inventory which inquires about anxiety symptoms, has been found to correlate .85 with Cattell and Scheier's trait-anxiety factor (1961).

that anxiety states will be manifested under circumstances involving varying degrees of stress. Thus, if Smith has an elevated trait-anxiety score, he is generally more disposed than the average person to respond with state anxiety, and, unless Smith lives in a very sheltered environment, he is likely to experience anxiety states more often than other people. It should be noted, however, that although Smith may be more disposed to react with anxiety states than other people, he may or may not be anxious *now*, and this will largely depend on whether or not he interprets his present circumstances as dangerous or threatening. While persons with extreme trait anxiety, such as acute, incipient schizophrenics and anxiety neurotics, are characterized by state anxiety much of the time, even they have defenses against anxiety that occasionally leave them relatively free of it. We have observed clinically that when such persons are occupied with a nonthreatening task as, for example, a noncompetitive but absorbing game, they may be diverted for a time from the internal stimuli that otherwise constantly cue state anxiety responses.

As a concept, trait anxiety appears to have the characteristics of a class of constructs which Campbell (1963) has called *acquired behavioral dispositions,* and which Atkinson (1964) labels *motives.* According to Campbell, acquired dispositional concepts, e.g., social attitudes, involve residues of past experience that predispose an individual *both* to view the world in a particular way and to manifest "object-consistent" response tendencies. Atkinson regards motives such as need-achievement as dispositional tendencies acquired in childhood which are latent until the cues of a situation arouse them. As an acquired behavioral disposition or motive, trait anxiety would seem to imply, on the one hand, a view of the world in which a wide range of stimulus situations are perceived as dangerous or threatening and, on the other hand, a tendency to respond to such threats with state anxiety reactions. The relation between state and trait anxiety may be conceived of as analogous in certain respects to the relation between the physical concepts of kinetic and potential energy. State anxiety, like kinetic energy, refers to an empirical process or reaction which is taking place *now* at a given level of intensity. Trait anxiety, like potential energy, indicates a latent disposition for a reaction of a certain type to occur if it is triggered by appropriate (sufficiently stressful) stimuli.

A TRAIT-STATE CONCEPTION OF ANXIETY

Research findings suggest that it is meaningful to distinguish between anxiety as a transitory state and as a relatively stable personality trait, and to differentiate between anxiety states, the stimulus conditions that evoke them, and the defenses that serve to avoid them. There is considerable general agreement that anxiety states (A-states) are characterized by subjective, consciously perceived feelings of apprehension and tension, accompanied by or associated with activation or arousal of the autonomic nervous system. Anxiety as a personality trait (A-trait) would seem to imply a motive or acquired behavioral disposition that predisposes an individual to perceive a wide range of objectively non-dangerous circumstances as threatening, and to respond to these with A-state reactions disproportionate in intensity to the magnitude of the objective danger.

In Fig. 29-1, a trait-state conception of anxiety is proposed which postulates two anxiety concepts, A-trait and A-state. This conception is not presented as a theory of anxiety, but rather as a means of clarifying the concepts of A-trait and A-state and as a conceptual framework for viewing theory and research on anxiety phenomena. Factors believed to be important in anxiety research are schematically represented and possible interrelationships among them are indicated. As may be noted in Fig. 29-1, A-trait and A-state are conceived of as independent of the threatening stimuli which

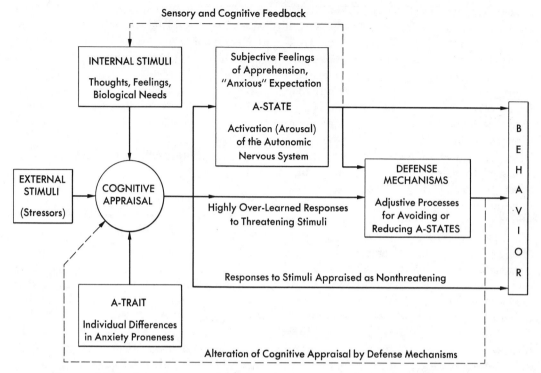

Figure 29.1 A trait-state conception of anxiety in which two anxiety concepts, A-trait and A-state, are posited and conceptually distinguished from the stimulus conditions that evoke A-state reactions and the defenses against A-states. It is hypothesized that the arousal of A-states involves a sequence of temporally ordered events in which a stimulus that is cognitively appraised as dangerous evokes an A-state reaction. This A-state reaction may then initiate a behavior sequence designed to avoid the danger situation, or it may evoke defensive maneuvers that alter the cognitive appraisal of the situation. Individual differences in A-trait determine the particular stimuli that are cognitively appraised as threatening.

evoke A-states and the defensive processes which are used to avoid them.

In essence, it is proposed that the arousal of A-states involves a process or sequence of temporally ordered events. This process may be initiated by an external stimulus, such as, for example, the threat of an electric shock in a laboratory experiment, or an internal cue—a thought or sensory representation of muscular or visceral activity associated with "feeling angry." If the stimulus situation is cognitively appraised as dangerous or threatening, then an A-state reaction is evoked. Through sensory and cognitive feedback mechanisms, the A-state reaction may serve as a signal that

initiates a behavior sequence designed to avoid or otherwise deal directly with the danger situation. The A-state may also activate cognitive or motoric defensive processes that have been effective in the past in reducing A-states by altering the cognitive appraisal of the danger situation. For example, an undergraduate subject in a psychology experiment may "deny" that the experimenter is really going to shock him, or "intellectualize" ("rationalize") that if he is shocked it won't hurt him because college officials would not permit this. The subject, in effect, reappraises the danger situation and finds it less threatening, resulting in a reduction in level of A-state.

A-trait is assumed to reflect residues of past experience that in some way determine individual differences in anxiety-proneness, i.e., in the disposition to see certain types of situations as dangerous and to respond to them with A-states. Those experiences that have most influence on level of A-trait probably date back to childhood, involving parent-child relationships centering around punishment situations. Level of A-trait is not expected to influence A-state response to all stimuli, only to particular classes of stimuli. Stimuli that have little or no threat value obviously would not be expected to elicit an A-state response. On the other hand, the threat of an objectively painful stimulus, like an electric shock, may be sufficiently general so that most subjects will respond with higher levels of A-state, irrespective of their level of A-trait. For such stimuli, however, individual differences in A-state reaction may vary as a function of other acquired behavioral dispositions. It has been observed, for example, that threat of electric shock produces significant increments in A-state that are unrelated to level of A-trait (Katkin, 1965), but which are markedly correlated with fear of shock (Hodges & Spielberger, 1966).

From the standpoint of a trait-state conception of anxiety, the most important stimuli are those which produce differential changes in A-state in individuals who differ in A-trait. There is as yet little experimental evidence that bears directly on the identification of such stimuli, since most experimental investigations of anxiety have been concerned either with A-trait or with A-state, but rarely with both. However, differences in the task performance of high and low A-trait individuals are most often found under conditions of failure or ego-involvement, or under circumstances which involve risk of failure such as that found in academic achievement situations (Mandler & Sarason, 1952; Spielberger, 1962). It may be speculated that A-trait involves a "fear of failure" motive as has been suggested by Atkinson (1964).

REFERENCES

Atkinson, J. W. *An introduction to motivation.* Princeton, N. J.: Van Nostrand, 1964.
Basowitz, H., Persky, H., Korchin, S. J., & Grinker, R. R. *Anxiety and stress.* New York: McGraw-Hill, 1955.
Campbell, D. T. Social attitudes and other acquired behavioral dispositions. In S. Koch (Ed.), *Psychology: a study of a science.* New York: McGraw-Hill, 1963. Vol. 6.
Castaneda, A., McCandless, B. R., & Palermo, D. S. The children's form of the manifest anxiety scale. *Child Develpm.*, 1956, **27**, 317–326.
Cattell, R. B., & Scheier, I. H. The nature of anxiety: a review of thirteen multivariate analyses comprising 814 variables. *Psychol. Rep.* 1958, **4**, 351-388.
Cattell, R. B., & Scheier, I. H. *The meaning and measurement of neuroticism and anxiety.* New York: Ronald Press, 1961.
Dollard, J., & Miller, N. E. *Personality and psychotherapy.* New York: McGraw-Hill, 1950.
Eysenck, H. J. *The dynamics of anxiety and hysteria.* London: Routledge & Kegan, 1957.
Freud, S. *Collected papers.* London: Hogarth Press, 1924. Vol. 1.
Freud, S. *New introductory lectures in psychoanalysis.* New York: Norton, 1933.
Freud, S. *The problem of anxiety.* New York: Norton, 1936.
Gantt, W. H. The origin and development of nervous disturbances experimentally produced. *Amer. J. Psychiat.*, 1942, **98**, 475–481.
Grinker, R. R., & Spiegel, J. P. *Men under stress.* Philadelphia: Blakiston, 1945.
Haggard, E. A. Psychological causes and results of stress. In *A survey report on human factors in undersea warfare.* Washington, D. C.: National Research Council, 1949.
Hanfmann, Eugenia. Psychological approaches to the study of anxiety. In P. H. Hoch & J. Zubin (Eds.), *Anxiety.* New York: Grune & Stratton, 1950. Pp. 51–69.
Hoch, P. H., & Zubin, J. (Eds.). *Anxiety.* New York: Grune & Stratton, 1950.
Hodges, W. F., & Spielberger, C. D. The effects of shock on heart rate for subjects who differ in a manifest anxiety and fear of shock. *Psychophysiol.*, 1966, in press.
Janis, I. L. *Psychological stress.* New York: Wiley, 1958.
Katkin, E. S. Relationship between manifest anxiety and two indices of autonomic response to stress. *J. Pers. soc. Psychol.*, 1965, **2**, 324–333.
Krause, M. S. The measurement of transitory anxiety. *Psychol. Rev.*, 1961, **68**, 178–189.
Lazarus, R. S., Deese, J., & Osler, Sonia F. The effects of psychological stress upon performance. *Psychol. Bull.*, 1952, **49**, 293–317.
Levy, L. H. Anxiety and behavior scientist's behavior. *Amer. Psychologist*, 1961, **16**, 66–68.
Liddell, H. S. Conditioned reflex method and experimental neurosis. In J. McV. Hunt (Ed.),

Personality and the behavior disorders. New York: Ronald Press, 1944. Pp. 389–412.

Malmo, R. B. Experimental studies of mental patients under stress. In M. Reymert (Ed.), *Feelings and emotions.* New York: McGraw-Hill, 1950. Pp. 169–180.

Malmo, R. B. Anxiety and behavioral arousal. *Psychol. Rev.,* 1957, 64, 276–287.

Mandler, G., & Sarason, S. B. A study of anxiety and learning. *J. abnorm. soc. Psychol.,* 1952, 47, 166–173.

Martin, B. The assessment of anxiety by physiological behavioral measures. *Psychol. Bull.,* 1961, 58, 234–255.

Masserman, J. H. *Behavior and neurosis: an experimental psychoanalytic approach to psychobiological principles.* Chicago, Ill.: Univer. of Chicago Press, 1943.

May, R. *The meaning of anxiety.* New York: Ronald Press, 1950.

Miller, N. E. Studies of fear as an acquirable drive. I. Fear as motivation and fear-reduction as reinforcement in the learning of a new response. *J. exp. Psychol.,* 1948, 38, 89–101.

Mowrer, O. H. A stimulus-response analysis of anxiety and its role as a reinforcing agent. *Psychol. Rev.,* 1939, 46, 553–565.

Mowrer, O. H. Preparatory set (expectancy): some methods of measurement. *Psychol. Monogr.,* 1940, 52, No. 2, 43.

Mowrer, O. H. *Learning theory and personality dynamics.* New York: Ronald Press, 1950.

Pavlov, I. P. *Conditioned reflexes.* London and New York: Oxford Univer. Press, 1927.

Sarason, I. G. Empirical findings and theoretical problems in the use of anxiety scales. *Psychol. Bull.,* 1960, 57, 403–415.

Sarason, S. B., Davidson, K. S., Lighthall, F. F., Waite, R. R., & Ruebush, B. K. *Anxiety in elementary school children.* New York: Wiley, 1960.

Schachter, S., & Singer, J. E. Cognitive, social, and physiological determinants of emotional state. *Psychol. Rev.,* 1962, 69, 379–399.

Spence, K. W. A theory of emotionally based drive (D) and its relation to performance in simple learning situations. *Amer. Psychologist,* 1958, 13, 131–141.

Spence, K. W. Anxiety (drive) level and performance in eyelid conditioning. *Psychol. Bull.,* 1964, 61, 129–139.

Spielberger, C. D. The effects of manifest anxiety on the academic achievement of college students. *Ment. Hyg., N.Y.* 1962, 46, 420–426.

Spielberger, C. D., & Smith, L. H. Anxiety (drive), stress, and serial-position effects in serial-verbal learning. *J. exp. Psychol.,* 1966, in press.

Sullivan, H. S. *The interpersonal theory of psychiatry.* New York: Norton, 1953.

Taylor, Janet A. The relationship of anxiety to the conditioned eyelid response. *J. exp. Psychol.,* 1951, 41, 81–92.

Taylor, Janet A. A personality scale of manifest anxiety. *J. abnorm. soc. Psychol.,* 1953, 48, 285–290.

Taylor, Janet A. Drive theory and manifest anxiety. *Psychol. Bull.,* 1956, 53, 303–320.

CURRENT THEORY AND RESEARCH ON CURIOSITY

30. Curiosity and Exploration *

D. E. Berlyne

A substantial portion of the activities of any organism must necessarily be devoted to the maintenance of biological well-being. In order to keep on living, all mammals must eat, drink, breathe, and satisfy other vital needs. It is commonly observed, however, that higher animals and man engage in a variety of investigative and exploratory behaviors even when no obvious biological needs are being served.

This general tendency to explore the environment, which appears to be aroused by novel stimuli and diminished by monotonous stimuli, has led D. E. Berlyne to suggest the existence

* Reprinted by permission of the author and the American Association for the Advancement of Science from *Science,* 1966, 53, 25-33. Copyright © 1966 by the American Association for the Advancement of Science.

of a *curiosity drive*. In the following article, Professor Berlyne reviews the theoretical issues and research findings relating to curiosity as a psychobiological drive state.

The experimental evidence cited by Berlyne shows that exploratory behavior is intensified in situations characterized by novelty, or complexity, or by lack of information, all of which lead to some degree of uncertainty. He also notes that, if an unfamiliar situation is too disturbing or too unpleasant, it may provoke fear and flight rather than curiosity and exploration.

Higher animals spend a substantial portion of their time and energy on activities to which terms like *curiosity* and *play* seem applicable (*1, 2*). An even more conspicuous part of human behavior, especially in highly organized societies, is classifiable as "recreation," "entertainment," "art," or "science." In all of these activities, sense organs are brought into contact with biologically neutral or "indifferent" stimulus patterns—that is, with objects or events that do not seem to be inherently beneficial or noxious. Stimulus patterns encountered in this way are sometimes used to guide subsequent action aimed at achieving some immediate practical advantage. An animal looking and sniffing around may stumble upon a clue to the whereabouts of food. A scientist's discovery may contribute to public amenity and to his own enrichment or fame. Much of the time, however, organisms do nothing in particular about the stimulus patterns that they pursue with such avidity. They appear to seek them "for their own sake."

Until about 15 years ago these forms of behavior were overlooked in the theoretical and experimental literature, except for a few scattered investigations. Recently they have been winning more and more interest among psychologists. They constitute what is generally known in Western countries as "exploratory behavior" and, in Eastern Europe, as "orientational-investigatory activity."

Early demonstrations of the prevalence and strength of these activities in higher animals were rather embarrassing to then current motivation theories. Animals are, of course, most likely to explore and play when they have no emergencies to deal with, but there are times when these behaviors will even override what one would expect to be more urgent considerations. A hungry rat may spend time investigating a novel feature of the environment before settling down to eat (*3*). A bird may approach a strange and potentially threatening object at the risk of its life (*4*). Even human beings are reported to have played the lyre while Rome was burning and to have insisted on completing a game of bowls after an invading armada had been sighted.

Under the influence of Darwin's evolutionary theory and later of Cannon's concept of homeostasis, it had come to be widely believed during the 1930's and 1940's that the motivation of behavior is bound up with clear-cut prerequisites of survival, such as eating, drinking, procreating, and avoiding bodily injury. Behavior is set in motion, it was thought, either by biological dangers or by events associated (through contiguity or through similarity) with biological dangers. Similarly, the goals for which animals and human beings strive were commonly assumed to have inherent or learned connections with biological gratification or relief. These assumptions, in different forms, were shared by the early neobehaviorists, physiological psychologists, and psychoanalysts.

As knowledge accumulated about the conditions that govern exploratory behavior and about how quickly it appears after birth, it seemed less and less likely that this behavior could be a derivative of hunger, thirst, sexual appetite, pain, fear of pain, and the like, or that stimuli sought through exploration are welcomed because they have previously accompanied satisfaction of these drives. The facts about exploratory behavior were especially hard to reconcile with the view once offered by Freud (*5*) and later espoused by neobehaviorists (6) that behavior is essentially directed toward minimizing stimulation and excitation, a view that anybody who has had to handle a child "with nothing to do" must have been tempted to question.

Being now compelled to recognize that higher animals put a great deal of effort into securing access to stimuli with no manifest ecological importance, we can discern two groups of reasons why this phenomenon may make biological sense. First, we know that spontaneous activity is constantly present within the central nervous system and that, during waking hours, the sense organs are ceaselessly bombarded with stimuli, all of which initiate excitatory processes within the brain. We also know that the brain is a highly intricate organ in which many processes can be initiated simultaneously and can interact to their mutual impediment. The only way in which the brain can perform its prime function of selecting adaptive responses is to allow one process to advance and complete itself while competing processes are held in check. To determine which process shall be granted priority, the brain depends on information about conditions inside and outside the organism, some of which enters through sense organs and some of which is stored after having been deposited by previous learning or by natural selection. The required information will often be lacking, in which case the brain will be unable to arbitrate between, or reconcile, the discrepant demands that are made on it. Reciprocal interference between processes going on within it and—if the organism is beset by an urgent call for action—conflict among incompatible response-tendencies may eliminate the effectiveness of behavior. So, in such cases, it is clearly useful for an organism to secure access to stimulus patterns that contain the information from lack of which it is suffering.

The second group of reasons is quite different. It seems that the central nervous system of a higher animal is designed to cope with environments that produce a certain rate of influx of stimulation, information, and challenge to its capacities. It will naturally not perform at its best in an environment that overstresses or overloads it, but we also have evidence that prolonged subjection to an inordinately monotonous or unstimulating environment is detrimental to a variety of psychological functions (7, 8). How much excitement or challenge is optimal will fluctuate quite widely with personality, culture, psychophysiological state, and recent or remote experience. But we can understand why organisms may seek out stimulation that taxes the nervous system to the right extent, when naturally occurring stimuli are either too easy or too difficult to assimilate.

With accumulating research, there have been more and more indications that exploratory responses can be of two distinct classes, corresponding to these two distinct biological needs. On the one hand, when an animal is disturbed by a lack of information, and thus left a prey to uncertainty and conflict, it is likely to resort to what we may call *specific* exploratory responses. These supply or intensify stimulation from particular sources—sources that can supply the precise information that the animal misses. The condition of discomfort, due to inadequacy of information, that motivates specific exploration is what we call "curiosity." In other circumstances, an animal seeks out stimulation, regardless of source or content, that offers something like an optimum amount of novelty, surprisingness, complexity, change, or variety. For this kind of behavior the term *diversive* exploration has been proposed. It is not preceded by receipt of partial information about the stimulus patterns at which it is aimed and thus seems to be motivated by factors quite different from curiosity.

SPECIFIC EXPLORATION

One of the earliest discoveries coming out of Pavlov's work on "higher nervous activity" was the phenomenon that he called the "orientational" or "investigatory" reflex (9). A dog would respond to any unusual or unexpected happening by desisting from whatever activity it might otherwise have been engaged in and turning its eyes, head, and trunk toward the source of stimulation. This was an unconditioned or innate reflex, and yet it was subject to many of the processes to which conditioned reflexes are subject, including extinction and disinhibition. If the stimulus evoking it were repeated at short intervals, the orientational response would gradually disappear. It would come back if the stimulus recurred, say, a day later, but, after several recoveries and extinctions the power of a particular stimulus to evoke the response might be permanently weakened (1, chap. 4). It was thus shown that novelty, especially short-term novelty, is a potent factor governing this reaction.

The influence of novelty was amply confirmed when specific exploratory behavior began to be studied in the West. It was found, for example, that a rat is more likely to walk up to and sniff at an object that it has not seen before than one to which it has been exposed during the last few minutes (10). When a rat is confined in a novel environment, the amount of wandering about that it does and the frequency with which it approaches a particular feature of the environment decline with time—that is, as the stimulus patterns that are present lose their novelty (11, 12). When the animal is put back into the situation after spending some time away from it, exploration will revive, but the revival will become less and less marked if the repeated exposures extend over several days.

Apart from the influence of novelty, the strength and direction of exploratory responses in animals have been shown to depend on stimulus properties of the kind usually denoted by words like *complexity*. More vigorous and prolonged exploration will generally be attracted by objects that offer more varied or more irregular stimulation (12, 13).

Similar variables have been found to govern specific exploration in the human adult.

We have used a number of techniques to compare the power of different visual patterns to attract and sustain inspection when subjects are given no special reason to attend to them. We have allowed subjects access to a switch controlling a tachistoscope, by means of which they could give themselves as many successive brief (0.14-second) glimpses of a pattern as they wished before calling for the next pattern (14). We have presented successions of patterns in an automatic projector, letting subjects look at each pattern for as long as they wished before pressing the button that replaced it with the next one (15). We have presented patterns side by side on a screen and measured how much time the subject spent fixating each of them; this measurement was made either by having eye movements observed by an experimenter who did not know which patterns were being exposed (16) or by recording them with an eye-movement camera (17). The influence of novelty is shown by one experiment (16) in which we showed a series of pairs of animal pictures, the picture on one side (the left and the right sides for equal numbers of subjects) being the same on every trial and the picture on the other side being changed from one trial to the next. Observation of eye movements (see Fig. 30-1) revealed that, as trials succeeded one another, the subjects spent a lower and lower proportion of the time inspecting the recurrent pattern and more and more time looking at the changing patterns.

All the techniques just mentioned have been used to study effects on exploration time of several stimulus properties that, although distinct, exemplify the kind of variable we mean when we use words like *complexity, irregularity,* or *incongruity*. In each of the pairs of patterns shown in Fig. 30-2, the member on the right is the more "complex" or "irregular" one, but the actual property that distinguishes it from its neighbor varies from one category of pairs to another. We have regularly found that the subject spends more time looking at the "more complex" than at the "less complex"

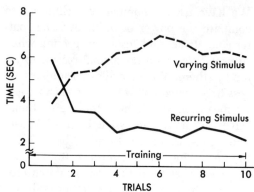

Figure 30.1 Mean time spent by subjects fixating a novel (varying) and a familiar (recurring) pattern when the two were presented side by side for 10-second trials with 20-second intertrial intervals. Adapted from Berlyne (14).

pattern of a pair. Since all these patterns are relatively simple, we have more recently added the patterns of Fig. 30-3 (*15, 17, 18*). These likewise comprise categories representing different "complexity" variables, but all of them contain notably more elements than the patterns in categories *A* through *D* of Fig. 30-2 and thus allow us to probe the upper reaches of the dimensions underlying judgments of "complexity." It has been demonstrated that the material in categories *XA* through *XC* (Fig. 30-3) is rated significantly more "complex" by adult subjects than the material in categories *A* through *D* (*17*). Experiments incorporating categories *XA* through *XC* have indicated that exploration time reaches a peak and declines as complexity becomes extreme. The point at which the peak is reached seems, however, to vary quite widely from individual to individual and from population to population.

An experiment (*19*) was carried out with 3- to 9-month-old babies, after casual observation of one infant suggested a strong predilection for looking at newsprint, maps, and the like. Spock (*20*) advises, in fact, that babies enjoy watching leaves and shadows. In the experiment, pairs of adjacent patterns were brought simultaneously

down into the field of vision, and it was found that patterns B3 and D3 of Fig. 30-4 were more likely than others in the same series to attract the subject's gaze first. These patterns seem to be more "complex" than the others in the sense that they possess more internal contour. There seemed to be some inconsistency between this result and Hershenson's finding (*21*) that newborn infants are inclined to spend more time looking at a 2 by 2 checkerboard than at a 4 by 4 or 12 by 12 checkerboard—that is, more time looking at the least complex stimulus pattern.

The discrepancy has since been resolved by Brennan, Ames, and Moore (*22*), who have shown that the preferred degree of complexity goes up with age: 8-week-olds prefer to look at a checkerboard of intermediate grain (8 by 8), whereas 20-week-olds prefer a 24 by 24 checkerboard to less complex ones. These investigators have also demonstrated that this development is not simply a matter of increasing visual acuity. Eight-week-olds can distinguish 24 by 24 checkerboards from gray rectangles. Other experiments have ascertained that novelty (*23*), surprisingness (a disparity between a stimulus event and expectation) (*24*), and regularity or irregularity of form (*25*) are other stimulus characteristics influencing infantile exploration.

In recent years, measurement of exploratory behavior has become a standard means of investigating not only motivational but also perceptual processes in subjects who are too young for traditional techniques, such as questioning and discrimination training. A difference in the power of two visual patterns to elicit exploration implies that the subject can tell them apart. By this means, it has become evident that some degree of visual form discrimination, presumably innate, exists before learning has had time to mould perception, a question that was formerly open to debate (*26*).

According to a theoretical view that suggests itself (*1, 27*), specific exploratory responses, whether unlearned or learned, are likely to result from an aversive condition

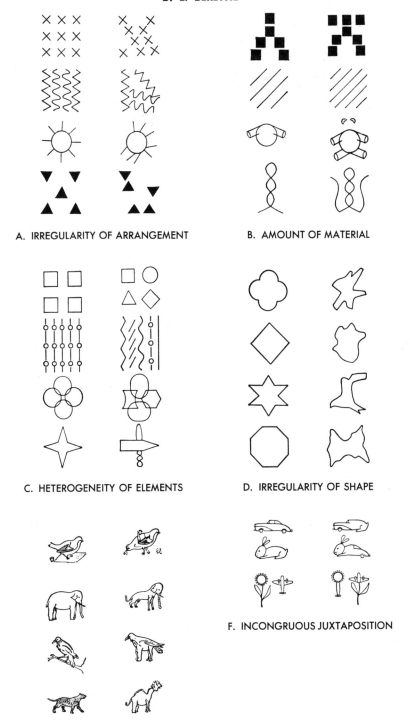

A. IRREGULARITY OF ARRANGEMENT

B. AMOUNT OF MATERIAL

C. HETEROGENEITY OF ELEMENTS

D. IRREGULARITY OF SHAPE

E. INCONGRUITY

F. INCONGRUOUS JUXTAPOSITION

Figure 30.2 Visual patterns, representing various "complexity" and "incongruity" variables, used in experiments on exploratory and related behavior in human adults. From Berlyne (16); some of the patterns were used in experiments reported in 14, 15, 17, 18, 30, 31, 39, and 40.

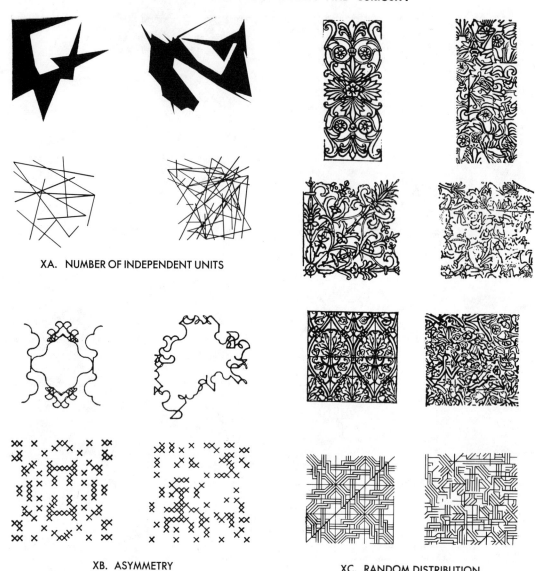

XA.   NUMBER OF INDEPENDENT UNITS

XB.   ASYMMETRY   XC.   RANDOM DISTRIBUTION

Figure 30.3   Visual patterns, representing various "complexity" variables, of a higher order of complexity than those of Fig. 30.2.   These patterns were first published in Berlyne and Lawrence (15), but some have been used for experiments reported in 17, 18, 30, 31, and 39–41.

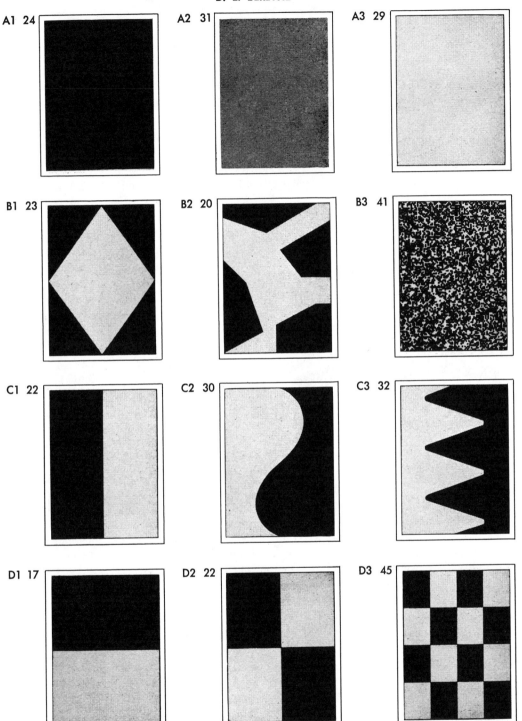

Figure 30.4 Four sets of three visual patterns used in experiments with 3- to 9-month-old infants. The patterns of a set were presented in pairs, and the member of each pair that first attracted the subject's gaze was noted. The numeral beside each pattern denotes the number of times out of 56 presentations (four with each of 14 subjects) that the pattern was fixated first.

or condition of heightened drive due to lack of information (subjective uncertainty). Such a condition, which may appropriately be called "perceptual curiosity," is apt to result from exposure to novel, surprising, highly complex, or ambiguous stimulus patterns.

TABLE 1

Mean Numbers of Responses in 15-Minute Session on Training Days

Reinforcing stimulus	Methamphetamine	Placebo	Mean
Familiar	9.0	4.8	6.8
Novel	3.9	11.7	8.2
Mean	6.6	8.2	

At present, my associates and I are engaged in experiments designed to test the hypothesis that subjective uncertainty is aversive—that its termination will reinforce an instrumental response. Presentation of blurred pictures is our means of inducing uncertainty. Our preliminary results have provided some tentative confirmation for our expectations. The replacement of a blurred picture by a clear version of the same picture seems, in at least some circumstances, to be a more effective reward or reinforcer (as shown by the rate at which a key is pressed to secure it) than the replacement of a blurred picture by an unrelated clear picture or by another blurred picture. Furthermore, we have some hint that a clear picture is most rewarding when it replaces a picture with an intermediate degree of blurredness. This seems to be a degree at which some differentiation is beginning to emerge but no objects or detail can be recognized, so that there is maximum scope for competing hypotheses.

COLLATIVE VARIABLES

The widespread attention that exploration and related forms of behavior are now receiving, after decades of relative neglect, seems justified when one considers the prevalence of such behavior in higher animal species. As psychologists are coming to recognize more and more, exploratory responses are indispensable adjuncts of many vital activities. When unlearned behavior patterns or discrimination learning have invested an external stimulus object with a special significance, an animal must initiate a segment of behavior by bringing its receptors into contact with the crucial cues that indicate what action is likely to have beneficial consequences. How sense organs are oriented must profoundly affect the form in which a stimulus pattern is perceived and represented in memory. But, as often happens with a new area of investigation, the examination of exploratory behavior has raised questions of a much wider import and reopened some fundamental theoretical questions that at one time seemed settled.

What is explored, and how vigorously, depends on many factors inside and outside the organism. Properties of external stimuli with which psychologists have long been concerned have an undeniably potent influence. They include psychophysical properties, closely dependent on specific physicochemical variables (for example brightness, loudness, color), and ecological properties, dependent on association with noxious events or visceral gratifications. It was, however, not long before experiments on curiosity and specific exploration had demonstrated the psychological importance of a third group of stimulus properties, which evidently outweighed the others in controlling this kind of behavior.

These are the properties for which I have suggested the term *collative* (1, 27), since they depend on comparison or collation of stimulus elements, whether they be elements appearing simultaneously in different sectors of a stimulus field or elements that have been perceived at different times. They comprise the properties that we designate by words like *novelty, surprisingness, incongruity, complexity, variability,* and *puzzlingness.* Just as the psychophysical properties are derived from distributions of energy and the ecological properties connect stimuli with the factors that govern natural selection, thus making contact with the two great unifying concepts of 19th-century science, the collative properties have close connections with information, the unifying concept responsible for some revolutionary developments in 20th-century science.

The technical language of information theory does not suffice for an adequate description of the collative variables, but its concepts can help a great deal in specifying and measuring them. Provided that certain assumptions are fulfilled, how "novel," "surprising," "regular," or "orderly" a structure is, how numerous its elements are, and how interdependent, determine its information content, uncertainty (from an external observer's point of view) regarding an organism's reaction to it, and the organism's degree of subjective uncertainty regarding what will happen next or regarding the nature of elements that have not yet been inspected.

What all the collative variables have in common to give them the motivational effects that they apparently share is an interesting but still debatable question. One hypothesis for which supporting arguments can be found (1, 27) is that these effects all depend on *conflict* between incompatible neural, and ultimately motor, reactions that are simultaneously mobilized.

The motivational effects of collative stimulus properties are by no means confined to occasioning and directing exploratory responses. They include the factors making for "good" or "bad" form, which were shown by the Gestalt psychologists to govern many perceptual phenomena. They include the factors constituting "form," "composition," or "structure" in the visual and performing arts, in literature, in music, and in humor.

Instead of eliciting exploration—which means approach and sustained contact—novel, surprising, and strange objects may provoke terror and flight (28). Approach

(for the sake of obtaining additional information or perhaps simply for the sake of relief through habituation) and escape are, after all, alternative ways of alleviating a disturbance due to a conflict-inducing sight or sound. Which will prevail seems to depend on many things, including how disturbing the stimulus pattern is, how agitated or relaxed a subject is, and what personality traits he possesses. Forms of behavior that apparently represent vacillation between curiosity and fear in the face of something unusual have frequently been observed in animals and in human beings. Whether something is experienced as pleasurable, annoying, or vapid often turns in an extremely subtle way on how much novelty, variety, or unpredictability it affords. This is true even when some extrinsic source of motivation is at work, as in the culinary and erotic domains.

AROUSAL

Still further ramifications come into view as we pursue the relations between exploratory behavior and arousal (1, 27). The concept of "arousal level" is an outgrowth of several developments in neurophysiology and psychology that have occurred during the last 15 years or so. It connotes a psychophysiological dimension, indicative of how "wide-awake," "alert," or "excited" an organism is at a particular time. Fluctuations in arousal are reflected by changes in the electrical activity of the brain, in electrical and thermal properties of the skin, in muscular tension, in the circulatory system, in the respiratory system, and in the diameter of the pupil, all of which can be recorded and precisely measured. A great deal has been learned, and more is coming to light, about the neural processes on which arousal depends, involving interactions among the brain-stem reticular formation, the hypothalamus, the diffuse thalamic system, and the cerebral cortex.

Few, if any, motivational aspects of behavior have been untouched by fresh thinking inspired by the concept of "arousal."

One particularly pregnant trend has been a progressive coalescence between the new concept of "arousal" and the concept of "drive," which has dominated discussion of motivation since the 1920's. If "arousal" can be identified with "drive" (and more refinement of both concepts is required before we can tell how far and in what sense it can be), the implications may be quite far-reaching. First, we shall have at our disposal more precise and direct techniques than we had before for measuring drive. Secondly, any factor that can be shown to raise or lower arousal will have to be included among the factors that induce and reduce drive, and thus among those that can motivate behavior and give rise to changes in behavior through learning.

The grounds for connecting exploratory responses with rises in arousal are twofold. First, a great deal of experimental work (largely, but not entirely, carried out in the U.S.S.R.) has shown at least some forms of exploratory behavior to be accompanied by pervasive psychophysiological changes, including several recognized indices of increased arousal (29). This work has led to a broadening of Pavlov's notion of an "orientational reflex" or orientation reaction. Pavlov used this term to denote the immediately visible bodily movements through which an animal focuses its sense organs on an unusual source of stimulation. It is now clear that these are accompanied by a whole network of processes, most of them not detectable without special amplifying and recording equipment, which seem to represent a mobilization of the animal's capacities to absorb information through its sense organs, process the information through its central nervous system, and act promptly and energetically.

Secondly, evidence is accumulating that the collative stimulus properties by which exploratory behavior is so profoundly influenced are capable of increasing arousal. Several experimenters have shown that a stimulus gradually loses its power to evoke an orientation reaction—that is, to raise arousal—as it loses its novelty through repetition (1, chap. 4). In our own research, my associates and I have been measuring the effects of various collative stimulus properties on the galvanic skin response (15, 30) (a transient increase in conductance or in potential difference between two points on the palms or soles) and on the duration of electroencephalographic desynchronization (31) (the replacement of alpha waves by an irregular, low-amplitude, predominantly high-frequency pattern, indicative of an alerted cerebral cortex) as indices of arousal or components of the orientation reaction. We have been able to show that the magnitude of the galvanic skin response declines not only as one visual pattern is repeatedly exposed but also as different patterns succeed one another.

We have found the intensity of the orientation reaction to increase with surprisingness (when surprising and nonsurprising stimuli are equated for novelty) and with the complexity and incongruity variables embodied in the patterns of Figs. 30-2 and 30-3. We have also demonstrated that the mean amplitude of the galvanic skin response increases with degree of conflict, which, as explained earlier, is suspected of

TABLE 2

Mean Numbers of Responses in 15-Minute Session on Test Days

Reinforcing stimulus	Methamphetamine	Placebo	Mean
Familiar	13.9	4.8	9.1
Novel	6.5	10.7	8.8
Mean	10.4	7.8	

being the common underlying factor responsible for the motivational effects of the collative variables. At present we are investigating electroencephalographic effects of various "complexity" variables descriptive of auditory stimuli. It has already become clear that white noise evokes longer desynchronization than equally loud sine-wave tones or combinations of two or three such tones.

EPISTEMIC CURIOSITY

Specific exploratory responses in human beings are, as often as not, "epistemic" responses as well as exploratory responses. The use of this term is proposed in order to indicate that they are aimed not only at obtaining access to information-bearing stimulation, capable of dispelling the uncertainties of the moment, but also at acquiring knowledge—that is, information stored in the form of ideational structures and giving rise to internal symbolic responses that can guide behavior on future occasions. Bringing sense organs into contact with appropriate external events is, of course, not the only means of accumulating knowledge. Thinking can be another form of epistemic behavior (32).

Extending the notion of perceptual curiosity suggested by studies of specific exploration, we may suppose that epistemic behavior is motivated by "conceptual conflict," or conflict between mutually discrepant symbolic response-tendencies—thoughts, beliefs, attitudes, conceptions (32, 33). Conflicting elements or requirements often characterize the "problems" that start us off inquiring or experimenting or thinking (32, chap. 10). Several experimenters have recorded variations in arousal level while subjects are engaged in thinking, and these variations are influenced by degree of "difficulty," in senses that seem to involve degree of conceptual conflict (32, chap. 11).

Unfortunately, the motivational aspects of epistemic behavior and of thinking in particular are only just beginning to receive study. We have made some preliminary investigations of the determinants of "epistemic curiosity" (as we may call a motivational condition favoring epistemic behavior) by presenting human subjects with a series of questions and simply asking them to specify a certain number of questions whose answers they would most like to know (34).

In one such experiment, questions about invertebrate animals were used. According to verbal reports, the most curiosity was induced by questions about the more familiar animals, by questions that subjects found surprising, and by questions that attributed to species characteristics they seemed unlikely to possess. These findings confirmed predictions from hypotheses regarding conceptual conflict. It had been argued that more familiar concepts would produce greater conflict than less familiar ones, by producing more numerous and stronger divergent associations.

In two later experiments, subjects were presented with quotations, each followed by the names of two or three possible authors. Each author's name was coupled with a number, purporting to show how many teachers out of a group of 100, had guessed it to be the correct name. One experiment provided evidence that curiosity was greater when there were three than when there were two alternative authors, and another demonstrated the influence of the distribution of supposed teachers' guesses: the more even the distribution, the greater the curiosity. These two variables—number of alternatives and nearness to equiprobability—are identifiable as the two principal determinants of subjective uncertainty, just as uncertainty in the information-theoretic sense is an increasing function of the two corresponding variables. Conceptual conflict is assumed to increase with subjective uncertainty.

Experiments in which other techniques were used have also confirmed the importance of such factors for epistemic curiosity (35). Novelty, surprise, and incongruity make children ask more questions and affect the content of their questions. Several investigators have found adult subjects more likely to seek symbolically expressed information as uncertainty and the gains and losses at stake increase, although there are signs that information-seeking may decline as these variables assume very high values.

DIVERSIVE EXPLORATION

There have been many reports from animal studies of exploratory behavior that seems to be aimed not at obtaining stimulation from a specific object or event about which there is a specific uncertainty but, rather, at obtaining stimulation from any source that can afford an optimum dosage of novelty, complexity, and other collative properties. For example, rats will, all other things being equal, tend to enter a maze arm that differs from the one they entered on the preceding trial or that has undergone some change since they were last in the maze (1, chap. 6; 36). Monkeys confined in a box will work hard, sometimes for as long as 19 hours at a stretch, at repeatedly opening a door so that they can see what is going on in the room outside (37). Human beings confined in a dark room with a minimum of stimulation will press buttons to make patterns of colored spots of light appear, preferring those sequences of pattern that offer the most variety and unpredictability (38). These and similar forms of behavior are classifiable, according to the proposed terminology, as "diversive" exploration, and it seems important to distinguish them at this stage of research from the specific exploratory responses that may be motivated by perceptual curiosity.

The advisability of drawing a distinction between specific and diversive exploration is supported by experiments with human subjects. When a subject is shown a pair of patterns from Figs. 30-2 or 30-3 and then asked to choose one of the two patterns for further viewing, which he is likely to choose depends on the duration of the initial exposure. If he has seen the two patterns briefly (for 1 second or less) before making his choice, he is more likely to want to see the *more* complex pattern again (39). Preliminary exposures of such brevity are presumably not long enough to allow him to see what the patterns are like and thus to relieve his curiosity. He chooses the more complex pattern, presumably because that is the one about which he has more residual curiosity. If, on the other hand, the preliminary exposures are long enough (3 seconds or more) to allow him to become adequately acquainted with the patterns, he is more likely to want another look at the *less* complex pattern (17, 39, 40). In this case, curiosity, having been largely eliminated by the initial exposures, must play a minor role. Factors akin to esthetic taste will presumably have more influence. Experiments in which verbal scaling techniques are used have, in fact, suggested that patterns attracting more specific exploration when perceptual curiosity is at work tend to be rated more "interesting," whereas patterns attracting more diversive exploration when a subject has no cause to wonder what a pattern is like tend to be rated more "pleasing" (15, 17, 39, 41).

There might seem to be a close affinity between specific exploration and activities such as science, philosophy, and mathematics, with diversive exploration more closely akin to entertainment and the arts. But this distinction is not absolute. The importance of pleasing structure in science, mathematics, and philosophy has been noted too often to be overlooked, while curiosity—wondering what will come next, trying to make sense of a work, and so on —certainly plays a part in esthetic appreciation.

Diversive exploratory behavior is likely to be especially strong after an animal or a human subject has spent some hours in an environment that is highly monotonous or devoid of stimulation (38, 42). The desperate craving of a bored person for a change of any kind is attested by everyday experience and by experiments on "sensory deprivation" (7).

One phenomenon that has been much investigated during the last 10 years and was particularly surprising when it was first discovered is the reward value that stimulus changes of no specific biological significance (for example, light coming on or becoming momentarily brighter, the sound of a buzzer or a click) can have, as shown by the power of such changes to reinforce a bar-pressing response in mice and rats (43).

Some recent experiments in which my associates and I sought factors governing diversive exploration (44) have confirmed the importance that the interaction between collative stimulus properties and arousal level has for this behavior also. The role of these variables in diversive exploration seems, however, to be somewhat different from their role in perceptual curiosity and specific exploration. Fortuitous circumstances compelled us to house some of the rats to be used for one experiment next to a room containing some extremely noisy printout counters. A quiet room became available later, and the remaining animals were housed in it. The experiment lasted for 8 days. On odd-numbered days (training days), each subject was placed in a Skinner box for a 30-minute pretraining period, during which no bar was present in the box. The pretraining period was immediately followed by a 15-minute training session, during which two bars protruded from the rear wall, and every time either was pressed, the illumination became brighter for 1 second or a buzzer sounded for 1 second. On even-numbered days (test days) there was a 15-minute test session during which the bars were present but no light change or buzzer sound occurred when one of the bars was pressed.

It turned out that, in animals maintained in the noisy quarters, a familiar stimulus (one that was presented every minute during pretraining periods) had a greater reward value than a novel stimulus (one not presented during pretraining periods), as evidenced by the rate of bar-pressing during both training sessions and test sessions. In animals maintained in the quiet room, on the other hand, novel stimuli were more rewarding than familiar stimuli.

These unexpected findings could be explained by making three assumptions: (i) that the rats subjected to noise between experimental sessions had a higher arousal level than the rats maintained in the quiet room; (ii) that the reward value of a stimulus resulting from diversive exploration is an inverted U-shaped function of the degree to which the stimulus raises arousal; and (iii) that the extent to which a stimulus raises arousal increases with its novelty and with the subject's initial arousal level. This explanation was corroborated by a subsequent experiment, in which injections of methamphetamine were used to raise arousal and a change in illumination served as reward. It was found, in accordance with predictions, that the drugged animals performed more responses with a familiar reinforcing stimulus, whereas control animals injected with saline solution performed more responses with a novel reinforcing stimulus (see Tables 1 and 2).

A number of experiments (18, 45) have indicated that conditions conducive to abnormally high levels of arousal (for example, hunger, pain, fear, noise, exposure to an incomprehensible tape-recorded message) make rats and human beings less eager than usual to seek out novel or complex stimulation. The findings just cited seem relevant to this phenomenon, among others.

CONCLUSIONS

Under the impact of experimental findings on exploratory behavior and cognate phenomena, motivation theory is undergoing some extensive remodeling. These findings have opened our eyes to the pervasive psychological importance of collative variables and arousal. We find ourselves forced to recognize that the disturbances that motivate behavior can come not only from external irritants, visceral upheavals, and deprivation of vital substances, but also from clashes between processes going on in the central nervous system. Related to these additional sources of motivation, there must be a wide range of hitherto overlooked reinforcing conditions that can promote learning of new behavior patterns. In opening up these new prospects, the study of curiosity, exploration, and epistemic behavior merges with developments in several other areas of psychological research (*1, 27, 32*), including personality theory, ethology, child development, education, attitude change, social interaction, esthetics, and humor.

REFERENCES AND NOTES

1. D. E. Berlyne, *Conflict, Arousal and Curiosity* (McGraw-Hill, New York, 1960).
2. W. I. Welker, in *Functions of Varied Experience*, D. W. Fiske and S. R. Maddi, Eds. (Dorsey, Homewood, Ill., 1961); H. Fowler, *Curiosity and Exploratory Behavior* (Macmillan, New York, 1965); L. G. Voronin *et al.*, Eds., *Orientirovochny Refleks i Orientirovochno-Issledovatel'skaia Deiatel'nost'* (Academy of Pedagogical Sciences, Moscow, 1958); D. E. Berlyne, in *Handbook of Social Psychology*, ed. 2, G. Lindzey and E. Aronson, Eds. (Addison-Wesley, Cambridge, Mass., in press).
3. A. Majorana, *Riv. Psicol.* **46**, No. 4, 1 (1950); M. R. A. Chance and A. P. Mead, *Behaviour* **8**, 174 (1955).
4. R. A. Hinde, *Proc. Roy. Soc. London* **B142**, 306 (1954).
5. S. Freud, *Intern. Z. Ärztl. Psychoanal.* **3**, 84 (1915).
6. N. E. Miller and J. Dollard, *Social Learning and Imitation* (Yale Univ. Press, New Haven, Conn., 1941).
7. W. A. Bexton, W. Heron, T. H. Scott, *Can. J. Psychol.* **8**, 70 (1954).
8. P. Kubzanski, in *The Manipulation of Human Behavior*, A. D. Biderman and H. Zimmer, Eds. (Wiley, New York, 1961).
9. I. P. Pavlov, *Conditioned Reflexes* (Oxford Univ. Press, Oxford, 1927).
10. D. E. Berlyne, *Brit. J. Psychol.* **41**, 68 (1950).
11. K. C. Montgomery, *J. Comp. Physiol. Psychol.* **46**, 129 (1953).
12. D. E. Berlyne, *ibid.* **48**, 238 (1955).
13. C. D. Williams and J. C. Kuchta, *ibid.* **50**, 509 (1957); W. I. Welker, *ibid.* **49**, 181 (1956).
14. D. E. Berlyne, *J. Exp. Psychol.* **53**, 399 (1957).
15. ——— and G. H. Lawrence, *J. Gen. Psychol.* **71**, 21 (1964).
16. D. E. Berlyne, *J. Exp. Psychol.* **55**, 289 (1958).
17. H. Day, thesis, University of Toronto, 1965.
18. D. E. Berlyne and J. L. Lewis, *Can. J. Psychol.* **17**, 398 (1963).
19. D. E. Berlyne, *Brit. J. Psychol.* **55**, 289 (1958).
20. B. Spock, *Baby and Child Care* (Pocket books, New York, 1946) p. 166.
21. M. Hershenson, *J. Comp. Physiol. Psychol.* **58**, 270 (1964).
22. W. M. Brennan, E. W. Ames, R. W. Moore, *Science* **151**, 354 (1966).
23. A. Saayman, E. W. Ames, A. Moffet, *J. Exp. Child Psychol.* **1**, 189 (1964); A. V. Zaporozhets, in "European Research in Cognitive Development," P. H. Mussen, Ed., *Monograph Soc. Res. Child Develop.* **30**, No. 2 (1965).
24. W. R. Charlesworth, paper read before the Society for Research in Child Development, 1965.
25. O. Graefe, *Psychol. Forsch.* **27**, 177 (1963).
26. R. L. Frantz, *Science* **140**, 296 (1963).
27. D. E. Berlyne, in *Psychology—a Study of a Science*, vol. 5, S. Koch, Ed. (McGraw-Hill, New York, 1963).
28. D. O. Hebb, *Psychol. Rev.* **53**, 259 (1946); K. C. Montgomery, *J. Comp. Physiol. Psychol.* **48**, 254 (1955).
29. E. N. Sokolov, *Perception and the Conditioned Reflex* (Macmillan, New York, 1963).
30. D. E. Berlyne, *J. Exp. Psychol.* **62**, 476 (1961); ———, M. A. Craw, P. H. Salapatek, J. L. Lewis, *ibid.* **66**, 560 (1963).
31. D. E. Berlyne and P. McDonnell, *Electroencephalog. Clin. Neurophysiol.* **18**, 156 (1965).
32. D. E. Berlyne, *Structure and Direction in Thinking* (Wiley, New York, 1965).
33. ———, *Brit. J. Psychol.* **45**, 180 (1954).
34. ———, *ibid.* p. 256; ———, *ibid.* **53**, 27 (1962).
35. ——— and F. D. Frommer, *Child Develop.* **37**, 177 (1966); F. Irwin and W. A. S. Smith, *J. Exp. Psychol.* **54**, 229 (1957); A. M. Becker, *ibid.* **55**, 628 (1958); J. M. Driscoll and J. T. Lanzetta, *Psychol. Rep.* **14**, 975 (1964); C. K. Hawkins and J. T. Lanzetta, *ibid.* **17**, 791 (1965).
36. M. Glanzer, *J. Exp. Psychol.* **45**, 387 (1953); K. C. Montgomery, *J. Comp. Physiol. Psychol.* **45**, 287 (1952); W. N. Dember, *Amer. Scientist* **53**, 409 (1965).
37. R. A. Butler and H. F. Harlow, *J. Comp. Physiol. Psychol.* **47**, 258 (1954).
38. A Jones, H. J. Wilkinson, I. Braden, *J. Exp. Psychol.* **62**, 126 (1961).
39. D. E. Berlyne, *Can. J. Psychol.* **17**, 274 (1963).
40. D. L. Hoats, M. B. Miller, H. H. Spitz, *Amer. J. Mental Deficiency* **68**, 386 (1963).
41. D. E. Berlyne and S. Pecknan, *Can. J. Psychol.*, in press.
42. R. A. Butler, *J. Comp. Physiol. Psychol.* **50**, 177 (1957); S. S. Fox, *ibid.* **55**, 438 (1962).
43. J. B. Girdner, *Amer. Psychologist* **8**, 354 (1953); H. M. B. Hurwitz, *Brit. J. Animal Behaviour* **4**, 31 (1956); G. B. Kish, *J. Comp. Physiol. Psychol.* **48**, 261 (1965); C. L. Roberts, M. H. Marx, C. Collier, *ibid.* **51**, 575 (1958).
44. D. E. Berlyne, P. H. Salapatek, R. S. Gelman, S. L. Zener, *J. Comp. Physiol. Psychol.* **58**, 148 (1964); ——— and I. D. V. Koenig, *ibid.*

60, 274 (1965); ——— and T. T. Hirota, *ibid.* in press.

45. R. M. Chapman and N. Levy, *J. Comp. Physiol. Psychol.* **50**, 233 (1957); W. R. Thompson and W. H. Higgins, *Can. J. Psychol.* **12**, 61 (1958); H. C. Hayward, *J. Personality* **30**, 63 (1962).

46. Research discussed in this article has been supported by grants from the Carnegie Trust for the Universities of Scotland, the Ford Foundation, the National Institute of Mental Health (U.S. Public Health Service), the National Research Council of Canada, and the Ontario Mental Health Foundation.

31. Selection of Unbalanced and Unusual Designs by Children High in Curiosity *

Wallace H. Maw and Ethel W. Maw

Everyone feels curious from time to time, especially when confronted with novel and interesting situations. The particular experience that one has at such times may be regarded as a *state* of curiosity. But some individuals are more active in seeking new experiences than others. Explorers and scientists, for example, are apparently motivated by a continuing desire to obtain new information. The particular personality *trait* which they seem to share may be regarded as a strong disposition to be curious. Thus, it is useful to recognize two curiosity concepts analogous to the concepts of state and trait anxiety that were identified by Spielberger in a previous selection.

In the following article, Professors Wallace H. Maw and Ethel W. Maw reason that children whose behavior is characterized by a high degree of curiosity should be more interested in discussing unusual things. They first identified children who were rated either high or low in curiosity by their teachers, their peers, and themselves. These children were then presented with a set of stimulus materials and asked to choose those about which they would prefer to be told a story. The results indicate that high-curiosity children are more interested in hearing about unusual designs and symbols than low-curiosity children.

This study was designed to test the hypothesis that children of high curiosity differ from children of low curiosity in their choice of unbalanced and unusual designs. It was undertaken as part of a larger study exploring the possibility of measuring curiosity with paper-and-pencil tests.[1]

If curiosity can be equated with the basic desire to know as postulated by Maslow (3) and if curiosity is aroused by the unusual and incongruous as shown by Berlyne (1), then it is reasonable to assume that persons with high curiosity will more often choose to hear about unbalanced and unusual designs than will persons with low curiosity. In other words, it is assumed that high-curiosity people are attracted to disequilibrium and unfamiliarity in their environments significantly more frequently than are their low-curiosity counterparts.

* Reprinted by permission of the authors and The Society for Research in Child Development, Inc., from *Child Development*, 1962, *33*, 917-922. Copyright © 1962 by The Society for Research in Child Development, Inc.

[1] The research reported herein was performed pursuant to a contract with the United States Office of Education, Department of Health, Education, and Welfare.

METHOD

In order to test the hypothesis that children with high curiosity choose the unbalanced and unusual more frequently than do low-curiosity children, the following steps were taken: (a) Children with high curiosity and children with low curiosity were identified. (b) An instrument composed of items allowing a choice between designs differing in degree of balance or familiarity was constructed. (c) The instrument was administered to a pilot group. (d) The results of the pilot study were analyzed and the instruments and procedures were modified in light of the findings. (e) The study was carried out with a larger sample.

Identification of Children with High and Low Curiosity

The procedure of identifying children with high and low curiosity is described in detail elsewhere (4). Briefly, it was as follows:

After analyzing philosophical and theoretical statements regarding curiosity and reports of investigations into the exploratory behavior of animals, a definition of curiosity was developed. According to the definition, an elementary school child is said to exhibit curiosity to the degree that he: (a) reacts positively to new, strange, incongruous, or mysterious elements in his environment by moving toward them, by exploring them, or by manipulating them; (b) exhibits a need or a desire to know about himself and/or his environment; (c) scans his surroundings seeking new experiences; and (d) persists in examining and exploring stimuli in order to know more about them.

On the basis of the definition, the children were rated by their teachers, their peers, and themselves. A separate instrument was used by each group of evaluators. Teachers ranked their pupils, peers used a modified "Guess-Who" test, and pupils rated themselves on an inventory. The judgments were found to be uninfluenced by age, race, popularity, or sex. Low positive correlations were found between teacher judgment and intelligence and between peer judgment and intelligence.

In the pilot study, regression equations were written for teacher judgment on intelligence and for peer judgment on intelligence. Pupils whose scores fell one half standard error of estimate above or below the regression line in both cases were used in the criterion groups. This procedure resulted in small groups—15 pupils in the high-curiosity group and 20 pupils in the low-curiosity group. It did not utilize self-judgment in the formation of the groups.

In the larger study, a composite rating was obtained by combining teacher, peer, and self-ratings in each classroom. On the basis of the composite ratings, pupils were ranked from high to low. The pupils ranking above the median were matched with those below the median on the basis of verbal and nonverbal intelligence. Two groups of 229 pupils each were selected by this method.

Development of an Instrument to Measure Acceptance of Unbalanced and Unusual Designs

A paper-and-pencil test consisting of 20 pairs of geometric figures and symbols was developed for the pilot study. In each pair, one figure was more balanced or familiar than the other. For example, two squares were shown. The balanced square had a dot in the center; the unbalanced square had a dot in the upper right-hand corner.

The pupils were asked to draw a circle around the figure or symbol in each pair which they would choose if they could hear a story about only one of the two signs. If an unbalanced or unfamiliar sign was marked, the pupil scored 1; if a balanced or familiar sign was chosen, the pupil scored 0.

The distribution of the scores of the pupils in the curiosity groups of the pilot study were negatively skewed. Therefore, the original test was modified in the hope of eliminating skewness. Instead of an either-or choice, the child was required to make a selection of one out of three. For some items, the pupils could earn 0, 1, or 2 points. In other items, it was possible to earn only 1 point. In a few cases, none of the figures was unbalanced or unusual. Inspection of the new distributions obtained in the major study indicated that the modification had eliminated some but not all of the skewness.

The coefficient of internal consistency of the test as used in the pilot study was estimated to be .90 based on 175 cases. The estimate for the revised test was .91 and was based on 232 cases from eight classrooms selected at random. Split-half correlation with the Spearman-Brown formula was used in both cases.

Samples

Fifth-grade children participated in the study. The fifth grade had been selected in order to avoid as many developmental reading problems as possible and to secure children before their interests crystallized to the degree so often the case with junior and senior high school pupils.

The 15 high-curiosity children and the 20 low-curiosity children of the pilot study were selected from 158 pupils in five classrooms of the New Castle Special School District in New Castle County, Delaware.

TABLE 1

Description of Subjects in Pilot Study

Group	N	CA (months) Mean	Vari- ance	Verbal IQ * Mean	Vari- ance	Nonverbal IQ * Mean	Vari- ance
High- curiosity	15	130.3	47.7	107.5	349.7	102.7	285.0
Low- curiosity	20	128.3	38.6	104.0	312.6	107.6	217.0

NOTE.—None of the differences between means or between variances of the two groups was significant.

* Lorge-Thorndike.

The pupils of the district came from many socioeconomic levels of society. Table 1 shows the mean and variance of age and of IQ for the pupils forming the criterion groups of the pilot study.

The 229 high-curiosity children and the 229 low-curiosity children of the larger study were selected from 749 pupils in 25 classrooms in four school systems in New Castle County, Delaware. The socioeconomic backgrounds of the pupils of the major study were on the whole higher than those of the pupils in the pilot study. Table 2 shows the mean ages and the mean verbal and nonverbal intelligence scores of the high- and low-curiosity groups in the larger study.

TABLE 2

Description of Subjects in Major Study

Group	N	CA (months) Mean	Vari- ance	Verbal IQ * Mean	Vari- ance	Nonverbal IQ * Mean	Vari- ance
High- curi- osity	229	130.7	20.4	115.5	148.4	110.2	168.7
Low- curi- osity	229	130.9	24.7	115.6	153.3	110.5	156.8

NOTE.—None of the differences between means or between variances of the two groups was significant.

* Lorge-Thorndike.

RESULTS

The results of the pilot study reported elsewhere (5) supported the hypothesis that high-curiosity children choose the unbalanced and unfamiliar more often than do low-curiosity children. As shown in Table 3, the Mann-Whitney U test yielded a U of 73.5 which is significant at the .02 level. The difference in variability of the scores of the high- and low-curiosity groups was not significant at the 0.5 level.

Table 4 shows the means and variances of scores on the revised "Which to Discuss" Test of high- and low-curiosity groups in

TABLE 3

Comparison of Scores on Which-To-Discuss Test
of High- and Low-Curiosity Groups
in Pilot Study

Group	N	Mean	Variance
High-curiosity	15	15.60	16.64
Low-curiosity	18	9.22	41.09
Significance of difference		$U^* = 73.5$, $p = .02$	$F = 2.44$, $p = .10$

* Mann-Whitney test.

TABLE 4

Comparison of Scores on Which-To-Discuss Test
of High- and Low-Curiosity Groups
in Major Study

Group	N	Mean	Variance
High-curiosity	222	44.70	104.40
Low-curiosity	218	41.31	135.09
Significance of difference		$z = 2.03$,* $p = .02$	$F = 1.29$, $p = .10$

* Mann-Whitney test.

the main study. Some of the pupils in the criterion groups were unavailable for testing, both when the instrument was first administered and during the make-up periods. Several pupils had transferred out of the schools. The mean ages and mean IQs of the resulting groups were not appreciably different from those originally calculated for the total criterion groups.

For the larger study, the Mann-Whitney U test was again used to test the significance of the difference between high- and low-curiosity groups. The difference was significant at the 0.2 level. This result supports the hypothesis of the study. Children in the high-curiosity group chose unbalanced or unusual designs significantly more often than did children in the low-curiosity group.

A difference in variability approaching significance was found between the two groups. This raises a question about overlap. Differences between groups are difficult to interpret when significant overlap is found.

DISCUSSION

Before discussing the implications of the study, it should be mentioned that the pupils were not asked which design they preferred, but which design they would prefer to hear about. The first implies evaluation in esthetics. When a test of this nature was administered to the children, no difference was found between the groups. Therefore, it is quite possible that a child desiring to know more about a particular unbalanced design would not choose it as the design for a decoration.

Perhaps the most important questions arising from this study are in the area of motivation. To what extent can interest be aroused by incongruous situations? It appears that, in the case of children with high curiosity, it would be advantageous to present material less rigorously balanced, less in line with their present status. In other words, high-curiosity children may be more willing to accept concepts that are disturbing.

The present study indicates that certain teaching materials and procedures may not be equally acceptable to all children. Even when children are divided into so-called homogeneous groups according to IQ, it is apparent that the kinds of stimuli that will produce interest differ for individuals within the groups. Children with identical IQs may desire different degrees of uncertainty in a learning situation.

The present study calls to mind the question regarding the relative effect of heredity and environment on curiosity. There is evidence from physiological psychology that the desire to seek knowledge of the unknown may be hereditary (2). It would be interesting to explore the question of the universality of the tendency of high-curiosity children to select the unbalanced. Would children living in another and very dissimilar culture react in the same way? An answer to this question might tell something indirectly about the influence of heredity and environment on curiosity.

The results of the study indicate that a test of designs could be developed that could be used to screen groups of children high in curiosity from those low in curiosity. The present instrument is only partially successful for this purpose, especially when the division between upper and lower groups is the median. With further modifications, the test may be acceptable for use in a battery with other tests that seem to measure other aspects of curiosity.

The questions raised by the study point out a need for more investigations in the area. Some are being planned with other groups and with instruments employing similar and different symbols.

SUMMARY

It was hypothesized that children with high curiosity would choose to hear about unbalanced and unfamiliar designs more frequently than would children low in curiosity. Fifth-grade children differing in curiosity were identified by their teachers, their peers, and themselves. Separate instruments, all based on the same definition of curiosity, were used by the three.

The choices of the peers and teachers were not significantly influenced by age, sex, and popularity. There were, however, low positive correlations between peer judgment and intelligence and teacher judgment and intelligence. Therefore, it was deemed necessary to control for verbal and nonverbal intelligence.

In a pilot study, 15 children with high curiosity and 20 children with low curiosity were selected from a sample of 158. In a larger study, 229 children with high curiosity were matched on the basis of IQ with 229 low-curiosity children. They were chosen from among 749 pupils.

The children of the high- and low-curiosity groups were given a test which allowed them to choose between balanced and unbalanced or familiar and unfamiliar designs. Differences in favor of the high-curiosity groups were found which were significant at the .02 level when the Mann-Whitney U test was used.

REFERENCES

1. BERLYNE, D. E. Conflict and information-theory variables as determinants of human perceptual curiosity. *J. exp. Psychol.*, 1957, 53, 399–404.
2. CARR, R. M., & WILLIAMS, C. D. Exploratory behavior of three strains of rats. *J. comp. physiol. Psychol.*, 1957, 50, 621–623.
3. MASLOW, A. H. A theory of human motivation. *Psychol. Rev.*, 1943, 50, 370–396.
4. MAW, W. H., & MAW, E. W. Establishing criterion groups for evaluating measures of curiosity. *J. exp. Educ.*, 1961, 29, 299–306.
5. MAW, W. H., & MAW, E. W. Nonhomeostatic experiences as stimuli of children with high curiosity. *Calif. J. educ. Res.*, 1961, 12, 57–61.

32. Reactive Curiosity and Manifest Anxiety in Children *

Ronald K. Penney

In a previous selection William James noted that both curiosity and fear are often aroused by strange and unfamiliar stimuli. When these emotional states are simultaneously evoked by the same stimulus object, there is often a tendency first to approach the object and then to avoid or withdraw from it. The strength of these antagonistic impulses seems to depend upon individual differences in anxiety and curiosity as personality traits.

In the following study, Ronald K. Penney investigated the relationship between curiosity and anxiety in elementary-school children. In a previous study, Professor Penney found that high-curiosity children tended to respond "true" to statements such as: "I would like to visit another country," and "It's fun to get mail." In the present study he shows that children with high trait-curiosity scores have lower trait-anxiety scores.

Professor Penney's results can be interpreted as indicating either that anxious children have less curiosity drive or that they tend to inhibit their exploratory behavior. If the latter explanation is correct, then we might also expect anxious children to be less creative. This complex interplay between creativity and anxiety is discussed by Wallach and Kogan in a later selection (see Selection 39 in Part VI).

McReynolds, Acker, and Pietila (1961) investigated sixth-grade children's object curiosity as it related to psychological ad-

* Reprinted by permission of the author and The Society for Research in Child Development, Inc., from *Child Development*, 1965, *36*, 697-702. Copyright © 1965 by The Society for Research in Child Development, Inc.

justment and reported that "the results raise the possibility that those aspects of classroom learning which depend on curiosity are hindered by the anxieties of the student" (p. 379). This conclusion was based on the negative correlations found between teacher's ratings of psychological adjustment and object curiosity. Object curiosity was measured by observing and recording children's manipulations of 35 different objects under controlled and free-play conditions.

Penney and McCann (1964) have constructed the Children's Reactive Curiosity Scale, (RCS) which purportedly measures the reactive curiosity of children in grades 4, 5, and 6. Penney's definition of reactive curiosity emphasizes the seeking of stimulus variation in a variety of situations, whereas object curiosity as defined by McReynolds et al. (1961) is limited to the exploration of specific objects. Object curiosity is part of the definition of reactive curiosity, however, and certain items of the RCS deal directly with object exploration. Moreover, McReynolds et al. (1961) found object curiosity to be positively related to teachers' ratings of sixth-grade children's originality and, similarly, Penney and McCann (1964) found reactive curiosity to be positively correlated with performance of sixth-grade children on the Unusual Uses Test.

The present study determined the relationship between reactive curiosity as measured by the RCS and manifest anxiety as measured by the Children's Manifest Anxiety Scale (CMAS; Castaneda, McCandless, & Palermo, 1956).

METHOD

Sample

The Ss were 178 children in grades 4, 5, and 6 of a single elementary school in Austin, Texas. There were 63 children in grade 4, 59 children in grade 5, and 56 children in grade 6. A total of six classrooms participated in the study.

Material

The RCS and its accompanying Lie Scale were employed. The RCS is a 90-item paper-and-pencil test, and each item is answered "true" or "false," depending on whether the statement is true for S or false. The Lie Scale is a 10-item paper-and-pencil test which is embedded in the RCS, and each item is also answered "true" or "false."

The CMAS was also utilized and consists of 53 items to be answered "true" or "false," 11 of these items being lie items and composing the Lie Scale. The Lie Scale embedded in the RCS is the same, minus one item, as that contained in the CMAS.

The lie items of both scales were designed to provide an index of S's tendency to falsify his responses. Neither the RCS or the CMAS correlate with the Lie Scale, however, and on this basis no Ss were discarded as a result of their lie scores. The lie items were maintained in both scales so as not to change the item context.

The Peabody Picture Vocabulary Test (PPVT; Dunn, 1959) was also administered as an untimed test for auditory comprehension of the spoken word. The test consists of 150 plates, each containing four pictures. The E provides the stimulus word orally, and Ss are required to identify from four pictures the one picture that represents the word or that best illustrates the meaning of the word. In the present study, the four pictures for each stimulus word were projected on to a screen, and the PPVT was administered as a group test to individual classes. The Ss were given booklets which contained 76 square line drawings. Each square was divided into four sections by a horizontal and a vertical line. The four quadrants of each square represented the four pictures projected on to the screen, and Ss were to place an X in the quadrant that represented the picture which illustrated the word orally presented by E. Norris, Hottel, and Brooks (1960) found the administration of the PPVT as a group test to be comparable to its administration as an individual test and give details concerning the group administration of the PPVT.

Procedure

Individual classes were taken from their classroom separately and brought to another room in the school where they were administered the PPVT, RCS, and CMAS, respectively. The classes were required to complete each test before they advanced to the next test.

Since the PPVT was administered as a group test, all Ss started at plate 25 and were taken through plate 80 in order to insure a basal of eight consecutive correct responses and a ceiling of six errors in eight consecutive responses. Since plate 25 corresponded to ages 4.3–5.5 and plate 80 corresponded to ages 13.6–15.5, it was assumed that children in grades 4, 5, and 6 would reach a basal after plate 25 and reach a ceiling prior to plate 80. The administration time was approximately 30 minutes.

The following instructions were read prior to the administration of the RCS and prior to the administration of the CMAS: "Read each of the following statements carefully. If the statement is true for you, put a circle around the T. If the statement is not true for you, put a circle around F." Four Es constantly observed the children to prevent copying. When the PPVT was administered, Ss were required to cover their answers with a sheet of paper as soon as they responded.

TABLE 1

Means and SD's of Manifest-Anxiety Scores for the High and Low Reactively Curious
Girls and Boys in Grades 4, 5, and 6

| | Girls | | | | Boys | | | |
| | High Reactive Curiosity | | Low Reactive Curiosity | | High Reactive Curiosity | | Low Reactive Curiosity | |
Grade [a]	Mean	SD	Mean	SD	Mean	SD	Mean	SD
4..........	19.55	10.49	26.56	6.50	14.44	3.92	24.33	7.23
5..........	21.67	9.16	23.22	9.52	16.56	9.94	20.11	7.03
6..........	16.89	7.43	24.67	7.93	13.11	5.36	15.44	8.21

[a] $N = 9$ girls and 9 boys for each grade.

RESULTS

Table 1 presents the means and SD's of manifest-anxiety scores according to grade level and sex for high and low reactively curious children. High reactively curious Ss were arbitrarily designated as those who scored 32 or more on the RCS while those Ss designated as low in reactive curiosity were those who scored 27 or less. As indicated in Table 1, there are nine Ss per cell, comprising approximately 60 per cent of the total sample. The RCS scores represent the scores obtained on the 40 items that discriminate between the high and low reactively curious children of the standardization sample (Penney & McCann, 1964). As Table 1 indicates for all grade levels and for both sexes, the children high in reactive curiosity tend to exhibit less manifest anxiety than those low in reactive curiosity.

A $2 \times 2 \times 3$ factorial analysis of variance was performed over the data of Table 1, and the main effects for both sex and reactive curiosity were significant beyond the 0.005 level ($F_{sex} = 8.62$, $df = 1,96$; $F_{RC} = 10.90$, $df = 1,96$). None of the other sources of variation was significant.

A similar $2 \times 2 \times 3$ factorial analysis of variance was performed using the intelligence scores derived from the PPVT. None of the sources of variation was significant, which implies that the group with high reactive curiosity possessed IQ scores

TABLE 2

Correlations between Manifest-Anxiety Scores and Reactive-Curiosity Scores for Girls and Boys in Grades 4, 5, and 6

| | Girls | | | Boys | | |
Grade	r	N	p	r	N	p
4....	−.38	34	<.025	−.49	29	<.005
5....	−.26	32	...	−.32	27	<.05
6....	−.42	32	<.01	−.17	24	...

equivalent to the group low in reactive curiosity.

In order to determine the *magnitude* of the relation between reactive curiosity and manifest anxiety, Pearson product-moment correlations were computed for the different grade levels and sexes. As in the previous analysis, the RC scores represented the scores based on 40 of the 90 items of the RCS. The results of this analysis are presented in Table 2. All the correlations in Table 2 are significant except the correlations for grade 5 girls and grade 6 boys.

When IQ scores derived from the PPVT were correlated with RCS scores (Pearson product moment), none of the correlations was significant for the girls and boys in the different grade levels. Two correlations were found to be significant, however, when the IQ scores were correlated with manifest-anxiety scores. Intelligence correlated −.37 and −.66 with manifest anxiety for grade 5 and grade 6 girls. All the other correlations between these two variables were negative but not significant.

DISCUSSION

The present results indicate that children's reactive curiosity is negatively related to their manifest anxiety. Children who are reactively curious exhibit less anxiety than children who are not as reactively curious. Although this negative relationship has been suggested by many theorists (Maddi, 1961; Woodworth, 1958), the present investigation is only the second empirical study that has been concerned with this relationship in children. The results of a previous study using children as subjects (McReynolds, Acker, & Pietila, 1961) are consistent with the results of the present study, although different measures of anxiety and curiosity were employed.

A negative relationship between curiosity and anxiety has also been reported in two studies at the adult level. Zuckerman, Kolin, Price, and Zoob (1964) have developed a Sensation-Seeking Scale (SSS) designed to quantify the construct: "optimal stimulation level." The SSS has a number of items pertaining to preference for the new and unfamiliar as well as items related to preferences for irregularity as opposed to regularity and routine. One aspect of reactive curiosity is the seeking of varied experience, and many of the items developed by Zuckerman et al. (1964) are highly similar to some of the RCS items. Due to this similarity it is perhaps not surprising to note that Zuckerman et al. report a significant negative correlation between SSS and anxiety as measured by the Multiple Affect Adjective Check List. The other study supporting a negative relationship between these two variables is another study by McReynolds (1958), who reports tentative evidence that curiosity and anxiety are negatively related in adult psychiatric patients.

The cause and effect direction of this negative relationship is at present unknown. Maddi (1961) has suggested that a high degree of need for variation may be in-

compatible with great overt anxiety. In other words, overt anxiety might tend to reduce approach behavior as anxiety would have associated with it behaviors that are incompatible with approach. On the other hand, a curious child may have his manifest anxiety reduced by curiosity or seeking stimulus variation. That is, the active variation of stimuli in the environment may tend to reduce manifest anxiety. There is no data to support either of these hypotheses at the present time.

IQ scores derived from the PPVT were found to be negatively correlated with manifest anxiety for girls in grades 5 and 6. These results are similar to those obtained by McCandless and Castaneda (1956), who studied sixth grade children and found a negative correlation between Otis IQ and CMAS scores for girls but not for boys. Feldhusen and Klausmeier (1962), however, utilized fifth grade children and reported negative correlations between manifest anxiety (CMAS) and WISC IQ for both boys and girls. Finally, Lunneborg (1964) employed grades 4, 5 and 6, and although IQ data were not reported, correlations between CMAS and reading and arithmetic achievement were presented. Over-all reading and arithmetic achievement correlated negatively with manifest anxiety but, as in the present study, only the correlations for girls in grades 5 and 6 were significant.

As in an earlier study (Penney and McCann, 1964), IQ was not related to reactive curiosity. The previous study utilized IQ scores which were derived from the California Test of Mental Maturity. It is encouraging to note the consistency of this relation, particularly since the present study used a different intelligence test which was administered in a group situation.

REFERENCES

Castaneda, A., McCandless, B. R., & Palermo, D. The children's form of the manifest anxiety scale. *Child Develpm.*, 1956, **27**, 317–26.

Dunn, L. M. *Peabody Picture Vocabulary Test manual.* Minneapolis, Minn.: American Guidance Service, 1959.

Feldhusen, F., & Klausmeier, H. K. Anxiety, intelligence and achievement in children of low, average and high intelligence. *Child Develpm.,* 1962, 33, 403–9.

Lunneborg, Patricia. Relation among social desirability, achievement and anxiety measures in children. *Child Develpm.,* 1964, 35, 169–82.

Maddi, S. R. Exploratory behavior and variation-seeking in man. In D. W. Fiske & S. R. Maddi (Eds.), *Functions of Varied Experience.* Homewood, Ill.: Dorsey Pr., 1961. Pp. 253–77.

McCandless, B. R., & Castaneda, A. Anxiety in children, school achievement and intelligence. *Child Develpm.,* 1956, 27, 370–82.

McReynolds, P. Exploratory behavior as related to anxiety in psychiatric patients. *Psychol. Rep.,* 1958, 4, 321–22.

McReynolds, P., Acker, M., & Pietila, C. Relation of object curiosity to psychological adjustment in children. *Child Develpm.,* 1961, 32, 393–400.

Norris, R. C., Hottel, J. V., & Brooks, Sadye. Comparability of Peabody Picture Vocabulary Test scores under group and individual administration. *J. educ. Psychol.,* 1960, 51, 87–91.

Penney, R. K., & McCann, B. The children's reactive curiosity scale. *Psychol. Rep.,* 1964, 15, 323–34.

Woodworth, R. S. *Dynamics of behavior.* New York: Henry Holt, 1958.

Zuckerman, M., Kolin, E. A., Price, L., & Zoob, I. Development of a sensation-seeking scale. *J. consult. Psychol.,* 1964, 28, 477–82.

INDIVIDUALITY : INTELLIGENCE AND CREATIVITY

In observing a group of people, one cannot fail to be impressed with how different they are. Some are taller, heavier, and fairer of complexion; others run faster, jump higher, and manipulate verbal symbols with greater facility. While each person is unique, he is still similar to others in many ways, and differences among people are of degree rather than kind.

Although concern with human differences and their effects on behavior can be traced to ancient China, the first systematic efforts to measure these effects date back little more than a hundred years. Scientific interest in the measurement of individual differences was stimulated by the great progress that was made in the physical sciences during the 18th and 19th centuries, and by Darwin's theory of evolution which fostered new concepts of human behavior. Advances in medicine and psychiatry and the many requirements for psychological tests in education and industry have made the need to develop sophisticated methods for measuring human differences ever more apparent.

Sir Francis Galton is generally regarded as the founder of *differential psychology*, which encompasses those fields within psychology that are centrally concerned with the study of individual differences. Galton believed that most important individual characteristics were inherited and he devised a number of objective procedures and instruments for measuring specific human differences. He also established the first Anthropometric Laboratory in England in 1884 where he obtained measurements of a large number of people on a variety of physical and mental tests.

Since Galton's time, psychologists have studied many human attributes, but none has been investigated more intensively than intelligence. In this research, the relative impact of heredity and environment on intellectual achievement has long been a question of central concern. Evidence bearing on this question is provided in the first three articles of this section. The selections by Galton and Thorndike, generally regarded as historical landmarks in the study of individual differences, support the view that intelligence is largely inherited. In the final article in this group, Asbell reviews research on children of comparable intelligence who subsequently lived in markedly dissimilar environments. The findings in the follow-up study of these children, conducted more than twenty-five years after the original measures of intelligence were obtained, dramatically demonstrate the degree to which environmental factors, particularly the environment of early life, can influence intellectual achievement.

The nature and measurement of intelligence is the main theme of the next three selections. In the first of these, Binet and Simon describe a classical experiment in which they compared the association of ideas in normal and mentally retarded persons. In the next article, Hunt reviews Piaget's theories of cognitive development in children, and he provides examples of the rich observational materials on which Piaget's conceptions of intelligence are based. Finally, in a rejoinder to the current criticism that intelligence tests discriminate against culturally-disadvantaged minority groups, Wechsler clarifies the nature of intelligence and how it is measured.

The last two articles are concerned with the combination of intellectual and personality factors that influence creative expression. Wallach and Kogan describe an experiment in which they developed procedures for distinguishing between intelligence and creativity in the thought processes of children. In the final article in this section, MacKinnon reports the findings of an entire research program that was designed to uncover the salient cognitive and motivational characteristics of creative persons.

HEREDITY, ENVIRONMENT, AND INTELLIGENCE

33. Hereditary Genius *

Francis Galton

The view that human intelligence is an inborn, inherited capacity, largely uninfluenced by training or experience, has been widely held by psychologist and layman alike. This notion has firm roots in Darwin's theory of natural selection which maintains that animals with adaptive characteristics will be better able to survive and reproduce.

The significance of the theory of evolution for the inheritance of mental abilities was first pointed out by Sir Francis Galton in his book *Hereditary Genius*, published in 1869. Galton believed that man's intellectual abilities were derived by inheritance through the operation of the same mechanisms that predisposed family members to resemble one another in their physical characteristics. In the following selection, Galton shows that men of outstanding reputation and eminence in Great Britain come from a relatively small number of distinguished families. On the basis of this fact, he then argues that genius is determined by inheritance and, consequently, environment has little real impact on the expression of intellect.

The arguments by which I endeavour to prove that genius is hereditary, consist in showing how large is the number of instances in which men who are more or less illustrious have eminent kinsfolk. It is necessary to have clear ideas on the two following matters before my arguments can be rightly appreciated. The first is the

* Excerpted from Chapters 2 and 4 of *Hereditary Genius: An Inquiry Into Its Laws and Consequences*, D. Appleton and Co., 1870.

degree of selection implied by the words "eminent" and "illustrious." Does "eminent" mean the foremost in a hundred, in a thousand, or in what other number of men? The second is the degree to which reputation may be accepted as a test of ability.

It is essential that I, who write, should have a minimum qualification distinctly before my eyes whenever I employ the phrases "eminent" and the like, and that the reader should understand as clearly as myself the value I attach to those qualifications. An explanation of these words will be the subject of the present chapter.

I look upon social and professional life as a continuous examination. All are candidates for the good opinions of others, and for success in their several professions, and they achieve success in proportion as the general estimate is large of their aggregate merits. In ordinary scholastic examinations marks are allotted in stated proportions to various specified subjects—so many for Latin, so many for Greek, so many for English history, and the rest. The world, in the same way, but almost unconsciously, allots marks to men. It gives them for originality of conception, for enterprise, for activity and energy, for administrative skill, for various acquirements, for power of literary expression, for oratory, and much besides of general value, as well as for more specially professional merits. It does not allot these marks according to a proportion that can easily be stated in words, but there is a rough common-sense that governs its practice with a fair approximation to constancy. Those who have gained most of these tacit marks are ranked, by the common judgment of the leaders of opinion, as the foremost men of their day.

The metaphor of an examination may be stretched much further. As there are alternative groups in any one of which a candidate may obtain honours, so it is with reputations—they may be made in law, literature, science, art, and in a host of other pursuits. Again: as the mere attainment of a general fair level will obtain no honours in an examination, no more will it do so in the struggle for eminence. A man must show conspicuous power in at least one subject in order to achieve a high reputation.

Let us see how the world classifies people, after examining each of them, in her patient, persistent manner, during the years of their manhood. How many men of "eminence" are there, and what proportion do they bear to the whole community?

I will begin by analysing a very painstaking biographical handbook, lately published by Routledge and Co., called "Men of the Time." Its intention, which is very fairly and honestly carried out, is to include none but those whom the world honours for their ability. The catalogue of names is 2,500, and a full half of it consists of American and Continental celebrities. It is well I should give in a foot-note [1] an analysis of

[1] *Contents of the "Dictionary of Men of the Time," Ed.* 1865:—
62 actors, singers, dancers, &c.; 7 agriculturists; 71 antiquaries, archæologists, numismatists, &c.; 20 architects; 120 artists (painters and designers); 950 authors; 400 divines; 43 engineers and mechanicians; 10 engravers; 140 lawyers, judges, barristers, and legists; 94 medical practitioners, physicians, surgeons, and physiologists; 39 merchants, capitalists, manufacturers, and traders; 168 military officers; 12 miscellaneous; 7 moral and metaphysical philosophers, logicians; 32 musicians and composers; 67 naturalists, botanists, zoologists, &c.; 36 naval officers; 40 philologists and ethnologists; 60 poets (but also included in authors); 60 political and social economists and philanthropists; 154 men of science, astronomers, chemists, geologists, mathematicians, &c.; 29 sculptors; 64 sovereigns, members of royal families, &c.; 376 statesmen, diplomatists, colonial governors, &c.; 76 travellers and geographers.

its contents, in order to show the exhaustive character of its range. The numbers I have prefixed to each class are not strictly accurate, for I measured them off rather than counted them, but they are quite close enough. The same name often appears under more than one head.

On looking over the book, I am surprised to find how large a proportion of the "Men of the Time" are past middle age. It appears that in the cases of high (but by no means in that of the highest) merit, a man must outlive the age of fifty to be sure of being widely appreciated. It takes time for an able man, born in the humbler ranks of life, to emerge from them and to take his natural position. It would not, therefore, be just to compare the numbers of Englishmen in the book with that of the whole adult male population of the British isles; but it is necessary to confine our examination to those of the celebrities who are past fifty years of age, and to compare their number with that of the whole male population who are also above fifty years. I estimate, from examining a large part of the book, that there are about 850 of these men, and that 500 of them are decidedly well known to persons familiar with literary and scientific society. Now, there are about two millions of adult males in the British isles above fifty years of age; consequently, the total number of the "Men of the Time" are as 425 to a million, and the more select part of them as 250 to a million.

The qualifications for belonging to what I call the more select part are, in my mind, that a man should have distinguished himself pretty frequently either by purely original work, or as a leader of opinion. I wholly exclude notoriety obtained by a single act. This is a fairly well-defined line, because there is not room for many men to be eminent. Each interest or idea has its mouthpiece, and a man who has attained and can maintain his position as the representative of a party or an idea, naturally becomes much more conspicuous than his coadjutors who are nearly equal but inferior in ability. This is eminently the case in positions where eminence may be won by official acts. The balance may be turned by a grain that decides whether A, B, or C shall be promoted to a vacant post. The man who obtains it has opportunities of distinction denied to the others. I do not, however, take much note of official rank. People who have left very great names behind them have mostly done so through non-professional labours. I certainly should not include mere officials, except of the highest ranks, and in open professions, among my select list of eminent men.

Another estimate of the proportion of eminent men to the whole population was made on a different basis, and gave much the same result. I took the obituary of the year 1868, published in the *Times* on January 1st, 1869, and found in it about fifty names of men of the more select class. This was in one sense a broader, and in another a more rigorous selection than that which I have just described. It was broader, because I included the names of many whose abilities were high, but who died too young to have earned the wide reputation they deserved; and it was more rigorous, because I excluded old men who had earned distinction in years gone by, but had not shown themselves capable in later times to come again to the front. On the first ground, it was necessary to lower the limit of the age of the population with whom they should be compared. Forty-five years of age seemed to me a fair limit, including, as it was supposed to do, a year or two of broken health preceding decease. Now, 210,000 males die annually in the British isles above the age of forty-five; therefore, the ratio of the more select portion of the "Men of the Time" on these data is as 50 to 210,000, or as 238 to a million.

Thirdly, I consulted obituaries of many years back, when the population of these islands was much smaller, and they appeared to me to lead to similar conclusions, viz. that 250 to a million is an ample estimate.

There would be no difficulty in making a further selection out of these, to any degree of rigour. We could select the 200, the 100, or the fifty best out of the 250, without much uncertainty. But I do not see my way to work downwards. If I were asked to choose the thousand per million best men, I should feel we had descended to a level where there existed no sure data for guidance, where accident and opportunity had undue influence, and where it was impossible to distinguish general eminence from local reputation, or from mere notoriety.

These considerations define the sense in which I propose to employ the word "eminent." When I speak of an eminent man, I mean one who has achieved a position that is attained by only 250 persons in each million of men, or by one person in each 4,000. 4,000 is a very large number—difficult for persons to realize who are not accustomed to deal with great assemblages. On the most brilliant of starlight nights there are never so many as 4,000 stars visible to the naked eye at the same time; yet we feel it to be an extraordinary distinction to a star to be accounted as the brightest in the sky. This, be it remembered, is my narrowest area of selection. I propose to introduce no name whatever into my lists of kinsmen (unless it be marked off from the rest by brackets) that is less distinguished.

The mass of those with whom I deal are far more rigidly selected—many are as one in a million, and not a few as one of many millions. I use the term "illustrious" when speaking of these. They are men whom the whole intelligent part of the nation mourns when they die; who have, or deserve to have, a public funeral; and who rank in future ages as historical characters.

Permit me to add a word upon the meaning of a million, being a number so enormous as to be difficult to conceive. It is well to have a standard by which to realize it. Mine will be understood by many Londoners; it is as follows:—One summer day I passed the afternoon in Bushey Park to see the magnificent spectacle of its avenue of horse-chestnut trees, a mile long, in full flower. As the hours passed by, it occurred to me to try to count the number of spikes of flowers facing the drive on one side of the long avenue—I mean all the spikes that were visible in full sunshine on one side of the road. Accordingly, I fixed upon a tree of average bulk and flower, and drew imaginary lines—first halving the tree, then quartering, and so on, until I arrived at a subdivision that was not too large to allow of my counting the spikes of flowers it included. I did this with three different trees, and arrived at pretty much the same result: as well as I recollect, the three estimates were as nine, ten, and eleven. Then I counted the trees in the avenue, and, multiplying all together, I found the spikes to be just about 100,000 in number. Ever since then, whenever a million is mentioned, I recall the long perspective of the avenue of Bushey Park, with its stately chestnuts clothed from top to bottom with spikes of flowers, bright in the sunshine, and I imagine a similarly continuous floral band, of ten miles in length.

*   *   *

Is reputation a fair test of natural ability? It is the only one I can employ—am I justified in using it? How much of a man's success is due to his opportunities, how much to his natural power of intellect?

This is a very old question, on which a great many commonplaces have been uttered that need not be repeated here. I will confine myself to a few considerations, such as seem to me amply adequate to prove what is wanted for my argument.

Let it clearly be borne in mind, what I mean by reputation and ability. By reputation, I mean the opinion of contemporaries, revised by posterity—the favourable result of a critical analysis of each man's character, by many biographers. I do not mean high social or official position, nor such as is implied by being the mere lion of a London season; but I speak of the reputation of a leader of opinion, of an originator, of a man to whom the world deliberately acknowledges itself largely indebted.

By natural ability, I mean those qualities of intellect and disposition, which urge and

qualify a man to perform acts that lead to reputation. I do not mean capacity without zeal, nor zeal without capacity, nor even a combination of both of them, without an adequate power of doing a great deal of very laborious work. But I mean a nature which, when left to itself, will, urged by an inherent stimulus, climb the path that leads to eminence, and has strength to reach the summit—one which, if hindered or thwarted, will fret and strive until the hindrance is overcome, and it is again free to follow its labour-loving instinct. It is almost a contradiction in terms, to doubt that such men will generally become eminent. On the other hand, there is plenty of evidence in this volume to show that few have won high reputations without possessing these peculiar gifts. It follows that the men who achieve eminence, and those who are naturally capable, are, to a large extent, identical.

The particular meaning in which I employ the word ability, does not restrict my argument from a wider application; for, if I succeed in showing—as I undoubtedly shall do—that the concrete triple event, of ability combined with zeal and with capacity for hard labour, is inherited, much more will there be justification for believing that any one of its three elements, whether it be ability, or zeal, or capacity for labour, is similarly a gift of inheritance.

I believe, and shall do my best to show, that, if the "eminent" men of any period, had been changelings when babies, a very fair proportion of those who survived and retained their health up to fifty years of age, would, notwithstanding their altered circumstances have equally risen to eminence. Thus—to take a strong case—it is incredible that any combination of circumstances, could have repressed Lord Brougham to the level of undistinguished mediocrity.

The arguments on which I rely are as follow. I will limit their application for the present to men of the pen and to artists. First, it is a fact, that numbers of men rise, before they are middle-aged, from the humbler ranks of life to that worldly position, in which it is of no importance to their future career, how their youth has been passed. They have overcome their hindrances, and thus start fair with others more fortunately reared, in the subsequent race of life. A boy who is to be carefully educated is sent to a good school, where he confessedly acquires little useful information, but where he is taught the art of learning. The man of whom I have been speaking has contrived to acquire the same art in a school of adversity. Both stand on equal terms, when they have reached mature life. They compete for the same prizes, measure their strength by efforts in the same direction, and their relative successes are thenceforward due to their relative natural gifts. There are many such men in the "eminent" class, as biographies abundantly show. Now, if the hindrances to success were very great, we should expect all who surmounted them to be prodigies of genius. The hindrances would form a system of natural selection, by repressing all whose gifts were below a certain very high level. But what is the case? We find very many who have risen from the ranks, who are by no means prodigies of genius; many who have no claim to "eminence," who have risen easily in spite of all obstacles. The hindrances undoubtedly form a system of natural selection that represses mediocre men, and even men of pretty fair powers—in short, the classes below D; but many of D succeed, a great many of E, and I believe a very large majority of those above.

If a man is gifted with vast intellectual ability, eagerness to work, and power of working, I cannot comprehend how such a man should be repressed. The world is always tormented with difficulties waiting to be solved—struggling with ideas and feelings, to which it can give no adequate expression. If, then, there exists a man capable of solving those difficulties, or of giving a voice to those pent-up feelings, he is sure to be welcomed with universal acclamation. We may almost say that he

has only to put his pen to paper, and the thing is done. I am here speaking of the very first-class men—prodigies—one in a million, or one in ten millions, of whom numbers will be found described in this volume, as specimens of hereditary genius.

Another argument to prove, that the hindrances of English social life, are not effectual in repressing high ability is, that the number of eminent men in England, is as great as in other countries where fewer hindrances exist. Culture is far more widely spread in America, than with us, and the education of their middle and lower classes far more advanced; but, for all that, America most certainly does not beat us in first-class works of literature, philosophy, or art. The higher kind of books, even of the most modern date, read in America, are principally the work of Englishmen. The Americans have an immense amount of the newspaper-article-writer, or of the member-of-congress stamp of ability; but the number of their really eminent authors is more limited even than with us. I argue that, if the hindrances to the rise of genius, were removed from English society as completely as they have been removed from that of America, we should not become materially richer in highly eminent men.

People seem to have the idea that the way to eminence is one of great self-denial, from which there are hourly temptations to diverge: in which a man can be kept in his boyhood, only by a schoolmaster's severity or a parent's incessant watchfulness, and in after life by the attractions of fortunate friendships and other favourable circumstances. This is true enough of the great majority of men, but it is simply not true of the generality of those who have gained great reputations. Such men, biographies show to be haunted and driven by an incessant instinctive craving for intellectual work. If forcibly withdrawn from the path that leads towards eminence, they will find their way back to it, as surely as a lover to his mistress. They do not work for the sake of eminence, but to satisfy a natural craving for brain work, just as athletes cannot endure repose on account of their muscular irritability, which insists upon exercise. It is very unlikely that any conjunction of circumstances, should supply a stimulus to brain work, commensurate with what these men carry in their own constitutions. The action of external stimuli must be uncertain and intermittent, owing to their very nature; the disposition abides. It keeps a man ever employed—now wrestling with his difficulties, now brooding over his immature ideas—and renders him a quick and eager listener to innumerable, almost inaudible teachings, that others less keenly on the watch, are sure to miss.

These considerations lead to my third argument. I have shown that social hindrances cannot impede men of high ability, from becoming eminent. I shall now maintain that social advantages are incompetent to give that status to a man of moderate ability. It would be easy to point out several men of fair capacity, who have been pushed forward by all kinds of help, who are ambitious, and exert themselves to the utmost, but who completely fail in attaining eminence. If great peers, they may be lord-lieutenants of counties; if they belong to great county families, they may become influential members of parliament and local notabilities. When they die, they leave a blank for a while in a large circle, but there is no Westminster Abbey and no public mourning for them—perhaps barely a biographical notice in the columns of the daily papers.

It is difficult to specify two large classes of men, with equal social advantages, in one of which they have high hereditary gifts, while in the other they have not. I must not compare the sons of eminent men with those of non-eminent, because much which I should ascribe to breed, others might ascribe to parental encouragement and example. Therefore, I will compare the sons of eminent men with the adopted sons of Popes and other dignitaries of the Roman Catholic Church. The practice of nepotism among ecclesiastics is universal. It consists in their giving those social helps to a nephew, or other more distant relative, that ordinary people give to their children. Now, I shall show abundantly in the course of this book, that the nephew of an eminent man has far less chance of becoming eminent than a son, and that a more remote kinsman has far less chance than a nephew. We may therefore make a very fair comparison, for the purposes of my argument, between the success of the sons of eminent men and that of the nephews or more distant relatives, who stand in the place of sons to the high unmarried ecclesiastics of the Romish Church. If social help is really of the highest importance, the nephews of the Popes will attain eminence as frequently, or nearly so, as the sons of other eminent men; otherwise, they will not.

Are, then, the nephews, &c., of the Popes, on the whole, as highly distinguished as are the sons of other equally eminent men? I answer, decidedly not. There have been a few Popes who were offshoots of illustrious races, such as that of the Medici, but in the enormous majority of cases the Pope is the ablest member of his family. I do not profess to have worked up the kinships of the Italians with any especial care, but I have seen amply enough of them, to justify me in saying that the individuals whose advancement has been due to nepotism, are curiously undistinguished. The very common combination of an able son and an eminent parent, is not matched, in the case of high Romish ecclesiastics, by an eminent nephew and an eminent uncle. The social helps are the same, but hereditary gifts are wanting in the latter case.

To recapitulate: I have endeavoured to show in respect to literary and artistic eminence—

1. That men who are gifted with high abilities easily rise through all the obstacles caused by inferiority of social rank.

2. Countries where there are fewer hindrances than in England, to a poor man rising in life, produce a much larger proportion of persons of culture, but not of what I call eminent men.

3. Men who are largely aided by social

advantages, are unable to achieve eminence, unless they are endowed with high
natural gifts.

*   *   *

To conclude: I feel convinced that no
man can achieve a very high reputation
without being gifted with very high abilities; and I trust that reason has been given
for the belief, that few who possess these
very high abilities can fail in achieving
eminence.

34. Measurement of Twins *

Edward L. Thorndike

To what extent do genetic endowment and life
experience contribute to man's intelligence?
The question of the relative impact of heredity
and environment (nature vs. nurture) on intellectual achievement represents a problem of
considerable importance. In fact, the answer
to this question influences the design of our
educational system, the manner in which we
deal with significant social problems, the nature
of our child-rearing practices, and perhaps
even the very ideals of our democratic society.

In the previous selection Galton observed that
eminent fathers are more likely to have eminent
sons and concluded that hereditary factors determine intellectual achievement. In the next
article, Thorndike approaches the nature-nurture
problem by examining the degree to which
specific intellectual qualities are related in members of the same family. His finding that "mental resemblances" among twins are greater
than those found among siblings leads him to
conclude, as did Galton, that intelligence is
largely determined by heredity. However,
Thorndike recognized the power of educational
and social institutions to produce differences in
the absolute achievements of men. But he believed that these differences were within the
"limits set by original nature to each individual."

The following is a summary of the results
of a study of the comparative importance
of original nature and training in the case
of fifty pairs of twins.[1] A detailed account
of the investigation will be published
shortly.

THE RESEMBLANCES OF TWINS AND OF SIBLINGS

From the information at hand, which is
not so satisfactory as information I hope
to obtain during the next few years, the
resemblance of twins in mental traits is
roughly twice that of ordinary siblings;[2]
according to the actual figures of my measurements of siblings, more than twice. I
have reason, however, to believe that the
correlation coefficients obtained for siblings
are affected by constant errors which make
them too low; namely, the selection of mentally unlike pairs by the conditions of the
methods of obtaining siblings and the absence of suitable data to make sufficient
correction for attenuation. Table 1 gives the
facts.

I use the words 'resemblance of' and 'likeness of' as synonyms for 'coefficients of correlation between.' A resemblance of .50

* Reprinted from the *Journal of Philosophy,
Psychology, and Scientific Method*, 1905, 2, 547-
553.

[1] The investigation here reported was made possible by a grant from the Esther Herrman Research
Fund of the New York Academy of Sciences.

[2] Karl Pearson has pointed out that the word
sibling is a convenient term to denote children of
the same parents.

TABLE 1

The Resemblances of Twins and Siblings Compared

Ability	Cofficients of Correlation	
	Twins	Siblings
A test	.69	.32
Word test	.71	.29
Opposites test	.90	.30

I give for siblings the obtained results. Since the correction for attenuation had to be made in an imperfect form, the true resemblances are probably somewhat higher, but not over .40.

means, then, a Pearson correlation coefficient of .50. I use the terms A test, word test, misspelled word test, opposites test, addition and multiplication to mean the tests, or at times the abilities measured by the tests, to describe which would take too much space.

THE RESEMBLANCES OF YOUNG AND OF OLD TWINS

The older twins show no closer resemblance than the younger twins, and the chances are surely four to one that with an infinite number of twins tested the 12–14 year olds would not show a resemblance .15 greater than the 9–11 year olds. The facts are given in Table 2.

THE RESEMBLANCES IN TRAITS LITTLE AND TRAITS MUCH SUBJECT TO TRAINING

The variations in the closeness of resemblance of the twins in the different traits show little, and possibly no, direct correlation with the amount of opportunity for environmental influences. The traits most subject to training (addition and multiplication) do show closer resemblances than the traits moderately subject to training (the "A" test and word test); but on the other hand show less close resemblances than the traits moderately subject to training (the misspelled word test and opposites test). The hypothesis that the true resemblance varies in amount inversely with the amount of opportunity for environmental influence would not be irreconcilable with the facts, and the hypothesis that the differences between the different traits are due to chance (including in that term the variable errors of the measurements and the possibility of the unequal inheritance of different traits) is the most probable of all. The difference between the traits most subject and those least subject to training is no greater than the median difference between any one trait of the six and any other. Surely there is no evidence here of any large contribution from similarity of training to similarity

TABLE 2

The Resemblances of Young and Old Twins Compared

	In corrected coefficients		In raw coefficients	
	Twins 9–11	Twins 12–14	Twins 9–11	Twins 12–14
(1) "A" test	.66	.73	.58	.67
(2) Word test	.81	.62	.62	.49
(3) Misspelled word test	.76	.74	.76	.74
(4) Addition	.90	.54	.83	.46
(5) Multiplication	.91	.69	.81	.53
(6) Opposites	.96	.88	.79	.78
Marks in (1), (2) and (3) combined			.71	.69
Marks in (4), (5) and (6) combined			.90	.75
Averages	.83	.70	.75	.64

TABLE 3

The Resemblances of Twins in Traits Little and in Traits Much Subject to Training

	Coefficients of correlation	Averages
(1) "A" test	.69⎫	.70
(2) Word test	.71⎭	
(3) Misspelled word test	.80⎫	.85
(6) Opposites	.90⎭	
(4) Addition	.75⎫	.795
(5) Multiplication	.84⎭	
Marks in (1), (2) and (3) combined	.70(raw)	
Marks in (4), (5) and (6) combined	.82(raw)	

of achievement. The facts are given in Table 3.

THE RESEMBLANCES IN MENTAL TRAITS COMPARED WITH THE RESEMBLANCES IN PHYSICAL TRAITS

It is highly probable from the facts so far given that the similarity of twins in ancestry and conditions of conception and birth accounts for almost all of their similarity in mental achievement,—that only a small fraction of it can be attributed to similarity in training. On general principles it is also highly probable that similarity of ancestry and conditions of conception will produce equal similarity in original physical nature and in original mental nature. Certain resemblances in original physical nature are in all probability neither increased nor decreased by such similarities and differences of home training as act upon twins and non-related children, respectively, within a group such as ours; e.g., resemblances in cephalic index, ratio of height sitting to total height, eye color and hair color. Other resemblances in original physical nature are increased and decreased slightly and perhaps not at all; e.g., circumference of head, length of head, width of head, length of forearm and length of finger joints.

If then, the resemblances of twins were almost entirely due to original nature, we should expect them to be only slightly in excess of the resemblances in physical traits. The existence of the latter as a fact may properly be taken as a partial verification of the former as a general hypothesis. The evidence of its existence is given in Table 4.

TABLE 4

The Resemblances of Twins in Mental and in Physical Traits

In mental traits		In physical traits	
1. "A" test	.69	11. Cephalic index	.76
2. Word test	.71	12. Ht. sitting/ht.	.76
3. Misspelled	.80	13. Height	.78
4. Addition	.75	14. Height sitting	.83
5. Multiplication	.84	15. Circ. of head	.75
6. Opposites	.90	16. Width of head	.86
7. Combined mark in 1–3	.70	17. Arm length	.72
8. Combined mark in 4–6	.82	18. Finger length	.71

7, 8 and 12–15 are raw correlations and the correction of attenuation might raise them by .01 or .02.

Median of 1–6	.78	Average of 11–12	.76 (possibly .77)
		" 13–18	.77 (possibly .78 or .79)
Average of 1–6	.78	Median of 13–18	.77 (possibly .78 or .79)
		" 11–18	.76 (possibly .77)
Average of 7–8	.76	Average of 11–18	.76 (possibly .77)
	(Possibly .80)		

SUMMARY AND CRITICISM

These facts prove that among one hundred twins living and attending school in New York City in 1903-4, the mental resemblances of a twin pair are about twice as great as those of a pair of siblings similarly chosen, are as great or nearly as great in the case of the younger as of the older half of the group, are as great or nearly as great in the case of the "A," word, misspelled word and opposites test as in the case of addition and multiplication, and are only slightly, if at all, greater than resemblances in physical traits which could have been caused, in some cases, only by original nature.

The facts are easily, simply and completely explained by one simple hypothesis: namely, that the natures of the germ-cells —the conditions of conception—cause whatever similarities and differences exist in the original natures of men, that these conditions influence body and mind equally, and that in life the differences in modification of body and mind produced by such differences as obtain between the environments of present-day New York City public school children are slight.

Certain other hypotheses seem possible at first sight, but become involved in great difficulties when one tries to explain all the facts by any of them. These difficulties I will point out briefly.

It may be said that all that has been proved of the twins is that they are alike in general mental maturity (i.e., in the points of development which they have reached).

Traits like those tested are of course influenced by maturity directly and indirectly through the relation between maturity and advance in school and the relation between the latter and certain of the traits tested. But maturity is by no means the total cause of efficiency in these traits. Nor is it a cause comparable in amount of influence with individual differences apart from ma-

turity. Nor is there any evidence that there is any greater resemblance of twins in maturity than in other factors, such as eyesight. If maturity were the total cause of efficiency in the six traits measured, these traits should in the same individual show perfect correlation with each other. They do not, nor, indeed enough correlation to assign maturity a very important place as a contributory cause. If resemblance in maturity were the cause of the resemblances found, these should be largest in the traits most subject to maturity. The opposite is the case.

It may be said that all that has been proved of the twins is that the environmental conditions from 9 to 14 years count little; that the similarities in environment in utero and during childhood are left as possible causes of the resemblances found; and that these are the real causes. But that the conditions in utero are the cause of the resemblances of related individuals is disproved by the fact that paternal is as great as maternal resemblance in the case of those traits where parents and offspring have been compared; and that similarities in environment from 0 to 9 years should produce a far greater effect on the children's abilities to add, multiply, mark misspelled words and write opposites than do similarities in environment from 9 to 15 is a notion utterly devoid of probability.

It is equally difficult to accept original nature as a cause of a moderate amount of the resemblance found and to explain the rest as due to training. Suppose, for instance, that some one assumes that the force of the germ-natures,—of the conditions of conception, is sufficient to produce a resemblance of .20 in siblings and .40 in twins in mental traits. He must be then willing to believe that the likeness in training of a twin pair is enough greater than the likeness in training of a sibling pair, two or three years apart in age, to make the .40 rise to .80, whereas the .20 rises only to .40 or less. He must also be willing to believe either that inborn mental make-up is inherited by a totally different law from that regulating inborn physical make-up or else that the similarities in training of twins will raise .40 to .80 in physical traits such as cephalic index, and that the similarities in training of siblings will raise the .20 only to .40 or .50. He must also place the bulk of influence of this training previous to the tenth year and assume that it is of such a generalized sort as would raise the resemblances in marking A's or words containing r and e as much as that in multiplication.

Doubtless we all feel a repugnance to assigning so little efficacy to environmental forces as the facts of this study seem to demand; but common opinion also feels a repugnance to believing that the mental resemblances of twins, however caused, are as great as the physical resemblances. Yet they are. I can not here discuss the general facts and detailed studies which bear upon the question of the amount of influence of such likenesses and differences in environment as existed in the case of these twins.

I shall also spend but little time in comments upon the application of the facts so far presented to theories of education and human action and to the practical problems of social control. The inferences with respect to the enormous importance of original nature in determining the behavior and achievements of any man in comparison with his fellows of the same period of civilization and conditions of life are obvious. All theories of human life must accept as a first principle the fact that human beings at birth differ enormously in mental capacities and that these differences are largely due to similar differences in their ancestry. All attempts to change human nature must accept as their most important condition the limits set by original nature to each individual.

We must be careful, however, not to confuse two totally different things: (1) the power of the environment,—for instance, of schools, laws, books and social ideals,—to produce differences in the relative achievements of men, and (2) the power of the environment to produce differences in absolute achievement. It has been shown that the relative differences in certain mental traits which were found in these one hundred children are due almost entirely to differences in ancestry, not in training; but this does not in the least deny that better methods of training might improve all their achievements fifty per cent, or that the absence of training, say in spelling and arithmetic, might decrease the corresponding achievements to zero. Similarly, the fact that Mr. Rockefeller has amassed one of the great fortunes of the age is undoubtedly due almost exclusively to his original capacity, not to circumstances; but this does not deny that it is almost exclusively circumstances which make the average wealth of men to-day greater than it was a thousand years ago or that future changes in the environment might, without any change in capacity make nine men out of ten the owners of automobiles, race-horses, tall hats and the other blessings of wealth.

The argument has been limited entirely to the causes which make one person differ from another in mental achievements under the same general conditions of life at the beginning of the twentieth century in New York City as pupils in its school system. If the resemblance of twins had been measured in the case of a group made up partly of New York City school children and partly of children of equal capacity brought up in the wilds of Africa, the variability of the group in addition and multiplication would have increased and the correlation coefficients would rise. They would then measure the influence of original nature plus the now much increased influence of the environment.

The relative impotence of such similarities of home training as existed in our fifty pairs of twins to create similarities of achievement does, however, make one suspect that the magnitude of the influence of the training given by schools, periods of civilization and the like has been exaggerated. For other reasons, also, I imagine this to be the case, but to prove or disprove it, one would need data quite different from the records of these hundred twins.

It is, then, folly to conclude that the inheritance of mental capacities from immediate ancestry implies the futility of education and social control in general—the wisdom of fatalism and laissez faire. Such studies as this merely prove the existence of and measure one determinant of human intellect and character and demonstrate that the influences of the environment are differential, the product varying not only in accord with the environmental force itself, but also in accord with the original nature upon which it operates. We may even expect that education will be doubly effective, once society recognizes the advantage from or need of wise investment. . . .

To the real work of man for man,—the increase of achievement through the improvement of the environment,—the influence of heredity offers no barrier. But to the popular demands from education and social reforms it does. For the common man does not much appreciate absolute happiness or absolute betterment. He does not rejoice that he and his children are healthier, happier and more supplied with noble pleasures than were his ancestors of a thousand years ago. His complaint is that he is not so well off as some of those about him; his pride is that he is above the common herd. The common man demands relative superiority,—to be above those of his own time and locality. If his son leads the community, he does not mind his real stupidity; to be the handsomest girl in the county is beauty enough. Social discontent comes from the knowledge or fancy that one is below others in welfare. The effort of children in school, of men in labor and of women in the home is, except as guided by the wise instincts of nature or more rarely by the wisdom of abstract thought, to rise above some one who seems higher. Thus the prizes which most men really seek are, after all, in large measure given or withheld by original nature. In the actual race of life, which is not to get ahead, but to get ahead of somebody, the chief determining factor is heredity.

35. The Case of the Wandering IQ's *

Bernard Asbell

Today there can be little doubt that both hereditary and environmental factors affect the development and expression of intelligence. Genetic endowment seems to determine the upper limit of intellectual achievement, while the stimulation provided by an individual's environment, especially early in life, markedly influences the degree to which this limit is approached. Acceptance of this view is reflected in remedial programs such as Head Start in which culturally disadvantaged pre-school children are given enriched educational experiences to offset the limited intellectual stimulation received at home.

But the critical significance of the role played by environmental stimulation in the development of intelligence has not always been recognized. In the following selection, Bernard Asbell presents a fascinating scientific case history that demonstrates how early views of the

* Reprinted by permission of the author and the McCall Corporation from the August, 1967, issue of *Redbook* magazine. Copyright © 1967 by McCall Corporation.

nature of intelligence at first led psychologists to underestimate the potential power of the environment. This selection also provides a dramatic illustration of how research on child development can contribute to the understanding and treatment of an important social problem such as mental retardation.

Thirty years ago in an Iowa orphanage a young psychologist, Dr. Harold M. Skeels, and his assistant, Dr. Marie Skodak, tested two infants, each a little more than a year old.

"They were miserable pieces of humanity," Dr. Skodak recalls. "They were scrawny little girls. They couldn't sit up, or make a sound except to whine or cry. If you tried to play with them or talk to them, all you got was a feeble 'Waaa.' Nothing! In simple tests of responding to words, locating the direction of sounds, picking up small objects, these babies functioned at the age level of three to seven months."

The children scored as hopeless imbeciles. They had IQs of 46 and 35.

The scores were hardly surprising. Both babies had been born to mentally deficient mothers, fathers unknown. On an IQ test one mother had been found to be feeble-minded; the other had been declared a "psychotic with mental retardation." It seemed to the young psychologists that these family histories clearly explained and corroborated their findings; the children were mental cripples. The psychologists did what seemed logical, necessary and routine. They recommended that the babies be committed to a home for the mentally retarded.

For thousands of babies before and since, similar decisions have marked the end of their sad stories. For these two infants, however, as well as for the two psychologists, that examination was a strange beginning.

The young professionals had no idea that they were soon to challenge two scientific beliefs which were then unquestioned. The first was that mental retardation (when

not caused by brain damage or other specific conditions) is inherited. The companion belief was that a child born an imbecile is fated to live and die an imbecile.

The challenge of these beliefs by Dr. Skeels and his young assistant was at first greeted by uproarious controversy among their colleagues, a controversy followed by rejection and then, after 30 years, by a dramatic vindication. This recent vindication—and the remarkable scientific detective story that led up to it—now throws wide-open some fundamental questions of what intelligence is, how it is nurtured and how it may sometimes be destroyed.

The evidence that first fell into the hands of Dr. Skeels and Dr. Skodak three decades ago in Iowa was not the result of purposeful research. It was produced by pure accident—the fact that Iowa's institutions for retarded children were filled to overflowing when the doctors examined the two mentally deficient babies. So they were sent from the orphanage to an adult institution, the Woodward State School and Hospital for the Mentally Handicapped.

As it also happened, Dr. Skeels and his assistant occasionally had to visit Woodward. On one such visit he and Dr. Skodak were making their rounds, giving tests in the women's wards, when they saw two jolly, pink-cheeked children about two years old at play. The two children looked strangely familiar, and the psychologists soon discovered that these were the two babies they had examined about eight months earlier.

"We could hardly believe it," Dr. Skodak recalls. "Here they were, bright, pretty, done up in hair ribbons, running around, playing, having a happy time with all kinds of toys. They just didn't look like the same children.

"We tested them again. A normal child of two can be expected to have a speaking vocabulary of at least a dozen words and to be beginning to put words together. He should understand simple commands like 'Bring me the shoe' and be able to draw something that can be taken for a circle. He should be able to thread large beads on a string, put a spoon in a cup and stir it—simple manual actions like that. On tests like these, the two little girls came out with IQs of seventy-seven and eighty-seven. This was about in the range of what we call 'dull normal,' a remarkable leap from the imbecile level at which they had tested before."

"I was unable to account for it," Dr. Skeels says now. "The change might have indicated some accident in the earlier testing if it had happened to only one child, but here were two. It was possible, of course, that the tests we'd just done were misleading; perhaps the improvement wouldn't last. We decided to leave the children just as they were and see what happened."

A year later the children were tested again—and the psychologists were astonished. The child who had first had an IQ of 35, then of 87, now showed an IQ of 88, only two points below the range of "average or normal." The other child, who had tested at 46, then 77, now scored a round 100, precisely the norm for American children her age. Clearly these children no longer belonged in a home for the feeble-minded; at least one of them was decidedly eligible for adoption. The immediate impulse of the psychologists was to transfer the children to an orphanage at once. But they decided first to find out what had happened to the two babies in the year and a half since the first tests had been made.

They learned that the infants had been placed in separate wards with women ranging in age from 18 to 50 years, women whose mentalities approximated those of five-to-nine-year-olds. Each baby had been "adopted" by one of the inmates, who became a kind of mother. Others in the wards, less actively attached to the children, became adoring "aunts." Since the adults themselves had the mentality of children, each ward had a dollhouse; and as the children joined in the women's play they were spoken to a great deal: "See?

This goes here. See the chair? Pretty chair."

Some of the inmates had been mothers and were quite competent in such motherly duties as bathing, feeding and diaper-changing; others enjoyed cuddling and singing to the children. The ward attendants, meanwhile, supervised the babies' diets and saw to it that they lived by a healthy routine.

Some of the inmates had spending money; they would give it to hospital employees for the purchase of small toys, pretty dresses and hair ribbons for the girls. Sometimes attendants on their days off would "borrow" the two children, give them automobile and bus rides or take them into stores to buy picture books that would then become the property of the ward. Most of the waking hours of all the people in the wards had begun to revolve around the two little girls.

"Here was a 'home' setting," points out Dr. Skeels, "abundant in affection, rich in wholesome and interesting experiences and geared to a preschool level of development."

A dilemma now confronted Dr. Skeels. Should he leave the three-year-olds among these feeble-minded women to whom they apparently owed their mental and emotional growth but where they certainly no longer belonged? Or should he transfer them to the state orphanage, which was crowded and understaffed and where they would receive only a minimum of attention? Dr. Skeels had seen many children of normal intelligence slide inexorably downhill in such institutions.

Unhappy with these alternatives, Dr. Skeels hit upon a third course, unusual but promising. He persuaded the orphanage staff to take special steps to find adoptive parents for the two little girls, even though most adoptions take place when babies are only a few weeks old.

"When adoptive parents were found," says Dr. Skeels, "I had a nice little explanation all prepared for them. I said, 'This is a fine youngster, but don't push her too far.' I still wasn't too confident of just what the potentials of these kids were. In case things didn't work out well, I had another lecture ready: 'Look, we made a ghastly mistake. This child wasn't supposed to be adopted. She's feeble-minded. Please let us take her from you and place her in an institution. We'll give you another fine, healthy child so you can start all over.' I'm happy to say, we never had to use the second explanation."

Dr. Skeels soon made an appointment with the chairman of the Iowa State Board of Control, which had charge of orphanages and homes for the retarded. Briefly he sketched for the board chairman the story of the two little girls and then put before him a bizarre idea. "I said to him, 'I would like permission to take eleven more feeble-minded babies less than a year old and put them in adult wards in institutions for the retarded, because I think that the babies will become normal.' As you can imagine, he looked at me queerly. He was not a professional, but an Iowa farmer who held his job by political appointment. He said, 'It sounds crazy to me, but tell me more.' "

Dr. Skeels then listed the depressing conditions for infant development in orphanages and other children's institutions at that time. Babies were kept in cribs surrounded by protective white sheeting, which shut out anything stimulating to look at. No toys dangled around them. The only adults they saw were preoccupied nurses who appeared for quick changes of diapers and bedding, for rapid bathing and medication, or to prop bottles into the babies' mouths with the use of efficient, impersonal holders. At six months of age the babies were moved into small dormitories, where for the first time they had a few playthings but if a ball rolled away, there was no friendly adult to retrieve it. When they were two years old the children were graduated to cottages housing 30 to 35 youngsters of the same sex in the charge of one matron and three or four untrained, often reluctant teen-aged girls, themselves

reared in the deadening environment of the orphanage. In homes for feeble-minded children, Dr. Skeels pointed out, life was, if possible, even more stultifying.

Continuing further with his unusual suggestion, Dr. Skeels hastened to explain that in placing the babies in wards for feeble-minded adults he would not be playing lightly with the fates of the children. Since their mentalities were already low and, as he and his colleagues had noticed, the IQs of children in orphanages and other children's institutions tended to go down, not up, what harm could come to them through a few months of affection from the feeble-minded women? On the other hand, he said, look what had happened to the first two little girls. If that were to happen to even one of the additional 11 children, the effort would be more than worthwhile.

But there was one hitch, Dr. Skeels added. After spending a year or two in a grownups' ward, the children would be two or three years old, an age that would make it hard to place them for adoption. If, in addition, their records showed that they had been in an institution for the feeble-minded, adoption would be impossible, if not illegal. So Dr. Skeels proposed listing the children as "house guests" at the institution, an informal designation that would require no marking on their records.

It seemed to be a gamble with only winning possibilities—no child could lose, but the lives of one or more of them might be improved—and at first Dr. Skeels had no other idea in mind. Then he realized that there might be another benefit. "Here was a gold mine for formal research—a situation that could not have been set up by choice. You can't play with human lives—especially with babies' lives—moving them from one environment to another just for the sake of research. But here, quite by accident, life itself had set up the proper conditions for us, and the results so far seemed to justify trying again on a more formal basis."

But to make the experiment valuable as research, Dr. Skeels would have to show that any benefits that might befall the additional 11 children would not have happened if these children had not been placed in wards with the feeble-minded women. He therefore proposed that 12 babies remaining at the orphanage be chosen as a "contrast group." Again, the children would not be harmed for the sake of the research; their lives would continue at the orphanage as if no research were being done. No one but Dr. Skeels and his assistants would know that their records of development were being observed in a special way, except for Harold B. Dye, M.D., superintendent of a state institution for retarded children, who helped Dr. Skeels develop his plan.

The 12 "contrast" children would resemble the "house guest" children as closely as possible in health records and family background. They would differ in only one respect. Their IQs would be higher than those of the "house guests." This was to test Dr. Skeels's earlier observations. Would their near-normal IQs decline at the orphanage in the way that Dr. Skeels had observed the IQs of others decline? If at the same time the IQs of the retarded "house guests" rose, how would the IQs of the two groups compare after, say, a year?

Dr. Skeels won permission to make his experiment.

The IQs of the 11 babies sent to the adult institution ranged from 36, or seriously retarded, to 89, or dull normal. Of the "contrast" babies remaining at the orphanage, the one with the lowest IQ scored 50, the one with the highest scored 103, or normal. Although nine of the contrast group were in the intelligence range considered adoptable, they were ineligible because of poor family histories or legal restrictions.

What had happened to the first two babies at Woodward now happened to nearly all the experimental 11. In almost every ward one inmate became a baby's

"mother" and others became "aunts." Each day, supervised by their "mothers" and "aunts," all the children frolicked together in a playground, riding tricycles and using the swings and slides. In the large living room of each ward there was plenty of space for indoor play. As soon as they could talk, the "house guest" children attended kindergarten and short daily chapel exercises that included group singing. When adults had dances and movies, the children went too. On the Fourth of July the residents put on a baby show. Each ward made a float upon which its baby rode, dressed in costume. Prizes were awarded for the nicest baby, most attractive costume and best float. Above all, there was the daily doting over the children by the "mothers" and "aunts."

The mental growth of the children was spectacular. The IQ of one child, originally 36, leaped to 81. Generally the greatest gains were made by those who had started lowest. Five of the 11 children attained IQs of 100 or higher. One boy astonished the psychologists by reaching 113. Every child gained, and the group's average rose from 64 to 92.

One child who leaped from 73 to 100 did so in only eight months. All the others, except one, made their gains in two years or less. The one exception, the girl who progressed from 36 to 81, took more than four years to do so. The doctors noted with interest that this child and one other originally had been placed in a ward with inmates whose average mental age was the lowest among the adults involved in the experiment. When these two children failed to show progress after many months, they were placed singly in other wards with brighter residents. After making new attachments with more active, attentive "mothers" and "aunts," they, like the other children, began to show marked gains in intelligence. Despite their later start, it wasn't too late to save them.

Of the 11 children, nine were placed in adoptive homes, just as the two girls who first went to Woodward had been. The remaining two, however, were returned to the orphanage. One of these, a child born to a 14-year-old mother, had been a guest in one of the brighter wards and had become the "daughter" of an inmate who was not only attentive but extremely possessive. The child's IQ had advanced from 57 to 94 in nine months. Her nursery teacher, however, felt the child was overdependent, and transferred her to a less-stimulating group of inmates. Here she received hardly more special attention than the grown inmates of the ward. Her IQ receded to 84, and soon afterward to 77.

The other "failure," born prematurely with congenital syphilis that was soon cured, had experienced a rise in IQ from 61 to 80 between her second and third birthdays. At this point a newly employed administrator sent her back to the orphanage, feeling the child no longer belonged in an institution for the retarded. The psychologists felt it impolitic at the time to fight the case. Before long the child's IQ declined to 63.

About two and a half years after the "house guest" children were adopted, Dr. Skeels visited them in their new homes for follow-up tests. He could hardly believe what he found. No child had an IQ of less than 90, and the average of all of the children was a normal 96.

Meanwhile the 12 "contrast group" children in the orphanage had sadly deteriorated over these three or four years. Having started at a near-normal average of 87, their group average had sagged to 66. The child who had started as the brightest, with an IQ of 103, had plummeted 54 points.

Thus while the retarded children sent to the home for the feeble-minded had now become normal, the near-normal children left in the orphanage had now become slow or feeble-minded.

Today it is hard to imagine with what shock these findings were regarded by the psychologists of nearly 30 years ago. But studies of human intelligence then were dominated by two assumptions: that intelligence, like the color of one's eyes, is built into the genes and remains forever fixed; and that the way in which a child lives is not a major factor in fixing his intelligence.

Yet it was precisely because their evidence to the contrary was so extraordinary that Dr. Skeels and his band of eager young helpers assumed it would be received with excited attention by their scientific colleagues.

On May 6, 1939, before the annual convention of the American Association on Mental Deficiency, in Chicago, Dr. Skeels read a report on his experiment. The report, coauthored by Dr. Dye, was greeted with stony silence—a silence to be followed by scathing criticism soon after the convention closed. One authority on intelligence, B. R. Simpson, mocked Skeels and Dye in print as inventors of a "wandering IQ." An even more eminent authority, Florence Goodenough, a designer of intelligence tests, denounced the Skeels-Dye study later the same year from no less distinguished a platform than that of the American Association for the Advancement of Science. Skeels and his associates were charged with distorting their facts, perhaps even falsifying them to attract attention. The facts couldn't be true because they violated what all psychologists *knew* to be true—that intelligence cannot be changed. Marie Skodak particularly recalls the AAAS meeting, in Columbus, Ohio, where Florence Goodenough read her attack.

"I happened to be the only one of our group there," recalls Dr. Skodak, who is now Director of Psychological Services for the public schools of Dearborn, Michigan. "I rose in the audience with all my youth and all my inexperience for that kind of debate among important professionals. I don't know all the things I said, but I remember that it was a long, long speech I gave. To this day, some people still remember me for that speech. But the criticism only got louder and worse. Pretty soon almost everyone in the field heard of 'that Iowa study' and that it was wrong. No one could say exactly *what* was wrong, but it was wrong."

The Skeels group, while wounded, remained unshaken. They were developing far more evidence than that derived from their study of a mere handful of children in an asylum. They were putting together a whole jigsaw puzzle of studies, all contributing to a single subject: the impact of environment on intelligence.

With Eva A. Fillmore, one of his assistants, Dr. Skeels studied families in which parents seemed to give their children inadequate affection and attention. Older children of such parents most often grew up with borderline intelligence or were mentally retarded. Their younger brothers and sisters, however, were generally of normal ability. This seemed to suggest that a younger child, even though lacking attention from a parent, benefited by the stimulaton of an older playmate in the house, even though not an intelligent one. Whatever the reason, this finding challenged the existing notion that the IQ score is fixed by heredity.

Meanwhile, Dr. Skeels worked on a broad-scale study to amplify his findings regarding the dozen children in the Skeels-Dye contrast group. This study showed that most children who remain for long periods of time in institutions supposedly for children of normal minds slowly but inevitably become retarded. The most revealing piece of the jigsaw puzzle was contained in still another study that Dr. Skodak coauthored with Dr. Skeels. When infants were placed for adoption, social workers, in matching children with adoptive or foster families, attempted to predict the mental level of the child. Because one can hardly test the mentality of an infant two or three weeks old, say, these predictions were based on the intelligence of their natural parents, which was usually low, and on the achievements of their older brothers and sisters. The Skodak-Skeels study, involving 100 children, found that a couple of years after adoption these children almost always surpassed the predictions of the orphanage social workers.

In all these studies, one thing seemed to account for a child's improvement. "The consistent element," wrote Dr. Skeels, "seemed to be existence of a one-to-one relationship with an adult who gave generously of love and affection, together with an abundance of attention and experimental stimulation from many sources. Those children who had little of these did not show progress. Those who had a great deal did show progress."

If any psychologist was inclined to share the Skeels heresy by further testing his findings, his plans were upset by the coming of World War II, which directed almost all professional skills into channels of national survival. Dr. Skeels himself was conscripted into an Air Force desk job.

When the war ended, Dr. Skeels discovered that the Iowa records section had discarded the detailed notes of his studies. As though to emphasize his disgrace, it was explained to him that the notes had taken up too much file space. All that was left were some rough data that his assistants had squirreled away on their own. Discouraged and apparently defeated, Dr. Skeels took a job as a clinical psychologist in a Veterans Administration hospital in Denver and eventually joined the United States Public Health Service. His work on children's intelligence seemed to be finished.

Yet the story was not ended. Shortly after the war, a graduate student at Northwestern University made a study of backward children in Chicago public schools and came up with evidence that IQs can be raised as a result of stimulating experiences. A few years later, however, a University of Illinois professor of education, Samuel A. Kirk, refuted the study by revealing some major errors in its methods. But in the course of preparing this refutation, Dr. Kirk restudied the published papers of Dr. Skeels and began his own large-scale research on mentally handicapped children. In 1958 he published a book, *Early Education of the Mentally Retarded,* advancing results almost identical with those of Skeels and Dye. The documentation put forth by Dr. Kirk, plus his eminence in the field, forced the professional establishment to sit up and take notice.

About five years later, in four classrooms of a Harlem public school, Dr. Martin Deutsch, supported by a grant from the Ford Foundation, produced remarkable rises in the scoring IQ of four- and five-year-old slum children by exposing them to highly charged stimulation in preschool classes. This accomplishment was duplicated in the public schools of Baltimore, also with financial help from the Ford Foundation. These experiments, widely publicized, rapidly led to the multimillion-dollar Federal effort known as Project Head Start. Soon research was launched in the malleability of intelligence in children under nursery-school age. Almost overnight the "wandering IQ" of young children became a subject of high fashion in educational and psychological research, although few of the professionals engaged in it had ever heard of Dr. Skeels.

One who had, however, was Dr. Robert J. Havighurst, of the University of Chicago. In 1961, attending a meeting one day at the National Institute for Mental Health, near Washington, he learned by chance that Dr. Skeels, now an administrator for the National Institute, had an office down the hall. Fired by an idea, Dr. Havighurst went to Dr. Skeels and introduced himself. Although Havighurst had never taken a position on the controversial work of Skeels, he realized that the early date of the study —more than a quarter century had gone by—presented a marvelous opportunity. These former imbeciles and dullards—the "house guests" and contrast group alike— were now adults. What had happened to them? Had the "house guests" who turned smart become dull again? Had those who

began by being smart and then turned dull in the orphanage found their "natural level" and turned smart again? Did any of them have children? And if so, what were *they* like? It was urgent that a follow-up study be made, he told Dr. Skeels.

Dr. Skeels's first reaction was one of resistance—but somehow hopeful resistance. How would he get away from his job? Who would pay the enormous cost of tracking down the children of the experiment? Who would assist him? But regardless of the difficulties, the job was not to go undone. He took the matter up with authorities at the Institute. He found them —to his surprise—interested, and also willing to pay the cost. The Institute would provide funds to find not only the 25 children in the Skeels-Dye experimental and contrast groups, but also the 100 children of the Skodak-Skeels study who had been placed in adoptive homes. Dr. Skeels called Dr. Skodak at her job in Dearborn.

As the two long-time colleagues began to plan, they realized the immense difficulties of their undertaking. After a quarter of a century, in modern, mobile America, how do you track down children who have grown into adults?

For instance, of the 25 children in the Skeels-Dye study (the 13 "house guests," including the first two girls, and the 12 in the contrast group), 14 were girls. If they had married, their names were changed. How could they be located? There were further problems. Adoption agencies do not keep long-range records of children they place. One or both of the adoptive parents—or even the child himself—might be dead.

The new study now became a detective story. The psychologists began their sleuthing by searching old telephone books, city directories and files of local credit bureaus in Iowa. Some of these directories were found in, of all places, the Des Moines office of the Animal Disease Eradication Division of the U.S. Department of Agriculture, which maintained old lists of people living on farms. Musty directories eventually turned up two thirds of the former orphanage children.

To find the rest, Drs. Skeels and Skodak visited small-town postmasters, bankers, old-time storekeepers, and elderly ladies with long memories. In calling upon these people, the psychologists could not save the project money by driving government cars. Those whom they hoped would be their informants about families long since moved away might jump to the conclusion that the inquisitive visitors were from the Federal Bureau of Investigation—or, even worse, from the Bureau of Internal Revenue. So, each in a rented car, Dr. Skeels and Dr. Skodak went their separate ways, driving from one town to another, from one house to another, each introducing himself as a friend of the family that was being sought.

Six of the "house guest" children were found to be still living in Iowa. The other seven were finally tracked down great distances away: two in Minnesota and one each in Wisconsin, Kansas, Nebraska, Arizona and California. Of the contrast group, nine of the 12 had remained in Iowa. One was located in Nebraska; another was traced to Florida, then to Montana and finally to California. One, Dr. Skeels learned, had died. Remarkably, not only all 25 children in the Skeels-Dye experiment but every one of the 100 children in the Skodak-Skeels study was located.

Now the two psychologists faced the problem of approaching the people they had traced.

"You can't write them form letters, or even call them on the long-distance telephone," Dr. Skeels points out. "After all those years, you just don't open that way. Only Marie Skodak or I could do it. At one time we were considered part of these families. We had had an understanding with the adoptive parents that we could come back periodically and give tests as the children became older, which we had done. Either of us could appear as an interested old friend and resume our relationship."

The search had taken 16 months. Now that they had been found, 95 per cent of the adopted children—now adults—were glad to co-operate. Co-operation meant hardly more than easy, informal conversation. Early in their planning, Drs. Skeels and Skodak had decided that there was little point in giving intelligence tests. What seemed far more appropriate was to get information on the real, demonstrated abilities of these adults: educational achievement, occupations and an estimate of their general social competence. Where it seemed appropriate, a suggestion would be made for giving IQ tests to their children.

If ability to hold a good job is a measure of a successful life, the 13 children who once were "house guests" in an institution for the mentally retarded had turned out astoundingly well. All had become self-supporting. One of the three boys in the group was a staff sergeant in the armed forces, another was a sales manager and the third was a vocational counselor on his way toward earning a master's degree.

The staff sergeant had been born to a 16-year-old mother whose IQ was 69. His father was unknown. With an IQ score of 113 after his period as a "house guest," he was adopted by a mechanic and his wife, both of them high-school graduates. As a teen-ager the boy dropped out of high school in his senior year, and after an act of vandalism spent a short time in a correctional school. He soon straightened out, joined the armed forces and later married a hospital technician, a high-school graduate. The couple have three small children whose IQs range from a bright 113 to a superior 125.

The sales manager was born to a houseworker who had quit school in the ninth grade; his father was believed to be a theater manager in a small town. After almost two years as a "house guest" he had an unimpressive IQ of 79, but was permitted to be adopted by a storekeeper and his wife. His childhood was marred by severe allergies. Recovering, he attended college for more than two years. He married. The IQs of the couple's three children range from 96 to 118.

The vocational counselor turned out to be one of the most remarkable of the "house guests." He had been a sickly baby. He was delivered by cesarean section to a woman whose IQ was 66; his father was unknown. At two years of age, with an IQ of 75, he spent hours incessantly rocking back and forth. He was one of the pair who had spent one and a half fruitless years among extremely dull inmates and then had been transferred to brighter "mothers" and "aunts." After attaining an IQ of 92, he was adopted by a college-graduate technician and his wife. The boy suffered severe asthma attacks as a small child, but these were brought under control. He completed high school and college, went on to postgraduate work at a good university and married a college-graduate commercial artist. They have no children.

Of the ten girls who were "house guests," eight married. One was subsequently divorced, but the others appeared to be enjoying stable, satisfying family lives. Of those who had been employed, one taught elementary school. Others in the group had become a registered nurse, a practical nurse, a licensed beautician and an office clerk. Two married without taking jobs. The two girls who had never been placed in adoptive homes wound up in the lowest-status jobs, as domestic workers.

The prize among the girls was one whose IQ during her "house guest" period had jumped from 65 to 104. She was adopted by an accountant and his wife, both college graduates. The girl, who grew to be unusually attractive and vivacious, completed high school and began training to be an airline stewardess. She left this training, however, to marry a meteorologist. The above-average IQs of their three children are 107, 110 and 114.

The "house guests" who married had a combined total of 28 children. The IQs of these children averaged 104. Lowest among them was 85; highest, 125. When one considers the early dullness of mind of their parents and the miserable mentalities of their known grandparents, these cold numbers appear to demolish old notions about the unchangeability of intelligence.

The success in adult life of the "house guests" was the shiny face of a two-sided coin. On the other side of the coin was the sad picture—with one startling exception—of the contrast group, the children who had remained in the orphanage.

Of 11 surviving members of this group —one died at 15 in an institution for the mentally retarded—none was adopted. Only two married; one of these subsequently was divorced. Four were still residents of state institutions and unable to hold paying jobs. The most promising of these had intermittently been paroled to his grandmother and hired himself out to mow lawns and shovel snow, but he could not function as an independent citizen. A fifth is employed as a gardener's helper in the institution in which he spent much of his life as an inmate. An attempt was made to get him an outside job, but he failed at it. He has no interest beyond his simple work, no known friends among either inmates or fellow employees. Of the six living on their own, three work as dishwashers. One folds napkins in a cafeteria and another, a male, is classed as a "floater."

This leaves one self-supporting member of the contrast group—known as Case 19. He was to be the ultimate surprise of the search conducted by Dr. Skeels. Dr. Skeels found him working as a skilled linotyper for a newspaper in a sizable Midwestern city. His earnings are greater than that of the rest of the contrast group combined. He is the only one with a stable marriage, a family and a home of his own.

Oddly, his good fortune can be traced directly to an affliction he had suffered since early childhood. As an infant, Case

19 underwent a mastoid operation that resulted in a moderate hearing loss. Between the ages of 15 months and four years, which he spent at the orphanage, his affliction brought him more sympathetic attention from adults than other children enjoyed. Still his IQ descended from 87 to 67. When he was five, old enough for Kindergarten, he was sent by the orphanage to a resident school for deaf children. His schoolmates, of course, were not "institutional" children as those at the orphanage were. They came from a normally wide range of homes and warm, concerned parents who kept close contact with their children. And like those in the "house guest" group, he informally acquired a "mother." The matron of his cottage took a special fancy to him, partly because he had no family. She often took him home with her for family meals, and so did her daughter and son-in-law.

"There was something unusually charming about him as a little boy," Dr. Skodak recalls. "He was the kind of child who responded to people—and to whom people responded. He openly sought affection and got it. During summer holidays he returned to the orphanage. Because he'd been away, he wasn't a real member of the group. So he'd hang around the orphanage office or parking lot. Staff members, seeing him there alone, often would take him along on trips to the post office or to do other chores. Sometimes they would buy him ice cream on the way back. The fact that he was deaf led him to more experiences of this kind than the other orphanage children had."

By another happy accident, during his year in kindergarten he was chosen for a special study in mental growth that was being conducted by a researcher from a state university. This placed him in an intensified program of individualized instruction and frequent trips. About two years after the Skeels-Dye experiment ended, when other "contrast" children at the orphanage almost all had deteriorated,

according to the scores of their follow-up tests, Case 19 showed a leap upward of 22 points.

At the school for the deaf, Case 19 was graduated from high school and went on to learn his trade as linotyper. Today he is an active leader in community organizations. His four children have IQs of 103, 107, 117 and 119. His surprising history as one of the "contrast" children—but resembling that of the more fortunate "house guest" children—indeed appears to be the exception that proves the rule.

May, 1966, was the 27th anniversary of Dr. Skeels's embarrassing appearance before the American Association on Mental Deficiency. Although irony was not intended, on that anniversary Drs. Skeels and Skodak appeared before the same association—in the same city, Chicago, and at the same hotel—to report on the unique 30-year aftermath of what is now recognized as a brilliant pioneering study in child development. The report this time was widely acknowledged in the professional press and applauded by the scientific world.

One importance of the recent follow-up search, Dr. Skodak points out, is verification that the early changes in the children who were placed with the retarded adults were not merely a scientific "fluke." The gains in intelligence made by the "house guests" held fast; those children grew up to be bright, contributing members of society. The "contrast" children, after early years of neglect, deprived of stimulating experience, grew to be not only of little worth to themselves but of great cost to society.

The cost in dollars was not left unexamined by Drs. Skeels and Skodak. They calculated that the 12 children in the unfortunate contrast group had spent an aggregate of 273 years in institutions at a cost of $138,000 in public funds. They are still young; the cost to the public of these dozen souls may yet more than double. On the other hand, the "house guest" children during one year alone—1963—paid

Federal income tax bills ranging from $38 to $848.

Another important point was made by the study, and in particular by the case of the "house guest" child who was transferred back to the orphanage by a new administrator and in consequence suffered a drastic decline in IQ. That point was also recently made when a study of Project Head Start showed that gains made by children in Head Start nurseries tend to be lost by those children who go on to inadequate schools.

"It's quite evident," Dr. Skodak points out, "that we can *create* people with severe mental handicaps, and, in fact, we do. The majority of mentally handicapped children don't come from orphanages, but grow up in disadvantaged homes and are educated in inadequate schools. Maybe society has more of a responsibility for the lives of these children than we have been willing to admit."

"Our little study made its point with only twenty-five children in an orphanage a long time ago," says Dr. Skeels, who is now retired and living in a seacoast town in southern California. "But there are hundreds of thousands of biologically normal babies born to cultural deprivation, social emptiness, maternal rejection or a combination of all of these. They grow up with the makings of juvenile delinquents, patients in mental hospitals, inmates of institutions for the mentally retarded or just unproductive, unhappy people. If we can bring them the Head Start kind of experience early enough, widely enough and with adequate follow-through to make sure it sticks, we'll find that most of these children can become successful high-school and college graduates instead."

THE NATURE AND MEASUREMENT OF INTELLIGENCE

36. The Association of Ideas Among the Feeble-Minded *

Alfred Binet and Th. Simon

Until the turn of the century, tests of intelligence measured simple sensory and motor functions such as thresholds for tones, the ability to make visual discriminations, or the time required to react to a stimulus. But scores on these tests proved to be unrelated to other measures of intellectual ability such as the academic achievement of school children. In 1889, Alfred Binet, now generally regarded as the founder of modern intelligence testing, established the first psychological laboratory in France, and began a systematic investigation of intelligence. He criticized sensory-motor tests of intelligence because the simple functions they assessed were too remote from the complex intellectual processes that he believed to be involved in thinking, reasoning, and problem-solving.

* Reprinted by permission of The Williams & Wilkins Co., Baltimore, Maryland, from *The Intelligence of the Feeble-Minded*, translated by Elizabeth S. Kite, 1916. First published in *L'Année Psychologique*, 1909.

In 1904, Binet was appointed to a commission to study mental retardation among children in the public schools of Paris. He and his colleagues were concerned with the pragmatic problem of measuring intelligence so that mentally retarded children could be diagnosed and assigned to special educational classes. They devised tests to evaluate intellectual functions such as memory, comprehension, and reasoning ability. One year later, in 1905, Binet and Simon published the first general intelligence scale.

Although Binet is best known for his pioneering research on the measurement of intelligence, he was also one of the foremost authorities of his time on the subject of "feeble-mindedness," or mental retardation as it is now called. The following selection illustrates Binet's genius for devising and interpreting mental tests. In this paper, Binet and Simon compare the association of ideas in normal and mentally retarded persons. They demonstrate that retarded persons differ from normals in the *organization* of their thoughts rather than in the words they use to express them.

Our object is to discover how association of ideas among defectives is formed, and if the mechanism of the production of ideas presents in them any particular traits worthy of psychological consideration. The procedure to be followed has been described by several authors; we have made only slight changes, which, however, were quite necessary. Here is the ordinary instruction given to our subjects. "We are going to say a word, and for every word you hear you are to say one, but the word that you say must not be the same as ours." Ordinarily the directions are more precise, the word is required to be in *relation* with the word of the experimenter but we cannot make this recommendation; our imbeciles would not understand it.

The young cook of twenty-three whom we have taken as a normal subject for comparison, is very much embarrassed by the vagueness of the instructions. This young woman was constantly annoyed and dissatisfied with her replies, asking us

what she ought to say, and if her words ought to relate to those given by us or not. And certainly she was quite right in asking. Her distress showed clearly the ambiguous character of the test. Of course, we did not reply to any of her questions, we made the experiment without explaining anything, and we give below the results. The times are extremely variable, between a minimum of 2 seconds and a maximum of 18. The median value, which is here much better than the average, is 5.5." The words that she gives are in the most diverse relation to the stimulus words; but all obeyed the fundamental law of completing the sense. Sometimes it might be a definition: "serpent—a creature that stings," or an effect: "shoe—for walking; water—refreshment; sun—warmth; garden—pleasure; paper—to write." Or the whole suggested by the part: "nose—face; hair—woman;" or supplementary connection "hat—coquetry;" sometimes a familiar association "knife—bread." This logical evocation, which was in no way demanded of her, however, proves that logic is easier to follow than chance; just as a worn path is easier to follow than a direct course over the fields. We consider it worth while to give the series of replies as a standard, although necessarily it bears the stamp of individuality, and does not present so general a bearing as one could desire.

Stimulus words	Time	Reaction
Singer	14"	Actor (after a moment of embarrassment)
I run	18"	The beautiful path
Revolt	5"	War
Hat	4"	Coquetry
Bottle	7"	Liquid
Picture	6"	Landscape
Moustache	7"	Chinaman
Knife	6"	Bread
Paper	6"	Write
Hair	9"	Woman
Red	4"	Flag
Dog	2"	Four feet
Rain	8"	Bad weather
Water	4"	Refreshment
Garden	3"	Pleasure
Omelet	3.5"	Food
Shoe	4"	For walking
Syrup	4"	Sweetened liquids
Tobacco	5"	It is dried leaves

Stimulus words	Time	Reaction
The nose	2.5″	Face
Sausage	9″	Food
The sun	4″	Warmth
Soldier	4″	Army
Newspaper	2″	Reading
Serpent	7″	A creature that stings
Misery	5″	The opposite of luxury
Justice	17″	To give what is right
Virtue	11″	It is a quality
Snow	5″	Rain
Handkerchief ..	7″	Cloth

Maximum time 18″, minimum time 2″. Median time 5.5″.

Our defectives are distinguished from normals by many characteristics, first of all by their general attitude. We have said that our normal subject was troubled and felt quite embarrassed. This embarrassment, so characteristic of a normal person who is a novice, was not in the least shared by our imbeciles, who showed the greatest serenity and evident satisfaction in all their replies.

All began by simply repeating the stimulus word; if no observation had been made to them they would have continued the repetition, which has no interest whatever. It is curious, but it is not peculiar to defectives. We have sometimes encountered normals in previous experiments who with good faith repeated the stimulus word without adding anything and who did not perceive the absurdity of this repetition.

We intervene after a certain time and urge our defectives to use a different word from the one pronounced by us. Sometimes it is necessary to insist quite a little in order to break up this habit. Some are embarrassed. They do not know what to say. For a time they are satisfied to repeat the words which they have already used at the beginning of the experiment; but this stock is soon exhausted; they must draw new words from their imagination. The words they find vary greatly and depend upon their mental level.

Let us first mention a high grade imbecile girl, Duguet. After having passed the preliminary period of repetition, which we have just described, she cites words which have no relation with ours, and

which probably she prepared beforehand. It can easily be seen because she always chooses from the same category of objects, either the names of garments or the names of objects present before her. She seems to have hesitated a little before following this direction; but it becomes evident towards the last, and the reaction times are very short, which is proof that she has prepared the word of reply.

Stimulus words	Time	Reaction
Singer	3″	Singer
I run	1″	I run
Revolt	2″	Revolt
Hat	8″	Hat

New explanations are given so that the subject may lose the habit of repeating.

Stimulus words	Time	Reaction
Bottle	35″	Don't know—ah—the table
Picture	4″	Chair
Moustache	4″	Bottle
Knife	4″	Plate
Paper	4″	Fork
Hair	3″	Knife
Red	5″	Spoon
Dog	5″	Carafe
Rain	4″	Umbrella
Water	4″	A boat
Garden	5″	Dress
Omelet	8″	Light
Shoe	3″	Carpet
Syrup	4″	On the floor
Tobacco	1.5″	Hat
Sausage	1″	A bed
Sun	16″	Hat
Soldier	2″	Dress
Newspaper	2″	Apron
Serpent	6″	Boot maker
Misery	1″	Stockings
Justice	2″	Slipper
Virtue	1″	Carpet
The snow	2″	The door
Handkerchief ..	3″	Square

Maximum time 35″, minimum time 1″, Medium time 3.5″.

From time to time, e.g., "rain" and "water," a slight associative influence let itself be felt, but more often there is no connection, as is seen with such couples as misery—stockings; justice—slipper. This absence of relation is quite characteristic. A normal would never think of replying thus, for he would realize that it rendered the experiment quite useless; at least, he would not unless as a result of an attitude of mockery. In the case of Duguet, the result proves the weakness of the association of words; the word pronounced by us does not stand out because she is looking for another. The times are shorter than those of a normal but we have explained the reason.

A middle grade imbecile, Victor, shows a form of transition. He commences like Duguet, by giving words without bearing upon those pronounced; then, beginning with the word tobacco, he changes his tactics. The associative influence of the words makes itself felt.

Stimulus words	Time	Reaction
Singer	3″	Singer
I run	3″	I run
Revolt	3″	Revolt
Hat	0″	Hat, a cap

We urge him not to repeat the word that we have said but to find another.

Stimulus words	Time	Reaction
Bottle	7″	Belt to put around the body
Picture	6″	Table . . . . girdle, cravat
Moustache	4″	Mous- . . . . a watch
Knife	5″	Kni- . . . . knife put in the post
Paper	5″	Ah . . . . socks
Hair	7″	Ah . . . . cravat
Red	4″	Ah . . . . shirt
Dog	5″	Socks . . . . night shirt
Rain	5″	Ah . . . . night shirt
Water	5″	Drawers
Garden	4″	A spade
Omelet	5″	A wheelbarrow to gather dirt
Shoe	5″	Spade—to dig
Syrup	5″	Rake—to gather dirt
Tobacco	4″	Tobacco to smoke in a pipe
The nose	4″	To put tobacco in his pipe
Sausage	0″	Sausage to light the pipe and tinder to light the pipe
The sun	4″	The sun to set up there
Soldier	4″	I never was a soldier
Newspaper	4″	Newspaper. To read the newspaper in bed
Serpent	4″	Siphon (?)
Misery	2″	Misery, yes (makes sorrowful countenance)
Justice	4″	Just for the saving (he means for the saving bank)
Virtue	8″	To put on ground, to eat in summer (understood lettuce, similar sound in French "vertu—laitue")
Snow	4″	The snow . . . . to fall on the world
Handkerchief	4″	To blow (gesture)

Maximum time 8″. Minimum time 2″. Median time 4″.

Victor's times are short, shorter than those of our normal (4″ instead of 5.5″). One might remark that the nature of his associations does not consist in grouping beside the spoken word a word having an entirely different sense, for instance, red-black, sun-moon, etc. Victor rather tends to develop the idea given to him, but he naturally employs very elementary processes.

With Albert, a high grade imbecile, after the preliminary period of repetition, all at once there is produced the association of ideas. There are here veritable associations, with heterogeneity of the elements. Let the reader judge.

Stimulus words	Time	Reaction
Singer		Singer
I run		I run
Revolt		Revolt
Hat		Hat
Bottle		Hat
Picture		Bottle
Moustache	12″	Cravat
Knife	5″	Fork
Paper	10″	Picture
Hair	9″	The head
Red	9″	White
Dog	5″	Cat
Rain		Ression (?)
Water	13″	The Seine
Garden	30″	There are flowers
Omelet	5″	Some eggs
Shoe	5″	Eggs
Syrup	5″	Cod liver oil
Tobacco	5″	Cigarette
The nose		Needles (probably had understood thimble (le nez . . . . le dé)
Sausage	8″	Pudding
The sun	5″	The moon
Soldier	5″	Military
Newspaper	35″	Magazine
Serpent	5″	serpe (pruning hook)
Misery	50″	Anger (?)

Stimulus words	Time	Reaction
Justice		The Justice
Virtue		Don't know what to say
The snow		The snow it falls, the snow
Handkerchief	20″	To blow one's nose

Maximum time 50″. Minimum time 5″. Median time 8″.

Albert's times are longer. The associations are of such ordinary character, or rather, so elementary, that one might have foreseen many of them. We have here results that do not seem to us clearly subnormal. An experimenter who was not forewarned might have attributed them to a normal. We will finish with the association of ideas of Griffon, a moron. These seem to us to be of an absolutely normal level, except for one or two improprieties of term or of thought.

Stimulus words	Time	Reaction
Singer	3″	Singer
I run	5″	To walk
Revolt	6″	Someone who jostles
Hat	7″	Hatter
Bottle	7″	Broken glass
Picture	3″	Images which represent landscapes
Moustache	6″	A man who has a moustache
Knife	12″	Which is made with a wooden handle
Paper	7″	It is made with rags from the factory
Hair	7″	Which is on the head of a man
Red	13″	A cloth that is red
Dog	6″	An animal that is cross
Rain	3″	That falls on the earth
Water	7″	Which is found in springs
Garden		Which is found in the fields
Omelet	3″	Which is made of eggs
Shoe	7″	Which is made of leather
Syrup	5″	Which is made in factories
Tobacco	7″	Which is made with tobacco from the Caroline Islands
The nose	7″	Which is above the chin
Sausage	7″	Which is made with fat of pork
The sun	10″	Which makes the earth go
Soldier	10″	Represents the earth
Newspaper	5″	Which is made in the printing shop
Serpent	6″	Which is found in the fields

Misery	2″	A man who is unhappy
Virtue	8″	A man who is good
The snow	3″	That falls on the earth
Handkerchief	6″	Which is made with rags

Maximum time 13″. Minimum time 2″. Median time 7″.

The replies of Griffon have the form of appreciations, of judgment, of definitions, much more than true associations. The times are quite long.

Let us sum up, now, what these experiments upon the association of ideas have taught us. The difference between the defective and the normal is seen constantly in the attitude taken, particularly in the beginning of the experiment. While the normal subject is embarrassed and protests that he does not know what is required of him, the imbecile and the moron, adapt themselves at once to the instructions of the new experiment. There is in this uneasiness at the beginning a mental state of higher order, which unfortunately cannot be written down with the replies of the subject, and which, so to speak, evaporates. It is a pity, for it forms a most characteristic difference. The length of the reaction times is also very significant. If we take the median times, we can see they are very much shorter with the defectives who are of low level, or who give reactions of an inferior quality; let us put these median times into a series; we have 3.5″–4″–8″–7″. This series is too short for us to be able to interpret it safely. We venture, however, to conclude from it that the time depends upon the more or less elementary character of the reaction, and that, considered separately, the reaction time signifies nothing more than the time required to do a certain problem when we are not told in what the problem consists. Let us add that similar studies upon eight normal school children, aged from ten to twelve years, have furnished us with the following median times, which represent each about thirty association experiments: 4″–5.3″–5.7″–6.7″–7.3″–7.5″–12.1″–19″ of which the median would be 7. This is a new argument to demonstrate that the association times are longer with normals than with imbeciles, without doubt because the former have more ideas to choose from. From this we can draw the following important conclusion in regard to the ideation of the imbecile.

When a normal reflects upon something, he does not content himself with evoking an image, but he has an end towards which he tends, and he tries to adjust his images to this end, and for this adjustment he chooses among his images, he seeks for, he rejects, and he retains. This work of selection is one in which the intelligence of the agent manifests itself. When asked to say a word after the word pronounced, he seeks more or less to find a suitable word; this causes frequent embarrassment and often rather long times before replying. With imbeciles, the work of ideation seems to be much more simple. The imbecile probably says the first word that comes to his mind; at all events if he rejects certain words as inappropriate, this work of selec-

tion is very short, very restricted; he does not possess much choice of words, he is not embarrassed, and consequently the work is more elementary, more rapid. If one gave a prize for rapidity it is the imbeciles who would win. As to the nature of the associations, it is evident that it can serve to distinguish only extremely low defectives like Victor and Duguet. We have seen that with them that which we have called "the associative action of words" does not take place for some time; but with Albert and with Griffon, the association formed present nothing peculiar, that is have no fixed relation to deficiency. One can conclude from this that it is not by the word of the inner language that the defective is differentiated from the normal; it is by the sentence rather than by the word; by the thought rather than by the image; by the organization rather than by the nature of the elements which are to be organized.

37. Piaget's Conception of Intelligence *

J. McV. Hunt

The crucial contribution of experience to intellectual development has now been amply demonstrated and, as a result, a conception of intelligence has emerged that emphasizes the continuous adaptive interaction between man and his environment. One of the outstanding contributors to this modern view of intelligence is Jean Piaget (Pee-ah-zhay). His work at the Rousseau Institute in Switzerland has been concerned with the development of logical thinking in children.

Piaget does not carry out experiments in the manner that has become characteristic of American psychologists who typically observe the performance of large groups of children on selected tasks. Instead, he makes frequent observations of the behavior of a few children in a variety of situations. Piaget's method consists of confronting a child with a problem and observing how the child attempts to solve it. As a check on the correctness of his interpretations, he varies the problem and the circumstances of his observations.

In the next selection, J. McV. Hunt reviews Piaget's major concepts and provides examples of the observational material on which Piaget's theories of intelligence are based. As noted by Professor Hunt, the thought processes that Piaget infers from his observation of children's

* Excerpted by permission of the author and the publisher from Chapter 5 of J. McV. Hunt, *Intelligence and Experience.* Copyright © 1961 The Ronald Press Company, New York.

problem-solving behavior are analogous in many respects to the procedures for processing information that are to be found in modern electronic computers.

A conception of intelligence as problem-solving capacity based on a hierarchical organization of symbolic representations and information-processing strategies deriving to a considerable degree from past experience, has been emerging from several sources. These sources include observations of human behavior in solving problems, the programming of electronic computers, and neuropsychology. It is interesting, therefore, to find such a conception coming also from Piaget's observations of the development of intelligence in children. The various lines of evidence appear to be coalescing to flow in one direction, a direction that makes interaction between the environment and the organism continuous. Piaget's observations of the homely interactions of the child with his everyday environment demonstrate empirically the formation of a vertical hierarchy of operations for the processing of information to guide action. His observations begin to show what these concepts of a vertical hierarchy of information-processing operations and a continuous interaction between the organism and the environment mean empirically in human development, where they most need to be understood.

For more than 30 years, Piaget and his collaborators at the Rousseau Institute in Geneva, Switzerland have been studying the development of intellectual functions and logic in children. Although he has not typically done "experiments" in the American manner, Piaget is a master at developing the theoretical implications of his observations. Moreover, his life's program constitutes research in the grand manner, both in scope and implications.

In his early studies of the child's language and thought (1932), judgment and reasoning (1924), conception of the world (1926), conception of physical causality (1927), and moral judgment (1932), Piaget based his observations almost completely on the language behavior of pairs of children in free-school situations. Out of this method came the well-known distinctions between egocentric and social language, between prelogical thinking and reasoning, and between animistic and symbolic forms of thinking. This portion of his work, and especially his propositions about the prevalence and ages of egocentric thought in children, have been severely criticized, and Piaget (1953a) has admitted that "my method of studying logic in the child was much too verbal at first, dealing particularly with the relation between thought and language" (p. 32).

Beginning, however, with his observation of the early origins of intelligence and reality constructions in his own children, Piaget (1936, 1937) revised his method of observation to focus on the child's actions in manipulating objects. He varied the objects and their arrangement to check his own interpretation of what central processes were implied by the child's actions. With older children he has set practical tasks and asked precise questions about the events taking place or about their own action.

PIAGET'S GENERAL CONCEPTIONS

Piaget (1936, 1947) conceives the adaptive interaction between organism and environment to involve two complementary processes, corresponding to inner organization and outer adaptation, which he calls *assimilation* and *accommodation*. Although such inclusiveness may be questioned, Piaget conceives these processes as common to both the physiological and psychological domains.

Assimilation occurs whenever an organism utilizes something from the environment and incorporates it. In the biochemical domain, it is exemplified by the ingestion of food which gradually transforms the somatic structures. In the psychological domain, assimilation operates whenever the organism sees something new in terms of something familiar, whenever it acts in a new situation as it has acted in other situations in the past, whenever it invests anything with familiarity (recognition), importance, or value. Thus, assimilation includes the phenomena which Pavlov (1927) called "conditioning," and also those which Hull (1943) and others have termed "stimulus generalization" and "response generalization." But where these terms have referred to associative or connective relations between observed stimuli and responses, Piaget takes the quite different view that the organism always acts in terms of the centrally organized, Gestalt-like structures which it has present (analogue of Hull's [1943] response repertoire). Moreover, these structures, which are observed as repeatable and generalizable pieces of behavior termed *schemata* and which are presumably mediated by neurophysiological processes of no immediate concern to psychology, warp receptor inputs to their own pattern and nature. It is thus that Piaget (1947) speaks of assimilation as "the action of the organism on surrounding objects, insofar as this action depends on previous behavior involving the same or similar objects" (p. 7).

Accommodation, the process complementary to assimilation, operates as the variations in environmental circumstances demand coping which modifies existing schemata. It is thus that the environmental circumstances act upon the organism, not by merely evoking a fixed response, not by getting a passive submission to circumstances, but rather by modifying the action or *schema* affecting them.

In the course of this dual adaptive process of assimilation and accommodation the ready-made reflexive schemata of the newborn infant become progressively transformed through differentiations and coordinations into the logical "organizations" (or operations for information-processing) of adult intelligence. This is the epigenesis of mind. As it proceeds, the child becomes capable of taking account of stimuli more

and more remote from him in space and time, and also of resorting to more and more composite and indirect modes of solving problems.[1] In this sense, "life is a continuous creation of increasingly complex forms and a progressive adaptation of these forms to the environment" (1936, p. 3).

The picture of the development of intelligence which emerges from the observations and experiments of Piaget and his collaborators is one of continuous transformations in the "organizations" or "structures" of intelligence. At birth the only "organizations" available are the congenital sensorimotor schemata, reflexes or instincts. The first period of intellectual development, the *sensorimotor*, lasts from birth till the child is roughly between 18 months and two years old. The reflexive sensorimotor schemata are generalized, coordinated with each other, and differentiated to become the elementary operations of intelligence which begin to be internalized and which correspond to the problem-solving abilities of sub-human animals. During this period, the child creates through his continual adaptive accommodations and assimilations, in six stages, such operations as "intentions," "means-end" differentiations, and the interest in novelty (Piaget, 1936). On the side of constructing reality, the child also develops the beginnings of interiorized schemata, if not actual concepts, for such elements as the permanence of the object, space, causality, and time (Piaget, 1937).

The second period of concrete operations in intellectual development, beginning when the child is about 18 months or two years old, lasts till he is 11 or 12 years

---

[1] Although Piaget (1947, p. 6) agrees that affective life can be distinguished from intellectual life, he regards them as inseparable because "all interaction with the environment involves both a structuring and a valuation . . . we cannot reason, even in pure mathematics, without experiencing certain feelings, and conversely, no affect can exist without a minimum of understanding or of discrimination." He concentrates on the intellectual aspect in his writings. These are the subject matter of this review, but elsewhere the writer (1960) attempts to utilize the implications of Piaget's observations for a theory of motivation.

old. It contains, first, a *preconceptual* phase during which symbols are constructed. This lasts to about four years of age, and during it the child's activity is dominated by symbolic play, which imitates and represents what he has seen others do, and by the learning of language. The accommodations forced by the variation in the models imitated along with the assimilations resulting from repetitions of the play-activities gradually create a store of central processes which symbolize the actions imitated (Piaget, 1945). As the images are established, the child acquires verbal signs for those which correspond to the collective system of signs comprising language. At this point the child comes under dual interaction with the environment, i.e., with the world of things and the world of people. The child's action-images greatly extend the scope of his mental operation beyond the range of immediate action and momentary perception, and they also speed up his mental activity, for the sensorimotor action is limited by the concrete sequence of perceptions and actions. This period contains, second, an *intuitive* phase. This is a phase of transition that lasts till the child is seven or eight years old. In the course of his manipulations and social communications, he is extending, differentiating, and combining his action-images and simultaneously correcting his intuitive impressions of reality (space, causality, and time). It contains, third, the phase of *concrete operations*. As the child interacts repeatedly with things and people, his central processes become more and more autonomous. Piaget (1945, 1947) speaks of his thought becoming "decentred" from perception and action. With greater autonomy of central processes come both differentiations and coordinations, or groupings, of the action-images into systems which permit classifying, ordering in series, numbering. These "concrete groupings" bring to the child's thought the properties of logical "groupings" or mathematical "groups." Piaget (1953) sees logic as the reflection of thought, and he finds in logical

operations the models that serve to explain what the child can and cannot do at various levels of development. The acquisition of these "concrete operations," which may be seen as analogues of both Harlow's (1949) "learning sets" and the operations for information-processing (Newell, Shaw, & Simon, 1958), bring a distinctive change in the child's concrete conceptions of quantity, space, causality, and time. This phase, and with it the second period, ends as the child spontaneously masters the multiplicative compensations that underlie the proportionality schema and the conservation of volume at about 11 or 12 years of age (Inhelder & Piaget, 1955).

The third period of *formal operations* starts at about 11 or 12 years when the child begins to group or systematize his concrete operations (classifications, serial ordering, correspondences, etc.) and thereby also to consider all possible combinations in each case. This period is marked by the beginning of ability to classify, order, enumerate, etc., in verbal propositions. In the period from age 11 or 12 to age 15 or 16, the child achieves the final steps of "decentring" and "reversibility" as his central processes become sufficiently autonomous to permit him to operate with the sum total of possibilities rather than merely the empirical situation. The child, become essentially adult, can now operate with the *form* of an argument while ignoring its *empirical content*. He can use systems of operations which permit him to deal with proportionality and probability. He can also use combinatorial analyses based on the logical structures which mathematicians call *lattices*. With these new-found thought structures, he need no longer confine his attention to existing reality. Not only do the hypothetico-deductive procedures of science and logic open to him, but he becomes concerned socially with seeing the world as it might better be and enters the roles of critic and social reformer.

It should be noted that in this picture of the epigenesis of the behavioral and thought structures comprising intelligence, those of each phase become incorporated and reorganized in the subsequent phase. The result is something analogous to the hierarchical arrangement of information-processes that have been postulated by the programmers of electronic computers (Newell, Shaw, & Simon, 1958) and that are beginning to be found within the brain (Pribram, 1960). Consider now the observational basis for this developmental picture. At about the beginning of the second month, Piaget observed variations in the sucking of his children. These activities occurred while the child manifested an expression of contentment. They included such acquired elaborations of sucking as the systematic protrusion of the tongue, which was accompanied later with licking the lips, actions with the saliva, and the sucking of the thumb. For instance, when Laurent was 30 days of age, Piaget observed him lying awake making sucking-like movements. Three days later, Laurent alternated between a sucking-like movement and passing his tongue over the lower lip. Two weeks later, his skill in this activity had increased, and he added grimacing as well as making a clapping sound when quickly closing his mouth after such exercises. Three more weeks, and Laurent added playing with his saliva, "letting it accumulate within his half-open lips and then abruptly swallowing it" (1936, pp. 51-52). A reciprocal coordination of arm movements and sucking came gradually. As the thumb and fingers came in contact with Laurent's face, his mouth grasped them. As thumb and fingers were thus discovered and rediscovered, a coordination between the arm movement and the sucking gradually emerged. In this process, the head could be observed to turn toward the hand, while the hand, in turn, moved irregularly toward the mouth. With repetition this coordination was perfected, and a circular response had resulted in an accommodative coordination of arm motion and thumb-sucking.

In the course of repeating routines, various positional, tactile, acoustic, and visual stimuli became assimilated into the ready-made schemata. These assimilations correspond to the phenomena of conditioning and stimulus generalization. For instance, by his ninth day, Laurent, who lay asleep in his crib, opened his mouth and began sucking the moment he was placed on his mother's bed. Later, being picked up by the nurse started both sucking and groping behavior. At three months of age, both Laurent and Lucienne stopped crying and made sucking motions at the sight of their mother unfastening her dress for nursing. At approximately five months, Jacqueline opened her mouth as soon as she saw the bottle. By seven months, she opened her mouth in one fashion at the sight of a bottle and in another fashion at the sight of a spoon. An accommodative differentiation was clearly evident.

A similar course of development appears for looking and its coordinations. Shortly after the child can follow a moving light by turning his head in coordination with his eye movements, objects of moderate brilliance are followed. At this point, Piaget observed his children staring at one object and then another for minutes at a time. When such staring behavior was in evidence, sucking-like movements and arm movements were absent. Just as the sucking schema generalizes from the breast to assimilate various other objects and signals, the looking schema generalizes. When several objects were hung from the hood of the bassinet, Piaget's children alternately examined one after the other. When new sights appeared, such as having the toys on the hood of the bassinet shaken, they looked with excited expressions, and they would actively look again and again as if attempting to repeat the experience by returning their gaze to the hood.

Reciprocal coordination between looking and hand movements grew directly out of these acquired elaborations and generalizations of looking to new objects. Such watching coordinations came about gradually, as is illustrated in the following quoted observation:

Observation 62: At age two months and four days, Laurent by chance discovers his right index finger and looks at it briefly. At two months and 11 days, he inspects for a moment his right hand, perceived by chance. At two months 14 days, he looks three times in succession at his left hand and chiefly at his raised index finger. At two months 17 days, he follows the spontaneous movement of his hand for a moment, and then he examines it several times while it searches for his nose or rubs his eye. At two months 19 days (please note for subsequent reference), he smiles at the same hand after having contemplated it 11 times in succession. I then put his hand in a bandage; as soon as I detach it (half an hour later) it returns to the visual field and Laurent again smiles at it. The same day he looks very attentively at his two clasped hands. At age two months and 21 days, he holds his two fists in the air and looks at the left one, after which he slowly brings it towards his face and rubs his nose with it, and then his eyes. A moment later the left hand again approaches his face, he looks at it and touches his nose. He recommences and laughs five or six times in succession while moving the left hand to his nose. He seems to laugh before the hand moves, but looking has no influence on the movement. Age two months and 24 days: at last looking acts on the orientation of the hands which tend to remain in the visual field (1936, pp. 96–97).

In the course of this development, the visual schema has assimilated the manual schema. This is to say that the eye tries to follow what the hand does, but the hand appears not to realize what the eye sees. Gradually, the accommodative effort of trying to see the hand brings the hand under visual control, and the child is thereby enabled to grasp the objects he sees. Something looked at becomes something to grasp. Similarly, as arm movements and the sucking become coordinated, as already noted, anything grasped becomes something to suck.

A similar coordination occurs between hearing and looking. Sounds heard gradually become something to look at. Consider the following abridged course of observations of Jacqueline:

Observation 43: At age one month, Jacqueline still limits herself to interrupting her crying when she hears an agreeable voice or sound, but she does not try to mark the sound. At one month, six days, same reaction. At one month 10 days, on the other hand, Jacqueline begins to smile at the voice. . . . At two months 12 days, Jacqueline turns her head to the side whence the sound comes. For example, on hearing my voice behind her, she turns in the right direction. At two months, 26 days, she localizes the source of sound quite accurately with her glance. She searches until she finds the person who is speaking, but it is difficult to say whether she identifies the source of the sound or whether this is simply accommodation to the sound (1936, pp. 80–81).

Development in Recognition

Recognition becomes, at this fourth stage, a genuine recognition of sign meanings. Each of Piaget's stages brings a characteristic type of meaning. At the first reflexive stage, the child recognizes whether he is merely sucking the skin of the breast or is really nursing the nipple by whether or not he is getting milk and swallowing. At the second stage, the recognition of sensory impressions is indicated by their evoking the act which they signify or by a smile. At the third stage, the recognition of an object may be shown by the child merely outlining the schema with which it is assimilated. At this fourth stage, the child's behavior indicates that he foresees an event which is quite independent of his own action. Consider these illustrations:

Observation 134: At age nine months 16 days, Jacqueline discovers complex signs in connection with her meal. She likes the grape juice in the glass, but not the soup in a bowl. She watches her mother's activity. When the spoon comes out of the glass she opens her mouth wide, whereas when the spoon comes from the bowl, her mouth remains closed. Her mother tried to lead her to make a mistake by taking a spoon from the bowl and passing it by the glass before offering it to Jacqueline. But she is not fooled. . . . At age nine months 18 days, Jacqueline no longer needs to look at the spoon. She notes by the sound whether the spoonful comes from the glass or the bowl and obstinately closes her mouth in the latter case. . . .

At age 11 months 15 days, Jacqueline cries as soon as her mother puts her hat on. This is not due to fear of the strangeness of seeing mother in a hat, but is due rather to the fact that "mother in a hat" signifies that mother is departing (1936, pp. 249–50).

In both of these instances, Jacqueline's behavior indicates that she recognizes what is coming even though the spoon and mother-in-a-hat have nothing to do with her own actions-in-progress at the time these signs are perceived.

The child's behavior in relation to phenomena which are new to him changes at this fourth stage. Whereas, at the beginning of the third stage a new obstacle only served to arrest his activity until such time as the child could find a way to utilize the object as an aliment for his habitual schemata, the child now not only looks at new objects for a much longer time, but he also engages in a series of exploratory movements relating to the object rather than to himself.

Discovery of New Means through Active Experimentation

Active experimentation is commonly motivated by the child's developing interest in novelty, and it leads to the discovery of new means. This process is to the tertiary circular reactions what the application of familiar means to new situations was to the secondary circular reactions. In these activities, the child begins to manifest the constructive, original element characteristic of intelligence, an element that is completely missed in the assumption of predetermined development and that is also largely missed in the stimulus-response theory of behavior.

One of the first manifestations of this original, constructive, discovering intelligence that Piaget observed in his children was what he calls "the behavior pattern of the support." Consider the following series of observations:

From Observation 148: Until age 10 months and 16 days, Laurent has not understood the relation "placed upon," hence the relation existing between an object and its support. . . . Numerous experiments repeated between ages seven months and 29 days and 10 months and 16 days have revealed that Laurent, until the later date, has remained incapable of utilizing it systematically. At seven months and 29 days, he succeeded, once in four attempts, in drawing a cushion toward him in order to grasp a box placed upon it; at eight months and one day he behaves in the same way. . . . But there it is still only a question of a coordination of schemata, analogous to that of the fourth stage. Being unable to grasp the box directly, the child instead takes possession of the first object encountered, while subordinating this act to the persisting desire to attain the objective. The proof in this case is the existence of the following reactions: . . . when I hold the objective in the air, 20 cm. above the support, Laurent pulls the latter toward him just as though the object were placed upon it. . . .

At age 10 months 16 days, on the other hand, Laurent discovers the true relations between the support and the objective and consequently the possibility of using the former to draw the latter toward him. Here are the child's reactions:

(1) I place my watch on a big red cushion and place the cushion directly in front of the child. Laurent tries to reach the watch directly and not succeeding, he grabs the cushion which he draws toward him as before. But then, instead of letting go of the support at once, as he has hitherto done, in order to try to grasp the objective, he recommences with obvious interest, to move the cushion while looking at the watch. Everything takes place as though he noticed for the first time the relation for its own sake and studied it as such. He thus easily succeeds in grasping the watch.

(2) I then immediately attempt the following counterproof. I put two colored cushions in front of the child, of identical form and dimensions. The first is placed as before, directly in front of the child. The second is placed behind, at an angle of 45 degrees, that is to say, so that the corner of the cushion is opposite the child. This corner is placed on the first cushion but I manage to flatten the two cushions at this place, where one is partially superimposed on the other, so that the second does not protrude and is not too visible. Finally I place my watch at the other extreme end of the second cushion. Laurent, as soon as he sees the watch, stretches out his hands, then grasps the first cushion which he pulls toward him by degrees. Then, observing that the watch does not move, he examines the

place where the one cushion is superimposed on the other, and he goes straight to the second one. He grasps it by the corner, pulls it toward him over the first cushion, and takes the watch. The experiment, when repeated, yields the same result the second time.

(3) I now place the two cushions next to each other, the proximal side of the second parallel to the distal side of the first. But I superimpose the first on the second on a strip about 20 cm. wide, the watch of course being at the extremity of the second cushion. Laurent immediately pulls the first cushion but, observing that the watch is not displaced, he tries to raise this cushion to reach the second one. At a certain moment he has succeeded in raising the first cushion, but without removing it, and he holds it against his chest with his left hand while trying to pull the second one with his right hand. He finally succeeds and takes possession of the watch, thus revealing his perfect comprehension of the role of the support.

(4) Finally I place the second cushion as in (2) but sidewise, the proximal corner of the second superimposed on one of the distal corners of the first. Laurent does not make a mistake, and at once tries to reach the second cushion. These four reactions combined reveal that the relationship between the objective and its support has been acquired (1936, pp. 282–84).

This observation epitomizes what Piaget means in his own methodology by an "experiment," namely, the varying of circumstances to make certain that a given interpretation is correct.

In his observations of such groping behavior wherein various schemata are subordinated as means to other schemata as ends, Piaget (1936) notes repeatedly how those elements which have no connection with the end are gradually eliminated. This observation corresponds to Thorndike's (1911) observation of the gradual elimination of unsuccessful responses in his chickens and cats in puzzle boxes and to Osgood's (1953) point that the "heavy" elements of response are gradually eliminated. It also corresponds to Hebb's (1949) short-circuiting among phase sequences as actions become autonomous central processes. Although Piaget sometimes uses the term *trial-and-error* to describe such groping behavior, he rejects

the concept of trial-and-error because, in his observations of his children in past situations, he has seen that the so-called "error responses" are actually schemata which they have used in a variety of earlier situations. The trying of one already assimilated response after another on unfamiliar objects, which Piaget terms *groping accommodation*, was characteristic of the fourth stage.

"Deferred Imitation" and Playful Make-Believe

Empirical intelligence becomes invention through mental combination presumably as central processes become more and more autonomous and can represent overt actions. This representational capacity shows also in those activities where accommodation is primary (imitation) and in those activities where assimilation is primary (play). The evidence for this assertion comes, first, from the fact that the child can immediately imitate new models, and second, from the appearance of "deferred imitation." In "deferred imitation," the child reproduces the actions of a model that is no longer present. Consider the following illustrative observations:

Observation 52: At 16 months and three days, Jacqueline had a visit from a little boy of 18 months whom she used to see from time to time, and who, in the course of the afternoon, got into a terrible temper. He screamed as he tried to get out of a playpen and pushed it backwards, stamping his feet. Jacqueline stood watching him in amazement, never having witnessed such a scene before. The next day, she herself screamed in her playpen and tried to move it, stamping her foot lightly several times in succession. The imitation of the whole scene was most striking. Had it been immediate, it would naturally not have involved representation, but coming as it did, after an interval of more than 12 hours, it must have involved some representative or pre-representative element (1945, p. 63).

Observation 54: At this same period of the behavior of her little friend, Jacqueline began to reproduce certain words, not at the time they were uttered, but in similar situations, and without having previously imitated them.

Thus, at 16 months and eight days, Jacqueline said *in step* as she was walking, although she had never uttered these words and they had not been said in her presence immediately before. It must thus have been a case of virtual imitation becoming real imitation in an active context . . . At 16 months and 10 days, Jacqueline pointed to her mother's nose, and said *nose,* again without having uttered the word before and without hearing it immediately before (1945, p. 63).

It should be noted that these instances of deferred imitation are either independent of language, as in the case of Jacqueline's imitation of her friend's tantrum, or else actually participate in the acquisition of language. This is an important fact for the issue of whether implicit speech is the basis for all thought.

38. The I.Q. Is an Intelligent Test *

David Wechsler

Psychological tests have recently come under attack because of claims that they are unfair to culturally-deprived minority groups and constitute an unwarranted invasion of privacy. For example, intelligence tests have been banned from the records of school children in New York City because members of minority groups tend to obtain lower scores on them. As a consequence of such actions, psychologists have been called upon to defend their tests and to clarify their concepts so that they may be more readily understood by the general public.

In the next selection, David Wechsler responds to the criticism that I.Q. tests discriminate against minority groups and discusses the nature of intelligence and how it is measured. (For a discussion of psychological tests and the invasion of privacy, see the article by G. A. Kimble in Part VII of this volume.) For more than three decades, Professor Wechsler has pioneered the development of scales for the measurement of intelligence, and the family of standardized tests that bear his name are generally accepted as among the most valid measures of I.Q.

Wechsler maintains that persons from culturally-disadvantaged groups score lower on intelligence tests because the tests accurately record the unfairness of life. He then argues that current criticism of I.Q. tests is misdirected, and that the real "culprits" are poor housing, broken homes, and a lack of basic opportunities, not biased intelligence tests.

It is now two years since the New York City school system eliminated the I.Q. from pupils' records. Banned under the pressure of groups that claimed the I.Q. was unfair to the culturally deprived, it has been replaced by achievement tests. Meanwhile, a great deal of effort is being put into developing new, nonverbal scales to measure schoolchildren's abilities while eliminating the troublesome factor of language.

Neither of these substitutes is an adequate replacement for the I.Q. In my opinion, the ban was misdirected in the first place and we should restore the I.Q. to its former position as a diagnostic tool as soon as possible. The substitutes simply do not test enough of the abilities that go to make up individual intelligence.

To understand what I.Q. tests do, and why they are valuable, we must first be

* Reprinted by permission of the author and the publisher from the *New York Times Magazine,* June 26, 1966. Copyright © 1966 by The New York Times Company.

clear about what intelligence is. This is a surprisingly thorny issue. Too much depends upon how one defines intelligence. In this respect psychologists are in no better agreement than the lay public. Divergency of view stems largely from differences in emphasis on the particular abilities thought to be central to the definition one envisages. Thus, an educator may define intelligence primarily as the ability to learn, a biologist in terms of ability to adapt, a psychologist as the ability to reason abstractly and the practical layman as just common sense.

One difficulty is similar to what a physicist encounters when asked to state what he means by energy, or a biologist what he means by life. The fact is that energy and life are not tangible entities; you cannot touch them or see them under a microscope even though you are able to describe them. We know them by their effects or properties.

The same is true of general intelligence. For example, we must assume that there is something common to learning to count, avoiding danger and playing chess which makes it possible for us to say that they are evidence of intelligent behavior, as against learning to walk, being accident prone and playing bingo, which seemingly have little if anything to do with it.

Intelligence, operationally defined, is the aggregate capacity of the individual to act purposefully, to think rationally and to deal effectively with his environment. Although it is not a mere sum of intellectual abilities, the only way we can evaluate it quantitatively is by the measurement of various aspects of these abilities.

Any test is primarily a device for eliciting and evaluating a fragment of behavior. An intelligence test is one by which an examiner seeks to appraise this bit of behavior insofar as it may be called intelligent. Various abilities can be used for this purpose because manifestations of ability are the means by which a subject can communicate and demonstrate his competences. To this end it is not so much the particular ability that is tested which is important, as the degree to which it correlates with posited criteria. A test is considered a good measure of intelligence if it correlates, for example, with learning ability, ability to comprehend evidence of capacity to adjust and so on. If it does so to a satisfactory degree it is said to be valid. But even when a test has been established as valid, there still remains a question: For what class of subjects is it valid? The answer will depend in a large measure upon the population on which the test was standardized—for example, middle-class white children, Southern Negro children or recently arrived Puerto Ricans.

Thus I.Q. tests are attacked on the ground that they are overweighted with items depending on verbal ability and academic information. Individuals with limited educational backgrounds are obviously penalized, and non-English-speaking subjects are admittedly incapable of taking the tests at all. This is an important stricture and test makers, contrary to some opinion, are fully aware of it. One way of "solving" the problem would be to provide separate normal or average scores for different populations, but apart from the practical difficulty of obtaining such norms, there is always the stricture that they bypass rather than meet the central issue. A compromise approach is practiced in some school systems, where intelligence tests continue to be used—under the more acceptable name of "aptitude tests."

Almost from the start, psychologists have sought to cope with the problem of literacy and language disability by devising nonverbal tests of intelligence. Thus, soon after the Binet tests were introduced more than a half-century ago, two American psychologists, Pintner and Paterson, developed the Non-Language Individual Performance Scale for non-English-speaking subjects. Similarly, when the Army Alpha (the main verbal test of World War I) was devised for the military services, a companion nonverbal test (the Army Beta) was prepared along with it.

The Pintner-Paterson scale required the subject to give evidence of his capacities by filling in appropriate missing parts on familiar pictures, putting together form boards, learning to associate signs with symbols, etc. The Army Beta consisted of such tasks as following mazes, reproducing picture designs, counting cubes, etc.—with directions presented to the subject by gesture or mime.

Many similar tests—the so-called "culture-free" or "culture-fair" tests—have followed. The most recent one reported is the Johns Hopkins Perceptual Test devised by Dr. Leon Rosenberg and associates at the Johns Hopkins School of Medicine. This test was initially developed for children who did not speak or who were handicapped by certain functional or organic disorders; it has also been recommended as a more effective intelligence test for the very young and for culturally deprived children.

The Johns Hopkins Perceptual Test consists of a series of designs from which a child is asked to choose appropriate patterns to match others shown to him. Its primary merit is that it eliminates the factor of language. It is also claimed to be less dependent than verbal tests upon acquired skills, which, of course, depend to some extent upon a child's environmental experience. But this test, like other performance tests, does not measure a sufficient number of the abilities that go to make up the total picture of intelligent behavior.

Contrary to claims, the results of performance tests have been generally disappointing. The findings indicate that while they may be useful in certain situations, and for certain diagnostic groups, they prove quite unsatisfactory as alternates for verbal scales. They correlate poorly with verbal aptitudes and are poor prognosticators of over-all learning ability as well as school achievement. Above all, they have turned out to be neither culture-free nor culture-fair.

Culture-free tests fail to attain their end because, in the first place, the items usually employed are themselves subject to particular environmental experiences. A circle in one place may be associated with the sun, in another with a copper coin, in still another with a wheel. In some places a dog is a pet, in others a detested animal. Pictures, in the long run, are just symbols and these may be as difficult to understand and recognize as words; they have to be interpreted, as anyone who has attempted to learn sign language knows. Putting together blocks may be a challenge or a threat, working fast a sign of carelessness or an incentive to competition. Nonverbal, even more than verbal tests, need to be related to particular environments and, from a practical point of view, are both limited in range and difficult to contrive.

Finally, many performance items when increased in difficulty tend to become measures of special abilities rather than having any significant correlation with over-all measures of intelligence. Thus, while tests of visual motor coordination may be useful items on intelligence tests for young children they are no longer effective at later ages. Copying a diamond is a good test at the 7-year level, but whether a child of 12 can reproduce a complicated design has little to do with his general intelligence and represents at most a special ability.

The effect of culture on test performance is a subject that demands serious concern, but here one deals with the problem of what one understands by the word "culture." In the United States there is a strong trend among contemporary writers to identify the term with socio-economic levels. This is in contrast to the historic and broader meaning of the term, which covers all human as well as environmental influences that serve to characterize the intellectual and moral status of a civilization.

Not all the poor are culturally deprived. Although standards may differ widely, "culturally different" does not mean "culturally deprived." The Jews and Italians who lived on the Lower East Side had their culture, and so have the Negroes in the slums of Harlem. They differ widely in respect to almost any variable one might employ, and culture is no exception. What this implies is that "culture" no more than color of skin should be a basis for assessing individuals.

The comments relating to the question of cultural impact apply with equal force to the problem of racial and national differences. One may start with the hypothesis that such differences exist and not necessarily be overwhelmed by their importance. This, in the writer's opinion, is a reasonable position.

This opinion is based on studies done in the field and, in particular, on data from World War I and World War II United States Armed Forces testing programs. The data from World War I included not only tables for the over-all draft population but for a great many subgroupings. Among these were separate test-score summaries according to national origin of the draftees, and a particularly detailed one comparing Negroes and whites. As might have been expected, differences between groups compared were found, and as might also have been expected invidious comparisons were immediately made and exploited. Particularly emphasized were the lower scores made by Negroes as compared with those made by white soldiers. Neglected, on the other hand, were the differences found between occupational levels and the more general ones between urban and rural populations.

It was not too difficult to correct the erroneous inferences made by the racists. But, in disposing of the racial claims, some authors went much beyond what the data warranted. Eventually, statements were made that other test findings revealed no significant differences between any national or racial groups—a fact which is equally questionable, and in any event still needs to be demonstrated. In the author's opinion, national and racial differences do exist—probably of both genetic and environmental origins, in varying degree. But the fact is that these differences are not large or relevant in the individual case.

We now come to the biggest bugaboo of intelligence testing—the I.Q. itself. The scientific literature on it is as large as its assailants are numerous. It has been attacked by educators, parents, writers of popular articles and politicians. During the Korean War it was investigated by Congress. Now that we are once more having trouble with draft quotas, the I.Q. will most likely be investigated again. It is doubtful whether the I.Q. can be brought into good grace at this time, but perhaps much of the fire sparked by the I.Q. can be quenched by an objective explanation of what it really is.

An I.Q. is just a measure of relative brightness. It merely asserts that, compared with persons of his own age group, an individual has attained a certain rank on a particular intelligence test. For example, a 10-year-old takes the Stanford-Binet test and attains a certain score, which happens to be that for the statistically average 8-year-old. We then divide the child's mental age (8) by his chronological age (10) and obtain a quotient, which we multiply by 100 simply to remove the inconvenience of decimal points. The result is called the Intelligence Quotient (or I.Q.) —in this case, 80. This particular figure tells us that, as compared with others in his age group, the child has performed below normal (which would be 100).

When this procedure of comparative grading is applied to a geography or bookkeeping test—when a teacher apportions class grades on a bell curve or a sliding scale—nobody gets excited. But when it is used with a mental test the reaction is quite different.

Opposition is generally focused not on the way that I.Q.'s are computed, but, more pointedly, on the way they are interpreted and utilized. One interpretation that has caused understandable concern is the notion that a person is "born with" an I.Q. which remains immutable. This is an allegation proclaimed by those who are opposed to the I.Q. rather than a view maintained by psychologists. What is asserted by psychologists, and supported by test-retest findings, is that I.Q.'s once accurately established are not likely to vary to any considerable degree. This does not mean that an I.Q. never changes, or that the conditions under which it was obtained may not have affected its validity.

The so-called constancy of the I.Q. is relative, but compared with other commonly used indexes, it is surprisingly stable. It is much more stable, for instance, than an individual's electrocardiogram or his basal metabolism level, which are accepted without question.

There are always exceptional cases which cannot be overlooked or bypassed. But one does not throw out the baby with the bath water. When for any reason a subject's I.Q. is suspect, the sensible thing to do is to have him retested. I.Q.'s, unlike the laws of the Medes and the Persians, are not irrevocable, but they should be respected.

While retest studies show that I.Q.'s are relatively stable, they also reveal that in individual cases large changes may occur —as much as 20 points or more. Thus, conceivably, an individual could move from the "dull normal" group to "average," or vice versa.

Much depends upon the age at which the original test was administered and the interval between testings. In general, I.Q.'s obtained before the age of 4 or 5 are more likely to show discrepancies between test and retest; those in the middle years least. Discrepancies are also likely to be larger as the intervals between retest increase. All this evidence points to reasons for not making a definitive intelligence classifica-

tion on the basis of a single test, and more especially on one administered at an early age. This precaution is necessary not because the tests are unreliable but because rates of mental maturity are often factors that have to be taken into account. Such variations tend not only to penalize slow developers but also to overrate early bloomers.

Various skills are required for effective test performance at different age levels. The fact that they are not present at a particular age level does not indicate that a child who lacks them is necessarily stunted. It may only be that these skills have not as yet emerged. Early training has a bearing on test readiness, but it is not true that if a child has not had this training at one age, he will not develop the skills required at a later age. On the other hand, deliberately teaching a child skills in order to have him "pass" an intelligence test, as now seems to be the vogue, is not the answer to acquiring a high I.Q.

An important conclusion to be drawn from the above is that more, rather than less, testing is needed. Unfortunately, when this is suggested, one encounters the objection that extended testing programs in public schools would be too costly. The expensiveness of school testing has been greatly exaggerated, especially when considered in relation to the over-all cost of keeping a child in school (an average of $600 to $700 per child per year in most parts of the country).

Particularly neglected is the individual intelligence examination, which at present is administered in most public schools only to "problem cases." In the author's opinion, an individual intelligence examination ought to be given to all children as they enter school. Most private schools require such an examination, and there is good reason why the public schools should also provide it.

Allowing $50 per examination administered once over a four-year period, the cost would be a minuscule addition to the school's budget. In return, a systematic individual examination could serve as a means of evaluating a child's assets and liabilities before he was subjected to the hazards of arbitrary placement. Finally, it must be borne in mind that intelligence tests are intended as a means not merely for detecting the intellectually retarded, but also for discovering the intellectually gifted.

In discussions of the merits and limitations of intelligence tests, one important aspect, frequently overlooked, is their basic aim. This objective is most effectively summed up in the late Prof. Irving Lorge's definition of what intelligence tests aim to measure—namely, "the ability to learn and to solve the tasks required by a particular environment."

This definition implies a multiple approach to the concept of intelligence and intelligence testing. In the latter process, one is of necessity engaged in evaluating an individual's particular abilities. Of course, in doing so, one obtains information regarding a subject's liabilities and handicaps. This information is both useful and important, but is really only an incidental aspect of what one wishes to discover from an intelligence test.

When it is asserted that intelligence tests are unfair to the disadvantaged and minorities, one must be mindful of the fact that they are simply recording the unfairness of life. They show also, for example, that our mental abilities, whoever we may be, decline with advancing age. . . . (Of course, this decline is in many cases counterbalanced by increased experience.)

Intelligence tests were not devised for the handicapped alone but for everybody. What then can be the reason for believing they may not be suitable for the major segments of our population—or for prohibiting their administration to the majority of children in a school system? The current New York City I.Q. ban is a case in point, and especially discouraging when one sees what is being used instead.

The tests that have been substituted are a series of achievement tests—in particular, reading tests. Of all the possible choices, one can hardly imagine a worse alternative. For of all areas in which the disadvantaged child is handicapped, reading heads the list. The main difference between an intelligence (or aptitude) test and an achievement test is that the former is less tied to curriculum content. If it is true that a low score on an intelligence test presents a misleading picture of a pupil's learning capacity, how much more unfair would be an even lower score on an achievement test. It is possible that the I.Q. was banned in New York because those who supported the ban wished primarily to combat what they believed to be a widespread view that the I.Q. is "somehow a fixed, static and genetic measure of learning ability." One may wonder, however, whether political pressures may not have played some role in the decision—and one may hope that the ban will soon be retracted.

The I.Q. has had a long life and will probably withstand the latest assaults on it. The most discouraging thing about them is not that they are without merit, but that they are directed against the wrong target. It is true that the results of intelligence tests, and of others, too, are unfair to the disadvantaged, deprived and various minority groups but it is not the I.Q. that has made them so. The culprits are poor housing, broken homes, a lack of basic opportunities, etc., etc. If the various pressure groups succeed in eliminating these problems, the I.Q.'s of the disadvantaged will take care of themselves.

CREATIVITY

39. Creativity and Intelligence in Children's Thinking *

Michael A. Wallach and Nathan Kogan

It is generally recognized that great artists and scientists possess something more than brilliant intellect. To be sure, high intelligence is usually an essential factor in their success. However, before outstanding results can be produced, intelligence must be combined with other qualities such as imaginative thought and motivation to achieve. This rare combination of intellectual and motivational factors is generally called *creativity*. But how do we measure creativity, and how is it to be distinguished from the more familiar concept of intelligence?

In the next selection, Professors Wallach and Kogan develop experimental procedures for differentiating between creativity and intelligence in children's thinking. By reference to the introspections of outstanding artists and scientists, the authors define creativity as the abundance of imaginative thoughts that a child can produce. In a gamelike situation, children were asked to suggest different ways in which various common objects could be used and, in addition, traditional measures of general intelligence were obtained. The measure of creativity was the number and uniqueness of the ideas that each child suggested.

The results of this study support the view that it is possible and worthwhile to distinguish between intelligence and creativity as two distinct kinds of cognitive excellence. They also demonstrate that a child is more likely to have imaginative thoughts in a play situation where his intellectual ability is not being evaluated by others.

While there has been a great deal of discussion in recent years concerning the importance of fostering "creativity" in our children, there is little solid evidence to support the claim that creativity can be distinguished from the more familiar concept of intelligence. To be sure, the word "creativity" has caught the fancy of the culture—frequent reference is made to creativity in contexts as diverse as education, industry, and advertising. Time and time again, however, the "proof" offered to support the existence of a type of cognitive excellence different from general intelligence has proven to be a will-o-the-wisp.

The logical requirements for such a proof can be put as follows. The psychological concept of *intelligence* defines a network of strongly related abilities concerning the retention, transformation, and utilization of verbal and numerical symbols: at issue are a person's memory storage capacities, his skill in solving problems, his dexterity in manipulating and dealing with concepts. The person high in one of these skills will tend to be high in all; the individual who is low in one will tend to be

* Reprinted by permission of the authors and the publisher from *Trans-Action* Magazine, 1967, *4*, 38–43, Washington University, St. Louis, Missouri. The illustrations are reprinted by permission of Holt, Rinehart and Winston, Inc., New York, from Figure 2 on page 34 of M. A. Wallach and N. Kogan, *Modes of Thinking in Young Children,* 1965.

low in all. But what of the psychological concept of *creativity?* If the behavior judged to be indicative of creativity turns up in the same persons who behave in the ways we call "intelligent," then there is no justification for claiming the existence of any kind of cognitive capacity apart from general intelligence. We would have to assert that the notion of greater or lesser degrees of *creativity* in people simply boils down, upon empirical inspection, to the notion of greater or lesser degrees of general *intelligence*. On the other hand, in order to demonstrate that there are grounds for considering creativity to be a kind of cognitive talent that exists in its own right, another kind of proof would be required. It would be necessary to demonstrate that whatever methods of evaluation are utilized to define variations in creativity from person to person result in classifications that are different from those obtained when the same individuals are categorized as to intelligence.

When we reviewed the quantitative research on creativity, we were forced to conclude that these logical requirements were not met. Despite frequent use of the term "creativity" to define a form of talent that was independent of intelligence, examination of the evidence indicated that the purported measures of creativity tended to have little more in common with each other than they had in common with measures of general intelligence. If one could do about the same thing with an IQ measure as one could with the creativity measures, (regarding who should be considered more creative and who should be considered less creative) it was difficult to defend the practice of invoking a new and glamorous term such as "creativity" for describing the kind of talent under study.

While varying conceptions of the meaning of creativity had been embodied in the measures used, they all shared one thing in common: they had been administered to the persons under study as *tests*. From the viewpoint of the person undergoing assessment, the creativity procedures, no less than an intelligence test, carried the aura of school examinations. They were carried out with explicit or implicit time limits in classroom settings where many students underwent the assessment procedures at the same time. Indeed, we even found that the creativity procedures had been described to the students as "tests" by the psychologists who gave them.

We were suspicious that such a test-like context was inimical to the wholehearted display of cognitive characteristics which could be correctly referred to as being involved in creativity. Hence we believed that creativity had not yet been given a fair chance to reveal itself as a different form of excellence than intelligence. These suspicions were reinforced when we considered what creative artists and scientists have said concerning creative moments in their own work.

THEIR CREATIVE ELDERS

In their introspections one finds an emphasis upon the production of a free flow of ideas—the bubbling forth of varieties of associations concerning the matter at hand. Einstein, for example, refers to the need for "combinatory play" and "associative play" in putting ideas together. Dryden describes the process of writing as involving "a confus'd mass of thoughts, tumbling over one another in the dark." Poincaré talks about ideas as having "rose in crowds" immediately prior to his obtaining a significant mathematical insight. These associations, moreover, range with high frequency into the consideration of unique, unusual possibilities, but ones which are nevertheless relevant to the issue rather than just bizarre. When we look into the conditions under which an abundant flow of unique ideational possibilities has been available, the artists and scientists indicate that the most conducive attitude is one of playful contemplation—if you will, of permissiveness. Creative awareness tends to occur when the individual—in a playful manner—entertains a range of possibilities without worry concerning his own personal success or failure and how his self-image will fare in the eyes of others.

With this in mind we formulated a research program that involved the extensive study of 151 fifth-grade children. They were of middle-class socio-economic status, and boys and girls were about equally represented in our sample. The work, which was supported in part by the Cooperative Research Program of the United States Office of Education, has been described in detail in our book, *Modes of Thinking in Young Children: A Study of the Creativity-Intelligence Distinction* (Holt, Rinehart and Winston, 1965).

From the introspections of scientists and artists arose some ground rules concerning what creativity might rightfully signify if in fact it constitutes a type of excellence different from intelligence. These ground rules might be put in terms of the following two injunctions:

First, study the flow of ideas—consider how unique and how abundant are the kinds of ideas that a child can provide when contemplating various sorts of tasks. One is talking here, of course, about relevant ideas, not about ideas that might earn the status of being unique only because they are so bizarre as to have no relevance at all to the task.

Second, provide an atmosphere that convinces the child that he is not under test —that the situation is one of play rather than one where his intellectual worthiness is under evaluation by others. This second injunction may be a particularly difficult one to fulfill on the American educational scene, where testing and the feeling of undergoing personal evaluation are ubiquitous. Yet if our considerations were correct, it obviously was essential to fulfill it if creativity was to receive a fighting chance to display itself.

Accordingly, we mustered every device possible to place the assessment procedures in a context of play rather than in the typical context of testing with which the children were all too familiar. There were no time limits on the procedures. They were administered to one child at a time rather than to groups of children seated at their classroom desks. The adults who worked with the children, moreover, had already established relationships in the context of play activities. We even took pains to avoid the customary vocabulary of tests and testing in connection with the research enterprise as a whole—in our talk with the children we described the work as oriented to the study of children's games for purposes of developing new games children would like.

The procedures involved such matters as requesting the child to suggest possible uses for each of several objects, or to describe possible ways in which each of several pairs of objects are similar to each other. For example, in one procedure the child was to suggest all the different ways in which we could use such objects as a newspaper, a cork, a shoe, a chair. "Rip it up if angry" was a unique response for "newspaper," while "make paper hats" was not unique. In another, he was to indicate similarities between, for example, a potato and a carrot, a cat and a mouse, milk and meat. "They are government-inspected" was a unique response for "milk and meat," while "they come from animals" was not unique. In yet another, he was to indicate all the things that each of a number of abstract drawings might be—such as the drawings shown in the illustrations (Fig. 39-1). For the triangle with three circles around it, "three mice eating a piece of cheese" was a unique response, while "three people sitting around a table" was not unique. For the two half-circles over the line, "two haystacks on a flying carpet" was a unique response, while "two igloos" was not unique.

Our interests were in the *number* of ideas that a child would suggest, and the *uniqueness* of the suggested ideas—the extent to which a given idea in response to a given task belonged to one child alone rather than being an idea that was suggested by other children as well. In addi-

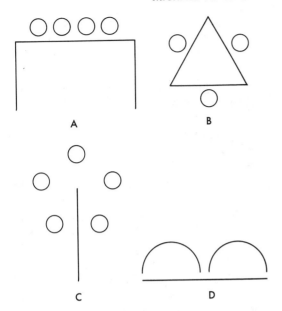

Figure 39.1 Children's responses to abstract drawings.

A. Unique: "Foot and toes."
   Common: "Table with things on top."
B. Unique: "Three mice eating a piece of cheese."
   Common: "Three people sitting around a table."
C. Unique: "Lollipop bursting into pieces."
   Common: "Flower."
D. Unique: "Two haystacks on a flying carpet."
   Common: "Two igloos."

tion, we used a variety of traditional techniques for assessing general intelligence with the same children.

When the results of the creativity assessment procedures were compared with the results of the intelligence measures, a definite divergence was obtained—the kind that had not been found in earlier studies. They had already shown, and so did our study, that a child who scores at the high intelligence end of one intelligence test will tend to score that way in other intelligence tests as well. In addition, however, our research revealed two further facts which tended to be different from earlier studies:

The various measures of creativity that we utilized had a great deal in common

with one another: a child who scored at the high creativity end of one of our creativity measures tended to score at the high creativity end of all the rest of these measures.

Of particular importance, the indices of creativity and the indices of intelligence tended to be independent of each other. That is to say, a child who was creative by our measures would just as likely be of low intelligence as of high intelligence. Likewise, a child who was relatively low in creativity by our measures would as likely be of high intelligence as of low intelligence.

In short, the obtained facts *did* support the view that in school children creativity is a different type of cognitive excellence than general intelligence. Such an outcome was especially striking in light of the fact that our procedures for assessing creativity of necessity called upon the child's verbal ability in some degree—and verbal ability is known to contribute substantially to performance on IQ tests. Despite this possible source of commonality, the chances that a child of high intelligence would also display high creativity by our measures were no more than about 50-50.

What are some of the characteristics, then, of children in our four categories: intelligent and creative; neither intelligent nor creative; intelligent but low in creativity; and creative but low in regard to intelligence? The composite pictures that emerged from the experiments and observations that we carried out are composites in the sense that some portions of the evidence upon which they are based were more clear for the boys, while other parts of the evidence were more clear for the girls. However, the general pictures that emerged for the two sexes tended to suggest the same underlying characteristics.

HIGH CREATIVITY— HIGH INTELLIGENCE

In many respects these children earn the most superlatives of any of the four groups.

For example, when they are observed in the classroom they tend to be particularly high in degree of attention span and concentration upon academic work. At the same time, their academic bent does not put them at a social disadvantage. Quite to the contrary, they are observed to be the most socially "healthy" of the four groups: they have the strongest inclination to be friends with others, and others also have the strongest inclination to be friends with them. (These observations were made during play periods as well as during class sessions.)

These children, in addition, are the least likely of all four groups to behave in ways that suggest disapproval or doubt concerning oneself, one's actions, and one's work. However, this isn't merely a question of behaving in a manner most in harmony with the society's expectations, for these children also demonstrate a strong inclination to engage in various sorts of disruptive activities in the classroom. It's as if they are bursting through the typical behavioral molds that the society has constructed.

What are some of the underpinnings of the general behaviors just described for this group? For one thing, they are likely to see possible connections between events that do not have too much in common. The members of this group, in other words, are more willing to posit relationships between events that are in many respects dissimilar. For another thing, these children are particularly good at reading the subtle affective or expressive connotations that can be carried by what goes on in the environment. These two matters are not entirely separate—a sensitive, aesthetic "tuning" to the possible expressive meanings conveyed by human gesture or by abstract design forms involves seeing possible linkages between quite different kinds of objects and events. The children high in both creativity and intelligence seemed to be most capable of all the groups regarding this kind of aesthetic sensitivity.

To illustrate how we studied the child's ability to read subtle expressive connota-

tions, consider the following example. We confronted the child with a picture of a straight line and asked him to imagine that he was looking down from above at a path that someone had made. The child was to tell us what sort of person made this trail. Our interest was in determining whether the child's response conveyed information about the kinds of emotional experience that might characterize the person in question, or on the other hand conveyed information only about the superficial character of what the person did. An example of a response showing sensitivity to possible expressive meanings was: "Someone very tense; because if he were relaxed he might wander all over; somebody mad." On the other hand, here is an example of a response that did not show expressive sensitivity: "Man was traveling on a highway; he met people in a huge car; it had a lot of people and it was crowded; they traveled together and got food in restaurants; when they got where they were going, they had a nice vacation."

Turning finally to the way these children describe their own feeling states, we find a tendency for them to admit to experiencing some anxiety, some disturbance—neither a great deal nor very little. It may be that experiencing some anxiety serves an energizing function for them: it is not so much anxiety as to cripple them, and not so little anxiety as to leave them dormant. Also, their total mode of adaptation does not minimize the experience of anxiety for them.

LOW CREATIVITY— HIGH INTELLIGENCE

In what respects are the children who are high with regard to general intelligence but low in creativity different from those who are high in both? Let us return first to behavior observed in classroom and play settings. While the high intelligence-low creativity children resembled the high creativity-high intelligence children in possessing strong capacities for concentration on academic work and a long attention span, in other respects they were quite different. Those of high intelligence but low creativity were least likely of all four groups to engage in disruptive activities in the classroom and tended to hesitate about expressing opinions. In short, these children seemed rather unwilling to take chances.

Parallel behavior was observed in their social relations with other children; while others had a strong inclination to be friends with them, they in turn tended to hold themselves aloof from interaction with other children. The high intelligence-low creativity children, therefore, seemed to be characterized by a coolness or reserve in relations with their peers. Others would seek out the high intelligence-low creativity children for companionship, possibly because of this group's high academic standing. The children in question, however, tended not to seek out others in return. Perhaps this group felt themselves to be on top of the social mountain, as it were —in a position where they could receive homage from others without any need for requital.

The observations regarding a tendency toward caution and reserve on the part of the high intelligence-low creativity children receive further corroboration in other areas of their functioning. For example, when asked to make arrangements and groupings of pictures of everyday objects in whatever ways they considered most suitable, they preferred to make groupings that were more conventional in nature. They tended to avoid making free-wheeling, unconventional arrangements in which there would be greater free play for evolving unique combinations of objects. For instance, a more conventional grouping would be assembling pictures of a lamppost, a door, and a hammer, and calling them "hard objects." A more unconventional grouping, on the other hand, would be putting together pictures of a comb, a lipstick, a watch, a pocketbook, and a door, and describing them as items that concern "getting

ready to go out." It is as if a greater fear of error characterizes these children, so that when left to their own devices, they tend to gravitate toward ways of construing the world that are less open to criticism by others.

We also found out that if you *request* these children to try to behave in a manner that involves establishing more free-wheeling linkages among objects, they are capable of doing so. It is not that they lack the ability to look at the world in this manner, but the inclination. When an adult in their environment comes along and makes it clear that they are expected to consider unusual and possibly bizarre ways in which objects can be linked, they are able to conform to this task demand with skill. But most of the time, their environment tells them that the more unconventional ways of proceeding are more likely to lead them into error and be criticized as wrong. Since the possibility of error seems particularly painful to these children, their typical behavior is to proceed in a manner that is less likely, on the average, to bring them criticism.

Another example of the same sort of process is provided when we consider how the high intelligence-low creativity group reads the possible affective meanings that can be possessed by the behavior of others. As in the case of arranging objects into groups, one can contrast more conventional, expected ways and more unconventional, unusual ways of construing what the behavior of others may signify. For example, an angry figure can be described as "angry" with little risk of error. It requires acceptance of unconventional possibilities, on the other hand, for the child to admit the idea that this figure might be "peaceful" or might be "searching." It turns out that the group in question is least likely to entertain the possibility of the more unconventional, unusual kinds of meanings. They seem locked, therefore, in more conventional ways of interpreting their social world as well as their physical world. Again, fear of possible error seems to be at work.

Since the high intelligence-low creativity children seem to behave in a manner that should maximize correctness and minimize error, we can expect them to be in particularly good standing in their classroom environment. Given their apparent tendency to conform to expectations, their mode of functioning should be maximally rewarding and minimally punishing for them. In short, there should be a high degree of fit between customary environmental expectations and their way of conducting themselves. We find, in fact, that this group admits to little anxiety or disturbance when asked to describe their own feeling states. Their self-descriptions indicate the lowest levels of anxiety reported by any of the four creativity-intelligence groups. Since this group behaves in a manner that should minimize worry or concern for them, their minimal level of reported anxiety probably represents an accurate description of how they feel. But at a cost, as we have noted, of functioning in a constricted manner.

HIGH CREATIVITY— LOW INTELLIGENCE

Turning to the group characterized by high creativity but relatively low intelligence, we find, first of all, that they tend to exhibit disruptive behavior in the classroom. This is about the only respect, however, in which their observable conduct in the usual school and play settings resembles that of the group high in both creativity and intelligence. Of all four groups, the high creativity-low intelligence children are the least able to concentrate and maintain attention in class, the lowest in self-confidence, and the most likely to express the conviction that they are no good. It is as if they are convinced that their case is a hopeless one. Furthermore, they are relatively isolated socially; not only do they avoid contact with other children, but in addition their peers shun them more than any other group. Perhaps, in their social withdrawal, these children are indulging fantasy activities. At any rate, they are

relatively alone in the school setting, and in many respects can be characterized as worse off than the group low in both creativity and intelligence.

It should be borne in mind that the high creativity-low intelligence children nevertheless give evidence of the same kind of creative thinking capacities as are found in the high creativity-high intelligence group. Again, for example, we find a greater likelihood of seeing possible connections between events that do not share much in common. The high creativity children, whether high or low regarding intelligence, are more willing to postulate relationships between somewhat dissimilar events.

Apparently, the kinds of evaluational pressures present in the case of intelligence and achievement testing as well as in the typical classroom environment serve to disrupt cognitive powers which can come to the fore when pressure is reduced. An interesting complementarity seems to exist with regard to the psychological situations found for the high creativity-low intelligence group and the low creativity-high intelligence group: while members of the former seem to perform more effectively when evaluational pressures are absent, members of the latter seem to work more adequately when evaluational pressures are present. It is as if the former children tend to go to pieces if questions of personal competence and achievement enter the picture, while the latter children have difficulty if they are denied a framework of standards within which they can evaluate what is required of them if they are to seem competent in the eyes of adults.

LOW CREATIVITY— LOW INTELLIGENCE

While the children in this group show the greatest cognitive deprivation of the four groups under study, they seem to make up for it at least to some degree in the social sphere. From observations of their behavior in school and at play they are found to be more extroverted socially, less hesitant, and more self-confident and self-assured than the children of low intelligence but high creativity. The members of the low-low group are particularly poor regarding the kinds of aesthetic sensitivity that were mentioned earlier—for example, they show the weakest tendencies to respond to the possible expressive meanings that abstract line forms may convey. Despite such deficiencies, however, this group does not seem to be the maximally disadvantaged group in the classroom. Rather, the low-low children seem to have worked out a *modus vivendi* that puts them at greater social ease in the school situation than is the case for their high creativity-low intelligence peers.

THE MOTIVATIONAL HURDLE

Now that we have characterized the four groups of children, let us finally consider the implications of the relative roles played by ability and by motivational factors in a child's thinking. The only group that looks like it is in difficulty with regard to ability—and even in their case we cannot be sure—is the group low in both intelligence and creativity. In the cases of the two groups that are low regarding one cognitive skill and high regarding the other —the low intelligence-high creativity group

and the high intelligence-low creativity group—our evidence suggests that, rather than an ability deficiency, the children in question are handicapped by particular motivational dispositions receiving strong environmental support. For the low intelligence-high creativity children, the difficulty seems to concern excessive fear of being evaluated; hence they perform poorly when evaluational standards are a prominent part of the setting. For the high intelligence-low creativity children, on the other hand, the difficulty seems to concern a fear of not knowing whether one is thought well of by significant others. The possibility of making mistakes, therefore, is particularly avoided. Further, if evaluational standards are not a clear part of the setting, so that the child does not know a right way of behaving in order to fulfill the expectations of others, performance will deteriorate because the problem of avoiding error becomes of prime importance.

In theory, at least, these kinds of motivational hindrances could be rectified by appropriate training procedures. If one could induce the low intelligence-high creativity children to be less concerned when evaluational standards are present, and the high intelligence-low creativity children to be less concerned when evaluational standards are absent, their thinking behavior might come to display high levels of both intelligence and creativity.

40. What Makes a Person Creative? *

Donald W. MacKinnon

Although the creative contributions of outstanding men mark the progress of civilization, the study of creativity itself is a relatively new area of psychological research. In the previous selection, Wallach and Kogan show that creative thinking in school children is not necessarily limited to those who possess high intelligence. In the next article, Professor MacKinnon describes the findings of a research program in which both the intellectual and personal characteristics of highly creative adults were investigated.

MacKinnon and his colleagues studied writers, architects, mathematicians, engineers, and scientists who had been nominated by their own professional groups as creative individuals. These persons were then intensively tested on a variety of tasks. The results of the study show that, in addition to high intelligence, creative persons have a number of personal qualities that contribute to their success. Among these are openness to new experience, relative freedom from restraints and inhibitions, and flexibility and independence in thought and action. It was also found that creative individuals possess an unquestioning commitment to creative endeavor as well as a very large amount of energy.

Six years ago, a group of psychologists began a nationwide study of human creativity. They wanted the scientific answers to the mystery of human personality, biology, intelligence, and intuition that makes some persons more creative than others.

* Reprinted by permission of the author and the publisher from *The Saturday Review*, New York, February 10, 1962.

Working under a grant by the Carnegie Corporation of New York, the researchers were faced with the usual stereotypes that picture the highly creative person as a genius with an I.Q. far above average, an eccentric not only in thinking but in appearance, dress and behavior, a Bohemian, an egghead, a longhair. According to these unproved stereotypes, he was not only introverted but a true neurotic, withdrawn from society, inept in his relations with others, totally unable to carry on a conversation with others less gifted than himself. Still others held that the creative person might be profound but that his intelligence was highly one-sided in a rather narrow channel, and that he was emotionally unstable. Indeed one of the most commonly held of these images was that he lived just this side of madness.

The psychological researchers who sought a more precise picture of the creative person conducted their investigations on the Berkeley campus of the University of California in the Institute of Personality Assessment and Research. At the Institute, the persons to be studied have been brought together, usually ten at a time, for several days, most often a three-day weekend. There they have been examined by a variety of means—by the broad problem posed by the assessment situation itself, by problem-solving experiments, by tests designed to discover what a person does not know or is unable to reveal about himself, by tests and questionnaires that permit a person to manifest various aspects of his personality and to express his attitudes, interests, and values, by searching interviews.

The professional groups whose creative

members were chosen for study were writers, architects, research workers in the physical sciences and engineering, and mathematicians. In no instance did the psychological assessors decide which highly creative persons should be studied. Rather, they were nominated by experts in their own fields; and to insure that the traits found to characterize the highly creative were related to their creativity rather than indigenous to all members of the profession, a wider, more representative sample of persons in each of the professional groups was also chosen, though for somewhat less intensive study. All told, some 600 persons participated.

As the study has progressed it has become abundantly clear that creative persons seldom represent fully any of the common stereotypes, and yet in some respects and to some degree there are likenesses. It is not that such images of the creative person are fantastic but that they are caricatures rather than characterizations, heightening and sharpening traits and dispositions so as to yield a picture recognizable, yet still out of accord with reality. There are, of course, some stereotypes that reflect only error, but more often the distortion of the reality would seem to be less complete.

As for intellectual capacity, it will come as no surprise that highly creative persons have been found to be, in the main, well above average. But the relation between intelligence and creativity is not as clear-cut as this would suggest, if for no other reason than that intelligence is a many-faceted thing. There is no single psychological process to which the term "intelligence" applies; rather, there are many types of intellective functioning. There is verbal intelligence, and on a well-known test of this factor creative writers on the average score higher than any of the other groups. But there is also spatial intelligence—the capacity to perceive and to deal with spatial arrangements—and on a test of this aspect of intelligence creative

writers as a group earn the lowest average score, while creative architects as a group are the star performers. There are, of course, many elements of intelligence in addition to these two.

If for the moment we ignore those patterns of intellective functioning which clearly and most interestingly differentiate one creative group from another, there are some more general observations that may be noted. It is quite apparent that creative persons have an unusual capacity to record and retain and have readily available the experiences of their life history. They are discerning, which is to say that they are observant in a differentiated fashion; they are alert, capable of concentrating attention readily and shifting it appropriately; they are fluent in scanning thoughts and producing those that serve to solve the problems they undertake; and, characteristically, they have a wide range of information at their command. As in the case of any intelligent person, the items of information which creative persons possess may readily enter into combinations, and the number of possible combinations is increased for such persons because of both a greater range of information and a greater fluency of combination. Since true creativity is defined by the adaptiveness of a response as well as its unusualness, it is apparent that intelligence alone will tend to produce creativity. The more combinations that are found, the more likely it is on purely statistical grounds that some of them will be creative.

Yet intelligence alone does not guarantee creativity. On a difficult, high-level test of the more general aspects of intelligence, creative persons score well above average, but their individual scores range widely, and in several of the creative groups the correlation of intelligence as measured by this test and creativity as rated by the experts is essentially zero.

Certainly this does not mean that over the whole range of creative endeavor there is no relation between general intelligence and creativity. No feeble-minded persons appeared in any of the creative groups. Clearly a certain degree of intelligence, and in general a rather high degree, is required for creativity, but above that point the degree of intelligence does not seem to determine the level of one's creativeness. In some fields of endeavor, mathematics and theoretical physics for example, the requisite intelligence for highly creative achievement is obviously high. But it does not follow that the theoretical physicist of very superior I.Q. will necessarily be creative, and in many fields of significant creative endeavor it is not necessary that a person be outstanding in intelligence to be recognized as highly creative, at least as intelligence is measured by intelligence tests.

Regardless of the level of his measured intelligence, what seems to characterize the creative person—and this is especially so for the artistically creative—is a relative absence of repression and suppression as mechanisms for the control of impulse and imagery. Repression operates against creativity, regardless of how intelligent a person may be, because it makes unavailable to the individual large aspects of his own experience, particularly the life of impulse and experience which gets assimilated to the symbols of aggression and sexuality. Dissociated items of experience cannot combine with one another; there are barriers to communication among different systems of experience. The creative person, given to expression rather than suppression or repression, thus has fuller access to his own experience, both conscious and unconscious. Furthermore, because the unconscious operates more by symbols than by logic, the creative person is more open to the perception of complex equivalences in experience, facility in metaphor being one specific consequence of the creative person's greater openness to his own depths.

This openness to experience is one of the most striking characteristics of the highly creative person, and it reveals itself in many forms. It may be observed, for example, in the realm of sexual identifications and interests, where creative males give more expression to the feminine side of their nature than do less creative men. On a number of tests of masculinity-femininity, creative men score relatively high on femininity, and this despite the fact that, as a group, they do not present an effeminate appearance or give evidence of increased homosexual interests or experiences. Their elevated scores on femininity indicate rather an openness to their feelings and emotions, a sensitive intellect and understanding self-awareness, and wide-ranging interests including many which in the American culture are thought of as more feminine, and these traits are observed and confirmed by other techniques of assessment. If one were to use the language of the Swiss psychiatrist C. G. Jung, it might be said that creative persons are not so completely identified with their masculine *persona* roles as to blind themselves to or deny expression to the more feminine traits of the *anima*. For some, of course, the balance between masculine and feminine traits, interests, and identifications is a precarious one, and for several it would appear that their presently achieved reconciliation of these opposites of their nature has been barely achieved and only after considerable psychic stress and turmoil.

It is the creative person's openness to experience and his relative lack of self-defensiveness that make it possible for him to speak frankly and critically about his childhood and family, and equally openly about himself and his problems as an adult.

One gets the impression that by and large those persons who as adults are widely recognized for their creative achievements have had rather favorable early life circumstances, and yet they often recall their childhood as not having been especially happy.

In studying adult creative persons one is dependent upon their own reports for the picture they give of their early years. Although they may often describe their early family life as less harmonious and happy than that of their peers, one cannot know for certain what the true state of affairs was. In reality the situation in their homes may not have been appreciably different from that of their peers. The differences may reside mainly in their perceptions and memories of childhood experiences, and it seems the more likely since one of the most striking things to be noted about creative persons is their unwillingness to deny or to repress things that are unpleasant or troubling.

The theme of remembered unhappiness in childhood is so recurrent that one is led to speculate about its role in fostering creative potential. In the absence of a sensitive awareness of one's own experience and of the world around one, without considerable development of and attention to one's own inner life, and lacking an interest in ideational, imaginal, and symbolic processes, highly creative responses can hardly be expected to occur. Something less than complete satisfaction with oneself and one's situation in childhood, if not a prerequisite for the development of a rich inner life and a concern for things of the mind and spirit, may nevertheless play an important contributory role.

There is no doubt, too, that some of the highly creative persons had, as children, endured rather cruel treatment at the hands of their fathers. These, to be sure, constitute the minority, but they appear today to be no less creative than those who could more easily identify with their fathers. There is some evidence, however, that those who were harshly treated in childhood have not been so effective or so successful in the financial and business (masculine) aspects of their profession as the others. There is in these persons more than a hint that they have had some difficulty in assuming an aggressive professional role because, through fear of their fathers their masculine identifications were inhibited.

Both in psychiatric interviews that survey the individual's history and present psy-chological status, and in clinical tests of personality, creative persons tend to reveal a considerable amount of psychic turbulence. By and large they freely admit the existence of psychological problems and they speak frankly about their symptoms and complaints. But the manner in which they describe their problems is less suggestive of disabling psychopathology than of good intellect, richness and complexity of personality, and a general candor in self-description. They reveal clearly what clinical psychologists have long contended: that personal soundness is not an absence of problems but a way of reacting to them.

We may resort again to Jung's theory of the psychological functions and types of personality as an aid in depicting the psychology of the creative person. According to this view it might be said that whenever a person uses his mind for any purpose he either perceives (becomes aware of something) or he judges (comes to a conclusion about something). Everyone perceives and judges, but the creative person tends to prefer perceiving to judging. Where a judging person emphasizes the control and regulation of experience, the perceptive creative person is inclined to be more interested and curious, more open and receptive, seeking to experience life to the full. Indeed, the more perceptive a person is, the more creative he tends to be.

In his perceptions, both of the outer world and of inner experience, one may focus upon what is presented to his senses, upon the facts as they are, or he may seek to see, through intuition, their deeper meanings and possibilities. One would not expect creative persons in their perceptions to be bound to the presented stimulus or object but rather to be intuitively alert to that which is capable of occurring, to that which is not yet realized; this capacity is, in fact, especially characteristic of the creative person.

One judges or evaluates experience with thought or with feeling, thinking being a logical process aimed at an impersonal analysis of the facts, feeling, on the other hand, being a process of appreciation and evaluation of things which gives them a personal and subjective value. The creative person's preference for thinking or for feeling in the making of judgments is less related to his creativeness as such than it is to the type of material or concepts with which he deals. Artists, in general, show a preference for feeling, scientists and engineers a preference for thinking, while architects are more divided in their preference for one or the other of these two functions.

Everyone, of course, perceives and judges, senses and intuits, thinks and feels. It is not a matter of using one of the opposed functions to the exclusion of the other. It is rather a question of which of them is preferred, which gets emphasized, and which is most often used. So also is it with introversion and extroversion of interest, but two-thirds or more of each of the creative groups which have participated in the study have shown a rather clear tendency toward introversion. Yet, interestingly enough, extroverts, though they are in the minority in our samples, are rated as high on creativity as the introverts.

Whether introvert or extrovert, the creative individual is an impressive person, and he is so because he has to such a large degree realized his potentialities. He has become in great measure the person he was capable of becoming. Since he is not preoccupied with the impression he makes on others, and is not overconcerned with their opinion of him, he is freer than most to be himself. To say that he is relatively free from conventional restraints and inhibitions might seem to suggest that he is to some degree socially irresponsible. He may seem to be, and in some instances he doubtless is if judged by the conventional standards of society, since his behavior is dictated more by his own set of values and by ethical standards that may not be precisely those of others around him.

The highly creative are not conformists in their ideas, but on the other hand they are not deliberate nonconformists, either. Instead, they are genuinely independent. They are often, in fact, quite conventional in matters and in actions that are not central to their areas of creative endeavor. It is in their creative striving that their independence of thought and autonomy of action are revealed. Indeed, it is characteristic of the highly creative person that he is strongly motivated to achieve in situations in which independence in thought and action are called for, but much less inclined to strive for achievement in situations where conforming behavior is expected or required. Flexibility with respect to means and goals is a striking characteristic of the groups we have studied.

On a test that measures the similarity of a person's expressed interests with the known interests of individuals successful in a variety of occupations and professions, creative persons reveal themselves as having interests similar to those of psychologists, architects, artists, writers, physicists, and musicians, and quite unlike those of purchasing agents, office men, bankers, farmers, carpenters, policemen, and morticians. These similarities and dissimilarities of interest are in themselves less significant than the abstractions and inferences that may be drawn from them. They suggest strongly that creative persons are relatively less interested in small details, in facts as such, and more concerned with their meanings and implications, possessed of considerable cognitive flexibility, verbally skilful, eager to communicate with others with nicety and precision, open to experience, and relatively uninterested in policing either their own impulses and images or those of others.

With respect to philosophical values—the theoretical, economic, esthetic, social, political, and religious as measured on one of our tests—there are two values most emphasized by all the creative groups. They are the theoretical and esthetic. One might think that there is some incompatibility and conflict between a cognitive and rational concern with truth and an emotional concern with form and beauty. If this is so, it would appear that the creative person has the capacity to tolerate the tension created in him by opposing strong values, and in his life and work he effects some reconciliation of them. Perhaps a less dramatic and more cautious interpretation of the simultaneous high valuing of the theoretical and the esthetic would be that for the truly creative person the solution of a problem is not sufficient; there is the further demand that it be elegant. The esthetic viewpoint permeates all of a creative person's work. He seeks not only truth but also beauty.

Closely allied to his strong theoretical and esthetic values is another pervasive trait of the creative, his preference for complexity, his delight in the challenging and unfinished, which evoke in him an urge, indeed a need, to discover unifying principles for ordering and integrating multiplicity.

In so brief a report, emphasis has had to be placed upon the generality of research findings. What needs to be equally emphasized is that there are many paths along which persons travel toward the full development and expression of their creative potential, and that there is no single mold into which all who are creative will fit. The full and complete picturing of the creative person will require many images. But if, despite this caution, one still insists on asking what most generally characterizes the creative individual as he has revealed himself in the Berkeley studies, it is his high level of effective intelligence, his openness to experience, his freedom from crippling restraints and impoverishing inhibitions, his esthetic sensitivity, his cognitive flexibility, his independence in thought and action, his high level of creative energy, his unquestioning commitment to creative endeavor, and his unceasing striving for solutions to the ever more difficult problems that he constantly sets for himself.

PERSONALITY AND
SOCIAL BEHAVIOR

Personality is an abstract term that refers to the characteristic ways in which people react to different life situations. Given the complex and changing demands of a hostile environment, practical concerns with differences in personality have necessarily absorbed man's interest since prehistoric times. Specific personality traits, such as aggressiveness, or dominance, or the ability to make decisive judgments and sound decisions, undoubtedly influenced the selection of leaders in stone-age societies, just as these same characteristics now help to determine our votes for mayor, congressman, or captain of the football team.

The scientific study of personality occupies a central position in psychology because it requires the integration of knowledge from many different areas. While research on personality is perhaps most closely related to the study of motivation and abnormal behavior, it also serves as a bridge between experimental psychology and social psychology. The study of personality shares with experimental psychology an emphasis on learning and underlying psychobiological processes. It shares with social psychology, and the related disciplines of sociology, anthropology, economics, and political science, the fact that most human behavior is determined and shaped by other persons and by the political and social institutions they create.

An individual's personality may be regarded as abnormal or disordered if his behavior is markedly different from that of other persons in a particular society. Sharply deviant behavior that in some manner poses a threat to life or property is not long tolerated either by other individuals or by society as a whole. Consequently, persons whose behavior violates the mores and basic values of a society are usually ostracized or committed to social institutions designed to control them and protect others. The personality of individuals whose behavior is characterized by deviant reactions to life and its circumstances is the central concern and essential subject matter of abnormal psychology.

325

It is customary to divide behavioral disorders into four main categories: psychoses, neuroses, psychosomatic disorders, and psychopathic personalities or character disorders. In psychoses, there is often bizarre behavior and an almost complete loss of contact with objective reality. In neurotic disorders, although there is no break with the real world, the patient suffers from inner conflicts, anxiety, irrational fears, and a variety of physical and psychological symptoms that reflect defenses designed to reduce the impact of these unpleasant emotional states. In psychosomatic disorders, the patient has a genuine physical illness caused, at least in part, by chronic conflict or other emotional disturbance. Finally, the delinquent or psychopathic individual tends to take his troubles out on society, violating laws and regulations and often leading a disorganized and useless life.

This section contains eight articles whose subjects range from abnormal behavior to social psychology. Although the topics of these selections seem to vary widely in scope, the concept of personality is basic to each. The first group of three selections is concerned with issues that bear on the nature of personality disorders and with diagnostic applications of psychological tests. Two types of personality disorders are described in the selections by Quay and Carr. In the first article, Quay analyzes the stimulation-seeking behavior of individuals diagnosed as psychopathic personalities and then suggests an interpretation of this behavior in terms of a pathological drive state. In the second article, Carr describes five kinds of psychological disturbance in schizophrenia and shows how these defects are reflected in intelligence and personality tests. In the final article in this group, Kimble clarifies the professional and ethical issues that are raised in current criticism of psychological tests.

The next group of three selections is concerned with the modification of deviant behavior. In a classic article relating learning theory and abnormal behavior, Jones describes methods for eliminating children's fears that are based on conditioning and extinction processes. Next, after outlining the general goals of psychoanalytically oriented psychotherapy, Colby describes some of the techniques and procedures used by psychotherapists in the treatment of emotional disorders. In the final article of this group, Kushner reports the treatment of a case in which an undesirable and debilitating symptom, chronic and intractable sneezing, was eliminated using a form of behavior therapy based on operant conditioning principles.

The last two articles in this section provide examples of the concepts and methods of modern social psychology. In the first, Aronson discusses Festinger's theory of cognitive dissonance and describes several recent experiments designed to evaluate it. He also suggests applications of dissonance theory to the practical problems of child-rearing. In the final article Haythorn and Altman describe the effects of social isolation on personal adjustment. In addition to demonstrating a number of ways in which social variables can influence behavior, these studies illustrate the complex interplay between the concepts and methods of research in social psychology and personality.

PERSONALITY AND BEHAVIOR PATHOLOGY

41. Psychopathic Personality as Pathological Stimulation-Seeking *

Herbert C. Quay

In a previous selection, Berlyne contends that novel or complex patterns of stimulation produce a condition of "subjective uncertainty" which is experienced as an aversive drive state. Since this drive state leads to investigative and exploratory behavior, Berlyne calls it "curiosity."

A somewhat different interpretation of the antecedents of exploratory behavior is based on the assumption that individuals are motivated to maintain an *optimal* level of stimulation or neural activity. In other words, either too much or too little stimulation will activate behavior designed either to reduce or intensify the stimulation that one is presently experiencing. Evidence supporting this interpretation comes from studies of sensory deprivation which demonstrate that absence of stimulation or continuous and monotonous stimulation produce an aversive drive state (experienced as subjectively unpleasant) that is strongly motivating.

In the following article, Herbert C. Quay applies the concept of an optimal level of stimulation to the interpretation of the behavior of individuals diagnosed as psychopathic personalities. Psychopaths are characterized by a high degree of impulsiveness, an inability to tolerate boredom, and a penchant for thrills and excitement. These qualities often lead them to antisocial behavior, immoral and illegal acts, and consequent difficulty with the law. Professor Quay suggests that this personality syndrome may reflect pathological stimulation-seeking in persons who experience normal levels of stimulation as unpleasant.

Theories about the nature and etiology of psychopathic personality [1] have had a wide range and, as might be expected, have reflected the pendulum swings from the organic to the psychodynamic and back again that have characterized theorizing about psychopathological conditions in general. The early theories emphasized "moral imbecility" (24) and constitutional inferiority (14). With the popularization of depth psychology came a variety of suggestions as to the psychodynamics of the disorder (1, 3, 12). A more recent return to the organic viewpoint has been bolstered mainly by EEG studies purporting to show a high percentage of abnormalities among psychopaths (5, 13).

Despite continuing controversy about many facets of psychopathic personality, certain behavioral features have now been described as central by a number of investigators (2, 3, 19, 21). The psychopath is almost universally characterized as highly

[1] In current nomenclature, sociopathic personality disturbance, antisocial reaction. This work was supported in part by Public Health Service grant MH 08437-01 from the National Institute of Mental Health. The author wishes to thank Professors J. McV. Hunt and Harry Munsinger for their critical comments on an earlier draft of this paper.

impulsive, relatively refractory to the effects of experience in modifying his socially troublesome behavior, and lacking in the ability to delay gratification. His penchant for creating excitement for the moment without regard for later consequences seems almost unlimited. He is unable to tolerate routine and boredom. While he may engage in antisocial, even vicious, behavior his outbursts frequently appear to be motivated by little more than a need for thrills and excitement. His deficits in learning, in terms of both avoidance and approach responses, are clinically obvious and have recently been documented by experimental study (11, 18, 25).

It is the impulsivity and the lack of even minimal tolerance for sameness which appear to be the primary and distinctive features of the disorder. In accounting for these and related features of the disorder this paper will attempt an explanation of psychopathic behavior in terms of the concepts of need for varied sensory stimulation, adaptation to sensory inputs, and the relationship of these to affect and motivation. The basic hypothesis is that psychopathic behavior represents an extreme of stimulation-seeking behavior and that the psychopath's primary abnormality lies in the realm of basal reactivity and/or adaptation to sensory inputs of all types.

A brief review of current motivational theory in order to point up recent conceptions of the relation between motivation and sensory stimulation seems relevant. For many years theories of motivation were based primarily upon the notion that an organism acts in such a way as to minimize stimulation—to reduce tension. More recent theory has taken cognizance of the fact that behavior may also be motivated by a need to increase rather than decrease stimulation. Hebb (9) was apparently first to emphasize that under certain conditions increases in stimulation were pleasurable and thus responsible for the institution of an adient drive. Since Hebb's first formulation of this notion, studies have demonstrated that animals will behave in such a way as

to provide increases or variations in stimulation. Dramatic demonstrations of the effect of severe attenuations of sensory stimulation on humans have been provided (10, 28). These studies show that not only is both the prolonged absence of stimulation and the prolonged presence of continuous monotonous stimulation subjectively unpleasant but that the effects of such experiences result in severe disruptions of affective and cognitive functioning. Thus, recent theory and experimental study have emphasized and demonstrated that both absences of and lack of variability of stimulation are affectively unpleasant and strongly motivating.

It may be possible, then, to view much of the impulsivity of the psychopath, his need to create excitement and adventure, his thrill-seeking behavior, and his inability to tolerate routine and boredom as a manifestation of an inordinate need for increases or changes in the pattern of stimulation. We are suggesting that the level and variability of sensory inputs which are necessary for the maintenance of pleasant affect are much greater for the psychopath than for the ordinary individual. It may be that under ordinary life conditions the psychopathic individual frequently suffers, in reduced intensity, from the unpleasant affect which is induced in such dramatic fashion by complete sensory deprivation or monotony.

What may account for this apparent pathological need for sensory input? Two possibilities suggest themselves. The first is that basal reactivity to stimulation is lowered so that more sensory input is needed to produce efficient and subjectively pleasurable cortical functioning. A second possibility is that there is a more rapid adaptation to stimulation which causes the need for stimulation variation to occur more rapidly and with greater intensity.

While there is a paucity of experimental research on psychopaths, the results of a number of studies seem relevant to the basic hypothesis. A smaller number of these studies also appear to bear on one or the other of the two possibilities suggested above. The studies, already cited, which have shown psychopaths to be deficient in conditionability can be interpreted in terms of the failure of either the unconditioned (avoidance learning) or reinforcing (approach learning) stimuli to have aroused excitatory processes in the organism. Some further evidence on learning in the psychopath has been provided by Fairweather (7), who investigated the learning of nonsense syllables in criminal psychopaths under three conditions of reward: no reward, certain reward and uncertain reward. His data indicated that the psychopaths learned best when reward was uncertain. If this reward condition can be interpreted as leading to an enhanced arousal due to the variability of stimulation induced by the uncertainty then the results can be seen as providing some support for the basic hypothesis. It is pertinent here to point out that Eysenck (6) considers the psychopath to be a highly extraverted individual and in turn considers the extravert to have a type of cortical organization which shows both a lowered reactivity to sensory input and a more rapid development of inhibition.

Studies of autonomic reactivity in psychopathic individuals appear to lend some support to the conceptualization offered here. In a study contrasting the autonomic responses of psychopaths with those of medical students, Ruilmann and Gulo (26) found that the psychopaths exhibited significantly smaller deflections and much more rapid recovery times under both neutral and emotion-inducing conditions. These results appear to indicate both a lowered reactivity and a more rapid adaptation to stimulation. Lykken (18) in the study of avoidance conditioning noted previously has demonstrated much the same phenomena. His psychopaths evidence both less sensitivity to noxious stimulation and a more rapid recovery to basal GSR after onset of such stimulation. Lind-

ner (16, 17) obtained somewhat different results in an earlier study. In his research the psychopathic group evidenced somewhat superior GSR reactivity to emotion-producing stimulation. However, the return to basal level was made more rapidly, indicating faster adaptation, a finding consistent with studies cited previously.

In a very recent study Fox and Lippert (8) compared the amount of spontaneous changes in GSR in a group of 10 male juvenile offenders who had been diagnosed as psychopathic with a group of 10 male offenders who had received diagnoses of inadequate personality. The psychopathic group exhibited very significantly less spontaneous activity. Of particular interest here is the fact that Mundy-Castle and McKiever (20) have shown that subjects, with few endogenous GSR responses adapted rapidly to a repetitive stimulus while those with more spontaneous GSR activity did not adapt. Fox and Lippert also demonstrated that mean basal resistance (computed once each minute for a 10-minute period) was not different for their two groups. This study does certainly suggest, when its results are considered in the light of the earlier findings of Mundy-Castle and McKiever, that the problem is one of rapid adaptation rather than diminished basal reactivity.

While the evidence for lowered basal reactivity is equivocal, the GSR studies almost uniformly indicate a more rapid adaptation process. Some further evidence is provided by Petrie, McCulloch and Kazdin (23). In a study carried out with juvenile delinquents (not necessarily psychopathic) they found that the figural aftereffects of delinquents were experienced in terms of reduced perceived size of the test object as compared with the stimulus object. They term this phenomenon "reduction." This phenomenon, it does appear, is related to adaptation to the stimuli provided by the original stimulus object. These investigators go on to suggest that the absence of sensation frequently experienced by the reducing individual is unpleasant and that he is motivated to change this state of affairs by seeking increased sensory input. In this respect they also note that earlier work on sensory deprivation suggested that those suffering most were inclined to diminish the intensity of environmental stimulation (22). Their theorizing is of course consistent with the stimulation-adaptation theories of motivation in general and serves further to point out the possible individual differences in terms of the need for stimulus input.

What we have suggested then is the notion that the psychopath, either due to a lessened basal reactivity or an increased rate of adaptation, quite frequently finds himself in a condition of stimulus deprivation. Since this condition is affectively unpleasant he is motivated to change this affective state by the seeking of stimulation. In a highly organized environment such as that in which modern man resides this seeking of either added intensity or added variability of stimulation may on occasion involve transgressions of both law and moral code. It is these transgressions, motivated by the search for added or more varied stimulus input, which most frequently bring the psychopath to public attention.

Assuming that this conception is at least partially explanatory of the behavioral manifestations of the disorder, one must then consider its possible origins. Here the situation is even less clear. Those who have argued for a constitutional origin have often cited the early appearance of precursors of the condition—in children of 4 and 5 years of age. Eysenck (6) also considers the cortical reactivity pattern of the extravert to be constitutional.

While the early childhood histories of psychopaths have never really been adequately compared to appropriate controls there seems general agreement that early childhood emotional trauma is frequently present. A variety of recent animal studies has indicated that traumatized (shocked) infant rats will exhibit less emotionality to

(or adapt more rapidly to) the effects of an unfamiliar situation than will animals not so traumatized (4, 27).

No matter what the origin it would seem fruitful to study highly impulsive, psychopathic behavior in terms of stimulation-seeking pathology. If decreased reactivity and/or rapid adaptation do produce in these persons an affective state of unpleasantness close to that produced by severe sensory deprivation or monotony in the normal individual, then new approaches to the diagnosis and treatment of the condition are needed. Experimental tasks measuring satiation, adaptation, marked preference for the highly novel, etc., may be used to investigate further the hypothesis presented here. Such tasks, if found to be associated with the clinical feature of the disorder, could then be employed in objective diagnostic batteries.

Treatment approaches might also be developed to attack the problem more directly. It may be possible to condition avoidance reaction using quite strong UCs and to condition approach reactions and secondary reinforcers using strong UCs coupled with reinforcement varied both temporally and qualitatively. The problem might also be approached through the development and use of drugs which increase reactivity or decrease adaptation.

REFERENCES

1. Alexander, F.: Neurotic Character, Int. J. Psychoanal. 11:292–311, 1930.
2. Caldwell, J. M.: The Constitutional Psychopathic State (Psychopathic Personality): I. Studies of Soldiers in the U. S. Army, J. Crim. Psychopath. 3:171–179, 1941.
3. Cleckley, H.: The Mask of Sanity. St. Louis: Mosby, 1955.
4. Denenberg, V. H.: Interactive Effects of Infantile and Adult Shock Levels upon Learning, Psychol. Rep. 5:357–364, 1959.
5. Diethelm, O., and Simons, D. J.: Electroencephalographic Findings in Psychopathic Personalities, J. Nerv. Ment. Dis. 102:611–614, 1945.
6. Eysenck, H. J.: The Dynamics of Anxiety and Hysteria. New York: Praeger, 1957.
7. Fairweather, F. W.: Serial Rate Learning by Psychopathic, Neurotic, and Normal Criminals

under Three Incentive Conditions. Unpubl. Ph.D. Thesis, University of Illinois, 1953.

8. Fox, R., and Lippert, W.: Spontaneous GSR and Anxiety Level in Sociopathic Delinquents, J. Consult. Psychol. 27:368, 1963.

9. Hebb, D. O.: The Organization of Behavior. New York: Wiley, 1949.

10. Heron, W.: The Pathology of Boredom, Sci. Amer. 196:52–56, 1957.

11. Johns, J. H., and Quay, H. C.: The Effect of Social Reward on Verbal Conditioning in Psychopathic and Neurotic Military Offenders, J. Consult. Psychol. 26:217–220, 1962.

12. Karpman, B.: Conscience in the Psychopath: Another Version, Amer. J. Orthopsychiat. 18:455–491, 1948.

13. Kennard, M. A.: The Electroencephalogram in Psychological Disorders: A Review. Psychosom. Med. 15:95–115, 1953.

14. Koch, I. L. A.: Kurzgefasser Leitfaden der Psychiatrie. Ravensburg, 1899.

15. Levine, S.: The Effects of Differential Infantile Stimulation of Emotionality at Weaning, Canad. J. Psychol. 13:243–247, 1959.

16. Lindner, R. M.: Experimental Studies in Constitutional Psychopathic Inferiority. Part I: Systemic Patterns, J. Crim. Psychopath. 4:252–276, 1942.

17. Lindner, R. M.: Experimental Studies in Constitutional Psychopathic Inferiority. Part II, J. Crim. Psychopath. 4:484–500, 1943.

18. Lykken, D. T.: A Study of Anxiety in the Sociopathic Personality, J. Abnorm. Soc. Psychol. 55:6–10, 1957.

19. McCord, W., and McCord, J.: Psychopathy and Delinquency. New York: Grune & Stratton, 1956.

20. Mundy-Castle, A. C., and McKiever, B. L.: The Psychophysiological Significance of the Galvanic Skin Response, J. Exp. Psychol. 46:15–24, 1953.

21. Pennington, L. A.: "Psychopathic and Criminal Behavior," in Pennington, L. A., and Berg, I. A.: An Introduction to Clinical Psychology, 3d ed., New York: Ronald, 1966.

22. Petrie, A.: Some Psychological Aspects of Pain and the Relief of Suffering, Ann. N. Y. Acad. Sci. 86:13–37, 1960.

23. Petrie, A., McCulloch, R., and Kazdin, P.: The Perceptual Characteristics of Juvenile Delinquents, J. Nerv. Ment. Dis. 134:415–421, 1962.

24. Prichard, J. C.: Treatise on Insanity. London: Gilbert and Piper, 1835.

25. Quay, H. C., and Hunt, W. A.: J. Consult. Psychol., in press.

26. Ruilmann, C. J., and Gulo, M. J.: Investigation of Autonomic Responses in Psychopathic Personalities, Southern Med. J. 43:953–956, 1950.

27. Salama, A. A., and Hunt, J. McV.: Fixation in the Rat as a Function of Infantile Shocking, Handling and Gentling, J. Genet. Psychol. 105:131–162, 1964.

28. Zubek, J. P., Pushkar, D., Sansom, W., and Gowing, J.: Perpetual Changes after Prolonged Sensory Isolation (Darkness and Silence), Canad. J. Psychol. 15:83–100, 1961.

42. Psychological Defect and Psychological Testing *

Arthur C. Carr

Schizophrenia is generally regarded as one of the most serious forms of mental illness. The psychological symptoms of this disorder include gross distortions in thinking, general inappropriateness in emotional expression, and extreme difficulty in interpersonal relations.

Our understanding of schizophrenia has been greatly facilitated by research into its causes and by the development of tests that provide sensitive measures of disturbance and deterioration in the psychological functions of schizophrenic patients. However, the behavioral pathology that occurs in schizophrenia differs markedly from case to case, and this fact has important implications for the diagnosis and treatment of individual patients.

* Reprinted by permission of the author and by Little, Brown & Company, Boston, from *International Psychiatry Clinics* (October, 1964), pages 773-789. Card I of the Rorschach Test, for which Professor Carr gives the verbatim response of a schizophrenic patient in this selection, is presented on page 583 of *Principles of General Psychology*, 3d ed., by Gregory A. Kimble and Norman Garmezy, The Ronald Press Company, New York, 1968.

In the next selection, Arthur C. Carr, an experienced clinical psychologist, discusses the use of psychological tests in the diagnosis of schizophrenia. Professor Carr describes the primary areas of psychological disturbance in schizophrenia, and he shows how defects in intelligence and personality are revealed in a patient's performance on tests such as the Wechsler Adult Intelligence Scale and the Rorschach Inkblots.

Psychological tests, when properly administered and interpreted by an experienced clinician, may make an important contribution to an understanding of the patient, clarifying aspects of classification, psychodynamics, and management. Although it is debatable whether psychological tests should ever be the sole basis for determining such issues, they nevertheless have come to play an increasingly important role in the diagnostic armamentarium available for evaluating psychological defects and have proved to be particularly sensitive in detecting underlying schizophrenic disorders.

Although there are many implicit assumptions regarding the utilization of test procedures, two important features should be elucidated briefly. In the first place, tests provide a fairly objective means for comparing a relatively controlled sample of the patient's behavior with available normative data representative of larger groups. Adequate standardization of tests has probably been achieved most extensively in the area of intelligence testing. For example, determining the patient's relative intellectual strengths and weaknesses, as well as his intellectual quotient (IQ), is made possible on the Wechsler Adult Intelligence Scale through the use of available normative data gathered from a sample selected as presumably representative of the general population of the United States. This standardization group was chosen in terms of such variables as sex, geographic region, urban-rural residence, race, and occupation, including seven age groups ranging from 16 to 64 years. Al-

though the degree of sophistication represented by this sampling procedure does not characterize the more limited standardization in the area of projective testing, there exists a substantial body of research and clinical data on all the major techniques which can serve as a basis for evaluating any individual patient's response patterns.

In the second place, in the test battery most widely utilized in clinical practice,* a broad range of stimuli on the continuum of structure-ambiguity is available for eliciting patient's response samples. In contrast to such specific or highly structured questions on the WAIS as "When is Washington's birthday?" and "How far is it from Paris to New York?" (to which there may be only one correct answer but many wrong ones), the projective techniques presumably have no "right" or "wrong" answers—"no two people see exactly the same thing,—just be sure to tell me *all* that you see." Thus, an essential characteristic of projective techniques is that they are unstructured in that cues for appropriate action are not clearly specified and the individual must give meaning to (interpret) such stimuli in accordance with his own inner needs, drives, defenses, impulses —in short, according to the dictates of his own personality. Whether the stimuli are inkblots (the Rorschach test) or ambiguous pictures (the TAT), the patient's task is to impose or project his own structure and meaning onto materials which have relatively little meaning or structure and which, in a purely objective sense, are only inkblots or ambiguous pictures.

It is not uncommon for patients with underlying schizophrenic disorder to function without apparent defect when they are in situations which offer obvious cues for social behavior. In structured situations, schizophrenics eventually classified as borderline, incarcerated, ambulatory, or pseu-

---

* The usual test battery includes the Wechsler Adult Intelligence Scale (WAIS), the Rorschach test, the Draw-a-Person test (DAP), the Bender-Gestalt test, the Thematic Apperception test (TAT), and the Sentence-Completion test (SCT).

doneurotic types may appear to function so well as to be regarded as "well adjusted." It is only when such persons are placed in relatively ambiguous or unstructured situations, where previous learning for behavioral cues cannot be utilized, that basic disturbances may become discernible.

The rationale for choosing tests of varying ambiguity stems from a recognition that social situations vary along this same dimension. A basic assumption underlying psychological testing is that individuals who show a certain kind of disturbance in a *test* situation of given degree of ambiguity would in all probability show a similar disturbance in a *social* situation of equal ambiguity. While it is difficult to specify the environmental counterparts for the varying projective test stimuli in terms of corresponding degrees of ambiguity, it is theoretically possible to do so. In the absence of such specification, there is, of course, no substitute for the clinician's training, experience, and knowledge of projective techniques as related to personality theory.

It might be added parenthetically that the typical verbal interview may also vary in its level of structure or ambiguity, through use of such techniques as the "blank screen," prolonged silences, selective reinforcement, inference from associative linkages, deliberate challenging of patient's contradictions, and so forth. Gifted interviewers undoubtedly utilize intuitively numerous techniques which establish a counterpart of projective tests within their own interviewing. Nevertheless, the psychiatric interview and particularly the standard mental status examination, as ordinarily conceived and executed, have tended to become a set of highly structured questions which implicitly carry with them some indication of the kind of response which might be appropriate. Research efforts within this Center are presently being directed toward the utilization of a standardized mental status examination which would tend to crystallize even further the interviewer's skills into a highly

structured, routinized technique. While the advantages which accrue from objectification of interviewing procedures are obvious, their inherent limitations seem to support the conclusion that the status of projective tests will not be diminished in the near future and that, on the contrary, it will probably be enhanced.

Recognizing then what appear to be major advantages of psychological tests, it must also be made clear that tests merely elicit behavior—the actual diagnosis of schizophrenia is made through the process of inference. Hence, tests do not offer any panacea or magical solution to the problems surrounding the diagnosis of schizophrenia. Although valuable clinical tools, tests are an adjunct and not a replacement for clinical knowledge. Regardless of how one chooses to elicit what presumably will be the most revealing sample of the subject's behavior, the judgments about the sample will still of necessity be based on one's conception of the behaviors that constitute schizophrenia. Thus, for example, the weight that the clinician chooses to give "poor reality testing" is reflected in his diagnosis of schizophrenia, whether he is using interview data or test data. This fact sometimes becomes obscured, particularly when one speaks of the presumed test signs of schizophrenia. In a real sense, there is no such thing as a "schizophrenic Rorschach," however useful such an abstraction may be. There are only schizophrenic persons!

It is not always easy to make the diagnosis of schizophrenia with absolute certainty. As long as the issue rests on such gross criteria as the presence of clear-cut thought disorders, delusions, hallucinations, and blatant reality distortions, the range of behaviors that identify schizophrenia are relatively easy to recognize. However, when the disorder is in a state of relative clinical muteness, in chronic schizophrenia, or when symptoms of the so-called "borderline states" are present, the traditional textbook definition and patterns are sometimes more difficult to apply.

The primary disturbances which may be detected through the use of psychological tests and subsequently related to the diagnosis of schizophrenia may be subsumed under the following headings: (1) variability in functioning; (2) distortions in thinking; (3) disturbances in affect; (4) disturbances in ego boundaries; and (5) difficulties in interpersonal relationships.*

VARIABILITY IN FUNCTIONING

Both as a group and as an individual, the schizophrenic is highly variable. This finding has been demonstrated with both simple and complex behavior (3). It has been repeatedly confirmed in an area where confirmation of results has not been the rule. The high variability both within the individual patient and between individual schizophrenics constitutes one of the major difficulties in attempting to isolate general characteristics of test responses in schizophrenics. An excellent review of the diverse findings is provided by Rabin and King (2). Paradoxically, this high variability itself may be diagnostic, for the quantity and quality of variability within the individual's test performance are often themselves one of the most reliable indications of whether or not the patient is schizophrenic.

It appears logical to assume that this variability in functioning is related to the nature of the disorder. Schizophrenia is basically a regressive disorder in which, unlike the more uniform regression characteristic of the organic psychosis, parts of

* Examples which may reflect disturbances not readily apparent in the more structured tests will generally be chosen from the Rorschach test. In reporting such examples, it must be made explicit that there are few or no single signs pathognomic of schizophrenia. Although the examples are chosen as being most consistent with schizophrenia, they may also occur in other disorders, particularly the organic brain syndromes and manic-depressive psychosis. Consequently, in actual practice, the total test battery must always be carefully evaluated in the context of the patient's present difficulties.

TABLE 1

WAIS Patterns in Four Patients

Subtest	Patient 1	Patient 2	Patient 3	Patient 4
Information	11	16	19	13
Comprehension	10	13	22	10
Arithmetic	13	12	13	17
Similarities	12	14	13	8
Digit span	9	12	15	14
Vocabulary	—	—	—	—
Digit symbol	11	7	19	14
Picture completion	6	11	12	10
Block design	14	11	17	17
Picture arrangement	5	13	8	13
Object assembly	9	12	11	18
Verbal IQ	106	122	125	116
Performance IQ	99	106	114	130
Full scale IQ	103	116	121	123

the ego regress at an uneven tempo and back to uneven points in the individual's developmental history. The essential characteristic of the regression itself is its variability in both quality and quantity. All manifestations of this regression and the anxiety and disorganization which it precipitates—whether reflected in affect, perception, language, or thought—will be as variable as the regression.

The quality of variability is often most dramatically illustrated in the relative intellectual strengths and weaknesses as reflected in the Wechsler Adult Intelligence Scale. Aside from qualitative aspects of the individual's performance, which may reveal disorders of thinking and conceptual difficulties, the mere quantitative aspects of the individual's profile often carry diagnostic implications. Marked discrepancies between verbal and performance IQ's, and variability in subtest scores are usual findings with schizophrenics. For example, four patients recently tested at the New York State Psychiatric Institute revealed the WAIS patterns shown in Table I. On the basis of a theoretical framework consistent with the nature of the relationships between personality and intelligence, and using the individual as his own baseline instead of placing reliance on schizophrenic group norms, the psychologist in each instance inferred the diagnosis of schizophrenia. It was also diagnostically revealing that, in each instance, there were examples of easy problems on the same subtest being missed while more difficult ones were successfully completed. Although any example taken out of context can be misleading, failing to know the number of weeks in a year or the date of Washington's birthday while responding with perfect accuracy to such questions as "What is ethnology?" and "What is the apocrypha?" is, for example, most consistent with the performance of a schizophrenic. Such variability is also prevalent on the Rorschach test, wherein clearly perceived, well-organized responses of perfect form accuracy will exist side by side with diffuse, poorly articulated responses of absurd form quality. Variability in tempo, sequence, and conventionality of response is also the rule.

DISTORTIONS IN THINKING

One of the signs traditionally considered pathognomic of schizophrenia is a breakdown and disorganization of the patient's thought processes.* The ordinary rules of

* Authorities differ in their emphasis on the relevance of the concept "thought disorder" for the diagnosis of schizophrenia. Some view it as basic to the disorder; others see it as a secondary phenomenon which actually may be present in varying degrees in a variety of disorders including both organic and manic-depressive psychoses. Some schizophrenics do show major difficulties in what are usually conceptualized as being "thinking" or "thought" disturbances. In others, the difficulties appear to be related more to other aspects of functioning. These are relative matters, however, with particular generalizations depending upon the observer's level of abstraction as well as upon basic differences in schizophrenics. I have subsumed some signs under "disturbances in thinking" which, strictly speaking, pertain more directly to "perception" (see under heading "Poor Contact with Reality") and "language" (see under heading "Peculiarities of Language"). Most authorities would take no exception to this, on the assumption that disordered language, for example, is a direct consequence of disordered thought. This is not a logical inevitability, however. As a matter of degree, thinking disorders may indeed be ubiquitous!

logic do not hold; rather, their thinking is much more like that of the child or of a dreamlike state. Illogical associations may prevail. Thinking may be autistic, condensed, highly symbolic, and bizarre. The capacity to make verbal abstractions may be deficient. There may be either a dearth of ideas and a slowing of the thought processes or an overproductivity of unrelated ideas.

Gross thinking disorders will usually be readily detectable in the patient's responses to the WAIS. In subtle forms, however, thinking disorders may become obvious only on the Rorschach test. Examples of the diverse ways in which such disturbance may be expressed are indicated in the following discussion.

Poor Contact with Reality

The best single Rorschach indicator of reality testing ability is the accuracy of form perception (F + %), reflecting the degree to which the person perceives with adequate critical capacity. In the schizophrenic, the poor form response is not caused by any visual-perceptual difficulty but is attributable to associational processes that are no longer subject to logical or critical control. Extremely poor responses in terms of form accuracy may alternate with accurately perceived responses.

Overgeneralization

Disturbances in thinking are sometimes reflected in the patient's tendency to overgeneralize or to make interpretations or conclusions based on inadequate or inaccurate inferences. Gross difficulties in making verbal abstractions may be reflected in response to the Similarities subtest of the WAIS, wherein abstractions may be extremely concrete or idiosyncratic ("A fly and a tree are alike because a fly has a penis sticking out and a tree has limbs") or on the Comprehension subtest ("One swallow doesn't make a summer means if you swallow something, watch out—winter can't be far behind").

Within the limits of the WAIS, however, many schizophrenics may make adequate, if not even superior, generalizations. In such instances, the difficulty may be reflected on the Rorschach test in which, for example, a tiny detail of the blot may be used for making an inaccurate generalization pertaining to the whole blot—e.g., Card VI: "It (the whole blot) looks like a cat because here are its whiskers" (tiny detail of the blot). In other instances, the spatial relationship between discrete areas of the blot is assumed to indicate an actual relationship, albeit highly unusual in terms of reality standards (e.g., Card X, center bottom detail: "This is a rabbit's head and these must be snakes coming out of the rabbit's eyes"). Such "contaminations" found in adults are most frequently schizophrenic, as are those involving the fusing of two separate responses to the same area into a single percept (e.g., Card I: "A butterfly woman with wings"). In so-called "positional responses," the association is derived solely from the fact that the area of the blot is located where it is (e.g., Card III, center detail: "These must be kidneys because they are in the middle"). In all such instances, the ordinary rules of logic are ignored; generalizations and conclusions are the product of illogical thought processes.

Unconventionality of Thinking

Alienation and estrangement from conventional thought, with inability to think along usual, conventional lines, may be reflected in a paucity of "Popular" (commonly given by normal groups) responses to the Rorschach test. In a record of average length, at least five or six "P" responses are necessary to indicate that the patient is sufficiently in contact with how other people perceive and think. While giving many unusual, even creative responses, the schizophrenic may fail to see what others feel is definite and obvious.

Idiosyncrasy of Thought

The schizophrenic's thought processes are often highly personalized and idiosyncratic. Thus, for example, although both schizophrenic patients and patients with organic disorders may perseverate the same response from one Rorschach card to another, the *perseveration* of the schizophrenic tends to be related to more bizarre, personalized material than that of the patient with organic disease, often dealing with sex, unusual anatomy, or other personal preoccupations. In some instances, the meaning given to the cards is so personalized and "private" as to suggest that the schizophrenic feels the blots were made, as they are, especially for him.

Peculiarities of Language

Language peculiarities may include obvious clang associations, neologisms, and "word salad." They may also, however, be extremely subtle. On the Rorschach test, they may be reflected in the tendency to resort to symbolic responses which have little relation to the blot itself—e.g., "This looks like the history of the struggle of good and evil" (Card VIII). Contaminated responses may give rise to highly unusual verbalizations (e.g., Card IV: "The back of a tree-bear"; Card V: "A bat-rabbit, no . . . I meant a rabbit-bat").

DISTURBANCES IN AFFECT

The term schizophrenia typically implies a "split" between the affective life and the ideational life of the individual, i.e., affect and feeling are not in harmony with the thought being experienced. Typical responses to emotional stimuli may reflect *inappropriate affect* (such as smiling while discussing a sad event), *blandness of affect* (apathy, aloofness, and dreaminess), or *rigidity of affect* (stereotyped emotional patterns).

Disturbances in affect may be readily apparent in the patient-tester relationship or in the manner in which the patient relates either to the test materials or to his own productions. In some instances, patients may be dealing with excessively gory, gruesome percepts without any indication of appropriate feeling or emotional reaction. In some instances, the patient will react with accompanying affect to his perceptions as if the blots were in reality the thing which he imagines them to be.

On the Rorschach test, affective contact is reflected particularly in how the color is utilized in quality and quantity and how it is related to other structural aspects of the blots, especially its relation to the form of the blot and the accuracy of the accompanying form perception. Adequate modulation of affect and social adaptability (reflected in the form-color response in which form is the more important determinant) are often lacking. The disruptive effect which affect may have on reality testing is indicated in diminished accuracy of form perception on responses in which color plays a determining influence. Complete absence of color may reflect apathy, emotional blunting, or a pathologic rigidity. Responses determined solely by color indicate impulsivity and a breakdown of controls. Color may evoke percepts related to "deterioration" responses—"dried urine," "blood stains," "burnt flesh," "cancerous tissue," and other gory, autistic responses. It should be noted that appropriate use of color on the Rorschach test is suggestive of favorable prognosis even in schizophrenic disorders.

DISTURBANCES IN EGO BOUNDARIES

The schizophrenic has great difficulty in differentiating stimuli from within or without the body, reality from fantasy, his own thoughts from those of others—in short, where he leaves off and outer reality begins. The absence of a firm sense of self-identity or ego boundaries is considered the basic disturbance in schizophrenia by some authorities. Whether a primary or secondary phenomenon, however, disturbances in this area underlie the difficulty which schizophrenics frequently have in properly evaluating or testing both inner and outer reality.

Disturbances in ego boundaries may be reflected in the Rorschach test through the adequacy with which the patient perceives movement in the blots, particularly human movement (M). An absence of human-movement responses may indicate defective empathic ability, while an overabundance of such responses may indicate withdrawal into fantasy and (in the context of poor form level) may suggest the presence of autistic features.

Disturbances in ego boundaries may also be indicated in the manner by which the patient gives his responses and his attitude toward them. In some instances, the blots may be reacted to as if they were "real" (e.g., "A vampire and it's coming right out after me"), reflecting a "loss of distance," basic to which is an inability to distinguish reality from fantasy. In other instances, the blots may be perceived as literally changing in front of the observer's eyes ("It's a larvae . . . now it's becoming a moth"). It is as though the observer were a passive participant in an event over which he had no control. Such response changes suggest alternating states of consciousness. In other instances, feelings of inner disintegration are projected onto the world (i.e., the inkblots) in such a way that things are seen as falling apart, exploding, rotting away, or decomposing. World-destruction fantasies may be implied, particularly if accuracy of form perception is poor. Restitutive efforts in the form of world-reconstruction fantasies are suggested by themes of rebirth, religiosity, power, strength, and so forth. Presence of numerous anatomy responses, particularly of the soft-organ variety, often of poor form quality ($F-$), are reflections of concern related to bodily integrity, fear of bodily damage, and/or preoccupation with bodily functioning. The anatomic content frequently pertains to digestive, birth, or sexual processes, and may be elaborated in a bizarre manner.

Directly related to the concept of ego boundaries is evidence suggesting that Rorschach content in terms of the degree to which definite structure is assigned to the periphery of the inkblot image may reflect how the individual perceives his body boundaries. Percepts in which the boundary is highlighted (e.g., "turtle with shell"; "man in armor") are labeled "barrier" responses; percepts emphasizing weakness and permeability (e.g., "a broken body"; "a torn rug") are labeled "penetration" responses. Such boundary scores have been correlated with a variety of behavior beyond mere psychopathology, including such diverse variables as psychosomatic symptom choice, reaction to surgery, and conduct in small group situations. Schizophrenic patients have been differentiated from normal and neurotic subjects in terms of low barrier, high penetration scores for the schizophrenics, as against high barrier, low penetration scores for the normals and neurotics (1).

The Draw-a-Person test may also be helpful in revealing similar disturbances. As an expression of the self or of the body in the environment, the projection of one's body image in the human-figure drawing has direct relevance to the concept of ego boundaries. Interpretative principles based on line quality, page placement, size relationships, distortions, unusual omissions, or peculiar emphases lead to specific inferences pertaining to how the body is perceived and experienced, and what the patient's relationship to his body and the relationship of the patient's body to the environment may be.

DIFFICULTIES IN INTERPERSONAL RELATIONSHIPS

The persistent inability to establish satisfactory interpersonal relationships is often considered one of the basic indications of a schizophrenic process. Underlying this inability may be found: (1) a marked *ambivalence* characterizing all aspects of the schizophrenic's life, often with accompanying difficulty around the appropriate expression and modulation of hostile impulses; and (2) *anhedonia* (a chronic defect in pleasure capacity), accompanied by inordinate social fear, distrust, and expectation of rejection which are present to a degree not generally found in other disorders.

One of the best single indicators of the individual's basic interest in and relation to other people is contained in the Rorschach human response, particularly when combined with movement which is appropriate to the form and is in the context of an activity appropriate to reality as experienced by others. Cards which typically elicit human-movement responses are II, III, and VII. "Withdrawal from interpersonal relationships," "lack of empathic ability," "inability to identify with others," "confused identification," and "overly critical in approach to other people" would be examples of inferences made on the basis of human percepts seen or rejected by the patient. Distanciation from others is suggested by responses of human beings from other cultures or worlds (e.g., "eighteenth-century dames," "Chinese ladies," "men from Mars"). In contrast to records with few or no human responses, an overabundance of these responses may reflect an extreme anxiety and overconcern the patient may have about other people. In the schizophrenic, human-movement responses often occur in the context of poor form level or are inappropriately attributed to tiny details of the blot or to unusual parts of the human body. The characteristics or activity attributed to perceived human beings will often be hostile in nature. Chaotic sexuality may be suggested by numerous sexual responses, often given in a bland, matter-of-fact way. Although the form qualities of certain blot areas elicit sexual responses even in normal subjects, schizophrenics tend to see sexual responses in atypical areas or delineate them with autistic elaborations. Estrangement from thinking like others is reflected in a low number of "Popular" responses.

DISCUSSION

If, on the basis of significant (1) variability in functioning, (2) distortions in thinking, (3) disturbances in affect, (4) disturbances in ego boundaries, and (5) difficulties in interpersonal relationships, the conclusion is made that the patient is schizophrenic, it may also be desirable to specify the type of schizophrenia in terms of the traditional categories: paranoid, simple, catatonic, or hebephrenic. This decision is made on the basis of the inferred clinical manifestations or overt expressions of the disorder, especially reflected in the defenses employed against further regression. In this Center, the "undifferentiated" or "mixed" types are frequently found, and involve marked conflict over the expression of impulses (catatonic) as well as tendencies to utilize projection as a defense (paranoid). Also prevalent are those individuals who function with minimal deficit on structured tests but reveal underlying schizophrenia on the least-structured techniques. If prominent hysteric or obsessive-compulsive defenses are apparent, this category may be classified as pseudoneurotic; otherwise, a borderline or ambulatory classification may be considered appropriate by the psychologist.

One practical question concerns the resolution of differences between clinical impression and test findings. Most frequently this discrepancy will be in the direction of the psychologist's conclusion that the patient is more disturbed than is consistent with the current clinical impression. This is not surprising; the statement that "the Rorschach provides an x-ray of the personality" is not a particularly good analogy except that the Rorschach, like the x-ray film that may show tooth cavities and bone defects even in the seeming paragon of health, may reveal defects in personality structure that appear to have no immediate correlates in overt behavior. Nevertheless, the psychologist should report the evidence as he finds it, without regard for consistency with clinical interview. The potentiality of today may become the actuality of tomorrow.

The psychologist will also do well, however, not to be exclusively preoccupied with the pathologic implications of Rorschach responses. Increasing awareness in recent years is being given to the cognitive aspects of personality functioning, stressing issues related to self-concept, personal values, and cognitive standards, as well as more conscious aspects of personality functioning. Whether or not a patient has a sense of humor may be a more important determinant of how and where he is accepted than many other deficits he may have, yet psychological reports rarely consider such a personality asset. Individuals can function productively and constructively with a surprising degree of pathology. Gauging the degree of control over primary process material might best be done by recourse to tests more directly related to cognitive functioning.

The psychologist can, of course, function best in those settings that do not violate the traditions of clinical medicine in regard to diagnosis. If the disorder of schizophrenia is imbued with unwarranted social or value judgments, if it is considered kinder or less stigmatizing to diagnose someone as manic depressive or neurotic, rather than schizophrenic, or even if one is intimidated by more subtle pressures related to a prevailing philosophy of schizophrenia, psychological tests cannot be utilized to their maximal benefit. In a setting in which proper diagnosis is considered merely the precedent for effective treatment, on the other hand, the test battery, properly utilized, may make an important contribution in the evaluation of psychological defect, particularly in the recognition of those disorders labeled schizophrenic.

APPENDIX

For readers generally familiar with the WAIS and the Rorschach test, the following profiles offer rich illustrative examples supportive of a schizophrenic diagnosis. The patient is a 19-year-old male, tested in the course of routine evaluation at the New York State Psychiatric Institute, prior to instigation of intensive psychotherapy.

TABLE 2

Test Results of WAIS

Information	16	Digit symbol	8
Comprehension	9	Picture completion	11
Arithmetic	11	Block design	7
Similarities	11	Picture arrangement	9
Digit span	9	Object assembly	7
Vocabulary	—		
		Verbal IQ	110
		Performance IQ	90
		Full scale IQ	101

The extreme variability in functioning—a 20-point discrepancy between verbal and performance IQ's; subtest scores which range from the dull normal (7) to the very superior (16) levels of intelligence—reflect a marked degree of impairment. Highest verbal score (Information) suggests use of intellectualization as a defense. The relatively high performance score on the picture completion subtest suggests possible overalertness to minute details, consistent with paranoid features. Intratest errors within this subtest, however, suggest variable reality testing ability. Lowest scores (Digit Span, Digit Symbol, Block Design, and Object Assembly) support the impression of affective features (anxiety and depression) with possible confusional states. Vocabulary was not given.

Rorschach Test
CARD I

1. A bat
(Whole) Its wings and these are its claws or antennas. This is the place where he goes to the bathroom (Dd31)—anus. Rest of body is here.

2. A lobster
(Whole) These wings could be claws, too. (?) Just its head is beaked sort of like a lobster. It's hard and stony-like. (?) Shading of the color.

3. Ugh! A monster of some kind. Whatever it is, I don't like it at all. That's just disgusting—horrible. Frightens me somewhat.

(Whole) It looks as if they are reaching for something, trying to engulf and eat it up. It looks like a big hand or something trying to engulf all around it. Just an ugly thing. They are all ugly. These (D5) are trying to close in on something.

Although the popular percept (bat) is given, the elaboration is highly unusual. Introduction of "anus" is idiosyncratic, forewarning of a theme which reaches greater intensity on subsequent cards. Anal responses or the tendency to see figures from the rear are often found in the records of paranoid patients.

With its central detail frequently seen as a female figure, Card I is sometimes assumed to elicit responses reflecting early attitudes toward the mother-figure. Note the incorporative characteristics attributed to aspects of this card, as well as "beaked . . . hard and stony-like . . . disgusting—horrible."

The theme of incorporation implied in the lobster response breaks through in blatant form in the last response. "Loss of distance" occurs ("Frightens me somewhat"). Such attributes as "disgusting," "horrible," and "frightening" connote significant projection, found in phobic, if not paranoid, patients. The departure from convention ("anus") and the disturbance in ego boundaries suggest as early as Card I that the patient is schizophrenic. In this context, the tendency throughout the test to give responses primarily to the whole blot is consistent with grandiose features.

❖   ❖   ❖

43. Psychological Testing and the Invasion of Privacy *

Gregory A. Kimble

There is presently a great deal of concern regarding the use and interpretation of psychological tests. The charge that intelligence tests are unfair to culturally-disadvantaged minority groups is answered by David Wechsler in a previous selection. (See Selection 38 in Part VI.) In the following paper, Gregory A. Kimble clarifies the current criticism regarding another aspect of psychological testing, namely, that requiring people to take personality tests constitutes an unwarranted invasion of privacy.

Professor Kimble suggests that much of the current concern about personality testing is based on a lack of understanding of the nature of tests and the scientific and practical purposes for which they are used. He points out that most critics of psychological testing confound scientific questions relating to the validity of tests as measures of psychological reality with ethical issues relating to what is done with the information that is obtained from tests. Thus, the problem boils down to the scientific validity of a particular test and the professional ethics of the tester.

Test findings which show, for example, that a child is inferior in intellectual ability, or that an individual has maladaptive personality characteristics, can provide a sound basis for more effective counseling and constructive action in schools and mental health clinics. But such information can also be used in unscrupulous and unethical ways, and care must be taken to protect against this danger.

* Reprinted by permission of the author from an unpublished paper presented by Professor Kimble at High Point College in 1966.

It is, of course, well known that certain of the activities of psychologists are raising an increasing number of moral and ethical questions and that currently these questions center on the use of psychological tests. The type of issue that has been raised has been expressed in a variety of ways. There have been articles in some of our most prestigious popular magazines denouncing the use of psychological tests; the Central Office of the American Psychological Association in Washington has been picketed by people opposed to testing; there have been full-length books such as *The Brain Watchers* that have held the procedures up to ridicule and there have been investigative hearings on the matter conducted by both Houses of Congress. From this it is perfectly clear that many people are worried about the use of tests by psychologists and others and there is an honest concern for the ethical implications of using such tests.

Now it seems to me that every ethical issue breaks down into two separate components: *First,* there is the fact, object, person or state of affairs toward which an ethical judgment is directed and *second,* there is the judgment itself. In making ethical judgments, I believe it is important to keep these two components separate. That is, if one is to reach a reasonable decision that any practice is good or bad, right or wrong, ethical or unethical, there must, as a precondition, be some understanding of what that practice is. In this particular case, one really ought to know what psychological testing is before he decides how he feels about it. Unfortunately, however, sound understanding has not often illuminated discussion of the matter and the conclusion that psychological testing is unethical has been reached without adequate knowledge of what actually is involved. What this paper has to offer is mainly an analysis of the facts of the situation. After you read it, you may still wish to conclude that the administration of psychological tests constitutes an invasion of privacy—or you may not. Whatever you conclude, however, will be an informed conclusion and not one based on lack of understanding.

CONCRETE ILLUSTRATION OF THE PROBLEM

So far this discussion has probably been too vague and general to do much more than to prove that a problem exists. To make the situation more graphic, consider this situation. Suppose that in some psychological study you or someone in your family were to be asked these five questions and required to respond "true" or "false" to each:

1. I have never indulged in any unusual sex practices.
2. During one period when I was a youngster, I engaged in petty thievery.
3. I go to church almost every week.
4. I have used alcohol excessively.
5. I have very few quarrels with members of my family.

These are all items in the MMPI, the Minnesota Multiphasic Personality Inventory, that has been the main object of the recent criticisms of psychological tests. The reasons for choosing these particular questions will be clear in a moment, but they are probably sufficient to present the problem in completely concrete terms. These questions seem to ask in order about the respondent's sex life, whether he can deny having been a juvenile delinquent, about his religious beliefs, his tendency to overindulge in alcohol and his personal rela-

tionships to members of his family. Given that the MMPI contains many questions of this type, it is not too surprising to find it referred to in the popular press as a "sex test," and a "religious test," or to discover that the question whether the psychologist should be allowed to meddle in such highly private matters has been raised. The psychological testers have been accused of having the motives of a professional Peeping Tom and it has been suggested that these activities should be subjected to some kind of legal control. Obviously, the question we are discussing is important and worthy of exploration in considerable depth.

ABSTRACT INTERPRETATION OF TEST RESULTS

In order to make matters clear, it will be necessary to approach the problem in a somewhat roundabout way. To begin, let us go back to our five items from the MMPI. Suppose a particular person responds to the questions in ways that say that his sex life is very ordinary, that he did not as a youngster engage in petty thievery, that he goes to church almost every week, that he has not used alcohol excessively and that he gets along very well with other members of his family. The question we want to ask next is how does the psychologist interpret these answers? How does he evaluate our hypothetical respondent? At this point it is worth noting that the answers might mean a number of different things but I rather suspect that the psychologist's actual interpretation is not exactly what you may have expected. The person who answered the questions as was suggested a moment ago would *not* be ticked off as a total abstainer, a religious zealot, a peaceful and honest person or someone whose sexual behavior would certainly be of little interest to Kinsey. The items are all from a scale on the MMPI that you might want to call a scale of self-control. If you think back over the questions you will see that they all relate, directly or indirectly, to a person's tendency to curb his impulses in a variety of situations. Responses to these questions contribute to an interpretation along these lines and say nothing about whether the man is sexy or sinful. Obviously, this interpretation of the test performance does not provide a resolution to the moral problem in that one may want just as jealously to guard himself from an invasion of privacy with respect to ego control as with respect to the details of his sex life and the dimensions of his religious beliefs. But if you are honest with yourself, you will probably have to admit that this interpretation places the matter in another light than that suggested by the content of the items on the test.

There are also several other lessons implicit in the example: *First,* the psychologist has little or no interest in, and almost never looks at, specific answers to specific questions. He looks instead to the number of answers that are diagnostic of a person's position on some abstract dimension of individual differences and, on most tests, he proceeds from there to a consideration of the pattern formed by the person's position on several dimensions.

Second, a test like the MMPI is actually made up of a number of scales. The individual items are often scored more than once and contribute to a variety of interpretations. This consideration is what accounts for the word "multiphasic" in the title of the MMPI.

Third, the interpretation of the test is quantitative and involves statements of *how much* of a certain trait a person has. The tests do not simply consign a person to a certain category. They seek instead to define a person's position on one or more dimensions.

SCIENTIFIC AND PRACTICAL PURPOSES OF TESTING

The discussion so far relates to the procedures employed by psychological testers.

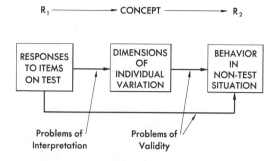

Figure 43.1 Diagram to illustrate certain points with respect to the use of psychological tests.

This also seems to be the point at which to mention another matter for the first time, namely the motives of those who use tests. In the main, these motives come down to one or both of the following: Either the psychologist is interested in the abstract scientific question of the dimensions along which individuals differ or else he has the purely practical objective of trying to predict how someone will perform in some important situation, such as in school, on a job or under stress. Next, let us consider these two purposes in some detail. The materials in Figure 43-1 will be useful in this connection.

The purpose of Figure 43-1 is to make certain logical points about the status of tests. The figure is to be read from left to right and, for some of you, the materials at the very top of the figure will serve as a useful reminder (cf. Kimble and Garmezy, 1968, Ch. 1). These materials simply indicate that the psychological tester is involved in a search for what we call "response-response laws" in which the personal traits of individuals figure as concepts or intervening variables. For those of you who have not been exposed to this way of thinking, the materials in the middle of Figure 43-1 will be more useful because they spell out the details of the abstract formula at the top. Beginning with the notation in the box at the left and moving across the figure, notice that the responses to test items, bits of behavior that are relatively neutral in and of themselves, are used on the one hand to make inferences about traits or dimensions of individual variation and, on the other, to make predictions about behavior in some nontest situation. To be more concrete about it, the responses a person gives to a set of test questions may be used to state that the person is introverted, extraverted, aggressive or whatever to such and such a degree. Or these same responses may be used to make some prediction such as that a person might be outgoing or retiring in a social situation. Or, finally, the psychologist may be interested in both of these matters and use the abstract dimensions of personality to make predictions about performance in a practical situation.

The chief reason for preparing this figure is that it will be useful in bringing a certain clarity to the confusing situation we are discussing. For, when the methods and purposes of the psychological testers are analyzed this abstract way, it turns out that different questions about, and criticisms of, testing are associated with the three main elements that emerge from the analysis. For example, one cluster of questions and criticisms is associated with the tests themselves. These are criticisms of the tests as measuring instruments and have to do with the types of questions on the test, the reliability of the measures obtained and so on. It is important to keep these questions separate from those associated with matters of interpretation or matters of validity.

ITEM CONTENT

The most frequent criticism of psychological tests falling in the first of these categories has to do with the types of questions asked on personality tests, specifically with the fact that many of them are embarrassing and offensive. As we have seen, the interpretations made of a particular test performance may not have much to do with the content of specific questions. This

fact suggests that it may be possible for those who construct psychological tests to use less personal questions. It was once thought that useful measures of personality could be obtained only by asking about very personal matters. This no longer seems so obviously the case. It may be that the same information can be acquired by asking people about less offensive things.

To illustrate this point in a little more detail, let us consider the Taylor Scale of Manifest Anxiety which is derived from the MMPI. Recently, in connection with certain problems associated with the relationship between anxiety and learning, we began to wonder whether anxiety were the critical thing and, as a part of trying to find out, decided to revise the anxiety test by removing the anxious content. In order to do this, we rewrote the questions in a way which left the form of each item the same but changed the content. For example, the anxiety scale contains the item to which a subject is to answer "true" or "false," "I am about as nervous as other people." The nonanxious translation of this item was, "I am about as gullible as other people." At several points in the test this meant changing items in ways that probably made their content less offensive. For example, Item 20 on the anxiety scale reads, "Often my bowels don't move for several days at a time" and we translated it into, "Often my luck is bad for several days at a time." We have now given this new test and the anxiety test to two different groups of about 100 subjects each and have compared the results. What we have found is that when both tests are scored by the same key, the scores are usually very similar. In one case, the correlation was over $+.80$ and in the other case over $+.70$. What this seems to suggest is that a large part of what is measured in at least some psychological tests can be measured in ways that do not require the subject to deal with materials he finds embarrassing.

THE QUESTION OF VALIDITY

We move now to the problem of validity. The immediate difficulty here is that validity is a very large and sometimes a very technical concept. It has many aspects and it is important to make certain distinctions. There will be several points on which to comment. The first is fairly close to matters we have just been discussing. Very often in popular discussions of the validity of, say, the MMPI, one finds statements like: "I do not see how questions like these can reveal anything important about a person." Technically, such a critic is saying, "I do not see how a test made up of questions like these can be valid." What is basic here is a failure to distinguish between what we sometimes call "face validity" and validity of other types. Face validity refers to what the questions on a test intuitively (or on the face of it) *seem* to measure. As it happens, a test can lack face validity and still have validity of other types. The MMPI is a test of this sort, a point to which we shall return after a brief comment on a second matter related to validity.

Another type of criticism one sometimes encounters entails the charge that tests are not valid because it is possible for a person to cheat on them. Please note very carefully that this is quite another matter from that we have just been discussing. That is, the word *valid* is now being used in a very different sense. About all one can say in response to this criticism is that it is very true of some tests and less true of others. The MMPI, for example, has built into it scales designed to tell whether a person is answering the questions honestly and responsibly. Other tests do not have this feature.

Returning now to the basic point, the most serious charge made against personality tests in particular is that they have little or no validity in the essential meaning of that term; that is, that they are useless in predicting performance in any important situation. For whatever reason, this criticism has sometimes been made by professional psychologists who really should know better. As with all blanket indictments, this one is far too sweeping. In general, it is true that personality tests do not have validity coefficients as high as those for intelligence and aptitude tests. On the other hand, it is possible to cite situations in which personality tests have been quite successful. In his testimony before the Senate Investigating Committee, for example, Dahlstrom (1965) made the point that the MMPI alone could detect the majority of adolescents who would later get into trouble with the law and that this information, supplemented by some very elementary knowledge about home backgrounds, could detect almost 90% of later juvenile delinquents. Obviously, then, personality tests can have a certain validity. The problem is to develop more tests that possess this feature, a possibility that cannot be ruled out by the mere proclamation that it is impossible.

THE DEMONSTRATION OF VALIDITY

In order to proceed further with our discussion of the issues involved in psychological testing, it will be useful to deal with the concept of validity in terms of the procedures used to evaluate this aspect of tests. In order to present the essentials, suppose someone believes that a certain score on the MMPI is a valid predictor of performance at some type of work and gives the test to 1,000 candidates for the job in question. The distribution of scores obtained would probably look something like that presented in Figure 43-2. The horizontal axis represents the range of scores on the test, from low to high, and the vertical axis represents the number of persons obtaining each score. In the graph, something called a *cutoff score* is indicated by a vertical line. The placement of this line will be clear in a moment. For the present just notice that, with such a score

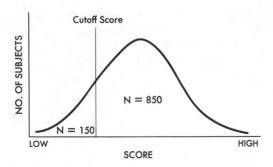

Figure 43.2 Theoretical distribution of scores on a test.

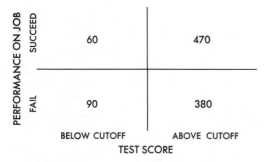

Figure 43.3 Materials of the type needed to determine the validity of tests.

established, we can define two groups of people, the relatively large group with scores above the cutoff score and the relatively smaller group below it.

The next step in our hypothetical study of validity would be to allow all of the individuals represented in this figure (those below the cutting score as well as those above it) to attempt the job for which we think the test has some validity. Then an indication of the validity of the test could be obtained by noting whether the people who failed and succeeded were below and above the cutoff score, respectively. The results might look something like what we see in Figure 43-3: Obviously, people above the cutting score tend to perform better in the practical situation than those who are below it but the relationship is very very far from perfect. Something like these hypothetical results is typical of the validity of most personality tests for most situations.

In passing it is possible, now, to explain a little about the placement of the cutoff score. It would actually be set at the completion of a study of the type just described and it would be placed at the point where it does as good a job as possible of accomplishing two things: of excluding as few as possible of the people who would succeed on the job and, at the same time, including as few potential failures as possible. No currently available test is capable of making a perfect discrimination between potential successes and potential failures. The tests are imperfect but note that they are imperfect to a degree and not totally worthless as has been claimed.

This leads to our next point. The obvious question to ask is why some people above the cutoff score on the test failed and why some below this score succeeded. The answer has probably already occurred to you. It is that other factors must play a part in determining performance in this situation. Once it is put in these terms, the point is so obvious that it is surprising that it even has to be made. For it is very clear that there will be no one-to-one correspondence between some element of personality and performance on any important task. But this is not to say that personality is not important; it is merely to say once more that the situation is not simple and, by implication, that assessment of a man for any important job requires more than just one type of evidence.

RELATED CONSIDERATIONS

A very practical illustration of the way in which personality variables can become important in situations where their predictive validity is notoriously low can be illustrated by reference to the current situation in many of our colleges. As you know, admission to college is becoming more and more difficult and college admissions officers are becoming more and more selective in their admissions policies, admitting only students who have high scores on the college board test. Now consider the logical last step in the application of this policy, in which the college admits only the people who have perfect scores on the test. Under these circumstances, the test score, which is normally a fairly good predictor of college performance, would have no predictive value at all (because everyone would have the same perfect score) and study habits, attitudes toward college, general morale, motivation and so on, all of which are personality factors rather than intellectual, would begin to make all of the difference. In many of our more prestigious colleges, the time has already come when a test of college adjustment predicts grades as well as the college board score, probably because these colleges are approaching the situation just described. Again this means that, for the prediction of performance in a complex situation, we need to use a variety of tests. Increasing the number of measures will increase the accuracy of prediction up to a limit that depends in known ways upon what it is we are trying to predict.

In order to illustrate something related to this last point, and one or two additional points as well, let us consider a study by Spielberger and his colleagues carried out over a two-year period at Duke University. During this period these investigators gave the Taylor Scale of Manifest Anxiety to all incoming freshmen on the assumption that anxiety might be related to performance at Duke. At the end of a semester it was possible to look at the students' grade point average as a function jointly of intelligence and anxiety. The results appear in Figure 43-4. Obviously, college grades depend both upon intelligence and anxiety, but the relationship is slightly complex: At the very lowest levels of ability, anxiety had no effect on grades; both anxiety groups have low grades presumably because these students lacked the ability for college work. At the very highest levels of intelligence, again, anxiety level makes little difference: these are all highly talented students whose grades are good. In the middle levels of ability, however, you see that anxiety makes

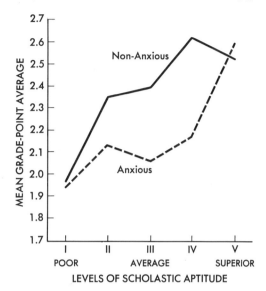

Figure 43.4 College grades as a function of anxiety and ability.

an important difference, about half a letter grade.

With all of this before us, we can now proceed to the final point about validity. It is that quantitative indexes of validity are not necessarily very good indicators of the value of the information obtainable from some test. One of the things that Spielberger and his associates found was that the dropout rate was higher among anxious freshmen than among nonanxious ones. They also found that psychological counseling not only reduced the number of dropouts but also raised the grades of these anxious students. In personal terms, the value of information about personality is not fully revealed by the magnitude of the validity coefficient. It is perfectly obvious that there would be some value in using the test and personal counseling if these procedures led to the salvaging of even one potential dropout in 100 students.

THE ETHICAL ISSUES

We have come a long way but we still have not faced up to the issues with which this talk intends to deal. We have felt it necessary to take so much preliminary time because it seems impossible to discuss an issue as big as this without laying a proper informational foundation. Turning now directly to some of the ethical problems, it has often been claimed that psychological tests are used as instruments of discrimination. The most notorious case of this type involved an electronics firm in the city of Chicago. This organization used a test that allegedly discriminated against Negroes because it did not, in the words of the court, "reflect and equate inequalities and environmental factors among the disadvantaged and culturally deprived groups." Verbal garbage such as this reveals how far the public can be from asking the simple and straightforward question that needs to be asked: Does performance on the test in question allow a valid prediction of performance on the job (if you wish, after a period of training)? If it does, it can be argued that management is entirely justified in excluding people who fail to achieve some cutoff score, whatever their color.

The reason for putting the matter this bluntly is that it points up something that people have not usually understood about the practical use of tests, namely, that it is practical. Tests are used in industry, not because of some voyeuristic interest in the private lives of personnel, but because the tests pay off. You may be absolutely certain that, whenever it costs more to buy tests, and to hire people to administer and interpret them, than they return in savings to a company, the tests will disappear from the scene very rapidly. And you may want to note in passing that this pretty well destroys the invasion-of-privacy argument, which turns out to be beside the point.

Another, less common, opinion about the use of psychological tests was once explained to me by an official in one of our major labor unions with whom I traveled from coast to coast by air. When the talk turned to the use of tests for hiring and firing, his point was that, in the history of the labor movement, it had always been very dangerous to concentrate this function in the hands of a few people because this power could so easily be misused. He was kind enough not to say that even psychologists might not be entirely trustworthy if they were in possession of such power. The important point to make here is that knowledge itself is ethically neutral and can be used for good or evil. Psychological knowledge is no different from any other kind in this regard. The charges are that it has been used mainly for bad purposes but it is actually easier to think of real cases in which the purposes have been good, for example: in demonstrating that women can do some jobs as well as men and, in this sense, supporting their entry into certain lines of work; in selecting underprivileged children who have the latent talent to profit from education; in choosing spacemen who can endure long periods of social and sensory deprivation. The list could go on and on. Of course, there are times when the use of tests is controversial. Suppose that someone is fired from a job on the basis of a test that says he is mentally ill. Does this not represent a misuse of the tests, as those who describe examples of this type have held? There are at least three points to make: *First*, it is obvious that mental illness incapacitates a man for certain types of work and that he must either be dismissed or given a long vacation. If the worker is mentally disturbed, the action is necessary whether the diagnosis was arrived at by way of a test score or some other way. *Second*, and on the other hand, it probably would be unwise to dismiss a man from a job on the basis of a single test score and nothing else. The validities of these tests are too low for that and other information should be taken into account. But, *third*, it does not follow from this that this will always be the case. Improvements in tests may make them quite valid and entirely useful for the purposes under discussion.

Considering Possible Alternatives

At this point it might be worthwhile to raise another question: If tests are not to be used for selection and retention of personnel, what alternatives are there? Obviously there are personal interviews, recommendations from friends, physicians and ministers and previous performance on the job in question or a related job. Although it may not have occurred to you before, it is possible to raise all of the questions about these types of information that are raised about tests. When these questions have been asked, one of the unfortunate facts to emerge is that, except for job performance, the other available kinds of evidence are even poorer than the psychological tests: Their reliabilities and validities are lower and, we might mention, probably more subject to misuse than the tests. Any information one gets about a person who is a candidate for any position can be interpreted as "invading his privacy" and laymen who are less sensitive to the issues are probably worse invaders of privacy than the psychological testers.

The Psychologist's Code of Ethics

What has been said so far about these ethical issues has been defensive and, in that sense, negative. There is, however, a positive side to the matter that requires some emphasis. As you know, the main users of psychological tests are the psychologists. What you may not know is that psychologists operate under a very carefully considered ethical code. This code covers such matters as the type of tests one may use, the competence necessary to administer and interpret tests and the confidentiality of test-information. Largely for this reason, in the hands of psychologists, tests are not widely misused. It is when they fall into the hands of people who do not understand them and are not covered by the psychologist's ethical code that

reasons for worry arise. But the problem, once more, is not with the tests but with their users.

THE ISSUE IN A LARGER SETTING

Finally we come to the most important part of the discussion and, in a way, the hardest to present. The main point here is that it seems very likely that recent reactions to tests are symptomatic of a great difficulty our society has in dealing with rapid advances in psychological knowledge. For it is becoming clear that the findings of psychology are going to require a sharper reorientation of our outlook than the advances in space technology. Moreover, this reorientation is going to be harder to achieve because it strikes closer to home and involves our most cherished and time-honored ways of thinking about human behavior. There are several aspects of the large problem. We need to rethink our positions on such questions as whether each man is unique, whether, in some sense, he is the same person from birth to death and what it peculiarly means to be a human being as opposed to some other kind. This is not to say that we will be required to do an about-face on these matters but rather that advances in the science of psychology are going to require their re-evaluation.

We might begin with the issues involving the permanence of a man's identity. To the psychologist it has been obvious for years that a man is not, as we have been taught to think, a constant, unchanging thing, guided from within by his will and entirely the captain of his own fate. He is, in part, a product of his environment. For any psychologist this is such a common way of thinking that most of us were surprised to find the validity of psychological tests challenged in the Senate hearings on the ground that test performance changed with changes in one's circumstances. For example, the fact that prison changes a man's responses to personality

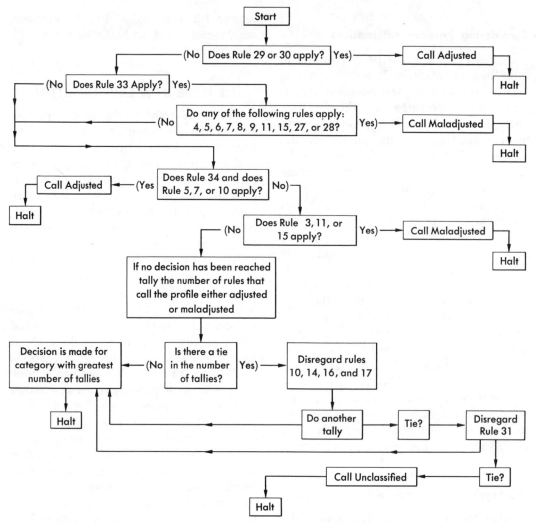

Figure 43.5 Flow chart illustrating how a computer may be used to diagnose adjustment of college students.

test questions was offered as evidence for the invalidity of the tests. If one stops to think about this charge even for the tiniest fraction of a second, he recognizes it as a remarkable testimony to the powers of the human mind to embrace incompatible ideas. On the one hand, we put a man in jail, presumably to change his behavior, and on the other, refuse to accept it when prison has the effect intended.

A second point, specifically about tests again, is that they have been criticized by some as a threat to the peculiarly human and unique individuality of a person. To make this point more concrete, consider the

following example: Suppose you are an applicant for some important position and that as a part of the battery of tests for the job you are given the MMPI. Suppose next that you are not afforded even the human dignity of having your test scored and evaluated by another human being. It goes, instead, to a machine for scoring and then to a computer for evaluation. Suppose, finally, the unkindest cut of all: that the computer calls you "maladjusted" and your application is denied.

In case you think this is sheer fantasy or science fiction, observe in Figure 43-3 the flow chart published by Kleinmuntz (1964) which accomplishes everything, including the final step in the example just used. If you are offended by a prospect such as this, it is not surprising but facts are facts and one does not deal with them by taking refuge in his emotions. It is up to you to ask yourself why you find this offensive and whether reasons you uncover really warrant your emotion.

If you are honest with yourself, you will probably discover that the reasons for your negative reactions involve some of the things mentioned earlier. It may seem to you, for example, that being put on to a punched card and then into a computer and finally into a category does violence to the uniqueness of man and that the violence would have been just as great even if the final category had been "adjusted."

The problem of uniqueness is a curious one. On the one hand we all recognize that some people are smarter than others; some are quicker to anger than others; some are shyer than others and so on. Each of these examples implies a common underlying dimension of variation. When we pursue this idea in common speech we abandon our faith in the uniqueness of man and say that "people are just about the same everywhere in the world." On the other hand, we also believe that each man is unique and that no two of them are alike. What needs to be said now is that these apparently incompatible ideas could both be true. There are general dimensions of individual variation but this does not rob an individual person of his uniqueness. For the number of dimensions on which men vary is enormous and the numbers of values of each dimension are also very large. For this reason, the numbers of combinations of positions on dimensions are literally billions of billions, so many that it is really unthinkable that two people would ever be exactly the same. At any rate, the psychological test is no threat to the conception of the uniqueness of man. To the extent that the tests are sound, they can determine the extent to which man is

unique and the extent to which he is not. These are questions of fact which the existence and use of psychological tests will do nothing to alter.

A further point that is easy to see in the flow chart on the screen is that the analysis of personality is a very complex business and this is always difficult. It is an unfortunate part of the personal makeup of most of us that we keep things simple as long as we can and prefer being given a pat answer by someone in a position of authority to being told that things are complex or that we might try to figure them out for ourselves. No doubt the placard carried by one of the ladies who picketed the American Psychological Association expressed this feeling. It said, "Don't be brainwashed by some Ph.D. See your clergyman or doctor." This attitude, in which negative reactions to psychological tests are only a minor part, is perhaps the most serious political and social issue we face today. Abstractly it is a crusade against intellectualism. More concretely, it is the attitude that says: "Accept the old cliches; don't face the fact that the world is changing; refuse to listen to the arguments of those whose positions we dislike; never criticize our President's foreign policy; keep the communists off our campuses; get the old-fashioned truth from your friendly politician, member of the American Legion or even the KKK instead."

CONCLUSION

So now we are at the end of what I have to say and I still have not told you what I think about psychological tests and the invasion of privacy. From what I have told you, however, you may be able to anticipate my position. At least now it can be put quickly. It is that the issues are exceedingly complex and that the charge, "invasion of privacy," is nothing but an evasion of the responsibility of facing up to a very very difficult set of problems. In our traditional and simplistic fashion, we have picked from the Constitution a catch-word and attempted to make it apply where it is not quite appropriate. In a way what is involved is like any other bit of prejudicial behavior: The fears created by a complex set of issues are directed against a simple, concrete thing such as a man's skin color, his religious practices, or in this case, a cliche "invasion of privacy." Please do not leap to the mistaken conclusion that I am coming out against privacy or in favor of its invasion. It is just that when the matter is looked at closely it turns out that neither the methods nor the motives of those who give psychological tests have much to do with this particular problem.

REFERENCES

DAHLSTROM, G. Testimony before Senate Investigating Committee. *American Psychologist*, 1965, **20**, 888–954.

KIMBLE, G. A., and GARMEZY, N. *Principles of general psychology* (3rd ed.). New York: Ronald, 1968.

KLEINMUNTZ, B. MMPI decision rules for the identification of college maladjustment: A digital computer approach. *Psychological Monographs*, 1964, **77** (Whole No. 577).

MODIFICATION OF DEVIANT BEHAVIOR

44. The Elimination of Children's Fears *

Mary Cover Jones

Because fear is an unpleasant and often painful emotional state, once it is aroused, it can have a profound and pervasive influence on behavior. Furthermore, since the tendency to fear certain objects persists over time and often generalizes to similar objects, a large part of an individual's mental life can be affected by fears developed in childhood. Thus, the elimination of children's fears, which is the subject of the next article by Mary Cover Jones, is a matter of considerable importance.

Professor Jones and her colleagues evaluated several different methods of controlling and modifying fear in young children. Although most of these procedures proved to be ineffective, two methods were discovered that did facilitate the elimination of specific fears. One of these involves conditioning a positive response (and pleasurable feeling) to the original fear-producing object. A second successful method involves presenting the fear-producing object to a child while he is engaged in social activity with other children who do not fear that particular object. Since both of these methods involve conditioning and extinction processes, they may be regarded as the forerunners of modern behavior therapy in which the treatment of emotional disorders is based on principles of learning.

The investigation of children's fears leads directly to a number of important problems in the genetic study of emotion. At the Johns Hopkins laboratory [1] Dr. John B. Watson has analyzed the process by which fears are acquired in infancy, and has

* Reprinted by permission of the author from the *Journal of Experimental Psychology*, 1924, 7, 382-390.

[1] Watson and Rayner, 'Studies in Infant Psychology,' *Scientific Monthly*, December, 1921.

shown that the conditioned reflex formula may apply to the transfer of emotional reactions from original stimuli (pain, loud noises, or loss of bodily support) to various substitute fear objects in the child's environment. This process has been further demonstrated by the author in the case of children from one to four years of age.[2] A study of how children's fears may be reduced or eradicated would seem to be the next point for an experimental attack. Such a study should include an attempt to evaluate, objectively, the various possible methods which laboratory experience has suggested.

The present research, an approach to this problem, was conducted with the advice of Dr. Watson, by means of a subvention granted by the Laura Spelman Rockefeller Memorial to the Institute of Educational Research of Teachers College.

The subjects, 70 children from 3 months to 7 years of age, were maintained in an institution for the temporary care of children. Admission to this institution depended as a rule upon conditions which made it difficult or impossible to keep the children at home: a case of illness in the family, the separation of father and mother, or an occupation which kept the mother away from home for a part of the day. As there was a charge for weekly care, those homes which were in actual poverty were not represented; the economic and social status of the parents, as well as the results of our intelligence tests (Kuhlmann and Terman) would indicate that this group of children was normal, and superior to the average for orphan asylums and similar institutions. As the danger of contagion is great in a group so constantly changing, a very thorough medical examination eliminated all those with symptoms of infection, and even those decidedly below normal in nutrition or general development. Our laboratory could not determine the admission and discharge of children, nor interfere in

[2] 'Conditioned Fear in Children,' published in 1924.

the prescribed routine of eating, sleeping and play. It was possible however for the experimenter to live in the building with the children in order to become acquainted with them in their usual environment, to observe them continuously for days at a time, and to take them daily, or oftener if desirable, to the laboratory where observations could be made under specifically controlled conditions.

In our selection of children from this group, we attempted to find those who would show a marked degree of fear under conditions normally evoking positive (pleasant) or mildly negative (unpleasant) responses. A wide range of situations were presented in a fairly standardized way to all of the children: such as being left alone, being in a dark room, being with other children who showed fear, the sudden presentation of a snake, a white rat, a rabbit, a frog, false faces, loud sounds, etc. This procedure served to expose fear trends if they were already present; it was not designed as a conditioning process, but merely as a method of revealing prior conditionings. In the majority of the children tested, our standard situations failed to arouse observable negative responses. This survey of children's fears is reported in another article.

When specific fears were demonstrated, our next step was to attempt their removal. By what devices could we eliminate these harmful reactions, which in many cases were subject to diffusion, and were interfering with the formation of useful attitudes and necessary habits? Our method or combination of methods depended upon the type of case presented and the manner in which treatment was received, as well as upon such external circumstances as quarantines, and the length of time the child was likely to remain in the institution.

THE METHOD OF ELIMINATION THROUGH DISUSE

A common assumption with regard to children's fears is that they will die out if left alone, *i.e.*, if the child is carefully shielded from stimuli which would tend to re-arouse the fear. "Elimination through disuse" is the name given to this process. The following cases from our records provide suggestive material:

Case 1.—Rose D. Age 21 months. General situation: sitting in play-pen with other children, none of whom showed specific fears. A rabbit was introduced from behind a screen.

Jan. 19. At sight of the rabbit, Rose burst into tears, her crying lessened when the experimenter picked up the rabbit, but again increased when the rabbit was put back on the floor. At the removal of the rabbit she quieted down, accepted a cracker, and presently returned to her blocks.

Feb. 5. After 2 weeks the situation was repeated. She cried and trembled upon seeing the rabbit. E. (the experimenter) sat on the floor between Rose and the rabbit; she continued to cry for several minutes. E. tried to divert her attention with the peg-board; she finally stopped crying, but continued to watch the rabbit and would not attempt to play.

Case 8.—Bobby G. Age 30 months.

Dec. 6. Bobby showed a slight fear response when a rat was presented in a box. He looked at it from a distance of several feet, drew back and cried. A 3-day period of training followed bringing Bobby to the point where he tolerated a rat in the open pen in which he was playing, and even touched it without overt fear indications. No further stimulation with the rat occurred until

Jan. 30. After nearly two months of no experience with the specific stimulus, Bobby was again brought into the laboratory. While he was playing in the pen, E. appeared, with a rat held in her hand. Bobby jumped up, ran outside the pen, and cried. The rat having been returned to its box, Bobby ran to E., held her hand, and showed marked disturbance.

Case 33.—Eleanor J. Age 21 months.

Jan. 17. While playing in the pen, a frog was introduced from behind her. She watched, came nearer, and finally touched it. The frog jumped. She withdrew and when later presented with the frog, shook her head and pushed the experimenter's hand away violently.

March 26. After two months of no further experience with animals, Eleanor was taken to the laboratory and offered the frog. When the frog hopped she drew back, ran from the pen and cried.

These and similar cases show that an interval of 'disuse,' extending over a period of weeks or months, may not result in eliminating a fear response, and that when other conditions are approximately constant there may be no diminution in the degree of fear manifested. From our experience, it would appear to be an unsafe method to attempt the cure of a fear trend by ignoring it.

THE METHOD OF VERBAL APPEAL

As most of our subjects were under four years of age, the possibilities of verbal analysis and control were very limited. We attempted to find how much we could accomplish toward breaking down a negative reaction by merely talking about the fear-object, endeavoring to keep in the child's attention, and connecting it verbally with pleasant experiences. This method showed no applicability except in the case of one subject, Jean E., a girl in her fifth year. At the initial presentation of the rabbit a marked fear response was registered. This was followed by ten minutes daily conversation about the rabbit; to hold her interest the experimenter introduced such devices as the picture book of 'Peter Rabbit,' toy rabbits, and rabbits drawn or modelled from plastocene. Brief stories were used, and there was always a reference to the 'real' rabbit as well. On such occasions she would say, "Where is your rabbit?" or "Show me your rabbit," or once "I touched your rabbit, and stroked it, and it never cried." (This latter was pure make-believe, and an interesting example of projection.) However, when the rabbit was actually presented again, at the end of a week, her reaction was practically the same as at the first encounter. She jumped up from her play and retreated; when coaxed, she reluctantly touched the rabbit while the experimenter held it; when the animal was put down on the floor she sobbed "Put it away," "Take it," and ran about the room frightened and distracted. She had learned to speak freely of rabbits, but this altered verbalization apparently was not accompanied by any change in her response to the rabbit itself. The experiment was interrupted after another three days of the same procedure, at the end of which time Jean left the institution with her initial fear patterns intact, so far as we could tell. It seems likely that many hours of training in the toleration of symbols may have little or no modifying effect on a mass reaction to the primary stimulus.

THE METHOD OF NEGATIVE ADAPTATION

This method is based on the theory that familiarity breeds indifference: if the stimulation is repeated often enough, monotonously, the subject finally becomes used to it and tempers his response accordingly.

Case 17.—Godfried W. Age 3 years.

A white rat was introduced from behind a screen. Godfried sat quietly for a few minutes, watching the rat with close attention. He then began to cry, made avertive movements with his hands and feet, and finally withdrew as far as possible from the animal. At the next presentation of the rat, Godfried did not cry; he advanced cautiously, making quick startled withdrawals whenever the animal moved.

A few days later when the same situation was presented, Godfried smiled and said, "Put it down on the floor." After three hours the rat was again brought in and allowed to run free in the pen. It scurried about and occasionally came very near him, but Godfried made no attempt to withdraw even when the animal advanced and touched him.

In this case, with practically no reëducative measures except repeated stimulation, Godfried conquered his specific fear. The experiment was not carried to the point where he showed a distinct positive reaction to rats, but he had developed a socially satisfactory attitude. As a strictly non-verbal approach, the method of negative adaptation is undoubtedly useful with infants and animals. In actual practice, however, we find very few fears in children of the pre-language period, and with the older children it is inefficient to eliminate

the degree of control, however slight, which language may afford.

Furthermore, with all but a few of our fear-objects the aim was not indifference, which negative adaptation implies, but something farther along the scale toward an acceptance reaction.

From our experience in general, it would appear that the repeated presentation of a feared object, with no auxiliary attempt to eliminate the fear, is more likely to produce a summation effect than an adaptation. With Godfried (the case just quoted) the loss of his resistance was possibly due to the fact that he had been afraid the animal would bite him. This fear, unrealized, was gradually overcome.

THE METHOD OF REPRESSION

In the home, as well as in the school and playground, social repression is perhaps the simplest and most common method of dealing with fear symptoms . . . a method, which, we may commonly note, often fails to remove the roots of the fear. As there are already too many examples of the maladaptive results of repression, we shall not attempt to add to their number. In our laboratory we used no repressive punishment, but within a group of children the familiar situations of ridicule, social teasing and scolding frequently appeared. Because of shame, a child might try to contain his fears without overt expression, but after a certain point had been reached, the reaction appeared notwithstanding.

Case 41.—Arthur G. Age 4 years.

Arthur was shown the frogs in an aquarium, no other children being present. He cried, said "they bite," and ran out of the play-pen. Later, however, he was brought into the room with four other boys; he swaggered up to the aquarium, pressing ahead of the others who were with him. When one of his companions picked up a frog and turned to him with it, he screamed and fled; at this he was chased and made fun of, but with naturally no lessening of the fear on this particular occasion.

Three boys standing around the aquarium each cried "Give me one," holding out their hands for a frog. But when the frog was offered they all precipitously withdrew. When two girls (4 years old) sang out to Sidney (age 3) "Sidney is afraid, Sidney is afraid," Sidney nodded his head in assent . . . illustrating what often happens in the use of social ridicule: the emotion is re-suggested and entrenched, rather than stamped out.

THE METHOD OF DISTRACTION

A convenient method, used frequently and with fair results, involves offering the subject a substitute activity. In order to capture a safety pin from the baby's hand and still preserve peace, its attention may be distracted with another toy, while you steal away the pin. Such a device, known to every mother, may be applied to the problem of eliminating fear responses. Arthur, whose fear of frogs had received some attention from us, wished to play with a set of crayons kept in the laboratory. We placed the crayons close to a frog on the table. Arthur stepped forward cautiously; keeping his gaze on the frog, he grabbed paper and crayons and showed alacrity in darting out of the danger zone. The experience, however, seemed to reassure him. "I ran over there and got it," he told us, "He didn't bite me. Tomorrow I'll put it in a little box and bring it home." At one stage of his fear of the rabbit, Sidney would whine whenever the rabbit was brought near, but he could readily be diverted by conversation about the rabbit's name, or some innocuous detail. For verbal distraction the constant presence of a grown-up is of course necessary; this introduces factors which are not always advantageous (such as reliance upon adult protection). Essentially, distraction soothes a fear response by inducing the child temporarily to forget the fear-object. (Substitution of an alternate stimulus-response system.) This may fail to result in any permanent reduction of the fear trend. Where the situation is properly managed, however, distraction passes over into a method which we have found distinctly useful, and which will now be described.

THE METHOD OF DIRECT CONDITIONING

It is probable that each of our methods involves conditioning in one form or another. Under this heading, however, we include all specific attempts to associate with the fear-object a definite stimulus, capable of arousing a positive (pleasant) reaction. The hunger motive appears to be the most effective for use in this connection. During a period of craving for food, the child is placed in a high chair and given something to eat. The fear-object is brought in, starting a negative response. It is then moved away gradually until it is at a sufficient distance not to interfere with the child's eating. The relative strength of the fear impulse and the hunger impulse may be gauged by the distance to which it is necessary to remove the fear-object. While the child is eating, the object is slowly brought nearer to the table, then placed upon the table, and finally as the tolerance increases it is brought close enough to be touched. Since we could not interfere with the regular schedule of meals, we chose the time of the mid-morning lunch for the experiment. This usually assured some degree of interest in the food, and corresponding success in our treatment. The effectiveness of this method increases greatly as the hunger grows, at least up to a certain point. The case of Peter (reported in detail elsewhere) illustrates our procedure; one of our most serious problem cases, he was treated by the method daily or twice daily for a period of two months. The laboratory notes for the first and the last days of the training period show an improvement which we were able to attribute specifically to the training measures used.

Case 30.—Peter. Age 2 years, 10 months.
March 10, 10:15 A.M. Peter sitting in high chair, eating candy. Experimenter entered room with a rabbit in an open meshed wire

cage. The rabbit was placed on the table 4 feet from Peter who immediately began to cry, insisting that the rabbit be taken away. Continued crying until the rabbit was put down 20 feet away. He then started again on the candy, but continued to fuss, "I want you to put Bunny outside." After three minutes he once more burst into tears; the rabbit was removed.

April 29, 9:55 A.M. Peter standing in high chair, looking out of the window. He inquired, "Where is the rabbit?" The rabbit was put down on the chair at Peter's feet. Peter patted him, tried to pick him up, but finding the rabbit too heavy asked the experimenter to help in lifting him to the window sill, where he played with him for several minutes.

This method obviously requires delicate handling. Two response systems are being dealt with: food leading to a positive reaction, and fear-object leading to a negative reaction. The desired conditioning should result in transforming the fear-object into a source of positive response (substitute stimulus). But a careless manipulator could readily produce the reverse result, attaching a fear reaction to the sight of food.

THE METHOD OF SOCIAL IMITATION

We have used this method extensively, as it was one of the first to show signs of yielding results.

Case 8.—Bobby G. Age 30 months.
Bobby was playing in the pen with Mary and Laurel. The rabbit was introduced in a basket. Bobby cried "No, no," and motioned for the experimenter to remove it. The two girls, however, ran up readily enough, looked in at the rabbit and talked excitedly. Bobby became promptly interested, said "What? Me see," and ran forward, his curiosity and assertiveness in the social situation overmastering other impulses.

Case 54.—Vincent W. Age 21 months.
Jan. 19. Vincent showed no fear of the rabbit, even when it was pushed against his hands or face. His only response was to laugh and reach for the rabbit's fur. On the same day he was taken into the pen with Rosey, who cried at the sight of the rabbit. Vincent immediately developed a fear response; in the ordinary playroom situation he would pay no attention to her crying, but in connection with the rabbit, her distress had a marked suggestion value. The fear transferred in this way persisted for over two weeks.

Feb. 6. Eli and Herbert were in the playpen with the rabbit. When Vincent was brought in, he remained cautiously standing at some distance. Eli led Vincent over to the rabbit, and induced him to touch the animal. Vincent laughed.

The second case illustrated a fear socially induced (this is perhaps the most common source of maladjustive fear trends) and the later removal of the fear by social suggestion. Many of the fears we studied pointed to an origin in a specific traumatic experience; it would probably have been a valuable aid in our procedure, had we been able to trace the developmental history of each of these fears. It was usually impossible to do this, however, in view of the institutional life of our subjects, and the fact that parents, even when they could be reached and consulted, were as a rule ignorant of their children's emotional mishaps.

SUMMARY

In our study of methods for removing fear responses, we found unqualified success with only two. By the method of direct conditioning we associated the fear-object with a craving-object, and replaced the fear by a positive response. By the method of social imitation we allowed the subject to share, under controlled conditions, the social activity of a group of children especially chosen with a view to prestige effect. Verbal appeal, elimination through disuse, negative adaptation, 'repression,' and 'distraction' were methods which proved sometimes effective but were not to be relied upon unless used in combination with other methods. It should be remarked that apart from laboratory analysis we have rarely used any of the above procedures in pure form. Our aim has been to cure the fear, by the group of devices most appropriate at any given stage of treatment.

45. Psychotherapy—Its Aim and Its Basic Theory *

Kenneth M. Colby

Mental illness has proved to be one of the largest problems of modern society. Two statistics reveal the depth of the problem. First, over twenty million people in the United States, or about one in ten, have emotional problems that require professional attention. Second, approximately one out of every two hospital beds is occupied by a mental patient. Thus, the care and treatment of persons with behavioral disorders has become an undertaking of such tremendous magnitude that substantial demands are now being made on the resources of our society.

Recently, efforts to modify the environmental conditions known to potentiate emotional disorders have increased, and discoveries of tranquilizing and activating drugs have helped to alleviate the suffering of mental patients. However, the major avenue of therapeutic assistance for most emotionally disturbed people, particularly those with neurotic disorders that do not require hospitalization, continues to be some form of individual psychotherapy.

In the following selection, Professor Colby outlines the general goals of individual psychotherapy. He also distinguishes between psychoanalysis and psychotherapy and provides an overview of the basic theory of personality on which psychoanalytically oriented psychotherapy is based. Finally, he describes the strategy and techniques of the psychotherapist as he puts these principles into practice in working with his patients.

* Reprinted by permission of the author and the publisher from Chapter 1 of Kenneth Mark Colby, *A Primer for Psychotherapists*. Copyright 1951 The Ronald Press Company, New York.

The goal of psychotherapy is to relieve the patient of distressing neurotic symptoms or discordant personality characteristics which interfere with his satisfactory adaptation to a world of people and events.

Sweeping as it sounds, this aim is actually a limited one, as the practicing psychotherapist well recognizes. Psychotherapy—including its most extensive form, psychoanalysis—is repair work. This view cannot be overemphasized. A psychotherapist should not expect great transformations equivalent to a psychological rebirth or a complete reorganization of the patient's personality. The results which can be achieved in this repair work are limited by the caliber of the original material (constitution plus young ego), the degree of damage (infantile traumas and adult frustrations), and what remains to be worked with (adult ego plus the reality situation). In people, as in clothes, some materials are finer to begin with and a repaired article is never as good as the new one. Since psychotherapy is confined to repair work, this limited aim may conflict with the beginning therapist's ambitions as well as with the patient's hopes.

The goal is further circumscribed by the aim of therapy to deal only with those areas of the personality producing major disturbances. Aspects of the patient's character which are ego-syntonic and which he wants to keep are better left alone unless they are inextricably bound up with his neurotic symptoms. For example, an overtly homosexual man who develops a phobia and who wishes to retain his sexual orientation can be treated for the phobia without seeking the goal of changing his homosexual character structure to a heterosexual one. Likewise, a deeply religious patient who desires relief from an anxiety neurosis without loss of his religious beliefs is entitled to psychotherapy devoid of the aim of altering these convictions. It sometimes does happen during therapy that patients change their views on what aspects of their personality they wish to retain, particularly when this appears necessary in order to be rid of unpleasant symptoms. However, such changes are secondary outcomes and not the initial sought-after goal.

In speaking of the goal of psychotherapy, the term "cure" frequently intrudes. It requires definition. If by "cure" we mean relief of the patient's current neurotic difficulties, then that is certainly our goal. If by "cure" we mean a lifelong freedom from emotional conflict and psychological problems, then that cannot be our goal. Just as a person may suffer pneumonia, a fracture, and diabetes during his lifetime and require particular minimizing and separate treatment for each condition, so another person may experience at different times a depression, impotence, and a phobia, each requiring psychotherapy as the condition arises. Our aim is to treat the presenting problems, hoping that the work will strengthen the patient against further neurotic difficulties but realizing that therapy cannot guarantee a psychological prophylaxis.

Finally, it is not the goal of psychotherapy to produce an ideal or model person. Everyone in life must learn to withstand a certain amount of emotional tension. That the patient who has undergone psychotherapy is one who is placid, emotionless, lovable, good-natured, and guiltless, no matter what happens to him, is an illusion in which neither the patient nor the therapist must invest, however strongly our culture insists on worshiping such a psychological saint.

All this, to be sure, is the therapist's concept of the goal, and it may differ widely from what some patients have in mind when coming to be helped. Since in our time and culture the psychotherapist has come to represent an amalgam of oracle, sage, and healer, those ridden by anxieties, who in other times might have relied upon other resources, now sometimes turn to him for "happiness" or a spiritual code to live by. There is much suffering and unhappiness in the world which psychotherapy can do nothing about. And establishing rules of conduct is not our province. Hence patients searching for happiness in terms of formulas or right-wrong precepts are certain to be disappointed by a psychotherapy which has the goal only of relieving neurotic or psychotic distress.

BASIC THEORY

We assume that, before a therapist attempts any psychotherapy, he will have acquired a familiar acquaintance both with the main clinical facts about neurotic and psychotic behavior and with convenient working concepts of a dynamic-genetic-structural-economic nature to use in understanding this behavior. These data are admirably, if tortuously, collected in Otto Fenichel's *Psychoanalytic Theory of Neurosis,* a book which must be read very slowly, in small doses, patiently and repeatedly. However, a few aspects of the theory can profitably be reviewed at this point. All the psychotherapeutic recommendations to be made are well founded in this logically uniform theoretical system as well as in practical experience.

Our theory begins with Freud's concept of the mind as an apparatus which attempts to deal with entering volumes of excitation in order to preserve the equilibrium of a rest state. The term "rest" is not to be taken in an absolute or static sense, but as implying a flux of energy changes within a limited range. As stimuli disturb the rest state by increasing tension, the mind seeks to discharge or bind this tension. Mental stimuli may be external or internal. External stimuli are those features of the surrounding environment perceived by the organism. Internal stimuli are those impulses (sexual and aggressive wishes) set going by biochemical energy changes. The young and growing mind learns, in integrating its internal needs with its environment, through thousands of reward-punishment experiences, to curb, moderate, channelize, displace, and postpone its wishes.

More specifically, a wish (internal tension-producing stimulus) may be totally gratified (tension discharged), totally denied (tension bound), or both gratified and denied (partially discharged, partially bound). The binding process is thought of in terms of defenses. In topographic terms, wish-impulses from the id are regulated by the defenses of the ego and superego.

In the normal state there is a harmonious relationship between wishes and defenses so that tensions are successfully managed with a satisfactory preservation of a relative rest state. A neurosis, on the contrary, is characterized (but not defined) by a neurotic conflict. That is, the compromise achieved by a wish and a conflicting defense has not successfully discharged or bound tension. Various clinical symptoms result from this type of conflict. We speak of a neurotic conflict, but there is usually more than one in a given neurosis. Since we treat them one at a time, it becomes a matter of convenience to speak of "conflict" in the singular. For the most part the patient is unaware of the nature, extent, or significance of his conflicts. Being unconscious and hence inaccessible, neurotic conflicts exert an all the greater influence on his mental life.

In theory, the goal of psychotherapy is to produce a favorable change in the disturbed balance of a conflictual wish-defense system, thus allowing a fuller gratification of the wish or at least a more suitable compromise. Since we cannot, to any great extent, influence by psychological means

the origin of biological processes per se (wish-impulses), in therapy we manage a wish-defense conflict by modifying the defense or ego component. Ideally we would like solely to attenuate or eradicate a pathogenic defense, but in actual practice, we probably annul some defenses while reinforcing others, the latter aiding binding rather than discharging functions. With the return of a relative equilibrium in a wish-defense conflict, tension diminishes and the symptoms decrease or vanish.

Next, let us consider the theory of the maneuvers by which this goal is reached. As the patient talks, the therapist listens and tries in his own mind to sort out, from the mass of thoughts, memories, and feelings the patient presents, an important neurotic conflict or group of conflicts. That is, the therapist attempts to see clearly the wish-defense system involved in a symptom-producing conflict. By various tactics (see below) he then brings this area to the attention of the patient in whom up until that time the ingredients of the conflict have been unconscious. As the defense of the conflict is brought to the patient's consciousness through verbalization, the motivation for the defense (affects of anxiety, guilt, shame, disgust regarding the wish) receives attention in terms of the patient's present and past life experience. Thereby the patient's "reasonable adult ego" is given the freedom to judge and relinquish this particular anachronistic defense as its motivation is seen to be of infantile origin.

Such is the strategy. The tactics by which the therapist influences a patient in this way now deserve comment. Statements by the therapist, i.e., interpositions and interpretations, are the chief tools used to change the defense or ego component of a neurotic conflict. These statements are made in reference to the patient's communications in two main areas, transferences and resistances, which represent the neurotic defenses in action in the therapy situation. By *transference* we mean the repetitious attempt, made unknowingly by the patient, to perceive and treat the therapist as an important figure of his childhood. *Resistances* are those defenses which operate in and against the therapeutic process to prevent an uncovering and a dissolution of the neurotic conflict. Thus, in theory, a transference is one form of resistance.

By now surely an important question has arisen. Isn't all this psychoanalysis? Freud said that any therapy which handles transference and resistance is psychoanalysis. Indeed, as presented, our theory of neurosis and our concept of the dynamics of cure are psychoanalytic. But though the theory is the same, the actual practice is somewhat different. These differences between psychotherapy and psychoanalysis are determined by several factors, the more important of which are mentioned below.

Time considerations are outstanding determinants in distinguishing psychotherapy from classical psychoanalysis. Since in psychotherapy both the therapist and the patient have less time available than is necessary for psychoanalysis, the frequency of interviews and the total duration of therapy are less. The time pressure prompts the therapist to be more active in questioning and in focusing the patient's attention on a significant conflict. This in turn means that the patient's communications are less in the nature of prolonged free association than they are a combination of conversation and associations. In psychotherapy, early childhood is less thoroughly explored and dreams are not exhaustively interpreted. The cases selected for psychotherapy differ in some respects from analytic cases, as may the degree to which a therapeutic goal is attainable. In psychotherapy probably more pathogenic defenses are strengthened, by support, guidance, and reassurance, than in psychoanalysis, which attempts primarily to eradicate defenses. Finally, whether the full transference *neurosis*, in which most or all of the patient's conflicts become centered about the therapist, theoretically can or should be avoided in psychotherapy is a much discussed question. In practice, though the transference neurosis may not develop to the degree observed in psychoanalysis, there is always a transference aspect and in some cases it may blossom with full intensity. Thus psychotherapy and psychoanalysis have a similar theory of neurosis and treatment, but they differ quantitatively and to some extent qualitatively in their theory, and hence practice, of technique.

46. The Operant Control of Intractable Sneezing *

Malcolm Kushner

At the turn of the century, Pavlov demonstrated that neurotic responses can be conditioned in animals. Since that time it has been generally accepted that learning plays an important part in the formation of neurotic symptoms in man. In fact, neurotic symptoms are now regarded by many as nothing more than conditioned responses that serve to reduce anxiety. If neurotic symptoms are indeed the result of learning, then it should be possible to eliminate them either by non-reinforcement (extinction), or by conditioning incompatible responses to the same stimuli that elicit them (counterconditioning).

In the past decade, new forms of treatment for emotional disorders have emerged. These treatment methods, collectively called the *behavior therapies*, make use of classical and in-

* This selection was written especially for this volume at the request of the editors and it is published here with Dr. Kushner's permission.

strumental conditioning procedures to modify or extinguish neurotic symptoms. In the next article, Malcolm Kushner, a psychologist who has pioneered the application of learning principles to clinical problems, reports a case in which an undesirable symptom was eliminated with behavior therapy.

At the time that treatment was begun, the patient was sneezing at the rate of about one sneeze every 40 seconds, and she had been sneezing for more than six months. The behavior therapy consisted simply of administering a strong electric shock every time the patient sneezed. This shock could be avoided only by not sneezing.

In a very short time, the sneezing was almost completely eliminated, but, as Dr. Kushner notes, the patient was not "cured." Even though the undesirable symptom was effectively eliminated, she remained the same anxious, awkward, immature adolescent that she was when the treatment for sneezing began. Consequently, the therapist's efforts were not terminated with the elimination of sneezing. Instead, a more conventional form of psychotherapy was then employed to uncover the underlying difficulty which had happened to manifest itself in sneezing.

The past decade has seen the introduction and widespread application of behavior therapy to the treatment of behavioral disorders (Wolpe, 1958). This approach holds that most behavior, normal or abnormal, is learned and therefore is understandable in terms of modern learning theory (Eysenck, 1960). In contrast to the views of psychoanalysts (who maintain that psychopathological symptoms represent unconscious complexes dating back to childhood and requiring lengthy analysis), the behavior therapist regards symptoms as nothing more than maladaptive, learned responses that may be directly eliminated or modified by new learning experiences. Consequently a direct attack upon the disturbing behavior itself should suffice to free or relieve the patient of his difficulties and enable him to live a more comfortable life.

Although learning in its various forms provides the theoretical base for behavior therapy, operant conditioning principles play a particularly important role in the techniques of the behavior therapist. This is true because the consequences of an individual's present behavior—the rewards and punishments that he receives—will determine a great deal of his subsequent behavior. The following case study illustrates how a behavior therapist deals with a complex clinical problem utilizing the methods of operant conditioning as well as more conventional dynamic treatment techniques (See Kushner, 1967, for a more detailed and technical account of these problems).

The patient was a 17-year-old high school sophomore who had been sneezing, vigorously and repeatedly, with no relief, for over six months. She was the third of five children in a modest, working class family. Her medical history revealed a series of frequent but relatively minor illnesses. The uncontrollable sneezing began in a hospital where she was being treated for a kidney infection. Just three days prior to being discharged the corridors outside her room were freshly painted and the sneezing began—at first moderate in intensity and not too closely spaced. Although the severity of her sneezing increased, she was discharged. However, when she returned home, her sneezing continued and she also began to experience severe headaches. Her concerned parents took her to a number of specialists who recommended hospitalization for a thorough medical work-up to determine the cause of the sneezing, which was now heavy and rapid.

Approximately three weeks after her initial discharge, the patient was readmitted to the hospital and given a series of intensive tests, including neurological, endocrinological, urological, allergic, and psychiatric examinations. She was given a wide variety of medications, some of which caused severe physical reactions, but the sneezing was unabated. She was seen regularly by a psychiatrist who used hypnosis as an adjunct to psychotherapy, but the sneezing continued. Finally trial exposure to other climates was prescribed and trips were made to different parts of the country, but these did not help. As a last resort, sleep was induced chemically for several days since it was noted that the patient did not sneeze at night when she slept. Upon awakening the sneezing resumed.

In sum, scores of consultants of various medical specialties examined the patient, but with no relief. During the six months prior to the treatment to be described, the patient spent all of her time in the hospital except for several brief periods of reduced sneezing and the trips in which she was exposed to different climates. She quickly became a public as well as a medical celebrity as her case received constant newspaper coverage and attracted national attention.

The patient resided in the same city as the writer and her case commanded special interest there, with extensive local newspaper and TV coverage in addition to the wire service reports. Since psychiatric and medical efforts were not successful and the sneezing appeared to have operant properties, the writer speculated that the patient's problem could be approached using

the methods of behavior therapy. It was felt that giving a brief non-convulsive electric shock contingent upon sneezing would bring this behavior under effective control. The writer contacted the patient's physician and offered to try this behavior therapy procedure with the patient and this offer was accepted.

THE BEHAVIOR THERAPY TREATMENT PROCEDURE

The patient was seen during the sixth month of her ordeal. Baseline data revealed an average rate of one sneeze every 40 seconds. At times, the sneezes occurred as frequently as every 15 seconds. The treatment consisted of placing a microphone around the girl's neck. This was connected to a sound-activated voice key and then to a shock source. Electrodes were attached to her fingertips via rubber finger coverings such as used by clerks for sorting papers. Sneezing activated the sound relay which in turn triggered a shock of approximately 3.5 milli-amperes intensity. The shock was contingent upon sneezing and could be avoided by the patient if she did not sneeze. Counters

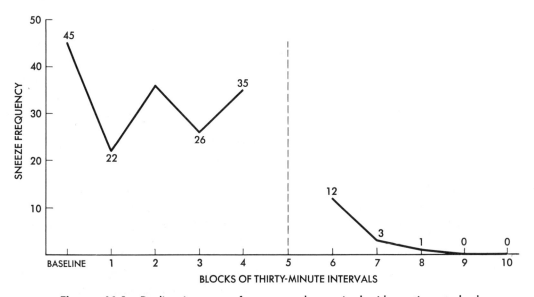

Figure 46.1 Decline in sneeze frequency when paired with contingent shock.

automatically recorded the frequency of sneeze responses for intervals of 30 minutes.

The frequency of sneezing for the baseline period and successive 30-minute intervals (Blocks) following this period are presented in Figure 46-1. During Block 3, the sneeze rate did not continue to decline in the manner expected. This failure prompted closer observation of the patient who was initially left alone in her room. It was discovered that the fingertip electrodes were not making good contact. Between Blocks 3 and 4 the patient was found holding the electrodes complaining that they kept coming off. Midway between Blocks 4 and 5, the electrodes again came off, forcing us to stop the procedure while they were taped on the patient's forearm. Once the electrodes were properly placed, effective control of sneezing was rapid, with an immediate reduction in sneezing and complete cessation by Block 9. There was no further sneezing the following day and two days later the patient was discharged from the hospital. Although this ended the most spectacular and unique phase of the treatment, much more was to follow.

THE FOLLOW-UP TREATMENT

In many cases, the disturbing behavior that resulted in the patient being referred for treatment appears to be functionally autonomous and maintained as the result of habit. In such cases, once the symptomatic behavior is modified, nothing further remains to be done, and the patient is usually able to carry on with the resources at hand. However, for patients who are actively engaged in the problem-solving phase of an emotional conflict, an alternate, more appropriate set of responses must be developed once the disturbing behaviors are modified. It was immediately obvious that the latter condition existed in the case of the patient with the sneezing problem, and that more conventional treatment methods were required.

In brief, the over-all picture revealed that the patient was an immature over-protected young lady with a poor opinion of herself and low self-esteem. Consequently, she was extremely anxious and uncertain of herself in interpersonal relations, particularly in dealing with males. She protected herself by limiting her social contacts, preferring to give most of her attention and affection to her numerous pets rather than people. She was also in conflict with her parents and siblings and this heightened her sense of vulnerability and dependence upon them. She expressed the idea that sneezing made her feel safe and secure, and that she would rather retreat to her world of animals and fantasy than live in the therapist's world which was so threatening. In effect, she was a frightened child in an unfriendly, threatening world, but she recognized, ruefully, that she must find her place in it.

The "meaning" or "reason" for the intense and prolonged sneezing is, of course, a question of considerable interest. It is the writer's opinion that the sneezing was initially elicited by the fresh paint in the hospital in a normal fashion, i.e., through irritation of the nasal mucosa. This occurred a few days before the patient was to be discharged, an event that she wished to delay as long as possible since she would be returning to the intolerable pressures that awaited her at home. In the hospital she not only escaped these pressures, but also became the object of concern and solicitude from her parents. Upon discharge from the hospital, the patient's sneezing was reinforced by her parents' concern and the fact that it permitted her to avoid family conflicts. When she was rehospitalized the escape contingency was again reinforced, thus contributing to the continuation of the sneezing behavior. As her condition became publicized, the patient began to receive many letters from well-wishers and cure-providers, and she was interviewed on TV and by other news media, etc. These added reinforcers firmly strengthened the sneezing. It is a well-established axiom of operant conditioning theory that successful escape or avoidance behavior is likely to be repeated, and this seemed to be the case with the patient's sneezing.

For a brief period following her discharge from the hospital, there were transitory attempts on the patient's part to reestablish her formerly successful escape-avoidance behavior. However, this time the contingencies were different. If she now sneezed the consequence was painful electric shock. Although she continued to have strong promptings to resume sneezing for a long time thereafter, she did not do so. When eventually the therapist pointed out to her the mechanism and motivation of her sneezing, she accepted this explanation and this gave added control for her sneezing.

The patient's verbalizations to the effect that she felt secure and protected when she was sneezing emphasized the successful escape-avoidance nature of that behavior and made absolutely necessary the establishment of more appropriate responses with which adaptively to resolve her many problems. In recognition of this need, the second phase of the treatment consisted of four major goals: (1) To enhance the patient's low self-esteem and encourage more assertive and independent behavior. (2) To provide her with additional activities outside of school and home. (3) To desensitize her anxiety when near boys and in social situations. (4) To help her family to understand her problems. It was anticipated that the development of greater self-confidence would result in the patient experiencing less anxiety, and that this would also help her to close the large gap which existed in the area of emotional maturity.

The conduct of the second phase of the treatment—the post-hospital phase—consisted essentially of conventional supportive psychotherapy. The therapist was fairly directive in his approach, particularly in encouraging more assertive and independent behavior. However, where applicable, further use was made of behavior therapy techniques, especially in attempting to desensitize the patient's disposition to experience anxiety in social situations. The desensitization procedure followed Wolpe's (1958) description of its use in phobic or allied states.

In order to help the patient develop self-confidence, she was encouraged to enroll in a modeling school where she obtained instruction in grooming, carriage, etc. During the summer, she was encouraged to take a position as a volunteer in a nearby hospital. The therapist also worked with the patient's family during this phase of treatment. In general, the focus of treatment was on the present behavior of the patient with emphasis given to helping her solve current problems. As of this writing (October, 1967), sixteen months have elapsed since the sneezing was stopped. Except for several brief efforts to resume sneezing that occurred early in this period, there has been no relapse nor substitution of other symptoms. The writer's efforts in assisting the patient to "grow up" and assume a responsible role in society are continuing, and it is likely that she will require treatment for at least another year.

In summary, this case demonstrates the application of behavior therapy to a specific clinical symptom in a patient who was attempting to resolve a current conflict. This symptom appeared to be a maladaptive, learned response that was effectively eliminated by a direct attack upon the disturbing behavior using behavior therapy techniques. The patient is also being helped to work through her basic conflicts through the use of a combination of behavior therapy and more traditional psychotherapeutic procedures.

REFERENCES

EYSENCK, H. J. (1960) (Ed.). Behavior Theory and the Neuroses. New York: Pergamon Press.
KUSHNER, M. (1967). Faradic aversive controls in clinical practice. In C. Neuringer and J. Michael (Eds.). *Behavior Modification in Clinical Psychology.* Appleton-Century-Crofts.
WOLPE, J. (1958). *Psychotherapy by Reciprocal Inhibition.* Stanford: Stanford Univ. Press.

SOCIAL BEHAVIOR

47. Dissonance Theory and the Formation of Values *

Elliot Aronson

The goals of social psychology are to understand and explain how people are influenced by the social stimuli that act upon them. In essence, the social psychologist wishes to know how an individual's thoughts, feelings, attitudes and actions are influenced by other human beings. The mores and values of the society in which an individual lives and the particular groups with whom a person spends his time are particularly important as sources of social influence.

The family is perhaps the most significant single group to which a person belongs. Personality development is influenced by family members through a process called socialization that begins in childhood and continues throughout life. This influence is mediated by subtle rewards and punishments that shape specific aspects of behavior and determine social values and attitudes. The goals of socialization are to help a child to develop a basic set of values that can guide his behavior when parents are no longer present.

The internalization of values is the focus of the theory of "cognitive dissonance" proposed by Leon Festinger. According to Festinger, when a person has two incompatible or inconsistent ideas (cognitions), he will experience a psychological state of tension called dissonance. This state (similar in some respects to a state of anxiety) has aversive drive properties that motivate the individual to reduce or eliminate the dissonance. In the following selection, Professor Aronson describes several experiments that were designed to evaluate dissonance theory, and suggests important applications of the theory to the practical problems of child-rearing.

Most parents are concerned with two basic goals in raising their children: To prevent them from performing destructive, dangerous and otherwise undesirable acts and to instill an enduring set of values that will enable them to live in society without breaking too many laws or violating too many cultural mores.

It would be wonderful if we could reason with the young child, if we could convince him by rational and persuasive argument that it is not nice to take away his baby sister's toys. But, as Aristotle observed 2,000 years ago, even many adults cannot be convinced by reason. This is true in spades when applied to the 4-year-old. Less rational techniques must be employed, techniques that involve rewards or punishments. Child psychologists generally agree that rewards, both in the form of concrete incentives and in the form of praise and approval, are an acceptable means of "reinforcing" desirable behavior and that rewarding desirable behavior is more effective than punishing undesirable behavior. Thus, they recommend that we should reward Johnny for being kind to his little brother as opposed to punishing him for being unkind to him. Parents, however, (even those of us who happen to be psychologists) are well aware that punishment or the threat of punishment is often necessary and, when judiciously used, can be an effective means of controlling the behavior of very young children.

Let us take a closer look at threats of punishment as a technique. These threats usually take the form of spankings or denial of privileges. A reasonable question is one of degree—in order to be most effective, how severe should a threat of punishment be? It stands to reason that if we want to prevent a child from performing a mischievous act, the more severe the threat, the greater the likelihood that he will comply—at least *while the threatening parent is standing there watching him.* And that's the rub. For while severe threats are effective in achieving the first major goal of parents (that of preventing momentary undesirable behavior), they have proved useless in helping the child develop a set of values. For example, child psychologists find that those parents who are most severe in punishing a child's aggressive behavior tend to have children who, although relatively unaggressive at home, are veritable hellions in the schoolyard where their parents are not present.

It is unfortunate that those techniques that are best for preventing momentary infractions are ineffective as a means of imparting basic values. Moreover, of the two goals, the latter is the more important, if for no other reason than the fact that it is more efficient. Once a child has developed a set of values, parents (and society) can afford to relax their vigil. If a child has not yet learned to respect the rights of others, we must be continually on our toes, armed with rewards or threats, to see to it that Johnny doesn't slug his little brother and abscond with his Batman doll. Once he has developed these values, he will refrain from these behaviors—not because of fear of punishment, but because he wants to. It would certainly be a much more efficient way to run a family (or a society) if we could imbue young children with complex values—if we could get them to stop slugging their brothers because they had come to dislike slugging smaller children.

Psychologists have been conducting experiments during the past few years that may have an important bearing on this problem. The experiments were derived from and inspired by the theory of "cognitive dissonance," which was first proposed in 1957 by Dr. Leon Festinger, a social psychologist at Stanford University. Stated in its simplest form, this theory suggests that when a person simultaneously holds two incompatible ideas (cognitions), dissonance occurs. This creates tension. Such tension is unpleasant, and the individual tries to diminish it by reducing the dissonance. This can be done by changing one idea (cognition) or the other to bring them closer together and make them more compatible.

For example, if a person has the cognition that he smokes cigarettes and reads that cigarette smoking leads to lung cancer, he experiences cognitive dissonance. His cognition that he is smoking is dissonant with his cognition that cigarette smoking might cause cancer. He can reduce this dissonance in a number of ways. Perhaps the most direct would be to stop smoking; the cognition that cigarette smoking causes cancer is perfectly compatible with *not* smoking. Although this is the most direct way to reduce dissonance, it is not the easiest course of action to take—as many of us have discovered. Consequently, most people attempt to reduce dissonance by working on the other cognition—that is, by making cigarette smoking seem less silly. They might belittle the evidence linking cigarette smoking to cancer ("Most of the data were gathered on rodents, not people"); or they might associate with other cigarette smokers ("If Sam, Jack, and Harry smoke, then it can't be very dangerous"); or they might smoke filter-tipped cigarettes and delude themselves that the filter traps the cancer-producing materials; or they might convince themselves that smoking is an important and highly pleasurable activity ("I'd rather have a shorter but more enjoyable life than a longer, unenjoyable one"); or they might actually make a virtue out of smoking by developing a romantic, devil-may-care image of themselves, flaunting danger by smoking. These behaviors are all acts of "self-justification" and, indeed, the cognitive dissonance theory is largely concerned with man's attempt to justify his own behavior, to make his actions appear to be reasonable and rational, after the fact.

What does all this have to do with instilling a permanent set of values in young children? Just this: Children are people, too; there is every reason to suspect that they experience cognitive dissonance and attempt to reduce it in much the same way that adults do.

Let us take as an example one that I used previously in a paper, prepared with the aid of a grant from the National Science Foundation, reporting on explorations of the applicability of the cognitive dissonance theory. This is the situation where a father comes upon his 5-year-old son hitting his younger brother. The parent threatens to punish the youngster if he ever catches him doing that again. Now, how can we utilize this episode to implant a permanent set of values in the child?

Each parent has at his disposal a range of punishments from the extremely mild (a stern look) to the extremely severe (a very stern look, a severe spanking, forcing the child to stand in a corner for two hours and depriving him of TV privileges for a month). The more severe the threat, the greater the likelihood that the youngster will mend his ways *while you are watching him*. But he may very well hit his brother again as soon as you turn your back.

Suppose instead that you threaten him with a very mild punishment. In either case (under threat of severe punishment or of mild punishment), the child experiences dissonance. He is aware that he is not beating up his little brother—and also aware that he wants to. When the child

has the urge to hit his brother and doesn't, he asks himself in effect, "How come I'm not beating up my little brother?" Under severe threat he has a ready answer—"I know why. I'm not beating him up because if I do my father is going to spank me, stand me in the corner and keep me from watching television for a month." The severe threat has given the child justification for not hitting his brother while he's being watched.

The child in the mild threat situation experiences dissonance, too. But when he asks himself, "How come I'm not beating him up?", he doesn't have a good answer, because the threat is so mild that it does not provide a superabundance of justification. The child is *not* doing something he wants to do—and while he has some justification, he lacks complete justification. In this situation he continues to experience dissonance. There is no simple way for him to reduce it by blaming his inaction on a severe threat.

Much like our cigarette smoker, the child must find a way to justify the fact that he is not aggressing against his little brother. The best way is to try to convince himself that he really doesn't like to beat his brother up, that he didn't want to do it in the first place, that beating up little kids is not fun. The less severe the threat, the less the external justification. The less the external justification, the greater the need for internal justification. Internal justifications are a long step toward the development of a permanent value.

To test this idea, I performed an experiment at the Harvard University nursery school in collaboration with Dr. J. Merrill Carlsmith. We did not try to change basic values like aggression, because parents might not approve of our changing important values. Instead, we chose a trivial aspect of behavior—toy preference.

We first asked 4- and 5-year-old children to rate the attractiveness of several toys; then we chose one that a child considered to be quite attractive, and we told him he couldn't play with it. We threatened half of the children with mild punishment for transgression—"I would be a little annoyed"; we threatened the other half with more severe punishment—"I would be very angry. I would have to take all of the toys and go home and never come back again. I would think you were just a baby." After that, we left the room and allowed the children to play with the other toys—and to resist the temptation of playing with the forbidden one. All of the children did resist the temptation—none played with the forbidden toy.

On returning to the room we remeasured the attractiveness of all of the toys. Our results were both striking and exciting. Those children who underwent a mild threat now found the toy less attractive than before. In short, lacking adequate justification for refraining from playing with the toy, they succeeded in convincing themselves that they hadn't played with it because they didn't really like it. On the other hand, the toy did not become less attractive for those who were severely threatened. These children continued to rate the forbidden toy as highly desirable— indeed, some even found it more desirable than they had before the threat. The children in the severe threat condition had good external reasons for not playing with the toy (the severe threat itself); they therefore had no need to find additional reasons (like that the toy was no longer attractive); consequently, they continued to like the toy.

Our experiment has been repeated by other psychologists at different universities across the country. The most dramatic of these experiments is one recently conducted by Dr. Jonathan Freedman of Stanford University. The exciting aspect of Dr. Freedman's experiment is that he showed that this effect is a long-lasting one. In his experiment, he repeated our procedure with minor changes. Freedman asked the children not to play with a highly desirable toy, using mild threats for some and severe for others.

After some 23 to 64 days had elapsed, different experimenters came to the classroom under totally unrelated circumstances to administer a psychological test. They tested the students in the same room that was used by Freedman—the original toys were rather carelessly strewn about. After each experimenter had administered one test to a child, she told him that she would have to score it and might want to ask him some questions about it later—and while he was waiting, if he wanted to, he could amuse himself by playing with some of the toys lying around.

Freedman's results are highly consistent with our own. The overwhelming majority of the children who had been mildly threatened weeks earlier did not play with this inherently attractive toy; on the other hand, the great majority of the children who had been severely threatened *did*, in fact, play with the toy. In sum, a severe threat was not effective in inhibiting subsequent behavior—but the effect of one *mild* threat inhibited behavior for 64 days. The beauty of this technique is that the child did not come to devalue this behavior (playing with the toy) because some adult told him it was undesirable; he convinced himself it was undesirable.

Parents who might be interested in applying this technique directly should be aware of the fact that the practical application of these results revolves around the subtle and difficult problem of finding precisely the correct amount of threatened punishment; a threat which is neither so mild that the child refuses to obey, nor so severe that he has ample justification for obeying. The control and precision that we have been able to achieve in the psychological laboratory is difficult to duplicate in the hurly-burly atmosphere of a complex family environment. Nonetheless, these difficulties are probably not insurmountable; accordingly, the technique presents an interesting possibility to the parent for dealing with transient disobedience while at the same time, hopefully, helping the child to develop a system of enduring values.

48. Together in Isolation *

William W. Haythorn and Irwin Altman

The eerie quality of a deserted city street in early morning is evidence of the comforting role played by familiar sights, sounds, and social interactions. Yet, most of us give little notice to the many stimuli that cause us to feel at home in our customary environment until, for some reason, these familiar and comforting stimuli are no longer present. Recent research on people confined in environments where stimulation is markedly reduced shows that men require a variety of stimuli in order to function effectively.

In the next selection, Drs. Haythorn and Altman describe the effects of social isolation on the adjustment of young sailors confined in a small room and isolated from outside contact for a 10-day period. The results of this study and others that are being carried out at the Naval Medical Research Institute provide scientific answers to questions concerning the potential effects of social isolation and personality factors on behavior. The success of future missions that will take man safely to the moon and beyond will depend on such information.

When Admiral Richard E. Byrd "wintered over" at an advanced weather station close to the South Pole in 1934-1935, he decided to go it alone because he felt that two could hardly be cooped up together for five months without seriously threatening each other's existence. He understood very well that he would face stresses of complete isolation. But isolation *with* another man—with all the personal conflicts and irritations that would inevitably result —seemed worse to Byrd.

* Reprinted by permission of the authors and the publisher from *Trans-action Magazine*, 1967, 4, 18-22.

The terrors of isolation are well known to explorers, prospectors, wardens, light-housekeepers—and, more recently, submariners, Arctic weather and radar station operators, and astronauts. Our earliest prisons were built so that the sinner might have solitude in which to meditate on and repent his sins; but they produced more suicides and psychotics than repentant sinners. "Cabin fever" and "going stir-crazy" are still potent expressions for the effects of loneliness.

A variety of psychological strains—apart from any physical dangers—are created when small groups are isolated from their fellows and confined to limited spaces, such as undersea stations and space capsules. Chief among these strains are *stimulus reduction, social isolation,* and *interpersonal conflict.*

Research on *stimulus reduction* shows that man needs a minimum level of stimulation—and variety of stimuli—to survive and retain his faculties. People confined to dark, quiet chambers—the traditional "solitary confinement" of the prisoner, or the sound-proof room used for training astronauts—often display bizarre stress and anxiety symptoms, including hallucinations, delusions, apathy, and the fear of losing sanity. Their performance deteriorates. In fact, recent evidence suggests that important changes may actually occur in the nervous system that will persist for some time after the isolate comes back to the normal world. Men in lonely military stations have shown similar reactions, if to a lesser degree. Men simply may not be built to adapt well to a closed-in world with too little stimulus or variety.

Social isolation creates other problems.

Man is a social animal. He needs other people; he gets emotional support from them; he understands and tests reality, and his feelings and beliefs, in large part through his interactions with them. Confined to a small group, his opportunity to get what he needs are strongly limited, and this can lead to frustration, dissatisfaction, and increased irritability. Without the normal ability to judge himself and his performance through the reactions of others, the accuracy and stability of his performance must fall, his emotional responses become less appropriate, and he may even become confused about what he really believes.

In isolation, *interpersonal conflict* becomes exaggerated—and there is less chance to go outside to blow off steam or escape from the difficulties of adjustment. In these circumstances irritations are likely to accumulate to the point of explosion. Such frictions are reported in histories of isolated groups almost without exception. In many instances, such conflicts have resulted in breaking up the group—even murder. Taken together, existing research and other evidence indicates that explorers of the future—in space and underseas—face socio-psychological hazards that may equal the physical threats of new environments.

WHO IS THE GOOD ADJUSTOR?

From the available literature, mostly anecdotal descriptions of what presumably took place in such environments as Arctic stations, we get some general descriptions of the persons who adjust well to isolation—and of those who do not. In temperament the poor adjustor to isolation is anxious, restless, individualistic. He wants a lot of activity and an ever-changing environment. He is intolerant of whatever he doesn't like. But the good adjustor *is* tolerant—of others, of authority, of tedium. He is more conformist, much less likely to do something considered against regulations, improper, or illegal.

But "good adjustor," of course, is a relative term, all men suffer in isolation. Even a good adjustor cannot be locked into a space capsule with just anybody—or even with just any other good adjustor. So what kinds of people can get along together with the least amount of open friction in isolation? What kinds can accomplish most work when locked up together? What kinds simply sentence one another to mutual tedium?

The literature on group composition, though not addressed specifically to isolated groups, sheds some light on interpersonal stresses and adjustments. It indicates that compatibility and team coordination can be strongly affected by proper choices of group members. A large variety of group characteristics have been examined, but for two-man teams they can be generally classified as:

—*competitive,* in which both cannot be mutually satisfied, as when both seek to dominate;
—*congruent,* in which both have similar needs, which can be satisfied from the same source, as when both like classical music, similar foods, or the same topics of conversation—or when both want to achieve a common goal;
—*complementary,* in which the needs are different, but mutually satisfied in the same situation, as when one likes to lead and one to be led, one is dependent and one likes to help others.

But ordinary group behavior is not necessarily the same as isolated group behavior. Specifically, what happens when pairs of men are locked together around the clock that would not happen if they were merely fellow workers or roommates who went their own ways at night? To answer this question the literature was not enough, a controlled experiment was necessary.

Eighteen pairs of men—young sailors in boot training—were selected to meet certain conditions of compatibility, in order to determine how much of the stress of isolation could be relieved by properly matching personalities. They were tested and rated in four personality dimensions:

Need for *achievement*. This was defined as the desire or need to accomplish some overall goal—a task-orientation, or work-orientation.

Need for *dominance:* the need or desire for control over others, for individual prominence—a self orientation.

Need for *affiliation:* the need and desire for affection, and association with others.

Need for *dogmatism:* the need to believe that one's own opinions and ideas are the only important ones; an inability to tolerate dissent; ethnocentric personality.

They were then matched in such a way that in one-third of the pairs both men were high in each of these dimensions, in one-third both were low, and in the final third one was high and one low.

Each pair in the experimental group was confined to a small room (12 feet by 12 feet) and isolated from outside contacts for 10 days. They were given a certain amount of work to do on a fixed schedule, but they were free to talk, read, play cards and checkers for several hours each day. They were not free to communicate in any way with the outside. They had no mail, radios, watches, or calendars.

The control group, composed of similar pairs, followed the same work schedule in identical rooms—but they slept in their regular Navy barracks, ate at the base mess, and were allowed to leave work for short breaks. In the evening they could use base recreation facilities.

The findings of the experiment will be presented in several categories:

Territoriality—the degree and intensity of the tendency to stake out certain areas, positions, and pieces of furniture as being exclusively one's own and off limits to others.

Disclosure—the intimacy with which each person confided in his partner and the extent of the confidence.

Performance—how well each personality type, in each condition of matching and environment did his tasks.

Personality interaction and social behavior—how well the different pairings got along with each other.

THIS LAND IS MY LAND

Many animals show a possessiveness about specific objects and places that has been called "territoriality." Early in the spring, for instance, male robins stake out individual areas to receive mates and will fight any other males that try to enter. Very little scientific evidence on territoriality exists for humans, but many parallels have been marked, and a few anthropological and social-psychological studies suggest that it operates in men. For instance, delinquent gangs fight to protect their "turf." Anthropologist Jules Henry in *Culture Against Man* describes a dreadful scene in a home for aged paupers in which the inmates, stripped of possessions and dignity, still fought to protect their final refuge of identification—their beds.

Possessiveness about pieces of furniture and equipment has been cited as one cause of friction in isolated groups. Through one-way glass we observed our experimental isolated pairs and control pairs to see how true this was, and whether and to what extent it really affected both the isolation and the clash of personalities.

We predicted that the isolates would be much more particular about staking claims to specific beds, chairs, and sides of the table than the non-isolated. This turned out to be true. Isolates established preferences for their beds quickly and definitely, with little intrusion into each other's sleeping space. This separation eased a little with time but not very much. Since beds are highly personal objects with fixed geographic locations, but chairs are non-personal and movable, territoriality about chairs and place at table developed more slowly, but it was definite after a few days.

The reverse pattern held for the non-isolates: they established early preferences for chairs and place at table, which declined with time, and relatively little personal preferences for bunks at first, but this increased with time.

GETTING TO KNOW YOU

We had anticipated that the isolated pairs would, over time, confide much more personal information to each other than those who left every evening and that this would increasingly include intimate information—in other words, both greater breadth *and* depth of disclosure. Literature about isolated groups had suggested that people use each other as sources of stimulation—and that they might use disclosure to speed up acquaintanceship.

Results, obtained from questionnaires, were pretty much as predicted. Isolated pairs gave each other more personal information of every kind, both intimate and non-intimate, than non-isolates. In contrast, the controls confided in each other about as much as they usually did with men in their regular training company, but much less than with their best friends. Confidences by isolates to their roommates, both intimate and general, were considerably greater than they gave to the usual barracks acquaintance. While less than "best friends," they could be considered the equivalent of relations with close friends.

It appeared that such extremely close contact and dependency produced pressures to learn about each other rapidly—a situation that does not necessarily lead to permanence (much like a fragile "summer romance," with too little time spent in "courtship"). The results showed that more intimate information is exchanged only after a certain amount of less intimate information has been sampled—as though the total information about a person is padded around a central core like the layers of an onion, and the social penetration process consists of cutting a wedge through the layers. Isolates did not achieve broad exchange at these deeper levels.

Were these greater exchanges due merely to the greater amount of time spent together? Not entirely. Observers reported that during free periods isolates generally talked, socialized, and played together more than non-isolates. They were rated as being more friendly, showing more social initiative, than the controls. There were exceptions, of course (as discussed below), and the pattern did vary somewhat with time. But, generally, the isolates seemed to be trying harder to get to know each other, realizing perhaps that they had little alternative.

Records were also kept of the extent to which the men engaged in solitary or joint activities. Isolated pairs at first, as noted, did many things together, but gradually drew apart, spending more time in solitary activities such as reading or lying on their bunks. It appeared as though isolates began to draw a "cocoon" around themselves as the pattern of isolation became firmly fixed, withdrawing into their own territories and dealing with each other less and less. This same "cocooning" has been reported in groups kept isolated by nature. The non-isolates, in contrast, started out spending more and more of their time alone, but this declined in the last days as joint activity increased.

TOIL AND TROUBLE

Questionnaire responses and performance scores on various tasks indicated that the isolated pairs experienced greater stress than the non-isolated—but nonetheless performed better. It has been known for many years that moderate levels of stress generally result in better performance. Nobody worked hard in the Garden of Eden.

But nobody can get much work done in the middle of combat either. Isolated pairs had far more trouble and personal conflict than controls. Two pairs were unable to complete the 10 days in the room, though it was comfortable enough, air-conditioned, and in no way physically threatening. Two other pairs showed great hostility—including extreme verbal abuse and some actual fighting. In one pair it reached such a pitch that the experimenters —who monitored the rooms day and night —had to step in to keep it from getting worse or being repeated. These results reflect closely not only the effects of isolation but the interactions of the personalities involved, exaggerated and made more dramatic by isolation.

As noted, one of the chief interests of the study was to determine the effects of the various combinations of different personalities. The characteristics—need for dominance, dogmatism, affiliation, and achievement—had been chosen because they had proved useful in previous studies of small groups. For every personality characteristic, at least one combination was incompatible. Two dominant men in the same room would be obviously incompatible. Those with different ways of thinking would not agree on how to face mutual problems; those with different needs for affiliation would expect contrasting things from each other, leading to a tense "climate" (the cool, laconic, independent man would obviously irk and be irked by the gregarious, loud, dependent one); and dissimilar needs to achieve could easily convince one man that the other was lazy, and the other that the first was an "eager beaver" "bucking" for promotion.

Of the four groups that had the most trouble, including the severe arguments and fighting, three pairs were both high in dominance, and two were strongly contrasting in their need for achievement— proving the hypothesis that putting together in isolation two domineering men, or one who was a driving "go-getter" and one who was not, would very likely lead to trouble. Territoriality was much more strongly marked in these incompatibles than in other isolated pairs.

However, "in isolation" is an important qualifier. Among the controls, who went home every evening, though there was obvious tension, fighting did not break out, and incompatibles actually performed better than the compatible—once more demonstrating the idea that a certain amount of tension is desirable for good performance.

While these two incompatible combinations showed similarity in conflict and territoriality, they also showed a fundamental difference. The high dominance pairs worked, played (and argued) together a lot—they could be termed active, competitive, and volatile, and their arguments were part of this picture. But those incompatible in achievement, when duty or circumstance did not force them into confrontation, tended to withdraw and avoid each other when they could.

The dogmatic isolates (who believed that only their opinions were worth considering) also had a lot of active social interchange, including arguments—but they were not so concerned with private territories.

But the isolated pairs with contrasting needs for affiliation were the most consistently passive and withdrawn of the lot, staking out private preserves to which they could retreat from each other. In this way they resembled closely those pairs with incompatible achievement needs. Generally, they had relatively subdued, quiet and private relationships, where members bore one another in relative silence, at a distance, and from their own territories. Their method of adjustment to incompatibility was social withdrawal—movement *away* from one another. This is in strong contrast with dominance incompatibility, which led to a noisy, volatile, aggressive relationship— movement *against* one another.

THE SELF AND THE SOCIAL

Perhaps these differences and similarities in personality adjustments and clashes can be better understood if we take the analysis a step further. Dominance and dogmatism are *egocentric* qualities—they reflect primary concern for the self—whether in relation to other persons (dominance) or to ideas and/or things (dogmatism). Need for affiliation and need for achievement are *sociocentric* qualities—they reflect concern for joint relationships between the self and others (affiliation) and as members of a group striving for a common goal outside the self (achievement).

The high dominance pair is competitive because each is trying to get the other to do what he wants. The highly dogmatic person regards his view as the only important one, whether in personal beliefs or in organization and performance of mutual tasks; and his partner is not likely to take this arrogance quietly.

Those with high need for affiliation, on the other hand, satisfy themselves *by* satisfying others, working to set up close and friendly relationships; and, similarly, a man with a strong need to achieve will work closely and enthusiastically with another who is in pursuit of the same goal. Thus self-fulfillment is achieved through joint effort, helping each other. In both need for affiliation and achievement the focus is more on what a person does *for others* than it is with either dominance or dogmatism. Where the pair is incompatible for affiliation or achievement—that is, a high affiliator or achiever combined with a low

one—they are incongruent rather than competitive or conflicting. They are frustrated more by the situation than the person—by what the other *doesn't* do rather than by what he does. Eager to cooperate, they depend on parallel eagerness. Faced by apathy, non-cooperation, or unfriendliness, they retreat and try to go their own ways. On the other hand the dominant or dogmatic do not really want cooperation (though they may use the word)—they want acquiescence.

This study demonstrates clearly that the stresses of isolation are considerably affected by the relations between personality types. Good adjustment may decrease or modify stress in constructive ways; bad adjustment may increase, exaggerate, or complicate it, sometimes in destructive ways.

Should interpersonal conflict therefore be avoided in today's space capsules, Antarctic stations, and sea labs? No. It can enliven an existence of otherwise deadly and crippling monotony. It can produce better performance. The questions we now have to answer are: How much stress? What kinds? How to assure that proper matches are made?